Tolstoy's Bicycle

Tolstoy's Bicycle

JEREMY
BAKER

ST. MARTIN'S PRESS
NEW YORK

For information, write: St. Martin's Press,
175 Fifth Avenue, New York, N.Y. 10010
Manufactured in the United States of America

Library of Congress Cataloging in Publication Data
Baker, Jeremy.
Tolstoy's bicycle.
1. Biography—Miscellanea. I. Title.
CT105.B26 920'.02 81-18497
ISBN 0-312-80866-6 AACR2
ISBN 0-312-80867-4 (pbk.) First Edition
Designed by Dennis J. Grasdorf

ACKNOWLEDGMENTS

I am most grateful to these two general libraries for their assistance: the London Library; and the Firestone Library at Princeton University. I am also grateful to these specialized libraries: Office of Population Censuses and Surveys; Morpeth, Northumberland; Kings School, Canterbury; Evangelical Library, London; Science Museum; Imperial College of Science and Technology; Jackson Library, Stanford University; International Labor Office; Royal Institute of British Architects; the Victoria and Albert Museum; Japanese Embassy; Kings College Hospital; LRC Ltd.; National Corporation for the Care of Old People; Geology Museum; and the National Advisory Centre for the Battered Child.

For permission to quote a poem by Boris Pasternak, I am grateful to the translators, Beryl and Joseph Aurak, and to the publishers, Thames and Hudson.

For initial encouragement, I am grateful to the Haimson family; R. L. M.; C. B. Handy; and David Chambers. For specific acts of assistance, I am grateful to N. M. Rowell; P. and R. Aikens; and the Alexander family. I am especially grateful to the Souccar family of Alexandria. For comments and information, I am grateful to Bernard Myers, Peter Evans, David Hoyle, Charles Schulz, and Elliott Morgan.

For general instruction, I wish to thank Husein Chung; and the Zen Center, San Francisco. For instruction in data handling, thanks go to Northern Electric, Montreal.

INTRODUCTION

Two terrible things were happening to me when I was **35**.

When at last I decided to tell my secrets to a friend, all he could say was, "And you're **35**!"

Thirty-five. Really. This made it all ten times worse. Thirty-five. This is the end, isn't it?

Obsessed by being **35**, I tried to look up the facts on age. It is well known that Mozart died at **35**. Didn't a lot of poets die in their **20**s? At **35**, shouldn't you be well ahead in your chosen occupation? On the other hand, isn't there hope—didn't some people start surprisingly late in life?

Previously, on my **30**th birthday, I had felt relief. It was now too late to do all the things that you should have done by the time you are **30**. It was rather like Christmas Eve, and the shops are shut, and it is too late to buy anything more.

But who said you had to do anything by **30**? Did anyone specifically give me instructions, or had these rules seeped into my brain? Answer: the latter. Somehow, we have allowed age rules to affect our lives without being scientific about it. If life can only be lived once, then by the time we know what's happening, it is too late.

This is what started me on the book. I had picked up the message of a certain life pattern, and it had not worked out as it should. The subconscious message had directed me on to this life pattern: decide on a career as early as **18**, when you are choosing a professional education; qualify professionally around **25**; get married and have children. At **40** to **50**, you can expect to be a partner in a reasonably successful professional business. (If you can make it work, quite a nice life, incidentally.)

That's it! That is the life pattern that I have always known I should follow.

What never happened is someone offering me a range of life patterns and allowing me to choose.

So, this is what this book hopes to achieve. Instead of one preferred way of being your age (**15**, **29**, **75**, whatever) I set out how various people have lived at that age. The variation is enormous.

By accumulating this information, the book lets the reader identify the basic life pattern of famous people. I show the turning points in their lives—both the successes and the failures. From this, you can say that X's life pattern was "late flowering," and Y's was "continuous achievement," and so on. Some discussion of these alternative life patterns occurs in short essays throughout the book.

SELECTION AND DATING TECHNIQUES

The original core of the text came from a flash of megalomania, in which all human achievement was divided up into twenty categories, and in each category an elite of twenty was chosen. For each of these resulting four hundred people, a profile was researched to show the shape of their lives—whether they were infant prodigies, late developers, and so forth. A life was written up under one or more key years, each of which made an entry. Obviously, the more important (or attractive) a personality is, the more entries he or she has been given. A "key year" may be the year of their greatest work, or of making a break, or even of disgrace.

As the book progressed, the simplicity of this scheme was eroded. Other names were added, as well as generalizations about aging itself. Now entries appear for one or other of these reasons:

—stories about the key years in the lives of the original four hundred people;

—single events/achievements/publications/etc. that are of great interest but which are not associated with the original four hundred (these are merely listed with no further data about the people involved);

—"moments"—the age of all those involved in a certain event; for example, the end of World War II is shown at the death of Adolf Hitler, **56*** (an asterisk refers to an entry at that age);

—summaries—grouping together similar entries, such as young athletes, gymnasts, at **15***;

—eligibility—these are rules that determine eligibility solely according to age, e.g., voting at **18***;

—general statements about changes in behavior as people become older; for example, in the section *Law, crime* there are statistics about your chances of being a criminal or victim in various age groups.

The main text refers only to individuals. Entries are written in the present tense, to show that "now" is a particular age. Age rules and generalizations about age are written in the past tense where appropriate.

The death of an individual does not rate an entry unless there is an unusual aspect to it; for death at an early age, see *Sport* or *Arts* at **35***. In general, I have avoided material that is already well covered, such as the childhood of famous people.

It would be impossible to include all major figures, however they might be defined. For example, in *Art,* Goya's life has several entries, but there is nothing about El Greco. This is not any comment about the relative merits of these painters. The criterion here is that we include a full range of life or career patterns, even though some leading personalities may be ignored. The book is about Life Patterns, and is not another dictionary of biography.

Any theorizing about this material would be premature, to say the least. If you were not careful, you would soon be speculating about "life." The aim of the book is hypothesis generation, not hypothesis testing. If there is any general approach in the book, it is that (1) any aspect of aging should be seen as having a social cause—not a biological cause—unless proved otherwise; and (2) where aging appears to have a biological cause, it is reversible, unless proved otherwise. Clearly people do grow older, and they/we do die, but the burden of proof must always be on anyone who seeks to make a culture-free generalization about aging.

About dating techniques: Any number in boldface type is an age, for example, **27**. **–1** is about life in the womb, and **0** is about life between birth and the first birthday. α is about immortality and life after death. An age with an asterisk, as mentioned, is a cross-reference to an entry at that age. Age is the difference between the date of birth and the date of the event; but this is not as simple as it looks. The birthdate is not always available, so, for example, medieval architects must be neglected in favor of architects of more modern times. Sometimes people simply keep their age out of public knowledge. Another difficulty is that an event may be more of a process than an action on a particular day. In order to make a fair comparison between ages in different occupations, the following rules have been adopted. In *Architecture,* the date of a building is here assumed to be the date at which construction commences, and where two dates are given (e.g., 1908–12), these represent the beginning and end of construction, with the architect's age being calculated from the first; if only one year is given, that is the best year available. In music, the date used is the date of the first performance unless there is an unusually long gap between composition and performance. In literature, the date of a book is the date of publication unless there has been another long gap between writing and publication. This rule applies to any book in any field. For elective offices, the date is the date of entering office and not the date of the election. In theater, a play is usually dated by its first performance. Films are listed under either the director or the most famous star; the age is calculated from the date of the first screening. Where several people are mentioned in an entry, their ages are all calculated from the date of the main event. Jail sentences are indicated by the age of the inmate at which his term expires; for example, for a convict of **20**, a twenty-year sentence is described as "until **40**." The lives of some U.S. Presidents are described every ten years, beginning at **5** and ending at **65**.

Subtracting one year/month/day from another is a difficult mathematical feat, and it would have made the past few years considerably easier for me if people had been born as early as possible in the year. I am grateful to Paul Revere (b. 1735, Jan. 1) and J. Edgar Hoover (b. 1895, Jan. 1) for their help on this point. Conversely, people such as Henri Matisse (b. 1869, Dec. 31) are uncooperative.

The division of individuals into "music—classical" versus "music—non-classical", is as uncontroversial as possible. People have been placed in the most obvious category. *Renaissance* (or polymath) is the heading for those who have contributed work of a world standard in two or more categories.

The sequence of sections has been governed by the overlaps between them. For example, *Science, technology* is followed by *Money, work* simply because it has sometimes been difficult to decide in which section an individual should be placed.

As a feminist, I have tried to get right the male-female ratio in the choice of subjects presented. Sometimes the facts of historical selection do not allow for a fifty-fifty ratio. Therefore, I keep to the belief that there is not any opposition between the two statements that (1) U.S. presidents have been one hundred percent male so far, and that (2) in our lifetime, that proportion can and should be fifty-fifty male/female. Within each year of age, information is shown under the following headings:

Health (including demographics)
History—World (excluding the U.S.A. and U.K.)
History—U.S.A.
History—U.K.

Religion, philosophy
Social science, education
Science, technology
Money, work
Renaissance (polymaths)
Architecture
Art
Music—classical
Literature
Plays, dance
Films
Music—non-classical (pop, rock, etc.)
TV, etc. (TV and any remaining show business)
Love, life (including sex, scandal, food)
Press
Exploration
Law, crime
Sports

−1

HEALTH

It's thought-provoking to observe that everyone in favor of birth control has already been born. —Norman Shumway (b. 1923), surgeon.

Louise Brown: conception (England, 1977). Her mother Lesley (**29**) has blocked fallopian tubes, and Dr. Patrick Steptoe (**65***) removes the tubes. He later takes an ovum from one of the ovaries and fertilizes it with sperm from father John Brown (**36**). Fertilization takes place in a laboratory dish, and Dr. Robert Edwards (**52**) then places the embryo in the mother's uterus. Louise is born by Caesarian section and weighs 5 pounds 12 ounces. She is the world's first "test tube baby."

The process of human life begins at the meeting of a sperm and an ovum in one of the fallopian tubes. The new organism, or zygote, now makes its way to the uterus.

Each year in England and Wales there are approximately 177,181,200,000,000,000 sperm ejaculated during heterosexual intercourse with women of fertile age; but of these sperm only 569,000 go on to become live births. (Assumptions: 60 million sperm per milliliter; 3 milliliters per ejaculation; 11.06 million females **15–49**; 89 sex acts per year per female.)

Each year in the U.S.A. there are 1,099,440,000,000,000,000 sperm ejaculated during heterosexual intercourse with women of fertile age; but of these sperm, only 3,300,000 go on to become live births. (Assumptions: 180 million sperm per ejaculation; 50.9 million females **14–44**; 120 sex acts per year per female.)

In the U.S.A. in 1978, more than 6,000 conceptions are the result of artificial insemination. The success rate for artificial insemination can be as high as 60 percent.

In London, the rate for providing semen is about £6 ($12) per ejaculation. Human sperm can be stored at low temperatures for later use. Males planning to have a vasectomy can build up a supply previous to surgery and have it stored as insurance. (A cartoon in London's *Private Eye* showed a famous male leaving an artificial insemination donor clinic where he had been "donating"; the caption read: "And I thought signing autographs was hard work.")

Your growth in the womb: During the first six weeks, you are known as an embryo; after that, you become a fetus. After 2 weeks, you are only 2 millimeters wide. After three months, you are 8 to 9 centimeters long and weigh 30 to 60 grams. After six months, you weigh around 800 grams. After seven months, you are about 33 centimeters long and 1,370 to 1,820 grams in weight. After nine months, you are 45 to 60 centimeters in length, and your weight is around 3,200 grams.

Your first movements that your mother could feel used to be known as the "quickening" of the baby—at around 16 to 18 weeks.

As different systems are formed in your body, you are temporarily highly vulnerable to diseases which are otherwise relatively harmless. The obvious example is rubella or German measles; if your mother has this during early pregnancy, you may be born deaf, blind, or have abnormalities of the heart.

About 1 in 5 pregnancies result in a miscarriage.

If a fetus dies in the first 27 weeks, this is a miscarriage, and the body is disposed of by medical staff; if the fetus dies at 28 weeks or later, this is a stillbirth, and the body must be given a proper burial.

In most countries, your health already depends on your social class. For example, 85 percent in the better off social class (U.K., 1975) receive prenatal preparation; but in the lowest social class, the corresponding figure is 21 percent. This is important because "if a mother has not reported her pregnancy by 16 weeks, her baby is five times more likely to die." And a study in Canada showed that "twice as many babies are born dangerously underweight if their mothers do not receive nutrition counseling until the 30th week than if counseling begins before the 20th week." And researchers Zigler and Hunsinger report in the U.S.A. that "over 30 percent of pregnant women receive no prenatal care during the first trimester."

It is better if your mother:

—is already linked to a prenatal health program;
—is a nonsmoker;
—is married;
—has not had 3+ abortions;
—is otherwise a healthy person;
—is average weight;
—takes no alcohol;
—is not diabetic;
—has not had a handicapped child;
—is on a diet which does not lack vitamins;
—has not had more than 2 children.

Your mother's drug-taking during pregnancy can have an effect on you for the rest of your life. Two extreme examples are (1) thalidomide; and (2) DES (diethylstilbestrol) in which females later are liable to cancer of the vagina, and males to sterility and cancer of the testicles.

AGE —1 YRS

In England and Wales (1977), there were 131,000 legal abortions and 545,400 live births.

Worldwide, 1 in 4 conceptions ends in abortion. In the U.S.A., out of every 3.8 conceptions, 1 is aborted; there are about 1.25 million abortions per year. Abortion rates vary widely from country to country: in East and West Germany 25 percent of all pregnancies are terminated; in France, it's 50 percent. In the U.S.S.R., Japan, and Italy more than half of all pregnancies end in abortion. And in some Latin American countries, there are twice as many abortions as births.

Aborted fetuses are nearly always aged three months or younger (around 89 percent); about 10 percent are in the second trimester; and 1 percent are in the third trimester. The typical abortion is by vacuum aspiration and takes around 5 minutes.

The average woman in the U.S.S.R. has six to eight abortions in her lifetime. It is not unknown for a woman to have fifteen abortions.

In cows, fertilized eggs are routinely taken from the mother, perhaps kept frozen at –196° centigrade, and later implanted in other cows. The same also happens with sheep. By the use of drugs, the mother is stimulated into superovulation, producing 8 to 12 eggs at one time. The success rate for each of these when reimplanted in a "host mother" is 40 to 59 percent. The deep-frozen embryos can be sold at auction, and the farmer buys them for implantation in his own cows.

The advantage of artificial insemination in animals is that use of the best bull can result in much higher productivity in the offspring—50 to 100 gallons more milk per lactation. In Ireland, the champion bull Bendalls Adema sired 212,000 offspring before his death at **14** (1978). The quality of his output was so great that farmers kept coming back for more semen. After his death, his stored semen continues to be available until stocks are exhausted.

The gestation period of an elephant is just under two years. A calf weighs 180 to 250 pounds at birth; it can stand almost immediately and walk or eat within an hour.

The gestation period of the common dolphin is 11 months; the killer whale, 11 to 12 months; common pilot whale, 15 to 16 months; and the sperm whale, 16 to 17 months.

The Repository for Germinal Choice is a California scheme by which potential mothers can have a supply of sperm produced by one of a panel of Nobel Prize winners. The first announced donor is William Shockley (**70**, in 1980), inventor of the transistor. Upon award of the Nobel Prize, males will be invited by the project chief, Robert Graham (**74**), to serve on the panel.

HISTORY—WORLD

Alexander the Great (b. 356 B.C.): his mother dreams of a thunderbolt falling on her and flames coming out of her. His father dreams that the new child shall be as strong as a lion. On the day of birth, an eastern temple is burned, and one of his father's generals wins a battle. These omens are clear to everyone: the baby will later win many battles in the east—which he does, from **20*** onward.

Nero, in 37 A.D.: his mother Agrippina (**20**) consults an astrologer about her fetus. The prophecy is that it will be a boy who will become Emperor but murder his mother. Agrippina, who is ambitious, replies: "Let him murder his mother but be Emperor!" Later, as a child, Nero hears another prophecy: a teacher tells him, "Your destiny is written in the skies." Nero goes on to become Emperor at **16** and does kill his mother at **21**. He commits suicide at **30***.

The future King Louis XIV of France, in 1638: his mother feels him kicking inside her for the first time, and a large fireworks display is immediately held in celebration. When he is born, free wine is dispensed from a city fountain. When he is two days old, members of Parlement come to pay their respects, and he is attended by seventeen personal servants. At **4***, his mother (**42**) kneels before him as he becomes King upon the death of his father (**42**).

HISTORY—U.S.A.

Human life shall be deemed to exist from conception.—Senator Jesse Helms (**59**) and Congressman H. J. Hyde (**56**) in 1981.

An angel flies into the room of Mary and tells her that she is pregnant with a child conceived by the spirit of God. The baby will be named Jesus. The angel says, "Hail thou that art highly favored, the Lord is with thee; blessed art thou among women. Fear not, Mary, for thou hast found favor with God . . ." Mary replies, "Behold the handmaid of the Lord; be it unto me according to thy word." (cf. **0***)

According to religious thinkers of the Renaissance, Mary received the news of her pregnancy with five successive emotions: (1) Disquiet (she was "troubled"); (2) reflection and prudence; (3) inquiry (how has this happened?); (4) submission (accepting the will of God); (5) merit—the very fact of being pregnant and being a mother.

You are already subject to Original Sin; this started at the Fall, with Adam and Eve, and it enters the new person during the act of sexual intercourse (early Christian teaching onward.) Only Jesus Christ and Mary were conceived without sin.

When does the soul enter the body? Aristotle believed that the potential soul entered the embryo with the semen, though he was later wrongly associated with the view that the soul entered at the fortieth day. According to Aristotle, the father contributes form, soul, and the higher order faculties to the fetus, conveyed through the semen; the mother contributes the material part of the fetus. The sex of the baby is a result of a battle between these two forces.

Another view: the soul that enters your body has come from another person. In a previous life, you were another person. You are now being reborn. Previously, you could even have been an animal (e.g., in Hindu philosophy).

Aphrodite was the Greek goddess of fertility.

To attack unborn life at any moment from its conception is to undermine the whole moral order which is the true guardian of the well-being of man. —Pope John Paul II (**59**, in 1979).

SCIENCE, TECHNOLOGY

Isaac Newton (b. 1642): his illiterate father (**36**) dies 2 months before Isaac's premature birth. At **3**, his mother (c. **30**) marries the Rev. Barnabas Smith (**63**), and she leaves Isaac to grow up with his grandparents until Smith dies when Isaac is **11**. He leaves school at **15** to work on the family farm, but returns to school at **17** and attends university from **18** to **22**. Because of a plague there, he returns home, and then, away from any intellectual equal, he creates a revolution in thought at **23***.

ARCHITECTURE

Frank Lloyd Wright, in 1869: his pregnant mother (c. **28**) takes ten engravings of old cathedrals and hangs them in the room that she is preparing for her baby. She has decided that this person will become an architect. Wright, in his late teens, goes to Chicago to train as an architect, and at **20** enters the office of Louis Sullivan (**33**). Wright marries his wife Catherine (**17**) that same year. His "Prairie Houses" are at **31*** onward.

MUSIC—CLASSICAL

Wolfgang Amadeus Mozart: his father Leopold (**37**) is writing a textbook on playing the violin. (Mozart is born January 27, 1756, and he is the seventh and last child, though only he and an elder sister survive into adult life.) (cf. **5***)

Percy Grainger (b. 1882): his mother looks at a Greek statue every night during pregnancy, so that her forthcoming baby will care for beauty. She is his piano teacher until he is **10**. At **25**, he is chosen by Grieg (**64**) to be the soloist in a performance of Grieg's Piano Concerto in A Minor.

LITERATURE

Our birth is but a sleep and a forgetting;
The soul that rises with us, our life's star,
  Hath had elsewhere its setting
  And cometh from afar;
  Hence, in a season of calm weather
  Though inland far we be,
Our souls have sight of that immortal sea
  Which brought us hither,
  Can in a moment travel thither,
And see the children sport upon the shore,
And hear its mighty waters rolling evermore.
—William Wordsworth, Ode (Intimations of
Immortality from Recollections of Early Childhood)

PLAYS, DANCE

Ben Jonson, in c. 1573: his father dies one month before the baby is born. Jonson has a confused upbringing and never goes to university. In his late teens, he takes part in military action in Europe and returns to London at **19**. At **22**, he joins the theater, and the breakthrough in his career is at **25***.

"The character of a child is already plain even in its mother's womb. Before I was born, my mother was in great agony of spirit and in a tragic situation. She could take no food except iced oysters and iced champagne. If people ask me when I began to dance, I reply, 'In my mother's womb, probably as the result of the oysters and champagne—the food of Aphrodite.' "—Isadora Duncan (b. 1878, San Francisco). She is quickly recognized as a deeply talented dancer and starts giving classes at **14**. She goes to Europe at **21**, and establishes herself as a performer. At **26**, she goes to Greece where she forms her artistic personality; she finds her sense of connection to the early civilization there, with its clothes and drama. Duncan becomes famous for her dancing and her dance schools; she also exemplifies the new "free spirit" approach to love and marriage. She dies at **49**, strangled by her own scarf which becomes caught in the wheel of her car. A few weeks earlier, she had completed her frank memoirs, *My Life.*

LOVE, LIFE

At the sixth week, gonads appear, but with no sense of their future as male or female. At the seventh week, it would be impossible to tell the difference between male and female fetuses. If male, testes appear at eight weeks onward, and if female, ovaries develop from the twelfth week onward.

In Tudor times, bonfires were often lit to celebrate the knowledge of a pregnancy in a rich family.

In Japan, a woman in the seventh month of pregnancy may wear a cotton abdomen band, the *iwata-obi,* and a small celebration is held when she begins to wear this.

The fetus's bones come from the father's sperm, and the flesh comes from the mother. Sperm flows from the marrow of the father's spine (ancient Egyptian belief).

LAW, CRIME

Lee Harvey Oswald, in 1939: two months before his birth, his father dies. Oswald has a stepfather between **5** and **8**. At **16** he leaves school and joins the Marine Corps. Coincidentally, his later killer, Jack Ruby, spends much of his childhood with foster parents, as his natural parents are separated. (cf. **24***)

Lee Kehos is injured during a road accident (Australia, 1972): owing to a lung injury suffered by his mother, there is a temporary loss of oxygen which results in his brain being permanently damaged. At **7**, after much legal argument as to his right to sue—the injury having taken place *before* his birth, before he would have become a person within normal legal assumptions—he is awarded $160,000 damages.

If a pregnant woman was condemned to be hanged in England (eighteenth century and earlier), the sentence would be postponed if she was 4½ months or more pregnant. But she would be hanged after the birth.

A disproportionately high amount of wife battering occurs to women who are pregnant.

The Justinian Code of the sixth century forbade abortions after the fortieth day, as the soul would then have entered the fetus.

In Britain, abortion was illegal after the "quickening." An Act of 1929 set 28 weeks as the last moment for an abortion.

Killing a viable fetus (after 28 weeks) is the crime of "child destruction," killing a person **0** to **2** is "infanticide," and killing a person **2+** is "murder."

The World Health Organization recommends an upper limit for abortions of 24 weeks.

0

HEALTH

Florence Nightingale (b. 1820): her mother (**32**) and father (**26**) give her the name Florence after the city in which she is born. He elder sister (**1**) had been born in Naples ("Parthenope" in Greek) and was thus named Parthenope Nightingale. In practice, the girls are called Flo and Pop. (cf. **16*** and **90***)

On average in England and Wales, there are 1,558 births per day.

Life expectancy in U.K. is now **69.5** (male) and **75.7** (female).

There are about 12 live births per year per 1,000 population. In Britain 13 percent of all live births occur to mothers born outside the U.K.; 8 percent of mothers (England and Wales, 1977) were themselves born in "NCWP," the new Commonwealth or Pakistan.

There are about 10.4 stillbirths per 1,000 live and stillbirths. For every 1,000 live births, there are 10.8 deaths within 4 weeks; and 15.9 total deaths in the first year; and .12 deaths of mothers (England and Wales).

About 9,000 people are born every day in the U.S.A. (1978).

The average citizen of the U.S.A. can now expect to live until **73.8**. More detailed figures are: white females, until **78.3**; all other females, until **74.5**; white males, until **70.6**; and all other males, until **65.5** (1979).

Out of 1,000 live births, c. 13.6 die before **1**, including 9.4 within the first 4 weeks. Out of 1,000 live births, there are only .09 maternal deaths (U.S.A., 1978). For comparison, the infant mortality rate in 1950 was 29.2 deaths per 1,000 live births.

The median live birth weight is 7 pounds 6 ounces (U.S.A., 1976).

In the U.S.A. (1976), nonwhite births are 18.9 percent of the total. Here are three comparisons of the differences between blacks and whites in the U.S.A.: Seventeen percent of white fetuses are aborted; the comparable figure for blacks is 25 percent (1974). The infant death rate (1976) was 15.2 for all races, but it was 13.3 for whites and 23.5 for blacks. Life expectancy at birth (1976) is **69** for males of all races, but black males can expect to live only until **64.1**.

Thirty-nine out of 40 babies are born without malformations. There are approximately 1.4 children born with Down's syndrome (mongolism) per 1,000 live births (England and Wales, 1971). The prevalence of severely mentally handicapped people is 100 per 100,000 of population **0** to **14**.

Depending on the hospital, a number of those born severely handicapped are "allowed" to die.

"It may be more important for a baby to have expert medical care during its first five or ten minutes of independent life than during the next 30 years," says the London-based Spastics Society. A campaign in France to reduce damage to health was partly based on the investment calculation that it was cheaper to provide elaborate prenatal and natal care than it would be to look after people who had been handicapped at birth. The cost of caring for one severely handicapped person during adult life, **16** to **65**, could be over $500,000.

In Britain and in the U.S.A., the higher your social class, the greater your chances now of survival. The perinatal death rate (England and Wales, 1970–72) was 32.1 for the lowest class versus 16.3 for the highest class. Also, the higher the social class, the less your chances of being born underweight. This is important because 45 percent of all cerebral palsy is associated with prematurity.

After one minute, your health is scored according to the Apgar Rating, which notes five factors: heart rate, respiratory effort, muscle tone, reflex irritability, and color.

Your heart beats per minute: during crying, 218; during sleep, 124. You sleep 18 hours per day.

Brain growth is the greatest ever between 3 and 11 weeks after birth.

Twins, etc.: 9.7 percent of all live births are multiple births. If your mother is under **20**, the rate is 5.5 percent; it rises to a maximum of 13.6 percent if she is **35** to **39**.

About 18 percent of births in the U.S.A. are by Caesarian section.

In the entire world (1977), there are about 350,000 births per day. The total population is about 4,124 million, and the growth rate is 1.9 percent per year.

Countries with a very high birth rate (1977) include Zambia, with 51.5 births per 1,000 population; Mali, 50.1; Angola, 49.9; and Ethiopia, with 49.4. Countries which have an unusually low birth rate in-

10 clude the U.S.S.R., 18; Japan, 16.3; the U.S.A., 14.7; the U.K., 11.6; Switzerland, 11.5; and West Germany, 9.5.

Mexico: in 1975 the birth rate was 42 births per 1,000 population. By 1979 this was believed to have dropped to 33 to 35.

In Bangladesh, there are 17.7 deaths of mothers per 1,000 births. The comparable figure in the West is about .1 maternal deaths per 1,000 births.

In France strenuous efforts are made to encourage large families. At the birth of the third child, the family is given "La Carte de Famille Nombreuse," which entitles them to many benefits. Mothers of 10 children are awarded the Gold Medal of the French Family. The worry of the "natalistes" is that France is not reproducing itself, since the average couple has only 1.8 children.

In China, the ideal family (1980) has only 1 child, since population has been increasing 1.4 percent per year. Parents have to obtain permission in order to have a second child. A third child results in significant loss of privileges and earnings. In the cities the minimum age for marriage is **27** (male) and **25** (female). And if the parents make a contract to have only 1 child, they receive extra earnings.

According to Plutarch, newborn Spartans would be examined by tribal elders to see if the infant was healthy. Sturdy infants would be returned to the parents for rearing. Sickly infants would be placed at the foot of Mount Taygetus to die from exposure. Killing off unwanted or sick babies was a normal practice in classical times. Unwanted babies in Imperial China were left outside on the doorstep at night, and a routine patrol carried them away for burial. In Paris (1758), 5,082 babies were left on doorsteps as foundlings, according to Jean-Jacques Rousseau (**46**).

Death rates for children are now given as per 1,000 births, but in the early days they were given as percentages since the numbers were so great. Rearranging data of 1829 and 1917, here are death rates for children in London who died before **5**:

1730–1749:	745	deaths	per	1,000 births
1770–1789:	515	"	"	"
1810–1829:	318	"	"	"
1911–1915:	168	"	"	"

It should be noted that these figures are for London, which in the eighteenth century was one of the most unhealthy places in England. The astronomic and unbelievable figures for that time are outside our experience, and can never be checked. Baby deaths were then so taken for granted that there would have been a great deal of underreporting. Stillbirths were not recorded, and babies who breathed a little before dying were often classified as stillborn to save on burial fees. Even the great Victorian William Farr, in his first report, had only one page on births, as opposed to 60 pages on deaths.

The future Japanese Admiral Yamamoto (b. 1885) is given the name Isoroku ("56") because his father is now aged **56**. Yamamoto launches the attack on Pearl Harbor (1941) when he is **56***.

Royalty and birth:

—Males born on the same day as the heir to the Pharaoh of Egypt would be taken away and educated with the heir.

—In the Ottoman Empire all boys born in the same year as the heir would later have their circumcision on the same day, at c. **7**.

—At the birth of a possible heir to the throne, it was essential that officials watched the moment of birth so that they could later confirm that there has been a true inherited line of descent. For example, the birth of Louis XVI (1754) was witnessed by the Chancellor and Keeper of the Seals of France.

—Queen Elizabeth II of England celebrates three birthdays per year, even though she was born on only one day in 1926! Her birthdays are (1) her chronological birthday in April; (2) her official birthday, at which she attends military ceremonies, in June; and (3) The Civil Service's Queen's Birthday holiday, in the spring. Another memento of the Queen's age is that on each Maundy Thursday gifts are given to pensioners, and the number of these recipients is equal to the number of years the Queen has lived.

HISTORY—U.S.A.

Calvin Coolidge is born on Independence Day, 1872. He goes on to become President at **51**. Coolidge makes his national reputation at **47**, when as Governor of Massachusetts he denies the right of public sector workers to take part in a strike. About Coolidge's infancy, Alice Roosevelt Longworth later comments that he looks as if "he had been weaned on a pickle." And when told of his death, several people are believed to have asked, "How could they tell?"

Nelson Rockefeller (b. 1908) is born on the sixty-ninth birthday of his grandfather, John D. Rockefeller, then the richest man in the world. At **15**, Nelson Rockefeller shoots himself in the leg with an air pistol while practicing a cowboy's "fast draw." At **20**, he visits Versailles, which his family is paying to be restored. After working for the family business at Rockefeller Center, he becomes Assistant Secretary of State at **36**, Governor of New York at **50**, and Vice-President at **66**.

Lyndon B. Johnson is born on August 27, 1908, in a small cabin in Texas. His mother writes: "Now the light came in from the east, bringing a deep stillness, a stillness so profound and so pervasive that it seemed as if the earth itself were listening. And then came a sharp, compelling cry—the most awesome, happiest sound known to human ears—the cry of a newborn baby; the first child of Sam Ealy and Rebekah Johnson was 'discovering America.' " (cf. **5***)

HISTORY—U.K.

You are an Englishman. That means you have drawn first prize in the lottery of life. —Cecil Rhodes (1853–1902).

Birth order, and succession as King or Queen: the succession to the throne goes to

[1] the sovereign's eldest surviving boy, and then to his male and female children;
[2] the next eldest surviving boy(s);
[3] the eldest surviving daughter(s);
[4] the brothers, and then the sisters, of the current sovereign.

The birth order of some kings and queens:

—*Only child:* Victoria (1819)
—*Only son:* Henry VI (1421), Henry VII (1457)
—*Elder or eldest son, or eldest son to survive childhood:* Henry III (1207), Edward I (1239), Edward III (1312), Henry IV (1367), Henry V (1387), Edward IV (1442), Edward V (1470), Edward VI (1537)
—*First daughter:* Mary I (1515), Elizabeth II (1926)
—*Second daughter, preceded by elder stepsister and younger brother:* Elizabeth I (1558)
—*Second sons:* Richard II (1367), Charles I (1600), Charles II (1630)
—*Third son:* Richard I (1157)
—*Fourth sons:* Henry I (1068), Edward II (1284)
—*Eleventh child out of twelve:* Richard III (1452)

The birth order of some British Prime Ministers:

—*Only child:* Ramsay MacDonald (b. 1866—unmarried parents), Stanley Baldwin (1867)
—*Elder or eldest son:* Lord Palmerston (1784—out of five), A. J. Balfour (1848), Winston Churchill (1874—one younger brother), Alec Douglas-Home (1903), Edward Heath (1916—one younger brother)
—*Second child, first boy:* Benjamin Disraeli (1804), David Lloyd George (1863—second child, but the *heir,* underlined by his family), James Callaghan (1912)
—*Second son:* William Pitt the Elder (1708), William Pitt the Younger (1759), Sir Henry Campbell-Bannerman (1836), H. H. Asquith (1852), Neville Chamberlain (1869), Harold Macmillan (1894), Anthony Eden (1897)

—*Younger of two daughters:* Margaret Thatcher (1925)
—*Other:* Sir Robert Walpole (1676) is fifth child and third son out of nineteen children; Lord John Russell (1792) is third son; Duke of Wellington (1769) is the fourth son; Clement Atlee (1883) is fourth son and seventh child out of eight; William Gladstone (1809) is fifth child out of six and the youngest son—but gradually becomes "the" son, as the elder brothers were not able enough to fulfill their father's ambition for them.

William the Conqueror (1027), Keir Hardie (1856), Ramsay MacDonald (1866) and Ernest Bevin (1881) are born to unmarried parents.

Ethelred the Unready is said to have urinated in his baptismal font (c. 968), thus foreshadowing an unsuccessful reign. This turns out to be true, because as King (from **10** onward) he has to pay tribute to the invading Danes—Danegeld.

Mary Queen of Scots: her father dies one week after her birth (1542, Dec. 7/8), and she becomes the sovereign. Her coronation ceremony is held at **9 months**. (cf. **5***)

Enoch Powell—an only child—later writes at **25**:

Mother, with longing ever new
  And joy too great for telling,
I turn again to rest in you
  My earliest dwelling. (cf **3***)

Margaret Thatcher is born (1925, Oct. 13) over the corner shop where her father (**32**) sells groceries and is a sub-postmaster. She is the second daughter, and later goes to Kesteven and Grantham Girls School, and to Oxford University. (cf. **21***)

Elizabeth II (b. 1926) is born by Caesarian section.

Charles Philip Arthur George (b. 1948) at birth receives the titles of Prince Charles, Duke of Cornwall, Earl of Chester, Duke of Rothesay, Earl of Carrick, Baron of Renfrew, Lord of the Isles, and Great Steward of Scotland. At **32,** he marries Lady Diana Spencer (**20**).

RELIGION, PHILOSOPHY

Athena is not born but springs from the head of Zeus; she is already fully armed, ready for her duties as Goddess of War.

After being born, Jesus is placed in a stable. As he is lying there, angels tell shepherds out in the fields to visit the baby and to worship him. Also, three wise men follow a bright star, and it leads them to Jesus, whom they worship. At **8 days**, Jesus is taken to the temple to be circumcised. An old man, Simeon, has been waiting for this moment; the new baby, he says, is a gift from God. Simeon's last ambition before dying is to see this baby, who is God's saving light for the whole world. Simeon is now ready to die, because he has seen the "light to lighten the Gentiles, and the glory of thy people Israel." (cf. **12***)

Buddha: at **5 days**, eight learned men examine the baby Prince Siddhartha, and they pronounce that he will become a Buddha. At **7 days**, Buddha's mother dies, and his aunt becomes his foster-mother. (cf. **2***)

Baptism of infants was a novelty introduced by St. Augustine (345–430 A.D.) who promoted the idea that you come into the world with Original Sin; therefore, without baptism, an infant who died would go to Hell. Previously, baptism had been for adults and was more of a "conversion experience." "Godparents" now promise that you will learn the details of religion as you grow up. Since the health of the newborns was often precarious, baptism took place as quickly as possible; the parish priest might come to your house late at night to make certain that no baby would die unbaptized.

Women in labor in ancient Egypt were protected by the god Bes.

Newborn children in ancient Rome were briefly placed on the ground, signifying the connection with the earth goddess, mother earth.

In astrology, your destiny is set by your "nativity"—the position of powerful planets at the moment of your birth. Until the seventeenth century, astrology was a serious science, corresponding to our psychology and even influencing public policymaking. Planets were God-made intermediaries between men and God. They influenced the four major constituents of the body. Your "nativity" does not fix your life, but it forever decides the best and worst times for you to take action.

Eligibility: Jewish males must undergo the ceremony of circumcision as a mark of the covenant between you and God.

Your afterbirth and umbilical cord may be used as important elements in religious or magical ceremonies. The place of its burial may be important. Your mother may have to be "churched" on reentry into the community after delivery.

SOCIAL SCIENCE, EDUCATION

Herbert Spencer (b. 1820) is one out of nine children, but he is the only one to survive to adult life. Later, he is an apostle of "survival of the fittest." (cf. **44***)

Adam Smith (b. 1723) and J. M. Keynes (b. 1883) are both born on June 5. Both publish their major works at **52***.

The baby's mind is a "tabula rasa," waiting for experiences to make their mark on its unblemished surface, according to John Locke (1632–1704).

The practice of noting birth dates is comparatively recent. We can assume that the first step was simply to record your place in the family. Noting dates of birth in Britain was uncommon until perhaps the nineteenth century. (It is not unusual for prominent figures in the Dictionary of National Biography to have only their date of baptism.) The reasons for recording genealogies and birth order, and later dates of birth include:

—inheritance of land, titles, or money;
—military—to list men of fighting ability;
—the development of Church administration at the end of feudalism;
—the promotion of insurance schemes in the eighteenth century;
—the Victorian interest in public health.

A possible scheme of stages in the growth in recording dates of birth: (1) the most simple method is to know only the birth order of siblings; (2) if the society has a method of naming a year, then you might know which year you were born in—you might think of everyone born in that year as members of a group, analogous to a class in a university (cf. Greece, **18***); (3) the children of the elite have their births recorded; (4) religious groups first record dates of baptism, and later the date of birth, but only for their members; (5) the national administration records the date of each birth.

The pioneer population statistics come from Scandinavia. For example, the first Norwegian figures relate to 1664–66, with a census in 1769. Other first national censuses were in the U.S.A., 1791; in England, 1801; in Ireland, 1813.

Much earlier, the registration of births and deaths had begun in parishes. The earliest full records are Spanish, from 1570 onward, with one parish register dating from 1394. In England, parish registers of birth, marriage, and death were directed in 1538, but this took decades to be implemented. Records on parchment were mandatory from 1598 onward. But dates of birth were not recorded by the state for the whole population until the Registration Act (1836).

For the elite, genealogies were of course started centuries and even millennia ago; the European royal families; or Abraham, in the Old Testament, at about 1300 B.C.; or the king lists of Egypt and Mesopotamia.

In 1639, the Massachusetts Bay Colony decided that statistics of birth, marriage, and death should be recorded, but this was inadequately performed. By 1833, only 6 percent of the U.S. population "had formal systems for routine registration of births and deaths" (according to demographer P. S. Lawrence).

The first two British censuses (1801 and 1811) had no columns to record the age of the people. An optional question on age was introduced in 1831. It was not until the 1851 census that everyone had to list his or her precise age. This showed, incidentally, that the mean age of the population was **26** for males, and **26.8** for females. Early "Bills of Mortality" (London, 1699) recorded the names of those who died; sex was always recorded and often the occupation of the person, but not the age.

Many African countries in the 1980s avoid taking a complete census. They are inhibited either by difficulties over cost and technique, or by fear of the results, for example, facts on excessive population growth. Also, by providing statistics about the relative numerical strength of tribes or ethnic groups, an accurate census may well upset a balance of power.

In China, your age was not counted from your birthday; instead, it was the number of calendar years in which you had lived. If you were born on the last day of the year, you were therefore the same age as someone born on the first day. Also, you were a year older than a person born on the first day of the following year.

The old custom in Japan was that you were **1** at birth. At your first birthday, you became **2**.

An interest in birth order and its effect on personality was a specialty of Alfred Adler (1870–1937). Put simply, as you grow up with a particular place in the hierarchy of that mini-society—your family—so later you will be more at ease if your adult relationships mimic this hierarchy; for example, the firstborn later becomes the boss.

SCIENCE, TECHNOLOGY

Genius-level creativity has typically been examined within the following causal models:

—inheritance of genes and genius, an approach associated with Francis Galton (1822–1911) and his book of 1869 *Hereditary Genius*;

—birth order within the siblings, certain positions being more likely to produce a stimulus to innovation and leadership;

—psychoanalytic forces—the love (or otherwise) received from father and mother;

—deprivation of parent(s) in early childhood, e.g., by death;

—early isolation, which may lead to daydreaming about basic questions concerning the world;

—benefitting from an affectionate and inspiring teacher;

—simply having a bigger brain; postmortems were sometimes performed on dead scientists to see if their brains were physically different from average; this happened to the body of Johann Gauss (1777–1855), German astronomer and mathematician. The brain weighed an unremarkable 1,410 grams, and is still preserved at Göttingen.

. . . today, only 9 percent of the very rich came from the bottom; only 23 percent are from middle-class origin; 68 percent came from the upper classes—C. Wright Mills, 1956.

Josiah Wedgwood (b. 1730) is the youngest of thirteen children (cf. **28***). Richard Arkwright (b. 1732) is also the youngest of 13 children (cf. **36***). Jean Paul Getty (b. 1892) is an only child (cf. **11***).

Laws on primogeniture were abolished in the U.S. through the initiative of President Thomas Jefferson (**57**); previously, primogeniture lead to the larger part of the parents' estate going inevitably to the older (male) child.

Depending on the society into which you have been born, your position for the rest of your life is influenced by your parents' status now when you are **0**. In the extreme case, your position may already be permanently determined at **0**, irrespective of almost any action that you may later take. Until comparatively recently, this may well have been the norm, and our assumption that we have a right to try for any position in society is new and surprising. Even today, people are born into the Harijans, the former untouchable caste in India, and this powerfully affects the rest of their lives. We in the West are shocked that a society continues to tolerate such a rigid form of tracking or streaming, whereby almost all opportunities for advancement are closed.

AGE 0 YRS

When a society is formally committed to abolishing favors inherited at **0**, there are often moments later in life at which you have a chance to enter a lifelong elite. In practice, there are moments at which you may join a class or group whose membership almost guarantees you a good status for the rest of your life. So, if you gain entry into Harvard, this is likely to be of permanent assistance to you. It is possible to trace the age at which these opportunities occur, when the gates shut against the majority, while only a tiny group takes a rapid trip upward. Where it is possible to see the moment at which entry to the elite is closing, then tremendous tension surrounds the process of selection. In France or Japan, where entry at **18/19** to the elite university-level institutions almost guarantees a life of success, poor performance at examinations is treated as a life-threatening event. Suicide is not unknown among Japanese students who fail to live up to their ambitions. In Britain, an elite life is believed to be the typical result after attendance at the right fee-paid schools, where entry is at **13**. Eighty percent of judges, 69 percent of a Conservative cabinet, and 68 percent of top civil servants were educated in these enclaves. Great controversy surrounds these schools, as it seems unfair to have such a powerful streaming effect at **13**.

18 In the U.S.A., "class, race, and sex are the most important factors in determining a child's future," according to author Richard de Lone. Comparing two children at **9** whose parents are at the top of the professional structure or at the bottom of the working class, de Lone asserts that one is four times more likely to enter college, twelve times more likely to complete college, and twenty-seven times more likely to end up in the top 10 percent income bracket. The weapons of a meritocratic society surprisingly perpetuate the inheritance of favorable positions in society. For example, SAT scores, used objectively for selection by universities, correlate with parents' income. Children from rich families tend to have better scores than those from poor families. According to de Lone, the fault lies less with the individual and his or her schooling, than with the overall outline of society, a pyramid. Even if access to the top is genuinely open to all classes, the shape of the society is still a pyramid. The very existence of a small number of privileged positions at the top of the pyramid necessarily leads to a vast number of unfulfilled people at the bottom.

RENAISSANCE

Benjamin Franklin (b. 1706): he is the youngest son of the youngest son, going back five generations. Born in Boston, he has to leave school at **10** to work in his father's soap business. At **12** he is apprenticed to a printer, and he works in London as a printer from **18** to **20**. After working in Philadelphia, he becomes owner of *The Pennsylvania Gazette* at **24**. From **26** onward he begins to acquire a reputation with his *Poor Richard's Almanack,* which runs until he is **51**. The first half of his life is spent developing his printing business and his writing skills; he uses his own need for education as the generator of his writing, so that both he and his readers are engaged in self-improvement. At **42**, he semiretires from the business and concentrates on his scientific interests—his famous kite experiment is at **46***.

ART

Salvador Dali (b. 1904): he is named after a late brother who died at **5**. Dali's parents are confused about their two sons and regard them as alternative versions of the same person. Dali later explains: "We'd be walking along the street, for example, and they would say to me, 'The other one sneezed when he passed by here; be careful.' " Not surprisingly, Dali later becomes a surrealist. His melted watches feature in his painting "The Persistence of Memory" at **27**; his powerful "The Crucifixion of St. John of the Cross" is at **47**.

MUSIC—CLASSICAL

Johann Sebastian Bach (b. 1685, March 21) is the eighth and last child. His father is **40**. (cf. **9***)

Ludwig van Beethoven (b. 1770, Dec. 16) is the second, but first surviving child, and he has a younger brother, Johann. (cf. **11***)

Franz Schubert (b. 1797, Jan. 31) is the thirteenth child out of fourteen. Only five survive into adult life. (cf. **18***)

Johannes Brahms (b. 1833, May 7): his mother Christiane is **43**, and his father is **27**. Christiane Brahms has her last baby at **46** and lives till **75**. (cf. **20***)

Benjamin Britten (b. 1913) is born on St. Cecilia's Day, the patron saint of music. (cf. **22***)

According to Dr. Michele Clements, newborn babies find pleasure in the music of Vivaldi and Mozart, but are indifferent to Beethoven, sleeping through recordings of his music. (This was learned in experiments done in 1977 at the Whittington Hospital, London, in tests to search out deafness as early as possible.)

LITERATURE

Honoré de Balzac (b. 1799) is wet-nursed by a policeman's wife. At **8**, he is sent away to boarding school and later complains that his parents never visited him between **8** and **15**. (cf. **20***)

Thomas Hardy (b. 1840) is put aside as being stillborn, until the nurse sees him move. (cf. **25***)

Scott Fitzgerald (b. 1896) is given the first names Francis Scott Key after a great-great-great-uncle who wrote "The Star-Spangled Banner." But his father is a salesman in the Midwest grocery trade. (cf. **18***)

Dylan Thomas (b. 1914, Oct. 27) is given the middle name of Marlais after a great-uncle who had been a poet and a bard. (cf. **19***)

PLAYS, DANCE

When the first baby laughed for the first time, the laugh broke into a thousand pieces and they all went skipping about, and that was the beginning of fairies.—J. M. Barrie (1860–1937) in *Peter Pan,* written at **44***.

August Strindberg (b. 1849) later writes: "My parents did not want me, and therefore I was born without a will of my own." He has an unpleasant and confused childhood. His father (**37**) is middle-class and his mother (**25**) is working-class at a time when these distinctions are crucial. From his birth onward, Strindberg seems doomed to be unhappy. At **13**, his mother dies, and his father quickly marries their housekeeper; Strindberg hates his new stepmother. After an erratic time in his **teens** and **20s**, Strindberg becomes a public figure with a novel at **30***.

Eugene O'Neill (b. 1888) weighs eleven pounds at birth. He later writes: "It was a great mistake my being born a man. I would have been more successful as a seagull or a fish." During his childhood, he spends nine months every year on theater tours with his family. His father is successful in only one role, the Count of Monte Cristo, and he is forced to play this role for twenty-five years. His mother is a drug addict. Appropriately, O'Neill is born at the location of the future Times Square, New York. O'Neill loses his virginity at **17** when his brother **(27)** forces him to come along to a brothel. At **18** O'Neill enters Princeton University; at **19** he is made to leave because of his poor grades and poor behavior. At **21** he goes on a long sea voyage to Buenos Aires; he obtains employment there with the Singer Sewing Machine Company, breaking up old machines with a sledgehammer. At **23**, he makes a suicide attempt. At **24**, he works for a few months as a cub reporter but has to enter a tuberculosis clinic. There, he reads Strindberg and starts writing plays. (cf. **25***)

Actors in Japanese Kabuki theater are selected only from males born into the existing Kabuki families, which go back to the origins of this art form.

FILMS

Lon Chaney (b. 1886): parents are deaf and mute.

Irving Thalberg (b. 1889) is born a blue baby, and his parents are told that his congenital defect will cause an early death. In his teens he is affected by asthma. At **19** he gets a job as a secretary at Universal Pictures, thanks to the help of Carl Laemmle **(51)**. Thalberg impresses Laemmle, who had also wished for a youthful success, since eight of his brothers and sisters had died in a scarlet fever epidemic. At **20** Thalberg is studio manager in Hollywood and represents Laemmle who stays in New York. At **22** Thalberg orders retakes on *The Hunchback of Notre Dame*; he calls back the company after shooting has been completed. He thus establishes his own method of working. At **23** he meets Louis B. Mayer **(37)**, and at **24** Thalberg becomes general manager of MGM. At **28** he marries, and the couple live in his mother's house. At MGM he produces one feature film per week, at the height of the star system. He dies at **37** of pneumonia. At the hour of his funeral, there is five minutes of silence on every set in Hollywood—partly because he has been the "Boy King," and partly because his leadership has often turned the routinely produced mass medium into an art form.

Donald O'Connor (b. 1928) (of *Singin' in the Rain*) appears on stage aged **3 days**, carried on by his father in an act entitled "The O'Connor Family—The Real Family of Vaudeville."

James Dean (b. 1931) is given the middle name Byron, after the poet.

"Ivory Snow Babies" win an award from the soap company. Previous winners have included Brooke Shields (who stars in the 1978 film *Pretty Baby*) at **12** and Marilyn Chambers, who later becomes a star of porn films.

MUSIC—NON-CLASSICAL

Frank Sinatra (b. 1915) weighs 13½ pounds at birth. At **21** he wins a talent contest on a local radio station and goes on to become (almost a punk-style) hero to teenage girls. He has his first hit record, "I'll Never Smile Again," at **24**, and he becomes the idol of wild "bobbysoxer" fans at **27**. This is before his permanent dominance of a certain area of music. (cf. **49***)

"Ain't She Sweet?"—this song is written by Milton Ager (**31**) on the birth of his daughter Shana Alexander in 1925.

Bette Midler (b. 1945), born in Hawaii, is named after film star Bette Davis (**37**). Her two sisters have been named Judy, after Judy Garland (**23**), and Susan, after Susan Hayward (**27**). By **28**, Bette Midler has a solo show on Broadway, *The Divine Miss M,* after having worked as a singer in a New York homosexual sauna. At **34**, she makes the film *The Rose* about the rise and fall of a rock star. This first film brings her a great deal of money, and she becomes a Goddess, providing "sleaze with ease."

LOVE, LIFE

There are now 105–106 males for every 100 females.

Place of birth: about 1.89 percent of babies are born at home, and the rest are born in a hospital (England and Wales, 1977).

Births by unmarried mothers: these are 1 percent in Japan; 8 to 9 percent in England and Wales (1977); about 33 percent in Scandinavia; 36 percent in Cuba. In the U.S.A., the figure is 14 percent, with 7.3 percent of white births and 49 percent of black births being outside marriage; these figures have greatly increased in the last quarter century—in 1940–44, 1.8 percent of white births and 16.8 percent of black births were outside marriage.

You now receive at least two names—the family name (surname), to show the family into which you are born and which you are expected to perpetuate; and your first name (forename, given name, Christian name), which is chosen because (1) it is a pleasant name in the view of your parents, or (2) it expresses some parental hope about you in the next seventy years, or (3) it commemorates a relative so that he or she may live on through your life.

Birthdays were first celebrated generally during the nineteenth century. Celebrating your own birthday depended on knowing the actual date of birth. This in itself meant that you had to be born into a culture that could and did record the date of birth.

Birthday cards: this is a subject which deserves further study. One authority has suggested that birthday cards were a derivative of Christmas cards, and that they started in the U.S.A. in the second half of the nineteenth century. There are dozens of books on Christmas cards but a comparative dearth of literature on the birthday card.

Since Old Testament times, gemstones have been given to the newly born to bring the particular quality that is associated with the stone. For example, a diamond given to you now is thought to bring you innocence and purity in later life.

Having a surname in an ancient society (for example, in Imperial China) indicated that you were a step above the bottom rank and that the government needed to take note of you as an individual. In a face-to-face society, a surname is not necessary, but it is essential in a society possessing a bureaucracy.

The most popular names in the U.K. (*The Times,* London, 1979) for females are: (1) Elizabeth, (2) Victoria, (3) Anna, and (4) Charlotte; and for males are: (1) James, (2) Nicholas, (3) Edward, and (4) Thomas.

In Russia, your name is registered at a ceremony in your local Baby Palace. You, and your parents, your Honorary Parents (similar to godparents) and grandparents are present, and a deputy from the Soviet hands your family a certificate enrolling you as a new citizen. In other parts of the U.S.S.R. little children add to the ceremony by giving their parents candles which they light. The ceremony typically ends with the song: "Let There Always Be Sunshine," the first verse and chorus of which is:

> The sun's circle, sky around—
> This is the drawing of a little boy.
> He drew it on a piece of paper
> And wrote in the corner:
> Let there always be sunshine
> Let there always be sky
> Let there always be mummy
> Let there always be me.

EXPLORATION

Out of the first 29 U.S. astronauts, 22 were firstborn, and five others were first sons.

LAW, CRIME

Charles Manson (b. 1934): his mother is a prostitute, and his father is one of her customers. The mother marries the father for convenience, but he disappears soon afterward. At 5, Manson has to move in with relatives, as his mother is arrested. At **14**, he lives on his own, and is then arrested for burglary. (cf. **35***)

John Doe is not born, but created by lawyers c. 1657—as are his later siblings, Jane Doe and Richard Doe.

In pre-Restoration Japan, infanticide was not described as killing the baby, but as "sending the baby back to the world of souls, instead of taking it into the world of men." Infanticide was not murder because babies were not yet accepted into the full human world.

SPORTS

Arnold Palmer's (b. 1929) first home is across from the third tee at the Latrobe County Golf Club, Pennsylvania, where his father is the professional. Palmer starts golf at **7**, and lives in Latrobe for the rest of his life. By **25**, he has won the U.S. Amateur Championship; he turns professional and is married—his wife Winnie is **20**. By **31***, he is the leader of a boom in golf.

The age of a race horse is determined similarly to the old Chinese system. Horses are assumed to be of equal age to all those born in the same chronological year. A foal is **0–1**; a yearling is nominally **1**; then a **2**-year-old. A colt or filly is **3** and **4**. A stallion or mare is **5** and over. In a race, a horse which is **6+** is described as "aged." Horses **4+** carry handicap weights, on a weight-for-age basis.

1

HEALTH

Helen Keller (b. 1882): born in Alabama, she suffers a disease which leaves her deaf and blind from the age of **19 months**. However, it gradually becomes clear to her mother (**23**) and father (**43**) that she is of exceptional intelligence. At **6**, she is taken to see Alexander Graham Bell (**39**), and he recommends a special teacher. At **7**, Keller meets "Teacher," Anne Sullivan (**20**) who immediately starts an intensive development of her student's senses. At **10**, Helen Keller is learning to speak, and at **19** she is accepted at Radcliffe College. Her first book, *The Story of My Life* is published at **23**. At **33**, she gives her first public lecture, and thereafter is a powerful supporter of handicapped people's rights. Though blind, her fingers constitute "ten eyes," and she says, "Every atom in my body is a vibrascope." She lives in the country as she finds city life extremely "noisy" in that she can feel so many vibrations. Both her optimism and her sensitivity to the world seem so contrary to the apparent defects of her body; when people meet her, they are struck by some special force, as if they have met a saint of their own times. Helen Keller's career lasts until a stroke at **81**, and she lives until **87**.

You should be congratulated on surviving to this age. The death rate **0–1** is so much higher than that for childhood and the early adult years that it is not overtaken until the **mid-50**s.

Since **0**, you have gained 15 pounds and 9–10 inches in length, on average.

The death rate in the first year is now about 15.9 per 1,000 live births (England and Wales). In the 1840s, the comparable figure was 153, and in the 1930s it was 62.

When orphans were boarded out in London in the eighteenth century, one parish gave a bonus to any nurse who managed to keep a child live until its first birthday. If such a scheme were not operated, the death rate in the first year could reach 40 or 50 percent. But if a nurse lost more than two children per year, she was dismissed from her duties.

Wet-nursing persisted in France until quite recently; almost a third of the babies in the Paris area were still being sent out to the country in 1907. "Frères de lait" ("brothers of milk") were two unrelated babies who were fed by the same wet nurse. In 1780 the police chief of Paris estimated that 80 percent of newborn babies were sent to the countryside to be wet-nursed.

The common hamster lives until **2**, and the golden hamster typically only until **1**. Some average life spans include: house mouse, **1–2**; dormouse, **2–3**; sardine, **3.3**; platypus, **5**; mongoose, **5**; rabbit, **5–6**. Some maximum life spans include: fruit fly, **.05–.1**; aphid, **.08**; grasshopper, **.2**; maggot in an apple, **.3**. The cricket lives to a maximum of **1**; the chameleon, until **3.5**; blue jay, until **4**; bluebird, until **4.5**; and the garden snail, until **4–5**. The commercial chicken is typically killed at **0.5**.

HISTORY—WORLD

Czar Ivan of Russia, in 1741: having been proclaimed Emperor-Autocrat of Russia at **3 months**, he is now deposed. The new ruler, Empress Elizabeth **(32)** sentences him to solitary confinement for the rest of his life. He is kept in a cage, inside a house, which is inside a prison. He grows up an imbecile. At **23** he is killed by guards during an abortive rescue attempt.

HISTORY—U.K.

The future King Edward VI (b. Mar. 1539) is given his own household at **1½** with a large number of appropriate officials. He becomes King at **8**, and the Book of Common Prayer is issued in his name at **12**. But he dies at **15**.

The future Queen Mary of England (b. 1516) is married in 1518 to the son of the King of France, the bridegroom (**9 months**) attending by proxy. The intention is that a repeat ceremony should be held when she is **14**, but this never takes place. At **5** she has an engagement ceremony to Emperor Charles V (**23**). At **8**, there is discussion of her possible marriage to the King of Scotland, James IV (**51**). At **9**, she becomes in effect the Princess of Wales by attending to legal proceedings there. At **10**, an effort is made to marry her to the current King of France (**32**). She becomes Queen in her own right at **37***, and later becomes known as "Bloody Mary." She is married at **38** to Philip II of Spain (**27**) and has no children. (cf. **27***)

LITERATURE

(Sir) Walter Scott (b. 1771) has polio at **1½**, which leaves him permanently lame in the right leg. (cf. **12***)

Leo Tolstoy (b. 1830, Aug. 4): his mother dies just before his second birthday. His father dies when he is **8**, and his grandmother dies the following year. The family is then split up into two groups, and Tolstoy is brought up by an aunt. He later writes about childhood: "What time could be better when the two highest virtues, innocent joy and a limitless need to love, are the only mainsprings of life." (cf. **18***)

FILM

Shirley Temple walks at **13 months** (1929). She attends dance classes at **3**; she is spotted by a talent scout and makes her first film. At **5** her song and dance routine in *Stand Up and Cheer* steals the picture, and she becomes a star; also at **5**, the studio publicity department announces that she is **4**. At **6**, in *Bright Eyes* she sings "On the Good Ship Lollipop"; she gains an Academy Award—the youngest person ever—and is said to put the Oscar with her dolls. At **8**, she is in *Who's Who,* again the youngest ever. At **12**, *The Blue Bird* is the first of her films to lose money. She goes to school for the first time. Later, after being a housewife and mother, she becomes a U.S. ambassador at **46**.

LOVE, LIFE

According to Masters and Johnson, gender identity is virtually fixed by **1½**. After this time, it is almost impossible to change your own sense of your gender, even if an accident or discovery about your sexual organs makes such a change appropriate. You are now set in seeing yourself as male or female.

LAW, CRIME

Delinquency starts in the high chair, and ends in the electric chair.—James D. C. Murray.

Charles Lindbergh, Jr., is kidnapped from his home in Hopewell, N.J. in 1932. His parents are "Lindy" **(30)** the aviator, and Anne Morrow Lindbergh **(25)**. The entire newspaper industry gives the kidnapping immense publicity, but the Lindbergh baby is found to have died shortly after the kidnapping. A number of states pass "Little Lindbergh Laws," increasing the penalty for kidnapping. Bruno Richard Hauptmann **(32)** is later executed in connection with this crime.

If you are murdered by your mother within the first twelve months, this is "infanticide" and is considered manslaughter, not murder (U.K.).

SPORTS

Muhammad Ali, at **1½** in 1943, swings an arm, and knocks out one of his mother's teeth. He takes up boxing at **12**; he is world heavyweight champion at **22***. In his **30**s, Ali comments on childhood: "What I like about children is kids are exiles from heaven. You can see God in children because they haven't had a chance to come into evil. That's why the first thing they do when they come onto earth is cry."

2

HEALTH

At **18 months**, 95 percent have walked, and spoken two or three words.

It used to be believed that malnutrition during the period of greatest growth of the brain **(–4 months** until **2)** would lead to permanent below-average intelligence; but it is now argued that humans are so resilient that they can recover even from the handicap of infant malnutrition. But for a variety of interrelated social and biological reasons, people who are starving or undernourished now **(2)** will never reach a proper size or intelligence for the rest of their lives.

A United Nations estimate is that 180 million children are not getting the bare minimum diet sufficient to maintain health and minimal physical activity. And 300 million children do not have access to clean water.

HISTORY—WORLD

Vladimir Ilyich Lenin does not learn to walk until he is almost **3** (1873). (cf. **37***)

Gerald Ford: his father leaves home in 1915 and is never seen again, except once, when Ford is **18**.

RELIGION, PHILOSOPHY

Hercules strangles two snakes which have been put in his cradle.

About this time, Buddha gains "samādhi" in meditation, the first ecstasy. (cf. **16***)

The future Dalai Lama is found in boys of this age group. His soul has come from the Lama who has recently died. The boy is selected because he recognizes sacred objects which are set before him, and which he has seen in his earlier incarnation as the previous Dalai Lama. His enthronement takes place at **3** or **4**; his coming of age is at **16–18**. From then onward, he would be the spiritual and political ruler of Tibet. From **2** onward, he meets few children of his own age and spends most of his time in meditation and listening to theological debates.

SOCIAL SCIENCE, EDUCATION

Sigmund Freud (1856) is sexually aroused by seeing his naked mother (**22**) as he recalls at **41** in a letter. At **1½** he had seen his younger brother (**8 months**) die which he later views as the not unwelcome loss of a rival to his mother's attentions. Freud is breastfed. As the eldest child, he is adored by his mother, and vice versa. She lives until **95**. He later writes, ". . . if a man has been his mother's undisputed darling, he retains throughout life the triumphant feeling, the confidence in success, which . . . brings actual success along with it. My strength has its roots in my relation to my mother." To his mother, Freud is always "my golden Sigi." (cf. **30***)

Carl Jung (**2** in 1878): later says: "My mother was a very good mother to me. She had hearty animal warmth, cooked wonderfully, and was most companionable and pleasant." At **3½** Jung has the first dream that he later remembers: he is nearly devoured by a one-eyed beast on a throne. (cf. **12***)

According to Glenn Dorman, the American author of *Teach Your Baby to Read* (1965), teaching your child to read "is more than a unique opportunity, it is a sacred duty." You should learn to read in the same way that you learn to hear. His advice is to start at **2**, and use big letters.

RENAISSANCE

Howard Hughes: in 1908 his father (**38**) develops a drilling bit that immediately becomes essential equipment in the oil business. The family rapidly becomes extremely rich, and the bit alone later brings Hughes three-quarters of a billion dollars between **18** and **66**. At **16**, his mother (**38**) dies, and at **18** his father (**54**) dies; Hughes quickly takes charge of the cash flow. In his **20**s he goes to Hollywood and makes his own films. At **24**, he makes *Hell's Angels,* starring Jean Harlow (**19**). At **36** he makes *The Outlaw,* starring Jane Russell (**22**). His special bra for Russell illustrates his publicity gifts as well as his engineering skill. Much of this film is shot in the evening as Hughes is currently engaged on aircraft production. Hughes develops a career in aeronautics simultaneously with his film career. At **29** he designs and pilots the fastest plane in the world; he achieves the U.S. transcontinental record at **31**, and at **32** he flies around the world in a record 91 hours. During this journey he sends messages about his progress to his current friend, the actress Katharine Hepburn (**29**). Hughes's genius takes a more bizarre and unproductive turn with his plane, the Spruce Goose, which he designs as an international troop carrier for World War II. Its first flight (at **41**) is two years after the war's end, and the plane is never flown again. Hughes's immense wealth, combined with his creativity and his concentration, brings him worldwide recognition in several fields, but gradually he loses his touch with reality and is virtually insane at the time of his death at **70***.

MUSIC—CLASSICAL

In the Suzuki method of learning the violin, you can now go to classes to watch and listen. A parent should accompany you. Around **3**, you start playing the violin, using a miniature instrument which is 1/16 adult size.

SHOW BUSINESS

Judy Garland (b. 1922) sings "Jingle Bells" on stage at **2½**.

LOVE, LIFE

In East Germany, 60 percent of people under **3** attend day care centers—part of a policy to maintain the population by reducing the difficulties of motherhood.

EXPLORATION

Eligibility: you are now too old to travel free on airlines; but concessions are usually available until you are **12**.

LAW, CRIME

Lizzie Borden, in 1862: her mother dies, and at **4** she gets a stepmother (**37**) whom Lizzie is accused of killing with an axe when she is **32***.

The median age for suffering from child battering is **2½**. The younger the victim, the more likely that the injury will be serious. The age group **0–1** suffer more from fractures, including skull fractures;

burns and scalds are more likely for older victims, reaching a peak at **9**. The rate of suffering is 1.5 per 1,000 in the age group **0–4** (U.K.) and .7 per 1,000 **0–15** (U.K.). Physical abuse of children was so normal in the past—as part of necessary "discipline"—that the first Act for the Prevention of Cruelty to Children was not passed in Britain until 1872.

SPORTS

Tracy Austin (1965) starts hitting tennis balls with a racquet. In the following year, at **3** she starts playing tennis with her family who are enthusiastic players. At **4** she is on the cover of *World Tennis*; at **13** she is on the cover of *Sports Illustrated.* Austin later advises: "**Six** is a good age to start, but children should never use their parents' racquets. It is vital that the racquet's grip and weight are chosen for an individual, and you don't have to spend a lot of money. But the most important thing is that tennis should never be a chore. It should always be fun." At **10**, Austin is U.S. No. 1 in the age group of 12 and below. At **14**, she is the youngest player to have appeared at Wimbledon. At **15**, she turns professional and immediately wins her first tournament—at Stuttgart—collecting $6,000 and a Porsche. At **16**, she is the youngest ever U.S. Open Champion, beating four-time winner Chris Evert-Lloyd (**24**). After winning this championship, Austin has to return to California to resume classes at Redondo Hills High School.

3

HEALTH

Brain growth is now largely finished. The growth spurt for the brain is between **–1** and **3**. The first alpha rhythm in the brain is at **2**.

HISTORY—U.K.

The future King Alexander II of Scotland, in 1201: the Scottish nobles are assembled to swear fealty to him, and he becomes King at **16**.

The future Henry VIII is appointed Lieutenant of Ireland, Duke of York, and Knight of the Garter in 1494. He is made Prince of Wales at **11** and becomes King at **17***.

30 Enoch Powell in 1915: his parents call him "Professor" as a nickname. He eventually becomes a full professor at **25**. (cf. **15***)

RELIGION, PHILOSOPHY

John Locke, the philosopher, speaking at **65** (1697) when he is a commissioner of the Board of Trade, proposes in a report that all working-class children should be in work at **3**, so that their maintenance is not a drain on parish resources. (cf. **58***)

John Stuart Mill can read in English and in Greek (1809); at **7** he is reading Plato. At **8** he speaks Latin and is tutor and father-figure to his brothers and sisters. Mill's education is the full-time project of his father, the philosopher James Mill (**36** when John is **3**). Mill does not know any other children as equals until **14**; his friends have been his father's friends, such as Jeremy Bentham (**61** in 1809). Later, Mill hits out at stuffing children with facts so that they become "mere parrots." But he himself does well out of the system. He goes on to become a powerful administrator, MP, and feminist, as well as philosopher.

Bertrand Russell, in 1875: his father dies (his mother had died when he was **2**) and he is sent to live with his grandfather, Lord John Russell (**83**), the former Prime Minister. At **0** Bertrand Russell's godfather had been John Stuart Mill (**66**). (cf. **38***)

You are now believed to be at your peak for extrasensory perception.

SOCIAL SCIENCE, EDUCATION

In Japan, if aiming for an elite job later on, you should now enter a prenursery school, so that you will do well in the entrance exam for nursery school at **4**. You will then be on course to do well at school, and so get into a good university at **18**.

Karl Pearson (b. 1857) in 1860 is ordered to stop sucking his thumb. On refusing to do so, he is told that his thumb will wither away if he does not stop sucking it. He puts his two thumbs together and points out that the sucked and unsucked thumbs are in an identical state of health. Karl Pearson goes on to become father of statistics. (cf. Galton, **47***)

MONEY, WORK

You would now be eligible to enter the London workhouse of Thomas Firmin, the philanthropist (1677 onward). By **10**, you would be fully trained and be sent out to regular employment. A small amount of education was provided—but only a minimum. Firmin explained that ". . . if whilst young they are taught to work, they would fall in love with it, and when old would not depart from it."

ART

Paul Gauguin, his widowed mother, and his sister leave Paris, and travel to Peru in 1851. They live there until he is **7**. (cf. **35***)

LITERATURE

Samuel Johnson (b. 1709) is taken to London in 1712 to have a cure from disease—the cure consists of being touched by the Sovereign, Queen Anne (**47**). (cf. **37***)

Alice Liddell (**3¾**) is introduced to Lewis Carroll (**24**), and he writes in his diary (1856, Apr. 25): "I mark this day with a white stone." (cf. **33***)

Joseph Conrad (b. 1857): his father is arrested in Poland in 1861 by Russian troops who are occupying the country. At **4**, the family is exiled to Siberia. At **7**, his mother (**32**) dies from the intense cold; at **11**, his father dies, and Conrad is sent to school for the first time. He becomes a sailor at **16**, and a novelist at **38***.

Dr. R. D. Laing has written: ". . . there is a brief time, before a child abdicates its ecstasy, when he or she will speak and think originally. The 'ecstasy' fades away; only poets and musicians keep it."

LOVE, LIFE

You now have egocentric speech and assume that any audience will be interested in what you have to say.

Your first "age of defiance" is **3–5**; the second is **12–15**.

4

HEALTH

Sleep: at **0**, you sleep 18 hours per day. At **4**, you sleep 11 hours per day.

Of the 122 million people born in 1979, 14 percent are expected to die at **4** or earlier (World Health Organization).

HISTORY—WORLD

Louis XIV becomes King of France in 1643. At **10** he has to be smuggled out of Paris for fear of a mob of the "Fronde"—a matter of considerable humiliation to him. At **13** he comes of age and is no longer subject to his mother's regency. By **22** he has full control upon the death of his powerful adviser, Cardinal Mazarin (**59**). By **40***, he has become the Sun King.

HISTORY—U.K.

The future King Edward V is appointed guardian of England (1475) in the temporary absence abroad of his father, Edward IV (**33**).

The future Queen Elizabeth II is modeled at Madame Tussaud's in 1930 and has a piece of Antarctica named after her. She becomes Queen at **25***.

SOCIAL SCIENCE, EDUCATION

John Evelyn (later, the diarist) starts reading Latin (1624). As an adult, he considers his education to have been deficient because he started Latin too late. He resolves that his own children will be able to do better, and at **4** they are writing in Greek.

Pre-Victorian children could be very knowledgeable by now at **4**, because schools operated with short vacations and began classes at dawn, continuing to bedtime with a bare minimum of interruption.

MUSIC—CLASSICAL

Itzhak Perlman loses the use of both his legs (1950) after a polio attack, and later goes on to become a concert violinist.

LITERATURE

Alastair "Mouse" Grahame in 1904: as a fourth birthday treat, his father Kenneth (**45**) invents a bedtime story about a river bank and the Wild Wood, and Rat and Toad of Toad Hall. Four years later, *The Wind in the Willows* is published. (cf. **49***)

FILMS

Bob Hope emigrates from Eltham, south London (his birthplace), to the U.S.A. in 1907.

Sammy Davis, Jr., joins his parents in their stage act in 1929.

Portland Mason, daughter of actor James Mason (**43**), appears in public in 1952 wearing make-up and high heels, creating a scandal.

5

HEALTH

Sweden is the first large-scale society in which your physical health in childhood is not influenced by your social class. In all other countries, your physical growth now is partly affected by the class in which you are growing up.

In eighteenth century London, 75 percent of children (who were featured in baptism records) died before **5**. Country deaths were appreciably lower. In any society not possessing modern medicine, you would by now have witnessed the death of another child.

HISTORY—WORLD

The future Cardinal Richelieu, in France (1590): his father dies and his family becomes "new poor." Richelieu, as a teenager, is trained for the Church and becomes both a priest and a bishop at **21**. He is appointed chaplain to the Queen of France at **29**. He is the country's leading nonregal power between **34** and his death at **57**.

HISTORY—U.S.A.

George Washington, in 1737, is growing up in Virginia. His family are wealthy landowners. His mother is now **28**. Washington has seven to eight years of schooling, received mainly from his father **(42)** and his half-brother Lawrence who is now **21**. (cf. **15*** for this and the following stories)

Abraham Lincoln in 1814 is living in Knob Creek, Kentucky, eight miles from the one-room log cabin in which he was born. At **7**, his family move to Indiana, and live in a cabin in the woods. Lincoln grows up with little formal schooling, and endures a Spartan frontier existence. At **9**, his mother dies, and his father **(39)** remarries shortly afterward.

Lyndon Johnson, in 1913: the family moves to Johnson City, Texas, a town with no electricity, no paved roads, and no trains. His mother gets a job teaching debating in the local high school.

Ronald Reagan is growing up in Illinois in 1916. He is the second son; he is having a relatively happy childhood, though his father is a sometime alcoholic. At **9**, the Reagans settle in Dixon, and Ronald Reagan later goes to Dixon High School.

Richard Nixon is growing up on a poor lemon farm with his parents at Yorba Linda, California, in 1918.

John Kennedy: his family is doing well in 1922; his father (**34**) is trading stocks on Wall Street and owns a small chain of movie houses. At **9**, Kennedy's family move from Boston to New York, traveling by private railroad car.

Jimmy Carter is growing up on a poor farm at the settlement of Archery in 1929, three miles west of Plains, Georgia. The family now consists of his mother (**31**), father (**35**), and his sister Ruth (**0**). The farm has an outdoor privy, no electricity, and no running water. Carter goes barefoot for over half of the year. His mother works as a nurse in Plains. At **12** Carter reads *War and Peace.*

HISTORY—U.K.

Richard Duke of York is married (1478, Jan. 15) to Lady Anne Mowbray (also **5**). He had become a Knight of the Garter at **2** and Duke of Norfolk at **4**. But at **11** he is one of the Little Princes in the Tower, murdered by direction of Richard III (**30**).

Mary Queen of Scots is engaged (1548, July 7) to the heir of the King of France—she herself has been Queen of Scotland since **9 months**. She now travels to France and is brought up at the French court, marrying at **15***.

The future Queen Victoria now in 1824 has her own personal governess who stays with her till **18***. The governess is said to never have a day's holiday in all that time.

SOCIAL SCIENCE, EDUCATION

"Growing up" is measured in terms of: physical size; physical dexterity; language—talking, reading, writing; sense of time; memory, intelligence, sense of logic and of numbers; creativity; ability to learn; sense of morality; social relationships; sense of identity of oneself and of others; motivation, ambition, curiosity; affection and happiness.

MONEY, WORK

Henry Ford is growing up on a small farm near Detroit (1868). He is the oldest son of a dominant mother who dies when he is **12**. Ford has to spend a lot of time looking after chickens and refuses to eat chicken as an adult. (cf. **16***)

If a lower-class person in a peasant society, you would now be employed in scaring birds or in looking after sheep. In the eighteenth century, orphans and the children of vagabonds would often be placed in parish workhouses and be employed at spinning or knitting, so that the workhouse would be self-financing.

ART

The painting "Las Meninas" by Velazquez (**57**, in 1656) is of a princess aged **5**. Velazquez's equally famous portrait of a boy on a prancing horse is of Prince Baltasar Carlos, also **5**.

MUSIC—CLASSICAL

Wolfgang Amadeus Mozart's first compositions are written when he is **5** (1761). He never goes to school and is taught music and mathematics by his father (**42**), who is his full-time coach and promoter. (cf. **6***).

Japanese children who have been learning the violin by the Suzuki method can now play Vivaldi concertos.

LITERATURE

Christopher Robin Milne has the first Winnie-the-Pooh stories read aloud to him in 1926 by his father A. A. Milne (**44***).

According to M. E. Smith, this is the typical increase in your vocabulary: at **2** you know 900 words; at **4**, 1,500 words; at **5**, 2,100 words; and at **6** you know 2,600 words.

PLAYS, DANCE

Tom Stoppard, in 1942: his father dies and Stoppard is brought to England. He was born in Czechoslovakia and has already lived in Singapore and in Darjeeling, India. Later, he does not go to university but works as a journalist. At **29** he makes an immediate impact with the play *Rosencrantz and Guildenstern Are Dead.* He writes *Jumpers* at **35**; *Travesties* at **37**; and *Dirty Linen* at **39**.

LOVE, LIFE

Until around 1800, there were no special designs for children's clothes. Babies of both sexes wore what we, today, would call dresses. Young people from **4+** were dressed as miniature adults.

FILMS

Charlie Chaplin appears on stage with his alcoholic father in 1894, who dies not long afterward. Chaplin is sent to an orphanage with his half-brother, as his mother can no longer look after them.

David Niven hears that his father has been killed at the battle of Gallipoli (1915).

Charles Bronson loses his virginity in 1926 at **5½** to a girl of **6**.

Natalie Wood: when the film *Happy Land* is made on location in her hometown of Santa Rosa, California, in 1943, Wood is discovered and shines as one of the local children.

Kornelia Ender is sent by her doctor for swimming lessons in 1964 as therapy for pains in her hips. By **17**, she wins two gold medals for swimming at the 1976 Olympics. By her mid-teens, she is in the world championship class. (cf. **15***)

Life Patterns

William Shakespeare (**35**) devised a seven-stage life pattern in *As You Like It.* His stages went from infancy through maturity, to a return to infancy in old age. Shortly before this, an influential Elizabethan book had been *The Differences of the Ages of Man,* by Henry Cuffe.

We should be careful about accepting these models at face value. Shakespeare, of course, could hardly be said to have had an average life, and Cuffe was executed at **38** (1601). Jacques, the speaker of the "seven ages," was a melancholy, pessimistic, and even eccentric figure in *As You Like It.* But models of life have an attraction.

Both Shakespeare and Cuffe helped to provide life patterns. The individual is faced with two problems here: (1) knowing the shape of their lives (for example, at what age to marry, have own house, and so on); and (2) having a causal model of life, so that action X today will lead to result Y when one is ten or twenty years older. Since time moves in one direction only (that in itself is a topic for numerous poets), we are liable to understand life only when it is too late to make the right decisions. Hence the interest in the "maps" that Shakespeare, Cuffe, and others might provide beforehand.

Not surprisingly, analogies from the plant world were used when it was necessary to explain changes in human life. The funeral service of the Book of Common Prayer says that man ". . . cometh up, and is cut down, like a flower. . . ." Growing, harvesting, and decay were obvious and unavoidable—in humans as well as in plants.

A powerful idea was that chance affected your life as much as any forceful action on your part. Medieval manuscripts, for example, showed a literal Wheel of Life (like a Ferris Wheel) in which those on the upside were grinning happily, and those on the downside were filled with despair and terror. The artist, and the observer, knew that soon both positions would be reversed.

For even the most graceful and powerful, there was always the final turn on the wheel—death. This could come at the peak of your worldly magnificence. Sometimes late medieval tombs emphasized this truth by showing two stone effigies; one would be of the person in full worldly robes, and the other would be of the corresponding decayed skeleton.

For everyday contemplation, there was the cult of "memento mori" (cf. religion, **30*** and α*). Hans Holbein, in his painting "The Two Ambassadors," showed a skull prominently in the foreground. Death was seen partly as a warning against excessive pride. It was only in 1978 that the Papal coronation service ceased to have a graphic version of this philosophy. Previously, toward the end of the ritual glorifying the new pope, sticks would be burned to ashes to the words "Sic Transit Gloria Mundi," thus passes the glory of the world.

Death would suddenly reduce even the grandest king or queen to a level far below that of even the cheapest vassal in his pigsty. Death was also the beginning of the greatest pressure for correct behavior, Judgment Day. However much your sinning had been performed with abandon, each action was being recorded in permanent form, so constructing a pattern of your life. Sooner or later, you would be introduced into the presence of God, the maker of the world and of the skies. Even though you may avoid seeing a shape in your life now, there would come a time when the thrust of your life would be held up for review—and for everlasting punishment or reward.

Until very recently, the shape of your life was heavily predetermined, and the only issue was one of survival as best you could. The idea of "life decisions" would have been difficult to explain to people who would live all their lives in one village. Even the choice of spouse would have been heavily influenced by elders and betters.

In a relatively static society, there were few options. Instead, you lived on a conveyor belt that transferred you from one status in life to the next. Childhood, apprenticeship, marriage, work, death, and decay all formed a pattern that was not open to much questioning. You were pushed along by basic and unsubtle forces, such as sexual desire, and aging brought about by hard physical work, and fear of starvation. Picturesque and/or frightening ceremonies marked your progress through the stages of life. With no formal training, people learned of the life pattern by watching these rites of passage, and by relating to role models. You absorbed your place in society and made the most of it. Lives of people in the previous generation followed patterns that you copied.

HAGIOLOGY, BIOGRAPHY, AND FICTION

When choice gradually became a reality (for those in the richer classes and as society became more mobile), the more formal training in life patterns became necessary. Three forms of this training were the reading of hagiology, of biography, and of fiction. Hagiology was the lives of the saints and martyrs, to be read in conjunction with the Bible itself. It was not unusual for one day of the week (Sunday) to be given over to examining the lives of these holy people, and so to draw conclusions about your own life.

For the well-educated, classical Greece and Rome provided models that had almost the same force as those of religion. In discussing the life and career of those around them, people would use a concept such as "hubris" or "Greek tragedy" by way of explanation. Other phrases from this source are still in use, such as genius, destiny, life force, fates, guardian angel, "favored by the gods," Achilles heel, and sometimes "Achilles sulking in his tent."

With increasing secularization (or at least with other fields of action besides the Church), biography began to provide instruction as to the possible paths available in life. Any school library today continues to have a large biography section, since people want to learn about their alternatives. And for the elderly, biography provides a mapping process to help us make sense of events that were a formless rush at the time they happened.

Biography provides a causal model for events in life; you see one person's early decisions and then observe how these worked out in the following decades. A series of biographies enables you to make models, often only semiconsciously, of the steps to be taken in order to gain a certain position in the world.

There are, of course, reasons of mere entertainment for reading biography—escapism, fantasy, nostalgia, and the pleasures of sitting in judgment on the subject of the book.

The exemplary figures were often quoted giving pieces of sage advice. For example, J. S. Bach has been quoted as saying, "Anyone could do as well, *if only he work as hard as I have.*" And Verdi has been quoted as giving useful advice to anyone in charge of a group project: "To trust is good; to mistrust is better." Similarly, it was entirely in order for biographers to pause in their story and advise the reader. Acquaintance with great figures gave them this right. For example, Hesketh Pearson commented in his book on Disraeli: "Fame and love are two main motives, but they oppose each other. Desire for fame is a will to conquer; desire for love is a wish to capitulate." Another example is Dorothy Parker's thought-provoking remark on Ernest Hemingway: "He has the most valuable asset an artist can possess—the fear of what he knows is bad for him."

In Samuel Smiles's *Self Help* (1859) and other works, this advisory aspect of the biography overflowed, and frankly became the center of the enterprise.

Although the ironic approach of Lytton Strachey is generally seen as a revolution in the writing of biography, the instructional aspect of biography did not change. Strachey was merely instructing the reader to take a new view on life. Now the quest for a certain kind of elite performance was to be seen as absurd and even as a disease. This view was as equally relevant in helping you form a view on your life as was the traditional hagiology. The debunking biography helped to answer the question that lurks in the back of every adult mind: *Why haven't I done better?* Answer: Because I am not, fortunately, as much of a thieving bastard as these people who have made it to the top. So, the more I can read biographies that show the elite to be unhappy and neurotic, then the happier I will be in my middle-level slot.

Creators of fiction also took time off to make comments on the patterns within the life span. Hogarth's paintings of "The Rake's Progress" defined forever a certain sequence of success and failure. And so did Milton's comment about pride going before a fall. Balzac once wrote: "Behind every fortune, there lies a crime." And Disraeli said in *Coningsby,* "Youth is a blunder; Manhood a struggle; Old Age a regret." One of Shaw's characters advised: "Getting patronage is the whole art of life. A man cannot have a career without it." Oscar Wilde is well known for his saying "Each of us kills the thing he loves"; Wilde is perhaps less well known for his decision-rule: "Take care of the luxuries, and the necessities will look after themselves."

Besides books, instruction about the life span has come from other sources which should be listed here for the sake of completeness—education theory, folk wisdom, astrology, sports, and show business. Typically, folk wisdom points to better mousetraps and the world beating a path to your door; or to "Early ripe, early rot," about the disadvantage of being an infant prodigy; or "shirtsleeves to shirtsleeves in three generations," about the loss of hunger and drive in a rich family. Both the sports and entertainment world have numerous theories of life, probably because the speed of your ups and downs is so much greater than in most other occupations. Sports training is often promoted for the very reason that it shows, in miniature, how commitments made today can have a desirable payoff later; this is "character building."

We now come to the formal and systematic approaches to the subject of life patterns, and the demand for these has come from the following: (1) the growth of large organizations with long-range planning of the careers of their members; (2) in a fast-changing society, individuals simply have more options in life and so look more often for advice; (3) changes in technology and in medicine have led to new life stages, and there is little traditional advice on being a teenager or about the new mass class of the **over-60s**.

DEVELOPMENTAL PSYCHOLOGY

Any full longitudinal research on the human life span would have to be funded for longer than the normal grant and published posthumously. So if you are looking for an explanation covering individual differences (not demographics and not sociology), and if you want to deal with human beings (not mice, fruit flies, or apes), then the whole subject must be divided up into manageable pieces. Typically the split is into either (1) researchable sequences within the human development; or (2) individual factors which can be researched at one moment in time for people of widely differing ages.

In the "sequences" approach, researchers look for a process that is long enough to illustrate human development, short enough to provide a research project, and that is repeated again and again by waves of new people, thus allowing replication of the test procedures. A typical sequence is the process of dying. Other sequences could be retirement; or, career planning and career choice; or selection and promotion and training within organizations; or university admissions policy, showing the growth from high school to graduation; or being a teenager. In most of these sequences people are moving through organizations (schools, hospitals, businesses) and thse provide a convenient base for the researcher. Within "child development," subjects include: do the events of any year(s) have a decisive effect over the next few years—or even the rest of your life; the most appropriate year(s) for learning various topics; development of conscience; physical growth of the brain; the competing contributions of home versus school; the effect, if any, of childhood trauma; the effect, if any, of maternal deprivation.

Working within the "factors" approach, you choose a factor of interest (for example sex, as measured by instances of intercourse per week) and you query people of all ages on this dimension. Roughly, you can see how this factor varies with age and you look for a causal explanation, and perhaps any possibility of arresting a decline that goes with aging. Other interesting factors include: creativity; memory; motivation; physical abilities such as running or agility; some measure of happiness, or unhappiness, such as suicide rate; in marketing, different purchasing habits, such as how your preference for various types of new cars changes as you get older.

One combination of these two approaches is to take one factor (for example, genius) and try to see the common factors among those who have this quality. Crudely, what were the similarities in the early days of Beethoven, Napoleon, John D. Rockefeller, and others? By reading a sufficient number of biographies, you can see (or not) that a certain position in the birth order, or an aggressive mother, or some other factor usually beyond the control of us readers, correlates with genius in adult life. In this approach, perhaps the most important factor to be investigated is "maturity". Here, the author (perhaps Freud or Maslow) sets out their own view of the mature person, and shows the steps necessary to get there.

ERIKSON/LEVINSON/"PASSAGES"

Lastly, we come to the attempt to integrate both the sequences and the factors approach into one single model of the human life span. This approach can be identified with Eric Erikson, Daniel J. Levinson and the bestseller "Passages," though there are of course others working in the same direction.

Typically, a study of this sort aims to (1) cover the whole period from life to death, particularly the adult years; (2) integrate both the internal psychological state with the individual's family and career position; (3) provide fairly precise chronological deadlines at which readjustments take place. Life is seen, plausibly enough, as a balancing act between competing external and internal demands; we develop stability, in a kind of coalition of forces; this lasts for maybe five to ten years until the coalition is upset and "crisis" ensues. The crisis is resolved with a realignment of the external and internal worlds.

For example, once you have a settled job and young dependent children, you have stability. The crisis occurs when children become less dependent, and simultaneously you reach a promotion ceiling at work. This is the "mid-life crisis" which has gained wide publicity. The neatness of the models, together with the fairly precise definition of crisis years, has made for an attractive package, and has led to testable hypotheses.

Probably what brought E/L/"P" its vast popularity was its suggestion that the adult person, particularly the adult male, was in almost a victimized group. In the 1970s, dignity had tended to come from being victimized. Previously, this adult male category had been the group against which all the others had rebelled. Now, thanks to E/L/"P," it too became another victim of society. The reader could believe himself to be as much of a sufferer as any of the other victim groups of that time, such as gays, Third World people, women, anyone with a mother, and on and on.

The defects of the Erikson/Levinson/"Passages" approach include the following: (1) the testable hypotheses do not sufficiently confirm the basic features of the model, when tested; although stability and crisis are a basic human cycle (not the only such cycle) they do not occur in the way that E/L/"P" predict. (2) Individual differences after childhood are so great that no single model of the adult can suffice. (3) Continuous changes in such diverse factors as medicine and the job market completely upset any static definition of the adult. (4) Similarly, the process of redefining "male" and "female" seems to have no end in sight, and so prevents a fixed view of the adult. (5) Adult stages are to a large extent, socially defined; E/L/"P" is coercive, stigmatizing, and stereotyping in the same old way, but uses more up-to-date language.

For the protagonists, the hope is that with sufficient data E/L/"P" can one day provide a detailed model of the stages in human life. But no amount of data will in fact provide this. They are attempting to lead developmental psychology off in search for the one model of the adult; but this type of search is a fundamentally misconceived enterprise.

6

HEALTH

Beginning of your permanent teeth; the last will appear anytime between **13** and **25**.

RELIGION, PHILOSOPHY

You must now start learning the catechism (England, sixteenth century.)

SOCIAL SCIENCE, EDUCATION

Montaigne (later the French essayist) speaks Latin (1539). Like Montesquieu (**6** in 1695), he is wet-nursed in a peasant family, and is always grateful for this experience of "how the other half lives."(cf. **32***, **39***, **59***)

MUSIC—CLASSICAL

Mozart begins touring Europe (1762), with his sister Nannerl (**10**), and they give concerts. (cf. **9***)

LITERATURE

James Joyce is sent away to a Jesuit boarding school, returning home only during the holidays (Sept. 1888–June 1891). (cf. **40***)

B. Traven has been brought up by his grandparents, as he was born out of wedlock. But his parents now marry (1888), and he has to move in with them. He "never feels at home" and adopts a series of secret disguises for the rest of his life. His best-known work is *The Treasure of the Sierra Madre.*

James Thurber is shot in the eye by his brother with a bow and arrow (1900). Thurber joins *The New Yorker* magazine at **33**. Among his well-known work, *Is Sex Necessary?* is at **35**, and *The Secret Life of Walter Mitty* is at **44**. At **45**, blindness forces him to give up his secondary career as a cartoonist. Thurber lives until **66**.

FILMS

Shirley Temple sings "On the Good Ship Lollipop" (1934); gets a special Oscar; earns $1,250 per week.

MUSIC—NON-CLASSICAL

Cole Porter starts music lessons (1897). His mother (**35**) encourages him to play the piano 2 hours per day, and at **11** she pays for a composition of his to be published. At **18**, he goes to Yale, and later Harvard. At **24**, he has his first song to be performed on Broadway. At **31**, his grandfather (**94**) dies and leaves him a fortune. Throughout his **20**s and early **30**s, Cole Porter is gifted, popular, but relatively idle. His career effectively begins at **37***.

Ray Charles has an illness which causes him to go blind (1936). But this does not prevent him from pursuing a successful career later. His hits start at **24** with "It Should've Been Me," and carry on throughout his **20**s. "Hit the Road, Jack" is at **31**, and he has more hits ten years later. One of Ray Charles's followers is Stevie Wonder, who is blind from birth (**0**, in 1950). Wonder makes his first hit record at **12**, "Fingertips Part 2," which goes on to sell one million copies. At **21**, he collects $1 million from a trust fund: his earnings since **12**. By **24**, he has sold over 40 million records, including at **23** "You Are the Sunshine of My Life."

Ringo Starr has appendicitis, and is in a coma for ten days.

SPORTS

Nadia Comaneci is one of 24 kindergarten pupils who are selected to start gymnastics training (Rumania, 1968). She now begins a program which builds up to 3–4 hours practice per day. By her mid-teens, she is world champion. (cf. **15***)

7

HEALTH

The fin whale is now sexually mature. Its length is approximately 20 meters.

HISTORY—U.K.

Henry VI: coronation ceremony (1429). He had become King of England at **0**, on the death of his father Henry V (**34**). Also at **0**, he had become King of France, on the death of King Charles VI (**53**) who himself had been crowned king at **11**. Henry VI goes on to receive another coronation, at **9** in Paris. When he makes an entrance into that city, he is greeted by a tableau vivant of three nude mermaids splashing about in a fountain which is dominated by the fleur de lys. The King starts to preside at councils at **12**; at **15**, the last of his preceptors or guardians dies, and from then on he acts on his own. Unfortunately, he is an ineffective ruler, and at **49** is murdered in the Tower of London.

(Lord) Palmerston and family (Aug. 1792) are virtually the last people to meet King Louis XVI (**38**) and Marie Antoinette (**37**), before the royal family is arrested and killed by the revolutionaries. The Palmerston family manages to escape, and travel to Switzerland, where they stay with Edward Gibbon (**55**) who has recently finished his *The Decline and Fall of the Roman Empire.* Palmerston first stands for Parliament at **21**, while an undergraduate; elected at **22**; offered the post of Chancellor of the Exchequer at **24**, but declines; Foreign Secretary at **46***.

In the sixteenth century, males would now have to start learning archery, as preparation for the military.

RELIGION, PHILOSOPHY

Give me the children until they are **7**, and anyone may have them afterward.—St. Francis Xavier (1506–52).

In the Roman Catholic church, you are now old enough to tell right from wrong; therefore old enough for confirmation and your first communion.

In the ancient Greek city-state of Sparta, males now left home and entered a state boarding school. Life was tough: discipline was by whipping, you had to go barefoot so that your feet would not soften, and only one garment was worn throughout the year (no extra clothes in cold weather).

In ancient Rome, males now left the "bosom of the mother" and became, in effect, an apprentice to the father. At **16**, with the "toga virilis," you became apprenticed to a male outside the family. Later, this system was replaced with schools: elementary, **7–11**; grammar, **12–15**; schools of rhetoric and law **16+**. The typical Greek schools were primary "paides," until **14**; secondary "epheboi," **15–17**; tertiary "neoi," **18+**.

In the past, French boys would now be taken from the supervision of women, and be supervised by men.

All girls in U.S.S.R. schools between now and **17** wear the same school uniform, and have done so since 1916. It consists of a dark brown long-sleeved dress, beneath a black pinafore.

Children who will do well in school at **16** can now be picked out by teachers, according to a study of the National Children's Bureau (London, 1979). The most accurate way of predicting success at **16** is to look at basic skills at **7**.

MONEY, WORK

Haroldson Lafayette Hunt is breastfed until he is **7** (1896). His family sees him as a brilliant child—at **3** he used to read the financial pages of the newspapers, and at **7** he is being educated at home. At **16** he leaves home and travels as a gambler for six years. In his **20**s, he starts drilling oil wells; he is very lucky and very hard working. By **59** he is the richest man in the world and starts another career as a publicist for extreme right wing views.

In pre-Victorian times, you would begin your apprenticeship at **7–12**. Your parents would pay a fee, and your master would provide food, clothing, discipline, and training. At the end of the period of indenture, you would be able to have a job in a trade which had restricted entry; that is, with any luck, you would have a lifetime of employment in that trade. Depending on the class of your parents, you would now be "bound" to a lucrative or a poverty-stricken craft. Thus your class in life is now fixed. "Parish apprentices" were orphans and others who received a minimal training in order to keep them out of the way and out of trouble.

MUSIC—CLASSICAL

Frédéric Chopin: Polonaise in G minor (1817)—his first published composition. He gives his first concert this year. He goes to the Warsaw Conservatory at **16**; first études around **19**; arrival in Paris at **21***, and triumph there.

Yehudi Menuhin makes his stage debut (San Francisco, 1923); and New York at **9**, London at **13**.

Daniel Barenboim gives his first public recital, in Buenos Aires (1950).

LITERATURE

Cedric Errol, an American, becomes heir to an Earl, and therefore moves to England with his widowed mother in *Little Lord Fauntleroy* (1886), by Frances Hodgson Burnett (**37**). She herself had emigrated in the opposite direction, from England to U.S.A., as a child.

Evelyn Waugh writes the first entry in his diary (Sept. 1911), which he keeps up almost continuously for another 53 years, and which is often the source for his later published writing. The first entry mentions his weekly attendance at Church—another habit of a lifetime. (cf. **20***)

FILMS

Buster Keaton is already a skilled acrobat (1902).

Orson Welles knows *King Lear* by heart (1922).

Margaret O'Brien gets a special Oscar (1944), for her performance in *Meet Me in St. Louis.*

LOVE, LIFE

In Tudor households of the upper classes, people at **7–10** would be sent away to be pages in other rich households. People born into the middle and lower classes would now begin their apprenticeships under which you would leave home and be indentured for seven years. In the Japanese Imperial household, the heir and other children would have left the family already, and would be living in another family; the fear of the adults was that too much affection would lead to the next generation being "soft."

In the sixteenth century and earlier, upper-class children could now be espoused in marriage. The minimum age for the marriage ceremony itself was **14** (male) and **13** (female). Parental consent was required for marriage until **21**.

In old Japanese society, funerals of people dying at **0–6** would be different from those for people dying at **7**+. There was an expectation that the young person may well die—as was common in any society before modern medicine. A saying explains, "Before **7** years old, the child belongs to God." Also at **7**, it was assumed that sexual differentiation has begun. On November 15, people of **7** are taken to shrines and are given special sweet food. In the past, boys had their heads shaved; today, traditional ceremonial costumes may be worn.

Charles Jean-Baptiste Sansom inherits the office of chief executioner of Paris (1726). Sansom has to employ an assistant for some years, but stands beside him during business. Twenty-eight years later, Sansom becomes too infirm to carry on working, and is succeeded by his son, Charles Henri Sansom (**15**), who begins work at once, and who in his **50**s becomes chief executioner during the French Revolution. (cf. **53***)

A girl (**7**) is hanged in London (1808), and a boy (**9**) is hanged in Chelmsford. Andrew Banning is hanged for stealing a spoon (1801). Hanging of this age group seems unremarkable in the eighteenth century and earlier, but is challenged at the beginning of the nineteenth century. However, a boy (**9**) is executed by hanging, in London (1833), for stealing printers' ink valued at two pence.

Albert DeSalvo (1939) sees his father (**30**) knock out all the teeth of his mother in one blow. Every night, DeSalvo and his brother get a beating from their father, a burglar. DeSalvo later becomes the Boston Strangler, when he himself is **30***.

This is approximately the age of criminal responsibility in sixteenth-century England; now eligible to be whipped, hanged, and so forth.

8

HISTORY—U.K.

Alexander III becomes King of Scotland (1249) on the death of his father (**51**). At **10**, he is married to Margaret (**11**), daughter of Henry III (**44**) of England. But he does not become free of a regency council until **21**.

RELIGION, PHILOSOPHY

René Descartes is sent to Jesuit boarding school (1604) for the next eight years. He later comments: "Those of high birth, whatever their sex, do not require to be old to surpass in erudition and virtue other people." (cf. **23***)

Mary Baker Eddy first "hears voices" (1829); later, she is the creator of Christian Science. (cf. **54***)

LITERATURE

Maxim Gorky leaves school (1876), and starts work. At **34**, he writes *The Lower Depths.*

Inspector Maigret: his mother now dies.

FILMS

Shirley Temple receives 135,000 birthday presents (1936).

Roman Polanski, in 1941: his parents are taken away to a Nazi concentration camp where his mother later dies. Polanski in his teens makes films in Poland, and his later work includes *Knife in the Water* at **29**; *Repulsion* at **33**; *Rosemary's Baby* at **36**; *Chinatown* at **41**; and *Tess* at **48**.

Margaret O'Brien: one of the top ten box office stars of 1945. At **9**, she also is in this list.

LOVE, LIFE

A girl dies in Bath, England (1830) and the parents put this message on her memorial stone: "Adieu, sweet blossom."

PRESS

In "Peanuts," no character is older than **8**.

EXPLORATION

Freddie Laker, in 1930: his father having left home, his mother remarries and Laker gets a stepfather. Laker is not sure what to call him, and tries "Dear"; he calls him Dear for the rest of his life. Laker does poorly at school, and becomes a salesman. At **25**, he sets up a tiny company dealing in war-surplus aircraft equipment. He suddenly becomes rich when at **26** the Russians blockade Berlin, forcing the Berlin Airlift, during which Laker planes fly night and day. After the emergency, he uses second-hand aircraft to provide vacation charter flights. This creates a revolution in mass vacations abroad. At **55**, his first Skytrain flight across the Atlantic causes another revolution, by breaking the power of the IATA cartel.

SPORTS

Bjorn Borg (1964) starts playing tennis. His father wins a racquet in a table-tennis competition, and gives it to him. By **15**, Borg has won his first Davis Cup match. He goes on to win the Wimbledon Singles title every year from **20** to **24**.

9

HISTORY—WORLD

Genghis Khan, in c. 1171: his father, the clan leader, is poisoned, and the rest of his family then lose their position. The boy gradually leads fighting groups of his own, and by **44** he has unified the Mongols. At **53**, he captures Peking. He is such a vicious fighter that opponents prefer to surrender immediately, rather than have a battle with him.

HISTORY—U.S.A.

Eleanor Roosevelt becomes an orphan (1894) on the death of her father (**34**). Her mother (**29**) had died when Eleanor was **8**. For the rest of her life, she remembers her father as a decent and brainy leader in the world. Other people have seen him as a drunk who precipitated his own death; to his daughter, he has been the source of love, companionship, and encouragement. She sees herself as "Father's own Little Nell" and sets herself the same high standard that she believes her father to have fulfilled. At **14**, she copies out this verse in her journal:

> To be the thing we seem
> To do the thing we deem enjoined by duty
> To walk in faith, nor dream
> Of questioning God's scheme of truth and beauty.

After an upper-class upbringing, she is married at **20**—on her mother's birthday—to her cousin Franklin D. Roosevelt (**23**). The ceremony is attended by President Theodore Roosevelt (**46**). Eleanor is a conventional wife and mother until her husband suffers from polio when she is **36**. This is the time of her emergence as a political force in her own right—partly because she has to represent her husband to advance his career, and partly because she has been wanting, in her housewife years, to be active in the outside world. When she is **48**, her husband becomes President. Though without executive power, she becomes one of the great influences in the development of liberalism. She is a leader in all the reforms of the day. Her gestures set the tone of the administration; for example, at **51** she invites the black contralto Marian Anderson (**34**) to sing at the White House. At **60**, her husband (**63**) dies, in the presence of his former lover, Lucy Mercer (**54**). At **61**, Eleanor Roosevelt is instrumental in the drafting of the Declaration of Human Rights. At **75**, she makes a speech supporting the nomination of Adlai Stevenson (**60**) as presidential nominee at the Democratic Party Convention. She lives until **78**. After her death her marriage is the subject of unpleasant controversy among some of her relatives.

HISTORY—U.K.

Henry III now becomes King (1216, Oct. 18), and is crowned at **12**.

Clement Atlee first goes to school (1892). Previously he has been educated at home by his mother. He is an ordinary, rather shy, middle-class person until **22**, when he visits the East End of London for the first time, and becomes converted to socialism by **24**.

SOCIAL SCIENCE, EDUCATION

Until now, it is said that you cannot conceive that time is irreversible.

MONEY, WORK

A Factories Act of 1833 said that children under **9** can no longer work in factories; but between **9** and **13** you can work up to nine hours per day.

ART

Titian arrives in Venice (1497), and is soon apprenticed in the studio of Giovanni Bellini (**62**). A fellow student is Giorgione (**22**). (cf. **33***)

MUSIC—CLASSICAL

J. S. Bach becomes an orphan (Jan. 1695) on the death of his father (**49**); his mother had died in the previous year. Bach is an able student but not an infant prodigy. He leaves school at **17**, and gets his first job at **18**, as violinist in the court orchestra of Weimar. (cf. **22***)

Mozart in London (1764–65): his six clavier sonatas are published and dedicated to Queen Charlotte (**20**), who gives Mozart's father (**45**) fifty guineas. Mozart is examined by a naturalist, Daines Barrington (**38**). He also composes his first symphony about now. (cf. **10***)

Mendelssohn: first public performance (1818). He comes from a rich, talented, and loving family, with extensive connections in the banking and musical worlds. Every day, he is made to start practicing at 5:00 A.M. At **11**, he makes a list of his compositions, and there are already 60 of them. (cf. **17***)

LITERATURE

Marcel Proust has his first asthma attack (1884), the beginning of his lifelong on-and-off illness, which separates him from a regular life. (cf. **18***)

Virginia Woolf starts the *Hyde Park Gate News* (1891), named after the street where her family live. At this time, she is also enthusiastic about cricket, and known as a "demon bowler." (cf. **13***)

PLAYS, DANCE

Ellen Terry makes her stage debut as the boy Mamilius (1856, Apr. 28) in *The Winter's Tale,* by William Shakespeare (**46**).

Matthew Prichard, in 1952: his grandmother, Agatha Christie (**61**) gives him the rights to a new play which she has just written. For each new play, it is her custom to give the rights to a different young relative; the plays usually run for six months, and the royalties form a useful nest egg for the child. Prichard's play is *The Mousetrap* which is still running thirty years later.

FILMS

Marilyn Monroe is taken to Los Angeles Orphans Home (staying there until she is **11**), following her mother's entry into a mental hospital (1935, Sept. 13). (Her father was always unknown to her.)

James Dean's mother dies of breast cancer (1939). He travels from Los Angeles to Indiana with the body, to the home of his grandmother, where he grows up on her farm.

Julie Andrews's family discovers that her voice has a range of over three octaves (1944) while she is singing during an air-raid.

Tatum O'Neal stars with her father Ryan (**32**) in *Paper Moon* (1973). She wins an Oscar.

LAW, CRIME

About 3.8 percent of murder victims are **9** or less (U.S.A., 1977).

Eligibility: Females may now be executed for offenses in Iran. In 1981, a girl (**9**) is shot for attacking revolutionary guards. Males are eligible for execution at **15**.

SPORTS

Jack Nicklaus (1949) starts playing golf. He accompanies his father (**36**) who has been told to do a lot of walking as therapy to recover from an ankle operation. By **22***, Nicklaus has won the U.S. Open, in his first year as a professional; at **24**, he wins six tournaments. He is later remarkable for the comeback in his game at **38***.

10

HEALTH

Your life expectancy now is **77.1** (female) and **71.1** (male) (England and Wales, 1973). Out of total deaths at all ages, only .42 percent (male) and .27 percent (female) occur in the ages **5** to **14**.

The causes of death for males **5** to **14** (England and Wales) are: (1) motor vehicle accidents; (2) other accidents; and (3) congenital abnormalities, leukemia, and other neoplasms. The causes of death for females are: (1) motor vehicle accidents; (2) congenital abnormalities; (3) other neoplasms apart from leukemia; (4) leukemia; and (5) other accidents. For people **5** to **9**, accidents and violence cause 38 percent of deaths. 57 percent of these are related to cars, and 14 percent associated with drowning.

Life expectancy in the U.S.A., 1976, is now **70.3** (male) and **77.5** (female).

The brain is 95 percent of its adult weight. At **0**, it is 25 percent; at **6 months**, it is 50 percent; at **3**, it is 75 percent; at **5**, it is 90 percent of adult weight.

Vaccines: diphtheria at **5**, BCG, against TB, at **10** to **13**; rubella for girls at **11** to **13**; polio and tetanus at **15** to **19**.

Some average animal life spans include: turkey, **6** years; cheetah, **6**; antelope, **8**; goat, **8–10**; porcupine, **8–12**; puma, **9**; squirrel, **9**; toucan, **9**; penguin, **9–10**; buffalo, **10**; fallow deer, **10**; sheep, **10–15**; tiger, **11**; hyena, **12**; alpaca, **12**; buzzards, **14**; giraffe, **14**; leopard, **14**; and jaguar, **14**.

Some maximum animal life spans include: earwig, **5** years; garter snake, **6**; mockingbird, **6**; anchovy, **7**; praying mantis, **8**; maximilian's parrot, **9**; electric eel, **11.5**; oyster, **10**; giant squid, **10**; robin, **12**; turkey, **12**; reindeer, **12**; salmon, **13**; codfish, **13**; crocodile, **13.5**; puff adder snake, **13.9**; and the seal, **14**.

HISTORY—U.S.A.

Amy Carter gets 300 letters each day at the White House (1978).

HISTORY—U.K.

Richard II becomes King (1377, June 21) on the death of his grandfather, Edward III (**64**). He is "beautiful as an archangel," all in white for his coronation. At **14**, he is instrumental in containing, and later crushing, the rebellion of peasants led by Wat Tyler. He marries at **15**, but is deposed at **32**, having pursued an overambitious policy against his enemies. He is murdered at **33**.

RELIGION, PHILOSOPHY

The world exists only for the breath of school children.—Rabbi Judah the Holy.

Except ye turn, and become as little children, ye shall in no wise enter the Kingdom of Heaven.—Jesus Christ, Matthew 18:3.

Anne Putnam (**12**), Betty Paris (**9**), Abigail Williams (**11**), and others accuse various people in Salem, Massachusetts (1692) of witchcraft. Nineteen people are subsequently hanged. The accusers are nearly all young girls; the witches are all old, of the parents' and grandparents' generations and they are nearly all female. An influential theoretician in the attack on witchcraft is the Reverend Cotton Mather (**29**); he is stimulated by observing Martha Goodwin (**13**) flying in his own home.

Some items on children and innocence:

In the Parthenon, Athens, the most sacred object during the religious ritual was carried by girls who were aged just below puberty. These girls are part of the procession, which is shown in the frieze around the building (now in the British Museum, known as the Elgin Marbles). The Parthenon was the temple to Pallas Athene, the maiden.

Between **6** and **10**, you were now eligible to be a vestal virgin—an assistant in the temple of Vesta, in ancient Rome. Your task would be to keep alive the sacred flame, which was devoted to the goddess of the hearth and of domesticity. At the end of five years service, you could leave and get married; if you lost your virginity during your period of office, you would be buried alive in a wall.

"Boy bishops" were children who were elected to act as bishop, in medieval times, at Christmastime.

In the ancient Roman Catholic church, the sacred leftovers from communion service were disposed of by giving them to "innocent children."

The most conspicuous singers in English cathedral ceremonies today are choir boys of **6** to **12**.

For the form of yoga which increases by having sexual intercourse without the emission of semen, the ideal partner is described thus: "Silver weighing fourteen ounces is desirable; it should never have been subject to smelting" or, in other words, a virgin girl of **14**.

Voting procedures in the republic of Venice included the drawing of lots, whenever it was necessary to ensure fairness in an arbitrary choice (e.g., in putting names in order on a ballot paper). The people who drew these lots were "ballottini," males of **11**, randomly chosen in an orphanage. Similarly, in seventeenth-century England, where punishment was to be given to one person out of a group of criminals, the straw was drawn by a child who was considered to be innocent. The one criminal would then be hanged.

Today, the Spanish national lottery has a boy (**13**) sing out the winning numbers.

SOCIAL SCIENCE, EDUCATION

The best education, according to Plato's *Republic,* is that the child should play among lovely things.

Jean Piaget writes his first scientific paper (1906) on an unusual bird seen in a local park. Soon, he does part-time work in a natural history museum. By **21**, he has published 20 papers. He gets his Ph.D. at **22**, and then goes to work at IQ testing. He becomes fascinated with children's "wrong" answers, and how they provide reasons for them. Some published papers on this lead to the post of Director of Studies at the J. J. Rousseau Institute, Geneva. In five books (written between **30** and **36**) he outlines his life work; how children grow up and develop their thinking ability.

"Gifted" children: a rough definition is an IQ of 140 and/or in the top two percent of the population in academic skills or in music or dance.

"Little Professor" is a concept in Transactional Analysis, of the Adult in the Child, or a premature adult.

In Elizabethan England, the lower classes entered the work force almost as soon as they could make a physical contribution. Education was reserved for those males born into families which could afford to keep them out of the work force between **7** and **10**. University education, for males in rich families, could begin at around **16**. According to researcher Margaret Spufford, "Between 1580 and 1700, 11 percent of women, 15 percent of laborers, and 21 percent of husbandmen could sign their names, against 56 percent of tradesmen and craftsmen, and 65 percent of yeomen."

UNESCO statistics of 1979 show that the percentage of children of primary school age who are not in fact attending school is: 22 percent in Latin America; 36 percent in Asia; and 49 percent in Africa. In India (1980) it is said that 62 percent of female children do not attend primary school, and that two-thirds of all children are unable to read or write.

MONEY, WORK

Robert Owen: end of his formal education (1781); he goes to work in a shop in Stamford, Lincolnshire. (cf. **28***)

John D. Rockefeller: his mother is given to tying him to a post and beating him (1849); his father is a salesman of quack medicine. (cf. **31***)

A third of U.S. black children are in families partly or wholly dependent on welfare (1978).

Eligibility: depending on waivers and local legislation, people **10** and **11** are allowed to do harvesting work in the U.S.A. for eight weeks in the summer, when school is not in session. They may work up to 40 hours per week.

ART

William Hogarth in 1707: his father (**44**) is sent to prison for debt, owing to failure of the latter's Coffee Shop. Hogarth and the whole family have to move into the prison, and they live within the compound for five years. At **16**, Hogarth is apprenticed to an engraver, and he sets up on his own at **23**. He becomes a successful portrait painter for the rich; but his most famous works are "A Rake's Progress" at **36**; and "Marriage à la Mode" at **46**. He helps to start a large London orphanage when he is **42**.

Many of the greatest hand-colored prints of the eighteenth and early nineteenth centuries were finished by children—only children could stand the boredom of the work. By **10**, their eyesight might be so damaged that they would have to retire.

MUSIC—CLASSICAL

W. A. Mozart stays briefly in Lausanne (1766) and a local journal says, "In young Mozart, the sensitiveness and the precision of his ear are so great that discordant, shrill, or too loud notes bring tears to his eyes." And a warning: ". . . is it not to be feared that, developing so young, he may grow old prematurely? It is only too true that precocious children have often been worn out in the flower of their youth." (cf. **12***)

It can show itself as the earliest [talent] because music is something you are born with, something interior, which needs no great exterior nurture and requires no experience derived from living.—Johann Wolfgang von Goethe (1749–1832), on infant prodigies and musical talent.

Claude Debussy enters the Paris Conservatoire (1872, Oct. 22) after the competitive entry examination. Generally his home life is poor and insecure—his father (**36**) is a drifter, and his mother (**35**) has an aversion to children, so that Debussy is brought up by an aunt. He does very well at the Conservatoire, and begins composing in his late teens. He writes *Clair de Lune* at **27***.

Percy Bysshe Shelley is sent to boarding school (1802) and for the first time he plays with other boys, as his family consists of four younger sisters. Though pushed around at school, he has a mystical revelation at **11**, that in his life he should choose only the pure and the lovely. (cf. **20***)

John Betjeman shows his poems to his schoolteacher (1916), but the latter offers no encouragement. The teacher is T. S. Eliot (**27**). (cf. **17***)

PLAYS

I would that there were no age between **ten** and **three-and-twenty**, or that youth would sleep out the rest; for there is nothing in the between but getting wenches with child, wrong the ancientry, stealing, fighting.—*The Winter's Tale*, William Shakespeare (1564–1616).

Youth is a wonderful thing. What a crime to waste it on children!—George Bernard Shaw (1856–1950).

FILMS

Charlie Chaplin's widowed mother is taken away to a mental institution (1899), and he returns home to a bare room which contains "a half-filled packet of tea, three halfpence, some keys, and several pawn tickets."

David Niven is expelled from his boarding school for sending a matchbox full of dog shit to a friend (**10**) who is ill with pneumonia (1920).

Charles Bronson: his father dies, probably from miner's black lung disease (1931).

Shirley Temple: *Rebecca of Sunnybrook Farm* (1938).

LOVE, LIFE

For a child of **10**, one year is 10 percent of his existence, but for an adult of **50**, the same period is only two percent. That interval of a year, therefore, is judged by the child as relatively long and by the adult as relatively short. . . .—Leonard Doob, following French philosopher Paul Janet in 1877, on the child's sense of time.

In a Devon village (England, 1688), 35.5 percent of the children had lost at least one parent. Death took away as many parents as divorce does today. Also, you had small chance of knowing your grandparents, as people married late, and had children late. But they died early, compared to the present. ". . . resident grandparents were uncommon, and conversation across the generations must have been relatively rare, much more so than it is today." The reason for this lack of communication was that your grandparents were dead.

Eligibility: males were now old enough to be married, according to the laws of Middle Assyria (1450 B.C.). But neighboring Babylonian codes did not fix any minimum age for marriage. In Old Testament times, Jews seem to have regarded **18** as the appropriate age for marriage, and **20** would be leaving it a little late.

In sixteenth century England, you would now probably kneel when talking to your parents. In Victorian times, you would almost certainly stand up.

In Japan, May 5 is a national holiday, "Tango-no-Sekku," in honor of children.

Eighty-one percent of children are now in two-parent families, and about 19 percent, or eleven million people, are now in one-parent families (U.S.A., 1979). A slightly earlier survey suggested that 15 percent of U.S. whites are now in one-parent families; for blacks the comparable figure is over 50 percent.

The aging of wines and spirits: whiskey is typically drunk when it is **5** to **15** years old; claret, **3** years; white wine, **0** to **2**; port at **3** to **7**, with very old port being **15** to **30**+.

EXPLORATION

David Livingstone leaves school, and is sent to work in a cotton factory, as a "piercer" (1823). With his first earnings, he buys Ruddiman's *Rudiments of Latin.* Later, perhaps his best-known moment as an explorer is at **58***.

In Hungary, you are now eligible to work on the "Young Pioneers" Railway of Budapest. This is a narrow-gauge system of eleven kilometers and eight stations. Apart from the drivers, all staff are **10** to **14**. You would work two-week tours of duty, and not attend school during that time. The railway follows a scenic route in the Buda Hills, and is a Hungarian tourist attraction.

LAW, CRIME

In Britain, this is the beginning of criminal responsibility. You can now be punished for a crime. Previously, you would be too young to have control over yourself.

In the child killings in Atlanta (1979–81), the victims are typically **7** to **15**, black and male.

SPORTS

Arthur Ashe (1953) is invited to the home of Robert Walter Johnson (**54**), a black M.D. who organizes tennis camps for promising blacks. At this time, there is effectively a color bar in most of the tennis world.

 At **14**, Ashe wins in his age group at the ATA National Championship. At **18**, he gets a tennis scholarship to U.C.L.A. At **25**, he wins the U.S. Open. At **32**, he wins the singles title at Wimbledon.

11

HISTORY—U.S.A.

George Washington: his father dies (1743, Apr. 12), leaving 10,000 acres and 49 slaves. The household in which he now grows up consists of his powerful (and impossible to fully please) mother, himself, and four younger children. (cf. **15***)

SOCIAL SCIENCE, EDUCATION

B. F. Skinner: first masturbation (1915); first knowledge of menstruation at **19**, and first sex at **23**. He discovers masturbation accidentally—the first touch reinforces his desire to continue the stimulus. (cf. **23***)

The "**11+**" exam was taken by English and Welsh children (1945–c. 1970), and it decided whether they would go to a Grammar School (leading to office and managerial jobs) or Secondary Modern schools (which led to blue-collar and laboring jobs).

MONEY, WORK

Jean Paul Getty: his lawyer father has to go on a business trip to Bartlesville, Indian Territory (later, Oklahoma) (1903). He gets caught up in the excitement of the new oil discoveries, and buys his first lease for $500. Paul Getty watches as the third well is successful. In his childhood, Getty's favorite reading is the adventure stories of G. A. Henty. (cf. **24***)

MUSIC—CLASSICAL

Beethoven is unpaid deputy to the court organist in Bonn (1782). He goes on the payroll at **13**. He is educated in music by his father, who is keen to be another "Mozart's father," but he lacks the ability and discipline to do this. Beethoven is obviously highly talented, but is not an infant prodigy. He does not establish himself as preeminent until his early **30**s. The father's drunkenness and poverty provide a humiliating childhood for Beethoven. His mother dies (at **40**) when he is **16**, and his father dies (at c. **52**) when Beethoven is **21**. (cf. **20***)

Franz Liszt gives his first concert in Vienna (1822, Dec. 1). At his second concert (also **11**), he is given a kiss of admiration by Beethoven (**52**).

LITERATURE

Charles Dickens moves from a country town, where he had enjoyed family life, to London, where the family is broken up (1823). His schooling ends, and his father is taken away to debtors' prison. Dickens starts work, and is employed in labeling bottles in a shoe-black factory, for seven shillings per week. (cf. **24***)

Walt Whitman leaves school, and becomes an office boy (1830). At **36***, he publishes his first book of poems, *Leaves of Grass.*

Agatha Christie, in 1902: her father dies. Up till now, the family had had an idyllic existence, with her father's only occupation being to play cards at his club. It now turns out that father has spent most of the family money. (cf. **29***)

PLAYS

Molière's mother dies (1633). His father remarries, but his stepmother dies when he is **15**.

Noel Coward has his first acting engagement in the professional theater (1911). He plays the part of a mussel in *The Goldfish,* an all-children matinee. Others in the cast include Michael MacLiammoir (**10**) and Ninette de Valois (**12**). At **12**, Coward goes on to play a mushroom in *An Autumn Idyll.* At **20**, Coward tells a friend that he will never have a settled income "because it would take away my ambition to succeed." At **24**, he stars in his own play, *The Vortex* which is attacked for the anger which it displays. At **25**, he has four productions running on the London stage. Later, his work includes *Private Lives* at **31**; the song "Don't Put Your Daughter on the Stage, Mrs. Worthington" at **33**; *Still Life* at **35**, later the film *Brief Encounter* at **44**; *Blithe Spirit* at **41**; and at **55** a season at Las Vegas, playing to what he calls "Nescafé society." In his **50**s, he is ignored as a has-been, but he manages to live past this until at **64** his *Hay Fever,* written at **24**, is successfully revived, and he becomes a "Grand Old Man" of the theater.

FILMS

W. C. Fields has a row with his father and runs away from home (1890).

Sabu: *Elephant Boy* (1936).

Elizabeth Taylor: *Lassie Come Home* (1943); and *National Velvet* at **12**, her sixth film and an enormous hit. Later, *A Place in the Sun* is at **19**; *Suddenly Last Summer* is at **28**; *Cleopatra* is at **30**; and *Who's Afraid of Virginia Woolf* is at **34**. By **44**, she has had seven marriages.

Nipper: death (1895). He is the dog who is portrayed listening to the brass horn of a phonograph; the painting of him is by his master, Francis Barraud (**43**) who sells the picture to The Gramophone Company, later known as His Master's Voice. Nipper dies now without ever knowing that he will become one of the most memorable images in the history of the trademark.

TV, ETC.

Robert Strom wins $224,000 by answering questions about electronics, in the TV quiz show "The $64,000 Challenge" (U.S. 1959). Shortly afterward, Teddy Nadler (**49**) earns $252,000 on the same show; previously, Nadler's highest income has been only $70 per week. The financing of these giant prizes is by Charles Revson (**53**) whose Revlon cosmetics company is booming, thanks to this TV exposure. Perhaps the most famous contestant of the program is Charles van Doren (**29**). Another famous winner is Dr. Joyce Brothers (approximately **30** in 1957).

LOVE, LIFE

Jacqueline Bouvier (Kennedy) is said to have read *Gone with the Wind* three times (1941).

LAW, CRIME

Mary Bell kills Martin Brown (**4**) and Brian Howe (**3**) (1968, in England); she is sent to prison for life.

SPORTS

Sonja Henie (1924) participates in her first Olympic Games, in ice skating, though with no success. But she gains Olympic gold medals at **15**, **19**, and **23**. She retires at **23**, turns professional, and makes the first of ten films, *One in a Million.* She dies of leukemia at **57**.

Billie Jean King (1955) saves to buy her first tennis racquet by doing odd jobs to accumulate the necessary $8. She goes on to win her first Wimbledon title at **17**, in the doubles. She wins the Wimbledon singles title for a record six times, between **22** and **31**. She also wins the U.S. championship four times, between **23** and **30**.

12

HEALTH

Al Capp is injured in a streetcar accident (New Haven, 1921) and his right leg has to be amputated above the knee. Capp later becomes a cartoonist, and does the "Li'l Abner" strip between **25** and **68**, and lives until **70**.

Puberty has dropped from around **17** to around **13**, in the past 100 years.

Females have a growth spurt around **12**, and males at around **14**. Between **12** and **16**, male strength doubles.

HISTORY—WORLD

Adolf Hitler attends his first Wagner opera, *Lohengrin,* at the Linz Opera House (1891). At **13**, his father **(65)** dies; at **17**, his mother **(47)** dies. At **19**, he is rejected for the second time in his application to the Vienna Academy of Art. At **20**, Hitler is a tramp in Vienna, for three months sleeping in the open. He moves into an institution for down-and-outs, and survives by painting watercolors of the city. At **24**, he is found "unfit" for the army, as being too weak; he moves to Munich, and makes money by selling his paintings from door to door. He is accepted into the army at the beginning of World War I, and finishes the war with the rank of corporal **(29*)**.

HISTORY—U.S.A.

Adlai Stevenson, playing with a gun, accidentally kills a cousin **(16)** (1916).

Jimmy Carter reads (1936) *War and Peace.* (cf. **15***)

HISTORY—U.K.

Edward V becomes King (1483, Apr. 9) at the death of his father, Edward IV **(41)**. But he and his brother, Richard, Duke of York **(11)** are kept prisoner—the Little Princes in the Tower—and smothered to death by order of Richard III **(30)**. Edward V would have achieved his majority at **14**, no longer being under the direction of a council which was set up for him at his birth.

Horatio Nelson enters the Navy (Nov. 1770).

Winston Churchill does badly in the entrance exam to Harrow, but is accepted anyway (1886). He goes on to do very badly at the school. (cf. **20***)

Shirley Williams auditions for the starring role in the film *National Velvet* (1944), but the part is given to Elizabeth Taylor (also **12**). Williams goes on to become a Labour cabinet minister.

RELIGION, PHILOSOPHY

Jesus is in the temple at Jerusalem, "sitting in the midst of the teachers, both hearing them and asking them questions." When asked why he has stayed so long, he replies "Knowst ye not that I must be about my Father's business?" (cf. **30***)

In the Anglican church, this is the approximate time for the confirmation service—to "confirm" the promises that were made on your behalf at baptism (**0**).

SOCIAL SCIENCE, EDUCATION

"The Wild Boy of Aveyron," in 1797: this is a boy who is found running wild in the forests of southern France. Eventually he is captured—he is naked, dirty, apparently a deaf-mute, and runs on all fours, as an animal. He is nothing like a Noble Savage. After capture he becomes a curiosity and a celebrity. He is named Victor, and is educated at a deaf institute in Paris. Unfortunately he is maintained all his adult life as a mental defective, and dies in Paris at about **43**.

Carl Jung, in 1887: three days of religious conversion. He has a dream of a divine turd falling from the sky and smashing a cathedral. His interpretation: this is the beginning of his integration of the dark side of life into the religious view. This integration has been lost in formal Christianity and lost most immediately to his father (**45**), a pastor. At **15**, Jung has his first communion; he is deeply disappointed, and never takes communion again. For him, Christianity has lost the acceptance of the fact of good and evil; it has therefore become a code in which it is impossible to win—your life is just varying degrees of sin. (cf. **25***)

SCIENCE, TECHNOLOGY

Thomas Alva Edison obtains employment selling newspapers on a train (1859). He soon develops the business so that he is employing two other people. He starts the *Weekly Herald* which he produces on the train. At **15**, he becomes a telegraph operator, and there follows a period in which he is an inventor, but also something of a wanderer. His first major invention is at **27**, and the effect is to quadruple the number of messages that can be sent over a telegraph line. He invents the phonograph at **30***.

Mozart: *Bastien and Bastienne* (1778); this is a one-act opera, and his first. (cf. **13***)

Artur Rubinstein: first European tour as a concert pianist (1898).

LITERATURE

(Sir) Walter Scott enters Edinburgh University (Nov. 1783). (cf. **42***)

Anthony Trollope starts a diary (1827) as an escape from his mad family. He is sent to boarding school, but is withdrawn at **15**, owing to his father's poor earnings. At **16**, finances improve when his mother Frances, publishes a best-selling book about a trip to the U.S.A. (cf. **28***)

Mark Twain leaves school (1847). He later becomes a licensed riverboat pilot at **22**. He deserts from the Confederate Army after one week (**25**), and eventually ends up as a reporter. At **29**, he writes *The Celebrated Jumping Frog of Calaveras County.* (cf. **48***)

John Masefield: his father dies (1890)—his mother had died when he was **6**. This is now the end of his childhood, and at **13** he is sent away to sea. He survives only three months, but continues traveling. He writes *Sea Fever* at **22**, while working as a bank clerk in London.

AGE 12 YRS

Denis Wheatley is expelled from Dulwich College, London (1908), a school which he hates for the rest of his life. At **80**, after a highly successful career as a writer, he publishes a lot of abuse about the school in his autobiography.

Lindsay Brown publishes *The Treasure of Dubarry Castle* (1978), a 30,000 word adventure story for children. Although this is her first published book, it is the thirtieth book which she has written since **5**.

FILMS

Katharine Hepburn: her brother Tom (**15**) dies (1921) by hanging.

Jane Fonda: her mother dies (1950, Apr. 14) by slashing her throat in a mental hospital. Eight months later, her brother Peter (**11**) nearly kills himself with a gun.

Tatum O'Neal: *The Bad News Bears* (1976). At **9**, she had been the youngest person to win an Oscar as Best Supporting Actress, for her part in *Paper Moon.*

Jodie Foster: a prostitute in *Taxi Driver* (1976). By **8**, she had completed 45 TV commercials. By **17**, she has made twelve films, and she enters Yale University.

12 is the average age of all the stars in the film *Bugsy Malone* (1976).

Brooke Shields: *Pretty Baby* (1978), directed by Louis Malle. She is Violet, a prostitute, who is auctioned off as "the finest delicacy New Orleans has to offer."

Giovanni Medici is secretly created a Cardinal of the Roman Catholic church (1489)—the youngest ever. He is the son of Lorenzo Medici, the Magnificent (**40**). Giovanni becomes Pope Leo X at **38**, and dies in office at **46**. He is not a good argument in favor of teenage cardinals as he is best remembered for his ineffective handling of the Reformation; at **45**, he excommunicates Martin Luther (**37**).

Jean-Jacques Rousseau is sent to work as an apprentice to an engraver (1725). This is a shock to him, following the pleasures of his upbringing. His hymn to childhood, *Émile*, is published at **50**. Paradoxically, Rousseau goes on to become a poor parent—he abandons his children at birth. In *Émile,* the ideal education is: no formal teaching until **12**, so that the person is a free child of nature; **12** to **15**, the formal education can all be fitted in here; **15+** is the time for any religious education, and you can then begin taking part in the world. Rousseau's reasoning is that individuals are born good, but corrupted by society, in the same way that the human race once had its own golden age of innocence and cooperation. With Émile, "Never command him to do anything whatever, not the least thing in the world. . . . Inflict on him no species of punishment." Émile does not need instruction: "All that he sees and hears attracts his notice, and he remembers it." About sex education: answer all his questions without embarrassment, as "Whoever blushes is already guilty; true innocence is ashamed of nothing." It is best to grow up in the country; if this is impossible, at least learn from country ways, as "Cities are the grave of the human species . . . peasants generally have more accurate minds." (cf. **38***)

Some early university entrants: Thomas Cranmer goes to Cambridge University at **14** (1503)—he is associated with the Book of Common Prayer at **59** (cf. **66***). David Hume enters Edinburgh University at **11** (1722) (cf. **28***). Jeremy Bentham enters Oxford University at **12** (1760), and he later dismisses it as full of "mendacity and insincerity."

Bar Mitzvah, for Jewish males; Bas Mitzvah for females. Confirmation is at **16** or **17**.

In the Spanish Inquisition, you would now be eligible for interrogation. From 1230 onward, the first step for inquisitors on arrival in a community would be to get males **14+** and females **12+** to swear that they believe the orthodoxy, and that they will betray anyone who is not a believer.

Following Rousseau's *Émile* (above), here is a listing of some adult attitudes toward childhood. Seeing children as:

—miniature adults; once out of breast-fed infancy, they can do all the things that adults do, but slower and less skillfully.

—in need of taming; severe whippings were necessary in early schools (e.g., sixteenth century) as children had to be broken, as you would break in a horse or other animal. This was the only way to tame the wild nature of a child; the alternative was anarchy.
—in preparation for adulthood; children are being trained for real life, which is seen as life between **21** and **65**. You train during your minority for life during your majority or adult time.
—dependent and vulnerable, and in need of protection.
—charmingly and enticingly dependent on us.
—people who can teach us; we adults learn from their freshness and spontaneity.
—an excuse for expressing informal feelings which we cannot express with our adult friends.
—an excuse for sentimentalization; we see their world as an escape from adult decisions and pressures.
—the subjects of jealousy and fear; children prevent us from indulging ourselves in our own lifestyle. Children seize both the privileges of dependency and the privileges of independence. Children are a nuisance and an irrelevance to the good life which we adults wish to lead for ourselves.
—as a reproach; they are straightforward and uncompromising; they remind us uncomfortably of the compromises (the giving-in) that we have had to make in order to survive and prosper as adults.
—part of our completeness as a mature adult.
—for good or ill, part of the endless process of nature; we are unavoidably programmed to want to conceive and look after children.
—our insurance policy against the future; we invest care in them now, and this pays off later, when they care for us and prevent us from getting lonely.
—your only true connection with the future; access to them is deeply valuable, and control of this access can be used as a bargaining counter.
—being gradually socialized into our culture, which will imperceptibly become theirs.
—people who have the same rights as any other people; being young should not lead to your being denied your rights; parents should not aim to change "their" children because they are not "theirs" in the first place.
—a chance for you to lead your life over again; this time, you can do better.
—the key to our psychological health as adults; the emotional

events in childhood determine our sanity later in life. And, therapy for adults is primarily a reworking of the emotional events during our childhood.

—a metaphor; the development of an individual child today is similar to the development pattern of the whole human race; civilization itself went through a gradual period of "growing up," etc.

—a source of knowledge; according to Margaret Mead, in a no-change society, children learn from adults; in a rapid-change society, the elders learn from the adolescents.

—an alternative: "Live fast, die young."

—unmalleable; genetic forces play a large part in forming their personalities, so adults should not waste time in trying to guide them in a specific direction; you should enjoy children as you find them.

—just a stage of life that should be as pleasant as possible, but no more or less so than at **20** or **60**.

SOCIAL SCIENCE, EDUCATION

For those few who went to university in sixteenth-century England and later, **12** to **14** would be an appropriate time to enter. For example, Thomas Hobbes, (**14**) at Oxford, in 1602; Adam Smith, (**14**) at Glasgow University, in 1737; by contrast, Henry George, later the economist, leaves school in California at **13** (1852).

At the University of Paris, in 1215, undergraduates could enter at **13** to **14**, and the faculty had to be at least **21**. At King's Hall, Cambridge, in 1380, the minimum age was **14**, but typical entry was at **15** to **17**, and law students might be up to **25**. In 1140, the age of students on entry to Bologna University was **18** to **25**, or older than undergraduates today on entry. People came to Bologna after they had already achieved some office or distinction at work. Early entry to university is dependent on two separate factors: (1) unusual ability in the student, and (2) differing conceptions of the place of the university in the educational system.

MONEY, WORK

George Eastman's education ends in the seventh grade (1861)—he later starts Kodak at around **30**. (cf. **32***)

Both John D. MacArthur and Daniel K. Ludwig leave school in the eighth grade; and later in 1976, are termed the two richest individuals in the U.S.

RENAISSANCE

Michelangelo is apprenticed to the painter Domenico Ghirlandaio (**39**, in 1488) and in the following year he is chosen to join the sculpture school organized by Lorenzo de'Medici (**40**). As a student there, he has his nose broken in a fight with Pietro Torrigiano (**17**, in 1489). The latter goes on to become the sculptor who brings the new Renaissance style to England, by making the first classical tomb in Westminster Abbey, at **40**. Michelangelo's first well-known sculpture is the "Madonna of the Stairs," at **17**. At **21**, he arrives in Rome, with introductions to leading personalities there, and at **24** he sculpts the St. Peter's "Pieta," of the Virgin Mary holding the dead Christ. Michelangelo's mother had died at **26**, when he was **6**. This sculpture is the only one that he signs—his name is on a band which crosses the breast of the Virgin. At **28**, he produces "David" in Florence, and a committee of artists is chosen to decide on the statue's location. This committee (1504) includes: Botticelli (**59**), Perugino (**54**), Leonardo da Vinci (**52**), Filippino Lippi (**47**), and Lorenzo di Credi (**46**). They choose to place "David" in front of the Palazzo Vecchio. Michelangelo later returns to Rome, and works on the Sistine Chapel from **33** to **37***.

ART

Renoir in 1854: he leaves school, and becomes an apprentice in a porcelain factory. (cf. **33***)

Henri Toulouse-Lautrec trips and breaks his leg (1878). At **14**, he trips again, and breaks the other leg. These injuries stunt his growth, and he is something of a dwarf for the rest of his life. He has his own painting studio at **21**, and begins developing his characteristic style around **24**. He dies at **37**, in a family chateau, suffering from drink and the effects of his self-destructive lifestyle.

MUSIC—CLASSICAL

Mozart receives from the Pope, the Knighthood of the Order of the Golden Spur (1769). He composes the opera *La Finta Semplice* and at **14** another opera *Mitridate.* By **13**, he has composed 558 pages of music. (cf. **16***)

Chopin writes his first mazurka (c. 1823.) (cf. **21***)

Daniel Barenboim plays, at his first concert in London, Mozart's A Major Concerto, with Josef Krips conducting (1956, Jan. 16). He is reputed to have memorized 300 solo piano pieces, and 14 piano concertos.

This is the average age of boys' voices to break. In the 1870s, it was as high as **17**.

LITERATURE

H. G. Wells is apprenticed to a draper (1879).

Virginia Woolf: her mother dies (1895), and her father cracks up, while she herself has a minor nervous breakdown. At **15**, her stepsister dies. At **22***, her father (**72**) dies, and she goes almost mad, cannot eat, and attempts suicide. At **24**, her elder brother (**26**) dies from malaria.

FILMS

The man who hates children can't be all bad.—W. C. Fields (1879–1946).

Norma Talmadge signs a contract with Vitagraph (1910). At **14**, she appears in *A Tale of Two Cities.*

Greta Garbo leaves school (June, 1919); her father is ill, and she looks after him until he dies, at **48** (1920, June 1), when she is **14**.

Judy Garland signs a contract with MGM (1935).

LOVE, LIFE

Minimum age for marriage: countries which set **14** (male) and **12** (female) as the legal minimum include Honduras, Panama, Colombia, Ecuador, Ireland, Bolivia, and Chile. In practice, not many people will in fact take advantage of this. For example, in Ireland half of marriages are by people **20** to **24**, only 13 percent are by people **19** and under, and in 1977 only two brides were **12** to **14**. Similarly, the birthrate for teenage mothers in Ireland is 10 percent of that for women **25** to **29**.

In ancient Rome, the minimum age for marriage was **12** (female) and **14** (male). Typically women were married before **16** and sometimes before they reached puberty. Men would be older, and if in the upper class might wait until they had achieved some office, in their early **20**s. Before her marriage, a girl would ceremonially say good-bye to the toys of her childhood, and place them on the altar of the household gods. In Europe of the middle ages, there would similarly be little time for women between puberty and marriage. In the French Revolution, the minimum marriage age was set at **12** (female) and **15** (male). In Belgium in the early nineteenth century, Adolphe Quetelet reported that women were typically married at **14** to **16**.

Beating, spanking, or smacking children is forbidden in Sweden. A child is like any other person, and so an assault is against the law, even if a parent is involved. The 1979 law states "A child may not be subjected to physical punishment or other injurious or humiliating treatment." Sweden maintains a parental education program, to help those parents such as immigrants and visitors who have been brought up to expect rights of physical and other punishment over their children. A new proposal would give children the right to their own attorney in any court proceedings at which their interests are being discussed, such as in divorce cases or other conflicts over access.

Males, **12** to **14**, watch about three hours twenty-two minutes of TV per day; and females watch three hours twelve minutes. This is the peak age of children's viewing. TV viewing is very age related. People **15** to **19** watch about two hours per day, roughly the same as at **5** to **7** (Greenberg, U.K., 1971). About violence and age: a survey of U.S. TV in 1967–69 showed that on prime time there were eight violent episodes per hour. Children's cartoons contain three to six times more of these violent episodes than the adult prime-time shows.

LAW, CRIME

Eve Postell is sent to prison until **127**, by a Florida court (1979) for second degree murder. She is one of five people, **12** to **17**, who rob the home of Ralph Germano (**85**). He later dies from the attack. The judge retains veto power over parole until Postell is **101**. In another case in Florida, Donald Palmer (**25**, in 1980) is convicted of causing the deaths of two people in a robbery, and he is sent to prison until he is **1,010**.

Males caught as vagabonds could now be sent into Royal Navy ships (U.K., eighteenth century), to act initially as servants of officers. People under **13** could be placed similarly in the merchant navy.

Boys **13** and under cannot be accused of a sex offense; they are assumed to be unable to perform sexually.

Over one third of the cars stolen in London are taken by people **10** to **16**.

14

HISTORY—WORLD

Ivan the Terrible starts to seize personal power (1544). At **3**, he had become Grand Prince of Moscow, the head of state, and he had been orphaned at **8**. Now, to demonstrate his determination, he has one of his enemies eaten alive by dogs. At **16**, he is crowned Czar. He is married, after inspecting 1,000 virgins who have been assembled for him in the Kremlin. But at **29** his first wife dies, and Ivan soon begins on a reign of terror. He dies at **53**, having killed (among others) his own son, and also an elephant who did not bow down to him.

Marie Antoinette is married (1770) to the future King Louis XVI (**15**) of France. They had first met two days previously, and it is another seven years before they first have sex. The marriage is expected to bring stability, as it unites France and Austria. They become King and Queen at **19** and **18**; but later they are guillotined during the French Revolution at **38*** and **37**.

Joseph Stalin enters the Tiflis Theological Seminary (1894), which he leaves at **19**. He goes to work in a geophysical survey, and makes his first speech at **20**. He organizes his first demonstration at **21**, and is first arrested at **22**. He is held in Siberia between **23** and **25**, and is arrested six more times between then and the Revolution at **37**. During these years, he is not a prominent figure in the Bolshevik movement. At **37**, he is the new Commissar for Nationalities. His period of power begins at **44***, with the death of Lenin (**53**).

HISTORY—U.S.A.

Eligibility: you may now become a page at the U.S. Congress, and join the Capitol Page School.

HISTORY—U.K.

The future King Edward I sails for Gascony (Aug. 1253), a part of France that was given to him at **13**. He marries at **15**, and becomes King at **33**.

Edward III is proclaimed King (1327, Jan. 13), as his mother has held his father, Edward II (**42**) prisoner—the latter is murdered nine months later. Edward III takes charge of the kingdom at **18**, by executing several of his father's murderers.

William Pitt the Younger enters Cambridge University (1773). He has been a sickly child, and has been educated at home by his father (**64**), the Prime Minister. Pitt graduates at **17**, and becomes an MP at **21**; Chancellor of the Exchequer at **23**. (cf. **22***)

Emmeline Goulden is taken to her first women's suffrage meeting (1872). At **21**, she marries Richard Pankhurst (**41**), and she supports him extensively in his campaigns for women's rights, socialism, and other causes. She has four children, and does not begin campaigning in her own right until after her husband's death. At **45**, she founds WSPU, the Women's Social and Political Union. She starts her first suffragette riot at **47***.

RELIGION, PHILOSOPHY

St. Pancras: martyrdom.

St. Bernadette: visions, at Lourdes (1858).

Kahlil Gibran conceives the idea of *The Prophet,* and works on it intermittently, until completion at **40**, in 1923.

Children's attitudes toward adults; adults can be seen as:

—gods, superhuman, faraway;

—pathetic traitors to their own youthful ideals; therefore only useful as models of how not to do it;

—an undifferentiated mass;
—not part of a continuum which might go from children–adult–old, but an entirely separate tribe;
—unbelievably old.

SOCIAL SCIENCE, EDUCATION

Adam Smith enters Glasgow University (1737); later, he goes to Oxford University, where the prevailing lassitude makes a lifelong impression on him—both the students and the faculty are insulated from the stimulus of the market, so that "In the University of Oxford, the greater part of the public professors have, for these many years, given up altogether even the pretence of teaching" (as he writes at **52***). Education is organized "for the interest, or more properly speaking, for the ease of the masters." The indolence of the faculty is caused by their income coming not from fees but from foundation emoluments. The indolence of the students arises from their being forced to spend time at college, simply to obtain an occupational qualification.

ART

The sculpture "Little Dancer at **14**" (1880) is by Degas (**46**).

LITERATURE

Beryl Bainbridge (later, the novelist) is expelled from school for being "a corrupting moral influence."

PLAYS

Juliet falls in love with Romeo (**16**), a few days before her **14th** birthday, in the play by William Shakespeare (**31**, in 1595). After being unable to stay together, they both die. Coincidentally, Juliet's mother had been **14** at the birth of Juliet. And in *The Tempest,* Miranda is **14**. *Romeo and Juliet* expresses the widespread sensation that young love is the most thrilling love of our lives, but also so passionate that it can end only in sadness. Significantly, the play has inspired more derivatives than any other work by Shakespeare. There are operas by Berlioz (**35**, in 1839); Gounod (**46**, in 1864); Delius (**28**, in 1900); and Leonard Bernstein (**39**, in 1957). Tchaikovsky's *Romeo and Juliet* Overture is written at **29** (1869). Prokofiev's ballet music is at **44** (1935). Films include those by George Cukor (**37**, in 1936) and by Franco Zeffirelli (**45**, in 1968).

FILMS

Charlie Chaplin leaves the theater for a short time, and becomes a messenger boy in the post office (1904).

Alfred Hitchcock leaves school, and gets a job in engineering drawing (1913).

James Cagney is a part-time office boy on the *New York Sun* (1913); at **15**, he works as a part-time assistant in the New York Public Library.

Cary Grant is expelled from Fairfield School, Bristol, for exploring the girls' lavatories (1918); he goes to work in a traveling theater show. Coincidentally, Dyan Cannon is said to get beaten by her headmaster for an incident in the boys' lavatories of her school.

Deanna Durbin: *Three Smart Girls* (1936); her first film.

Donald Sutherland is Canada's youngest radio announcer (1948).

MUSIC—NON-CLASSICAL

Helen Shapiro: "Please Don't Treat Me like a Child," and "You Don't Know," and "Walking Back to Happiness" (1961). The last two became number one. But by **16**, she is called a has-been. In adult life, she continues as a performer in clubs, but never again achieves the prominence she had at **14**. She is so often used as an example of rise-and-fall in the pop world that her adult nonfame continues to keep her famous.

TV, ETC.

The average person in the U.S.A. has, since **5**, seen thirteen thousand deaths on television.

LOVE, LIFE

King Louis XIII of France is married, in 1615, to Anne of Austria (also **14**). They do not have sex for three years, until a couple of friends show them how it is done. The first child is born when they are both **37**.

Scottish orphans traditionally now have the right to name their own guardians.

EXPLORATION

Bill Cody sets a Pony Express record (1860)—he rides 320 miles at an average speed of 15 m.p.h. At **37**, he starts "Buffalo Bill's Wild West Show," and he tours the U.S.A. and Europe; in this show, he defines the image that is later permanently attached to the Wild West. At **67**, Buffalo Bill Cody starts a new career, by appearing in silent movies.

LAW, CRIME

Robert Earl May, Jr., is sent to Missouri State Penitentiary, on four counts of armed robbery (1978). He had used a shotgun in a theft, and helped beat up a grocery store saleswoman. According to his sentence, he would not be eligible for parole until **62**.

In Roman times, this was the age of majority for males, for property and other purposes. Males could now marry; females could marry at **12**.

In Britain until the nineteenth century, you were now eligible for punishment by transportation to a penal colony.

This is the peak age for convictions (U.K., 1965). Half of the people found guilty of crimes are aged **10** to **21**. Roughly, the favorite crime per age group is: **10** to **14**, larceny; **14** to **16**, breaking and entering; **17** to **20**, violence; **21** on, sex, fraud.

SPORTS

Mikhail Botvinnik (1925) beats the current chess champion, José Capablanca (**36**), when the latter is giving a simultaneous display. Botvinnik is a Soviet Master at **16**, and wins the Russian national championship at **20**.

Ilie Nastase (1960): his first tennis "incident." He hits the son of his coach during an argument. At **17**, he receives his first suspension. And at **32**, he is banned from the Davis Cup because of his bad behavior; he also has to miss the U.S. Open because of another three-month suspension. Nastase is otherwise a highly skilled player; for example, he gets to the Wimbledon singles final at **26** and **30**.

15

HEALTH

On the advantages of being with youth: Hermippus is a Roman schoolteacher who lives until **115**. All his pupils had been girls; this was seen as the cause of his longevity, because you should "breathe the air of young girls night and morning, and . . . by doing so the vital forces will be strengthened and preserved, as adepts know well that the breath of young girls contains the vital principle in all its purity" (from a book by Elie Metchnikoff, a researcher on longevity, cf. **100***).

Teenage mothers: countries with a high fertility rate for women **15** to **19** include Cameroon, where there are 297 births yearly for every 1,000 women **15** to **19**; U.S. Virgin Islands, 230; Liberia, 187; Honduras, 162; and El Salvador, 149. Countries with a low teenage mother rate include: Japan, 13.7; Holland, 11.3; Switzerland, 12.4; and Hong Kong, 17.6. For comparison, the U.S. figure is 57.5; Canada, 33.8; and England and Wales, 32.4.

For mothers **15** and under, there were 1,338 illegitimate births and 3,526 abortions (U.K., 1975). In the same age group, about 600 girls each year have gonorrhea.

In a developing country, it is typical to have half the population in their mid-teens or younger. For example, Mexico (1977) had a population in which half were **16.8** or younger. In Western Europe in 1865, about one third of the population was **14** or below. The figure for England was 36 percent between **0** and **14**, and France 27 percent. In 1820, the median age of the U.S. was **17**; in 1860, **19.4**; and it reached **25** in 1920.

HISTORY—WORLD

Clovis: crowned King, at Tournai (481 A.D.); he lives until **45**.

The future King Henry IV of France: at **15**, in charge of his own army (1569); he becomes King at **35**.

The future Catherine the Great is married to Peter III (**16**) of Russia. When she is **32**, her husband becomes Czar; but at **33**, she is proclaimed Empress, and her husband is by chance killed almost immediately afterward. Catherine becomes sole ruler of Russia until her death at **67***.

HISTORY—U.S.A.

George Washington, in 1747, is living in Virginia. At **17**, he becomes county surveyor for Culpeper, Virginia, and explores the frontier. At **20**, his half-brother Lawrence (**36**) dies, and the estate of Mount Vernon is in effect left to George Washington. His expedition and fighting around Fort Le Beouf and Fort Necessity take place at **22**, and make him well known in North America and in Europe. At **23**, his prowess as a fighter leads to him being put in charge of Virginia's forces. By his early **20**s, with his campaigns on the frontier against French forces, he has already distinguished himself as a military leader. (cf. **25***)

Abraham Lincoln, in 1824: he and his family are living in Indiana. At **19**, he makes a trip to New Orleans. At **21**, the family moves to Illinois, and he lives at New Salem, **22** to **28**. He is self-educated. He gains a place in the state legislature at **25***.

Lyndon Johnson graduates from Johnson City High School (1924). In a road accident he totally wrecks the family car and his father buys a new one. At **18**, he enters South-West State Teachers College, in San Marcos, Texas, and works as a caretaker to pay his expenses. At **23**, he becomes secretary to Congressman Richard Kleberg (**44**), the heir to the King Ranch of 1.25 million acres.

Ronald Reagan, in 1926: he is attending Dixon High School, Illinois, where he later becomes president of the student body. In the summer, he is a lifeguard at a local pool. After high school, he goes to Eureka College, Illinois, where he studies economics and sociology. Here he is also president of the student body. Upon receipt of his B.A., he becomes a sports announcer at a radio station.

Richard Nixon, in 1928, is growing up in California. At **20**, he is told by his football coach at Whittier: "Show me a good loser, and I'll show you a loser." Nixon is student body president at Whittier. He moves to Duke University Law School where he is also elected president of the student body, and from where he graduates at **24**.

John F. Kennedy is at Choate School (1932). His father (**44**) buys Scotch whiskey franchises in anticipation of the repeal of Prohibition; later, these are sold for a profit of $8 million. At **18**, John F. Kennedy is voted "most likely to succeed" by his classmates at school. At **23**, he publishes his first book, *Why England Slept,* on appeasement.

Henry Kissinger and family flee from Nazi Germany (Aug. 1938) to the U.S.A. (cf. **35***)

Jimmy Carter graduates from high school in Plains (1940). There are only 24 in the graduating class. He gets a last whipping from his father (**45**)—the sixth in eleven years—for shooting his sister in the buttocks with a BB gun. At **15**, he owns five small houses, which he rents out as an investment, bought with money he had earned himself. (cf. **25***)

HISTORY—U.K.

Lady Jane Grey is married (1553, May 21) and proclaimed Queen of England in the following month as the tool of her ambitious relatives. But Queen Mary I (**37**) quickly asserts herself and Jane is arrested. Following an unsuccessful rebellion on her behalf by Sir Thomas Wyatt (**23**), she is executed at **16**, having been forced to see the decapitated body of her husband, executed minutes before her.

Mary Queen of Scots is married (1558, Apr. 24) to the future King of France, Francis II (**14**). Her mother-in-law, Catherine de Medici (**39**) has had a similar childhood to Mary's in that she was orphaned at **0** and married at **14**. After Mary's wedding, her relative, Queen Mary of England dies (at **42**), and Mary claims the throne. At **16**, her father-in-law dies, and she becomes, nominally, Queen of France, Scotland, Ireland, and England. But at **17**, her husband dies, and a year later she has to travel back to Scotland. At **22**, Mary marries Lord Darnley (**19**), who in the following year participates in the murder of her secretary, David Rizzio (**33**). Darnley himself is murdered at **21**. Mary is captured by the English when she is **25**, and is kept in prison until **44***.

The future Duke of Wellington is taken away from Eton (1784) by his mother (**42**) owing to lack of money. A year's tutoring in Brussels marks the end of his formal education. His father had died at **45**, when Wellington was **12**. At **17**, Wellington is an army officer, and advances to full colonel at **27**, when he goes out to India. By **35**, he has made a name for himself there. His Peninsula campaigns in Spain and Portugal are from **39** to **43**; Waterloo is at **46***.

Benjamin Disraeli leaves school (1819) and has two years private study before becoming apprenticed to solicitors. He later rejects the idea of a university education—"The idea of Oxford to such an individual was an insult." At **20**, he fails in an attempt to start a newspaper, but writes his first novel *Vivian Grey*. Throughout his **20**s, he is a traveler and a novelist; he is an MP at **32**, and married at **34***. (cf. **30***)

Enoch Powell (1927) "discovers Germany"—a world both of high romantic fantasy and also of careful scholarly logic. After a brilliant (though solitary) career at university, he becomes Professor of Greek at Sydney University, and publishes his first book of poems, both at **25**. He joins the Army at **27**, and moves from private to brigadier by **32**—partly achieved by reading Clausewitz in the original German. He is an MP at **37**. (cf. **55***)

James Callaghan leaves Portsmouth North Secondary School (1927) and, on the instruction of his mother, gets a job with a pension at the end of it. This is as a clerk in the Department of Inland Revenue, where he earns 33 shillings and 6 pence. His father had died when he was **9**, and his mother then had to live on 10 shillings per week. Callaghan goes into the Navy at the beginning of World War II, and becomes an MP at the end of the war, when he is **28**.

In a sample of 20 consecutive British prime ministers, 60 percent had lost one or both parents before they reached **15** (in Lucille Iremonger's *The Fiery Chariot*, 1970).

Eligibility: at **15 years 8 months**, you are old enough to join the Army, as a junior. The effective upper age limit for entry is **25**.

SOCIAL SCIENCE, EDUCATION

. . . the season when the tide of animal spirits flows fast, and the froth of insolence rises to the surface. . . .—Xenophon (c. 388 B.C.) about the Spartans.

If male, and if at a fee-paying school in England up till the middle of the nineteenth century, you would be studying only Latin, Greek, and some Christianity. One lesson per week might be given on modern history; one more lesson per week might be on mathematics. Corporal punishment would be the rule, as it was at most times since the Romans and the Greeks. "Utilitarian" topics were despised, though gradually accepted. Roman education similarly had a heavy anti-utilitarian bias—indeed education and direct utility could well be seen as directly opposite in past educational theory. Directly useful education was for the lower classes, in the apprenticeship system.

Corporal punishment in English schools—in Croydon, outside London, 1,046 people **(12–17)** were caned in 1977–78. At Purley High School for Boys, there were 394 canings yearly, for 900 boys in the school. Corporal punishment is available for a narrow age range—typically for **11–16/17**, and sometimes for **8–11**. It is not now in the criminal justice system for any age.

Corporal punishment of children has been taken for granted, as obvious and necessary, until very recently. The first surviving description of a schoolroom is from Mari, Mesopotamia (c. 2000 B.C.) and it gives the details of caning.

You are advised to stay in school until you have graduated. In 1979, in the **16** to **24** age group, the unemployment rate for high school dropouts was 16.4 percent for whites and 29.7 percent for blacks. The unemployment rate for high school graduates was 6.4 percent for whites and 20.3 percent for blacks.

SCIENCE, TECHNOLOGY

Michael Faraday puts his head through some iron railings of a house (1806) and asks himself if he has achieved a mind-body separation. At **13**, he had left school, and worked as an errand boy. At **14**, he becomes an apprentice bookbinder. At **20**, he obtains work as a laboratory assistant. At **30**, he does remarkable work on electromagnetic lines of force, and at **40*** he invents the electricity generator.

Georg Cantor, in 1860: at his confirmation into the Lutheran Church, he receives the following letter from his father (c. **51**).

> Dearest Georg; Through the goodness of the Almighty, the Creator of the universe and Father of all living creatures, may this day be of blessed influence upon your entire future life. May you constantly and unremittingly keep before your eyes the virtuous resolutions which you have no doubt made today. . . . How often the most promising individuals are defeated after a tenuous, weak resistance in their first struggle following their entry into practical affairs. . . . But they *lacked* the *steady heart,* upon which everything depends! Now, my dear son! *Believe me,* your *sincerest, truest* and *most experienced* friend—this sure heart, *which must live in us,* is: a *truly* religious spirit.
>
> . . . to the many-sided development of the mind in many humanistic disciplines—and of this you must always be thoroughly conscious!—to all this, the second period of your life, your *youth,* now just beginning, is *destined,* in order first to *equip yourself with dignity* by means of all this for *those struggles* yet to come. . . .
>
> . . . your parents and all other members of the family have their eyes on *you* as the eldest, and expect you to be nothing *less* than a [distinguished teacher], and God willing, later perhaps a *shining star* on the horizon of science.

Georg Cantor goes on to become perhaps the leading mathematician of the nineteenth century. (cf. **50***)

William Morris (Lord Nuffield) leaves school (1893), and sets up his own bicycle repair business. At **19**, he is one of 23 cyclemakers listed in the city of Oxford. (cf. **26***)

Early nineteenth-century factory workers were typically children, teenagers, and young adults. For example, in a Lancashire cotton mill (England, 1837, according to Farr) 37 percent of the workers were **15** and under; 57 percent were **20** and under; and 82 percent were **30** and under.

Child labor became a "problem" when people outside the family began to have the capacity to exploit children during the industrial revolutions. Previously, it was thought natural that children should contribute to the family economy from an early age, for example, by being a bird scarer in the fields at about **5**.

The International Labor Office has set **15** as the minimum age for entering employment. In 1944, the ILO set **14**, and their current aim is to have **16** as the minimum working age. Often, for those **12–15**, there is legal permission to work part-time, perhaps in harvesting, or in shops on the weekends. However, the reality is that today there is a vast amount of child labor. The ILO estimates that 52 million people at **14** and under were at work in 1979. In some ways, this is not surprising, given the pattern of our own industrial revolutions. But since children have such little power, they are often given jobs which are dangerous and which may permanently incapacitate them. Employers are more willing to risk industrial accidents with children than they are with adults.

One reason that child labor persists, according to ILO researcher Elias Mendelievich, is that in poor societies there is nothing else for young people to do. In India 83 percent of those **6–10** are in school, but at **11–14** only 36 percent are in school. If the employed children suddenly reported for instruction, there would be no buildings or teachers to receive them.

In the U.S., the first federal attempt to restrict child labor was the Child Labor Law of 1916. It was immediately declared unconstitutional, and the U.S. had to wait until 1938 for child labor legislation, when an almost identical act was passed and upheld by the Supreme Court. The 1916 act barred **under-14**s from work in factories; and the under-**16**s from work in mines and quarries. Between **16–18**, the work day was a maximum of 8 hours, and the work week was no more than 48 hours. In 1938, the U.S. had 850,000 people **15** and younger in employment.

Perhaps the first attempt in England to fight the abuse of child labor was in 1788; chimney sweeps could not employ "climbing boys" (the people who climbed up inside the chimney to dislodge the soot) until the boys had reached **8**, according to a new law. In 1834, this minimum age was raised to **10**. For workers in the cotton mills, an 1819 law set **9** as the minimum age; between **9** and **15**, you could not work more than twelve hours per day. From 1833, people **9–12** could not work more than eight hours per day, or 48 hours per week; at **13–17**, you could not work more than twelve hours per day, or 69 hours per week. A law of 1842 set **10** as the minimum age at which a male could work in a coal mine; an investigatory committee had found children as young as **3** down the mines—young people were useful in mines as their small size enabled them to pull wagons of coal through tunnels which were too low for the animals that would otherwise be used.

MUSIC—CLASSICAL

Claudio Monteverdi publishes his first book of motets (1582); he has published the fourth book by **19**. (cf. **43***)

The heroine of *Madame Butterfly* is **15** at the start of the opera, but commits suicide at **18**. (cf. **41***)

Ernest Lough is the soloist for a recording of "Oh for the wings of a dove," in the Temple Church, London (1938). This later sells two million copies.

PLAYS

George Bernard Shaw becomes a clerk in the office of a Dublin land agent (1871). He has been highly unsuccessful at school and hated both the lessons and the sports. Later, as an adult, he always speaks contemptuously of schools. At **19**, Shaw resigns from the agency and moves to London. He does not return to his home city until **48**. He lives in London with his mother (then **44**) and she supports him. In his **mid-20**s, Shaw sets himself the task of writing five pages per day. But the resultant novels gain him only sixty rejection slips. At **26**, he is converted to socialism at a lecture by the American economist Henry George (**43**). Throughout his **20**s, Shaw is virtually an unemployed person pursuing self-education. He earns only a tiny amount from his writing. He loses his virginity at **29**, with a widow (**44**); previously he had said that self-respecting adults could not face each other after sex, so sex should be between strangers who would never meet again. At **29**, he makes £112 ($230) from journalism. The first production of one of his plays is at **36**, and Shaw immediately starts writing several plays per year. These include: *Mrs. Warren's Profession* at **37**; *Arms and the Man* at **38**; *The Man of Destiny* at **39**; and *The Devil's Disciple* at **40**. At **42**, he marries Charlotte Townshend (**41**), a virgin who stays a virgin. By **42**, Shaw can support himself as a playwright, and at last the world is accepting him in the way that he has always seen himself—as a creative person of great importance. (cf. **50***)

Alfred Jarry: *Ubu Roi* (1888). The first version is a marionette play. At **23**, he creates a theater version but keeps many of the marionette features. This play is later seen as a foundation of modern drama. Jarry continues to write in a highly eccentric style, but never again with the same influence. He dies at **34**, partly from the effects of alcohol.

FILMS

Greta Garbo is a lather girl in a Stockholm barber shop (1921).

Lana Turner is noticed by Billy Wilkerson of the *Hollywood Reporter,* as she has a soda in Schwab's Drugstore, Los Angeles (1936). He puts her in contact with an agent, who gets her a small part in a film—having a soda in a drugstore. (The film is *They Won't Forget,* 1937).

Charles Bronson becomes a miner (1936) in his Appalachia home town.

Deanna Durbin: *One Hundred Men and a Girl* (1937); she stars opposite Leopold Stokowski (**55**).

Judy Garland sings in *Broadway Memory of 1938* (1937), and becomes a star.

Sue Lyon: *Lolita* (1962).

MUSIC—NON-CLASSICAL

Paul Anka: "Diana" (1957). Later, he pays $250 for the right to translate the song "Comme d'habitude" into English; he is not altogether unsuccessful, with "My Way."

LOVE, LIFE

Giacomo Casanova, in 1740: after a meal of bread, Parmesan cheese, and Cyprus wine, he loses his virginity to two sisters, Nanetta (**16**) and Marta (**15**), in a wide bed on the fourth floor of their aunt's (**60**) house in Venice. Shortly afterward, he seduces a bride (**19**) who is afraid of thunder; their orgasm occurs at the thunderclap, and he tells her that she has been cured of her fears. Now begins Casanova's full-time pursuit of sex. He is too keen on novelty to be satisfied with marriage; and he is against masturbation as it, by "irritating nature, provokes her to vengeance, which she takes by redoubling the desires of the tyrant who has subdued her." Casanova makes a living throughout Europe by being an expert on the new financial institution of the lottery. In his **50**s, this and other endeavors gradually fail, and at **60** he accepts employment as a librarian in an obscure central European castle. Here from **65** onward he relieves his frustrations by writing his memoirs; in doing so, Casanova transforms himself into the permanent symbol of desire and the thrill of the chase. By spending many pages, and indeed whole chapters, on developing characterization, he transforms a repetitive story of conquest into a genuinely arousing book. This is published posthumously, and immediately recognized as a work of art. Casanova dies at **73**, in comparative obscurity, his body weakened by eleven attacks of sexually transmitted disease.

Photographs of girls at about **15** are often associated with David Hamilton (**33**, in 1966) who has produced several best-selling books of his work. Having been a magazine art director, at **33** he concentrates on one obsession—girls on the eve of losing their virginity. David Hamilton makes this subject his own artistic property. In each of his pictures, girls are wistfully approaching an unknown pleasure; by implication, it is the viewer who is going to help them into the next stage of life.

One person in three now has acne.

The FBI estimates that there are one million teenage runaways from American families.

A third of all the smokers in Russia are **14** to **17**. In West Germany, it is estimated that of all those on heroin, perhaps 20 percent are **12** to **16**.

It has been reported that in the U.S. there are 264 magazines which are devoted to pedophiliac sex.

EXPLORATION

In the great era of sailing ships (eighteenth and early nineteenth centuries), crews were young. A typical career might be: **13/14**, go to sea as an apprentice or junior clerk; by **21**, you could be first mate if you were intelligent and had worked hard; by **25**, you could have your own command. It was possible, in the eighteenth century, to be a sea captain before you were old enough to vote. For example, Nathaniel Silsbee of Salem, Massachusetts, went to sea at **14** (1788); he was a captain at **18½**, and retired at **28**, to live off the fortune which he had earned. This structure continued even up till the 1890s, though captains were usually appointed older and continued for longer—but even at this time there were captains in their **20**s. This emphasis on youth was due to: (1) increasing demand for crews, as transportation expanded; (2) the horrific nature of the work, which could not be endured for many years; (3) the senior officers' ability to accumulate an equity interest in ships, thus quickly leading to the equivalent of a pension.

LAW, CRIME

Dick Turpin is caught stealing cattle (c. 1721); he joins a band of smugglers and deer thieves. Later, he is hanged at **33***.

Al Capone joins a New York street gang, the "Five Pointers" (c. 1914). He becomes a bouncer, owing to his great physical strength and his belligerence. At **20**, he is called to Chicago, to become number three in a gang there. Prohibition begins when he is **21**, and Capone quickly becomes an equal partner in the new business of bootleg liquor. By **26***, he is head of the gang.

Males must now (England, thirteenth century) turn out to pursue any felons and other enemies of the community. This is the law of "posse comitatus" (force of the county), and eventually leads to the "posse" of the American Wild West.

According to the National Education Association, 50,000 to 60,000 U.S. teachers are physically assaulted each year in school (1979).

SPORTS

W. G. Grace (cricket, 1863) scores 32 for a side against the England team. At **18**, he scores 224 not out for England. He continues as the most impressive player of his time until his retirement from international cricket at **50***

Lottie Dod is the youngest-ever Wimbledon champion (1887)—this is the first of her five Wimbledon singles titles. In a recent Wimbledon (1978), 17 of the top 50 women players are **20** and under. But the world top players are about **24***. Some teenage tennis champions include the following: Suzanne Lenglen (1914) is the Paris singles champion at **14**. Maureen Connolly is U.S. singles champion at **16** (1951); she wins the Grand Slam at **18**; but she dies from illness at **35**, having had to retire at **19**, due to a broken leg in a riding accident. Pam Shriver reaches the final of the U.S. Open at **16** (1978). Tracy Austin is the youngest-ever winner there, at **16** in 1979 (cf. **2***). Ken Rosewall wins the French and Australian singles titles at **18** (1953)—the youngest ever in both cases. Christine Truman wins the French and Italian tennis championships at **18** (1959). And Wilfred Baddeley is the youngest-ever winner of the men's singles at Wimbledon, in 1891, at **19**.

Bobby Fischer (1958) becomes the youngest-ever International Grandmaster. At **16**, he leaves school to take up chess full time. At **19**, he reveals an unusual temperament by being the only person to accuse the Russian Olympic team of cheating. At **29**, he achieves international fame by beating Boris Spassky (**35**) in Iceland—after another unpleasant but highly effective display of temperament. Fischer appears to retire from the game in his **mid-30**s, while devoting his energies to a religious organization in Los Angeles.

Julian Hodgson (1978) defeats two chess grandmasters in successive games—a record.

Pele (1955) scores four goals for the Santos second team. At **16**, he is promoted to the Santos first team, and also makes his first appearance for Brazil. He helps Brazil win the World Cup three times running, at **18**, **22**, and **26**. He is Brazil's most famous player until his retirement at **34***.

Lorraine Crapp (1956) breaks four swimming records in one day;

two months later, she again breaks four swimming records. She retires at **21**. Kornelia Ender (1973) is the fastest sprint swimmer in the world, at **14**. Shane Gould (also **15**) wins three gold medals for swimming at the 1972 Olympics: she also gains a silver and a bronze; she retires at **16**, after a public career that began at **14**. John Konrads (also **15**, in 1958) holds three world records at the same time; so also does Tim Shaw (**16**) in 1974. Sharron Davies (also **15**) wins all seven finals which she enters—a record—at the British national swimming championships (1978). Debbie Meyer gains three golds at the 1968 Olympics, at **16**. Shirley Babashoff gains two world records at **17** (1974). And Don Schollander gains four golds in the 1964 Olympics, at **18**. Tracy Caulkins wins her thirty-first U.S. swimming title at **18** (1981).

Three gymnastics champions:

Nadia Comaneci (**14**, in 1976) is awarded seven scores of a perfect 10, for her gymnastics displays at the Olympics—a record which brings her three gold medals. But at **16**, she has difficulty in maintaining this standard; at the World Gymnastics Championships, she takes fourth place. From **14** to **16**, she grows four inches taller, and adds 21 pounds.

Olga Korbut, at **17**, wins three gold medals in the 1972 Olympics. But she slips (and cries), and the overall champion is Ludmila Turitscheva (**20**). Olga Korbut is so attractive that she personally starts a worldwide boom in gymnastics. But by **23** she is photographed appearing as an exhausted and even ugly has-been.

Olga Bicherova; first, in the 1981 World Gymnastics Championships, one month after reaching the minimum age, **15**.

1. VARIETIES OF SUCCESS

READY

To decide that you are good enough for an elite position.

Being marked for success; having a star; a sense of destiny. "Hungry" and eager.

The moment when you know that you are going to do well, that it is all going to work out, even better than you had hoped.

TITLES

A.A., B.A., M.Sc., Ph.D.

KCVO; the Honorable you.

The Principal's entrance—not the chorus entrance—at La Scala; VIP lounge at the airport; the Archbishop of Cyprus is the only person on the island who can write in purple ink; your personal flag; "Hail to the Chief" whenever you arrive.

Open Champion. Vice-President in charge of the sales division.

GENUINE ACHIEVEMENTS

Paradigm creation, versus normal science. Creating a world view or consciousness. In architecture, the "formgiver." Setting the public agenda, and forcing people to face certain issues.

History and you, together. Some force of society, of today, flows through you.

Creating a structure out of anarchy. Inventing a whole society and social system, out of nothing.

Expert; the authority.

Exploring the most difficult of problems, without taking soft options. Living with an amount of tension which others would find intolerable. Looking for the truth, however obscure, or painful, or embarrassing. Ready to give yourself totally to your current activity; to risk burning yourself out.

PUBLIC ATTENTION

Your name is associated with a societywide process; your name by itself is enough—Picasso, Dylan, etc.

You go to your old school—and the whole organization comes to a standstill so as to welcome you. For example, at Winchester, the whole school comes to the gates in order to welcome a distinguished alumnus.

As organizer, director, etc., a whole organization responds to your views. In the same way that a family or house may reflect the dreams of one ordinary person, so an organization or even a country can be identical with your own personality.

You are asked for your views on your subject. Later, you are asked for your views on any subject. People need you to speak to them. Talk shows. Or as guru, your theories give a meaning to the lives of many followers.

"Legendary"; you enter, and people are thrilled; people are electrified to know that you are in the building. You are so well known that strangers recognize you in public places. Your presence generates hysteria; you connect with a deep and powerful feeling in your audience. You have done something so great ("awesome") that people are overwhelmed by being near you.

REVENGE

Someone had previously doubted your ability—you now let them know of your success; they had humiliated you, and now they regret it. You take over the organization, and move in your own people; there is a new message for anyone who disagrees with you—Goodbye!

To smash the opposition; to crush the opposition; to beat them into a pulp. To settle the scores of a lifetime. To conduct a merciless bloodbath of the opposition. To see fear and defeat in their eyes.

PHYSICAL SUCCESS

A large amount of money. Someone else takes care of the trivia and secretarial chores in your life. Expense account. Surrounded by assistants, flacks, go-fers, and so on. Physical space; your own territory, or estate, or "kingdom." Beautiful clothes; fresh sheets every night.

Able to manipulate an organization, so that you can get roughly what you want.

The peaks connect.—William Zeckendorf. Having reached the peak of your profession, you now meet others who have reached the peak in other fields.

Part of an "informal college"; becoming part of a network of powerful and mutually-admiring people. You no longer have to sell yourself or sell your ideas. New jobs and opportunities flow in your direction.

Green awning syndrome.—Mel Brooks. Your record of achievement is so good that any project you propose will be accepted and funded—even a film about a green awning.

SEX

Coming to terms with your own sexuality.

You look at someone and they smile back at you; they are excited that you talk to them.

When you arrive, people are pleased that you've come; everything is organized—bright lights, loud music, food, drink, clapping, you're here! It's you! (People want to sleep with you; it's up to you to decide.)

Alpha ape. As much sex as you like, with the person(s) of your choice.

You read the news on TV; literally millions of viewers dream of sleeping with you.

MORAL

You have done what is right, and no other justification is required.

Top-most point of being.—R. L. Stevenson.

Tingling with excitement; every aspect of you is now happening; finding your voice; hitting on your own personal style; authentic. Your work and behavior in public exemplifies your inner feelings, whims, affections. You do well at what you have chosen to do.

"At ease with yourself."

The thrill of uncovering a secret aspect of yourself, and living it out with other people.

"Indestructible"; bouncing back from failure or a reverse—you recover because of your inner certainty and sense of direction.

CONTENTMENT

Enough money; never having to bother for the rest of your life. When you consider the other people at your school, and how they have done recently, you realize that life is okay. (Ambition is infinite, and can never be fully satisfied.)

At home in your own body.

When you were in bed this morning, you played with your own child.

Two happy children, a dog and a cat, a house and a garden, and someone who cuddles you when you wake up in the middle of the night.

To be true to someone for years and years; not to throw them away as you change. You are together for ever and ever, whatever your differences.

2. VARIETIES OF FAILURES

BASIC DEFECTS

Ugly. Lacking in skill, talent, self-confidence, intelligence. You mumble, so no one can hear your ideas.

No resilience—unable to recover from reverses.

Ambition seems tasteless to you. Your ethnic group does not deserve success.

NAMES

Loser; steer clear of; has-been; a remember-when; never fulfilled your potential; liar; dead loss; dead-and-alive; half-baked; pathetic;

bit of a poor old thing; a shame; a reject; desperate; sick; not worth knowing; not up to much; not up to the mark; redundant; dead wood; burnt out; skid row; on the skids; shopping bag lady; vagrant; old and worn out; suicidal; professional suicide; political or artistic suicide; throw in the towel; rejection slip; banished; impeached; eliminated; sent to Siberia; don't call us, we'll call you.

MECHANICS

You try, but never quite make it.

You try various things, but can never decide which direction is suitable for your commitment; you want to be committed, but it has not worked out that way.

On a losing streak; a vicious circle—nothing goes right, and so you acquire the reputation as a loser; you are shunned.

You do not have the power to acquire proper services and assistance—this slows you down more than ever.

You cannot handle organizations. You are always up against some vague organizational requirement that you cannot understand, and which prevents you from fulfilling your aims. You have good ideas, but are unable to sell them. You are frustrated because you cannot reach the decisionmakers.

You have been held back by lack of opportunities—at last, you obtain the right conditions, but you are unable to make full use of this chance.

FEARFUL OF SUCCESS

A champion is afraid of losing; everyone else is afraid of winning.—Billie Jean King.

You see yourself as a victim. You do not feel the possibility of doing well, of being happy. You have no right to success.

OTHER PEOPLE

Someone who was your equal at college—that person is now doing much better than you.

You fail to join an up-and-coming group; you are excluded from the more interesting meetings. Not only do you lose contacts, but you miss the stimulus—so you become less and less worthy of joining this interesting group.

You work hard, but fail to publicize yourself. An acquaintance produces less useful work, but their self-publicity brings greater rewards than you obtain.

You do not have the strength to stand up for ideas. You get taken for granted.

Sheer exhaustion—success has been achieved at vast cost to your personal life, and this cannot continue any longer. In your profession, achievement cannot merely be maintained, but must be fought for continuously; you can no longer do this.

Losing contact with the earthy roots of your achievement. Losing your own fresh vision; losing this "splendor in the grass."

Type-cast; in a rut; losing your flair. People indulge you, and so your standards gradually slip. Surrounded by yes-men. Didactic; sentimental; repetitive; tired.

The change from creative, intuitive person into the analytical commentator.

Out of touch. The world moves on, and you are left high and dry. Your unique skill/insight/sensitivity is no longer appropriate.

Success comes from questioning ideas; you are unable to repeat this painful process.

SELF-BETRAYAL

A life of quiet desperation.

A boring job which pays well; your creativity sort of goes into your home, pastimes, vacations, and so on.

Your public career is a facade—behind it, you have inexpressible desires and emotions; you cannot find a channel for these.

Giving in to the "real world"; not holding on to your best ideas. Prostituting your talent. Not living up to your potential. Living a lie.

Not being taken seriously; not being accepted at your own evaluation.

Unsatisfiable needs. However good you are, it is never enough; it never will be.

Basic conflicts, never resolved. You are much older, but you still have the same problems. You fail to see that "I have discovered long since that it only needs a little courage to fulfill wishes which till then have been regarded as unobtainable."—Sigmund Freud, at 62.

No sense of identity; no feel for the ethnic basis to your self; no links with your family heritage.

Wasted years; wanting to have your time over again—but it is too late.

LOVE

Success in the outside world, but at the expense of your own personal life; thousands of fans, but no one that you love.

Never having loved with truth.

You have lost touch with your children. They used to love you, but their interests are now elsewhere.

Now, not being in love. Today, no one loves you, no one cares about you.

Trying to pick up someone, you become friendly, but they don't realize that you are wanting to be seductive (laughter); you don't pursue the matter any further.

3. GREATNESS

Each person chooses success or failure. But greatness is not within your choice. You must fight for greatness. You fight for it, and will probably fail. You strive, and you will probably be crushed.

You can choose success, and make contentment into your own true success. But to choose great achievement is to walk a path of cruelty—to yourself, and to others. To imagine greatness without cruelty is to deceive yourself. Greatness and cruelty are inseparable, however much the greatness blinds us to the cruelty. As we embark on a great journey, let no one fool themselves as to its immediate consequences—before greatness, there will come sadness, suffering, and cruelty.

Even to observe greatness is an achievement.

To see greatness is to be smashed in the face. To feel the greatness of an achievement is to suffer an overwhelming blow to your own body.

To understand the changes caused by a great act is itself a great enough achievement.

To feel the greatness of a great art work is to suffer a devastation of your own mind.

To truly watch a great performance is to risk the ending of your own personality.

To surrender yourself in great love—this is something that no sane person can ever willingly do.

To enter into the full force of a great work is to scream and scream and scream until your own personality is gone, destroyed.

Each person is tinged with greatness, however small, however short-lived, however tangential, however much disowned. Each person has seen a second in which they were great; but the possibility of prolonging this seems beyond them. Do not pretend that this greatness will necessarily return.

Greatness comes by being part of the waves; greatness comes

through flying with the wind; greatness comes when events flow through you; history makes itself felt in you, before touching the rest of the world.

Be ruthless with your ideas. Test each idea to destruction. Burn each idea. The direction you now assume to be obvious—this is wrong.

Get on board the speeding train. Fight your way forward, and cling to greatness. In a moment, you will be gone; others will be destroying themselves, to reach your position. Let the desire of your heart take precedence over all other things; let us hear you sing with beauty. Let us see you transfigured with the shining light of greatness. Let beauty flood your body, as you connect yourself with power.

No position lasts for longer than a moment. For a brief span, you may listen to the applause; then, you must defend yourself. Greatness is nobody's gift. Greatness must be defended and defended, for ever and ever, for each day and throughout the day, until you are tired and exhausted, and you resign yourself to former greatness.

All friendship, self, kindness, goodness, wealth, and prospects, all these must be consumed in the fire, if need be. And the result may be that you have nothing, except the memory of your attempt at greatness.

16

HEALTH

Florence Nightingale receives a mystical vision of her future (1837). She writes in her diary "God spoke to me, and called me to his Service." At this time, Florence Nightingale is a highly unusual person, having been brought up to be independent. She benefits from: (1) a good education from her father, now **42**; (2) in her mid-teens, being the vehicle of the ambition of her mother, **48**; (3) a sense of destiny and uniqueness; (4) being introduced to the intellectual and social elite of the times; (5) meeting a small number of role models, such as Julia Ward Howe (now **17**). Unfortunately, having created this independent figure, her parents cannot accept that she will want a career. So, for the next sixteen years, she is highly frustrated; she has a regular upper-class life of indolence, but is privately obsessed by dreams, God, and by her unfulfilled ambitions. Her parents are dismayed by their child; her mother comments, "We are ducks who have hatched a wild swan." (cf. **30***)

HISTORY—WORLD

Joan of Arc offers her services (1428) to the King of France, Charles VII (**25**), to help defeat the English forces occupying their country. She is sent back to her village, even though she says that her guidance comes from divine voices. At **17**, she repeats her offer, and is placed in charge of a French army. For a year, she is successful in defeating the enemy, and in beginning the process of liberating her country. She is captured at **18**, and burned to death at **19**—but survives as an inspiration, and later as a saint.

Czar Fedor II becomes the new ruler of Russia (1605) on the death of his father, Czar Boris Godunov (**53**). But supporters of a rival czar, "False Dimitri," arrange for Fedor to be killed—he is strangled, after having his genitals ripped off.

King Hussein: King of Jordan (1952), under a regency; and full power as king, at **17**.

HISTORY—U.K.

Edward the Black Prince fights at the battle of Crécy (1346). His father (**33**) is told that the son is in danger, but he refuses to rescue him—"Let the boy win his spurs."

Ramsay MacDonald leaves school (1882)—first job is lifting potatoes on a farm. MP at **40**; Prime Minister at **57–58**, and from **62** to **68**.

Stanley Baldwin is given a beating when discovered reading pornography at boarding school (1883). His father is summoned, and Baldwin later has to leave school a year early. He gets a third class degree at university, and his father comments: "I hope you won't get a Third in life." He is forced to work in the family ironworks, but becomes MP at **41**, and Prime Minister at **55**.

Eligibility: if a Page of Honour to the Queen, you must now retire. Eligibility for pages is **13½** to **16½**. Your task will have been to attend the Queen when she is wearing state robes, for example, at the opening of Parliament.

RELIGION, PHILOSOPHY

Prince Siddhartha (Buddha) is married, to his cousin Yashodhara (also **16**). (cf. **29***)

Blaise Pascal: *Essai pour les Coniques* (1639). He is an infant prodigy, whose education has been pushed continuously by his father. Pascal is famous by **22**, for his invention of a calculating machine. He later makes experiments about the nature of a vacuum, and is a pioneer in probability theory. At **31**, he has a frightening vision of himself as one of those who had denied Jesus Christ, and then helped in His crucifixion. Pascal's *Pensées* are written from **35** onward, and say that belief in God is (crudely speaking) a better bet than atheism, given that (1) we cannot know until we are dead, and (2) the infinity of reward if Heaven does in fact exist. Pascal dies at **39**, a practicing and passionate Christian.

Billy Graham: conversion experience (1934), and beginning of his preaching career.

SOCIAL SCIENCE, EDUCATION

In the Russian Revolution (1917), **17** was set as the new minimum school-leaving age—this was the aim, though not the immediate achievement.

In Britain, the minimum school-leaving age was fixed in 1908 at **14**. A survey in the 1860s showed students left upper-class schools at **18**, middle-class schools at **16**, and working-class schools at **14**. Students from very poor families left even earlier, assuming that they had gone to school in the first place.

Do not leave school now. For the average person, those who stay in the educational system tend to have higher total lifetime incomes. Your temporary gains now in employment will be overtaken by those who go on to obtain school qualifications and perhaps a degree.

Here is some advice for those who are now thinking of dropping out of the educational system to take up physical work instead of joining the managerial elite:

I am told that you forsake writing, that you give yourself up to pleasures. . . . Do you not recall the indolent one whose name is unknown? He will be loaded like an ass. . . . Put writing (learning) in your heart, that you may protect yourself from hard labor of any kind, and be a magistrate of high repute!—Egyptian, c. 1340 B.C.

Phillips Academy, Andover, Massachusetts: the fees in 1979 were $4,975 per year. Fees at Eton College are £3,150 ($6,300) per year (1980); and at Le Rosey, Switzerland, the cost is $15,000 per year.

In West Germany, alarm has also been expressed at the high pressure placed on people at school. With the need to gain good results so as to be able to compete in the job market, some people are being destroyed by the stress. Suicide among school children is no longer newsworthy, as young people kill themselves by hanging or throwing themselves under trains. Annually, 500–700 people at school kill themselves; 18,000 make a suicide attempt; and 600 die from drugs.

In California, school attendance is for 180 days per year. In Japan, you go to school for 220 days annually. Japanese colleges require math beyond trigonometry, but only five percent of California high school students study trigonometry.

SCIENCE

Charles Darwin leaves school (1825) and is sent to Edinburgh University, to study medicine. In this, he is a failure, and at **19** he is sent to Cambridge to prepare for the priesthood. Again, his performance is indifferent, and he later says that "my time was wasted" at both universities. "I was considered by all my masters and by my own Father as a very ordinary boy, rather below the common standard in intellect. To my deep mortification, my Father once said to me: 'You care for nothing but shooting, dogs and rat-catching, and you will be a disgrace to yourself and all your family.' " Charles Darwin's third attempt at a career begins with his journey on the ship HMS *Beagle,* which he decides to join, as the result of "a trifle," when he is **22***.

MONEY, WORK

G. F. Swift borrows $25 from his father to buy a live heifer (1855), sells the resultant beef to neighbors for a total of $35, and develops this later into multimillion-dollar meat packing business in Chicago.

Henry Ford leaves school (1879) and gets a job as an engineer, in which he shows considerable native skill from the beginning. At **21**, he attends a commercial "business university" for a few months, but that is the extent of his formal business education. (cf. **24***)

Aristotle Onassis: a Turkish army takes over in his home town of Smyrna (1912), and his father—a successful trader—is imprisoned. Onassis and his family survive by his trading, and his negotiating with the occupying army. But after a family row, Onassis leaves for Argentina. (cf. **17***)

RENAISSANCE

Leonardo da Vinci, in 1468: he becomes an apprentice in the workshop of Andrea del Verrocchio (**33**), the painter and sculptor in Florence. Leonardo was born illegitimately, and was kept by his natural mother for only a brief period; he was then brought up by stepmothers in the house of his father. Leonardo's apprenticeship is completed at **20**, and he begins a period of exploration and general discovery. He is a physically attractive person, of unusually wide interests; he does impressive paintings, but he is not an infant prodigy. His first major work is "The Adoration of the Magi," at **29** which he does not finish. At **30**, he leaves his home area and goes to the court of Ludovico Sforza (also **30**), the ruler of Milan. Leonardo presents himself as a musician who has great expertise at military fortifications—art is hardly mentioned in his letter of application. While at Milan, he starts on his uniquely wide-ranging interests, including town planning, fortifications, guns, and the design of stables. He leaves Milan at **47**—he had arrived at **30** as just one of many talented people of the time—and leaves with a national reputation. This is due mainly to two projects, the giant equestrian statue of Ludovico, the design of which is completed at **41**, and his painting "The Last Supper," finished at **45**. Later, this is rivaled only by his "Mona Lisa," at **51***. A note on Ludovico: he obtained power in Milan at **28**; at **39**, he marries Beatrice d'Este (**16**) and then enjoys a peak of magnificence and creativity at his court; he is captured by the French at **48**, and dies in a French prison at **56**.

ARCHITECTURE

Palladio enrolls in the Guild of Stone Masons and Brick Layers, in Vicenza (1524). (cf. **28***)

ART

Elizabeth Siddal is found working in a London hat shop (1850) and taken away to be a model for the Pre-Raphaelite Brotherhood. She represents the new ideal of beauty, and is soon commemorated in "Ophelia," the painting by Millais (**22**). At **26**, she marries Rossetti (**32**). She kills herself at **28**, with an overdose of the drug laudanum.

MUSIC—CLASSICAL

Mozart: eight symphonies (1772), and the opera *Lucio Silla*. (cf. **22***).

Benjamin Britten: *Hymn to the Virgin* (1930)—this is sung at his funeral, 47 years later.

LITERATURE

Tess Durbeyfield is seduced, or raped, by Alec d'Urberville, and she becomes pregnant. The baby dies, and Tess becomes a milkmaid. Later, to escape from d'Urberville, Tess stabs him; but she is convicted for this, and hanged.—from the book (1892) by Thomas Hardy, **52**.

PLAYS, DANCE

Margot Fonteyn dances Odette, in *Swan Lake* (1935); she dances *Giselle* at **17**, and stars as Princess Aurora, in the *Sleeping Beauty* at **19**. Later, at **43**, she dances for the first time with Rudolph Nureyev (**24**), in *Giselle*.

FILMS

Lilian Gish: *The Birth of a Nation* (1915).

Clark Gable runs away from home (1917); goes to work in an automobile tire factory; later, works in oilfields.

Greta Garbo makes her first two films (1921). They are advertising shorts; the first is for the department store in which she is a shop assistant; the second is for the Stockholm Cooperative Society's bakery department. She then wins a scholarship to the Royal Dramatic Academy, Stockholm.

Dorothy Lamour is elected "Miss New Orleans" (1931); but goes to work as an elevator operator in the Marshall Field store, Chicago.

Debbie Reynolds is elected "Miss Burbank" (1948); enters the film industry.

MUSIC—NON-CLASSICAL

"Sweet Little **16**" is by Chuck Berry (**32**, in 1958). A similar song is "Go Away Little Girl (Before I Ask You to Stay)" by Mark Winter (1962).

LOVE, LIFE

Eligibility: it is now legal for you to have sex.

It is impossible to give one age at which people have lost their virginity. Instead, it is possible to find the proportion of people in successive age groups who report having had sex. For example, Kinsey in 1953 found that 20 percent of females **16** to **20** reported having lost their virginity. In 1978, researchers Zelnik and Kanter found that 41 percent of people **15** to **19** reported having had sex. At **19**, 55 percent of unmarried females reported having had sexual experience.

A 1980 survey at Stanford University showed that 32 percent of sophomore females reported having had sex while in high school; the comparable figure for their mothers was 6 percent. The typical student was said to have lost her virginity at **17**.

Penalties for breaking the law on the age of consent are severe, and so the authorities do not enforce the law where a female **15** or younger makes love to a slightly older male, or vice versa. If the male were **21**+ and the female **15** or under, then the full rigor of the law would be applied. In effect, there is a powerful difference between the law as written, and the law as routinely applied. But a recent attempt in New Jersey to bring these two into line with each other provoked an outcry. A 1979 law allowed sex below **16** as long as the age difference between the partners was four years or less; that is, the new law would be the same as the application of the old law. A public outcry caused the age of consent to be raised back to **16** without any loopholes.

In Holland, the age of consent is **16**; but sex with females **12** to **15** is only prosecuted if the female lodges a complaint. Also, penal code 249.1 protects people under **21** from any lascivious acts (e.g. "touching up") by employers, or by parents or foster-parents. In Britain, the age of consent is **16** for heterosexuality, and **21** for homosexuality. Also, at **16**, you are allowed to leave home without your parents' permission.

In England, a male at **24** or less has a defense against a statutory rape charge if he can show that he honestly believed the female to be **16** or over.

In England, there is no law forbidding an adult woman from making love to a male under **16**. However, if a woman touches a boy's penis, she is guilty of indecent assault.

LAW, CRIME

Christopher Craig and Derek Bentley (**19**) are caught by London police while in the middle of a burglary (1952). Craig shoots a policeman, and kills him. Bentley is Craig's accomplice, and is too stupid to be able to read his own statement about the crime. Both are found guilty of murder. But owing to an age rule that you are only eligible to hang at **18**, Bentley (the accomplice) is executed, and Craig (the actual killer) is sent to prison. Craig is released in his late **20**s. This anomaly becomes a powerful argument in the anti-hanging campaign.

In San Diego (1979), Brenda Spencer kills the head teacher and the custodian of her school, and wounds eight fellow students with rifle fire. She is quoted as explaining that "Monday gives me the blues." She has a history of violence, including setting fire to cats. The rifle was a Christmas present from her father.

The Children's Act (U.K., 1908) abolished hanging as a punishment for people under **16**. Later, the limit is raised to **18**, where it stayed until the complete abolition of hanging, in 1965.

When corporal punishment was legal in Britain (until 1948), the instrument was a bundle of birch sticks; these weighed nine ounces for people **15** and under, and 12 ounces for **16** and above. The Larceny Act (1916) consolidated a wide variety of Victorian laws, and it defined that males **15** and under could get 25 strokes; **16** and over could get 50 strokes. For simple larceny, birching was only for **15** and below. No lower age limit was mentioned in this act.

In France in the early nineteenth century, you would now be eligible for the full range of adult punishments—death, solitary confinement, galley slave, and so forth. At **15** and under, you would merely be "confined by way of correction."

SPORTS

Jonathan Vowles (U.K., 1978) survives a drop of 2,660 feet. Both his main parachute and his emergency parachute fail to open—and he falls the whole distance. He happens to hit the plastic skylight of an aircraft hangar, and this breaks his fall. He injures a knee ligament, but is otherwise unhurt.

The manager of Arsenal's first division soccer team (U.K., 1971) was quoted on the chances for someone wanting to play top class soccer—he gave odds of 160,000 to 1. Every year, 80,000 boys are watched by talent scouts. Out of these, 40 are invited to play at the club headquarters. Five of the 40 are signed as apprentices. And every other year, one apprentice makes it to the first team. Seventy-five percent of the apprentices cannot get a job anywhere in the game after their training ends—and they do poorly in the rest of the job market, as they have neglected their studies in their attempt to move into professional sport. (See also American football, at **21***.)

17

HISTORY—WORLD

Peter the Great begins taking control as Czar (1689); he had received the title at **9**, but lived under the regency of his sister. He now governs a land area of 5.7 million square miles. At **25**, he inspects new developments in Europe, and spends much of the rest of his life in implementing these ideas within Russia. At **31**, he founds St. Petersburg, later the capital; at **37**, he defeats King Charles XII (**27**) of Sweden, and so opens up the western edge of Russia. Czar Peter dies in office at **52**.

Lenin, in 1887: his brother Alexander (**21**) is hanged, after taking part in a bungled assassination attempt of Czar Alexander III (**32**). At **15**, Lenin's father (**55**) had died; the family has been well off, and in the upper-middle class. Lenin now becomes a law student, and graduates at **23**. He works as a lawyer. He travels abroad at **25**; he is then arrested for the first time, and is sent to Siberia. Conditions are relatively comfortable, and his time here (until **29**) is spent on self-education on revolutionary theory. "What Is to Be Done?" is written around **31**. Lenin is then becoming the most prominent and active theorist of the coming revolution. He works full-time at this, supported by family money and payments from the revolutionary organization—itself supported by gifts and bank robberies. At **37***, a conference of leaders confirms Lenin as the first among equals.

HISTORY—U.K.

Henry VIII becomes King (1509, Apr. 22) and afterward marries Catherine of Aragon (**23**)—who is both a widow and a virgin. (cf. **41***)

Winston Churchill fails the entrance exam (1891) to the Royal Military Academy, Sandhurst, for the second time; but is admitted at the next attempt. (cf. **20***)

SOCIAL SCIENCE, EDUCATION

If we have chosen the position in which we can accomplish the most for humanity, then we can never be crushed by the burdens because these are only sacrifices made for the sake of all. Then it is no poor, restricted egoistic joy that we savor; on the contrary, our happiness belongs to millions, our deeds live on calmly with endless effect, and our ashes will be moistened by the ardent tears of noble men.—Karl Marx at **17** (1835) writing on the problem of career choice. (cf. **29***)

King Henry VI of England begins the foundation (1439) of both Eton College, Windsor, and of King's College, Cambridge. At **24**, he lays the foundation stone of King's College Chapel.

MONEY, WORK

Henry Royce loses his engineering apprenticeship (1880) on the death of the aunt who had been supporting him. But at **20** he becomes chief electrical engineer of the (small) Electric Light and Power Company, installing the first electrical facilities in Liverpool; starts his own company at **21**. At **17**, the Hon. C. S. Rolls is at Eton (1894); decides to become an electrical engineer, and goes to Cambridge University. (cf. **32***)

William Hill collects betting slips in the factory where he works (1920)—later becomes the world's first (legal) multimillionaire bookmaker.

Aristotle Onassis arrives in Buenos Aires (1923, Sept. 21) with about £60 ($120). After a year of odd jobs, he becomes a telephone repairman, on the night shift. During the day, he starts his own export-import business. Millionaire at **23**. (cf. **25***)

ART

Auguste Rodin fails the entrance test, for the third and last time, at the École des Beaux-Arts, Paris (1857). After temporarily becoming a novice monk, he begins work as an assistant in a sculpture practice that produces external decorations for buildings. Usually this work is signed by the chief sculptor, not Rodin. He produces his own first major work at **35**—"The Age of Bronze"—and starts on his giant project, "The Gates of Hell," at **39***.

MUSIC—CLASSICAL

Mendelssohn: overture to *A Midsummer Night's Dream* (1826). The rest of the incidental music is written at **34***. (cf. **20***)

Rudyard Kipling is a journalist in India (1865) for the next seven years—the most exciting time of his life, and the source of his inspiration.

Jack London works on board ship (1893), sailing off the coast of Russia. At **27**, he publishes *The Call of the Wild*.

Ernest Hemingway is an ambulance driver in World War I, but is seriously wounded (1918). He goes home, before returning to Paris at **22***.

Alfred Lord Tennyson publishes his first book of poems (1826), with those of his brother.

Georgette Heyer publishes her first book *The Black Moth* (1921).

Susan Sontag is married at **17**, and divorced at **24**. (cf. **33***)

Seventeen—this novel is by Booth Tarkington (**47**, in 1916).

FILMS

Edna Purviance visits the studio of Charlie Chaplin (**22**) (1911), and he offers her a star part.

Lilian Gish: *Intolerance* (1916).

Errol Flynn works as a shipping clerk (1926–27).

Deanna Durbin, child star, has her first screen kiss, in *Three Smart Girls Grow Up* (1939).

Judy Garland: *The Wizard of Oz* (1939).

Sabu: *The Jungle Book* (1942)—marks his virtual retirement as a star.

Jean Seberg, in 1956: in a national talent search among 17,000 people, she is chosen to star in *Saint Joan,* directed by Otto Preminger (**50**). She is taken from an obscure town in Iowa, and made into a celebrity. But after the excitement of her discovery, the film is disappointing, and her performance is derided. She goes on to make a number of films, and is well reviewed in the French *Breathless* at **20**. Later, at **31**, she becomes pregnant; in order to attack the work she has been doing for radical causes, the FBI and J. Edgar Hoover (**75**) put out a rumor that the child has been fathered by a Black Panther. The distress over this causes her to go into premature labor, and the baby—white—is lost. On each anniversary of this event she tries to commit suicide, and at **40** she is found dead in her car in Paris. In the following year, Romain Gary (**66**), her ex-husband, also commits suicide.

MUSIC—NON-CLASSICAL

Booker T and the MGs: "Green Onions" (1962). The group goes on to exploit this success with songs that feature onions again, and also potatoes.

LOVE, LIFE

In any one year, about .22 percent of people **0–17** become dependency and neglect cases in court (U.S.A., 1974).

Queen Charlotte's Ball, in London: this was the dance which marked the coming out of rich or high status girls. The practice of presentation at Buckingham Palace ended in 1958, and the last Queen Charlotte's Ball was held in 1976. At the great moment of the ball, approximately 200 girls, **16–18**, would walk in procession, pulling a large birthday cake, and moving toward the guest of honor. The band would play music from Handel's (**62**, 1747) *Judas Maccabeus,* the favorite music of Queen Charlotte. As the guest of honor came forward to cut the cake, the debutantes, dressed all in white, would perform a deep curtsy. This was the beginning of their "season."

PRESS

Seventeen magazine: this is started by Walter Annenberg (**36**) in 1944. At **45**, he starts *TV Guide.*

LAW, CRIME

Jack Archer-Shee is cleared of stealing a five shilling postal order while a cadet officer at the Royal Naval College, England (1912). This incident is later made into a play, *The Winslow Boy,* by Terence Rattigan (**35**, in 1946). Archer-Shee's father spends all the family money on legal costs in establishing Jack's innocence but the son is killed at **19**, in World War I.

The first U.S. institution for juveniles' "correction" was opened in New York in 1824. Previously, there had been no age segregation, and children were punished in the same prisons as adults. During medieval and Tudor times, it is noticeable that two reviews of the law then have no mention of children as such, or of separate punishments for younger people. Until the early nineteenth century, everyone from about **9** mingled in the same institution, and received the same basic sentences. There were distinctions in prison, but these were between male versus female, debtors versus violent criminals, and divisions between social class. "Borstal," the English system of positive training for young criminals, did not begin until 1908.

A "juvenile" is **17** or younger in most states. Sometimes there is a status of "youthful offender," between the juvenile and the adult criminal. Punishments for juvenile delinquents include probation, and doing time in a range of training schools, halfway houses, ranches, and forestry camps. A British study showed that the cost of keeping someone in a residential center is about £100 ($200) per week; probation costs £3 ($6) per week, and "community service orders" cost £5 ($10) per week.

CINS, PINS, or MINS are children/persons/minors in need of supervision. They have not broken any adult laws, but are uncontrollable, runaways, and the like.

Of people **10** to **17**, 3.75 percent appeared at juvenile court in any one year (U.S., 1974).

SPORTS

Maia Chiburdanidze (1978): women's world chess champion. She has been playing chess since **4**, and entered her first tournament at **9**. At **13**, she is an international woman master, the youngest international master of either sex. In the world championship she now defeats Nona Gaprindashvili (**37**) who has held the title since **21**.

18

HISTORY—WORLD

Tutankhamen: death (c. 1352 B.C.). He has been ruler of Egypt since about **9**.

Mehmed II becomes Ottoman Sultan (1451) at the death of his father (**46**). Mehmed had first received sovereign power at **12** when his father abdicated at the time of his **40**th birthday. But the boy was unable to exercise power with sufficient competence, and at **14** he was replaced by his father. Now at **18** Mehmed goes on to create the Ottoman Empire, an achievement which earns him the name Mehmed the Conqueror. At **21**, he captures Constantinople (Istanbul) and he changes Hagia Sophia into a mosque. Under his leadership, the city becomes an imperial capital and an important world center. At **41**, he wins a battle which extends his control over the Balkans. At **48** he has his portrait painted by the Venetian, Gentile Bellini (**51**). At the time of his death (**49**) he is planning a westward extension of the empire, with a proposed invasion of Italy.

In China, the minimum age today for voting and participation in parliamentary proceedings is **18**; military service liability is **18–23**.

In France, the minimum voting age is **18**; Members of Parliament must be at least **23**, and the same rule applies to the President.

In West Germany, voters must be at least **18**, and you are eligible for election to the Bundestag at **18**. The Federal President must be at least **40**.

In Italy, for the Chamber of Deputies, a voter must be at least **18**, and a Deputy must be at least **25**. For the Senate, a voter must be at least **25**, and a Senator **40**. The President must be at least **50**.

In Cuba, in the nineteenth century, the age of majority was **25**.

A proposal in Finland is that at **15** to **17** you should enjoy a half-vote in any election.

For voting ages in history, see Plato at **60***.

A note on military conscription:

In ancient Greece, you would now be eligible for conscription. Your age is determined by your age class to which everyone born in the same year belongs (something similar to a university's Class of '42). This age class is named after (eponymous with) the person who holds the political position of "archon" during the year of your birth; the archon changed annually. In order to stimulate the militaristic spirit, teenage males in Sparta would annually take part in a tough competition—they would submit to being publicly flogged, to see how long they could endure it without moving or screaming.

If a Roman male, you would be liable for military service at **17**. During the three centuries before Christ (during the creation of the empire), you would not be able to hold high office until you had completed 10 military campaigns. During the first century B.C., tertiary education slowly developed for the upper class, in oratory, law, and philosophy. Later, when the boundaries of the empire were more settled, elite males would serve one year in the military, then a period in administration, and could enter the Senate by inheritance at **25**.

Imperial China, from 200 B.C. onward: you would have to register for military service at **20** (equivalent to our **19**), and serve four years. From **24** to **56**, you were in the reserves, and eligible to serve in an emergency.

In the Ottoman Empire, males were liable for enrollment in a form of elite slavery. Every three to seven years, commissioners would visit each village, and males **8** to **20** would be lined up for inspection. The most able, typically **14** to **18**, would be taken to Constantinople where they would be trained either as soldiers, the Janissaries, or as future top civil servants. They all went on to become the administrative corps of the empire. Since these boys came from poor families, their only loyalty was to the Sultan, whose favor caused them to have a privileged status.

Israel today: eligible for military service at **18**—males for three years, and females for two years.

Switzerland today: all males must undergo 21 weeks of military training at **20**. Between **21–32**, they have a total of 160 days of training; at **33–42**, a total of 10 days; and at **43–50**, a total of 13 days. Until **50**, they must accept annual inspections of their equipment readiness and shooting skill.

Australia in the 1960s and 1970s operated a call-up system which used birthdays to regulate the supply of conscripts. Males were liable for service at **20**. Since a whole age group was never required, selection was by lottery; marbles were drawn, each having a birthday on it. The military authorities calculated how many birthdays' worth of conscripts were needed for their purposes. In the first of the six monthly lotteries, 96 birthdays were called up, but only 38 in the fourth lottery.

HISTORY—U.S.A.

Hubert Humphrey has to drop out of the University of Minnesota (1929), to help in his father's drugstore; but he gets his B.A. at **28**. (cf. **34***)

Edmund Brown spends the next three and a half years (1956) in a Jesuit seminary. (cf. **32***)

Eligibility: you may now vote in elections. You can be elected to the House of Representatives at **25**, and to the Senate at **30**.

Eligibility: males must now register for the draft.

In Virginia, 1642, all males **16** to **60** had to be "armed with arms," and willing to go "to the wars."

In the colonies, voting was so restricted by property, religious, and gender qualifications that an age rule was superfluous. But in 1647 Massachusetts set **24** as the voting age for nonfreemen.

The U.S. voting age was changed from **21** to **18** in 1971.

HISTORY—U.K.

Queen Victoria is awakened at dawn (1837, June 20) to be told that she is now Queen. William IV (**71**) had succeeded in his aim to delay his death till she was past her **18**th birthday, so that her mother (**50**), whom he hated, would never be regent. Victoria is now guided by Lord Melbourne (**58**), who is both Prime Minister and her private secretary. (cf. **20***)

Eligibility: you may now vote in elections. You may be elected to Parliament at **21**. Military conscription used to begin now.

In a survey of Scotland in 1743, fighting personnel were seen as males aged **18** to **56**.

Electoral power was originally a privilege, not a right. The sovereign had all the power, and this was gradually shared with assemblies of notables. Prior to having a set minimum age for membership (**21**) in Parliament, a representative had to hold an official role, such as knight, property owner, priest, or head of family, and this gave him adult status. There was thus no need to define adult status through an age qualification, and **21** came to be formalized in the more open and fast-moving circumstances of the seventeenth century.

In Magna Carta (1215), paragraphs two to six deal with inheritance, and differentiate between "heirs who are of full age," and "heirs who are under age," the latter needing a guardian to supervise their inheritance. There is no further definition of "full age." But in 1216, Magna Carta was revised, and coming-of-age was formally set at **21**. A voting age was not needed in Magna Carta since the qualifications to take part in the political process were so numerous that only a full rich adult male would be able to become a member of the Great Council. Richard II became King at **10** (1377) and his actions were supervised until he "was of age to know good and evil." In practice, Richard's supervising council was disbanded at **13**, and he took independent action from **14** on.

Another version of the age of majority is the age at which you can be held fully responsible for your own actions. In 1536, it was enacted that a king at **24** could repeal any laws passed between his accession and **24**. Presumably these might be the result of undue pressure on the juvenile ruler. In 1830, it was decided that **18** should be the age of majority for the sovereign, even though **21** was the voting age. Before **18**, the sovereign's power would be held by a regency.

In 1657, during the Protectorate or republican period of government, an age rule was devised for the first time on the subject of membership in Parliament. The minimum age was set at **21**.

When women first received the vote (1918), the minimum age was set at **30** for women, but it was already **21** for men. In 1928, both sexes could vote at **21**.

For males **20–24** in 1914, there was a 30.6 percent chance of being killed in World War I; and for males **13–19** in 1914, there was a twenty-eight percent chance of death in the war. One comment on these dead is on the war memorial outside Canterbury Cathedral:

True love by life
True love by death is tried.
Live thou for England
We for England died.

RELIGION, PHILOSOPHY

Gregory XI becomes a Cardinal (1347); and Pope at **41**; death at **49**.

Odet de Coligny: Cardinal (1535).

According to Michael Argyle, this is the peak age for religious involvement. From now onward there is a decline until the lowpoint at **30**; then, a gradual rise until old age.

SOCIAL SCIENCE, EDUCATION

In Japan, if aiming at a top job in later life, you must now secure admission to one of the leading ten universities. With "employment for life," and employers' selection based on the university you attend, this is a key moment in your life. Suicide among exam failures is high—about 800 suicides per year for the under **20**s. Depression is common; attendance at "crammers" is high, as is studying for 11 hours per day.

MONEY, WORK

Frederick W. Taylor leaves Phillips Exeter Academy (1874) and deliberately avoids university; becomes a shop-floor apprentice in rebellion against the unreal, overeducated society in which he has been brought up; between **22** and **33**, develops his theories of scientific management, an extreme and influential system of rationalizing production. He sets up his own business at **37***.

SCIENCE, TECHNOLOGY

Commonsense is the deposit of prejudice laid down in the mind before the age of **18**.—Albert Einstein (1879–1955).

William H. Perkin: first production of an aniline dye (1856). He now starts on large-scale manufacture, and he achieves this by **23**. This is the beginning of the synthetic dye industry.

Norbert Weiner: Ph.D., at Harvard (1913.) Later, his best-known work is *Cybernetics* at **53**.

ARCHITECTURE

Nicholas Hawksmoor becomes clerk to Sir Christopher Wren (**47**) (1679).

Louis H. Sullivan visits the Sistine Chapel (1874). (cf. **38***)

ART

Ansel Adams, in 1920: as a music student, he gets a summer job in Yellowstone National Park, and becomes attracted to the spectacular views there. By **28**, he has dropped music, and become a full-time photographer. He works for the rest of his life in this field.

MUSIC

Schubert: *The Erl King* (1815)—one of his 189 compositions this year. (cf. **31***)

Guiseppe Verdi applies to the Milan Conservatorium (1832), but is turned down, because of lack of ability, and not having the appearance of a musician. A businessman in his home town now pays for him to have tuition in Milan, and Verdi writes operas—his third, *Nabucco,* is produced at La Scala at **28**. Verdi marries his patron's daughter, and they have two children; but both the children and the wife die when Verdi is in his **20**s. Verdi writes continuously, and his sixteenth opera is *Rigoletto,* at **37**. Years later, when the patron is minutes before death, he asks Verdi (now **54**) to play a tune from *Nabucco.* At **85**, Verdi is asked if the Milan Conservatorium can now call itself the Verdi Conservatorium—Verdi takes pleasure in refusing. (cf. **37***)

LITERATURE

Paul Baumer: his entire class at school volunteers for service during World War I. Their parents call them heroes and the Iron Youth. But by **19** Baumer says, "We are all old folks," and most of his friends have been killed or have had arms and legs amputated. He himself is killed at **20**, on a quiet day toward the end of the war.— in *All Quiet on the Western Front* (1929), by Erich Remarque, 1898–1970.

Tolstoy later says of himself: "Men of genius are incapable of studying when they are young, because they unconsciously feel that they must learn everything differently from the mass." At **16**, he had lost his virginity, having been forced to accompany his elder brother to a brothel. As a teenager, he is alternately overserious and overambitious; then a failure; then writing a book of rules so as to reform his behavior; and then repeating this cycle. (cf. **23***)

Marcel Proust has a year of military service (1889–90); he passes 59th in a class of 60. (cf. **39***)

F. Scott Fitzgerald is accepted by Cottage (1914), apparently one of the top four eating clubs at Princeton. This is the key time of his life, which he describes in *This Side of Paradise* at **24***—though in fact he never graduates from Princeton, because of World War I. He dies at **44***, while reading the Princeton Alumni Weekly. Although Princeton has a timeless air, the Cottage Club is only **27** in 1914.

PLAYS

Georges Feydeau: *Wooed and Viewed* (1880). This is his first play. He makes his name with *Amour et Piano* at **21**, and proceeds to write sixty more farces abut bedrooms, sex, lack of sex, rooms with lots of doors, and so on. These include *Un Fil à la Patte* at **32**; *L'Hôtel du Libre Échange* or in English, *Hotel Paradiso,* at **34**; *The Girl from Maxim's* at **37**; *Occupe-toi d'Amélie* at **46**; and *A Flea in Her Ear* at **48**. Feydeau keeps writing farces until his death at **59**.

FILMS

Humphrey Bogart is expelled from Phillips Academy, Andover, Massachusetts (1918, May 15).

Cary Grant has a summer job as a stilt-walker at Coney Island (1922).

Greta Garbo: *Gösta Berling's Saga* (1924)—a four-hour period drama of high intensity, directed by Mauritz Stiller (**41**) who gives her the name of Garbo. The film is an enormous success, and they both sign with Louis B. Mayer (**40**).

Deanna Durbin signs a new contract (1940)—she is now to receive $400,000 per picture.

Lauren Bacall starts work on *To Have and Have Not* (1945), with Humphrey Bogart (**46**), to whom she says, "You know how to whistle, don't you?" They marry the following year.

Elizabeth Taylor makes her first romantic movie: *Conspirator* (1950), and receives the Harvard Lampoon award for "so gallantly persisting in her career, despite a total inability to act."

Claudia Cardinale wins a contest, "Most beautiful Italian girl in Tunisia" (1957); the prize is a trip to the Venice Film Festival.

Eligibility: You may now see adult movies.

MUSIC—NON-CLASSICAL

Chubby Checker: "The Twist" (1960). For a brief period, the entire Western world is now dancing the Twist.

Marianne Faithfull: "As Tears Go By" (1964). Later, at **28**, she announces that she has slept with three of the Rolling Stones, and that Mick Jagger (**30**) is best.

The Who: first performance at which they smash their equipment (1964). They have been playing together for a couple of years, originally as the High Numbers. Now, at the end of a performance at the Marquee, one of The Who gets angry and attacks his guitar. Soon equipment smashing becomes an obligatory feature of their act—many in their audiences are coming principally to see this last moment of destruction. "My Generation" is at **19**. "Tommy" is three years later, by Roger Daltrey at **23**, and it also ends the interest in smashing, which eventually costs them £300,000 ($600,000) in lost equipment.

LOVE, LIFE

Most men want girls of **18**.—an expensive call girl in the book *Working* by Studs Terkel.

Cleopatra, in 51 B.C., becomes joint ruler of Egypt, on her marriage to her brother Ptolemy XIII (**12**). At **22**, she has a child whose father is Julius Caesar (**53**), and she is forced to marry another brother, Ptolemy XIV (also **12**). At **29**, she gives birth to twins, and the father is Mark Antony (**43**). Later, Antony at **53** fails in a rebellion against Rome and he commits suicide. Rather than submit to Antony's conquerors, Cleopatra (**39**) holds a poisonous snake to her breast and dies.

PRESS

William Randolph Hearst is at boarding school (1891), and hating it. Later he says, "It takes a good mind to resist education." (cf. **22***)

This is the age of majority: as a minor, contracts you make can later be repudiated, as if you did not really make them. Minors' property is generally held for them by a trustee or similar person. In U.K. law, a "child" is **0–13**; a "young person" is **14–17**. You can now sue, and be sued. You can sit on a jury.

In a survey of British people **15–21**, 90 percent wanted tougher sentences for vandals and hooligans; and 64 percent wanted hanging for any murder (National Opinion Polls, 1978).

SPORTS

Maribel Atienzar (1978): first woman bullfighter in 40 years at Madrid's central bullring.

Steve Cauthen (1978) wins racing's Triple Crown, and is U.S. Sportsman of the Year. At **17**, he rode horses to win a total of $6 million. Cauthen has been brought up on racetracks, as his father worked as a blacksmith, shoeing horses. Cauthen was first put on a horse at **1**; he is riding ponies at **2**; by **5**, he can ride bareback at top speed. His parents gradually devote themselves to his career. He turns professional at the earliest possible moment—on his **16**th birthday—and completes his high school graduation by correspondence course. At **18**, he goes on to disconcert his fans by moving from New York to California, and suffering a 110-race losing streak.

19

HEALTH

Elaine Dale gives birth to her first child, Sara Louise (England, 1979) and proceeds to look after her by herself, changing her and feeding her in the usual way—even though Elaine was herself a thalidomide baby. Elaine had been born without arms, and does all her household jobs with her feet. She comments: "I wouldn't know what to do with arms if I had them—so far as I'm concerned they're a blooming nuisance."

HISTORY—WORLD

Augustus is appointed head of Rome (44 B.C.) in the will of his great-uncle, Julius Caesar (**56***). This succession is disputed, but after leading his armies in fighting Augustus secures his position by about **23**.

He now begins the transformation of the Republic into the Empire, which he accomplishes in two ways—the stabilization of the borders, and the reform of colonial administration. His systems last for 200 years. Augustus dies in office at **67**, and immediately lives for ever, having been voted a god.

Gavrilo Princip assassinates Archduke Ferdinand at Sarajevo (1914) and thus starts World War I. Later, owing to an age rule that he is too young to be executed, Princip is sent to prison—even though millions of teenagers are now dying in battle. He himself dies of disease, in prison, at **23**.

Jean Claude Duvalier becomes the president-for-life of Haiti (1970), the youngest head of state in the world at this time. He had inherited this position.

HISTORY—U.K.

William, Duke of Normandy, in 1048: some townspeople jeer at him, because of his illegitimate birth, so he cuts off the hands and feet of two of them. (cf. **39***)

SOCIAL SCIENCE, EDUCATION

The proportion of the U.S. population in college (1977) at **18** and **19** is 30 percent; at **20** and **21**, it is also 30 percent; and at **20–24**, 16 percent; **25–29**, 11 percent; and at **30–34**, it is 7 percent. The proportion of the U.S. population (1977) in school at **3** and **4** is 32 percent; at **5** and **6**, it is 96 percent, and at **7–13**, it is 99.4 percent.

The age participation rate is the percentage of people entering higher education. For example: in the U.K. (1978–79), it is 13.5 percent and for Japan it is 35 percent.

In China there are 300,000–500,000 people in higher education of a total (all age) population of 850 million. There are said to be 146 million in primary education; Peking University has only about 10,000 students (1979), but this is increasing rapidly.

MONEY, WORK

Typically, teenage unemployment is three to five times greater than the rate for workers **25+**; the unemployment rate at **20–24** is 2.5 times the rate at **25+**. For minority groups (e.g., blacks in the U.S.A.), these rates are at least doubled in each age group. Although this excess black unemployment has become accepted as inevitable, it is a recent phenomenon. In 1948 (U.S.A.) and in the 1950s, black teenage unemployment was not of a different order from white unemployment. In some years, black teens had less unemployment than white teens.

Attitudes to teenage unemployment include the following: (1) that it is a cruel interruption of the transition from school to work; (2) that it will lead to bitterness, alienation, and crime; (3) that it is unpleasant, but unemployment at **40–60** has far more serious consequences; and (4) that it is partly caused by the overambitious job expectations of teens.

Special programs are often designed for teenage unemployment. They include job-creation programs during the summer, and training programs to provide job skills for school-leavers. Professor Walter E. Williams has suggested that youth unemployment in the U.S.A. could be powerfully attacked by not applying the minimum wage laws below a certain age. The accidental effect of a relatively high minimum wage is greater teen unemployment; since teens have less to offer and since employers cannot hire them at their true (temporarily) low value, then unemployment takes place. In West Germany, where teenage unemployment is low, **under-18**s are paid only 25 percent of the adult wage.

RENAISSANCE

John Buchan, at Glasgow University (1894), draws up a list of books that he wants to write soon—three novels, a collection of essays, and poems about fishing. They are all published by **24**. At **21** he makes a formal life plan, "List of Things to Be Done." This describes achievements for subsequent years, arranged in columns for Literary, Academic, and Practical fields. Many of the immediate aims are shortly achieved. After university, Buchan simultaneously pursues two careers, in politics and writing. At **26**, he is a member of "Milner's **(47)** Kindergarten," an elite group of civil servants who plan the reconstruction of South Africa after the Boer War. At **51**, Buchan becomes a Member of Parliament, and he is Governor General of Canada from **59** until his death there at **64**. Out of his 64 books published, probably his most famous is *The Thirty-Nine Steps* at **39**, which is filmed three times. Other books include *Prester John* at **34**; *Castle Gay* at **54**; and *Sick Heart River* at **64**.

ARCHITECTURE

Buckminster Fuller is expelled from Harvard for the second and last time—first time for excessive partying, and second time for not showing any interest in the educational process (1914). (cf. **32***)

MUSIC—CLASSICAL

Richard Wagner has a symphony performed (1832). (cf. **29***)

Johann Strauss the Younger starts his own orchestra (1844) which becomes a rival to his father's **(40)**, the current Waltz King. The father dies at **45**, and the two orchestras become one. At **42**, the younger Strauss writes "The Blue Danube." He then begins writing operettas, of which the most famous is *Die Fledermaus* **(49)**. He continues to compose until the year of his death, at **73**.

Toscanini in 1886: as a cellist in an opera orchestra, he takes over the conducting of *Aïda*—the principal conductor, the assistant, and the chorus master all being indisposed, for various reasons. Toscanini conducts entirely from memory, and the performance is a success. Next day, he is appointed principal conductor. At **32**, he is appointed to La Scala, Milan, and at **41** to the Metropolitan Opera Company, New York. He becomes conductor of the NBC Symphony Orchestra at **70***.

LITERATURE

William Makepeace Thackeray leaves Cambridge (1830), without a degree.

Enid Blyton publishes her first poem (1917).

Dylan Thomas writes: "A born writer is born scrofulous: his career is an accident dictated by physical or circumstantial disabilities" (1933). He had been a reporter from **16½**, but at **18** becomes a full-time poet. (cf. **34***)

Françoise Sagan: *Bonjour Tristesse* (1954).

PLAYS

Beatrice Tanner elopes, and becomes Mrs. Patrick Campbell (1884). She establishes herself as a great actress when at **28** she stars in the premiere of *The Second Mrs. Tanqueray,* by A. W. Pinero (**38**). At **49**, she creates the part of Eliza Doolittle, in *Pygmalion,* written by her friend George Bernard Shaw (**57**).

FILMS

Harold Lloyd: a movie company comes to his home town, San Diego, California (1912), and he gets a job as an extra. Within four years, he has made 100 films himself.

Sergei Eisenstein is training to be an architect (1917). So is James Stewart, at Princeton (1927), and James Mason, at Cambridge (1928). Ronald Colman wants to train as an architect, but his family can't afford the tuition (1910).

Jean Harlow: *Hells' Angels* (1930); this is her first starring role, and the film is directed by Howard Hughes (**25**).

William Hanna and Joseph Barbera (**28**) create Tom and Jerry, in *Puss Gets the Boot* (1939).

Elizabeth Taylor: *A Place in the Sun* (1951). She has been making films solidly throughout her teenage years.

Jane Fonda leaves Vassar without graduating (1957). At **20**, she succeeds in the acting classes of Lee Strasberg (**57**); film debut at **21**, as a cheerleader in *Tall Story.*

Candice Bergen: *The Group* (1966); her debut.

Jerry Lieber, words, and Mike Stoller (also **19**), music: "Kansas City" (1952); also, "Hound Dog" when they are both **20**; "Jailhouse Rock" at **23**; "Love Potion No. 9" at **27**; and "I'm a Woman" at **30**.

Elvis Presley: "That's All Right, Mama" (1954)—his second recording. He has had his first recording contract after an executive heard him singing on a record-your-own-voice machine. This second record does well, and by **20** his versions of "Hound Dog" and "Heartbreak Hotel" are international hits. Presley's career is organized by Colonel Tom Parker (**45**). Presley's military service begins at **23**, by which time he is already the greatest person ever in rock 'n' roll. His hits are too numerous to mention; they continue after his army time, with a revival in his career at c. **34–38**. He is married at **32**. In his lifetime he sells 600 million records.

Everly Brothers: "Wake Up, Little Susie" (1957). "Cryin' in the Rain" is at **24**. Their career ends at **35**.

Paul and Paula: "Hey Paula" (1962). This is a permanent hit, but they can never repeat this success. They are examples of pop stars who have one monument in history, and then are never heard again.

The Chiffons: "He's So Fine" (1963).

The Crystals: "Da Doo Ron Ron" (1963). This is produced by Phil Spector (**22**) and is one of the big sellers which make him a millionaire this year. Spector can afford to go into semiretirement before he reaches **30**. At **30**, he is the producer of "The Concert for Bangladesh." Later, another version of "Da Doo Ron Ron" is made, very successfully, by Shaun Cassidy (**21**, in 1977).

Mike Oldfield: "Tubular Bells" (1973).

Kate Bush: "Wuthering Heights" (1978).

TV, ETC.

Josephine Baker: "La Revue nègre" (Paris, 1925). Strong men weep at her clothesless dancing.

LOVE, LIFE

Ulrike von Levetzow, at Marienbad in 1823: J. W. von Goethe (**74**), a family friend, who is also one of the most famous men in the world, falls in love with her, and wishes to marry her. Her mother (**36**) tactfully declines. Ulrike lives until **95** without ever marrying. (cf. Renaissance, **24*** and **100***)

PRESS

Henry Luce and Briton Hadden: editor and publisher of the *Yale Daily News* (1917). (cf. **24***)

Patty Hearst is kidnapped (1974, Feb. 4) by SLA, the Symbionese Liberation Army, which includes William Harris (**29**) and Emily Harris (**26**). Hearst is the daughter of the rich newspaper owner (**58**). She is kept for 57 days in a closet $5\frac{1}{2} \times 2$ feet, and threatened with further violence if she does not join the SLA. She joins, and as "Tania" she is photographed carrying a gun at a San Francisco bank robbery. At **20**, she is caught and initially given a sentence until **55**. But this is later reduced, and she in fact leaves prison at **24**. At **25**, she marries a policeman (**33**). William Harris is sent to prison until **44**; Emily Harris until **42**.

The typical person arrested for burglary is a male **15–19**; 84 percent of those arrested are **24** or younger. The typical age for larceny-theft is **17**: 60 percent of such arrestees are **20** or younger. The typical person arrested for robbery is a male **16–20**. The typical person arrested for aggravated assault is a male **18–22** (U.S. [FBI] 1978).

SPORTS

Bobby Orr (hockey, 1967) is named Defenseman of the Year, and holds this title for 8 years in succession. At **28**, his knee gives him trouble, and prevents him from winning again. This medical condition forces him to retire at **30**, at a time when he is earning $600,000 yearly.

20

HEALTH

You can now expect to live until **77.2** (female) and until **71.4** (male) (England and Wales, 1975). Out of total deaths at all ages, only 1.1 percent (male) occur in the age group **15** to **24** and .46 percent for females.

The causes of death for males **15–24** (England and Wales, 1977) are: (1) motor vehicle accidents; (2) all other accidents; (3) suicide and self-inflicted injuries; (4) miscellaneous other cancers not in the main sites; (5) other external causes, for example, violence; (6) leukemia. Note that a large proportion of these deaths are preventable. The causes of death (female) are (1) motor vehicle accidents; (2) miscellaneous other cancers; (3) suicide and self-inflicted injuries; (4) other external and violent causes; (5) congenital abnormalities; (6) all other accidents.

Life expectancy in the U.S.A. (1976) is now until **70.9** for males and until **77.8** for females. The causes of death for people **15–24** (males) are: (1) and by far the largest, auto accidents; (2) suicide; (3) cancer; (4) diseases of the heart; (5) pneumonia and flu; (6) cerebrovascular. For females, the causes are: (1) and by far the largest, auto accidents; (2) cancer; (3) suicide; (4) diseases of the heart; (5) pneumonia and flu; (6) cerebrovascular.

In sixteenth century England, half the population was under **20**. In the British census of 1831 it was still true for males that half were **20** or below. In 1820 the median age of the U.S.A. was **16.7**. It first reached **20** in 1870, and reached **30** in 1950. In 1977, the median age was estimated to be **30.3** (whites) and **24.1** (blacks).

Teeth: a surprisingly large number of people already have poor teeth.

Some average animal life spans (in years) include: both the domestic cat and the domestic dog, **13–17**; ostrich, **15**; rhesus monkey, **15**; llama, **15**; chimpanzee, **15–20**; polar bear, **16**; cockatoo, **18–30**, depending on the species; sacred ibis, **19**; stork, **19**; kite, **20**; emu, **20**; grizzly bear, **20**; ox, **20–25**; lion, **20–25**; domestic horse, **20–30**; zebra, **22**; Amazon parrot, **24**; and African parrots, **17–22**.

Some approximate life spans (in years) for animals include: starling, **15**; bull frog, **15.6**; kangaroo, **16**; egret, **16**; herring, **18–19**; trout, **18**; rattlesnake, **18.6**; parakeet, **20**; periwinkle, **20**; California newt, **21**; cardinal bird, **22**; flamingo, **22**; corals, **22–28**; boa constrictor, **23**; cormorant, **23**; canary, **24**; striped bass, **24**; and the camel, **25**.

HISTORY—WORLD

War would always exist because there will be boys of **20** to bring it into existence, by dint of love.—Henry de Montherlant (1896–1972), French novelist.

Alexander the Great in 336 B.C.: on the death of his father (**46**), he becomes King of Macedon. His father had unified Macedonia with the Greek city states such as Athens. Alexander at **13** had been tutored by Aristotle (**41**); at **16**, he had been temporarily head of the country while his father was abroad. Alexander now uses his inherited war machine to create a vast empire. He first conquers Palestine and Egypt; he then moves against the Persian empire, farther east; finally he goes as far as the northwest of India. He dies at **32**, in Babylon, at the peak of his conquests, but having weakened himself by doing so much.

20 to **25**! These are the years! Don't be content with things as they are.—Winston Churchill.

Canute becomes King of England (1014).

Queen Victoria marries (1840, Feb. 10) Prince Albert (also **20**). The Queen had made the proposal. She goes on to have nine children. She is a mother at **22**, grandmother at **39**, and great-grandmother at **59**. She is widowed at **41**, and lives till **81**.

Winston Churchill, in 1895: death of his father Randolph (**45**); death of his grandmother Clarissa Jerome (**70**); and death of his nanny and de facto mother, Mrs. Everest (**62**), also known as "Woom." Churchill had been born in an ugly but impressive family palace, and has had an erratic and unsuccessful education. At **13**, he just managed the entrance to his next school, and at **18** he needed three attempts to enter military academy. Now at **20** begins twenty years of continuous upward movement. He enters the Army where he starts on a campaign of self-education. At **22**, he fights on the frontier between India and Afghanistan; at **23**, he writes this up in his first book *The Story of the Malarkand Field Force.* He publishes other books at **24** and **25**. Also at **25** he leaves the Army and becomes a journalist in the Boer War. He escapes from imprisonment there, and becomes a national celebrity. At **26**, he enters Parliament. At **31**, he publishes a biography of his father, and becomes a government minister. At **33**, he enters the cabinet, and he marries Clementine Hozier (**23**). He is a leader in the great social reforms at the beginning of the twentieth century. At **35**, he is the second youngest home secretary. At **37**, he campaigns for Irish Home Rule, and is a pioneer in the development of the airplane. At **39**, he is in charge of the Navy at the start of World War I, having built it up into a uniquely strong force. But the failure of a risky military campaign at **40*** forces him to resign.

RELIGION, PHILOSOPHY

Become the one you are.—Friedrich Nietzsche (1844–1900).

SCIENCE, TECHNOLOGY

Jeremiah Horrocks: first observation of the transit of Venus (1639). He dies 13 months later.

Guglielmo Marconi: his first experiments in transmission by radio (1894). Almost immediately, he senses the vast commercial possibilities. He takes out his first patent at **22**. At this time, Marconi is working entirely on his own, financed by his family; he is not attached to a university or any other organization. At **23**, he starts his own radio company. At **26**, he sends the first radio message across the Atlantic. By **50**, he has a worldwide chain of shortwave transmitters. Marconi's success is due to his commercial vision, and to his self-confidence, which allows him to hire elite talent—for example, at **25**, he employs J. A. Fleming (**49**) who at **55** develops the rectifier. Marconi dies at **63**, on the fortieth birthday of his original company.

MONEY, WORK

Sir Thomas Grosvenor marries Mary Davies (**11**) in 1676—a moment that leads to the Grosvenors afterward becoming one of the richest landowning families in Britain. Her marriage dowry includes land near the execution ground of Tyburn (later the Mayfair estate), and Ebury Farm (later the Belgravia estate). Sir Thomas dies at **44**; Lady Grosvenor goes mad at **59**, and dies at **65**.

Helena Rubinstein emigrates to Australia (1902), having dropped out of medical school in Europe. She maintains her clear complexion with face cream made by her mother. People ask her how she looks so good; she gets formula from her mother and starts selling it. Makes enough money to set up a beauty salon in London (**25**), Paris (**29**), and New York (**32**).

RENAISSANCE

Lorenzo de' Medici becomes the ruler of Florence (1469) on the death of his father (**53**). Lorenzo goes on to become "Il Magnifico" and to combine a knowledge of architecture, painting, sculpture, and philosophy with an ability to maintain calm government in Florence, and to keep the republic relatively independent during a period of upheaval. Lorenzo benefits from the enrichment of Florence and the consolidation of the Medici family by his father and grandfather (d. **77**, in 1464); but at Lorenzo's death (**43**), the perfection of Florence begins to disappear. At **29**, Lorenzo is the victim of the Pazzi conspiracy, organized with the probable connivance of Pope Sixtus IV (**64**). During High Mass in Florence Cathedral, to welcome a new Cardinal, Raffaello Riario (only **16**), Lorenzo is injured, and his brother Giuliano (**25**) is killed. Many of the conspirators are hanged that same evening, and Lorenzo employs Sandro Botticelli (**33**) to record the scene. A year later, another of the murderers is brought back from Turkey; his executed body is sketched by Leonardo da Vinci (**27**). Pope Sixtus IV is later better remembered for his creation of the Sistine Chapel, consecrated at **69**. Lorenzo marries at **20**, and goes on to father ten children; at **34**, his daughter Madalena (**14**) is married to a papal son, Francesschetto Cibo (c. **40**); and at **40** his son Giovanni (**13**) is privately created a Cardinal, who later becomes Pope Leo X at **38**. And a nephew born when Lorenzo is **29** later becomes Pope also—Pope Clement VII (**45–56**). At the moment of Lorenzo's assumption of power in Florence (1469), Leon Battista Alberti is **65**; Fra Filippo Lippi, the painter, has just died at c. **63**, and his son Filippino, also a painter, is c. **12**; Benozzo Gozzoli, the painter, is **49**; Lorenzo's mother, Lucrezia Tornabuoni, is **45**; Marsilio Ficino, the philosopher, is **36**; Andrea del Verrocchio is **34**; Sandro Botticelli is **24**; Luca Pacioli, the codifier of double-entry bookkeeping, is **24**; Domenico Ghirlandaio, the painter, is **20**; Leonardo da Vinci is **17**; Girolamo Savonarola, the priest, is **17**; Amerigo Vespucci, later the Florentine explorer whose name is given to America, is **15**, and living next door to Botticelli; Pico della Mirandola, later the philosopher who attempts a synthesis of Plato and Christianity, is **6**; Niccolò Machiavelli, later the civil servant and political scientist, is **0** and **7 months**; Pisa University is about **130**; and later Michelangelo is born when Lorenzo is **26**.

ARCHITECTURE

Saul Steinberg is studying architecture in Milan (1934), but from **27** onward he becomes a cartoonist, in New York. He later says: "The study of architecture is a marvellous training for anything but architecture. The frightening thought that what you draw may become a building makes for reasoned lines." Le Corbusier (1887–1965) never qualifies as an architect, but in later life he receives one of Steinberg's certificates—highly impressive, though illegible. Charles Eames (1907–78) is another unqualified architect.

ART

Dante Gabriel Rossetti: foundation of the Pre-Raphaelite Brotherhood (1848). Other members include John Millais (**19**) and William Holman Hunt (**21**). At first, they are bitterly attacked, but soon become accepted. They do their best work in the next decade, and then for the most part their inspiration flagged. Millais had been an infant prodigy; he now goes on to paint "Ophelia" at **22**, and "Autumn Leaves" at **27**. This is his best period. Later, he does landscapes and portraits, which are popular—particularly "Bubbles" (**57**), used in advertisements for Pears Soap. Rossetti had also been precocious; he now does poems and paintings, and some wonderful sketches of Elizabeth Siddal (**16** when they meet). His work later becomes highly repetitive; as he grows accustomed to a vast income, he is trapped into cranking out picture after picture. Holman Hunt produces "The Hireling Shepherd" at **22**, "Light of the World" at **26**, and the searing "Scapegoat" at **27**—but afterward nothing dramatic until his memoirs of the "PRB" at **78**.

James McNeill Whistler flunks out of West Point—later says, "Had silicon been a gas, I would have been a major general." At **21**, he moves to Paris to become an artist. He has his first solo show at **40***.

Pablo Picasso: Blue Period (1901–04); and Rose Period from **24**. (cf. **26***)

Andy Warhol: B.A. (Pictorial Design), Carnegie Institute of Technology, Pittsburgh (1949). He now works on *Glamour* magazine in New York. By **29**, his drawings of shoes have made him the leading commercial artist of his time. His pictures of Campbell's Soup cans start at **34***.

MUSIC—CLASSICAL

Beethoven in 1790 writes: "My youth, yes I feel my youth is just beginning." (cf. **32***)

Mendelssohn and others revive the *St. Matthew Passion* of J. S. Bach (**44**) (1829, March 11). He now writes *Calm Seas and Prosperous Voyage;* and also *Fingal's Cave,* while on a tempestuously successful tour of Britain, still at **20**. He next goes to Italy, and starts the writing of the *Italian* Symphony. At **26**, he is in charge of musical activities in Leipzig. (cf. **34***)

Brahms in 1853 reads this article about himself, written by Schumann (**43***): "I always thought that there would arise, that one day there must suddenly arise a man who in an ideal form would incarnate the supreme expression of his epoch, someone who would achieve mastery not by progressive development, but who would spring fully armed like Athena from the brain of Zeus. And he has come!" (Schumann is taken off to a mental hospital a few months later.) Brahms writes *A German Requiem* at **34**, and his four symphonies from **43*** onward.

William Walton: *Façade* (1922); and *Belshazzar's Feast* at **29**; *Crown Imperial* March at **35**.

LITERATURE

The imagination of a boy is healthy, and the mature imagination of a man is healthy; but there is a space of life in between, in which the soul is in ferment, the character undecided, the way of life uncertain, the ambition thick-sighted: thence proceeds mawkishness.—John Keats (1795–1821).

Percy Bysshe Shelley publishes his rejected manuscripts (1812) by putting them into bottles, and sending them out to sea. Since being expelled from Oxford at **18**, he has had difficulty in promoting his views, owing to their extreme atheistic and egalitarian nature. (cf. **29***)

Mary Shelley: *Frankenstein* (1818)

Honoré de Balzac: his parents agree to support him for two years, while he becomes professional writer (1819). He writes a play about Oliver Cromwell, hoping that this will bring him instant fame. The play is hopeless, and Balzac is forced to enter a series of money-making schemes (also disastrous) and to produce pulp fiction. (cf. **30***)

Arthur Rimbaud: end of his career as a poet (1874). Since **16**, he has written some of the greatest French poems of his time. Inexplicably he now stops writing. At this moment, his supporter and lover, Paul Verlaine, is **30**. In his **20**s, Rimbaud travels in Africa. At **30**, he learns that he is gaining something of a reputation as a poet. But he dies at **37**, from cancer.

Boris Pasternak accompanies his artist father (Nov. 1910) who is to make a deathbed portrait of Tolstoy (**82**). Pasternak himself later publishes *Dr. Zhivago* at **68**.

Evelyn Waugh graduates from university with minimal qualifications (1924). He has a couple of teaching jobs in boys' boarding schools, but is dismissed. He makes a suicide attempt, but is stung by jelly fish, and so chooses not to drown. He is saved at **24** by the enormous success of his *Decline and Fall,* and he publishes continuously from then onward. (cf. **50***)

PLAYS

Bertolt Brecht: *Baal* (1918), and *Drums in the Night* at **21**. Early in his **20**s, he establishes himself as a powerful force in the theater. *The Threepenny Opera* is at **30**; *Rise and Fall of the City of Mahagonny* is at **32**; and *St. Joan of the Stockyards* is at **34**. Brecht is driven out of Germany by the rise of the Nazis, and he writes three great plays while in exile during his late **30**s, viz., *Galileo, The Good Woman of Setzuan,* and *Mother Courage and Her Children.* For a time, he lives in the U.S., and there completes *The Caucasian Chalk Circle* at **50**. After further travel, he returns to Germany, and at **51** is given his own theater, the Berliner Ensemble. Here he directs all the plays that he has written during his exile. Brecht has been close to some of the most powerful events in contemporary history. As a playwright in his **20**s and **30**s, he has been so innovative that his productions in his **50**s seem revolutionary to most theater people. But he lives only until **56**.

FILMS

John Ford has a small part in *The Birth of a Nation* (1915), by **D. W.** Griffith (**40**).

Irving Thalberg is in charge of production at Universal Studios (1919).

Jean Harlow: *Platinum Blonde* (1931).

Judy Garland: *For Me and My Gal* (1942).

At the age of **20**, I had grabbed at the sky, and had touched some stars. And who but a **20**-year-old would think you could keep it?—Lauren Bacall, in her memoirs. At **19**, she met Humphrey Bogart (**45**,* 1944) to make the film *To Have and Have Not.* They are later married—his fourth and last—and he lives until **57**. The story of *To Have and Have Not* is taken from the book of the same name, by Ernest Hemingway (**38**, in 1937).

 Norma Jean Baker goes to 20th Century-Fox studios, and obtains an appointment with the head of casting; he gives her a contract, and also her new name, Marilyn Monroe (1946, July 16).

Jeanne Moreau joins the Comédie Française on her twentieth birthday.

Debbie Reynolds: *Singin' in the Rain* (1952).

Shirley MacLaine is in the chorus of *The Pajama Game* (May 1954) and understudy to the star; after five performances, the star breaks her ankle, and Shirley MacLaine takes over. She is offered a film contract that night, by a Hollywood producer who happens to be in the audience. Two months later, she stars in *The Trouble with Harry,* directed by Alfred Hitchcock (**55**).

Richard Dreyfuss is a conscientious objector; does two years work, as a filing clerk on the graveyard shift, at Los Angeles County General Hospital (1967–69).

Nastassia Kinski: *Tess* (1981), directed by Roman Polanski (**48**). Tess herself was **16**.

MUSIC—NON-CLASSICAL

Bob Dylan: "Bob Dylan" (1962), his first album. This is recorded 14 months after he has arrived in New York, after leaving the University of Minnesota. At **21**, he records "Blowin' in the Wind," and makes himself both a musical and a political figure. At **22**, he records "Girl of the North Country"; at **23**, "Mr. Tambourine Man"; at **24**, "Like a Rolling Stone"; at **25**, "Blonde On Blonde," which includes "Sad Eyed Lady of the Lowlands"; and at **26** "I Shall Be Released." Bob Dylan sets himself up as a person who "knows where it's at," that is, he can intuitively read the truth about society as it changes. In this, Dylan is successful, at least until **30**. But later, should he ever make a mistake (cf. **38***), there are endless critics who will jeer at him for losing his touch and for failing to keep up with changing times.

Billy J. Kramer and the Dakotas: "Bad to Me," and "Want to Know a Secret" (1963).

Prince: "Dirty Mind" (1981).

LOVE, LIFE

Youth is a continuous intoxication; it is a fever of good health, the riot of reason.—La Rochefoucauld, 1613–80.

He who reaches the age of **20** and has not married spends all his days in sin. "Sin" actually? Say better "all his days in thought of sin."—The Talmud.

Here is the inscription on the tombstone of a Greek girl who dies now, unmarried, in Egypt, sometime around 300 B.C.:

> For twice ten years my father provided for me,
> Nor did I even complete the rite of the bridal chamber and bed,
> nor did my body lie in the couch,
> nor was there an allnight knocking by the girls of my age on
> the cedar doors.

Nell Gwyn: birth of her first child (London, 1670). The father is King Charles II (**39**) who had seen her on stage at **18** and had fallen in love with her. Before her acting career, she had sold oranges in the theater. This first child is given the title of Duke of St. Albans, and the family name of Fitzroy. Nell Gwyn dies at **37**, from apoplexy.

In the age group **15–29**, there are 100.3 males for every 100 females (U.S.A., 1976).

63 percent of U.S. women (1977) at **20** have never married.

50 percent of unmarried mothers are **19** and younger. The age group which is next most likely to be unmarried mothers is **20–24**; and then, **25–29** (U.S.A., 1976).

In Japan, January 15th is a national holiday in honor of all those who are coming of age, **20**, this year. The holiday is derived from "gempuku," the old coming-of-age ceremony which used to be held at **12–15**. You are at the center of family celebrations. It is likely that your food today will represent the family's hope for your future; for example, rice and red beans, white and red, for good fortune. Also, food may be cut out in the shape of the pine tree which as an evergreen is a symbol of long life, or in the shape of a plum blossom, the first blossom in spring and the symbol of freshness and vitality. In the Imperial Royal Family, the coming-of-age ceremony for the Crown Prince's heir, Prince Naruhito (**20** in 1980), included the presentation of a coronet from the emperor; the prince publicly committed himself to his grandfather to devote his life to Japan. The prince also visited the shrines and sanctuaries of the emperors from the past, to make reports to them on the attainment of his manhood.

EXPLORATION

In motor accidents, it is said that the highest death rates occur at **19** for motorcyclists, at **24** for car occupants, and at **6** for pedestrians.

Insurance premiums for car drivers are highest now; they decline quickly by about **35**, and they are lowest at **60+**. By **35**, the premium is cut in half, and with a no-claims bonus it may well be one fourth of the rate at **20**. Drivers at around **20** have a high exposure to risk, since they typically drive at high speed, often at night, and they also lack experience. Reaction speed, which may perhaps favor the younger driver, is ignored by insurance companies, in view of the risky lifestyle. Insurance companies can offer special programs for the **60+**, since at that age experience is greater, the individual drives fewer miles, more often during daylight, and he or she has a less risky lifestyle.

LAW, CRIME

Ninety percent of people executed by hanging were aged **20** or less (U.K., 1785).

Today, 51 percent of people arrested in London are **20** or below.

SPORTS

Dwight F. Davis (1900): creation of the Davis Cup in tennis, the international tournament. Davis is a Harvard undergraduate who plays for the first-ever U.S. side, and who wins his match. For three years, **19–21**, Davis is a U.S. national doubles champion.

Pancho Gonzalez: U.S. tennis champion (1948). John McEnroe (also **20**) wins the same tournament in 1979.

Chris Evert (1975): U.S. Open champion, for four consecutive years, **20–23**. At **19**, **20**, and **21**, she is the champion at Wimbledon. At **20**, she earns $413,000; and at **22**, she makes another $453,000. As a child, Evert has been taught by her father, a professional tennis coach in Florida; and at **14** she was number one in her age group. At **24**, she marries John Lloyd (**24**)—also a tennis star, but in the $50,000 class.

Nancy Lopez (1977): she turns professional, and in the next two years she wins seventeen major golf tournaments.

21

HEALTH

Karen Ann Quinlan goes into coma after being hurt in a road accident (New Jersey, 1975). She is put on life-support machinery. At **22**, medical, legal, and religious authorities agree that she is irreversibly brain damaged, and that it would be right to withdraw the life support equipment. This is done, and contrary to expectation, Karen continues to live.

Simón Bolívar is an observer of Napoleon's (**35**) self-coronation, in 1804. Bolivar is both stimulated and repulsed by this spectacle, and he goes home to Venezuela, to lead a revolt against the Spanish occupying forces. At **30**, he is briefly the leader of his country, but has to return to guerilla fighting. At this time, he develops his vision of a free South America, in *The Letter from Jamaica.* He captures Bogotá at **36**, Ecuador at **39**, and Peru at **41**. A new country is named after him at **42***.

HISTORY—U.K.

Catherine Howard becomes the fifth wife of Henry VIII (1540, June 10), but is executed by his order when she is about **23**.

Douglas Bader loses both legs in a flying accident (Dec. 1931) and has to leave the Royal Air Force at **23**. But he returns to the service at **29**, flying in the Battle of Britain, and becoming a wing-commander.

Margaret Thatcher works in the research department of a plastics factory (Sept. 1947), having recently obtained her B.Sc. in chemistry. She now becomes Secretary of the Colchester Young Conservatives, and reaches the finals of the Home Counties (North) Area public speaking competition. She first addresses the party's national conference at **23**, and first stands for Parliament at **24** (youngest woman candidate at that election). She gradually switches careers to being a barrister, and is first an MP at **33**, having earlier married and had twins. (cf. **44***)

Eligibility: you are now old enough to be a member of Parliament (since the Parliamentary Election Act of 1695). If a peer, you are now old enough to be summoned to the House of Lords (since 1685).

RELIGION, PHILOSOPHY

St. Clare: the foundation of the Poor Clares (1215), the Franciscan order for women.

MONEY, WORK

Edwin Land drops out of Harvard in his first year (1930)—invents Polaroid by **23**. He invents his one-step photographic system by **38**, and is in charge of his own firm for the whole of his working life.

Yves St. Laurent is appointed head of the House of Dior (1957).

SCIENCE, TECHNOLOGY

Humphry Davy: discovery of nitrous oxide, laughing gas (1800).

Thomas J. Watson, Sr., joins National Cash Register (1895); becomes a leading salesman. (cf. **39***)

Steven P. Jobs and Stephen G. Wozniak (**29**): the first Apple microcomputer (1976), which they manufacture in Jobs's garage. Soon they are joined by Mike Markulla (**34**) and within four years they have built up the company so that it goes public. After that, the principals in the firm are rich.

ART

Edvard Munch: "The Sick Child" (1885). At **4**, he had seen his mother die of tuberculosis; when he is **13**, his sister (**15**) dies of the same disease. Munch later writes about this painting, "With 'The Sick Child' I opened up new paths for myself—it became a breakthrough in my art. Most of my later works owe their existence to this work." At **30**, Munch paints "The Scream"—a woman screaming, under a sky of blood.

MUSIC—CLASSICAL

Orlando Gibbons becomes organist of the Chapel Royal (1605), and continues in office till his death at **42**. Also at **21**, Henry Purcell becomes organist of Westminster Abbey (1680).

Chopin gives his first concert in Paris (1832, Feb. 26), and immediately enters the social and intellectual elite there. (cf. **28***)

Enrico Caruso achieves prominence for his singing of Rodolfo in *La Boheme* (1894).

LITERATURE

A writer's art must be racial—which means, in plain words, that it must be based on the accumulated sensations of the first **twenty-one** years.—T.S. Eliot (1888–1965).

Jane Austen writes *Pride and Prejudice* (1796); it is rejected by a publisher, and not published until she is **38**. She now begins *Sense and Sensibility.* (cf. **33***)

Leslie Charteris leaves university without a degree (1928), but immediately writes a best-seller, *The Saint.* After 40 books, he publicly hires ghostwriters to write new Saint books.

PLAYS, DANCE

The action of the ballet *Swan Lake* takes place on the **21**st birthday of Prince Siegfried. He has to choose a bride, and he falls in love with Odette, a fragile and virginal woman. But shortly afterward he also expresses his love for Odile, a woman of daring and lust. Siegfried has destroyed the love between himself and Odette, and they both die on the following morning—perhaps to live on in another world.

Brigitte Bardot: *Doctor at Sea* (1955).

MUSIC—NON-CLASSICAL

Joan Baez is on the cover of *Time* magazine, as a symbol of the folk-song movement (1962). At **18**, she made her first appearance at the Newport Folk Festival, and sang to 13,000 people. At **24**, she sets up the Institute for the Study of Non-Violence, in Carmel Valley, California. At **27**, she marries David Harris (**22**), a resistance worker against the Vietnam War. (cf. **38***)

Cilla Black: "Anyone Who Had a Heart" (1964).

Mary Wells: "My Guy" (1964).

The Supremes: "Where Did Our Love Go?" (1964); and at **22** "Stop! In the Name of Love." At this time they dominate pop music so effectively that they have five number one records in a row. And at **23** "You Can't Hurry Love."

Procol Harum: "A Whiter Shade of Pale" (1967).

Sid Vicious, the guitarist of the Sex Pistols (1979), the preeminent Punk group, dies in New York from a heroin overdose. He has been out on bail from a charge of murdering Nancy Spungen (**20**), a girl friend who had been stabbed to death. The records of the Sex Pistols have been extensively banned. Shortly after Vicious's death, his mother (**46**) herself faces a drug charge, in connection with 15 pounds of marijuana.

TV, ETC.

David Sarnoff, a radio operator with the Marconi Company (1912) keeps in radio contact with the S.S. *Titanic* for 72 hours while it sinks. This makes him briefly world famous. Sarnoff had joined Marconi at **15**, and worked his way up from filing clerk; he made sure to read all documents before filing them, thus gaining a unique insight into the company's operations. At **26**, he is commercial manager of Marconi when it is bought up by RCA, the Radio Corporation of America. At **30**, he is general manager of RCA, and President at **39**. Though a radio pioneer, Sarnoff is able to see that TV will become dominant, so he leads his company, now NBC, into television, with the first programs being transmitted when he is **48**.

LOVE, LIFE

Lucrezia Borgia: her third marriage (Rome, 1501); her new husband is Alfonso d'Este (**24**). Her first marriage had been at **13**, to Giovanni Sforza (**28**), and had been dissolved at **17**, when she married Alfonso of Aragon (also **17**). At **19**, her second husband dies, probably strangled by order of her brother, Cesare Borgia (**24**). Now, at **21**, her third marriage is by direction of Pope Alexander VI (**70**), her father and lover. She goes on to carefully perform her new duties as Duchess of Ferrara. She dies in childbirth at **39**.

Eligibility: you are now allowed to bet. Gambling is legal between **18–21**, depending on local legislation. The age range with the highest rate of betting is **18–24**; betting decreases fairly slowly until **65**, and then falls away rapidly.

PRESS

Herbert Block adopts the name "Herblock" (1930) while drawing cartoons for the Chicago *Daily News.* Later, at **41**, he is one of the first to attack Senator Joseph McCarthy (also **41**). At **70**, he continues to be a cartoonist.

Ronald Searle: cartoons of girls and teachers at "St. Trinian's" school (1941), until **33**.

Jann Wenner begins *Rolling Stone* magazine, in association with columnist Ralph Gleason (**44**) (1967)—it sells 6,000 copies, and requires an investment of $7,500. At **33**, Wenner takes control of *Look* magazine, at a time when *Rolling Stone* has a circulation of 600,000.

Tony Elliott starts *Time Out* (London, 1968) with £70 ($150). Elliott is a university student, but now drops out. Ten years later, the magazine is still the best weekly about London.

LAW, CRIME

Andrew Medosa, in New York (1979): during a gasoline shortage, he has an argument while disputing priority at a pump. Another driver (**23**) pulls out a gun, and kills him.

In a survey of all the lynchings in one year (U.S., 1930), the lynchers were typically white males, late **teens** to **25**. There were no females of this age taking part, but a number of middle-aged women who were said to incite the mob to greater brutality. Of the 21 mob victims, two thirds were **24** or under, and only three were over **45**, one being **70**.

SPORTS

Paul Murphy (U.S.A., 1858) suddenly appears from nowhere to beat the three greatest chess players in the world. But by **23**, he has completely dropped out of chess. His life is disrupted by the U.S. Civil War, after which he sets up as a lawyer in Louisiana. His life is one long decline, from **23**, until his death at **47**.

Floyd Patterson (1956) wins the world heavyweight boxing championship. He is the youngest to do so. The second youngest is Muhammad Ali (**22***).

Virginia Wade later writes: "During my **21**st year, I began to create a multifaceted dream; I would celebrate my **21**st birthday, get a first class degree in mathematics, and win Wimbledon—all within a matter of days. In fact, I got a third at university, and lost in the first round at Wimbledon. The only part that actually worked out was my birthday coming and going on July 10th." It is not until **32** that she manages to win this championship.

Dick Fosbury: The Frosbury Flop, at the 1968 Olympics. He travels head first, on his back, to win the high jump.

In American football, each season there is a pool of former college players who are aiming for professional status in the NFL, the National Football League. This pool contains 4,000 players, who go to summer training camp; at the end of camp, only about 225 have survived the cuts. Even so, only about 10 percent of these will make it to the starting lineup at the first game.

22

HEALTH

Caspar Bartholin: discovery of Bartholin's glands (1677); and at **30**, Bartholin's duct and gland.

Recently in the U.S.A. there has been a decline in the number of mothers in this age group. For example, out of all ever-married women aged **20–24** there were 24 percent without children in 1960; but there were 43 percent without children in 1977.

In the U.S.A., mothers having abortions are roughly one third **teenagers**, one third **20–24**, and one third **25+**.

In London in 1830, the laboring classes died on average at **22**; tradesmen and their families at **25**; and the gentry at **44**. Life expectancy in classical Rome could be around **22**, and in western Europe in the eighteenth century it might be around **36**. By the beginning of the twentieth century, the roughly comparable figure would be a life expectancy of **52–55**.

HISTORY—WORLD

Ivan III becomes Grand Prince of Moscow (1462). By his death (**65**), he has earned the title "Ivan the Great" by throwing out the invaders—the Tartar Horde—and so in effect establishing the independent nation of Russia.

Alfred: King of England (871–99).

King Henry I personally pushes a conquered enemy (1090) off the top of a high tower.

Robert Walpole leaves Cambridge without a degree (May 1698), owing to the death of his eldest brother. He begins managing the family estates; MP at **24**, and Secretary of War, at **31**. (cf. **34***)

William Pitt the Elder enters the army (Feb. 1731). He had left Oxford without a degree. He becomes an MP at **26**, and makes his first well-known and patriotic speech at **30**. (cf. **48***)

William Pitt the Younger, in 1782: in a speech to the House of Commons, he lets slip that he "would never accept a subordinate situation," that is, any junior job. He is Chancellor of the Exchequer, his first job, at **23**, and Prime Minister from **24** to **41***, and **44** to **46**, dying in office.

Luke Hansard begins printing the *House of Commons' Journals* (1774), later known just as *Hansard*.

William Gladstone enters the House of Commons (1832, Dec. 13). He had got a double first at Oxford, and had been president of the Union. At **28**, he publishes his first book, which says that the Church of England and the state are linked together for all time. He enters the Cabinet at **33**. At **29**, he marries Catherine Glynne (**27**), who is related to five former prime ministers. (cf. **45***)

Clement Atlee meets poor people for the first time (1905), when visiting the East End of London. He almost immediately becomes a Socialist, and is an out-of-work organizer and do-gooder for the next nine years. He becomes Mayor of Stepney at **36**; MP at **39**; in the Cabinet at **57**; Prime Minister at **62**.

NOTE: as some evidence of marriage practices, here are the ages of English kings and queens upon marriage, from 1100 to 1486:

Henry I (**32**) marries Matilda of Scotland (**21**) in 1100;
Stephen (**29**) marries Matilda of Boulogne (**20**) in 1125;
Henry II (**19**) marries Eleanor of Aquitaine (**30**) in 1152;
Richard I (**34**) marries Berengaria of Navarre (**28**) in 1191;
John (**21**) marries Isabel of Gloucester in 1189;
Henry III (**28**) marries Eleanor (**19**) in 1236;
Edward I (**14**) marries Eleanor (**10**) in 1254; at **60**, he marries Marguerite (**20**) and has his last child at **66**;
Edward II (**24**) marries Isabelle (**13**) in 1308;
Edward III (**15**) marries Philippa (**15**) in 1328;
Richard II (**15**) marries Anne of Prague (**15**) in 1382;
Henry IV (**13**) marries Mary de Bohun (**10**) in 1380/81;
Henry V (**32**) marries Catherine of Paris (**18**) in 1420;

Henry VI (**23**) marries Margaret of Anjou (**16**) in 1445;
Edward IV (**22**) marries Elizabeth (**27**) in 1464;
Richard III (**19**) marries Anne Neville (**16**, a widow) in 1472;
Henry VII (**28**) marries Elizabeth (**20**) in 1486;
and for Henry VIII, cf. **41***.

RELIGION, PHILOSOPHY

St. Wenceslas: death (929 A.D.). He became the ruler of Bohemia at **15** and had begun a pious anti-pagan administration. But he is now killed by his brother. He is later canonized, and much later still is commemorated in a fictitious story in a Christmas carol.

SCIENCE, TECHNOLOGY

Charles Darwin: voyage on HMS *Beagle* (1831), to South America and the Pacific. He is unpaid naturalist on board, and the main purpose of the expedition is to make charts for navigation. The voyage lasts until **27** and Darwin collects numerous botanical and geological records. Upon return, he sets about writing up this data, and he gradually develops the ideas of (1) mutable, not fixed, species; (2) the development of species through natural selection, not through any conscious effort by God or animal. He is so struck by the revolutionary nature of these ideas that he first publishes three books on geology, at **33**, **35**, and **37**. After work on barnacles he begins again his work on species at **45**, and the first paper is given at **49**. The ideas which he first sketches out at **29–30** are not fully published until **50***.

George Westinghouse: invention of the air brake, for trains (1868).

Frank Whittle: first patent for a jet engine (1930). Whittle is a low-ranking apprentice in the air force, and his work on jets is mostly ignored. At **27**, the British Air Ministry allows the patent to lapse. Whittle's first test engine runs at **29**, and his first jet-engine plane flies at **33**. The time lag is due to: technical difficulties in producing new metals to withstand the heat and loading; the tiny amount of investment money allocated to him; the time he has to spend on his regular career to become a pilot; and poor health due to overwork. After the first successful flight, Whittle is disappointed to find that his previously ignored project is now taken over by several giant organizations, and he himself is almost ignored in the rush. At **41**, he virtually retires from the field, disappointed by the continuous intrigue necessary to implement his ideas. But during his retirement he is consoled by a stream of honors and awards.

Brian Josephson: prediction of the Josephson Effect (1962), soon confirmed by others, and later proposed for use in computers.

MONEY, WORK

Duke of Bridgewater; after a scandal over the family into which he has been going to marry (1758), he retires to his country estates, ignoring London life, and starts developing his properties; hires James Brindley (**43**) to cut the first canal in Britain. The events at **22** result in a lifelong hatred of women, and a lifelong obsession with canals; he dies a very rich bachelor at **67**.

Cyrus H. McCormick invents his reaper (1831), but time needed for farming, a bankruptcy, and other hazards prevent him from exploiting his invention until he is **38**—but he then creates his own company.

ART

Samuel Palmer, in 1827: he goes to Shoreham, Kent, and between now and **26** produces a series of lovely and influential landscapes. Previously he had been a visionary and a child prodigy. He lives until **76**, but never again produces anything that is quite comparable.

Paul Cézanne fails the entrance test for the École des Beaux-Arts (1861), and goes to work in the family bank. Supported by family money, he soon returns to painting, and works steadily, mainly on his own. He is said to develop his mature style from **37** onward; he has his first one-man show at **56***.

Vincent van Gogh, in 1871, comments on an old, semifailed uncle: "In most men, there exists a poet, who died young, whom the man survived." At **20**, van Gogh starts a two-year stay in England. At **23**, he returns, and teaches languages and mathematics at a small boarding school for boys in Ramsgate. After leaving, he determines to become a priest, and at **25** is a preacher in a coal-mining region of Belgium. (cf. **35***)

MUSIC—CLASSICAL

J. S. Bach obtains employment as an organist (Sept. 1707) and marries Maria Barbara (also **22**). At **23**, he becomes organist at Weimar, and now begins his great period as composer of organ music. This lasts till **32**, when he becomes Kapellmeister at Köthen. The organ pieces that are later remembered are composed between **23** and **32***. The choral music typically comes from his time at Leipzig, from **38*** onward.

Mozart: *Paris* Symphony (1778). His mother (**58**) dies while the two of them are on a visit to Paris. Mozart comes home for his last two years in Salzburg. He writes *Idomeneo* at **24**. This is sometimes said to be the beginning of his adult life regaining the momentum that he had had as an infant prodigy. (cf. **25***)

Edward Elgar becomes bandmaster at the Powick lunatic asylum, near Worcester (England, 1879). This job in music therapy occupies one day a week, and augments his income from working in his father's music shop. He had left school at **15**, and received little formal musical education after that. He gradually develops his skill as a composer, but it is still almost 20 years before he first produces anything that is memorable—viz., the *Enigma Variations* at **41***.

Benjamin Britten: music for the film *Night Mail* (1936). This work is for the Post Office Film Unit, and at **24** he does more background music, for a film on the telephone dial. At **23**, he begins his lifelong relationship with Peter Pears (**26**), and buys a house near Aldebrough—where they start their first Festival at **34**. Britten writes *Ceremony of Carols* at **28**. (cf. **48***)

ARCHITECTURE

Giles Gilbert Scott wins the competition for the design of Liverpool Cathedral (1903)—not completed until after his death at **80**.

LITERATURE

Virginia Woolf and her family move to Bloomsbury (1904), and begin having their friends (e.g., Lytton Strachey, also **22**) 'round to the house—this is the beginning of what came to be known as "Bloomsbury." (cf. **33***)

Ernest Hemingway moves to Paris (1921), as correspondent for a couple of North American papers; there, he makes friends with Ezra Pound (**24**), and Gertrude Stein (**47**), who afterward writes, "They were all **23**: later, they were all **26**." Hemingway also meets Scott Fitzgerald (**26**), and James Joyce (**40**). Unlike many of the "artistic" people who had moved to Paris, Hemingway practices his work all the time, and at **27** publishes *The Sun Also Rises,* and *A Farewell to Arms* at **29**. (cf. **50***)

Kurt Vonnegut is a prisoner-of-war in Germany, and watches the Anglo-American firebombing of Dresden (1945, Feb. 13). He becomes a full-time writer at **27**, but does not become well known until *Cat's Cradle* (**40**). His *Slaughterhouse Five* (**46**) is inspired by the bombing of Dresden.

FILMS

Merle Oberon: *The Private Life of Henry VIII* (1933); instantly becomes a star.

Charles Bronson is drafted (1943); becomes a tail-gunner in a B-29; on leaving, at **27**, decides not to return to previous occupation (coal miner in Appalachia), and instead drifts into acting.

Judy Garland: *Meet Me in St. Louis* (1944).

Jean-Luc Godard starts writing for *Cahiers du cinéma* (1952).

Brigitte Bardot: *And God Created Woman* (1956), directed by Roger Vadim (**28**); this film makes her an international star, as "BB."

Isabelle Huppert: *The Lacemaker* (1977).

Bing Crosby: "I've Got the Girl" (1926), his first commercial recording.

Buddy Holly: death, in a plane crash (1959). His career had begun at **16**. "Peggy Sue" and "That'll Be the Day" are at **19**. His posthumous releases include "Raining in My Heart" and "It Doesn't Matter Any More." After his death, his reputation climbs even higher than it has been during his lifetime (cf. **35*** for other early deaths of music stars). Buddy Holly's replacement at his last concert is Bobby Vee (**16**) who goes on to make at least ten hit records, including "Take Good Care of My Baby."

The Beatles: "Please, Please Me" (1963). This is their first number one hit. Their original core group, The Quarrymen, had begun five years previously, and they played a season in Hamburg at **20**. At **23**, they tour the U.S.A., and Beatlemania sweeps the country. "A Hard Day's Night" is at **23**; "Help" and "Rubber Soul" at **24**; "Sergeant Pepper" is at **25**, the same year as the death of their manager, Brian Epstein (**32**). The "White Album" is at **27**, and the group disbands at **29** (cf. **38*** for their subsequent life). At the moment when the Beatles are **22**, Little Richard is **28**, and Chuck Berry is **37**.

Barbra Streisand: *Funny Girl* (1964–65).

Jim Morrison and the Doors, in 1966: the beginning of their three years at the top of the rock world. For example, "Light My Fire" is at **23**. But during a rave tour at **25**, Morrison shows his penis to an audience, and the resulting legal complications seem to make any further musical activity impossible. Morrison dies in his bath at **27**, perhaps from respiratory problems and a heart attack.

The Cream, in 1966: the beginning of their two-year existence as the best rock group in the world. At this moment, Eric Clapton is **21**, Jack Bruce is **22**, and Ginger Baker is **25**. Clapton and Bruce are two out of many stars who have worked with John Mayall (**32**) and the Bluesbreakers.

David Bowie: "Space Oddity" (1969); and "The Rise and Fall of Ziggy Stardust and the Spiders from Mars" at **25**. He makes the film *The Man Who Fell to Earth* at **28**.

Andrew Lloyd Webber: "Jesus Christ Superstar" (1970); and "Evita" at **30**; "Cats" at **32**.

Cat Stevens: "Tea for the Tillerman," and "Where Do the Children Play" (1971). "Morning Has Broken" is at **24**. Later, Stevens takes up a religious career, and virtually withdraws from the world of the star. He changes his name to Yusef Islam.

TV, ETC.

Harry Houdini: first escape from a hospital straitjacket (1896). This is the beginning of his career as one of the most remarkable people of his time. Houdini maintains his prominence by constantly presenting himself with greater and greater escaping problems (from a straitjacket, *underwater*) from which he always survives. He dies as the result of an accident, at **52**.

Goldie Hawn: "Laugh-In" (1967–70); other stars are Judy Carne (**28**) and Dan Rowan **46**. Goldie Hawn makes the film *Cactus Flower* at **24**, and *There's a Girl in My Soup* at **25**. She has her own TV specials in her **30**s. She stars in *Shampoo* at **30**, and in *Private Benjamin* at **35**.

LOVE, LIFE

Jean Shrimpton: appearance at Ascot Races, Melbourne (1965) in a dress which reveals part of her thighs. This shocks the other racegoers, but leads to a brief international craze for the miniskirt.

James Stare (1979) breaks the world disco-dancing record—he dances in New York for 330 hours, over 15 days.

Marriage: you promise to look after each other for the rest of your lives. Two people become one, and they start to form a new small community. Both of you wear a ring, so that everyone can instantly recognize your status. You swear that you will have sex with only one person, "till death us do part," or, for about 58 years.

In India, the marriage age was raised in 1978, to **18** (female) and to **21** (male), minimum, in an attempt to lower the birthrate. In China today, the preferred age for marriage is **26–28** (male) and **24–26** (female).

In the U.S.A., the marriage age has steadily become lower since the last century, but it is now moving very slowly in the direction of older marriage. In 1890, the typical couple was **26.1** (male) and **22** (female); in 1956, the couple was **22.5** and **20.1**, the youngest average couple in modern times. In 1979, the typical couple at marriage was **24.4** and **22.1**.

In the U.S.A. (1976), the median age at first marriage is **22.9** male, and **21** female. The median age at divorce after first marriage is **30.3** and **28.2**. And the median age for remarriage is **35.1** and **31.7**. Here are the percentages of people who are married per age group (U.S.A., 1977):

age	male	female
18–19	5.9%	19.8%
20–24	34.6	51.3
25–29	68.5	75.8
30–34	82.0	82.8
35–44	86.2	83.1

In the U.S.A. (1978), there are about 2.2 million marriages each year, and 1.1 million divorces. In California (1977), marriage and divorce were almost equal. In several states, there were more divorces than marriages—Illinois, Kentucky, Maryland, Nebraska, and Washington.

In England and Wales, the mean age for women at first marriage is **22.7** in 1971–75; and it was **24.6** in 1941–45.

In 1851 (England and Wales), the legal minimum age for marriage was **14** male, and **12** female. But the mean age at first marriage was in fact **25.8** male, and **24.6** female. In 1861, only 33 percent of women **20–24** were married; the corresponding figure in 1971 had risen to 60 percent. In Elizabethan and Jacobean times, the marriage age was typically **24** female, and just under **28** male; in view of the short life expectancy, these are quite old ages (from research by Peter Laslett).

Eligibility: for the minimum age for marriage, Austria and West Germany set **21** (male) and **16** (female). In Poland, the minimum is **21** (male) and **18** (female).

According to Gail Sheehy, the author of *Passages,* losing interest in sex begins at a surprisingly early age. In a survey, she asked males at what age they began to lose interest in sex; she says, "I looked in astonishment at the ages—**23**, **21**. Ages like that."

PRESS

William Randolph Hearst fails to complete his junior year at Harvard (1886) and goes to work as a reporter at the New York *World,* owned by Joseph Pulitzer (**39**). When Hearst is **23**, he is given his own newspaper by his father (**67**). The paper is the San Francisco *Examiner.* Hearst loses $300,000 in the first year, but signs up Ambrose Bierce (**45**) as a columnist. Circulation begins to increase rapidly. At **32**, Hearst buys the New York *Journal.* Hearst comes from a very rich family, and since **0** all his whims have been satisfied by his mother and father. At **23**, he begins building an organization which will respond to his every desire, however grand or trivial. (cf. **35***)

(Lord) Northcliffe: first issue of his weekly magazine *Answers to Correspondents* (London, 1888). This is a journal which combines entertainment with general knowledge; the idea is borrowed from his previous employer, George Newnes (**37**). The magazine is part one in Northcliffe's "Schemo Magnifico"—his plan to create a publishing empire. By **24**, he has two other magazines—*Comic Cuts* and *Chips*—and *Answers* has a circulation of 200,000. At **25**, he buys a manor house. At **30**, he starts the *Daily Mail,* Britain's first good cheap newspaper. In his childhood, Northcliffe had suffered from genteel poverty—his father (now **50**) a barrister, had been unable to obtain work, and dies at **52**, suffering from drink. At **22**, Northcliffe leaves a humiliating existence behind for a life of indulgence. His leadership in the only mass media of the time gives him the sensation of immense power; he appears to be directing the political and cultural life of the country. (cf. **30***)

Norman Rockwell does his first cover for the *Saturday Evening Post* (1916). He goes on to do 317 more covers, soon becoming nationally famous. His "Four Freedoms" covers are done at **47**. (cf. **82***)

LAW, CRIME

Thirty percent of rapists arrested are **18–22**; 56 percent are **24** or younger. (U.S.A., FBI).

The danger age for rape victims is **20–24**; the next most dangerous age is **16–19**. After **24**, the chances of being a rape victim diminish with age.

In a survey of a typical midwestern medium-security prison, the inmates had an average age of **22.6.** Over half had sentences of 8–10 years.

The victims associated with the "Yorkshire Ripper" (England 1975–80) are eleven women at **16–28**, one at **32**, and one each at **41** and **42**. The murderer is Peter Sutcliffe **(29–34)**.

SPORTS

Don Bradman (1930) scores 974 runs in the cricket test matches between Australia and England.

Len Hutton (cricket, 1938) scores 364 runs in one Test match, for England, against Australia.

Jack Nicklaus becomes U.S. Open golf champion (1962), beating Arnold Palmer **(33)**. Also at **22**, Jerry Pate wins the U.S. Open in 1976.

Muhammad Ali (1964) defeats Sonny Liston **(35)**, and so becomes the world heavyweight boxing champion. He explains his technique: "Float like a butterfly, sting like a bee." At **23**, he smashes Floyd Patterson **(30)**. Formerly Cassius Clay, he now converts to the Black Muslim faith, and takes up his new name. At **25**, he refuses induction into the military, saying that "I ain't got no quarrel with them Viet Cong." It is not until **29** that the Supreme Court overrules his draft conviction. Ali is now one of the best-known people in the whole world. He retires at **37**, having won back his title for the third time at **36***.

Mark Spitz (1972) gains seven gold medals in the Olympic games—a record. Each gold is earned in a record time. He is later encouraged to exploit his worldwide fame, but turns out to be too shy for the commercial life. His agent charges $12,500 for each appearance by Spitz—but the swimmer prefers to spend his time on his yacht.

23

HISTORY—WORLD

Ho Chi Minh, in 1911, is working in the kitchen of the Carlton Hotel, London, under the direction of the leading French chef, Escoffier (**67**). He had left his homeland, Vietnam, at **21**, and has been working for two years as a sailor. At **27**, he moves to Paris where he starts his political writing. At **29**, he tries unsuccessfully to have the problem of his country's independence discussed at the Versailles Peace Conference. He spends his **30**s and **40**s in the planning of the decolonization of Vietnam. He returns home at **51**, during World War II. At **55**, the northern half of the country obtains independence. At **64**, the French are defeated at Dien Bien Phu, and start decolonization of the south. But at **71** U.S. military influence begins to grow rapidly. At **79**, the first U.S. withdrawals take place, but Ho dies at **79** with his dream of a united and independent country unfulfilled.

Chou En-lai, in 1921, is living as a student in Paris, and supporting himself by occasional low-paid work. Here Chou helps establish the European branch of the Chinese Communist party, meeting in a room of an obscure hotel. Chou returns to China at **26**. By **29**, he is head of the military side of the party. He takes part in the Long March at **36**. By **37**, he has become number two to Mao's (**41**) number one. At **51**, at the end of the civil war, this partnership becomes the leadership of China.

HISTORY—U.S.A.

Theodore Roosevelt: State Assemblyman in New York (1881). He becomes Assistant Secretary of the Navy at **38**; Governor of New York, at **40**; Vice-President, and then President at **42**. (cf. **39***)

RELIGION, PHILOSOPHY

Descartes has a dream of revelation (1619, Nov. 19). He recites two Hamlet-style Latin poems by Ausonius, about Pythagoras and the best road to pursue in life. He is convinced that the Spirit of Truth is speaking to him. This moment is the beginning of his great insights, and he resolves to go on a long pilgrimage, on foot, as a thanks-offering to the Blessed Virgin. At this time, he is a traveler, and in the military. Fairly rich through inheritance, he spends the rest of his life working out his ideas. The famous sentence "I think therefore I am" appears at **41***.

SOCIAL SCIENCE, EDUCATION

B. F. Skinner leaves college (1927) and sets aside a year in which to become a writer. He is encouraged in this by a letter from Robert Frost (**53**). But the year is a failure. After reading *Behaviorism* by J. B. Watson (**47**), he signs up for graduate school in psychology.

MONEY, WORK

George Westinghouse invents the air brake (1869) for use on trains; sets up his own company, which successfully exploits this huge improvement. But his second major step, the Westinghouse Electric Company (at **40**) is not such a great success.

Armand Hammer graduates from medical school (1921); sells the family drug firm (which he has been running part-time) for a profit of $1 million; goes to Moscow, and negotiates U.S.-U.S.S.R. trade deal with Lenin (**51**). (cf. **58***)

SCIENCE

Isaac Newton, in 1666: he watches an apple fall, and this starts him speculating on gravity and its effect on the motion of the planets. He is living at home, away from any university colleagues, and he is working by himself. He now completes work on gravity; on the nature of light; and on calculus. He later says, "I was in the prime of my age for invention and minded mathematics and philosophy more than at any time since." At **26**, he is appointed Professor of Mathematics at Cambridge, following the departure of Isaac Barrow (**38**). At university, he pursues his three main interests, as well as work in chemistry/alchemy. Newton works incredibly hard, and has to train himself to take time off for sleeping. His important book results from these insights at **23** onward, and it is published at **44***.

Ernest Solvay: the Solvay process for the production of sodium bicarbonate (1861).

Paul Héroult and Charles Hall (both **23**): invention of the electrolytic process to make aluminum (1886).

ARCHITECTURE

James Wyatt wins competition for the Pantheon, Oxford Street, London (1770), and this leads to endless commissions.

King Ludwig II of Bavaria: start of the castle at Neuschwanstein (1868). He had become King at **18**, on the death of his father (**53**). He starts Herrenchiemsee at **23**, and completes Linderhof at **34**. This castle begun at **23** is the one which is later featured in a million travel posters. Ludwig drowns at **40**, shortly after being removed from power. He is **27** when he first arranges to have an opera performed with himself as sole member of the audience.

MUSIC—CLASSICAL

Gioacchino Rossini: *The Barber of Seville* (1816, Feb. 20). This is his sixteenth opera. He has been a paid musician since early teens, as his parents are both poor musicians, and the family needs his earnings. Rossini writes *La Cenerentola* at **24**, and *La Gazza Ladra* at **25**. He retires at **37*** after writing 38 operas, and he lives in luxury for the rest of his life, till **76**.

Peter Ilyich Tchaikovsky resigns from the Civil Service (1863, May 13) to learn composition full-time at the St. Petersburg Conservatory. Previously he has been at the Ministry of Justice, having received almost all his education at the St. Petersburg School of Jurisprudence. He explains his fears about his career switching: "Now I am firmly convinced that, sooner or later, I shall exchange my work for music. Don't think that I imagine I'll become a great artist. It's simply that I want to do that to which my calling draws me. Whether I shall be a famous composer or an impoverished teacher, my conscience will be easy—and I shall have no painful right to grumble at fate or people." He writes the first version of the *Romeo and Juliet* Overture at **29**; and it is not until **33** that he has a popular success, with his opera *The Oprichnik.* He composes only during the summer months—the rest of the year is spent as an "impoverished teacher." (cf. **37***)

LITERATURE

James Boswell meets Dr. Johnson **(54)** for the first time (1763). Boswell now travels by himself for several years, and the period of their recorded friendship is when Boswell is **32** to **44**. His *Life of Johnson* appears when he is **51**, and he dies at **55**.

John Keats writes "Endymion" (1818). (cf. **26***)

Tolstoy in 1851: having some leisure while waiting to enter the army, and while he recovers from the side-effects of a VD cure, he starts his first book, *Childhood.* It is immediately taken seriously by the reading public. But Dostoevsky prophecies that Tolstoy will not write much of anything else. (cf. **27***)

Stephen Crane: *The Red Badge of Courage* (1895). Crane dies at **28**, from the effects of tuberculosis, debt, and overwork.

PLAYS

Christopher Marlowe: *Tamburlaine the Great* (1587); and at **24**, *The Tragicall History of Dr. Faustus.* At **29**, a warrant is issued for his arrest, because of his revolutionary views; but, before he can be found, he takes part in a fight in a tavern, and is killed.

R. B. Sheridan: *The Rivals* (1775), with the creation of Mrs. Malaprop. At **25**, he writes *The School for Scandal.* After this, he moves into theater direction and into politics. He lives until **64**.

FILMS

Mary Pickford signs a two-year contract (1916); it guarantees her $1,000,000.

Rudolph Valentino: *Alimony* (1918); he is an extra and a dancer.

Clark Gable marries his acting coach Josephine Dillon (**37**) (1924, Dec. 31). He gets a three-day job as a film extra.

Frank James Cooper is a door-to-door salesman in Los Angeles, selling to mothers to have their babies photographed (1924); he becomes an extra in silent Westerns; changes his name to Gary Cooper, after his agent's home town.

Cary Grant is a musical comedy star on Broadway (1927).

Katharine Hepburn: *A Bill of Divorcement* (1932); this is her successful debut. She gets her first Oscar at **24**, in *Morning Glory.*

Marlon Brando, on stage: *A Streetcar Named Desire* (1947); and stars in the film at **27**.

Marilyn Monroe poses for some calendar photos, with "nothing on but the radio" (1949); receives $50 for a day's work.

Natalie Wood and Warren Beatty (**24**): *Splendor in the Grass* (1961).

Julie Christie: *Billy Liar* (1963).

Catherine Deneuve: *Belle de Jour* (1966).

Mia Farrow gives birth to *Rosemary's Baby* (1968).

Rainer Werner Fassbinder makes *Why Does Herr R. Run Amok?* (1969); this establishes him as a director.

MUSIC—NON-CLASSICAL

Eric Burdon and the Animals: "The House of the Rising Sun" (1964).

The Byrds: "Mr. Tambourine Man" (1965).

The Beach Boys: "Good Vibrations" (1966).

Bobbie Gentry: "Ode to Billie Joe" (1967).

Elton John: "Your Song" (1970).

TV, ETC.

Orson Welles: radio play announcing that Martians have landed in New Jersey (1938). So realistic are the mobilization scenes that the nation is thrown into panic. (cf. films, **25***)

LOVE, LIFE

Marie Duplessis coughs herself to death, watched by her lover, Alexander Dumas fils. Later, at **44** (1848), Dumas writes her story as *The Lady of the Camellias.* Verdi at **39** presents the story in *La Traviata*

(1853), and Greta Garbo stars as Camille in a film version at **31*** (1936).

Isabella Beeton publishes the first monthly installment of her *Book of Household Management* (1859) which she completes at **25**. This book ("Mrs. Beeton's") has over 500,000 words and besides cooking recipes it provides instruction for the eighteen grades of servant in her ideal household. She also discusses etiquette, economy, and recipes for "Useful soups for benevolent purposes," that is, for giving to the poor. Her motto is "A place for everything, and everything in its place." At the center of it all there should be the mistress of the house, "The Alpha and Omega in the government of her establishment." The book is an instant best-seller. Mrs. Beeton has learned household management as the eldest in a family of 21 children and step-children; but in her fourth confinement, she dies, at **28**.

Mrs. Lillie Langtry: debut in London (1876) in which she quickly becomes a dazzling success. At **26**, she is the mistress of the Prince of Wales (**37**). At **28**, she gives birth to a daughter whose father is Prince Louis of Battenberg (**27**). Two years later, Prince Louis marries a niece (**21**) of the Prince of Wales. Afterward, the Prince of Wales becomes King of England (Edward VII), **59–68**; Prince Louis's wife lives until **87**, and their son becomes Earl Mountbatten of Burma (d. **79**, 1979); and Mrs. Langtry's granddaughter becomes a well-known TV announcer.

PRESS

Marchamont Nedham: "Mercurius Britanicus" (U.K., 1643)—an early and famous anti-establishment newspaper.

Benjamin H. Day: start of the *Sun* (1833). This is the first successful mass-market newspaper in the U.S.A. Its price is one cent against other papers' six cents. At **28**, Day sells out, and lives in comfortable circumstances for the rest of his life, dying at **79**.

John Delane becomes editor of the *Times* (London, 1841). He is appointed by the proprietor, John Walter (**65**), on the death of the previous editor, Thomas Barnes (**56**), who had himself been appointed at **32**. Delane is now editor through the peak years of the newspaper's power. At **28**, he makes his name by editorializing against the excesses of the railway boom, even though railway companies provide the paper with extensive advertising. At **37**, Delane attacks the mismanagement of the Crimean War. He is never married; instead, he sees his mother, or writes to her, on every day of his life, until she dies when he is **52**. Delane is editor until **60**, and lives until **62**.

LAW, CRIME

Parents who batter their child and do serious injury have a median age of **22** (female) and **25** (male). Parents who inflict mild battering are about two years older.

The Marquess of Queensberry (1867): the Queensberry Rules for boxing.

Bobby Hull (hockey, 1961–62): 50 goals in one season; and 54 at **27**; and 52 at **28**. He retires at **39**.

Wilfred Benitez now holds the light-welterweight, the welterweight and the light-middleweight world boxing championships (1981).

24

HEALTH

The mean age for women at their first live birth is **24.2** (England and Wales, 1971–75).

HISTORY—WORLD

Napoleon helps win a decisive battle at Toulon (1793) for the forces of the French Revolution. At **26**, he helps quell a counterrevolutionary riot in Paris. He is recognized as a military genius who is on the side of the revolution. With the old commanders deposed or guillotined, Napoleon becomes commander-in-chief in Italy, and begins a wave of conquests throughout Europe; these he consolidates by establishing new and modernizing regimes. By **30***, he returns to Paris.

Namik Kemal and others: the "Young Ottomans" (1865), which becomes the Young Turks. They constitute a vigorous reform movement within the decrepit Ottoman or Turkish Empire. At this time, there was a fashion for "Young" movements—Young England, Young Czechs, Young Germany, Young Ireland, and both Young Maoris and a Young New Zealand party.

This was the average age for passing the first-level exam in the old Chinese civil service—the archetypal bureaucracy of the scholar-official or mandarin. Exams were in three grades, signified by the place in which you took them: (1) in your district (at average **24**); (2) at the provincial capital (at average **31**); and (3) in Peking. You could enter at any age, and if failing, you could repeat the exam as often as you wished. On passing the district exam, you would now be known as "beautiful talent." The mandarin system began around 200 B.C. Retirement was not strictly enforced, and there was no age rule on retirement until 1757, when the basic system had been running for almost 2,000 years. There was no time limit on the years spent in top appointments—it averaged eight years, but could be longer or shorter than this. The elite exam in Peking consisted of essays written during three days of solitary confinement. Should you die during this time, your body would have to be lifted out through a hole in your cell's roof, as the gates to the examination compound were sealed shut. Exams were held every three years, between 1067 and 1900. Mandarins formed a hierarchy which was devoted to the emperor, and independent of the military, the hereditary landowners, and the merchants. Mandarins wore special buttons, showing their grade, and faced south when acting in authority. Following Confucius, your achievements as a mandarin would be reviewed every three years, and you would be promoted or demoted.

HISTORY—U.K.

Prince Charles Edward, Bonnie Prince Charlie, leaves Rome, his birthplace, and travels to the Hebrides, off Scotland (1745, Aug. 2), where he begins his rebellion against England. But after losing the Battle of Culloden, he is forced to leave Scotland at **25**, and spends the rest of his life as a wanderer, political refugee, and a drunk. He dies in Rome at **67**.

MONEY, WORK

Henry Ford marries Clara Jane **(20)** (1888, Apr. 11). He calls her "The Believer," because she always believes that he will do well in the end.

Jean Paul Getty: first million dollars (1915); retires. He had been oil prospecting since **22**, with his millionaire father as banker.

Ralph Nader graduates from Harvard Law School (1958), having concentrated on the need for legal redress in auto accidents; later gets a job in Washington investigating this issue. (cf. **31***)

SCIENCE, TECHNOLOGY

Lord Kelvin: the concept of absolute zero, −273° centigrade (1848).

RENAISSANCE

Johann Wolfgang von Goethe: *The Sorrows of Werther* (1774). This novel is written out in four weeks; it is the story of a man **(25)** who kills himself after failing in love. The book has a devastating impact throughout Europe, and Goethe is instantly famous. At **23**, he had published *Gotz,* a leading work in the new *Sturm und Drang* (Storm and Stress) movement in Germany. At **26**, he becomes a government official in Weimar, at the invitation of its Duke **(18)**. Goethe is there occupied both with poetry and theater direction, and also with entirely practical matters such as roads, finance, and mining. Supervision of mines leads him to his scientific work which is on geology and plants;

he attempts the outline of a complete synthesis of nature. Although he fails in this, he does interesting work on color, morphology, and gestalt. Goethe takes a trip to Italy, **37–39**, and it is later suggested by a psychoanalyst that he loses his virginity at **38** with a Roman woman, Faustina (**23**). On his return to Weimar at **39**, he meets Christiane Vulpius (also **23**) and they live together. Their first child is born when he is **40**, and they marry when Goethe is **57**. At **45**, Goethe begins his famous and productive friendship with the poet Schiller (**35**); this lasts until the latter's death at **46**. In his **mid-20**s Goethe writes his work on *Faust,* a project that occupies him intermittently for the whole of his life (cf. **100***).

ARCHITECTURE

Le Corbusier goes on a long sketching tour (1911), covering eastern Europe, parts of Asia, Rome, and the Acropolis. He had left school at **13** and ended any formal training in art at **16**. At **27**, he designs "Maison Domino," his first project for mass-produced housing. At **33**, he writes the book *Vers Une Architecture;* this later becomes a bible as it contains statements such as "A house is a machine for living in." At **38**, he designs a house for an exhibition, "Pavillon de L'Esprit Nouveau," and this is one of his first projects to be actually constructed. At **39**, he sends in designs to the competition for the League of Nations headquarters; his work is rejected but it is so controversial that he then becomes a notorious figure, inside and outside the architectural profession. His attractive Villa Savoie is at **41**, and his Swiss Dormitory, Paris, is at **43**. Throughout his **40**s and **50**s he continues to make gigantic plans for new cities, but these typically gain only publicity. Very little is constructed as he is seen as an impossible visionary. The breakthrough in his career can be said to occur at **57***.

ART

Jasper Johns destroys all his existing work (1954). He has his first one-man show at **28**, when he exhibits his "Target" and "American Flag."

MUSIC—CLASSICAL

Alexander Borodin receives his Ph.D. in chemistry (1858, May 15), and becomes Professor of Chemistry at **29**. He continues in this occupation all his working life, and his music has to be fitted in as best he can. As a result, his later reputation is based on a comparatively small number of compositions.

Constant Lambert: *The Rio Grande* (Dec. 1929)

LITERATURE

Beatrice: death (Florence, 1290). When she was **8**, the future poet Dante (**9**) had fallen in love with her. Soon after her death, Dante writes *Vita Nuova,* a collection of poems and prose writings in her honor. And at **43*** he begins his great *Divine Comedy* in which Beatrice is a principal figure—the Light of Grace, "donna beata e bella," and "questa gloriosa Beatrice," the woman who leads the poet to Paradise.

John Milton graduates from university (1632). Instead of getting a job, he chooses further study, and travel, with the formal ambition of making a great contribution to national life—as he writes at **29*** "Fame Is the Spur." He is willingly supported by his father (**70**). Milton is a poet and traveler until about **30**; he then becomes a political writer, and later a senior civil servant in the revolutionary government of Oliver Cromwell. He returns to poetry in his mid-fifties, completing *Paradise Lost* around **56***.

Lord Byron publishes the first two Cantos of "Childe Harold" (Mar. 1812). It is a public success; he "wakes up one morning, and finds himself famous."

Charles Dickens publishes *Pickwick Papers* (1836) and it is an almost instant national success. He marries, and starts work immediately on *Oliver Twist,* another instant success. Previously he had been a journalist, and worked on the reporting of Parliament and of the Law Courts. From **24** on, he continues at the top of his profession. (cf. **46***)

Jack London: *The Son of the Wolf* (1900)—his first book and an immediate success. By the time of his death at **40** he has written fifty books. *The Call of the Wild* is at **27**.

Rupert Brooke: *The Old Vicarage, Grantchester* (1911). (cf. **27***)

F. Scott Fitzgerald: *This Side of Paradise* (1920), and *The Beautiful and the Damned* at **26**. (cf. **29***)

FILMS

Greta Garbo: *Anna Christie* (1930)—her first talkie (advertised as "Garbo speaks!!")

Joan Crawford: *Grand Hotel* (1932).

Marilyn Monroe: small parts in *The Asphalt Jungle,* and *All About Eve* (1950).

James Dean: *East of Eden* and *Rebel Without a Cause* (1955). Two weeks before the release of the latter, Dean dies in a road accident (1955, Sept. 30). A few weeks previously, he had starred in a road safety commercial.

John Travolta: *Saturday Night Fever* (1978).

In the U.K. in 1978, 55 percent of filmgoers are in the age group **16–24**—even though only 18 percent of the population are in this age group.

MUSIC—NON-CLASSICAL

The Association: "Never My Love" (1967)—one of the greatest records ever made.

Simon and Garfunkel: "Parsley, Sage, Rosemary, and Thyme," and "Sounds of Silence" (1967). Also "Bookends" and "Mrs. Robinson" at **25**, and "Bridge over Troubled Water" at **27**.

Barbra Streisand; concert attended by 135,000 people (New York, 1968).

LOVE, LIFE

William Beckford is alleged to have a homosexual relationship with William "Kitty" Courtenay (**11**, in 1787); because of this, Beckford spends the rest of his life (d. **84**) as a social outcast from English society, though his fortune enables him to live in dramatic and extravagant surroundings. Beckford had been brought up with extreme wealth, and had received nothing but the best—at **5**, he was given piano lessons by W. A. Mozart (**8**). Beckford has a major achievement with his Gothic novel *Vathek* which at **22** he writes nonstop in 60 hours.

Thomas Crapper sets up his own plumbing business (London, 1861). This is shortly after the opening of the city's first main sewers; and at **35** the Metropolitan Water Act guarantees an adequate supply of piped water. Crapper is "in" at the beginning of a W. C. (water closet) and faucet boom; he perfects a toilet cistern which discharges a large amount of water at high speed. One of his designs flushes automatically when you arise from the seat. Crapper lives until **73**, and is deeply proud of his business; but it is not until World War I, when he would have been **80**, that he is immortalized by U.S. servicemen who find that his name is on every toilet in Europe.

Calamity Jane is the only woman at Fort Laramie (1876), together with 1,500 men who are assembling to kill off the Sioux tribe.

Roger Vadim: marriage to Brigitte Bardot (**17**, in 1952). At **30**, he marries the actress Annette Stroyberg; at **36**, he has a relationship with Catherine Deneuve (**20**); at **39**, he marries Jane Fonda (**29**); and at **47** he marries Catherine Scheider.

Eligibility: this is the last year in which you can enter the "Miss World" competition. You must be female, single, and **17–24**.

PRESS

Edward Scripps: the Cleveland *Penny Press* (1878)—the first of his many newspapers.

Henry Luce and Briton Hadden (also **24**): start *Time* magazine (1923). Their first employee is Roy Larsen (**23**)—who retires 56 years later. Luce's genius is to organize the week's news into a fixed arrangement of "departments." Luce (**24**) is also the patron saint of those who wish to put an age after every name. Later, Hadden dies at **31**. Circulation of *Time* reaches one million when Luce is **44**. He starts *Fortune* at **32**, *Life* at **38**, and *Sports Illustrated* at **56**.

About the *Time* cover: the youngest person to be featured is Jesus Christ at **0**; the oldest person is Amos Alonzo Stagg (**96**).

Richard Ingrams and others: *Private Eye* magazine (London, 1961); at this time, Gerald Scarfe is **25**; Paul Foot is **23**; Peter Cook, and William Rushton, also **23**. Ingrams (**14**), Foot (**13**), and Rushton (**13**) were at boarding school together, and collaborated on the school magazine.

EXPLORATION

Matthew Flinders: first person to sail around Tasmania, off Australia (1798–99).

Chuck Yeager: first person to fly beyond the speed of sound (California, 1947).

LAW, CRIME

Bonnie Parker (**23**) and Clyde Barrow (**25**) are shot to death in their car, as they return to their country hideout in Louisiana (1934). Their Ford V-8 contains 15 guns. The police are directed by Detective Frank Hamer (**50**) who has been brought out of retirement to organize their capture. Bonnie and Clyde's main career has lasted only two years, and consists of robbing grocery stores, filling stations, and small-town banks—and 12 murders. They become famous by sending their photographs and poems about themselves to the police. Frank Hamer is famous for the rest of his life, until his death at **71**.

Lee Harvey Oswald shoots President John F. Kennedy (**46**) (1963, Nov. 22), and is himself shot soon after by Jack Ruby (**51**). The latter is a Dallas nightclub owner, who claims he wishes to save the Kennedy family any further suffering.

The last-ever criminals to be hanged in England are **24** and **21** (1964, Aug. 13). They had killed someone of **53**.

Myra Hindley and Ian Brady (**28**) are the "Moors Murderers" (England, 1964). They murder three people (**10**, **12**, and **17**) and bury two of the bodies in bleak moorland. Before one murder, they tape-record the victim (**12**) begging to be allowed to go home.

Richard Speck shoots eight nurses in Chicago (1966, July 14). The victims are **20**, **20**, **20**, **21**, **22**, **22**, **23**, and **24**. Speck has had ten arrests in his teens, and now faces imprisonment until at least **424**.

David Berkowitz kills six people, wounds seven more, and causes extensive damage by arson (New York, 1977). Owing to letters with which he publicizes himself, he is known as "Son of Sam." His victims are typically around **20**. Berkowitz has been working as a postal clerk; previously he has been in the Army, from **18** to **21**. He is sentenced to serve in prison until he is **340**, but he will be eligible for parole at **55**.

Steven Judy: execution, in the electric chair (Indiana, 1981). He had raped and killed a mother (also **24**) and killed her children, **5**, **4**, and **2**. He had committed his first rape at **13**, and since then spent two years in a mental hospital. Judy was abandoned by his own parents, and now at death seems content: "I've lived my life the only way I knew how, and I'm just kind of glad it's over with now."

Other recent executions include: murderer Jesse Bishop at **46** (Nevada, 1979); murderer Gary Gilmore at **36** (Utah, 1977); murderer John Spenkelink at **30** (Florida, 1979).

In the 1960s urban riots in the U.S., roughly 50 percent of the typical participants were aged **15–24**; 25 percent were **25–34**, and the rest were predominantly older. The **14**s and younger were not much present—or at least were not often arrested, which is the source of these figures.

73 percent of people arrested for major crimes are **24** or younger (U.S., FBI).

The most likely murder victim is a male **20–24**. The most likely murderer is a male **18–22**. From **24** onward, your chances of being a murder victim are less and less. Over half of murder victims are **15–34**. About one third are in their **20s** (U.S., 1977 [FBI]).

The majority (32 percent) of murderers who are sent to death row are **20–24**. The probability of a murderer receiving the death sentence diminishes from now on. About 14 percent on death row are **19** or under (U.S., 1978).

SPORTS

Rod Laver (1962) wins six national tennis championships in one season. At **31**, he wins the Grand Slam for the second time—a unique achievement.

The top tennis players (1978) are around **24**; viz., Connors (**26**), Borg (**22**), and Vilas (**26**); and Evert (**24**), Navratilova (**22**), and Cawley (**27**). In 1978, the last 16 men and women at Wimbledon include seven who are **30** or more, the oldest being Billie Jean King (**34**). In the same tournament, of the most successful 32 women in the singles, 14 were teenagers.

Trevor Francis (U.K., 1979): first soccer player to be traded for £1 million ($2 million).

Bjorn Borg (tennis, 1980): Wimbledon champion, for the fifth successive year. In the final, he stops the challenge of John McEnroe (**21**). But in the following year he succumbs to McEnroe's terrorist-style assault.

25

HEALTH

Motherhood: here are the most fertile age groups of women, listed in decreasing order of fertility (U.S.A., 1978):

age group	births per year per 1000 women
20–24	112
25–29	108
30–34	54
15–19	53
35–39	19
40–44	4
10–14	1

HISTORY—WORLD

Suleyman the Magnificent becomes head of the Ottoman Empire (1520), on the death of his father, Suleyman the Grim (**50**). He is now the ruler of Turkey, Greece, Palestine, and Egypt. He goes on to extend the empire. At **26**, he conquers Belgrade; at **31**, he defeats the King of Hungary, Louis II (**20**). At **34**, he conducts an unsuccessful siege of Vienna. At **39**, he conquers Iraq, as part of a general eastward expansion. At **56**, he conquers Tripoli. At **59**, he puts a stop to the rebellion of his eldest son—he personally supervises the son's execution by three mutes. Suleyman the Magnificent dies at **71**, at a time when he is in charge of an army of 200,000, during another campaign in Hungary.

In Imperial Rome, this was the age at which you could enter the Senate, if you had inherited a position.

HISTORY—U.S.A.

George Washington, in 1757, is in charge of Virginia's military forces. He retires at **26**, with the rank of brigadier. At **27**, he marries Martha Dandridge Custis (also **27**), and he takes a seat in the Virginia House of Burgesses. At **27**, he begins fifteen years in which he is a country gentleman attending to the needs of his large estate at Mt. Vernon. (cf. **35*** for this and some of the following stories.)

Betsy Ross: adoption of the Stars and Stripes as flag of the United States (1777, June 14).

Abraham Lincoln, in 1834: election to the Illinois state legislature. At **27**, he becomes an attorney, and is busy and prominent in his profession. At **33**, he marries Mary Todd **(23)** and they have their first child in the following year.

Lyndon Johnson, in 1923: he continues as secretary to a rich local congressman, Richard Kleberg **(45)**. At **26**, he joins a New Deal job-creation scheme, as state director of the National Youth Administration. At **29**, he is elected to Congress.

Ronald Reagan, in 1936: he is a sports announcer in Des Moines. At **26**, this job takes him to Los Angeles, where a talent scout offers him a job in films because of his attractive voice. He works for Warner Brothers at $200 per week. His first part is in the film *Love Is on the Air* in which he plays a radio announcer. This is the start of a busy film career in which he features in fifty films, typically being a nice guy who never manages to get the dream girl. At **29**, he stars in *Knute Rockne—All American;* at **31,** in *King's Row.* At **31**, during World War II, he receives a commission in the military, and makes training films. At **34**, he leaves the military with the rank of captain. Reagan's first marriage is at **29**, to Jane Wyman **(26)**.

Richard Nixon, in 1938: he is now in law practice. During World War II, he is in the Navy, and leaves at **33** with the rank of lieutenant commander. He is elected to Congress at **33**.

John F. Kennedy enters the Navy (1942). At **26**, his PT boat is sunk by the Japanese, and he survives for five days on a Pacific island before he is rescued. At **27**, his elder brother Joe **(29)** is killed in the war. At **28**, his father **(57)** extends his property empire by purchasing the largest building in the world, the Merchandise Mart, Chicago. At **29**, John F. Kennedy is elected to Congress.

Jimmy Carter, in 1949, is in the nuclear submarine service of the Navy. At his job interview, he confesses to Admiral Hyman Rickover **(49)** that, although doing well, he has not always done his best; Rickover bleakly terminates the interview by asking "Why not?" For Carter, this question creates an ambition that is overwhelming and ultimately unattainable. At **28**, his father **(58)** dies, and Carter resigns from the submarine service, to carry on with the family peanut farm in Georgia. At **31**, he becomes chairman of the Sumter County School Board.

Elizabeth I becomes Queen (1558, Nov. 17—cf. **54***)—as does Queen Elizabeth II, also at **25** (1952). But the public career of Mary Queen of Scots effectively ends at **25**. (cf. **15***)

The Duke of Cumberland defeats Bonnie Prince Charlie, the "Young Pretender" (also **25**) at the Battle of Culloden (1746, Apr. 16), and goes on to viciously attack the Scottish clan system. He dies at **44**, having developed the Ascot races.

William Wilberforce travels on the continent (1784–85), and has an experience of religious conversion. Previously he has been self-indulgent and a gambler. He had inherited a fortune, and used it to obtain election to Parliament at **21**. He takes his first public steps against slavery, and succeeds in the abolition of the slave trade when he is **48**.

Eligibility: in the Army, this is the last year for joining. Certain exceptions are made until **33**, but rarely.

RELIGION, PHILOSOPHY

George Berkeley: *Treatise Concerning the Principles of Human Knowledge, Wherein the Chief Causes of Error and Difficulty in the Sciences, with the Grounds of Scepticism, Atheism, and Irreligion, are inquired into* (1710). This is his major work, and is permanently admired as a complete philosophical system. He does not develop his ideas any further; for the rest of his life, he is successful as a missionary and a bishop. He dies suddenly at **67**.

Joseph Smith: *Book of Mormon* (1830)—the foundation of the Church of Jesus Christ of Latter-Day Saints. Smith suffers death at the hands of a mob, at **38**.

A. J. Ayer: *Language, Truth, and Logic* (1936).

SOCIAL SCIENCE, EDUCATION

Friedrich Engels: *The Condition of the Working Class in England* (1845). His first publication on the fate of the working class had been at **19**. When he is **24**, he first meets Karl Marx (**26**). (cf. **29***)

Booker T. Washington: head of new school at Tuskegee, Alabama (1881). He retains this position until **59**; it is his base, from which he puts forward his ideas on minority education.

Carl Jung graduates from medical school (1900) and suddenly decides on psychiatric training. He later advises against using your will in career choice—don't force yourself into a mold, but in effect take the simplest path. (cf. **45***)

Werner Erhard is "turned off" from his old lifestyle (c. 1959); he changes his name, and becomes sales manager for a door-to-door encyclopedia company. By **36**, he has left, and started his own religion—"est."

Charlie Schwab: superintendent of the Homestead steel works (1887), under Andrew Carnegie (**51**). At **19**, Schwab had been Chief Engineer at Homestead. At **30**, he is a force for reconciliation after the destructive Homestead strike. (cf. **39***)

Aristotle Onassis buys six freighters (1931). This is his first move into shipping; he has had his own export-import business in Argentina; millionaire at **23**. (cf. **40***)

SCIENCE, TECHNOLOGY

Werner Heisenberg: uncertainty principle (1927).

ARCHITECTURE

Abraham Darby III and T. F. Pritchard (**52**): the Iron Bridge at Coalbrookdale, England (1775–81). This is the first cast iron bridge in the world, and a symbol of the Industrial Revolution. Darby took over the family business at **18**, and is a whiz-kid third generation ironmaster. Pritchard is a professional architect who has here reached the peak of his life after a process of steady innovation.

Joseph Paxton is appointed Head Gardener at Chatsworth House (1826). (cf. **49***) AGE 25 YRS

A. W. N. Pugin: Scarisbrick Hall (1837).

ART

Lorenzo Ghiberti wins competition (1403) to make the north door of the Baptistry, in Florence. This is completed at **46**, and he makes the east door from **47** to **74**. He does a small number of other works, but mainly spends his entire life in making two doors—but the most famous doors in art history.

Raphael, in 1508: having made his name in Urbino and Florence, he travels to Rome and is introduced into the papal court. Almost immediately, he begins frescoes for the Pope, decorating the first of seven large rooms at the Vatican. Raphael's first attempt is so good that his client removes existing frescoes by people such as Piero della Francesca. This project continues until his death at **37**. His designs (cartoons) for seven tapestries in the Sistine Chapel are done at **31**.

Giovanni Piranesi: first "Carceri" etchings (1745)—14 etchings of vast imaginary prisons, full of threatening punitive equipment. This is his brilliant debut, which he is later unable to surpass. He almost never achieves his ambition to be an architect, and supports himself by his distinguished pictures of Rome. He lives until **58**.

Aubrey Beardsley dies of tuberculosis (1898). He had got a break at **18** by showing his portfolio to Edward Burne-Jones (**57**), who advised him to give up his job in an insurance office. By **21**, Beardsley has created a scandal, with his drawings of "Salome."

Marcel Duchamp: "Nude Descending a Staircase" (1912); and at **30**, "Urinal, by R. Mutt," a urinal which is rejected for exhibition as an art work.

MUSIC—CLASSICAL

George Frederick Handel arrives in London (1710), his new home for the rest of his life. Previously he has been traveling as a musician in Italy, after leaving his home in Germany at **18**. He now settles into a career as prolific composer of operas, and he is also enthusiastic for the business aspects of arranging such things as subscription concerts. Besides these numerous works (later forgotten), he writes the *Water Music* at **33**. His oratorios begin in his **50**s, and the *Messiah* is written at **56***.

Mozart rows with his patron (1781, May 9), and is literally kicked out by the latter's chamberlain (**38**). Mozart writes *Die Entführung aus dem Serail* at **26**, and is also married—to Constanze Weber (**19**). They live in Vienna, and get their money from his subscription concerts, and lessons; Mozart composes in the morning, and gives lessons in the afternoon. (cf. **30***)

Beethoven writes on his birthday (1795): "Courage! My spirit shall rule, even though my body be weak. Twenty-five years have gone. This year must decide what the man shall be. Nothing must be left undecided." He writes his first symphony at **29**, and the *Moonlight Sonata* at **30**. His career can be said to become secure in his early **30**s. (cf. **32***)

Edvard Grieg: Piano Concerto in A Minor (1868), and *Peer Gynt* Suite at **32**. Grieg lives till **64**.

Leonard Bernstein at 1943: as assistant conductor of the New York Philharmonic Symphony Orchestra, he has to step in for Bruno Walter (**67**) who is indisposed. Bernstein is famous overnight.

LITERATURE

John Donne writes his *Elegies* while a law student at Lincoln's Inn, London, and while on military expeditions against the Spanish (c. 1597). Ben Jonson writes that Donne "[had] written all his best pieces ere he was **25** years old." But the love poetry for which he is later famous is written around **28** to **33**, and not published during his lifetime—as he thought it would detract from his career prospects, in the government, and later in the Church at **50***.

S. T. Coleridge writes "Kubla Khan" in a dream (1797).

Richard Henry Dana: *Two Years Before the Mast* (1840)—from his journal as a seaman, having taken time out from his Harvard degree. He spends the rest of his life as a lawyer.

Thomas Hardy has been working as an architectural assistant since **16**, and has published only one small article, on building. On his **25**th birthday (1865), he writes: "Feel as if I had lived a long time and done very little." He now starts to try his hand at part-time writing, and publishes his first novel at **30**. His publishers force him to make up the losses on this, but his *Under the Greenwood Tree* (**31**) makes a profit, and he becomes a professional writer. He writes *Far From the Madding Crowd* at **33**. (cf. **53***)

Franz Kafka graduates as a lawyer (1908), but gets a job dealing with workmen's accident compensation. This turns out to be, in effect, a bureaucracy which prevents people from obtaining their just desserts. In order to support himself while writing, he has avoided getting a semiwriting job as "writing is a form of prayer," so it must not be diluted. He falls in love with a barmaid, but complains that "whole regiments of cavalry have ridden over her." (cf. **40***)

Dorothy Parker and Robert Benchley (**29**) start lunching at the Algonquin Hotel (1918)—later, the management provides them with a round table. (cf. **29***)

Success turns to ashes—Joe Lampton is forced to marry the boring heiress whom he had once craved, in *Room at the Top*, 1957, by John Braine (**35**).

Colin Wilson: *The Outsider* (1956). The success of this enables him to become a full-time writer, having previously worked in a plastics factory.

PLAYS

Ben Jonson: *Every Man in His Humour* (1598). The actors in the premiere include William Shakespeare (**34**). The play is such a hit that Jonson is acclaimed as one of the leading writers of the day. Earlier in the year, he had killed a man in a duel, but later escaped the appropriate punishment. At **28**, he writes *Poetaster* which is soon banned because it insults lawyers and others. At **32**, he writes his first masque, and his greatest work is done in his **30**s, *Volpone* at **32**, and *The Alchemist* at **37**. He later continues to write masques, but is not such an admired and fashionable figure. He lives until **64**, and his tomb is marked "O Rare Ben Jonson."

Eugene O'Neill, in 1913, has his first volume of writings published, by a vanity press with the cost being met by his father (**67**). O'Neill starts a one-year course in drama at Harvard, under George Pierce Baker (**48**). In the next two years, O'Neill writes eleven one-act plays, three full-length plays, and a number of other projects. At **27**, he has the first production of a play on a public stage—*Bound East for Cardiff,* at the Wharf Theater, Provincetown. He quickly moves to the center of theater attention. By **31**, he has his first play on Broadway—

 Beyond the Horizon. It is well reviewed and his proud father (**73**) cries in the audience. At **33**, he consolidates his reputation as the leading American playwright with *The Hairy Ape.* He writes *Anna Christie* at **34**; and *All God's Chillun Got Wings* at **35**, this causing controversy when the leading actress kisses the hand of Paul Robeson (**26**). O'Neill writes his own favorite play at **37**, *The Great God Brown.* At **42**, he writes the thirteen-act *Mourning Becomes Electra.* (cf. **51***)

FILMS

Charlie Chaplin has his first big success: *Tillie's Punctured Romance* (1914); he invents his character of The Tramp while working at Keystone Films (1914–15). He works at Essanay **26–27**; and Mutual **27–28**.

Darryl F. Zanuck (1928) decides that *The Jazz Singer* should have spoken dialogue, in addition to recorded singing. This is the beginning of "talking pictures."

Errol Flynn apparently acts in the Northampton Repertory Theatre, England (1934).

Katharine Hepburn returns from being a star in Hollywood (Oscar at **24**) to a disaster on Broadway—in *The Lake* (1934). About this performance, Dorothy Parker (**41**) says, "She runs the gamut of emotion from A to B."

Dorothy Lamour makes the first of the "Road" pictures (1939), with Bob Hope (**36**) and Bing Crosby (**38**)—the last is made thirteen years later.

Vivien Leigh: *Gone With the Wind* (1939).

Orson Welles: *Citizen Kane* (1940)—this is probably the most brilliant first film ever made. At **23**, his fake radio newsflash had caused millions of listeners to believe that the Earth was being invaded by Martians. At **26**, he makes *The Magnificent Ambersons,* and he stars in *The Third Man* at **34**. But he never again achieves the drama and control that he exhibits at **25**. In his career, he exemplifies the person who never fulfills their early promise. Admirers believe that the film industry should be blamed for not adjusting itself to his talent; detractors of Welles believe that he has made no effort to move forward from a state of brilliant adolescence.

MUSIC—NON-CLASSICAL

Benny Goodman's orchestra decides to improvise for the last number of its last foreseeable engagement, as they have nothing to lose—and the audience goes crazy. Overnight, Goodman becomes the King of Swing (1935).

The Four Seasons: "Big Girls Don't Cry" (1962).

The Band: "Music from Big Pink" (1968).

At the Woodstock Festival (1969), in Woodstock, New York, at the farm of Max Yasgur (**50**), the performers include: The Who (**23**); Joe Cocker (**25**); John B. Sebastian (**25**); Sly and the Family Stone (**25**); Richie Havens (**28**); Joan Baez (**28**); and Crosby (**28**), Stills (**24**), Nash (**27**), and Young (**24**).

PRESS

James Gordon Bennett II becomes editor of the New York *Herald* (1866), the leading paper of its time. He dies in office at **77**. Bennett is famous for his enterprise; at **28**, he sends H. M. Stanley to Africa, and later to explore for Dr. Livingstone (**58**).

C. P. Scott becomes editor of the *Manchester Guardian* (1872–1929). This is the period of the paper's major development; the paper is a supporter of all progressive causes, and a conscience of the Empire. Scott stays in office until **82**, and keeps fit by bicycling to work. He is appointed to the editorship by a cousin, J. E. Taylor (**41**); on his retirement, he is succeeded by his son, E. T. Scott (**46**).

EXPLORATION

Charles A. Lindbergh: first nonstop solo flight across the Atlantic, in his plane "Spirit of St. Louis" (1927). Until now, he has been employed as an airmail pilot. His great flight is greeted with worldwide adulation, partly because the feat has required both technical skill and personal bravery. Lindbergh's life is permanently transformed by his hero status. He continues to be an aviation pioneer, working for Pan American Airways.

LAW, CRIME

Timothy Evans is hanged in London (1950) for the murder of his baby (**1**) and also of his wife (**20**)—though it is not thought necessary to have a second trial to prove that he strangled his wife. Evans is illiterate and something of a mental defective. The main witness against him is Reginald Christie (**51**), formerly a part-time policeman, who has been living downstairs in the same house. Three years after Evans's execution, detectives find a number of strangled women buried in Christie's garden. Christie confesses to having murdered seven women, including Mrs. Evans, and he himself is hanged at **54**. It is later believed that if Christie's guilt had been known at the trial of Evans, then it is somehow unlikely that Evans would have been hanged.

Charles Whitman shoots 46 people from a tower at the University of Texas (1966). Eleven die. On the previous day, Whitman has stabbed his mother and his wife. Whitman is killed by police shots.

According to a Los Angeles police indictment, Kenneth Alessio Bianchi kills ten to thirteen women (**12–28**) in 1977. He is alleged to be the "Hillside Strangler."

The longest sentences are typically given to the **22** to **25** age group.

After **25**, sentences diminish (U.S., 1975). The U.S. Law Enforcement Assistance Administration supports local U.S. police programs that focus exclusively on "career criminals." The latter are typically in their **20**s, and the administration is thinking of focusing on career criminals in their late teens.

SPORTS

Patrick Davies (**22**) and John Errington (**27**) break a world record—they play squash without stopping for 107 hours 15 minutes (London, 1979). By the end, they have temporarily turned themselves into zombies; the supervising doctor warns against this kind of record attempt, as it might cause brain damage.

Suzanne Lenglen (1925): Wimbledon champion for the sixth and last time.

Jean-Claude Killy (skiing, 1968) wins all three Alpine events at the Olympics—the Downhill, the Slalom, and the Giant Slalom. He becomes a household name throughout the world, and is known even to those who have never been skiing.

Evel Knievel (1974): motorcycle leap at Snake River Canyon (Idaho), which is almost a mile wide. The attempt fails, but Knievel survives.

STRATEGIES FOR SEEING YOUR OWN LIFE

What is your general approach when seeing your own life? How do you react to opportunities? In what style do you make decisions about yourself?

Planning: a formal set of aims, timing, contacts, experiences; seeing your resume or curriculum vitae as a valuable object which you construct over the decades.

Today: to be happy today; that is enough. Things will be okay; we will all survive. No need to go crazy in trying to foresee the future.

Only the best: "Aut Caesar aut nihil"; the best, at whatever cost to yourself. Either Caesar's job or nothing. Like Anna Karenina, and like Greta Garbo, you are not going to compromise. Either the position allows for you to do your best, or you leave.

Balance: over a typical day or week, you achieve a good balance of earnings, interesting work, family life, fun, sex, and so forth.

Praxis: your everyday life exemplifies your basic ideals. The little details of your life fit in with a very large religious or political theory—because there is no point in having a grand theory unless you can work it out in your own life. Alternatively,

> A man must choose
> perfection of the life
> or of the work.—W. B. Yeats

Your work exists even at the expense of your personal life. It does not matter about the mess of your everyday life—what is important is what you produce. Like Nietzsche, you may be a nobody, but you produce material of interest.

One area of excellence: you have one peak activity and the rest of your life does not matter. Creativity, or nothing. If you are the top in one activity then you are happy to be "getting by" at everything else.

Role model: you choose one admirable person, and model yourself on that person. When you have to make a decision about your own behavior you ask yourself what this person would do or advise in the circumstances.

The list: in my life I aim to go to Venice; see the Pyramids; have all the major sexual experiences, and so on. It would be wrong, when it is too late, to look back on your life, and feel that you had missed out on these adventures. Now, when you can cross an adventure off your list ("completed") you lose interest and want to move onto something else.

Loose: never getting trapped; free; able to drop out of the rat race; not so tied to financial or family commitments that you cannot take time off should you feel like it. Not getting stuck—having a major change in your life about every seven years; "Don't do anything too bloody long."—Ernest Hemingway.

Jungle: life is cruel and competitive, and you must be able to survive. Any look at history shows revolutions, depressions, chaos; you must be ready for any of these. "Look after number one"—yourself. Be brainy, cunning, sly, crafty, whatever; endure humiliation but survive. If necessary, break the rules. Like Freud (**44**), be a "conquistador."

Sheer hard work: this clearly has a payoff; as in the saying "one percent inspiration, 99 percent perspiration."

Tough: you can cope with life's adversities. You can recover from disappointment.

Fully involved: you keep busy, and don't sit around. Whatever happens you are moving; not stationary, and not at a loss for things to do. Every day you do something interesting.

Be your age: in the past, you behaved in a certain way. Now, you are acting in the way appropriate to your current age. You have different desires at each age.

Family: nothing matters compared with this. There is no deeper pleasure.

Health: keeping healthy. There is no greater priority.

Steady accumulation: paying off your house, or working your way up the organization. Every day, you become a little more favored.

Waiting: you are waiting for an opportunity. Nothing much is happening at present. You are "doing time." But you are prepared; should an opportunity present itself, you will spring into action.

Realistic: you can't afford to be romantic. You have to scale down your ambitions and learn from your mistakes. It hurts; but it works.

Last chance: you must hurry; you have little time to spare; you must make up for lost time.

Destiny: whatever happens, you will do well in the end. You have this feeling inside you that you will be okay.

Morality: you are behaving correctly and decently, whether or not this brings any so-called success.

Luck: this is so decisive that conscious aims are absurd. Alternatively, luck is important, but you gain luck by working hard at making opportunities.

Contracyclical: willing to look at unfashionable or even unpleasant ideas. When everyone is going one way, you know that there must soon be a backlash of some kind.

Dry run: I am only here on a dry run. I am learning the rules of life. Next time around, when I have to live my life over again, I will know how to do it properly.

Confused: you do not know what is happening; you can't decide about priorities; you cannot make sense of events (a nonstrategy).

Defeated: doomed; a "victim"; not in control. You have done all you could but it has not brought you any luck. You are resigned. Everything is against you.

26

HEALTH

Theodor Bilharz, in 1851: description of the disease which is later named bilharziasis. He dies from typhoid at **37**, before either he or his contemporaries realize the significance of his discovery.

Crawford W. Long: first use of ether in surgery (1842). Long does not immediately write up this advance and it is discovered again by William T. G. Morton (**27**, in 1846) whose use of ether in dentistry opens the gates to the widespread use of anesthesia in surgery.

HISTORY—WORLD

Hannibal: commander-in-chief of the Carthaginian forces (221 B.C.)—later famous for his use of elephants during campaigning.

Charlemagne: King of the Franks (768), until his death at **72**.

Emperor Henry IV, in 1077: his rebellion against the papacy having failed, he travels to Canossa, Italy, to do penance. The Pope, Gregory VII (**56**) forces Henry to stand for three days outside in the snow, wearing the clothes of a penitent. Then, Henry is admitted, and given the Sacrament, as an end to his excommunication. Henry had become King and Emperor at **6**. Later, both men die while fleeing from their enemies—the Pope dies at **64**, having been driven out of Rome; and the King dies at **55**, escaping from Henry V (**20**), his own son.

Fidel Castro: with only 150 supporters, he makes a frontal attack on the Moncada barracks, in Cuba (1953). This is a failure, and he is imprisoned by the regime of President Batista (**52**). He is released at **28**; he returns with a tiny guerilla group at **30**, and he achieves power, with Che Guevara (**28**), at **32**. Castro then begins his lifelong rule of Cuba. Che Guevara dies fighting in Bolivia at **39**.

HISTORY—U.S.A.

Robert Kennedy is campaign manager (1952) for John Kennedy's (**35**) election to the Senate. (cf. **42***)

HISTORY—U.K.

Edward the Black Prince wins the Battle of Poitiers (1356, Sept. 19). At **15**, he had distinguished himself at the Battle of Crécy.

Samuel Phillips: foundation of Phillips Academy, Andover, Massachusetts (1778).

Alice Freeman: President of Wellesley College, Massachusetts (1881–87).

Beatrice and Sidney (**27**) Webb: founder-members of the Fabian Society (London 1884).

Margaret Mead: *Coming of Age in Samoa* (1928). This makes her famous, and she gets her Ph.D. at **27**. She publishes *Growing Up in New Guinea* at **28**, and is probably the best-known anthropologist for the rest of her life. (cf. **40***)

SCIENCE

Tycho Brahe: *De Nova Stella* (1572).

Eugen Goldstein: first use of the concept "cathode rays" (1876).

Albert Einstein publishes five papers in physics (1905). One of these is on the Special Theory of Relativity. Each is revolutionary; in a different area of physics; and probably all are worthy of the Nobel Prize—which he is given at **42**. Einstein's approach to work is (1) to attempt the most difficult problems of the time; (2) to imaginatively link concepts and facts which have never previously been linked together; (3) to concentrate in tranquillity for as long as necessary, ignoring the trivia of daily life. All this work is done outside office hours, in his own time, and independent of any university. At this time, he is working in the Swiss Patent Office. He does not obtain a junior faculty position until **30**. He now builds on this work at **26**—at **28** he writes a paper which includes the equation $E = mc^2$. He goes on to develop the General Theory of Relativity by **36***. At this moment in 1905, Ernst Mach is **67**; E. W. Morley (**67**); A. A. Michelson (**52**); Henrik Lorentz (**52**); Max Planck (**47**); Herman Minkowski (**41**); Ernest Rutherford (**34**); Max Born (**22**); Niels Bohr (**20**); Otto Stern (**17**); Louis de Broglie (**13**); and Werner Heisenberg (**3**).

Donald A. Glaser: first bubble chamber (1952). This is an extension of the cloud chamber, on which C. T. R. Wilson had completed his major work by **42**, in 1911.

MONEY, WORK

Jean Paul Getty comes out of retirement (1917)—is worth $3 million by **30**. (cf. **37***)

Charles Revson is refused promotion in the nail polish company where he works (1932), so starts his own company, with the help of his brother, a friend, and $300 which becomes Revlon.

Walter Reuther is fired as a foreman at the Ford Motor Company (1933), for promoting the union. He goes on a two-year round-the-world visit to auto plants; at **28**, works full time for the United Autoworkers Union. At **34**, Ford recognizes the UAW.

William Morris (Lord Nuffield): his Oxford automobile and cycle agency goes bankrupt (1904)—Morris had been the partner in charge of the technical side. (He makes his first car for sale at **36***.)

ARCHITECTURE

Gaudí: Casa Vicens, Barcelona (1878–80)—his first house to be built. (cf. **32***)

ART

Masaccio: "Expulsion from Paradise" (1427) and other frescoes in the Brancacci Chapel, Florence—some of the most influential art ever made. Masaccio dies at **27**; his coworker Masolino is then **45**.

Rembrandt: "The Anatomy Lesson of Dr. Tulp" (1632).

Canaletto: "St. Marks Square, with the Basilica" (1723). This is one of the first of his pictures to achieve his unique style. By maintaining his skill and style, he is able to travel extensively, and to be in work as long as he lives. He lives until **71**.

Pablo Picasso: "Les Demoiselles d'Avignon" (1907). (cf. **56***)

MUSIC—CLASSICAL

Giovanni di Palestrina is appointed director of music for the services of St. Peter's Rome (1551). He dies in office, at **68**. (Unfortunately, it is very difficult to attribute work to Palestrina in this book, as dates of his composition are not clear.)

Jeremiah Clarke: *Trumpet Voluntary* (1700).

Hector Berlioz: *Fantastic Symphony* (1829). This is written in honor of an Irish actress whom he adores from afar. They marry when he is **29**, and she in fact makes him very unhappy. (cf. **35***)

Pietro Mascagni: *Cavalleria Rusticana* (1889). He is now transformed from obscure country piano teacher into an internationally famous "man of the future." But despite a large number of opportunities, he never again does anything that is memorable. He dies at **79**, having done well from "Cav" for the whole of his life. Ruggiero Leoncavallo writes *I Pagliacci* at **34** (May 1892) and for him too it is the only composition which survives; he dies at **61**.

Henry Wood conducts the first of the Promenade Concerts (1895); these occupy him for the rest of his life. At **72**, they are moved to the Royal Albert Hall, and he conducts his last concert at **75**, shortly before his death.

Zubin Mehta: conductor of the Los Angeles Philharmonic Orchestra (1962).

LITERATURE

Thomas Gray begins writing "Elegy in a Country Churchyard" (1742), and finishes it when he is **34**.

Samuel Taylor Coleridge publishes "Lyrical Ballads" (1798), with William Wordsworth (**28**). It contains Coleridge's "The Rime of the Ancient Mariner." He had written "Kubla Khan" at **25**. He dies at **62**, having spent the rest of his life as a literary personality, not writing much more poetry after his late **20**s.

John Keats dies (1821, Feb. 23), in a house by the Spanish Steps, in Rome. His death is caused by tuberculosis.

Edgar Allan Poe marries his cousin Virginia Clemm (**13**) (1835); he publishes *The Fall of the House of Usher* at **30**, and *The Murders in the Rue Morgue* at **32**; but he dies at **40**.

D. H. Lawrence leaves schoolteaching (1911) on the publication of his *The White Peacock*. He writes *Sons and Lovers* at **28**, and *Women in Love* at **35**. (cf. **43***)

Aleksandr Solzhenitsyn is sentenced to eight years imprisonment (1945); he is released at **34**, but is kept in exile in Siberia until **37**. (cf. **43***)

PLAYS, DANCE

Anna Pavlova creates the role of *The Dying Swan* (1907) from choreography by Mikhail Fokine (**27**). At **27**, she begins her travels around the world, and these tours continue until her death at **50**.

John Osborne: *Look Back in Anger* (1956); also, *The Entertainer* at **27**, and *Luther* at **30**. *Inadmissable Evidence,* about the horrors of middle age, is at **34**.

Arnold Wesker: *Chicken Soup with Barley* (1958); also *Roots* at **27**; and *I'm Talking About Jerusalem* at **28**.

FILMS

Rudolph Valentino: *The Sheik* (1921); he receives continuous adulation from now onward, until his death at **31**.

Greta Garbo: *Susan Lenox: Her Fall and Rise* (1931).

Fay Wray is rescued from *King Kong* (1933).

Errol Flynn: *Captain Blood* (1935)—makes him famous.

Jean Harlow dies (1937, June 7) of natural causes, complicated by lack of medical attention—her mother was a Christian Scientist. The funeral is attended by her first and third husbands, but not by her second, Paul Bern; he had previously killed himself, at **33**.

Betty Grable has her legs insured for $500,000 (1942).

Grace Kelly: *Dial M for Murder;* and *Rear Window* (1954).

Elizabeth Taylor: *Cat on a Hot Tin Roof* (1958); and she stars in *Suddenly Last Summer,* at **28**.

Shirley MacLaine: *The Apartment* (1960), with Jack Lemmon (**35**).

Sophia Loren: *The Millionairess* (1960).

Jane Fonda: *Cat Ballou;* and *La Ronde* (1964). At **27**, she marries the producer of the latter, Roger Vadim (**37**).

Barbra Streisand: *Funny Girl* (1968); her first film; Oscar.

Sharon Tate is murdered at 10050 Cielo Drive, Los Angeles (1969, Aug. 9). She is stabbed to death by the followers of Charles Manson (**35***).

Liza Minelli: *Cabaret* (1972), with Michael York (**30**), and Joel Gray (**40**); the director is Bob Fosse (**47**).

Rainer Werner Fassbinder: *The Bitter Tears of Petra von Kant* (1972).

Maureen Teefy: *Fame* (1980). On those striving to achieve fame, the film says, "If they've got what it takes, it's going to take everything they've got."

MUSIC—NON-CLASSICAL

Tim Hardin: "Reason to Believe" (1966).

John Denver: "Leaving on a Jet Plane" (1969).

Rod Stewart: "Every Picture Tells a Story" (1971). He is now number one rock singer.

EXPLORATION

Bryan Allen: first human-powered flight in a figure-eight course (1979). He is a cyclist, and he pedals powerfully enough to provide in effect a motor for a very light plane. This plane, "Gossamer Condor," is designed by Paul MacCready (**53**). Later, Allen powers a similar plane for 22 miles across the English Channel.

PRESS

George Plimpton: editor, the *Paris Review* (1953). His book *Out of My League* is at **34**, and *Paper Lion* is at **39**.

LAW, CRIME

John Wilkes Booth shoots President Lincoln (**56**) (1865, Apr. 14) and is himself later killed while escaping. Three other men are executed (**20**, **22**, and **29**), and also Mrs. Surratt (**45**). She is almost certainly innocent, and her son John (**20**) is almost certainly guilty—but he manages to escape any punishment. Later, the assassin of President McKinley is Leon Czolgosz (**20**). The assassin of Senator Robert F. Kennedy is **23**. The attempted assassin of Governor George Wallace is **21**; and of President Reagan, **25**.

J. Edgar Hoover becomes Assistant Director of the (Federal) Bureau of Investigation (1921), and works here for the rest of his life. He becomes acting Director at **29**, and dies in office at **77***. His success is due primarily to a new systematic attention to detail; he initiates nationwide collecting of criminals' fingerprints.

Al Capone becomes head of his gang in Chicago, when the previous number one departs, leaving everything to Capone (1925). Only Capone is vicious enough to survive as a leader in Chicago in Prohibition. He now gets himself a seven-ton customized bulletproof Cadillac. He runs a complex organization, with assistants for bribery, alcohol, brothels, gambling, and violence, as well as subsidiary gangs. At **28**, he is instrumental in securing the election of a mayor of Chicago who is sympathetic to "gangland." Capone's methods include mobs, shootings, and the instruction to his supporters, "Vote early, and vote often." (cf. **30***)

Lucky Luciano becomes "King of Booze" (1928), the head of a huge illegal alcohol organization in New York. At **22**, he had begun selling liquor to the garment trade in New York, after the beginning of Prohibition. At **33**, he kills the "Capo di Tutti Capi," and is himself the Boss; he moves into the Waldorf-Astoria Hotel.

This is the average age of people transported from Britain to penal colonies in Australia (1788–1868). There were about 150,000 in all, the vast majority having had previous convictions. Political protesters tended to be about five years older than criminals. You were eligible for punishment by transportation when you reached **14**.

SPORTS

Joe DiMaggio (baseball, 1941) has a 56 game hitting streak—perhaps the greatest achievement in the history of the game. Earlier in the season, he had suffered a batting slump. He retires at **36**, and coaches until **51**. He is a well-known TV personality afterward. (cf **61***)

Joe Namath (1969) leads the New York Jets to victory in the Super Bowl, beating the Baltimore Colts. At **32**, Namath earns $420,000 from the New York Jets, and he also makes $250,000 in TV commercials for Fabergé. At **34**, he retires, and begins a career in films.

27

HISTORY—WORLD

Albert Speer, an architect (1932), meets Adolf Hitler (**43**) who turns him into one of his favorites. Speer is employed to make gigantic architectural designs for the Third Reich. During World War II, Speer (then **36**) is made Minister for Armaments. His skill and energy are such that Germany's survival in the war is extended. But afterward, Speer is imprisoned (**40–60**) for his use of slave labor.

HISTORY—U.S.A.

Martin Luther King is leader of a bus boycott in Montgomery, Alabama (1956), where he is a minister. This is his first major confrontation, and it leads to a Supreme Court decision, outlawing Jim Crow laws. (cf. **34***)

HISTORY—U.K.

The future Queen Mary I—"Bloody Mary"—attends the sixth and last marriage (1543, July 12) of her father, King Henry VIII (**52**) to Catherine Parr (**31**). She herself becomes Queen at **37***.

Group Captain Leonard Cheshire, VC is the British observer at the dropping of the atomic bomb on Nagasaki (1945). Almost immediately afterward, he sets up the first of his Cheshire Homes, for the dying and for the incurably sick.

RELIGION, PHILOSOPHY

John Calvin: *The Institutes* (1536)—a powerful text of the Reformation. At **32**, he begins his attempt to turn Geneva into a Christian commune; well before his death (**55**), he has succeeded in this.

C. T. Russell: approximate beginnings of the Jehovah's Witnesses (1879).

SOCIAL SCIENCE, EDUCATION

Edward Gibbon, while visiting the Forum in Rome (1764), decides to write a history of the decline and fall of the Roman empire. He publishes the first volume at **39**, and the last three volumes at **50***.

Adolphe Quetelet, in 1823: he visits Paris to discuss his own subject of astronomy, but happens to meet the leading figures in the emerging science of "moral statistics," that is, the mathematical analysis of people's choices on moral questions, such as crime, marriage, and so on. At **35**, he publishes *Research on the Propensity to Crime at Different Ages;* he is the first to show systematically that crime rates rise to early manhood, but then steadily fall as people get older. This volume helps to make him the true founder of sociology. However, he himself always believes that this is a relatively minor interest of his, compared with his original interest in astronomy. Later, Quetelet achieves permanent fame for his minor interest, and is ignored for his major interest.

(Lord) Acton, the historian, writes that "Power tends to corrupt, and absolute power corrupts absolutely. Great men are almost always bad men. . ." (1861).

Max Weber completes his thesis (1891). At the end of the examination, the examiner (**74**) congratulates him thus: "When the time comes for me to descend into the grave, there is no one to whom I would rather say, 'Son, here is my spear, it has become too heavy for my arm' than Max Weber." Weber becomes Professor of Economics at **30**; his *The Protestant Ethic and the Spirit of Capitalism* is published at **40***; and *Economy and Society* is begun at **49***.

MONEY, WORK

F. W. Woolworth: sets up first store (1879), selling a large variety of goods, at only one price—five cents. (cf. **60***)

SCIENCE, TECHNOLOGY

Elias Howe: the first sewing machine (1846).

Richard Dedekind: the Dedekind Cut, in mathematics (1858).

The mean age for a Ph.D. in physics is **26**; for a Ph.D. in sociology it is **28** (U.S.A., according to researcher Stephen Cole, 1979).

RENAISSANCE

Queen Christina of Sweden, in 1654: she abdicates from her throne, and now sails away from her native country. (Later, her last look at Sweden is the subject of a famous film scene, by Greta Garbo, also **27**, in 1933.) At **6**, she had inherited her position, on the death of her father, King Gustavus Adolphus (**37**); at **14**, she attends her first regency council meetings, and she receives full power at **18**. She is both a skilled political figure, and a great patron of arts, literature, and philosophy. At **22**, she hires René Descartes (**52**) to be a member of her new Swedish Academy, but she inadvertently causes his death in the following year. At about **27**, she converts to Catholicism, and is unable to continue her rule over her Lutheran country. At **28**, she arrives in Rome and makes her entrance in a ceremonial carriage designed by another polymath, the architect and sculptor Gianlorenzo Bernini (**56**); she is confirmed into the Catholic church by the Pope himself, Alexander VII (**56**). In Rome, she pursues her political and her artistic interests—she makes a bid to become Queen of Naples at **30**, and she tries to become Queen of Poland at **40**. Her choirmaster at **53** is the composer, Alessandro Scarlatti (**20**), and he serves her for three years. After her death, Christina is commemorated in three ways: by her large tomb in St. Peter's; by her extensive library bequests to the Vatican library; and by the Accademia dell'Arcadia, which her friends set up in the year following her death and which formalizes the artistic and learned salon which she has maintained at her palace.

Louis Tiffany begins his experiments in glassware (1875). His first patents are at **33**, and he starts his own factory at **44**.

Buckminster Fuller, in 1922: following the death of his daughter (**4**), he has a nervous breakdown, and later spends two years in withdrawal from the world. But during this time, he produces his most forceful early work, the modular bathroom, and Dymaxion House. At **34**, he emerges from "exile" with these and other designs.

Moshe Safdie: Habitat '67 (1965–67)—the precast concrete box housing scheme at the Montreal's Expo '67 world's fair. He obtained the commission by proposing the building when he was a staff architect on the Expo organization.

ART

Naum Gabo is the leader of the Constructivist movement at the beginning of the Russian Revolution (1917). He has to leave at **32**, because of changes in the political climate. He spends the rest of his life working out these ideas of **27–32**.

MUSIC—CLASSICAL

Hugo Wolf in 1887: his father dies at **59**, and this depresses him. But a friend pays for the first-ever publication of a group of his songs, and this seems to open the floodgates—he now watches himself pour out a stream of songs which are masterpieces. The songs for which he is later famous are nearly all written between **27** and **29**, numbering 160 in that time. At **29**, he begins on what he considers to be a greater ambition, which is to write operas. In this, he is a failure. At **39**, he goes mad, and dies in a mental hospital at **42***.

Claude Debussy: *Clair de lune* (1890). He writes *Prélude à l'après-midi d'un faune* at **31**, and *Pelléas et Mélisande* around **34**. (cf. **46***)

LITERATURE

Robert Burns: "The Kilmarnock Poems" (1786). These poems had been written while he was a farmer, and they now make him an overnight success. He dies at **37**.

The Grimm Brothers: *Fairy Tales* (1812–15). This is a break from their usual work, which is about linguistics and philology.

George Sand: *Indiana* (1831), her first published book.

Henry David Thoreau moves to Walden Pond (1845, July 4), and lives by himself, self-sufficient and observing nature. His stay of two years two months costs him 27 cents per day, and results in *Walden* at **37**. At **28**, he is jailed for one night for not paying his taxes, and two years later he writes *Civil Disobedience.*

Tolstoy meets Sonya Behrs (**11**) (1856, May 26); they are married six years later. (cf. **35***)

H. G. Wells leaves teaching, and becomes a writer (1893).

Upton Sinclair: *The Jungle* (1906). This is written after a seven-week trip to Chicago, and it transforms him into a nationally known author. An act of Congress remedies the abuses in the meat-packing industry that his book has revealed. He writes powerfully for the rest of his life.

Rupert Brooke: "If I should die, think only this of me. . ." (1914). He dies in the following year, from blood poisoning which originated from an insect bite on the lip.

T. S. Eliot chooses not to complete the last stage of the Harvard Ph.D. program (1915), even though he has finished his dissertation. His first poem "The Love Song of J. Alfred Prufrock" (written at **22**) is published, and is an immediate success. Eliot has very little money, and at **29** begins work in the Colonial and Foreign Department of Lloyds Bank, in London. He stays there until **37***, when he has become an expert on foreign currency problems. While working full-time at the bank, he establishes himself as a major literary critic through his spare-time writings. He writes "The Waste Land" at **33**.

PLAYS

Nikolai Gogol: *The Inspector General* (1836).

FILMS

Rudolph Valentino: *Blood and Sand;* and *The Four Horsemen of the Apocalypse* (1922).

Sergei Eisenstein: *The Battleship Potemkin* (1925).

Walt Disney: *Oswald the Lucky Rabbit* (1928)—his first real cartoon success. Also, he invents Mickey Mouse this year; and he does the first of his *Silly Symphony* films at **28**.

Bing Crosby appears as a solo singer in a series of Mack Sennett (**51**) comedy films (1931).

Cary Grant moves to Hollywood, from New York (1931), and joins Paramount. At **28**, he is demanded by Mae West, as her leading man in her first film, *She Done Him Wrong.*

Greta Garbo says, "I want to be alone," in *Grand Hotel* (1932).

Errol Flynn: *The Charge of the Light Brigade* (1936).

Ingmar Bergman directs his first film, *Crisis* (1945).

Deanna Durbin, ex-child star, retires (1949), and goes to live in Paris, having amassed a large fortune from her 22 films.

Grace Kelly marries Prince Rainier of Monaco (**33**, in 1956), and retires from films.

Richard Lester: *The Running, Jumping, and Standing Still Film* (1959).

François Truffaut: *Les Quatre Cent Coups*; and *Tirez le Pianiste,* at **28**.

Julie Andrews: *Mary Poppins* (1963); her first film; Oscar.

Richard Dreyfus: *Jaws* (1975); from script by Peter Benchley (**33**).

MUSIC—NON-CLASSICAL

Jerry Jeff Walker: "Mr. Bojangles" (1968).

Abba (**24**, **27**, **28**, **29**) wins the Eurovision song contest (1974). Under the guidance of their manager, Stig Anderson (**43**), they go on to sell almost 150 million records; within five years, they employ 50 people, and have a yearly turnover of £12 million ($24 million), half of which is profit.

TV, ETC.

"Charlie's Angels" (1976) are Kate Jackson (**26**), Jaclyn Smith (**26**), and Farrah Fawcett-Majors (**28**). Ms. Fawcett-Majors goes on to sell eight million posters of herself in a bathing suit; although her body gives the appearance of perfection, she was in fact born with a tumor obstructing her digestive tract.

LOVE, LIFE

Irving Robbins: opening of the first Baskin-Robbins ice cream store (1945). The first day's turnover is $35.

Hugh Hefner: start of *Playboy* magazine (1953). The first centerfold is Marilyn Monroe (**23**). At **44**, he presents the first centerfold with pubic hair, Marilyn Cole (**25**). At **54**, sample centerfold ages in three successive issues are **20**, **21**, and **23**.

Marc Quinquandon: death (France, 1979). He has been training for a new record in snail eating—he eats 72 snails in three minutes, and collapses.

EXPLORATION

John Smith: first settlement at Chesapeake Bay, and the exploration of Virginia (1607). In this year his life is saved by Pocahontas (**13**) who intervenes when he is about to be killed by natives. Later, at **34**, Smith does careful mapping of New England, before returning home to England at **35**. He never again sees the New World. Instead, he publishes mouthwatering descriptions of the empty lands awaiting development, and so he creates intense interest in colonization. He is **40** at the time of the *Mayflower,* and he lives until about **51**.

Z. M. Pike: discovery of Pike's Peak, Colorado (1806). Later, as a brigadier-general in the U.S. Army, he is killed in battle at **34**, on the future site of Toronto, Ontario.

Yuri Gagarin: first human in space (1961, Apr. 12).

Garry Trudeau: honorary degree, Yale University (1976)—youngest ever recipient—for his "Doonesbury" strip. This originated at **20** when he was a student at Yale.

LAW, CRIME

Caryl Chessman is sentenced to death (1948) as the Red Light Bandit, a cruel rapist, kidnapper, and armed thug. By working at the appeals system, he puts off his execution until **39**. During this time, he writes two best-selling books; he had learned to type at **20**, in the prison secretarial school, when serving a previous five-year sentence for armed robbery. Chessman is still typing when the warden (**61**) arrives to take him up to the "Big Sleep," or gas chamber.

SPORTS

Captain Matthew Webb (1875) is the first person to swim the English Channel. He takes 21 hours 43 minutes, for the distance of 21 miles. Since his effort, only around 200 people have managed the crossing, out of at least 1,000 attempts. Later, the oldest person to swim the Channel is **58***, and the youngest is **12***. At **35**, Webb drowns, while trying to swim across the waters above Niagara Falls—an attempt to exploit his fame as a swimmer. A memorial stone to Webb carries this inscription: "Nothing Great Is Easy."

Bill Tilden (1920) wins Wimbledon for the first time. At **25** and **26**, he had lost the U.S. championship in the finals—but he reforms his play and now begins a ten-year domination of tennis. He wins Wimbledon again at **28** and **37**, and wins the U.S. championship seven times. At **23**, Tilden had risen only to seventieth place in the U.S. amateur rankings—at a time when there were few other players. But his public career comes to a disastrous end at **53***.

Sandy Koufax (baseball, 1963): he breaks his own National League strike-out record, bringing the total to 276. He also has his eleventh shut-out, a major-league record for a left-hander.

Dawn Fraser (swimming, 1964) wins the Olympic 100 meters; she had previously won this gold medal at both **19** and **22**.

Johann Cruyff: soccer star of the 1974 World Cup. By 1978, he has retired.

Niki Lauda (1976): accident at the Nurburgring motor racing circuit. He is burned about the body and face, and is given the last rites. But he literally comes back from the dead, and wins the world championship at **28**—his second win, having previously been champion at **26**. Lauda retires from racing at **30**, having started on developing his own small airline.

28

HEALTH

Andreas Vesalius: *De humani corporis fabrica* (Basle, 1543). This book is the start of anatomy. Vesalius's breakthrough has been to do his own dissection of bodies, and he has ignored medical theories which have been accepted for more than 1,000 years.

HISTORY—WORLD

Gaius Caesar Caligula: assassination (41 A.D.). Caligula became Roman Emperor at **24**, following the death of Tiberius (**79**) whose will Caligula manipulates to obtain sole power. As Emperor, his dynastic ambitions cause increasing resentment; at **26**, his sister Drusilla (**22**) dies, and he consecrates her as a diva or goddess. It is this kind of behavior that leads to his assassination; Caligula is vicious, incestuous, and autocratic. He is killed at **28**, as is his wife—his fourth.

Frederick the Great: King of Prussia (1740) until his death at **74**.

Rudi Dutschke: a leader of the student riots in Europe in 1968. He gains the name "Red Rudi," but is severely injured in an assassination attempt. Similar groups: the Italian "Red Brigade" is founded (1969) by Renato Curcio (**27**) and others; also Baader (**27**) of the Baader-Meinhof gang.

Colonel Qaddafi: revolutionary takeover in Libya (1969) and appointment as head of state.

Samuel Doe: head of the nation of Liberia (1980). He achieves power in a coup d'etat, having previously served as a master sergeant in the Liberian army.

HISTORY—U.S.A.

Mary Jo Kopechne dies at Chappaquiddick (1969, July 18), in a car driven by Senator Edward Kennedy (**37**).

As an attempt at compromise in the arguments over slavery, Pennsylvania voted in 1780 that slaves born after that date should be slaves until **28** and then should have their freedom.

HISTORY—U.K.

Henry V: Battle of Agincourt (1415).

Henry VII defeats Richard III (**32**) at the Battle of Bosworth Field

 (1485, Aug. 22) and then literally receives the crown. Also at **28**, he marries Princess Elizabeth (**20**)—this is the uniting of the Lancaster and York sides in the Wars of the Roses, and the beginning of the Tudors. Henry VII lives until **52**.

Lord George Gordon: the Gordon Riots (May 1780). Huge riots take place in London, with Newgate Prison wrecked, and the Bank of England threatened. 20,000 troops are required to restore order. The original grievance was a proposal to remove restrictions against Catholics. Gordon himself later becomes a Jew, and dies, mad, in the rebuilt Newgate Prison at **41**.

Eligibility: entrants into the administrative branch of the British Civil Service (the top layer) are typically **28** or under.

RELIGION, PHILOSOPHY

St. Catherine of Siena persuades the Pope to leave Avignon, and move the papacy back to Rome (c. 1375).

David Hume: *Treatise of Human Nature* (1739). This has little immediate public impact, and by **40** he turns to the writing of history and economics. The majority of his philosophical ideas have been initiated when traveling abroad between **23** and **26**. (cf. **30***)

SOCIAL SCIENCE, EDUCATION

Franz Boas, the anthropologist: first contact with the Kwakiutl peoples, who become his lifelong source of data (1886).

Noam Chomsky: *Syntactic Structures* (1957). Later, he writes on public policy: *American Power and the New Mandarins* (**40**).

SCIENCE, TECHNOLOGY

Carl Linnaeus: *Systema naturae* (1735)—the start of the modern classification system in botany. Linnaeus sees God in nature, and becomes God's Registrar. Linnaeus is a man of great self-confidence and he says of his book: "a masterpiece that can never be read and admired enough." At **46** he writes a book which he says is "the greatest in the realm of science." About his work in general, he says: "I do not know whether anyone now can venture forward without being led by my hand." Linnaeus's self-admiration is not entirely unjustified. He lives until **70**.

Antoine Lavoisier deposits a sealed note (1772) with the Secretary of the Academy, in Paris, on the subject of his new theory of combustion. At **29**, this is read in public, and by **36** he is able to give the name oxygen to the gas which he has discovered. At **39–40**, he discovers the composition of water. He goes on to become a leader in the new scientific approach to agriculture, but he is executed at **50***.

James Joule: completion of his work on the mechanical equivalent of heat (1847).

Rudolf Clausius: second law of thermodynamics (1850). Later, he is the first to use the word "entropy."

Chester F. Carlson, in 1934: he is a patent lawyer who has previously been laid off from scientific work at Bell Telephone Laboratories. On his own, he now starts to design the ideal office copier. By **31**, he has completed the basic design. By **39**, he retires and lives off his earnings from the Xerox process for the rest of his life.

Roy J. Plunkett: discovery of Teflon (1938).

MONEY, WORK

Josiah Wedgwood starts his own business, at the Ivy House Works (1758, Dec. 30). He is the brainiest in a family devoted to pottery, in an area in which the pottery industry is suddenly expanding greatly. By **38**, he is able to open a large new factory, at Etruria, to which he later adds a model village, and a mansion for himself—Etruria Hall.

Robert Owen marries the daughter of the owner of New Lanark Mill (1799, Sept. 30). Previously he had been a highly energetic employee of other mill owners. He now takes over New Lanark, and it continues speedy growth. But it is not until **49*** that Owen publishes his *Report to the County of Lanark* for which he is later famous.

E. I. Du Pont emigrates to U.S., and sets up company to manufacture gunpowder (1800), at Wilmington, Delaware.

Henry Ford gets a job as engineer with the Edison Illuminating Co. in Detroit (1891, Sept. 25) and stays there until he is **36**. He works part-time on his automobile interests, and produces his first car at **32**. At this time, he is one of several hundred people in the U.S.A. who are making their own self-propelled carriages. (cf. **36***)

Juan Trippe: Pan American Airways (1927).

Henry Ford II: head of the Ford Motor Company (1945).

ARCHITECTURE

Palladio gives up work as a bricklayer, and his patron Giangiorgio Trissino starts to give him a wide general nonarchitectural education (c. 1536) (cf. **39***)

Philip Webb: Red House, Bexleyheath, Kent (1859).

Charles Rennie Mackintosh: Glasgow School of Art (1896), won in competition. For the next few years he is able to produce brilliant work, particularly in furniture and interior design. But the strain forces him to resign his practice at **45**, and he dies at **60** having produced little other work of value.

ART

A court painter in London (1732) is told to paint King George II as **28**, and the Queen as **25**. Both in fact are **49**.

Chopin: 24 Preludes (1838). He writes these and other pieces while in Majorca, with his lover, George Sand (**34**). They then return to her country house; their friends include Delacroix (**40**) and Liszt (**27**). The major period of Chopin's compositions is his **20**s and early **30**s. He dies from consumption at **39***.

Ralph Vaughan Williams: *Linden Lea* (1900).

Igor Stravinsky: *The Firebird* (1910, June 25). It is an immediate and permanent success. He writes *Petrouchka* at **29** and *Rite of Spring* at **31**. (cf. **48***)

Jacqueline du Pré, the cellist, is told that she has multiple sclerosis, after she gradually falls sick on a concert tour of the U.S.A. (1973).

LITERATURE

Anthony Trollope begins his first novel (Sept. 1843) while working as a rural administrator in the Irish postal service. Although he now publishes constantly, he is not well known until his *Barchester Towers* at **42**. (cf. **40***)

Dostoevsky is put in front of a firing squad (1849) for having discussed revolutionary topics. But the execution is a hoax, and he is sent to Siberia for 10 years. (cf. **45***)

Conan Doyle writes *A Study in Scarlet* (1887), his first Sherlock Holmes story. At this time, Doyle has a medical practice near Portsmouth. It is not booming, and he has plenty of time for writing. He becomes a full-time writer at **31**. (cf. **44***)

Lytton Strachey: *Eminent Victorians* (1918). This establishes (1) his writing style, used in a number of similar works; and (2) his permanent fame.

Judy Blume starts writing her first children's book (1966). She is a frustrated American housewife. By **40**, she has sold five million copies, of eleven titles, and she publishes her first adult novel, *Wifey*—about a frustrated American housewife.

PLAYS, DANCE

Sophocles defeats Aeschylus (**57**) in the Athens festival drama contest of 468 B.C. Later, his plays include *Antigone* at **56**; *Oedipus Rex*, probably at **69**; *Electra* at **87**; and *Oedipus at Colonus* at **90**. Sophocles writes 124 plays, and lives until **90***.

William Shakespeare is by now a well-known figure in the theater world (1592). At approximately **26** to **29**, he writes *Henry VI, Richard III, The Comedy of Errors,* and *The Taming of the Shrew.* At **30** to **33**, he writes *The Two Gentlemen of Verona, Love's Labour's Lost, Romeo and Juliet, Richard II,* and *A Midsummer Night's Dream.* At **34** to **37**, he writes *Much Ado About Nothing, Henry V, Julius Caesar, As You Like It, The Merry Wives of Windsor,* and *Hamlet.* The 154 sonnets are written at various times between **29** and **36**. (cf. **38*** and **48***)

Harold Pinter: *The Birthday Party* (1958); *The Caretaker* at **30**.

FILMS

Mary Pickford: *Little Lord Fauntleroy* (1921)—both the little lord, and his mother.

Mack Sennett joins the new Keystone Company (1912), and makes his famous contribution between now and **33**. He develops the Keystone Cops at **28**, and works with Fatty Arbuckle **(31)**.

Buster Keaton makes ten feature films between now and **33** (1923–28).

Alfred Hitchcock: *The Lodger* (1927); this is his first film, and already shows his characteristic style.

Gary Cooper: *The Virginian* (1929); this establishes him as a star.

Marlene Dietrich: *The Blue Angel* (1930).

Johnny Weismuller retires as an Olympic swimmer (1932), and becomes Tarzan.

Paulette Goddard: *The Great Dictator* (1939).

Trigger dies; he was the horse associated with Roy Rogers.

Ingrid Bergman: *Casablanca* (1943), with Humphrey Bogart **(44)**.

Stanley Donen: *Singin' in the Rain* (1952), starring Gene Kelly **(40)**, Debbie Reynolds **(20)**, and Donald O'Connor **(27)**.

Louis Malle: *Zazie dans le Métro* (1960).

Julie Andrews: *The Sound of Music* (1964).

Rainer Werner Fassbinder: *Fear Eats the Soul* (1974).

MUSIC—NON-CLASSICAL

Dr. Jules Stein resigns his position as chief resident in ophthalmology at Cook County Hospital (Chicago, 1924), and he starts his own agency to book bands. He invents the "one-night stand," to book a band for a night and not for the then-conventional period of a week. Stein's organization, the Music Corporation of America, grows to become an industry leader.

Woody Guthrie: "This Land Is Your Land" (1940); and "Bound for Glory" at **31**. He is ill with Huntington's disease from about **43**, and dies at **55**.

Stewart Copeland, and the Police: "Zenyatta Mondatta" (1980).

TV, ETC.

Henry Winkler: as the Fonz **(18)** in the TV program "Happy Days" (1974).

Christina Onassis, the shipping tycoon: divorce (1979), her third. Her marriages have been at **18**, **23**, and **27**. She is said to be worth at least $200 million, and is sometimes known to headline writers as "Thunderthighs."

PRESS

Tom Driberg starts his "William Hickey" column in the London *Daily Express* (1933)—a pioneer in gossip columns.

Charles M. Schulz: "Peanuts" (1950); this strip cartoon contains no one over the age of **8**. The pioneer strip is "The Yellow Kid" (1896) by Robert F. Outcault (**33**). "Mutt and Jeff" (1907) is by Bud Fisher (**23**). Chic Young (**29**) draws the Bumsteads, Blondie and Dagwood (1930). Al Capp (**26**) draws "Li'l Abner" (1935). "Superman" (1938) is invented by Jerry Siegel (**24**) and Joe Shuster (**24**).

EXPLORATION

Louis Joliet: voyage of discovery down the Mississippi River (1673). He is accompanied by Jacques Marquette (**36**), who dies at **38** after spending a winter on the site of the future Chicago.

René Caillé: first European to visit Timbuktu, and survive (1828). He dies at **38**, from diseases contracted in Africa.

George Willig: ascent of the New York World Trade Center (1978), on the outside. This building is 1,350 feet high, and he climbs it in 3½ hours, taking advantage of a rail which is part of the window cleaning equipment. In 1981, Daniel Goodwin (**25**) climbs the oustide of the Sears Tower, Chicago—he takes seven hours to work his way up 110 stories.

LAW, CRIME

Ruth Ellis murders her ex-lover David Blakely (**24**) (1955), shortly after she has had a miscarriage. She is hanged for murder—the last woman to be hanged in Britain.

David Hickock and Perry Smith (**31**) shoot Herbert Clutter (**48**), Bonnie Clutter (**45**), and their children Nancy (**16**) and Kenyon (**15**) (1959). Hickock and Smith had met as roommates in Kansas State Penitentiary. The murders are later the basis of the book, *In Cold Blood* (1965) by Truman Capote (**41**), and the murderers are hanged five years after the crime.

SPORTS

Lord Derby: the first Derby horse race (1780). The horses must be **3**.

Babe Ruth (baseball, 1923): opening of Yankee Stadium, sometimes known as the "House that Ruth Built" (owing to the huge crowds that he attracts). His career in the major leagues is between **19** and **40***, and he lives until **53**. Babe Ruth is also something of a sexual athlete; even during his most successful period he arrives every morning at the stadium in a state of exhaustion, from time spent in seduction. His manager once queried the wisdom of this: "You mean you spend from eight in the evening until four-thirty in the morning working to have pleasure for only two minutes?"

Jack Dempsey (b. 1895) is knocked out of the ring in a fight, but gets back in again, and goes on to win. He is world heavyweight champion between **24** and **31**. He then loses his title to Gene Tunney (**29**). In a second match, Dempsey knocks out Tunney for about 14 seconds, but loses the bout. However, Dempsey is able to retire with gigantic winnings. Gene Tunney retires at **30**, marries a steel heiress, and becomes the favorite boxer of the intellectuals.

Harold Larwood (cricket, 1932–33)—the "body-line" tour of Australia.

29

HEALTH

William Farr: article "Vital Statistics" (London, 1837). This is the beginning of his contribution to the new subject of medical statistics. He uses the newly available census data to make causal models of disease patterns. At **31**, he is appointed first-ever compiler of abstracts in the General Register Office. Farr is self-taught—there would have been no one to teach him—and he becomes the essential link between the emerging wealth of demographic data and the increasing interest in the public health of large cities of the nineteenth century. At **44**, he proves to the general public that there is a link between cholera and polluted water supply. Farr goes on working until **72**, and dies at **75**.

Frederick Banting: discovery of insulin (1921), in association with Charles Best (**22**).

The median age of the U.S.A. (1977) is **29.4**.

HISTORY—WORLD

Adolf Hitler, at the end of World War I (1918): he has reached only the rank of corporal, but his bravery has been recognized by an impressive number of medals. He now becomes part of the mass of unemployed; he makes his first speech at **30**, and becomes president of the minuscule National Socialist party at **32**. His Munich Beer Hall putsch at **34** is a failure, and he spends nine months in prison, where he starts *Mein Kampf.* On his release, his Nazi party fails to expand, until the economic chaos following the 1929 crash, when Hitler is **40***.

HISTORY—U.S.A.

Lyndon Johnson: Congressman (1937, Apr. 10). He becomes Senator at **40**; Vice-President at **52**; and President at **55**. (cf. **59***)

John F. Kennedy: Congressman (1947). (cf. **35***)

HISTORY—U.K.

The Duke of Clarence is drowned in a butt of malmsey wine (1477, Feb. 18) at the Tower of London—by order of his elder brother, King Edward IV (**34**).

Charles II—becomes King (May 1660), at the Restoration. He had been **18** at the execution of his father, King Charles I (**48**).

RELIGION, PHILOSOPHY

Prince Siddhartha, later the Buddha, leaves his wife and newborn son, to become a penniless wanderer. (cf. **35***)

St. Francis of Assisi: *Friars Minor* (1210)—the beginning of the Franciscans.

Wittgenstein: *Tractatus Logico-Philosophicus* (1918). (cf. **47***)

SOCIAL SCIENCE, EDUCATION

Karl Marx and Friedrich Engels (**27**): the Communist Manifesto (Feb. 1848). The party is one of many radical groups operating at this time. Marx establishes his ascendancy within the party by his energy, brilliance, and all-encompassing theories. At **31**, Marx is forced to go into exile, and settles in London. This is his British Museum period, in which he does his research in the reading room there. From **33–44**, he is European correspondent for the New York *Tribune. Grundrisse* is written at **39**. All during this time, Marx and his family are poor, sick, quarrelsome, and having to live in cramped conditions. Eventually he is rescued by payments from Engels. The first volume of *Capital* is published at **49***.

SCIENCE, TECHNOLOGY

James Watt: his sudden insight for the design of the steam engine (1765). In one to two days, he produces almost all the basic principles of the future power source. Previously he has had neither a university education nor even an apprenticeship. At **28**, he had been given the task of repairing a precursor of the steam engine, and its defects in design had been brought to his notice. There now follow ten years before an engine is commercially available. This time lag is due to his lack of money, and to the difficulty of producing adequate quality metal products with the existing technology. At **39**, Watt establishes a partnership with the manufacturer Matthew Boulton **(47)**, and from then on the steam engine gradually helps to create the Industrial Revolution. Watt and Boulton form a classic partnership in the history of technology—their talents provide a useful balance to each other, since Watt is science oriented and Boulton is strong on marketing and on production (cf. **52***). Later, George Stephenson **(44)** opens the first passenger-carrying railway, in 1825, and the famous steam locomotive "Rocket" is constructed at **48**.

Charles Babbage: his first attempt to invent a calculating machine (1822); he dies at **77** with this pioneering work in computers still unfinished.

Alexander Graham Bell: patent on the telephone (1876). The first message ever sent by telephone is "Mr. Watson **(22)**, come here. I **(29)** want you."

Ernest Lawrence: cyclotron (1930).

MONEY, WORK

Eli Whitney: patent for the cotton gin (1794), which mechanically separates cotton seeds from the fiber. Owing to copying of his design, and to difficulties with patent law, he fails to make a fortune out of this. But life improves at **33***.

Bruce Barton: BBDO (1919)—foundation of Batten, Barton, Durstine, and Osborn, the advertising agency.

Robert S. McNamara: one of the "Whiz Kids" (1946). After World War II, the top ten experts in military management form themselves into a team and offer their services as a package to Henry Ford II **(28)**. The latter is eager to bring new control techniques into the then chaotic Ford Motor Company. The ten ex-officers **(26–34)** are lead by C. B. "Tex" Thornton **(32)** and they make an immediate impact on the company. Their searching approach causes them to be known as the Quiz Kids which is later softened to Whiz Kids. McNamara goes on to become president of the company at **44**. At **45**, he becomes U.S. Secretary of Defense, and at **52** he is made president of the World Bank.

ARCHITECTURE

Robert Adam surveys the Emperor Diocletian's palace at Split (1757), taking only five weeks to do so—this is the starting point for his own distinctive style.

Alfred Waterhouse: wins competition for the huge Manchester Assizes (1859), with a design in Venetian Gothic.

 Giuseppe Sacconi: Victor Emmanuel II monument, Rome (1884)—won in competition, but not fully complete at his death (**50**).

Peter (**31**) and Alison (**26**) Smithson win competition for Hunstanton School, England (1954)—start of the "New Brutalism."

ART

Lawrence Alma-Tadema develops his lifelong style around now (1865)—sunny classical buildings of marble, filled with luscious figures, draped and undraped. (cf. **76***)

MUSIC—CLASSICAL

Richard Wagner: first performances of *Rienzi* (1842), and of *The Flying Dutchman;* and of *Tannhäuser* at **32**. In his **20**s, Wagner has been musical manager of various small opera houses. The score of *Rienzi* is finished in debtors' prison, as Wagner is already in debt through extravagance—a condition that lasts for the rest of his life. (cf. **37***)

Mozart: Piano Concerto in C Major, K. 467 (1785)—later used in the film *Elvira Madigan.*

LITERATURE

". . . fame is the spur . . ."—John Milton (1637). (cf. **56***)

Isaac D'Israeli: *On Some Characteristics of a Youth of Genius* (1795).

Percy Bysshe Shelley: death (July 1822). He drowns in a sailing accident in the Mediterranean. His body is found with a volume of Keats (d. **26**, 1821) in one pocket, and of Sophocles (d. **90**, 406 B.C.) in the other. The body is burned on an Italian beach, with Lord Byron (**34**) as one of the witnesses. The ashes are buried in Rome, close to the burial place of Keats himself. Shelley's last poem is "The Triumph of Life"; he had written "Ode to the West Wind" at **27**. At his death, hardly any of his poems are publicly known, as people have been offended by his scandalous lifestyle. Shelley's first wife has already drowned herself; his sister-in-law has also drowned herself. At **20**, Shelley meets Mary Godwin (**15**) and one and a half years later they elope. Mary writes *Frankenstein* when she is **20**. Her father, William Godwin, lives until **80**; Shelley's father lives until **91**.

Emily Brontë publishes *Wuthering Heights* (1847), but dies a year later. Anne Brontë dies at **29**, having published novels at **27** and **29**. Charlotte Brontë publishes *Jane Eyre* at **31**, but dies at **39**, a few months after her first marriage. Their brother, Branwell Brontë, dies at **31**. Their father, Patrick, survives them all, dying at **85**.

James Elroy Flecker: *The Golden Journey to Samarkand* (1913); but he dies at **30**, from tuberculosis.

Agatha Christie: her first book, *The Mysterious Affair at Styles*

(1920). She had learned about poisons during work in a hospital dispensary. The book is still in print at the time of her death (**84**).

Dorothy Parker slashes her wrists, but survives (1923). At **32**, her first book of poems "Enough Rope" makes her rich and famous; and she does another volume at **34**. She had started writing by doing captions for *Vogue* at **23**. (cf. **70***)

F. Scott Fitzgerald: *The Great Gatsby* (1925). (cf. **44***)

Jack Kerouac writes *On the Road* in three weeks (1951). It is published six years later, and Kerouac dies at **47**.

FILMS

Louis B. Mayer collaborates (1924) with Samuel Goldwyn (**42**) to form MGM, or, as it should be known, Metro-Goldwyn-Mayer (**29**). Mayer becomes studio head, a position he holds until he is **56**.

W. H. Auden: script for *Night Mail* (1936), the film on the overnight mail train between London and Scotland; the music is by Benjamin Britten (**23**).

Douglas Fairbanks, Jr.: *The Prisoner of Zenda* (1937).

Errol Flynn: *The Adventures of Robin Hood* (1938).

Alan Ladd: *This Gun for Hire* (1942)—makes him a star.

Trevor Howard: *Brief Encounter* (1945), with Celia Johnson (**37**).

Marlon Brando: *The Wild One* (1953).

Doris Day: *Calamity Jane* (1953).

Marilyn Monroe: *The Seven-Year Itch* (1955).

Clint Eastwood is in "Rawhide," on TV (1959), for the next seven years.

Delphine Seyrig: *Last Year in Marienbad* (1961).

François Truffaut: *Jules et Jim* (1961), starring Jeanne Moreau (**33**) and Oskar Werner (**39**). In the film, Jim is **29**, and Catherine, cause of all the trouble, is **32**.

Elizabeth Taylor: *Butterfield 8* (1961); Oscar.

Roman Polanski: *Knife in the Water* (1962)—his first feature.

Claude Lelouch: *A Man and a Woman* (1966); with music by Francis Lai (**33**).

Mia Farrow asks the reference book *International Film and Television Year Book* to delete her age from subsequent editions (1977).

Meryl Streep: *Kramer vs. Kramer* (1979).

MUSIC—NON-CLASSICAL

Sigmund Romberg: *The Desert Song* (1926).

Sammy Davis, Jr., loses an eye in a road accident (1954); at **31** he converts to the Jewish faith, and from then on he sometimes describes himself as "a one-eyed Negro Jew."

Bill Haley: "Rock Around the Clock" (1954). When this is used as the background for a film at **30**, audiences destroy the theaters in their enthusiasm. "See You Later, Alligator" is at **31**, as is "Rock-a-Beatin' Boogie." Later, after a long period of obscurity, Haley enjoys a rediscovery in his early **50**s, and continues to perform these pioneer rock numbers until his death at **55**.

Glen Campbell: "By the Time I Get to Phoenix" (1967), written by Jim Webb (**21**).

Carole King: "Tapestry" (1971).

Barry Manilow: "Mandy" (1974), and "Trying to Get the Feeling" at **31**. By appealing across age barriers, he becomes the most successful solo artist in the world.

Linda Ronstadt: best female vocalist (1975); and again at **30** and **31**.

TV, ETC.

Sid Caesar and Imogen Coca (**43**): "Your Show of Shows" (1951). Scriptwriters include Mel Brooks (**24**) and Larry Gelbart (**23**) who later is the producer of "M* A* S* H" at **44** and "Marriage" at **52**. Later, Caesar at **35** employs such writers as Woody Allen (**22**) and Neil Simon (**30**).

LOVE, LIFE

Cheryl Tiegs: best-selling poster of herself (1977).

Erno Rubik: Rubik's Cube (1974).

The peak years for moving home are **20–29**; after **29**, your chances of moving home decrease as you get older (U.S.A., 1977).

PRESS

Henry Mayhew, Mark Lemon (**32**), and others: *Punch* magazine (London, 1841).

Stewart Brand and others: *Whole Earth Catalogue* (1968–71).

Bob Woodward and Carl Bernstein (**28**): reports on the break-in at Watergate of the Democratic party headquarters (1972). Their chief at the Washington *Post* is Benjamin C. Bradlee (**51**). At **31** and **30**, they publish their story of the reporting—*All the President's Men;* at **33** and **32**, they publish *The Final Days,* another best-seller. Carl Bernstein leaves the *Post* at **34**, and Bob Woodward continues to be a reporter there.

EXPLORATION

John Alcock (**26**) and A. W. Brown (**32**): first nonstop flight across the Atlantic (1919). Their Rolls-Royce engine is by Henry Royce (**56**).

Naomi James breaks the record for sailing solo around the world—she does it in 272 days (1978).

Jesse James: raid on the First National Bank, Northfield, Minnesota (1876). He and his gang kill several people, and lose three of their own members. This raid is an attempt at a once-and-for-all robbery, to provide enough money to last the rest of their lives. James's gang is well known and popular; they rob small-town banks and cross-country trains. Jesse James is killed in his own home at **35**, by a young man who is in contact with the forces of law and order.

SPORTS

John B. Kelly (rowing, 1920): Olympic golds in both the single and the double sculls. At **33**, he retains the gold in the doubles. His daughter Grace is born when he is **38**, and she becomes a princess on her marriage, in Monaco, when he is **65**.

Eddy Merckx (cycling, 1974) wins the Tour de France, for the 5th and last time. At **30**, he comes second, and he is sixth at **32**. In a typical recent Tour de France (1977), the winner is Bernard Thevenet (**29**), and the next five are **22–32**.

Jean-Marc Boivin: descent in a hang-glider from the peak of the highest mountain in the Americas—23,000-foot Aconcagua, in the Andes. He glides down 10,000 feet in twenty minutes.

Nelson Piquet: world motor racing champion (1981).

30

HEALTH

Florence Nightingale in 1850: she writes in her diary: "Today I am **30**—the age Christ began his mission. Now no more childish things. No more love. No more marriage. Now Lord let me think only of Thy Will, what thou willest me to do. Oh Lord, Thy Will, Thy Will." At **29**, she had declined a second proposal of marriage, since she thought that marriage would conflict with her career—even though she did not then have any career. She now wants to enter the hospital world, but family and social pressures have prevented her from taking much action. She gets up before dawn to study public health; at breakfast she resumes the normal life of an upper-class woman. It is not until **31** that she has hospital training. At **33**, she is appointed head of a small institution for the care of sick gentlewomen. At **34***, she suddenly becomes a major figure in history, with her nursing at the Barrack Hospital, Scutari, in the Crimean War.

H. L. Marriott (**35**) and Alan Kekwick (**26**): first blood transfusion by continuous drip (1935).

Life expectancy in the U.S.A. (1976) is now until **71.8** for males, and until **78.2** for females. At the present time, you are now in the largest growing age group in the U.S.A. Comparing 1977 with 1970, the **25–34** people have increased 32 percent and the **65+** have increased 18 percent.

For U.S. males **25–44**, the causes of death are: (1) auto accidents; (2) heart diseases; (3) cancers; (4) homicide; (5) suicide; (6) cirrhosis of the liver. For black males, homicide is the first cause of death, as it is for all males in New York City, in this age group.

Out of total deaths at all ages, only 1.1 percent (male) occur in the ages **25–34**, and 0.7 percent (female) (England and Wales, 1977). You can now expect to live until **77.5** (female) and until **71.8** (male).

The causes of death for males **25–34** (England and Wales, 1977) are: (1) motor vehicle accidents; (2) suicide and self-inflicted injuries; (3) miscellaneous "other" cancers; (4) other accidents; (5) ischemic heart disease. The causes of female death are (1) miscellaneous "other" cancers outside the main sites; (2) suicide and self-inflicted injuries; (3) breast cancer; (4) motor vehicle accidents; (5) other forms of violence; (6) cerebrovascular disease.

Countries with a very low life expectancy include Chad, **29** male and **35** female; Togo, **31** and **38**; Upper Volta, **32** and **31**; Bangladesh, **35** for both sexes. In the U.S.A., 1900–02, the life expectancy at birth of the black population was until **32.5** (male) and until **35** (female). By 1976, the comparable figures were **64.1** and **72.6**

It is not too early to check yourself against risk indicators of future ill health. Typically you are scored against such factors as weight, inheritance, smoking, diet, exercise, and blood pressure, so that you can work out your probable life expectancy. Now is the time to ensure that you are settling into a healthful lifestyle.

You are most vulnerable to multiple sclerosis when in your early **30**s. The disease is unlikely to affect anyone before **17**, and after the early **30**s your chances of being affected will diminish continuously. MS strikes three women for every two men. The farther you live from the equator, the more likely you are to be affected. At any one time, 25–50 people per 100,000 population will be afflicted by it.

Some average life spans for animals include: African elephant, **24**; arctic whale, **24–37**; dolphin, **25–30**; condor, **26**; American vulture, **32**; goldfish, **25**; king penguin, **26**; trumpeter swan, **29**; Canada goose, **32**; domestic pigeon, **35**; Bengal tiger, **26**; brown lemur, **31**; and the lobster until **33**. Tree growth: the Norway spruce, or Christmas tree, is now 41–58 feet high; the Douglas fir, 60–80 feet; and the Sitka spruce, 74 feet high.

HISTORY—WORLD

Nero: suicide (68 A.D.), following the failures of his policies as Roman Emperor. He had held office since **16**; the Great Fire of Rome had occurred when he was **26**. He now puts a knife to his throat, and has a secretary push it. His last words are: "What a great artist dies!"

Napoleon arrives back in Paris (1799) after four years of terrifyingly successful campaigning abroad. He had first made his name at **24***. After ten years of the French Revolution, there is still no clear permanent power structure. Napoleon has himself made First Consul, and effective dictator. He now consolidates the revolution by introducing a wide range of administrative reforms, transferring power to the new professional classes. At **35**, he crowns himself Emperor, in the presence of Pope Pius VII (**64**). By **38**, his military skill gives him control of virtually all mainland Western Europe. At **42***, he overreaches himself by marching on Moscow.

Yassir Arafat: beginning of his influence with the Palestine Liberation Organization (1959). Arafat was born in Jerusalem, and grew up there and in Gaza.

HISTORY—U.S.A.

Nat Turner leads the bloodiest slave rebellion of the pre-Civil War period (1831, Aug. 21); but he is caught, and executed at **31**.

Paul W. Tibbets: pilot of the B-29 bomber which drops the atomic bomb on Hiroshima (1945, Aug. 6).

HISTORY—U.K.

Elizabeth I is publicly asked by Parliament to get married (1564).

Disraeli in 1835 tells Lord Melbourne (**55**) that he, Disraeli, will one day be Prime Minister. (cf. **34***)

RELIGION, PHILOSOPHY

Jesus begins preaching; he spends 40 days in a far-off wilderness, and is tempted by the idea of wordly fame, power, and riches. Afterward, he is baptized by John the Baptist; the Holy Ghost is represented by a dove in the sky. (cf. **32***)

Dogen Zenji (founder of Soto Zen) retires to a small temple in Japan, and begins his writings on Zen (1230). at **12**, he had entered the Buddhist priesthood; at **23**, he left his homeland, Japan, to study in China.

David Hume writes: "Beauty in things exists in the mind which contemplates them" (1741).

 Schopenhauer: *The World as Will and Idea* (1818)—his central book.

G. E. Moore: *Pincipia ethica* (1903). This is seen as his best work; it establishes him as a distinguished philosopher. He lives until **85**, always seen as a great philosopher, but without a large development from his position at **30**. Moore is later believed to have lost his virginity at **43**, on the occasion of his marriage.

It is better to write a short good book later than a bad long book earlier.—advice to a Ph.D. student by the philosopher Gilbert Ryle (1900–76).

Eligibility: you are now old enough to become a bishop of the Anglican Church. The minimum age for a priest is usually **24**.

"Memento mori" was the idea that you must not forget that one day you will die. In the excitement and carelessness of youth, you are liable to forget death. "The Three Dead People" were medieval pictures of three persons in the prime of their life—who, while happily riding through the forest, suddenly come upon three skeletons. They are seeing themselves in the future. Another example of memento mori: the rosary beads belonging to Louis XIV were each carved in the shape of a skull. And, in the painting "The Ambassadors," by Holbein, one of the ambassadors (**29**) is pictured in front of a skull.

SOCIAL SCIENCE, EDUCATION

John Harvard: death (1638). In his will he leaves £779 and 400 books to a small local college (**2**) which has recently been established in Cambridge, Massachusetts. In honor of his gift, the college is renamed Harvard. Also, Yale University receives its name in 1718, after a substantial gift by Elihu Yale (**69**) who made his fortune in India and who lives until **72**. Also, Stanford University is set up in 1885, by Leland Stanford (**61**), the railroad pioneer, to commemorate his only child who died the previous year at **15**. And, the Smithsonian Institution is set up after a bequest by James Smithson (d. **64**, in 1829).

Alexis de Tocqueville: *Democracy in America* (1835). The first part of this work immediately establishes him as a prominent social scientist. The last part is published at **35**. He goes on to become a politician in France. At **44**, he is briefly his country's foreign minister, but never again reaches such heights. He restores his reputation with *L'Ancien Régime* at **51**, and dies at **53**.

Sigmund Freud is married (1886), to Martha Bernays (**25**). They have been engaged for four and a half years; Freud has had to repress his intense desire for her, as his career and financial problems have made marriage impossible. Freud is an M.D. with a small reputation for his experiments on the nervous system. He is set on joining the intellectual elite, the "upper ten thousand," but it is not until **36** that he begins analysis of a patient. (cf. **39***)

Karl Mannheim: *On the Interpretations of "Weltanschauung"* (1923). And, *The Problem of a Sociology of Knowledge* at **32**; *Ideology and Utopia* at **36**.

Wilhelm Reich: *The Discovery of the Orgone* (1927)—on the function of orgasm for a balanced life. Reich never wins mass support, but he does develop a cult. At **60**, he dies in jail, having been imprisoned as a charlatan.

Robert Hutchins: president of the University of Chicago (1929)—beginning of his "Chicago Plan" of education, centered around the "great books."

SCIENCE, TECHNOLOGY

Robert Hooke: *Micrographia* (1665). This includes the first use of the word "cell" in biology.

Heinrich Lenz: Lenz's Law (1834).

Thomas Alva Edison: invention of the phonograph (1877). The first recording is "Mary Had a Little Lamb." Edison's greatest period of invention is roughly **27–39**. He now goes on to pioneer mass electric lighting in cities. At **39**, he marries his second wife (**20**), and he becomes less obsessive about his work, and also less successful. He does, however, go on to inventions in cinematography, but he loses $2 million in a failed process to extract iron ore. Edison lives until **84**.

C. A. Parsons: first steam turbine (1884).

Herman Hollerith: invention of the punched card for analysis of large quantities of data (1890). At **36**, he organizes the Tabulating Machine Company which later becomes IBM.

Hans Geiger: the Geiger counter (1913).

MONEY, WORK

Jean Paul Getty marries Jeanette Demont (**18**)—his first (of five) marriages. (1922). Divorced after one and a half years.

Alexei Stakhanov digs out 102 tons of coal in one night (1935), thus becoming the first "Stakhanovite" of Russia.

John Stephens owns 10 shops on Carnaby Street, London (1966).

Larry R. Williams: having made $1 million in commodity speculation, he retires; but later says that he comes back to work after only six days; writes book *How I Made a Million Dollars.*

RENAISSANCE

T. E. Lawrence: entry into Damascus, having advanced from the Red Sea, during World War I (1918). He has been military adviser to a brilliant guerilla campaign by Arab forces against the Turkish empire. At **30**, Lawrence is now unknown, but at **31** a series of lectures by Lowell Thomas (**27**) bring him an incredible fame, and he becomes the legendary "Lawrence of Arabia." Lawrence is both a scholar and a man of action. The Arabian campaign is the culmination of many aspects of his nature—his asceticism, his bravery, his caring for the Arabs, his study of military history, and also his outsider status, as a person born illegitimately. In his **20**s, Lawrence has done archeological work in Arabia, and this had given him his knowledge of the desert. At **31** and **32**, he works unsuccessfully for Arab independence, to prevent Turkish rule being followed merely by French and British rule; in this he is unsuccessful, and his desert campaign begins to appear as something of a cynical manipulation of the Arabs. At **33**, he completes a wonderful book on the campaign, *The Seven Pillars of Wisdom,* and he writes poetry which is published afterward. Later, Lawrence becomes permanently famous because of his ambiguity about the elite world: having at **30** and **31** become such a magical figure, he enters the military at **34** and chooses to occupy the lowest possible rank. On the one hand, he has strived for elite performance, at the greatest personal cost, and he also embellishes his exploits so that they become even more admirable than they deserve to be; on the other hand, he appears to back away from fame, and he spends ten years working as an anonymous figure in military workshops. T. E. Lawrence is killed in a motorcycle accident at **46**, at a time when he is paralyzed with doubt concerning his modest/striving and austere/voluptuous nature.

ARCHITECTURE

Francesco de Sanctis: the Spanish Steps, Rome (1723–25).

ART

David Hockney: "A Bigger Splash" (1967); "Mr. and Mrs. Clark & Percy" (London) at **33**; and "My Parents and Myself" at **38**. At **38**, he also designs the sets for Stravinsky's (**69**) opera *The Rake's Progress.*

MUSIC—CLASSICAL

Mozart: *The Marriage of Figaro* (1786). This is so good that the orchestra applauds him in the middle of the first rehearsal. At **29**, he had written six string quartets dedicated to Haydn (**53**), who believes him to be the greatest of composers, and tells him so. (cf. **32***)

Robert Schumann marries (1840, Sept. 12), and composes almost half of his 250 songs in this one year. He and Clara (**20**) are composers as well as musicians. At **29**, he had written "Träumerei" (Dreaming) in *Scenes from Childhood*. But he goes permanently mad at **43***.

Henry Howard, Earl of Surrey, one of the two people who had brought the sonnet to England, is executed (1547), for incorporating the king's symbols into his own coat of arms.

Honoré de Balzac publishes *Les Chouans* (1829), a historical novel, which is his first success. He immediately produces two more successes. He now settles into the lifestyle which he maintains for the rest of his life: writing all night, being highly productive, and constantly engaged in unsuccessful affairs and money-making schemes. Though these schemes usually fail, they bring him the knowledge of French life which he uses in *La Comédie humaine* **(33–50)**.

Hans Christian Andersen: first volume of fairy tales (1835).

Guy de Maupassant: *Boule de Suif* (1880).

H. Rider Haggard: *King Solomon's Mines* (1886); and *She* at **31**.

Jerome K. Jerome: *Three Men in a Boat* (1889).

P. G. Wodehouse begins writing about Jeeves (1911).

James Joyce leaves Ireland (Sept. 1912), and never returns.

e e cummings: *Tulips and Chimneys* (1924). This is his first book of poems; he goes on to have a lifelong career in poetry.

W. H. Auden is a stretcher bearer in the Spanish Civil War (1937).

Doris Lessing: *The Grass Is Singing* (1950)—her first book.

Joseph Heller (1953) begins work on his novel *Catch-22.* He is currently working at *Time* and later at *McCall's* magazine. He writes one hour per day, and the book is published at **38**. He later says: "You see, when I was writing *Catch-22,* I had dreams of glory, and *every one* of them has come true."

Sylvia Plath: *The Bell Jar* (1963). She commits suicide this year.

PLAYS

Pierre Corneille: *Le Cid* (1636).

August Strindberg, in 1879: his novel *The Red Room* establishes him as a prominent writer. Much of his **20**s has been spent rewriting an unsuccessful historical play. With this novel about contemporary Stockholm, he hits on a style that expresses his bitterness and his dislike for the culture of the times. At **28**, he had married Siri von Essen **(27)**; at **35**, his short stories, *Married,* arouse disgust, and he has to face court proceedings. The conflicts in his life find expression in his naturalistic plays, *The Father* at **38**, and *Miss Julie,* a sensation, at **39**. Also at **39** he is a pioneer, for his generation, in confessional writing, with his autobiography, *The Son of a Servant.* Strindberg exemplifies the popular idea of the creative person as maniac; much of the time he is in fact mad. But he also keeps writing throughout his life, and later creates other plays of permanent value. (cf. **52***)

A man has more character in his face at **30** than at **20**—he has suffered longer.—Mae West.

Any woman who tries to change a man, particularly after he's reached his **30**s, is a fool. The only thing she can do is make him worse. His views, his habits, his ideas, everything you know about him are part of him. You can either love him as he is, or you don't love him at all.—Lauren Bacall.

Sergei Eisenstein: after the success of *The Battleship Potemkin* (**27**), he travels in Europe, U.S.A., and Mexico for the next four years—starts many projects, but never satisfactorily completes any of them.

Theda Bara, silent film star, is released from her contract with the Fox studio (1920), and is never seen in another film.

John Gilbert makes his first talking picture (1929, *His Glorious Night*), and everyone laughs at his squeaky voice. His career is virtually ended, and he dies at **38**, from the effects of drink.

Clark Gable: *A Free Soul* (Mar. 1931)—he smashes Norma Shearer (**27**) in the face, and establishes himself as a "tough" actor. He makes twelve pictures in this one year, including *It Happened One Night.* In this, he doesn't wear an undershirt, and retail sales of them drop by 75 percent, causing a recession in the U.S. undershirt industry.

Greta Garbo: *Anna Karenina* (1936), with Fredric March (**38**), and Basil Rathbone (**43**).

Errol Flynn stars in *The Private Lives of Elizabeth and Essex* (1939)—this is the peak of his popularity.

Charles Bronson has his first acting lessons (Feb. 1950)—at the Pasadena Community Playhouse; gets his first (small) part in a film, *You're in the Navy Now* (1951).

Mario Lanza: *The Great Caruso* (1951)—makes him a celebrity, but he dies of a heart attack at **38**.

Elizabeth Taylor signs to make *Cleopatra* (1962–63), with Richard Burton (**37**); she is paid $10,000 per working day.

Peter Watkins: *The War Game* (1965)—a documentary about Britain after an atomic bomb attack; too horrific (and truthful) to be shown by its sponsors, BBC-TV.

Peter Fonda and Dennis Hopper: *Easy Rider* (1969), with Jack Nicholson (**32**).

Rainer Werner Fassbinder has so far directed sixteen feature films (1976).

In the film *Logan's Run* (1976), a futuristic society decrees that everyone must be killed ceremonially on reaching **30**.

Sylvester Stallone: *Rocky* (1976).

75 percent of U.S. filmgoers are under **30**.

Thomas Arne: "Rule, Britannia" (1740).

George Cory: "I Left My Heart in San Francisco" (1953).

Lionel Bart: "Oliver" (1960).

Judy Collins: "Who Knows Where the Time Goes" (1969). "From Both Sides Now" was at **29**. Her album "Whales and Nightingales" is at **32**.

TV, ETC.

Ken Loach: "Kathy Come Home" (U.K., 1966).

Joanna Lumley: as Purdey, in "The New Avengers" (1976).

LOVE, LIFE

"Never trust anyone over **30**."

Archduke Rudolph: death, at Schloss Mayerling, outside Vienna (1889, Jan. 30), after killing his lover, Baroness Marie Vetsera (**18**) in a suicide pact. Rudolph is Crown Prince of the Austro-Hungarian Empire; he had married at **23**, and has been frustrated in his wish for divorce. His mental balance has been affected by a venereal disease. The archduke and Marie first made love seventeen days before their suicide; in a last letter to her sister, the baroness asks that a gardenia be placed each year at her tomb, on January 13th. Soon after the tragedy, Mayerling is converted into a convent, by Rudolph's father, Emperor Franz Joseph (**49**) who lives until **86**. Marie Vetsera's sister dies at **32**, from a miscarriage; her brother is killed at **43** in World War I; her mother (now **43**) survives until **79**.

Seven percent of U.S. women (1977) aged **30–34** have never married. At **20**, the figure was 63 percent; at **24**, 27 percent; at **28**, 12 percent.

In Europe in the nineteenth century, people married late, by today's standards. For example, in France, 1856, by **30** only 30 percent of males and 47 percent of females were married. By **40**, 74 percent of males and 78 percent of females were married.

PRESS

Horace Greeley: editor, the New York *Tribune* (1841).

George Newnes: *Tit-Bits* magazine (1881). Having produced the dummy, he has no capital left to print the first issue, so he starts a vegetarian restaurant which generates the necessary cash flow. *Tit-Bits* leads to a magazine empire: *The Strand* at **38** onward, featuring Sherlock Holmes; and *Country Life* at **46**. Newnes is made a baronet at **43**.

Ottmar Mergenthaler: first patent for Linotype (1884).

Lord Northcliffe: *Daily Mail* (London, 1896). (cf. **42***)

William F. Buckley: founder-editor, *National Review* (1955).

 Norris and Ross McWhirter: *Guinness Book of Records* (1955).

About some U.S. magazines: *Scientific American* (1845) is started by Rufus Porter (**53**), an inventor; after a year, he sells it to Orson D. Munn (**22**) and Alfred E. Beach (**20**), and they are the managers during its early period of growth. *Harper's* (1850) is started by Fletcher Harper (**44**), and the first editor is Henry J. Raymond (**30**). *Atlantic* (1857) is founded by Francis H. Underwood (**32**) and the first editor is James Russell Lowell (**38**). *Ladies' Home Journal* (1883) is started by Cyrus H. K. Curtis (**31**). *Collier's* (1888) is started by P. F. Collier (**39**). The first editor of the *National Geographic* magazine (1888) is Henry Gannett (**42**). The first editor of the *New Republic* (1914) is Herbert D. Croly (**45**); the editorial board includes Walter Lippman (**25**), and the magazine is subsidized by Willard Straight (**34**) and his wife Dorothy Whitney Straight. John Johnson (**27**) starts *Ebony* magazine in 1945. *Seventeen* is started by Walter Annenberg (**36**).

EXPLORATION

Francisco Coronado: leader of the expedition in which Europeans first see the Grand Canyon (1540).

LAW

Al Capone: the St. Valentine's Day Massacre (1929). Seven members of a rival gang are killed by Capone's gang, at the warehouse of the S-M-C Cartage Company, Chicago. Capone is not charged with this, and now serves one year in jail on another charge. During this time, he runs his organization from a telephone in the office of the prison warden. But at **29**, his income tax had come under special investigation by a group of IRS staff including Eliot Ness (**28**) and others who are all under **30**. At **32**, Capone gets eleven years for tax evasion, shortly before Prohibition ends. He is kept at Alcatraz, which he leaves at **40**, suffering from advanced syphilis which has caused his brain to deteriorate. He dies at **48**.

Dr. Carl Austin Weiss kills Senator Huey Long (**42**) (1935). Weiss, an M.D., had been horrified by fascism, when on a visit to the Europe of Mussolini.

Albert DeSalvo murders Anna Slesers (**55**) (1962), and becomes the Boston Strangler. In 18 months, he kills 11 women; they come in two age groups—**75**, **69**, **68**, **67**, **65**, **58**, **55**; and **23**, **23**, **23**, and **19**. Previously, DeSalvo has had convictions for breaking and entering, and for sex offenses. Throughout his childhood, DeSalvo would get a belting each night from his father, a burglar. DeSalvo now spends the rest of his life in a prison mental hospital.

Danny DeSouza is sent to jail (1976) until **60**, for bringing five kilos of hashish into Turkey. Other people have received similar sentences. A Pakistani in the same Bayram Pasha jail is there for 100 years for drug offenses. In Bangkok, Rita Nightingale (**24**) is sent to prison until **44** for trying to smuggle drugs out of Thailand (1978). In practice, long sentences are often mitigated by revolutions and by amnesties (for example, "I got twelve years in Franco's Spain, but actually did two and a half years, because of amnesties for the new pope, et cetera"). However, jails holding prisoners on lifelong and beyond-life sentences typically use torture, because no other remaining sanction is available against uncooperative prisoners.

Eligibility: now old enough to be a juror in ancient Greece.

Eligibility: in South Africa, you are now too old to be sentenced to a flogging.

The mean age of a woman at a battered wives hostel was **30.66** (London, 1977); the husband was **33.9**. The couple had had a relationship for 8.76 years, and violence started when the wife was about **24**, and the husband **27**.

Crime statistics are often attacked because of the large number of unreported and undetected crimes. So, statistics showing a high proportion of youths as offenders might be suspect. It is interesting to note, therefore, that in the crime having the highest clear-up rate—murder of law enforcement officers—70 percent of the killers are **30** and younger. The police officer victims are **25–30** (32 percent of the total killed); 28 percent are **31–40**, and 29 percent are **41** and over (U.S. [FBI]).

SPORTS

Diana Nyad (1979): first person to swim from the Bahamas to Florida—89 miles in 27½ hours.

Pittsburgh Pirates: winner of the World Series (baseball, 1979). Their average age is **30.4**, ranging from **22** to **38**. The captain and most valuable player is Willie Stargell (**38**), and the manager is Chuck Tanner (**50**).

Anatoli Karpov: world chess champion (1981). He defeats Victor Korchnoi (**50**).

31

HISTORY—WORLD

Atahualpa, king of the Incas: death by strangulation, at the hands of the Spanish invaders (1533).

RELIGION, PHILOSOPHY

Pico della Mirandola: death (Florence, 1494).

Soren A. Kierkegaard: *The Concept of Dread* (1844). (cf. **42***)

Sabine Baring-Gould: "Onward, Christian Soldiers" (1865).

SOCIAL SCIENCE, EDUCATION

Germaine Greer: *The Female Eunuch* (1970).

Ellen Futter: president of Barnard College (New York, 1981).

SCIENCE, TECHNOLOGY

Claus Roemer: the first reasonably accurate calculation of the speed of light (1676).

Heinrich Hertz: discovery of radio waves (1888).

Marie Curie: discovery of radium (1898). For this, she receives the Nobel Prize at **36**. For further discoveries, she receives a second Nobel Prize at **44**.

Louis de Broglie: his contribution to wave theory, in physics (1924). In 1926, Erwin Schrodinger (**39**) writes a key paper on wave mechanics. In 1928, P. A. M. Dirac (**26**) predicts the positron, which is first observed in 1932 by C. D. Anderson (**26**). The neutron is discovered in 1932 by James Chadwick (**40**).

Richard G. Drew: invention of adhesive transparent tape—Scotch tape, or Selotape (1930).

MONEY, WORK

John D. Rockefeller: Standard Oil Co. (Ohio) (1870)—to take over the oil interests which he has built up in the previous seven years. At **42**, Rockefeller and associates control 90 percent of the entire U.S. oil industry. (cf. **43***)

Herbert Dow: the Dow Chemical Company (1897).

Elizabeth Arden opens her first beauty shop on Fifth Avenue, New York (1910). This is the beginning of her cosmetics empire. She changes her name from the original Florence Nightingale Graham, partly influenced by the death in this year of the original Florence Nightingale (**90***). On the day before the shop opens, she mails a letter to herself: "Dear Elizabeth Arden, good luck (signed) Florence Nightingale Graham."

W. O. Bentley: the first Bentley car (Sept. 1919)—3 litre, Ex-1. Up to this time, he has been a London distributor for French sports cars. At **36**, one of his cars wins the second-ever Le Mans 24-hour race.

Conrad Hilton buys his first hotel, for $5,000 (Texas, 1919). He builds up a small chain, but suffers heavily during the Depression. During World War II (**53–57**), he is able to buy hotels when no one else wants them. The great expansion of his empire occurs in his **60**s, with the postwar growth in travel. At **79**, he sells the international side of the Hilton business, and he retires from day-to-day management of his U.S. chain at **80**, at a time when his corporation runs 185 hotels. Conrad Hilton has straightforward rules for success. Two of them are: (1) "Dig for gold"; and (2) "Be big. Think big. Act big. Dream big."

Ralph Nader publishes *Unsafe at Any Speed* (1965). At **35**, his "Nader's Raiders" force wholesale consumer changes. At **36**, he receives considerable damages from General Motors, for invasion of privacy, due to their attempt to obtain damaging information about his private life.

Lynn Salvage is the youngest president of a U.S. bank (First Women's Bank, in New York City, 1977).

RENAISSANCE

Prince Albert: the Great Exhibition (1851).

ARCHITECTURE

John Nash goes bankrupt (1783), having been an architect in private practice for three years. (cf. **46***)

George Basevi: Belgrave Square, London (1825).

Frank Lloyd Wright, in 1900: his "Prairie Houses" are typically built in his **30**s. Wright starts young (cf. – **1***) in architecture, and is quickly seen as a highly creative force. The Larkin Office Building, Buffalo, New York, is at **35** and it is the most original office building of its time. The Robie House, Chicago is at **39**. At **40**, he abandons his wife (**37**) and children, and goes off to Europe with a neighbor's wife. In doing this, he is mimicking an incident in his own childhood when his father had disappeared forever. At **46**, Wright designs the Imperial Hotel, Tokyo, and at **54** he gets a telegram saying that the hotel has survived a major earthquake "thanks to your genius." At **55**, his mother (**83**) dies, as does his father figure, Louis Sullivan (**68**). His home/office at Taliesin East, Wisconsin, is destroyed by fire for the second time, and at **56** he starts on the rebuilding. At **60** he inaugurates the Taliesin Fellowship—in future, drawing-office staff have to pay him for the privilege of being part of his office, thus reversing the more conventional arrangement. Wright has a highly productive old age, starting at **66***.

ART

Edouard Manet: "Déjeuner sur l'herbe" (1863). (cf. **49***)

Claude Monet exhibits his painting "Impression: Sunrise" (1874), which leads to the name Impressionism. Renoir (**33**) is in the same exhibition. At this time, Pissarro is **44**, Manet is **42**, Degas **40**, Cézanne **35**, Morisot **33**, and Mary Cassatt is **29**. Also, Bonnard is **7**, and Matisse is **5**. The last Impressionist exhibition is held 12 years later.

Man Ray: the iron/flatiron with tacks sticking out of its smooth surface (1921).

Bridget Riley: first solo show, of Op Art (1963).

MUSIC—CLASSICAL

Schubert dies (1828, Nov. 19) from typhoid. In his last year, he has been very productive, as usual—including the last series of the song cycle *Die Winterreise* (Winter Journey), and his Ninth Symphony, the *Unfinished;* his Eighth was written at **25**. Schubert has always been poor and destitute, not managing to gain anything from his large number of compositions. At **31**, he is a torchbearer at the funeral of Beethoven **(56)**, and, a few months later, he is buried beside him.

Richard Strauss: *Till Eulenspiegels* (Sept. 1895), and at **32**, *Also Sprach Zarathustra,* later the theme music for the film *2001.* Strauss is said to have started composing at **6**; he is a conductor in his early **20**s, and composes from now till his late **70**s. (cf. **45***)

Jean Sibelius is given a pension for life (1897) by the Finnish government, so that he can be, in effect, the Finnish national composer. He writes *Finlandia* at **33** and had written the *Karelia* Suite at **27**. He is fairly prolific (and also distinguished) until around **60**, and dies at **91**.

LITERATURE

"No, life is not over at thirty-one," says Prince Andrei Bolkonsky, a widower of **31**. Later this year, he sees Natasha Rostov **(17)**, at her first ball. Andrei is intrigued by her. Two days later, he hears her sing, and he almost cries in public; her voice reminds him of the powerful, lovely feelings within him, and the drab, efficient exterior that he presents to the world. Even she exhibits some of this contrast. Soon afterward, Andrei and Natasha are awed to find that they are falling in love.—*War and Peace* (cf. **35***)

Antony Hope: *The Prisoner of Zenda* (1894).

Elinor Glynn: *Three Weeks* (1907)—she becomes a total success.

Frank Richards creates Greyfriars School, Billy Bunter, and company (1908).

Henry Williamson: *Tarka the Otter* (1927).

E. M. Forster: *Howard's End* (1910); this is his fourth novel, and he publishes his fifth and last at **45**—*A Passage to India.*

Erich Remarque: *All Quiet on the Western Front* (1929).

William Faulkner: *Sartoris,* and also *The Sound and the Fury* (1929). He publishes three novels in the next three years.

Erica Jong: *Fear of Flying* (1973). This sells 5.5 million copies. She has previously made a reputation as a poet.

Ivan Turgenev: *A Month in the Country* (1850). This is the first "psychological" Russian play and it makes no impact when first performed; it is not an acclaimed success until the end of Turgenev's life. He lives until **64**. At **61**, he sees a revival of his great play, and he has his last love affair—with the actress (**26**) who plays the part of Vera (**17**). But, as in the play, the affair never catches fire.

Ferenc Molnar: *Liliom* (1909); and *The Guardsman* at **32**.

Vaslav Nijinksy: end of his career as a dancer (1919). Since **21**, he has established himself as the leading male dancer of his time. He is now pronounced to be incurably insane, and he lives as a recluse until his death at **72**. Parts of his famous diary are published at **49**. His wife Romola (now **27**) lives until **86**.

David Hare: *Plenty* (1978).

FILMS

Rudolph Valentino dies from an ulcer (1926), and $1\frac{1}{4}$ million women try to attend his funeral.

AGE 31 YRS

James Cagney: *Public Enemy* (1931). Inspired by the marital problems of the director William Wellman (**35**), Cagney pushes a grapefruit in the face of actress Mae Clarke (**21**). This is the film that makes Cagney a star. He goes on to become the most famous film crook of all time, in *G-Men* at **31**; *Angels with Dirty Faces* at **34**; *Each Dawn I Die* at **35**; and later films such as *Love Me or Leave Me* at **51**. Before his screen breakthrough, Cagney has been a singer and dancer. This side of him appears in another great success, *Yankee Doodle Dandy* at **38**.

Greta Garbo: *Camille* (1936), with Robert Taylor (**25**), directed by George Cukor (**37**), and produced by Irving Thalberg (**37**). Garbo plays the part of Marguerite Gautier, who had originally died from consumption at **23**.

James Stewart: *Mr. Smith Goes to Washington;* and *Destry Rides Again* (1939). At **32**, *The Philadelphia Story.*

Katharine Hepburn: *The Philadelphia Story* (1940).

Dustin Hoffman gets $17,000 for his first starring role (*The Graduate,* 1968); but gets $250,000 for his next performance, in *Midnight Cowboy,* at **32**.

Natalie Wood: *Bob and Ted and Carol and Alice* (1969); she is given a percentage, as the film is not expected to do very well. But it becomes a minor cult picture, and she is said to collect $2 million.

Oliver Reed: *Women in Love* (1969)—has naked wrestling match with Alan Bates (**39**).

Peter Bogdanovich: *The Last Picture Show* (1971).

Sissy Spacek: *Coal Miner's Daughter* (1980). She wins an Oscar.

Bruce Springsteen: "The River" (1980).

TV, ETC.

Jack Webb: "Dragnet" (1951). The last episode is at **49**, when he goes on to become a busy TV producer.

Nigel Kneale: script of "The Quatermass Experiment" (U.K., 1953). The storyline is that if you are contaminated by a certain organism from outer space, then you gradually turn into a blob. Kneale makes a career out of exploiting this horrific idea, with Quatermass films at **33**, **35**, and **45**, and more Quatermass on TV at **56**. The terrifying theme music is by Gustav Holst (**40**, in 1914).

LOVE, LIFE

Alma Maria Schindler: widowed (1911) by the death of her husband, the composer Gustav Mahler (**50**). She had married him at **22**, and had been at the center of Viennese life, at a time when the world's best artists and writers seemed to be living there. Now at **31** she falls in love with the painter Oskar Kokoschka (**28**) and they live together for the next three years. At **35** she meets the architect and polymath, Walter Gropius (**32**); she goes to a station to say good-bye to him, but there, "overwhelmed by his ardor, Gropius simply pulled me up into the moving train." They soon marry. Almost at once, she falls in love with the playwright Franz Werfel (**26**), and they begin a relationship; at **49**, she marries him. At **55**, her daughter (**19**) by Gropius, dies from infantile paralysis, and Alma's friend Alban Berg (**50**) dedicates his violin concerto to the girl, "to the memory of an angel." Later, Werfel at **52** writes the script for the film *The Song of Bernadette,* which wins five Oscars. At **66**, Alma is widowed again, and she writes her memoirs: here she explains her life with a new saying, "Amo ergo sum"—I love, therefore I am.

PRESS

Henry J. Raymond starts the *New York Times* (1851). In 1896, Adolph S. Ochs (**38**) buys the paper, and this is the beginning of its preeminent position. At **20**, Ochs had started the *Chattanooga Times.*

Joseph Pulitzer purchases the St. Louis *Evening Dispatch* (1878) at a bankruptcy sale, for $2,500. Pulitzer had started as a poverty-stricken immigrant, but soon does well as lawyer and politician. His associates on the newly named *Post-Dispatch* are John A. Dillon (**34**), John J. Jennings (**25**), and Henry W. Moore (**29**). They rapidly make the paper into a leader in journalism—through sensationalism, crusades against all evils, and by hiring the best writers for good wages. Pulitzer is the first person to give journalists a paid annual vacation. At **36**, he buys the New York *World,* and there duplicates his success, but on a wider scale. Later, the Pulitzer Prizes are set up under the terms of his will, following his death at **64**.

DeWitt Wallace and Lila Wallace (also **31**): start of the *Reader's Digest* (1921).

Frank Hampson: "Dan Dare" (1950, until **40**), the prize-winning science fiction strip.

EXPLORATION

John H. Speke: first European to see Lake Victoria, the source of the River Nile (1858).

LAW

Allan Pinkerton starts Pinkerton's National Detective Agency (1851).

SPORTS

Arnold Palmer (1960) wins the U.S. Open, and is elected Athlete of the Decade. He has been instrumental in bringing golf to an enormous popularity. At this time, he has an administrative assistant and his own full-time pilot for his plane. He advertises Heinz Ketchup, as well as lines of toiletries and sportswear that carry his own name. Although his game begins to deteriorate a little, he still reaches the third position in money earning, at **37**. Palmer continues as a popular and rich public personality. At **42**, he is still 25th in earnings. He plays in his last Ryder Cup at **44**, and at **46** wins the Spanish Open, and the British PGA championship.

Jonah Barrington (1972)—British Open champion in squash. He has been the champion continuously since **25**. At **37**, he reaches the quarter-finals, but the championship is won by Geoff Hunt **(31)**. Previously, Barrington had been thrown out of university for drunkenness. The historian of squash, Rex Bellamy, describes him as ". . . a born fighter. But not a born champion . . . his pride and burning ambition was never satisfied with one outstanding performance in a tournament. He had to keep on winning until there was no one left to play. . . . Because of his intelligent approach to the task, his intensity of effort, his loathing of failure, he became a rare winner in a nation of good losers. He had the nerve to believe it was possible." At **33**, after his greatest days are perhaps over, Barrington describes the feeling of success: "There is a fantastic and savage and unrivalled and unbelievable satisfaction the moment you know you have beaten your opponent. You look into his eyes and see the defeat, the degradation, the humiliation, and there isn't anything in the world like it."

This is the typical age for a world motor racing champion. In a recent year, the top ten drivers were evenly spread between **27** and **34**, except for one at **37** (Mario Andretti).

32

HEALTH

T. R. Malthus: *An Essay on the Principle of Population* (1798). In this landmark publication he states that there will always be population pressure, unless population checks are institutionalized. Food supply increases arithmetically but population increases geometrically, owing to "passion between the sexes." Malthus lives until **68**, and is survived, appropriately enough, by two adult children, a son and a daughter.

Robert Koch: paper (Breslau, 1876) saying that anthrax is caused by bacteria. At **34**, he discovers that the infection of open wounds is caused by bacteria. At **38**, he discovers the bacillus which causes tuberculosis. For his work on TB, he receives the Nobel Prize at **61**. He dies at **65**.

Karl Landsteiner: discovery of the three basic blood groups, ABO (1900–01); and at **72**, discovery of the Rh factor.

HISTORY—WORLD

James Wolfe defeats the Marquis of Montcalm (**47**) at the battle of the Plains of Abraham, Quebec (1759). Both had started their military careers early—Wolfe became an officer at **14**, and Montcalm at **12**. Both die immediately after the battle.

Ch'iu Chin: execution (1907). She is one of the first revolutionaries in China, and becomes a heroine to Mao Tse-tung (**14**). At her trial, her last words are:

> Autumn rain
> and autumn wind
> will make me die of sorrow.

Later, her body is reburied, and Mao builds over her grave the Wind and Rain Pavilion.

HISTORY—U.S.A.

William Bradford, and other members of the Plymouth colony: the first Thanksgiving dinner (1621).

William Clinton: Governor, Arkansas (1978)—the youngest governor in 40 years.

Edmund Brown: Secretary of State of California (1970–74). Previously he had been an attorney in Los Angeles. He becomes Governor at **36** (1975).

HISTORY—U.K.

Henry IV becomes King (1399, Sept. 29) by crushing Richard II (**31**), and later murdering him.

RELIGION, PHILOSOPHY

Jesus: crucifixion, at this age, or perhaps in his late **30**s. (The Turin Shroud is of a man **30–35**.)

Medieval theologians believed that at the Resurrection, your body will return to the state at which it is now, **32**, because this was the age of Jesus Christ at his death and resurrection.

SOCIAL SCIENCE, EDUCATION

Montesquieu: *The Persian Letters* (1721). This is an ironic description of contemporary France, allegedly as seen by two Persian tourists—equivalent to our "visitors from outer space." The book is spiced with the Persians' worries on the administration of their harem back home. Montesquieu is here a pioneer in (1) cultural relativism, and (2) soft porn. His major work is *The Spirit of the Laws* at **59**.

Henry George: *Our Land and Land Policy* (1871).

Ferdinand Tonniës: *Gemeinschaft und Gesellschaft* (1887).

SCIENCE, TECHNOLOGY

Leonardo Fibonacci: *Liber abaci* (1202); this book causes the switch from Roman to Arabic numerals.

Charles Lyell: *The Principles of Geology* (1830); the three volumes are published between now and **35**.

T. H. Maiman: the first laser beam (1960).

Ray Dolby: first sale of Dolby noise-reduction equipment, in hi-fi (1965).

Clive Sinclair: first genuine pocket electronic calculator (1972). At **36**, he completes his design for a pocket televsion set.

MONEY, WORK

George Pullman: his first-ever sleeping car is an immediate success (1863), and he goes on to develop his own profitable railroad carriage business.

J. Pierpont Morgan: his first big break (1869)—over the reorganization of a railroad (the Albany and Susquehanna). He had arrived in Wall Street at **20**, as a junior accountant. In his **40**s, "Morganization" brings him fortunes, out of the reorganizing of other railroads. (cf. **55***)

George Eastman: first patent on his own Kodak roll film (1886)—the beginning of his virtual monopoly in the photographic film market. (cf. **77***)

C. S. Rolls is killed in a plane crash (June 1910). Having been a pioneer in cars—Silver Ghost at **29**—he had then become a pioneer in the new aircraft business. (c. f**41***)

David E. Lilienthal: appointed to the board of the Tennessee Valley Authority (1933), where he is the driving force.

RENAISSANCE

Jim Zockoll sets up a domestic drain clearing business (1963) while keeping his job as a pilot for Pan American Airways. As a small landlord of investment property on Long Island, he has noticed that blocked drains are a vexing problem and that plumbers are slow and inefficient. He buys some drain clearing equipment and starts his own specialized company. At first he has to subsidize the company from his pilot's salary. Later the company does well, and he starts selling franchises. By **48**, he is a millionaire, with an international business, and he is still a half-time pilot with Pan Am.

ARCHITECTURE

Jules Hardouin-Mansart: Galerie des Glaces (Hall of Mirrors), Versailles (1678).

A. W. N. Pugin starts work on designing the interiors for the Houses of Parliament (Sept. 1844). He designs every aspect, and they are the finest Gothic Revival interiors in the world.

Antonio Gaudí designs a small chapel for the crypt of the Sagrada Familia church in Barcelona (1884–85)—the beginning of his lifelong commitment. The crypt chapel is in a fairly conventional Gothic style. (cf. **38***)

Gerrit Rietveld: design for a chair (1918)—this is the definitive De Stijl chair, made of timber without any joints, and painted in primary colors.

Buckminster Fuller: Dymaxion House project (1927). (cf. **68***)

ART

Giorgio de Chirico, in 1922: this is now the beginning of the end of his career at the forefront of painting. Since **23**, he has made his name with paintings of piazzas and buildings, all of which are both classical and surreal. At least one of these paintings appears later in every art history of the times. But now he renounces this, and for the next 58 years paints old-fashioned work which is virtually ignored. He has had his ten years "in history," and he now departs.

Robert Smithson: his earthwork "Spiral Jetty" (1970).

J. S. Bach is appointed Kapellmeister, at Köthen (1717, Aug. 5). At **35**, his first wife dies, and at **36** he marries Anna Magdalena (**20**). He completes the Brandenburg concertos at the time of his second marriage. (cf. **38***)

Mozart writes his last three symphonies, in approximately six weeks (1788). He had written *Eine Kleine Nachtmusik* at **31**, and writes *Così fan tutte* at **33**. But this is the period in which poverty and the lack of commissions begin to hurt—he is now ignored in favor of composers who are later unknown. (cf. **35***)

Beethoven: Symphony no. 3, *Eroica* (1803). This is the time at which he establishes himself as the composer of overwhelming achievement. Previously, he has been seen as talented and energetic, but perhaps somewhat mad. His *Moonlight Sonata* is at **30**. At **31**, his deafness rapidly overcomes him, and he sees it as a deathlike challenge which turns him into an exile from the community. *Fidelio* is at **34**. Symphony no. 4 is at **35**; no. 5 at **36**; and no. 6, the *Pastoral,* at **37**. At **38**, he completes Piano Concerto no. 5, the *Emperor.* Symphony no. 7 is at **41**, as is no. 8. Beethoven composes little at **44–49**. His Mass in D is at **52***.

LITERATURE

Sir Philip Sydney dies (1586).

Herman Melville: *Moby Dick* (1851). He exhausts himself by writing seven novels in the next seven years, and he becomes a customs officer, from **47** to **66**. He dies at **72***.

Henry James settles in Europe (1875).

Richmal Crompton publishes *Just William* (1922), the first of her William (**11**) books. Illustrations are by T. Henry (**43**). At **34**, polio forces her to give up her job as a schoolteacher, and so she becomes a full-time author.

Hart Crane kills himself (1932, Apr. 27), by jumping off a ship which is traveling in the Atlantic. Around **27**, he had written *The Bridge,* his hymn to the Brooklyn Bridge.

André Malraux: *La Condition humaine* (1933).

J. D. Salinger: *The Catcher in the Rye* (1951).

PLAYS

J. M. Synge: *In the Shadow of the Glen* (1903). This is his first play. He follows it with *Riders to the Sea* at **33**, and *The Well of the Saints* at **35**. His last complete play is his best-known work, *The Playboy of the Western World* at **36**. Synge dies at **38**.

R. C. Sherriff: *Journey's End* (1928).

Rolf Hochhuth: *The Deputy* (1963).

Charlie Chaplin makes his first visit home, after his career in films (1921), and he is greeted with hysterical, nationwide adulation.

Edna Purviance retires (1926), with her last film, *The Sea Gull,* never shown.

Louis B. Mayer helps start the Academy of Motion Picture Arts and Sciences (1927).

Antonin Artaud acts in *The Passion of Joan of Arc* (1928).

John Wayne: *Stagecoach* (1939), directed by John Ford (**44**). This is Wayne's transition from small-part player into a star. John Wayne's career is remarkable in that from now on he spends the rest of his life at the center of public attention. Films include *Red River* at **41**; and *The Man Who Shot Liberty Valance* at **55**. His acting roles change as he ages; he even manages to incorporate his experience of cancer (at **57**) into a film role, in *True Grit,* at **62**.

Judy Garland: *A Star Is Born* (1954).

Kenneth More is the war hero in *Reach for the Sky* (1956).

George C. Scott: *The Hanging Tree* (1959)—his film debut.

Audrey Hepburn is Holly Golightly, in *Breakfast at Tiffany's* (1961); the song "Moon River" is by Henry Mancini (**39**).

Jean-Luc Godard: *Vivre Sa Vie* (1962); and *Les Carabiniers* and *Le Mépris* at **33**.

Alan Bates: *A Kind of Loving* (1962)—his first starring role.

Richard Lester: *A Hard Day's Night* (1964), with the Beatles (**23**).

Michael Caine: *The Ipcress File* (1965); this is his first big success, and he makes *Alfie* in the following year.

Jane Fonda: *They Shoot Horses, Don't They?* (1969).

Bernardo Bertolucci: *Last Tango in Paris* (1972); with Marlon Brando (**48**).

MUSIC—NON-CLASSICAL

Francis Child: "English and Scottish Ballads" (1857–58). Child is a teacher of literature at Harvard, and this publication is a detour outside his official career—but by accident he has hit on his life's main achievement, the preservation of folk music. He now continues in his official work, with a book on Chaucer at **38**, and he becomes Professor of English at **51**. At **47**, he begins the collection of U.S. folk music, and the resulting ten volumes are not all published until his death at **71**.

Jerome Kern and Oscar Hammerstein II (both **32**): *Show Boat* (1927), including such songs as "Ol' Man River." *Show Boat* is the beginning of the modern musical. Kern's composing career runs from **17** to **44**, and he dies at **50**.

Richard Rodgers: "Blue Moon" (1934).

Michael Bennett: *A Chorus Line* (1975).

Steve Winwood: "Arc of a Diver" (1981).

TV, ETC.

Ned Sherrin: "That Was the Week That Was" (1963, and sequels). The show's host is David Frost (**24**) who is relentlessly anti-establishment. Frost's own attitude changes so much that at **38** he makes a controversial interview series in association with former President Richard Nixon (**64**).

LOVE, LIFE

Regnier de Graaf: first use of the word "ovary" (1673). At **27**, he was the first to make a careful investigation of the testicles.

Giuseppi Cipriani: opening of Harry's Bar (Venice, 1931).

PRESS

J. A. MacGahan: reporting of Turkish atrocities in Bulgaria (1876). This is an early example of the power of a war correspondent; the reports lead to war, which leads to the liberation of Bulgaria. MacGahan is called "The Liberator"; but at **33** he dies of disease, when still abroad.

Harold Ross: *The New Yorker* (1925). Ross dies at **59**, and is succeeded by William Shawn (**44**). When Ross is **33**, he signs up George Ryall (**38**) to do a column on racing, as "Audax Minor." Ryall continues to write this until **91**.

EXPLORATION

Bartholomew Diaz: first European to land at the Cape of Good Hope (1488)—his approximate age. Vasco da Gama is also about **32** when he is the first European to sail around the Cape of Good Hope, in 1497.

Meriwether Lewis (**30**) and William Clark (**34**): the great Lewis and Clark Expedition, from St. Louis, Missouri, to the Pacific, and back (1804–06). Lewis becomes Governor of Louisiana Territory at **34**, but dies a violent death at **35**. Clark becomes Governor of Missouri Territory at **43**, and lives until **68**. The Lewis and Clark Expedition is funded by direction of Thomas Jefferson (**61**).

Thor Heyerdahl: He and some companions sail on a small raft, "Kon-Tiki," constructed with primitive technology, from South America to Polynesia. Kon-Tiki proves the possibility of human migration in ancient times (1947). Later, after a book and a film about the expedition, Heyerdahl makes a similar trip from Morocco, in "Ra," at **54**.

LAW

King Henry II holds the Clarendon Assize (Feb. 1166) which promotes widespread reform of the criminal justice system. This is the beginning of the Grand Jury.

Lizzie Borden kills Andrew Borden (**70**) and Abby Borden (**65**) (1892). Her father gets 10 wounds with an axe, and her step-mother gets 20. Lizzie Borden escapes conviction, and lives relatively happily, on the proceeds of her inheritance. She dies at **67**, leaving a quarter of a million dollars.

John Dillinger is shot dead by the FBI (1934). In only the past 18 months, he has become famous nationwide by robbing banks and evading the FBI. Dillinger's death mask is sent to J. Edgar Hoover (**39**) who keeps it in his office for the rest of his life.

The Great Train Robbery of 1963: 12 people steal £2½ million ($5 million) in used banknotes, from an overnight train going between Scotland and London. The organizers are **34**, **32**, **32**, and **31**; they each make £¼ million. The subsidiary members are mainly in their early **30**s, ranging from **44** to **28**; they each make £100,000. The majority get prison sentences of 30 years, but are paroled long before that. One of the robbers, Ronald Biggs (**34**) soon escapes from prison, and ends up in Brazil. By getting a local girl pregnant, he avoids extradition, and is said to live happily ever after.

Stanley Rifkin steals $10.2 million from the Security Pacific National Bank (1978), by directing its computers to transfer money to his account in Switzerland. He uses knowledge gained in his work as a computer consultant.

Daniel James White shoots the Mayor of San Francisco, George Moscone (**49**), and Supervisor Harvey Milk (**48**). White is a former policeman and supervisor. He had campaigned against homosexuality, and in favor of the death penalty for murder (1978).

SPORTS

A. J. Foyt (1967): wins the Indianapolis 500, for the third time; and winner of the Le Mans 24-hour race.

Heather McKay (1973) holds the Australian and British squash championships for the last time. She has been Australian champion continuously since **20**, and the British champion since **19**. After a semi-retirement, she returns to win the World Open title at **38**.

Alan Reeter (1979) breaks the hang-gliding distance record. He glides for 67 miles in Nevada, sometimes reaching a height of 14,000 feet.

33

HISTORY—WORLD

Ch'ung-chen: suicide (1644). He is the sixteenth and last Ming emperor of China. He has been unable to resist the invasion of his country by people from Manchuria, to the northeast. As the Manchus enter Peking, Ch'ung-chen takes off his Imperial robe, and writes this message: "I, feeble and of small virtue, have offended against Heaven.... Ashamed to face my ancestors, I die. Removing my Imperial cap and with my hair disheveled about my face, I leave to the rebels the dismemberment of my body." The emperor then strangles himself, as does his one remaining aide, a eunuch.

Mao Tse-tung, in 1927: as a Communist who had cooperated with Nationalist forces, he is now forced underground, when right-wing Nationalists gain power. Mao is a guerilla fighter from now until **55*** when the People's Republic of China is formed. The Long March occurs at **41**; his *Red Book,* as it is later known, is written between **42** and **46**.

Eva Peron: death, from cancer (1952). Her husband is Juan Peron (**56**), President of Argentina. She had married him when she was **26**. Juan Peron is President from **50** to **59**, when he is overthrown and exiled to Spain, later accompanied by the remains of his late wife. He dies at **78**, after a brief come-back period as President. Eva Peron is famous for becoming inordinately rich while genuinely promoting socialism.

HISTORY—U.S.A.

Henry Clay becomes Speaker of the House of Representatives (1810), on his first day as a member.

Susan B. Anthony, in 1853: it is about this time that she fixes on women's suffrage as the central cause of her life. At **19–29**, she has worked as a teacher, and she has taken part in the main reform causes of the time, for example, abolition, temperance, and women's suffrage. At reform meetings, she finds her path blocked because of her sex, and this leads to her decision to focus on feminist issues. She now begins strenuous campaigning, which leads, at **49**, to the formation of the National Woman Suffrage Association, with Elizabeth Cady Stanton

(**53**). At **50**, the first voting with women eligible takes place in Wyoming Territory. At **52**, Anthony votes in a presidential election, and is fined $100. Throughout the middle part of her life she is a dedicated campaigner; at **70**, she lives in her first real home since childhood, having spent all the intervening years staying in hotels. Susan B. Anthony lives until **86**. In middle age, she is constantly attacked as being austere, humorless, and ridiculous; in old age, she becomes almost a saint. But she would have had to live until **100** to witness the success of her life's work, the granting of votes to women.

Jody Powell is appointed press secretary to President-elect Carter (**52**, 1977).

HISTORY—U.K.

Sir William Wallace in 1305: after fighting Edward I (**66**), King of England, for the independence of Scotland, he is betrayed, captured, and taken to London. There he is hanged, drawn, and quartered; parts of his body are exhibited in Scottish towns, in order to inhibit any further opposition to Edward I.

Edward III wins the battle of Crécy (1346, Aug. 26) and then institutes the order of Knights of the Garter, sometime between now and **36**.

Winston Churchill: first cabinet post (1908). He now marries Clementine Hozier (**23**)—and later says that they "live happily ever after." They are married for 57 years. (cf. **20*** and **40***)

Mairead Corrigan and Betty Williams (**34**) receive the Nobel Peace Prize (1977), for launching the "Peace People," a movement that combines Roman Catholic and Protestants in Northern Ireland. In the previous year, three of Williams' children (**0**, **2**, and **8**) had been accidentally killed as the result of a gun battle, and horror at this had lead to the peace movement. Betty Williams never fully recovers from her grief, and at **37** she commits suicide. In the following year, her widower, Jack (**37**), is married to Mairead Corrigan.

RELIGION, PHILOSOPHY

St. Augustine: conversion, and baptism (387 A.D., Easter Eve).

SOCIAL SCIENCE, EDUCATION

Mary Wollstonecraft: *Vindication of the Rights of Women* (1792).

Nikolai Kondratieff: *The Long Waves in Economic Life* (1925). This is used by Joseph Schumpeter whose life work culminates in *Business Cycles* at **56** (1939). Later, this topic is reworked by Gerhard Mensch (**38**, 1975) in his *Stalemate in Technology: Innovations Overcome the Depression.*

Alfred Schutz: *The Phenomenology of the Social World* (1932).

George Gallup starts the American Institute of Public Opinion (1935), to conduct "Gallup polls." At **47**, he predicts the victory of Thomas Dewey (**46**) in the 1948 presidential election.

Paul Samuelson: first edition of his textbook, *Economics* (1948).

SCIENCE, TECHNOLOGY

Joseph Henry: design of the first electric motor (1831).

Lee de Forest: invention of the triode, making the tube/valve into an amplifier (1906).

MONEY, WORK

Eli Whitney receives contract for 10,000 muskets from the U.S. government (1798); beginning of his "interchangeable part" system of manufacture. Although taken for granted later, this is a basic foundation of mass production. Previously each finished object was made one-at-a-time, from parts whose dimensions fitted only that one object; specialized repetitive manufacture of individual components is not therefore possible until Whitney comes along. He dies at **59**, in comfortable circumstances, but without really cashing in on the change that he has created.

John Deere moves to Illinois, and begins developing the steel plough (1837), which is literally instrumental in developing the North American prairies. He is president of his own company, Deere and Company, until his death at **82**.

Akio Morita buys the license (1954) to manufacture transistors in Japan; the U.S. inventors charge him $25,000. At **25**, he had founded the Sony Corporation with Masoru Ibuka (**38**) and only $500. Morita first exports from Japan to the U.S.A. when he is **37**. By **57**, total annual sales of Sony are $2.7 billion.

RENAISSANCE

Christopher Wren: five days after the Great Fire of London (1666) in which the city is substantially destroyed, he produces a design for the complete rebuilding of the city along modern lines. Wren's first career has been as a scientist; at **24**, he became professor of astronomy, and had produced significant work on navigation, instrumentation, and anatomy. The Royal Society, the scientific organization, was formed by people meeting after one of his lectures. Wren did his first architectural design at **30**. Now at **33** he confronts the opportunity of his lifetime with unrivaled energy and creativity. His proposals for the new city establish him as the key new architect. At **36**, he makes his first design for the city's cathedral; work commences on St. Paul's at **40**, and the first service is held there at **64**. Wren also designs 52 churches, and the last is begun in the year of his death, **90**.

Thomas Jefferson: chief author of the Declaration of Independence (Philadelphia, 1776). At **14**, Jefferson had become head of his wealthy family on the death of his father (**49**). The household then consisted of his mother (**37**), a younger brother, and four sisters, and 100 slaves working on the estate. After college, Jefferson is apprenticed at **19** to "my second father," George Wythe (**36**) and he spends five years nominally learning the law, but in fact also studying the classics, philosophy, and many other subjects. Afterward, he does legal work and attends to the management of his estate. At **28**, he marries Martha Skelton, a widow with a son of **4**; she dies ten years later. At **30**, another inheritance brings his total wealth to 135 slaves and 11,000 acres. At **25**, Jefferson entered the Virginia House of Burgesses; at **31**, he published *A Summary View of the Rights of British America;* this has resulted from long, intense reading of political theory. Although the publication does not have a sudden success, being one out of many printed at the time, it helps him at **32** when he attends the Continental Congress. Here he meets the leaders of the future revolution, and he is a member of 34 committees. He is the second youngest member of the Congress. At **33**, when a committee has to be set up to write the Declaration, Jefferson's reputation as a writer and learned person make him the inevitable choice for a leading position. Also at **33** he drafts the constitution of the state of Virginia. The factors allowing him now at **33** to take such an important historical role include: (1) a wide education, and the wealth which has allowed him to pursue his reading; (2) sheer talent at writing prose; (3) his work in committee has brought him to the notice of many influential people; (4) his responsibilities as a landowner and slaveholder have forced him to consider the dilemmas and temptations of power; (5) his feeling for historical change has brought him to the center of this important historical event. After the drama of 1776, Jefferson serves unsuccessfully as Governor of Virginia, **36–38**, but later becomes President, **57–65***.

ARCHITECTURE

Baldassare Longhena: S. Maria della Salute, Venice (1631).

Giuseppe Mengoni: the Galleria, the influential shopping center in Milan (1862).

Hector Guimard: the standard entrances for the Paris Metro (1900)—the Art Nouveau classic.

Ludwig Mies van der Rohe returns to Berlin (1919), after four years in World War I, the whole time being spent as a private in an engineering regiment. This return is the beginning of a "creative explosion." His first project is for a glass-walled skyscraper on a prismatic plan, for Friedrichstrasse, Berlin (1919). This project contains the definitive design of an all-glass curtain wall. (cf. **36***)

It has been said that the people who built Stonehenge (2900 B.C.–2300 B.C.) would have been young. The men typically died by **36**, and the women by **30**.

Titian: "Man with a Glove" (Louvre) (1520). (cf. **51***)

Renoir: "The Loge" (1874). (cf. **73***)

Filippo Tommaso Marinetti publishes the Futurist Manifesto (1909); this is a hymn to speed, danger, the industrial future, and war. In fact, World War I comes when Marinetti is **39**, and it effectively kills the movement, including several of its members. Futurism survives only as an influence on other groups. In his **40**s and **50**s, Marinetti has a less publicized career, as a leader in the development of Fascism. He dies at **70**, in the same year as the end of Fascism.

Alexander Calder meets Mondrian (**49**) (1931), and this leads to Calder's invention of mobiles—a kind of oscillating Mondrian painting.

Claes Oldenburg: first soft sculptures (1962), for example, "Soft Typewriter"; his gigantic monuments are from **36**. His "Monument for Yale University: Lipstick" is done at **40**.

MUSIC—CLASSICAL

Arthur Sullivan writes the music for *Trial by Jury* (1875) to words by W. S. Gilbert (**37**). Up till now, Sullivan has been a distinguished up-and-coming member of the serious music world. The two of them now collaborate for the next 14 years and more as Gilbert and Sullivan on *The Mikado* when Sullivan is **43**, and *The Gondoliers* at **47***. Both Sullivan and Gilbert are classic cases of serious artists who do their most memorable work as a sideline—what they considered to be trivia has turned out to be unique, and the serious material has been almost forgotten.

LITERATURE

James Boswell goes on a tour of the Highlands of Scotland, with Dr. Johnson (**64**) (1773).

Jane Austen moves to Chawton, in Hampshire, where she lives for the rest of her life (1809). (cf. **36***)

Lewis Carroll: *Alice's Adventures in Wonderland* (1865); and *Through the Looking Glass* at **40**. He is a lecturer in mathematics from **23** to **49**.

Horatio Alger is dismissed from his position as minister at the Unitarian Church, Brewster, Massachusetts (1866) because of his sexual activity with boys in the "Cadets for Temperance" class. Alger now goes to New York. The dismissal resolves a dilemma, as he has not been able to decide between the two careers which he has been pursuing simultaneoulsy—minister and writer. He has been a fairly successful part-time author since **22**, and has already published two boys' books. In New York, he notices the vast number of orphans, and at **35** he writes about them in *Ragged Dick; or Street Life in New York.* He instantly becomes famous and rich. He goes on to write virtually the same story repeatedly and he publishes 100 books, selling as many as 250 million copies. In any of these "our hero" is typically a newly poor boy who, by taking advantage of a lucky break, brings himself back to the world of wealth and success. Alger's emotional life is confined to his friendships with boys. He never marries and he describes only one kiss in the whole of his writing. He dies at **67**, and sums up his life in this verse which includes five of his book titles:

> Strive and Succeed! The world's temptations flee;
> Be Brave and Bold! and Strong and Steady be!
> Shift for yourself, and prosper then you must;
> Win Fame and Fortune while you Try and Trust.

Virginia Woolf recovers (1915) from a suicide attempt and nervous breakdown that followed her marriage (**30**), and now begins the highly productive period in her life. She publishes *The Voyage Out* at **33**, and *Night and Day* at **37**. At **35**, she and her husband start the Hogarth Press, and never again have to submit their books to publishers—they publish their own. (cf. **45***)

Susan Sontag: *Against Interpretation* (1966).

Erich Segal: *Love Story* (1970). He subsequently has to leave his teaching job at Yale University, perhaps for appearing too often on TV talk shows. "I confess I wasn't as cool and reserved as I should have been. . . . No one told me when to stop."

PLAYS

William Wycherley: *The Country Wife* (1673); and *The Plain Dealer* at **34**. Wycherley writes no more plays after this. His work has been a vigorous satire on the people around him, and these two plays are of permanent value. Wycherley lives until **76**. He has been a brilliant young man, but from **34** on, his life can be seen as a struggle without much reward. In his **40**s, he spends five years in debtors' prison. He is on the fringe of the elite world, but exists on its charity which is not always enough.

Jean-Georges Noverre: publication of the book *Lettres sur la danse* (1759) in which he names forever the basic positions in classical ballet.

Arthur Miller: *Death of a Salesman* (1949). Also, *All My Sons* is at **31**; and *The Crucible* at **37**. At **40**, he marries Marilyn Monroe (**30**) and he writes the screenplay of *The Misfits* at **44**.

Brendan Behan: *The Quare Fellow* (1956).

D. W. Griffith, in 1908: he now starts work as a director in the film industry. Until now he has been a poorly paid actor and author. He views the current film scene with distaste, and is driven into the industry because of his failure in the more established and admired art forms. But Griffith now becomes stimulated into an amazing burst of energy. He makes 400 short films between **33** and **38**. In these he invents many of the basic features of film. At **40**, he makes *The Birth of a Nation,* the first film that equals the greatest drama to be found in painting or on the stage. It is both a critical and a financial hit. At **41**, he makes *Intolerance.* This too is mostly a critical success, but its gargantuan sets cause Griffith financial problems. He keeps working, but his moment in history ends in his early **40**s. His last admired film is at **49***.

Sam Taylor does the only thing for which he is famous—he receives this credit for his work on "*The Taming of the Shrew*" (1928): "By William Shakespeare, with additional dialogue by Sam Taylor."

Buster Keaton: *Spite Marriage* (1929); this is his last film, as his career comes to a stop after rows with studio boss Louis B. Mayer (**44**).

Norma Talmadge: *Du Barry, Woman of Passion* (1930)—she now retires, having accumulated a great deal of money. AGE 33 YRS

George Cukor directs his first film—*One Hour with You* (1932).

Clark Gable: *It Happened One Night* (1934)—causes him to be called "King of Hollywood."

Walt Disney invents Donald Duck (1934); Mickey Mouse had been invented when Disney was **27**.

Marlene Dietrich: *The Devil is a Woman* (1935).

Marilyn Monroe: *Some Like it Hot* (1959).

Jeanne Moreau: *La Notte,* and also *Jules et Jim* (1961).

Dustin Hoffman: *Little Big Man* (1970).

George Lucas: *Star Wars* (1977); *American Graffiti* was at **29**, and *The Empire Strikes Back* is at **36**.

MUSIC NON—CLASSICAL

Liberace: weekly TV show (1952). He now places a candelabra on his piano, and thus establishes his permanent trademark and identity.

Roberta Flack: "The First Time Ever I Saw Your Face" (1972).

TV, ETC.

Bruce A. Peterson: crash landing of a NASA experimental plane (1967). This is filmed, by chance, and is later used as the opening shot for "The Six Million Dollar Man."

Jim Henson: the Muppets, on "Sesame Street" (1969).

Dick Cavett: "The Dick Cavett Show" (1969).

PRESS

Joe Rosenthal: photograph of five marines and a naval corpsman raising the U.S. flag at Iwo Jima (1945, Feb. 23). The photograph is later reproduced in the form of a bronze statue. This is probably the most famous war photograph of the 1940s. Perhaps the best-known war photograph of the 1930s is that of a soldier apparently at the moment of death, in the Spanish Civil War, 1936, by Robert Capa (**23**).

EXPLORATION

Thomas Cook: organization of a special train, from Leicester to Loughborough, in England, to attend a temperance meeting (1841). Cook has been a missionary until now, but he gradually switches his career into the travel business, which he has accidentally discovered. He becomes a pioneer in the package tour. He goes on to change the travel clientele, from being rich individuals into being middle-class people, organized by the trainload. Cook lives until **83**, by which time he has seen a revolution in the travel world.

Amelia Earhart: first woman to fly solo across the Atlantic (1932). At **36**, she is the first person to fly from Hawaii to California. She disappears while flying over the Pacific when she is **38**.

LAW

Dick Turpin, the highwayman, is executed at York (1739) for stealing a black mare.

Glenn Turner starts Koscot Interplanetary (1967), a company designed to sell cosmetics derived from mink oil. Turner's motto is "Dare to be great." His method is pyramid selling, or the principle of the chain letter. His achievement: allegedly to defraud 100,000 people out of about $40 million, within the next five years.

John MacLean: end of his career in which he has stolen $150 million, and become America's most successful lone burglar (1980).

SPORTS

Jaroslav Drobny (1954) wins Wimbledon for the first and only time. He had been seeded eleventh. In the final, he beats Ken Rosewall (**20**.) Earlier in the championship, he had won the longest-ever Wimbledon match, against Budge Patty, 6–8, 18–16, 6–3, 6–8, 12–10.

Rocky Marciano (1956): retirement from boxing. He has won 49 victories in 49 fights. He dies at **46**, in a plane crash.

Joop Zoetemelk (cycling, 1980): winner, Tour de France.

34

HEALTH

Florence Nightingale arrives in the Crimea with a small party of nurses (1854). At this time there has been a complete breakdown in medical services, during the fighting between Russia and Britain, France, and Turkey. The Crimean War is a fiasco, and Nightingale stands out as one of the few competent people associated with it. On her return home, she receives complete adulation, and this gives her the influence to fulfill her dream of changes in nursing. Previously hospital workers had mainly been either doctors or domestic servants. Florence Nightingale brings about a new profession; she emphasizes sanitation, kindness, good character, and medical education—she thus creates nurses, and angels. Besides nursing, she promotes other powerful causes—reform of the Army; sanitation, particularly in India; pauper administration; the design of hospitals; district nurses, to promote healthy practices in the home. Her *Notes on Nursing* is published at **39**. Her first nursing school is opened at **40**. Her public career extends until around **80**, and she lives until **90***. The first superintendent of the new Nightingale School of Nursing is another remarkable woman, Sarah Wardroper (**48**) who had been widowed at **28** and left with four children. Mrs. Wardroper continues as superintendent until **75** and dies at **80**.

HISTORY–U.S.A.

Herbert Hoover: in charge of the U.S. economic relief for Europe (1918). He is President, **44–48**.

Hubert Humphrey: Mayor of Minneapolis (1945)—his first elective office. He becomes U.S. Senator at **37**; and Vice-President at **53–57**.

Martin Luther King, Jr. leads march on Washington (1963), and makes a speech from the Lincoln Memorial to about 500,000 people—"I have a dream. . . ." (cf. **39***)

David Stockman: Director of the Office of Management and Budget (1981). His task is to oversee a budget currently at $739,000,000,000.

HISTORY–U.K.

Robert Walpole is imprisoned for six months in the Tower of London (1711) for his corruption while in charge of the finances of the military. But at **39** he becomes Chancellor of the Exchequer; and first-ever Prime Minister from about **44***.

Benjamin Disraeli marries Mary Anne Wyndham (**46**) (1839, Aug. 28) and at **37** he is prominent in the "Young England" group in the House of Commons. His novels *Sybil: or the Two Nations* (**40**) and *Coningsby* (at **39**) illustrate his views. He becomes party leader at **41**; Chancellor of the Exchequer at **46**; Prime Minister at **63***.

RELIGION, PHILOSOPHY

Martin Luther: his attack on the indulgences system of the Roman Catholic Church (1517). He nails a list of 95 arguments on the door of the castle church, at Wittenberg, thus mobilizing the energies of the Reformation. He had been ordained a priest at **24**; and received a vision of his own greater future at **30**. He is excommunicated at **37**; marries at **41**; dies at **62**.

Ann Lee: while in prison for Shaker practices (1770), she receives a vision that sexual intercourse is the cause of human sin. From now on, she becomes a leading member of the Shaker movement, setting up communities in which sex is banned. She founds the first American Shaker Society at **40**, and dies at **48**.

SOCIAL SCIENCE, EDUCATION

Erving Goffman: *Presentation of Self in Everyday Life* (1956); and *Asylums* at **39**.

SCIENCE, TECHNOLOGY

Wilbur Wright (**36**) and Orville Wright (**32**): the first powered plane flight (1903).

A. A. Michelson, and E. W. Morley (**49**): the Michelson-Morley experiment (1887), on the speed of light. This turns out to be constant, in all directions. Michelson continues to measure the speed of light until the day before his death, at **78**.

Federico Faggin: start of the Zilog microchip company (1975). By **38**, its turnover is $20 million per year.

MONEY, WORK

A. P. Giannini opens his Bank of Italy (San Francisco, 1904). He employs three people. At **31**, he had gone into retirement, having built up sufficient capital for his needs, through real estate dealing. At **32**, he accidentally became director of a local bank as part of his duties as executor of an estate. Now at **34** his innovation is to make banking available to a mass public. He opens his first branch at **37**, and first Southern California branch at **43**. By **57**, he controls the third largest bank in the U.S. At **60**, it becomes the Bank of America. Giannini manages to survive the San Francisco earthquake at **36**, and the Great Crash at **59**. He lives until **79**.

Gilbert Trigano joins the Club Mediterranée (1954) in its fifth year of operations. He is appointed Managing Director. Up till now he has been a supplier of camping equipment to the Club. This moment is at the beginning of a worldwide boom in travel; the Club offers low-cost vacations in straw huts situated in faraway places. At **34**, the Club has 7,000 clients per year; at **44**, it has 90,000; at **54**, it has 432,000 clients, and owns over 100 hotels and villages.

RENAISSANCE

Leon Battista Alberti begins to study architecture (1438). Previously, at **20**, he has written a distinguished comedy in Latin; at **28** onward, he has been writing the lives of the saints, and has gone on to become a priest. At **31**, he writes *On Painting,* a landmark text in the development of perspective. In his new career, he becomes architectural adviser to the papacy at **43**; at **48**, he publishes *Ten Books on Architecture,* an important contribution to the subject; and at **49** he is in charge of the first renewal of the Trevi Fountain in Rome, though his work is later overlaid by that of Nicola Salvi (**35**, in 1732). At **52**, he commences one of his best-known designs, the front of Santa Maria Novella, in Florence. After working as an architect in his **50**s, he returns to writing, and produces a work on grammar, and a pioneering book on cryptography, systematic codes for transmitting secret messages. At **64**, he publishes his final book, *On the Man of Excellence.* As if to illustrate his own topic, he is at this moment designing the church of St. Annunziata, in Florence. Alberti lives until **68**.

ARCHITECTURE

Robert Adam: Syon House, London (1762).

James Gandon: Four Courts, Dublin (1776–96).

William Thornton: the original design for the U.S. Capitol (1793). The dome, as seen today, is by Thomas Walter (**47**, 1851).

Victor Horta: Hôtel Solvay (1894)—his best Art Nouveau house.

Walter Burley Griffin: first prize in the competition to design the new city of Canberra, Australia (1911). He does the drawings with his future wife, Marion Mahoney, while they are both assistants in the Chicago office of Frank Lloyd Wright (**42**).

Antonio Sant'Elia publishes *Manifesto of Futurist Architecture,* (1914), including his highly influential sketch for urban complexes or "megastructures"; but he is killed in the war, at **36**.

Berthold Lubetkin and others: Highpoint Flats, London; and the Penguin Pool, London Zoo (both 1935).

 James Stirling (**33**) and James Gowan (**35**): Engineering Building, Leicester University (1959–63).

ART

Andy Warhol: "Campbell's Soup Can" (1962); and "Brillo Pads" at **36**. At **35**, he makes an eight-hour movie of the Empire State Building. At **39**, he and others make the films *Flesh* and *Lonesome Cowboys;* he is also stabbed by a member of SCUM (Society for Cutting Up Men).

MUSIC—CLASSICAL

Carl Maria von Weber: *Der Freischütz* (June 1821).

Mendelssohn: incidental music for *A Midsummer Night's Dream* (1843). He writes his second oratorio, *Elijah* at **37**, but dies at **38***.

Brahms: *A German Requiem* (1867). (cf. **43***)

Léo Delibes: *Coppélia* (1870).

Nellie Melba, the opera singer, has a new dessert created in her honor—Peach Melba (1894). (cf. **65***)

LITERATURE

O. Henry spends three years and three months in jail on an embezzlement conviction (1896). But while there he writes short stories that make him a professional writer on release; his jail companions contribute to the topics of his later stories.

Simone Weil kills herself (1943, Aug. 24), through starvation.

Dylan Thomas is discovered to have not paid income tax for the past 16 years (1948); but he spends the next (and last) five years of his life under the financial control of the income tax authorities. (cf. **35***)

PLAYS, DANCE

Tennessee Williams: *The Glass Menagerie* (1944). He goes on to write *A Streetcar Named Desire* at **36**; *The Rose Tattoo* at **39**; *Cat on a Hot Tin Roof* at **44**; *Suddenly Last Summer* at **47**; and *The Night of the Iguana* at **50**. His next play *The Milk Train Doesn't Stop Here Anymore* at **52** is the first of several which are poorly received.

Terence Rattigan: *Separate Tables* (1945); also, *The Winslow Boy* at **35** and *The Browning Version* at **37**. Rattigan had first made his name with *French Without Tears* at **25**.

Edward Albee: *Who's Afraid of Virginia Woolf* (1962).

Joe Orton: death (1967). His head is smashed in by his lover Kenneth Halliwell (**41**), an actor who has known Orton since before the playwright's success. This fame has made Halliwell jealous and insecure. Orton's plays have been *Entertaining Mr. Sloane* at **30**; *Loot* at **33**; and *What the Butler Saw* at **34**. After the murder, Halliwell, who at **23** had seen his own father's suicide, now kills himself.

Alan Ayckbourn: *Absurd Person Singular* (1973). From **20** on, Ayckbourn writes a farce per year, including *The Norman Conquests* at **35**; *Bedroom Farce* at **38**; and *Sisterly Feelings* at **41**.

FILMS

Cecil B. DeMille: *Carmen* (1915), his first spectacular.

Fatty Arbuckle, earning $7,000 per week, has his career destroyed by three trials for manslaughter, after the death of a girlfriend at a party. Although acquitted, he never does any more good work, and dies at **46**.

Fred Astaire and Ginger Rogers (**22**): *Flying Down to Rio* (1933); this is the first film in their partnership. Another is *Top Hat,* at **36** and **24**.

Greta Garbo: *Ninotchka* (1939); her first comedy, and advertised as: "Garbo laughs."

David Lean and Noel Coward (**43**) codirect: *In Which We Serve* (1942).

Carole Lombard, wife of Clark Gable (**41**), is killed in a plane crash (1942). She had recently completed *To Be or Not to Be.*

Danny Kaye: *The Secret Life of Walter Mitty* (1947).

Marilyn Monroe: *The Misfits* (1961)—screenplay by Arthur Miller (**46**), her husband; divorce shortly afterward.

Stanley Kubrick: *Lolita* (1962), with James Mason (**53**) as Humbert Humbert (**37***), and Sue Lyon (**15**) as Lolita.

John Frankenheimer: *The Train* (1964).

Clint Eastwood: *For a Fistful of Dollars* (1964); and *For a Few Dollars More* (**35**), and *The Good, the Bad, and the Ugly* at **36**.

Shirley MacLaine is a delegate at the Democratic Party Convention, Chicago (1968).

Dustin Hoffman: *Straw Dogs* (1971).

Seventy-five percent of filmgoers (U.K., 1978) are aged **16–34**, even though only 36 percent of the population are in this age group.

MUSIC—NON-CLASSICAL

Burt Bacharach has a string of hits around this time (1962). He has so many that it is difficult to make a choice, but they include "Don't Make Me Over" at **34**; "Anyone Who Had a Heart" at **35**; and the shattering "Walk On By" at **36**, sung by Dionne Warwick (**23**).

Bill Graham: the first concert which he promotes (1965). Until recently, he has had such employment as statistician with a railroad. He now builds an empire in rock music. His closing of the Fillmore East and Fillmore West concert halls is at **40**, but his career continues as an impresario, albeit at a less hectic pace.

Kris Kristofferson: first performance as a singer (1970). He had been a Rhodes Scholar at **22**, followed by five years in the U.S. Army as a helicopter pilot. He moved to Nashville at **29**.

TV, ETC.

John Reith is appointed General Manager of the new British Broadcasting Company (1922). At this time, the BBC has three other employees and is virtually ignored by the established media of the day. Reith is convinced that he is at the beginning of a very great success; he has been looking for exactly this kind of pioneering job. He now writes in his diary: "I am profoundly thankful to God for his goodness in this matter. It is all His doing." By **38**, the BBC has grown to 773 people and Reith is well on the way to establishing his ideal organization. He sets a messianic tone for the BBC, allowing no interference by government or business, and emphasizing the cultural life of the nation. He insists that radio newsreaders wear formal clothes when performing their unseen duties. The shiplike headquarters building, Broadcasting House, is opened at **42**. Reith leaves the BBC at **48**, and has a number of top government positions, before his death at **82**. Not surprisingly, after the BBC he never finds another job which gives him the exhilarating and slightly mad sensation of being "fully stretched."

Dorothy Malone: "Peyton Place" (1964–68), also starring Mia Farrow (**19**).

Mary Tyler Moore: "The Mary Tyler Moore Show" (1970), until **38**.

LOVE, LIFE

Vic Bergeron: opening of "Hinky Dinks" restaurant, in Oakland, California (1934). He soon changes the name to "Trader Vic's." At **51**, he opens in San Francisco, and this is the beginning of his worldwide chain of restaurants.

EXPLORATION

Captain William Bligh: the mutiny on H.M.S. *Bounty* (Pacific Ocean, 1789). Bligh is deposed by his deputy, Fletcher Christian (**24**); 18 loyalists and Bligh are put in a 23 foot longboat and they sail 3,600 miles, an incredible feat. Bligh arrives home in England after eleven months travel, and he receives promotion. Later, at **50**, he is appointed Governor of New South Wales, Australia. But at **53** he suffers the second full-scale rebellion of his life, and the colonists imprison him for two years. On returning home to England, he is again promoted, and becomes Vice-Admiral by **59**. He lives until **63**, when he dies in Bond Street, London. Fletcher Christian is killed at **29** by fellow mutineers, when they quarrel over women, on their island paradise, Pitcairn Island.

Richard M. Hoe: first rotary printing press (1846). This revolutionizes the speed of printing, particularly when at **59** he is able to incorporate continuous rolls of paper, as invented by William Bullock (**52**).

William Howard Russell lands in the Crimea (1854) and begins his reports on the war there, for the *Times,* London. His horrific descriptions of army inefficiency make him the most effective of pioneer war correspondents. Russell goes on to report on wars for the next thirty years, including the American Civil War. His last war is in Egypt at **64**, and he lives till **86**.

Allen Lane founds Penguin Books Ltd (1936), the paperback pioneers.

Tom Wolfe: *The Kandy-Kolored Tangerine-Flake Streamline Baby* (1965), a collection of his magazine articles. At **39**, he invents the phrase "radical chic"; at **41**, he invents the phrase "The Me Decade," about the 1970s. His book on the space program, *The Right Stuff,* is at **48**.

LAW

Adolf Eichmann becomes head of office IV B 4, of the RSHA, the Reich Security Service head office in Berlin (1940). This is the Gestapo organization for "Endloesung," the Final Solution, or holocaust of 6 million Jews. At **28**, Eichmann had by chance become a guard in the Jewish museum at SS headquarters. There, he developed a uniquely systematic obsession about the Jews. At **32**, he is head of a program to remove all Jews from Austria. It is not until **54*** that Eichmann is captured and executed.

Julius Rosenberg (**32**) and Ethel Rosenberg (**36**) face trial (1951) for sending atomic bomb secrets to the U.S.S.R. at the end of World War II. They are found guilty, and are sent to the electric chair two years later.

Robert Vesco acquires control of IOS, Investors Overseas Services, in a reverse takeover (1970). This signals a downturn for IOS founder Bernie Cornfield (**42**) who had built up the organization using the slogan "Do you sincerely want to be rich?" Over $2 billion had been collected from individuals, and used for investment. Vesco now travels in a private 707, equipped with a discotheque and a sauna. He begins the illegal transfer of perhaps a quarter of a billion dollars from IOS to banks in Panama and the Bahamas. He gets away with this by appointing a new bank as trustee for IOS investors—but Vesco controls this "independent" bank. He also delays investigation by the Securities and Exchange Commission, by making contributions to CREEP, the Committee to Re-Elect the President (Nixon). At **36**, Vesco moves to Costa Rica, a country which has no extradition arrangements with the U.S.A.

 George Davis is sent to prison (1975) until **54** for London robberies, due to evidence based on identification. His wife (**31**), mother (**56**), and other relatives organize a huge campaign in the East End and elsewhere, using the slogan "George Davis is innocent, OK." This is successful, and Davis is released at **35**. But at **36** he is caught while assisting in a bank raid; he is sent to prison until **51**.

SPORTS

Pierre Coubertin (1896): organizer of the first Olympic Games of the modern era. He comes from a wealthy background, which perhaps leads to his insistence on the amateur status. Coubertin lives until **75**.

Pele (1974) retires from soccer, amid national mourning in Brazil. But he makes a comeback at **35**, playing for the New York Cosmos, until **37**. In his last match, he scores the 1,281st goal of his career.

David Steele (1975) plays in his first international cricket match, for England, against Australia. Up to this moment he has been an obscure gray-haired figure who has been playing in his "benefit" season to provide money for his forthcoming retirement. The England side has been suffering devastation from the terrifyingly fast bowling of Denis Lillee (**26**) and Jeff Thomson (**25**). Steele, on his third ball, scores a boundary, and goes on to successfully resist the Australian bowling. In a paroxysm of relief (at this national deliverance), Steele is voted "Sports Personality of the Year."

Alan Jones: Grand Prix world motor racing champion (1980).

35

HEALTH

Motherhood: although there is an increased risk of congenital abnormalities in a baby as the mother's age increases, an important factor is social class. "A class I [the top class] mother of **35** has exactly the same possibilities of having a normal pregnancy and a normal baby as a [lowest] class V mother of **22**."—U.K. researcher Professor Richard Beard (1979).

When mothers in the past had numerous children, it was of course likely that fertility would extend to the late **30**s. For example, in Sweden, 1776–80, out of a total 72,400 births, almost 13,000 were to women **35–40**. This compared with about 19,000 births to the most prolific age group, **25–30.**

Motherhood and twins: the peak years for having multiple births are **35–39**.

Women from now on are recommended not to take the contraceptive pill, especially if they are smokers. A combination of smoking, the Pill, and being **35+** leads to significantly greater chance of death from stroke or heart attack.

HISTORY—WORLD

Alfred Dreyfus is convicted in France of selling military secrets to the Germans (1894), and is sent to the penal colony of Devil's Island, off South America. After a controversy which rocks the nation, he is found (**46**) to have been entirely innocent. Pro- and anti-Dreyfusards see the case as exemplifying the weaknesses or strengths of the country. Literally without doing anything, Dreyfus becomes a central symbol of the dilemma facing the country at this time—between conservatism and modernization. After acquittal at **46**, Dreyfus leads a relatively quiet life, and dies at **75** in decent obscurity. In 1894, his most prominent supporter, Émile Zola, is **54**.

HISTORY—U.S.A.

George Washington, in 1767, is a country gentleman who is developing his rich estate of Mt. Vernon. In his late **30**s, the political situation becomes more confused, and at **42** the first Continental Congress is held, to which Washington, a landowner and former military leader, is sent as a delegate. Also at **42**, he is the organizer of the military for five Virginia counties. By **43**, he has been appointed the chief of the revolutionary forces, and his great skill is to build an amateur group into a fighting force. The Declaration of Independence is signed when he is **44***. Washington organizes a cunning guerilla campaign against the numerically superior British army. His crossing of the Delaware River is at **44**, and he forces a significant retreat of the enemy. (cf. **45***)

Francis Scott Key: "The Star-Spangled Banner" (1814, Sept. 14).

Abraham Lincoln, in 1844: he is self-employed as a country lawyer in Illinois. He is a member of the U.S. Congress at **38–40**, after which he returns to his legal career in Illinois.

Lyndon Johnson (1943) continues as a congressman. At **40**, he is elected to the Senate.

Ronald Reagan, in 1946: having recently left the military, he now returns to his film career, but begins also to take an interest in the organizational and political side of movies. He now supports liberal and left-wing causes, for example, the Americans for Democratic Action. At **39**, he supports Helen Gahagan Douglas (**49**), a screen star turned politician, in her unsuccessful campaign versus Richard Nixon (**37**) for a seat in the U.S. Senate. At **36–41** he is president of the Screen Actors Guild. He makes $3,500 per week at Warner Brothers; his films include *Bedtime for Bonzo* (**0–1**) at **40**. At **43**, Reagan's film career ends, and he works as TV host for the General Electric Theater, until **51**. In this position he is also employed to give lectures on the capitalist system to General Electric employees. Reagan's first marriage ends in divorce at **37**, and at **41** he marries Nancy Davis (**30**); they go on to have two children, the last when Reagan is **48**.

Richard Nixon, in 1948, continues as a member of Congress. At **37**, as a member of the House Un-American Activities Committee he becomes a national figure, for the first time, by forcing the further investigation of Alger Hiss (**45**). This leads to Hiss's imprisonment for three years eight months. Also at **37**, Nixon is elected to the Senate. At **39**, he is candidate for vice-president. During this campaign, he makes his famous "Checkers" speech about a dog (**1**) which has been a gift for his daughter Tricia (**6**). Nixon is elected Vice-President.

John F. Kennedy is elected to the Senate (1952). He has been a congressman since **29**. He is a bachelor until **36** when he marries Jacqueline Bouvier (**24**). At **39**, he gets a Pulitzer Prize for his book, *Profiles in Courage.* He is elected President at **43***.

Henry Kissinger is in charge of the Defense Studies Program (1958–68) at Harvard, where he had completed his Ph.D. at **31**. (cf. **45***)

Jimmy Carter, in 1959, continues as a peanut farmer in Plains, Georgia. He also continues as chairman of the Sumter County School Board, and he leaves this position at **36**. He is a Georgia State Senator, **38–42**, and holds only county-level positions on leaving the state senate. At **42**, he fails to obtain the Democratic nomination as candidate for governor, and he becomes a born-again Christian.

Cesar Chavez starts his own organization, the National Farm Workers Association (1962), in California; forms the United Farm Workers Organizing Committee at **39**—UFWOC.

Eligibility: it is now too late to enter the military.

HISTORY—U.K.

Guy Fawkes tries to blow up Parliament (1605, Nov. 5), but is caught in the act, and later executed.

RELIGION, PHILOSOPHY

Prince Siddhartha, Shakyamuni Buddha, the founder of Buddhism, becomes enlightened while meditating under a tree, having developed a Middle Way between self-indulgence and asceticism. "I was enlightened simultaneously with the universe."

John Wesley, and Charles Wesley (**31**): new conversion, and beginning of Methodism (1738).

SOCIAL SCIENCE, EDUCATION

Emperor Frederick I, Barbarossa: *Habita* (1158), the constitution of Bologna University, and the document from which flows the doctrine of academic freedom.

Theodor Herzl: *Des Judenstaat* (1896). The first Zionist conference is held at **37** and Herzl is the chairman. He dies from pneumonia at **44**.

Bruno Bettelheim: in the concentration camp at Dachau (1938). He is unexpectedly released at **36**, and emigrates to the U.S.A., where he becomes a professor of educational psychology. His first two major books are published at **47**. And later, *The Empty Fortress* (**64**); *The Children of the Dream* (**66**); *Surviving and Other Essays* at **75**.

SCIENCE, TECHNOLOGY

Robert Boyle: Boyle's Law, on the inverse relationship between the pressure and the volume of a gas (1662). At **34**, he had published *The Sceptical Chemist*, which marks the foundation of chemistry as a separate subject.

Amadeo Avagadro: Avogadro's hypothesis, on gases and molecules (1811). He dies unknown and unrecognized, at **80**.

V. K. Zworkin: first demonstration of television (1924).

C. G. King: the isolation of vitamin C (1932).

Gordon Moore: "Moore's Law" (1964), that the capacity of an electronic chip will double each year, for at least the next ten years.

MONEY, WORK

James Fisk and Jay Gould (**33**) make $11 million in one day—"Black Friday" (1869, Sept. 24). They sell short on gold, anticipating the release of Federal gold onto the market by President Grant (**47**), whose brother-in-law is a party to the scheme.

G. William Miller becomes President of Textron Inc. (1960), largely because of his handling of their new acquisition, Bell Helicopter. At **53**, he becomes Chairman of the U.S. Federal Reserve Board.

Eligibility: at the end of this year, you must resign from the Jaycees.

In Japan, there is pressure on females to retire early from work. For example, office workers may be called "office flowers" in their **20**s, but soon afterward become "wilting office flowers." After marriage, the pressure to retire is considerably increased, even before children arrive; since your husband will be a workaholic, he will be too tired to help in the home, and so all domestic work will have to be done by the wife. Although it is illegal, some firms even give financial inducements to retire at **30**.

Niccolo Salvi: the Trevi Fountain, Rome (1732).

Charles Bulfinch: Massachusetts State House (1798).

William Butterfield: All Saints, Margaret Street, London (1849).

Frederick Law Olmsted, and Calvert Vaux (**33**) win competition for the design of Central Park, New York (1857).

Charles Garnier: Paris Opera House (1860–75).

Frank Lloyd Wright: the Larkin Building, Buffalo, New York (1904).

ART

Emanuel Leutz: "Washington (**44**) Crossing the Delaware" (1851)—later, this is said to be the most popular painting in the Metropolitan Museum of Art, New York.

Paul Gauguin is let go from his lucrative job with a firm of Paris stockbrokers (1893). His departure is caused by a downturn in the economy. Gauguin has been an amateur painter who has done some good work on the fringe of the Impressionist movement. He now begins to pursue his painting; but initially he suffers an extreme of poverty, and is unable to support himself or his family (five children; oldest is **10**). At **39**, he moves to Brittany and there becomes a leader in a new philosophy and a new painting style. At **43***, he takes himself to Tahiti.

After a dispute with Gauguin (**39**) in Arles, Vincent van Gogh slashes off the lobe of his right ear (1888, Dec. 23). He takes the piece round to a nearby brothel. At **32**, van Gogh had briefly enrolled in art school, his only period of formal training. At **36**, he voluntarily commits himself to a mental hospital. Later at **36**, he sells "Red Vineyard" for 400 francs—the only sale during his lifetime. He writes to his mother: "[T]his is how things go in a painter's life; success is the worst thing that can happen." At **37**, he leaves mental hospital, the head doctor writing "Cured" on his file. But two months later, van Gogh shoots himself, and dies.

Henri Matisse: first Fauve exhibition (1905). The other "wild beasts" include Vlaminck (**29**); Dufy (**28**); Derain (**25**); and Braque (**23**).

Francis Bacon: "Three Studies for Figures at the Base of a Crucifixion" (1944). He later comments: "I began with this painting."

Jackson Pollock: first of his drip or "action" paintings (1947). He becomes instantly famous, either as an artist or as a curiosity.

NOTE: here follow some early deaths.

Aubrey Beardsley dies at **25** (1898); Richard Parkes Bonington, the landscape painter, dies of brain fever at **26** (1828). Masaccio dies at **27**

(1428); Georges Seurat dies at **31** (1891); Giorgione dies at **35** in 1510; Amedeo Modigliani dies at **35** (1920); Caravaggio dies at **36** (1610); Toulouse-Lautrec dies at **36** (1901); Raphael dies from fever at **37** (1520); Watteau dies from tuberculosis at **37** (1721); Van Gogh dies at **37** (1890); and Jackson Pollock dies in a car crash at **44** (1956).

Some alternative explanations for "early genius, early death" include:

(1) since people typically died earlier than today, it is not surprising that some geniuses suffered in what was then the normal way; (2) the knowledge of their forthcoming death, the signs of tuberculosis, for example, may have spurred them on to greater creative efforts; (3) intense effort weakened them, and made them susceptible to the diseases of the times; (4) some people have had a hatred of aging, and so take risks with their life. Another explanation is by the poet, Byron (d. **36**, 1824): "Those whom the gods love, die young." Another view is that in some sense those who die young are the lucky ones; the poet Rupert Brooke (d. **27**, 1915) was described as "a golden-haired Apollo, magnificently unprepared for the long littleness of life."—Frances Cornford.

MUSIC—CLASSICAL

Mozart composes two operas *La Clemenza di Tito* and *The Magic Flute,* and much other music—but dies (1791, Dec. 5, at five minutes to one in the morning) from uremia, rheumatic fever. He composes his *Requiem* almost up to the moment of his death, and it is completed by his pupil, Franz Xaver Süssmayr (**25**). Mozart has recently been very poor, and his funeral is attended by almost no friends; his grave is not marked by any stone, and later cannot be identified. Out of his roughly 650 compositions, 144 have been printed in his life—but soon after his death there is a flood of printed scores, as public taste catches up with him. His wife (**28**) lives for another 51 years, and is treated as something of a holy relic, as people try to compensate for virtually ignoring Mozart during the last years of his life. As a musician, Mozart had obviously made the transition from infant prodigy to adult composer—but he never regained his childhood fame until after his death.

Berlioz, at a concert of his works in 1838: Paganini (**56**) comes out of the audience, kneels before him, and hails him as the only possible successor to Beethoven. Berlioz had written the *Fantastique* Overture at **26**; he writes *The Damnation of Faust* at **42**; and *The Childhood of Christ* at **50**. (cf. **59***)

Modest Petrovich Mussorgsky: *Pictures at an Exhibition* (1874). His opera *Boris Godunov* was first performed at **34**. Mussorgsky could never make a career as a professional musician, and so most of his life is spent as a civil servant. He dies at **42**, partly from the effects of alcohol.

 Frederick Delius: *Koanga* (1897), and *A Village Romeo and Juliet* at **38**.

NOTE: here follow some more early deaths.

Franz Schubert dies at **31** (1828). Mozart dies at **35** (1791). Mendelssohn dies at **38** (1847). Carl von Weber dies at **39** (1826). Chopin dies at **39** (1849). Hugo Wolf dies at **42** (1903). Robert Schumann dies at **46** (1856).

LITERATURE

Thomas Hughes: *Tom Brown's Schooldays* (1857). He is a barrister, and ends as a judge, at **60**. He keeps writing books, though none as good as this.

Tolstoy begins work on *War and Peace* (1863–69); his helper and secretary is his wife Sonya (**19**). Sometimes they rewrite the manuscript seven times. Up to now, Tolstoy has been in the army, has wasted much family money through gambling, fathered one illegitimate son, but he has been a writer since **23***. The last volume of *War and Peace* is published when he is **41**; *Anna Karenina* takes him from **45** to **49***.

Gustave Flaubert: *Madame Bovary* (1857).

Louisa M. Alcott writes *Little Women* (1868) in six weeks, with the aim of making money. It is a picture of happy, rewarding family life, of a kind that she has never experienced—nor does she experience later, when she is rich and famous. She had previously written *Hospital Sketches* at **31**, about her horrific nursing experiences during the American Civil War. For the rest of her life, she continues as a grim but successful writer of happy children's books.

Beatrix Potter publishes (1901) her first Peter Rabbit book—from a story originally written to a child eight years previously. There now follows a stream of similar books. But at **47** she marries her lawyer, and concentrates on real animals for the next 30 years—she had bought a farm and much of a Lake District village with her earnings. As a farmer, she dislikes anyone to refer to her time as an author.

Margaret Mitchell: *Gone with the Wind* (1936). She has been a reporter, **22–26**, but had been forced to resign because of an ankle injury. She stays at home and writes the book in secrecy. Her friends commiserate with her for not fulfilling her potential. "GWTW" is an instant success, and for the rest of her life she has to keep two secretaries to deal with contracts and fan mail. She lives until **49** and never has the time to write another piece.

George Orwell: *Homage to Catalonia* (1938), derived from his experiences in the Spanish Civil War. This is the first work that demonstrates his main idea—that the Left, though morally superior, can in practice be as autocratic as the Right. (cf. **46***)

Dylan Thomas watches the last illness of his father (1949), and writes, "Do not go gentle into that good night . . ." Dylan Thomas dies at **39***.

Iris Murdoch publishes her first novel, *Under the Net* (1955); previously she had been a lecturer in philosophy. Angus Wilson also starts writing about now, while an employee of the British Museum.

Thomas Chatterton, a poet, kills himself at **17** (1770), after the rejection of his work; he is later regarded as a martyr to creativity, and is commemorated by a well-known painting; he is also the subject of an unsuccessful opera, by Leoncavallo (**18**, in 1876).

John Keats dies of tuberculosis at **25** (1821).

Rupert Brooke dies at **27** (1915).

Stephen Crane dies at **28** (1900).

Percy Bysshe Shelley drowns accidentally at **29** (1822).

Emily Brontë dies at **30** (1848).

James Elroy Flecker dies at **30** (1914).

Sylvia Plath kills herself at **30** (1963).

Hart Crane drowns himself at **32** (1932).

Simone Weil kills herself through starvation at **34** (1943).

Lord Byron dies at **36** (1824).

Adam Lindsay Gordon, the Australian poet, shoots himself at **36** (1870).

Robert Burns dies at **37** (1796).

Arthur Rimbaud dies at **37** (1891).

Thomas Wolfe dies at **37** (1938).

Jules de Goncourt dies at **39** (1870).

Dylan Thomas dies at **39** (1953).

Edgar Allan Poe dies at **40** (1849).

Jack London dies at **40** (1916), after an overdose of morphine.

Franz Kafka dies at **40** (1924).

Guy de Maupassant dies at **42** (1893).

F. Scott Fitzgerald dies at **44** (1940).

Yukio Mishima commits ritual suicide at **45** (1970).

PLAYS

Friedrich Dürrenmatt: *The Visit* (1956).

Christopher Marlowe dies at **29** (1593). Alfred Jarry dies at **34** (1907). Joe Orton is killed at **34** (1967). Otto von Horvath dies at **36** (Paris, 1938) when a tree falls on him during a storm as he is walking along the Champs Elysées; his best-known work is *Don Juan Comes Back from the War,* described as a work of "harsh pessimism." J. M. Synge dies at **38** (1909). Brendan Behan dies at **41** (1964). Anton Chekhov dies at **44** (1904). Oscar Wilde dies from meningitis at **46** (1900).

Charlie Chaplin marries Lita McMurray Grey (**16**), because he has got her pregnant (1924). He met her when she was **12**, and he had cast her as the angel in *The Kid* (1920). They are married for two years, and apparently have sex six times a night.

Alfred Hitchcock: *The Man Who Knew Too Much* (1934).

Gary Cooper: *Mr. Deeds Goes to Town* (1936).

Bob Hope: *The Big Broadcast of 1938*—his first picture as a star; and *Don't Look Now* (also 1938), his first picture with Bing Crosby (**37**).

John Huston directs his first film—*The Maltese Falcon* (1941), with Humphrey Bogart (**42**).

Alec Guinness plays eight different people in *Kind Hearts and Coronets* (1949).

Ingrid Bergman has a child by Roberto Rossellini (**44**), when she is still married to someone else. Her pregnancy creates a scandal, which temporarily halts her career.

Doris Day: *Pillow Talk* (1959), with Rock Hudson (**34**).

Stanley Kubrick: *Dr. Strangelove: Or How I Learned to Stop Worrying and Love the Bomb* (1963), with Peter Sellers (**38**).

Tony Richardson: *Tom Jones* (1963), with a script by John Osborne (**34**), starring Susannah York (**22**), David Warner (**22**), Albert Finney (**26**), Hugh Griffith (**51**), and Edith Evans (**75**).

Jean-Luc Godard: *Alphaville* (1965).

Mike Nichols: *Who's Afraid of Virginia Woolf?* starring Elizabeth Taylor (**34**), and Richard Burton (**41**).

Sherry Lansing: head of 20th Century-Fox (1980).

NOTE: here are some premature deaths in films.

James Dean dies in a car crash at **24** (1955).

Jean Harlow dies at **26** (1937).

Rudolph Valentino dies at **31** (1926).

Jayne Mansfield dies in a car crash (1967), at **35**.

Marilyn Monroe dies of a drug overdose at **36** (1962).

Irving Thalberg dies at **37** (1936).

John Gilbert dies at **38** (1937).

Natalie Wood dies at **43** (1981).

Montgomery Clift dies at **44** (1966).

MUSIC—NON-CLASSICAL

"I'm **35**—it's just the body I carry is **69**."—Frank Sinatra.

Find something you like doing, and do it till it kills you.—Keith Richard.

NOTE: here are some premature deaths in the music industry:

Buddy Holly dies in a plane crash at **22** (1959, Feb. 3).

Duane Allman, lead guitarist of the Allman Brothers, dies at **24** (1971); he is killed in a motorcycle accident; coincidentally, Berry Oakley, another member of the same group, dies in an almost identical motorcycle accident, a year later, also at **24**.

Brian Jones drowns in a swimming pool at **25** (1969), a few months after leaving the Rolling Stones; Jones had been busted three times in one year for drug offenses, and had made love to 64 women in one month.

Otis Redding is killed in an aircraft accident at **26** (1967), accompanied by four other musicians, **18**, **18**, **18**, and **19**.

Janis Joplin dies at **27** (1970) from a drug overdose; from **24** on, she has been the leading female personality in rock; her ambition has been to "get high and get laid."

Jimi Hendrix dies of a drug overdose at **27** (1970).

Jim Morrison, of the Doors, dies at **27** (1971).

Brian Cole, of the Association, dies of a drug overdose at **28** (1972).

Ron "Pig-Pen" McKernan, of the Grateful Dead, dies at **28** (1973), of a liver complaint.

Bon Scott, of AC/DC, the leading heavy metal group, dies at **28** (1980); a postmortem reveals that he has 690 milligrams of alcohol in his blood; for comparison, 370 milligrams is said to be lethal, and 690 is the equivalent of drinking five bottles of brandy in ten hours.

Sam Cooke dies at **29** (1964) in a shooting incident; his big run of hits had started at **23**, including "Chain Gang" at **25**; after his death, his records continue very strongly in the charts, as with Buddy Holly.

Marc Bolan, of T. Rex, dies in a car crash at **29** (1977), the driver being his girl friend (**30**) who survives.

Keith Moon, of the Who, dies from drugs at **31** (1978), a few days after announcing his engagement; in his life he is believed to have caused $400,000 worth of damage to hotel rooms, and other places; coincidentally, Keith Moon had spent his last night watching a film about Buddy Holly; another coincidence is that he dies in the same London apartment in which Mama Cass (Elliot) had died. Two more coincidences: a year after Moon's death, 11 teenagers are trampled to death at a concert given by the Who; and there is a song by the Who, "Hope I Die Before I Get Old."

Brian Epstein, manager of the Beatles, dies at **32** (1967).

Cass Elliot, of the Mamas and the Papas, dies at **32** (1974).

Florence Ballard, ex-Supreme, dies at **32** (1976) at a time when she is living on welfare.

John Bonham, drummer with Led Zeppelin, dies at **32** (1980) after inhaling his own vomit; he had drunk 40 shots of vodka in the previous 12 hours.

 Glenn Miller at **33** disappears over the English Channel, while flying to France (1944).

Phil Ochs hangs himself at **35** (1976); he had been a big songwriter during the 1960s, but had recently begun to worry about lack of inspiration.

Gene Vincent dies at **36** (1971).

Bob Marley, the reggae leader, dies of cancer, at **36** (1981).

Mike Bloomfield, sometime of the Electric Flag, dies at **37** (1981), perhaps from the effect of drugs.

George Gershwin, composer of *Porgy and Bess,* dies at **38** (1937).

Mario Lanza dies at **38** (1959).

Claude François, the leading French singer, dies at **38** (1978); he accidentally electrocutes himself while changing a lightbulb in his bathroom.

Alan Freed, leading rock industry entrepreneur, dies at **42** (1965); he had been scapegoated for all the payola sins of the record industry, and his career and life had been destroyed.

Elvis Presley dies at **42** (1977).

Billie Holiday dies at **44** (1959).

Judy Garland dies of a drug overdose at **47**.

Long-term careers in rock music are unlikely, since rock stars are expected to live "on the edge" during their working life. Rock musicians are employed by society to act out the fantasies which it is too scared to live out for itself. Consequently, the logic of the performer's position leads inexorably toward self-destruction; to be old would seem to be the complete antithesis of the performer's identity. So an early death is almost part of the job (cf. Janis Joplin's comment about **70***). Putting it more matter-of-factly, Pete Townshend of the Who is quoted as saying at **35**, "I really do feel that there's a certain age beyond which you can't—no matter how much your audience might will you to—do the standard rock 'n' roll thing." Pop music has to be the music of the moment. But the moment passes, and the performer is left without a career.

A rock career, after the first peak, can end or continue in these ways:

—to be a "one hit wonder"; to have one moment in music history, and then return to being an average person;

—a drug bust or other legal trouble can break the momentum of a group; you then drift apart, perhaps to join groups, or perhaps to leave the music profession altogether;

—you develop as a person, and you let your music reflect the changes in your life; you hope your public will empathize, and even change with you, for example, from pure rock into religion;

—you crack up; you go bankrupt, or become homeless; you have to be moved into a mental hospital; the monetary savings of your peak earnings years have disappeared or have been stolen;

—you die, either from drugs or drink, or from an accident in traveling to a concert, or are somehow burned out by your extravagant or rootless life;

—you make a farewell film, and then stop; you exit at a peak, as did the Band (**35**) in its film of its last concert, "The Last Waltz" (1978);

—you make a "comeback" album;

—you produce the same music, but in a more relaxed way, for example, at clubs or in cabaret; your audience will enjoy hearing the standards performed by a great old name; in this alternative, you move into a less confrontational atmosphere—for example, Chuck Berry (**46**, in 1972) made a success in a Las Vegas hotel, where he had previously made his name with hits such as "Johnny B. Goode" at **32**;

—you appear at revival or vintage or Golden Oldie shows; you do not change, but continue as a figure out of history; as an example, Bill Haley continues to perform "Rock Around the Clock" (originally at **28**) for 25 years;

Rapid turnover is such a feature of rock and punk music that we forget how unusual it is in other forms of popular entertainment. People such as Sophie Tucker (1884–1966), Frank Sinatra (b. 1915), Sammy Davis, Jr. (b. 1925), and Liberace (b. 1919) have had lifelong careers.

Tom Jones is an example of a performer who has managed the move from man-of-the-moment to someone with a permanent audience; his early successes included "It's Not Unusual" (1965), and he is still charismatic, to his followers, at **40** (1980). Another long career is that of Burl Ives, who first appeared on Broadway at **29** (1938); he starred as Big Daddy in the film of "Cat on a Hot Tin Roof" at **49**, and he made a big concert tour of Europe at **69**. Cliff Richard (b. 1940) manages to keep on appealing to the same age range, even as he himself gets older. More typically, other stars appeal to the same generation, and the star and the audience grow old together. Cliff Richard had a number one in the charts at **38** (1979)—his first hit had been at **17**, and he has had 64 hit records since then.

Different types of music have different traditions. Rock stars age rapidly; country and western singers are allowed by their audiences to go on forever ("Worse luck."—Peter Evans).

TV, ETC.

Blondin: crossing of Niagara Falls on a tightrope (1859). This makes him suddenly world famous. He uses his fame to develop a long and successful career in music halls. He dies at **73** from natural causes, at his London suburban home, named "Niagara Villa."

Leonard Nimoy and William Shatner (also **35**): "Star Trek" (1966–68). Nimoy has pointed ears in the show, as he is half descended from an alien species. Nimoy never quite repeats this success, but perhaps he does not need to do so—from now on he becomes a cult figure, and he also publishes several books of poetry. Showing the typecasting pressures, Nimoy's autobiography is called "I Am Not Spock." The genius behind "Star Trek" is Gene Roddenberry (**45**).

LOVE, LIFE

Dick Price and Michael Murphy (both **35**): Esalen Institute, Big Sur, California (1965). At this moment, Fritz Perls is **72**, Ida P. Rolf is **68**, and William Schutz is **40**.

PRESS

When one hears of a poet past **35**, he seems somehow unnatural and even a little obscene; it is as if one encountered a graying man who still played the Chopin waltzes.—H. L. Mencken, the journalist (1880–1956).

John Milton: *Areopagitica* (1644)—an early plea for freedom of the press. It is heavily influenced by Milton's visit at **29** to the recently censored Galileo (**74**).

William Randolph Hearst is instrumental in creating the Spanish-American War (1898) over Cuba. Hearst now owns two newspapers, and he has made their circulations zoom by the manufacture of news. This war is the extreme example of his ability to create news out of events that happen only because he himself has orchestrated them. Among the staff ("commissioners") that Hearst employs in Cuba are the writer Stephen Crane (**26**) and the artist Frederick Remington (**36**). Hearst now attempts to enter politics. By **45**, this proves to be a failure, and he is permanently wounded by the antagonism aroused by his candidacies. (cf. **56***)

Gloria Steinem, and others: *Ms.* magazine (1972).

EXPLORATION

George Vancouver: exploration of the area later known as Vancouver, in British Columbia and in Washington (1792). He names Puget Sound after one of his officers, Peter Puget (**30**).

Hiram Bingham: rediscovery of Machu Picchu, the lost city of the Incas (1911).

Reinhold Messner: solo climb of Mt. Everest, without oxygen (1980)—perhaps the greatest achievement in the history of mountaineering.

Early retirement for stewardesses was a feature of the airline industry at the beginning of passenger carrying. The first stewardesses were ex-nurses who had to retire on marriage or at **32**, whichever came first. Today such a rule would generally be illegal, and cabin personnel can work until **65**, while pilots have to retire at **60**.

LAW CRIME

Wyatt Earp: the gunfight at the O.K. Corral (1881, Oct. 26). This is between Earp, Doc Holliday (**32**), and friends, versus a rival gang. Each side is mainly a bunch of vicious gamblers who are competing in the robbery of stagecoaches. Later, after a fairly law-abiding career as a gambler, Earp dies in Los Angeles at **84**.

Robert F. Kennedy: Attorney-General of the U.S. (1963). He is the third youngest to hold this office.

Charles Manson organizes the murder of film star Sharon Tate (**26**) (1969). Manson's associates include Linda Kasabian (**20**), Patricia Krenwinkel (**21**), and Charles Watson (**24**). Leslie van Houten (**19**) and others kill the Labianca family on the following day. At **26**, Manson had received a ten-year sentence for forging checks, and he was released at **32**. He then acquired a following at the San Francisco "Summer of Love," and later sets up his own commune, from which these murders at **35** are based.

The Kray twins are sent to prison (1969) until **65**—in the 1960s, they had attempted to become Britain's answer to Al Capone (**26***, **30***).

Brian Cooper and Nigel Maidment are publicly given 80 strokes of the cane (1978) in Saudi Arabia. They are working on an engineering contract there, and are found to have manufactured alcohol in their hotel bedroom.

SPORTS

Agathos Daimon: he dies during a boxing match at one of the original Olympic Games in classical Greece. His tombstome is erected near Olympia, and it says:

Here he died, boxing in the Stadium,
Having prayed to Zeus for either the Wreath (of victory) or death,
Aged **35**. Farewell.

Some examples of boxers and their retirement: John L. Sullivan makes a comeback out of retirement at **46** (1904), and wins his first contest in two rounds; but he then decides on complete retirement. Joe Louis first retires at **34**, but financial difficulties force him into making a comeback; he loses his world heavyweight title for the last time at **36**, and is knocked out at **37** by Rocky Marciano (**28**). Sugar Ray Robinson retires as world middleweight champion at **32** (1952); he makes a comeback at **34**, and is forced out at **39**. Muhammad Ali is forced to retire at **38**.

José Capablanca (1924) is perhaps the best-known person in chess history—his period of greatest ability is from **31** to **39**. He dies at **53**, after a stroke suffered while watching a chess game.

David Parchment (1979) breaks a world record—he performs 233 parachute jumps in 18 hours. He had started in the sport of parachuting at **31**. Each jump is from about 1,500 feet, and takes 40 seconds; in breaking the record, he falls a total of 65 miles.

Rodney Marsh (1979) plays his last soccer game; he has been a star for England and in Florida. He comments: "It's the best time for me to quit. I'm at the peak of my profession. I'm the captain of my team, and only last week I scored two great goals."

NOTE: here are some examples of early death in the world of motor racing:

Mike Hawthorn (**29**, in 1958) wins the world motor racing championship, and decides to retire. His decision is prompted by the death of his friend Peter Collins (**27**) in an accident in the German Grand Prix. But Hawthorn himself is killed, a few months after retirement, in an accident on an ordinary public road. Hawthorn won the 1955 Le Mans race in which he narrowly missed death in the greatest disaster of motor racing history—83 spectators die when a car flies off into the grandstand. About the dangers of racing, Niki Lauda (**28**) has been quoted as saying: "I accept that there is perhaps a twenty percent chance that I may be killed in a race." Deaths among motor racers include the following: Jochen Rindt dies at **28**, at Monza (1970), a circuit in which 50 people have been killed in the track's history. Tom Pryce (**28**) is killed in a 1977 Grand Prix. Jim Clark (**32**, in 1968) is killed at Hockenheim; later there is a memorial race to Jim Clark, and in 1980 Markus Hoettinger (**23**) is killed in a practice for this. Bruce McClaren (**32**, in 1970) is killed in a test drive at Goodwood. Carlos Pace (**32**, in 1977) is killed in a plane crash; at **30** he won the Brazilian Grand Prix. Ronnie Peterson dies at **34** (1978) after an accident at the start of the Italian Grand Prix at Monza.

Peter Gregg kills himself with a gun at **40** (1980); he had been the champion driver of Porsches. Graham Hill (**46**, in 1975) is killed in a plane crash; he had been world champion driver at **33** and **39**. Luigi Fagioli (**53**, in 1952) is killed practicing for the Monaco Grand Prix. Motorcycle racing is more dangerous than driving; in a typical recent season (U.K., 1978) four people were killed—**18**, **29**, **33**, and **35**.

Age and Peak Performance in Sports

A list of the factors which contribute to sports success includes the peak years for the following:

—reaction time;
—physical strength;
—endurance;
—physical dexterity and coordination;
—maturity during competition;
—experience in your particular sport (for example, being the "Old Fox" who always happens to be in the right place at the right time);
—and ambition.

In adulthood, experience increases with age; physical abilities decrease; and ambition varies independently of age.

Some of these sports factors rise and fall quickly—by **20**, you may have peaked in reaction time. Others may take years to acquire—maturity during competition, for an example, so that you can psych out your opponents with increasing success. In the main, sports ability is dependent on relatively age-specific factors, even in such cerebral sports as chess. Ambition is unique in the above list, as it can rise and fall, and increase again.

Where these factors do simply rise and fall with age, the peaks will probably not coincide. Top performance in each sport needs a different combination of these abilities. At the end of this essay, there is a table showing the peak years for each sport.

Sports vary as to how age-specific they are. The peak years for swimming are very short—Shane Gould's career at the top was only from **14** to **16** (cf. **15***). In other sports, like baseball and cricket, you can stay at the top for two decades. Declining ability in, say, quick reflexes, is balanced by increasing experience in the game.

THE PRE-PEAK AND THE POST-PEAK YEARS

In the original Olympic Games, boys were **12–17**, and the championship eligibility began at **18**, the same age as military conscription. These junior events were always an integral part of the games.

Any well-organized sport today has a system of age-stratification, so that you can compete against people of roughly your own age—in the same way that there are different leagues or divisions for people of different skill. In the pre-peak years, age-stratification gets you into the habit of winning; in the post-peak years, age grouping helps to keep you active in your sport.

In U.S. competitive swimming, the pre-peak years are divided into four age groups: **0–10**; **11** and **12**; **13** and **14**; **15**, **16** and **17**. The introduction of this age-grouping was one source of the amazing postwar improvement in swimming in the U.S.A. Incidentally, this very precise age-grouping in the early teens indicates the rapid changes that take place in swimming ability around these years. In contrast, it would hardly make any sense to divide the early **20**s, for example, swimming races for **20–21**, **22–24**, and so on.

Here are some typical names for the age-group: the *pre-peak years* are for juniors, colts, novices, futures junior varsity, or designated simply by age, such as the **under-21**s. The *peak years* are for the Olympics, seniors, professionals, world records, and World Series.

The post-peak years are for seniors, veterans, masters, vintage. Confusingly, "seniors" can be used for either the peak or the post-peak years, as can "champion." Here, "peak" is used for the age at which you are capable of breaking the absolute world record, or playing on the best team. In horse racing, there is a further difficulty for outsiders—jockeys are always called "boys" in America, and "lad" is a stable helper of any age.

Obviously, the chronological ages that are pre-peak or post-peak will vary from sport to sport, and even within a sport. For example, in soccer, a defender lasts longer than a forward. For skiers using the NASTAR system, the peak age is **16–19**. If you are **15** and below, or **30**+, you benefit in the handicapping. Bowls is a sport generally played by older people; the Welsh have a league to bring new blood into the game—the pre-peak or "Junior" league is for the **under-35**s.

PARTICIPATION

The problem of peak performance is not one that faces most of us. Who cares about Bjorn Borg or Mark Spitz? What truly matters is how fit you yourself are today and tomorrow. Look at this table for record times in running two distances:

	100 meters	*10,000 meters*
men aged 40	10.8 sec.	28 min. 33 sec.
50	11.4 sec.	32 min. 30 sec.
60	12.0 sec.	36 min. 16 sec.
70	14.6 sec.	41 min. 21 sec.
80	20.5 sec.	48 min. 19 sec. (at **79**)
90	19.9 sec.	

Although it is clear that performance deteriorates with age, what is surprising is how little fall-off there is. The fact that anyone of **80** can run 10,000 meters in less than one hour is amazing—I would have guessed two days to be the record. So what we must look at is the applicability of the sport to a particular age. How open is a sport to participation when you are in the post-peak years?

Running is fairly age-specific for championships—but you can jog at any age. Swimming is both the most age-specific for peak performance, and the least age-specific for participation. Swimming can begin before you learn to walk and continue until **81*** and beyond. Conversely, there are some sports in which the peak performance years extend beyond the years of participation. These sports often involve a high risk of danger, such as boxing, motor racing, and bullfighting. If you cannot make it into the top class, then there is little point in persisting. A mediocre-ability boxer is likely to retire earlier than a champion.

As you get older, the suitability of a sport depends on these factors:

—quantity of time required to keep a minimum of performance (you may now have much less, or much more, time available);

—time in coordinating the sport into the rest of your life. It is easier to organize team sports for people at school; it is easier for a family person to jog alone, or to play tennis with one other person;

—physical factors; beyond a certain age and level of skill, a sport may be impossible;

—how much can you vary the sport to fit in with your (declining) level of performance? For example, in weight training, you can vary your effort from high to the almost infinitely low level. This is good for long-term participation, but in a team sport such as football, you must reach a medium-high threshold of performance before you can get anything out of the game. Swimming and jogging are two other sports which are good for participation because they do not have this high threshold for participation. As you get older, you swim or jog slower and slower and that's okay.

People respond to these difficulties over participation in the following way:

—give up participating and become a spectator—the "sad sack" syndrome;

—change sports as you get older—move from football into golf, or from gymnastics into weight training;

—transfer into a less strenuous aspect of the same sport—move from player to coach, and from coach to administration.

To watch a tennis championship is to observe an event which is age-stratified with precision: ball boys and girls, **13–16**; players **16–35**; umpires **35–55**; and senior officials **55–70**.

This pattern of age grouping is common. For example, in soccer's peak event, the World Cup, referees were typically aged **36–46** (1978). Similarly, the chief administrator of the Olympic games (1980) was Peter Killanin (**66***).

One explanation is that umpires are ex-players, and the top officials are ex-umpires. Another explanation is money—the job of referee is often time-consuming, yet few sports are so rich that they can afford good salaries for a host of umpires, linesmen, and so forth. Such officials therefore tend to be either retired, or ex-military, and so older than the players.

TABLE OF SPORTS AND AGE

"Peak" = absolute peak achievement in a sport, irrespective of any handicapping for age. "Participation" = taking part in this sport for your own personal benefit or enjoyment only. The ages below are the beginning and ending ages for taking part in each sport, at either "peak" or "participation" level. Where there are two figures, for example, the tennis peak starts at **16/19**, this means that the record earliest peak is around **16**, but that most peak performances begin around **19**. Note that the table is about typical ages; we are less interested in oldest-ever and youngest-ever record performances.

	Years peak	Years participation
Peak Typically in Mid-Teens		
gymnastics	**14/16–16/25**	**6/10–25/30**
swimming	**14–18/25**	**1/5–18/100**
Peak Typically in Early **20**s		
roller skating	**15/18–30/35**	**10/20–30/40/50**
rugger	**19–30/35**	**9–28/39**
surfing	**18–35**	**10/14–21/30/40**
table tennis	**18–29**	**7–70**
tennis	**16/19–33/41**	**7/10–45/60**
track & jogging	**17/21–27/34**	**3–93**
Peak Typically Around Late **20**s, Early **30**s		
archery	**18–39**	**15–45/65**
badminton	**17–33**	**12–45**
ballroom dancing	**17/21–30/40**	**13–70/80**
baseball	**19/23–33/43**	**5/8–28**
bobsled	**20–35**	**15/18–30/45**
boxing*	**21/24–35/39**	**7/12–29**

bullfighting	**18/21–34**	**11/15–21**
cricket	**20/24–35/40**	**7–67/87**
cycling	**21–32/35**	**5–95**
fencing	**19/21–35**	**10–40/60**
hang gliding	c.**18**–c.**35**	**14/19–40/**
hockey	**18/22–28/35**	**12/15–28/35**
horse racing	**16/17/21–35/45**	**5–65/95**
golf	**20/25–37/43**	**9/30–60/95**
motor racing	**21/25–35/40/46**	**17/21–25/35**
mountaineering	**20/25–35/45**	**14/20–40/50**
parachuting	**20–40**	**16–73**
rowing	**18–32**	**12–30**
skiing	**16–29**	**5/15–40/80**
soccer	**18/21–33/39**	**5/10–28/40**
squash	**19/25–31/43**	**12–40/50**
stock car racing	**18/22–30/32**	**15/18–25/40**
wrestling	**21–30/39**	**15–30**
weight training	**21–35**	**10–40/90**
Peak Typically in **20**s, **30**s, or **40**s		
angling	**20–50**	**5/10–70/90**
ballooning	**25–45/60**	**18/25–40/60**
caving	**21–41**	**16–45**
rifle shooting	**21–41**	**15–60/90**
yachting	**15/20–45/55**	**10–50/80**
No Precise Peak Age		
bowling	**20–60**	**5–95**
bowls	**18/40–50/60**	**18/50–70/100**
bridge	**14/27–50**	**10–99**
chess	**15/23–39/49**	**5/15–90**
croquet	**18/30–40/60**	**15/50–99**
darts	**21–52**	**16–88**
fox hunting	**30–60**	**15–50/80**
frisbee	**15/50**	**6/10–50/**
gliding	**21/25–57**	**16/18–40/60/70**
powerboat racing	**21–55**	**17–40/65**
snooker	**25–55**	**10–80/100**

*In boxing, the number of rounds you can box is limited by age: **18+**, six rounds; **19+**, eight rounds; and **21+**, full bout.

PARTICIPATION

The sports can be grouped together for the ease of participation as you get older.

Good for participation: angling, archery, ballroom dancing, bowls, bridge, chess, cricket, croquet, cycling, dance, darts, fox hunting, frisbee, gliding, golf, martial arts, parachuting, rifle shooting, skiing, snooker and billiards, squash, swimming, tennis, track and jogging, weight training, yachting.

Okay for participation: baseball, fencing, gymnastics, hang gliding, hockey, mountaineering, polo, roller skating, rugger, rowing, soccer, surfing, wrestling.

Bad for participation: (here the participation age often stops earlier than the peak championship age) American football, boxing, bullfighting, motor racing, stock car racing.

Retirement and Sport

Retirement from the sports world presents these problems:

—it is likely that you have now completed the greatest success of your life;

—you may well be finishing the peak earning years of your life;

—it is very exhausting, physically and emotionally, to continue to keep yourself at peak competitive performance;

—if you hang on, you can only go downhill; if you do not retire gracefully, you may be driven out by a hot young thing—perhaps you yourself reached championship level by driving out an older person, and you could now be on the receiving end of this process;

—in some sports, injury and even death is a statistical possibility—therefore the temptation is to retire as soon as you have reached a clearly visible peak (cf. motor racing, at **35***);

—but, when you retire, you will join "normality," and leave an exciting, elite occupation; you leave the peak of one career and have to start at the bottom of another; on retirement, you will miss the ego trip, the earnings, and your sense of identity;

—you may have to start a new career at a time when others in it are already well established;

—is it ever possible to retire at the moment of your greatest performance? There is always someone older than you who has reached a new peak—so you are tempted to postpone retirement;

—one force for retirement is that sport itself begins to seem a nonadult goal in life. For example, Niki Lauda who retired from motor racing at **30** (1979) commented: "There I was going round the track at God knows what speed when I suddenly thought: Why am I doing this? It's daft. There are other things in life I want to do. . . . Racing doesn't mean anything to me anymore. . . . It is the kind of thing that happens to a racing driver. One minute you want to race. The next you know you want out."

After retirement from professional sport, here are some options for the rest of your life:

—to take a job associated with your sport, as coach, manager, administrator, sports shop owner, and so on.

—to live off your earnings for the rest of your life; for example, Joe Frazier, the boxer, is said to have retired at **32** with $2.5 million earned, and James Hunt, world motor racing champion at **29**, retired also at **32**, having earned approximately £1.5 million (3 million dollars).

—alternatively, to spend the remainder of your life in paying off the debts which you have accumulated in your bid for championship status (apparently this was a not uncommon fate for sportsmen in the original Olympics).

—to collect money from a "benefit" season, or from a "testimonial" match in your honor; and/or now to collect from a pension fund or players' retirement scheme, which pays up at about **35**.

—to stop retiring, and make a comeback; for example the soccer star Pele retired at **34** (cf. **15***) and made a comeback at **35**. See also boxers at **35***.

—to return to the game, but move down from major league to the minors—as did Jim Bouton (**39**, in 1979), the former Yankee player and baseball author.

—to take up another activity in which your existing fame and skill will be useful; for example, Sonja Henie (cf. **11***), the ice-skater turned film star; or Johnny Weismuller, the former Olympic swimming champion, who at **28** retired, and enters the film industry in the part of Tarzan. When he retired from films, he went to work for a swimming pool company in Florida.

—to survive on your endorsements of sports products; for example, Fred Perry's tennis clothes continue to be bought long after his playing career has ended.

—to continue in the public mind as a symbol of decency, reliability, and achievement; Joe DiMaggio (cf. **26***) is an example.

—to get a complimentary seat in the grandstand for the rest of your life.

—to continue as a public "legend" and to keep playing at exhibition games, golf tournaments, and so forth. People will come to see the legend, even if your playing standards are somewhat diminished.

—to achieve success at an entirely different occupation; for exampel, Jack Lynch (b. 1917) was Ireland's leading track athlete between **21** and **34** and also a record breaker in hurling and in Gaelic football. At **31**, he became a member of Parliament, and at **61** he was Prime Minister of the Republic.

—to suffer withdrawal symptoms; after the loss of fame, admiration, cash, et al, you get physically out of shape, and you become aimless.

—to try to recapture the form of your peak days—but fail in this attempt and become a pitiful embarrassment to your ex-admirers.

—to suffer physically for the rest of your life; boxers, whose career has been spent in taking punishment, or the rugger player who is a paraplegic after breaking his neck in a game.

—to die soon afterward in some other activity (for example, flying) which you have taken up in your continuous pursuit of living dangerously.

—if a champion in the original Olympic Games, to expect to go on to high office in the military and political system. Success at sports was seen as indicative of general leadership ability.

—sex: male champion racehorses probably have the most pleasant retirement. A successful horse can retire after just two seasons (**2** and **3**) and be put out to stud. The stallion must now have sexual intercourse with an endless stream of mares who are brought to be serviced. The horse's death occurs roughly around **25–33**. During the mating season, a male may have relations with 80–120 females.

36

HEALTH

F. J. Lewis: first use of hypothermia in a heart operation (1952).

Alick Isaacs, with Jean Lindenmann (**33**): discovery of interferon (1957). Isaacs dies at **45**.

Jean Henri Dunant: the Red Cross organization (1864).

HISTORY—U.S.A.

William Penn: Pennsylvania (1681).

William Jennings Bryan: his "cross of gold" speech at the Democratic Convention (1896); he wins the nomination, but loses the election, to William McKinley (**53**).

HISTORY—U.K.

Arthur Onslow is made Speaker of the House of Commons (1728)—holds office for another 33 years.

David Lloyd George delivers his "Peoples' Budget" (1909, Apr. 29)—a landmark in the development of the welfare state. He had been an MP at **27**, and Chancellor at **35**; Prime Minister at **54**; resigns at **59***.

RELIGION, PHILOSOPHY

G. W. F. Hegel: *Phenomenology of Mind* (1806)—pioneer in the dialectical method, and later the favorite of Karl Marx.

William Booth starts a mission in the East End of London (1865)—this is the beginning of the Salvation Army. Previously, he had been a traveling preacher and Methodist. By the time of his death (**83**), he is the General of a worldwide Army.

Georges Gurdjieff returns to Moscow, after having disappeared in Asia for the past 20 years. He now begins teaching such people as P. D. Ouspensky.

SOCIAL SCIENCE, EDUCATION

J. B. Say: *A Treatise on Political Economy: or, the Production, Distribution, and Consumption of Wealth* (1803)—start of supply-side economics.

Maria Montessori: opening of her first "Casa dei Bambini" (1906), where children can discover for themselves the nature of geometry, numbers, music, and so forth. Montessori lives until **82**.

C. A. van Gennep: *Rites of Passage* (1909). Although this makes him later a permanently famous person, he now leaves this topic, and moves into other areas of anthropology.

J. M. Keynes: *The Economic Consequences of the Peace* (1919). As an official of the British Treasury, Keynes attends the Versailles Conference at the end of World War I. Here he meets, or observes, the elite of the Western world; he is disappointed, and says so in this book. He also prophecies here that victory over Germany will be followed by an economic depression. (cf. **52***)

Betty Friedan is a journalist (1957); she surveys her classmates from Smith about their life since leaving college, and receives many difficult-to-verbalize complaints—the "problem that has no name." By **42**, she is able to write this up as *The Feminine Mystique*. She helps start the National Organization of Women at **45**.

Franz Fanon: *The Wretched of the Earth* (1961), and death at **36**. On hearing that he has leukemia, Fanon hurries to finish this book before dying.

Theodore Roszak: *The Making of a Counter-Culture* (1969).

Kate Millett: *Sexual Politics* (1970).

Christopher Jencks: *Inequality* (1972).

Douglas Hofstadter: *Gödel, Escher, Bach* (1980).

SCIENCE, TECHNOLOGY

Antoine Lavoisier: identification of oxygen (1779).

Dmitri Mendeleev: publication of his periodic table of the elements (1871). He predicts the existence of three more elements. These are discovered when he is **41**, **45**, and **51**, and he himself is seen as a giant among scientists. He now lives for another 36 years.

Ernest Rutherford: Nobel Prize (1908) for work which effectively sets out the basic architecture of the atom. He later goes on to perform equally important work on the first nuclear reaction, between **45** and **52**.

Frederick Soddy: the concept of isotopes in atomic physics (1913).

Albert Einstein: the General Theory of Relativity (1915), following from his Special Theory, at **26***. At this time, he is known only to a tiny elite within the world of physics. Two of the predictions in relativity are that (1) light would be deflected by gravity, and (2) time, as measured by a clock, would change in the presence of changing gravitational fields. At **40**, the first prediction is confirmed by Arthur Eddington (**36**) and others—Einstein overnight becomes the most famous scientist in the world. The second prediction, about clocks, now becomes famous; it is so foreign to commonsense that it helps to present Einstein's physics as an entirely new intellectual event. People are shocked, and delighted, that such a fixture as Newton (**23***, **44***) has to be modified. Einstein now becomes a general-purpose genius; having solved the problems of space/time in the universe, more mundane problems should be easy to solve. He therefore uses his fame to support certain vital issues, especially pacifism and his idealistic view of world government. His time is often taken up with traveling, the giving of lectures, and the receiving of honors. But in physics, there is a growing gap between him and the mainstream. At **48**, he is in disagreement with the "uncertainty principle" of Werner Heisenberg (**25**). For the rest of his life, Einstein is a world figure, and he intervenes in the development of the atomic bomb, at **60***.

Sir Richard Arkwright designs his spinning frame between **33** and **36** (1767–69); he has his own wig and barber business, and is a part-time inventor. Although he is unable to defend his patents, he makes a good deal of money out of textiles through his skill and inventiveness at organizing some of the first-ever factories. (cf. **50***)

Henry Ford leaves the Edison Illuminating Company (Aug. 1899) and forms the Detroit Automobile Company. His backers are some of the leading rich people in Detroit. But the company lasts only a year, and Ford concentrates on designing racing cars, believing that this is the best way to develop car technology. (cf. **38***)

William Morris (Lord Nuffield): first Morris Oxford car (1913); but he does not achieve mass sales until his late **40**s. The new car is a novelty as it aims at the lower end of the market (existing cars have been for the rich); where possible, the car is assembled from parts brought in from other manufacturers.

William B. Walton teams up with two others to start a corporation owning motels—his first office is in an abandoned workshop, and they go $37,000 into debt (1956). This is the beginning of Holiday Inns; at **48**, he opens the 1,000th motel, and is worth around $150 million.

RENAISSANCE

Samuel Pepys: last entry in his diary (London, 1669); he is suffering from eyesight problems, and stops the diary which he had begun at **26**. Later, his diary is the achievement for which he is permanently famous; but now at **36** his public career is still ahead of him. He is a civilian administrator in the Navy, and at **33** he had written an important policy document on the poor state of the service. Pepys is, in effect, civilian chief at the Navy, at **40–46**, and **51–56**; he initiates the construction of thirty large ships which transform the fleet. At **51**, he is also appointed president of the Royal Society, the organization of scientists, and his imprimatur appears on the title page of *Principia* by Isaac Newton (**44***). Pepys lives until **69**; his wife Elizabeth, who figures prominently in the diary, dies at **29**, when he is **36**; Pepys is a widower for the rest of his life. The diary is written in a kind of shorthand and is never read during his lifetime. It is first decoded and published when he would have been **192**.

William Blake: *Songs of Innocence, and of Experience* (London, 1794). Blake is a workaholic and also is gifted in several directions. In his books he routinely combines: his own poetry; illustrations of biblical figures in a Michelangelesque style; thoughts on political revolution; and a mystical symbolism that fights against the new industrial rationality; all of this is typically engraved, colored, and produced by himself and his wife. His best-known poems are "Tiger! Tiger! burning bright . . ." at **36**, and "And did those feet in ancient times . . ." at **47**.

In his old age, Blake is surrounded by a group of young people, paradoxically known as "The Ancients," who are anxious to learn the complete philosophical and artistic system which he has developed. Blake dies at **69** and is said to be singing at the moment when he "passes from one room to another."

Walter Gropius: opening of the Bauhaus school of design (Germany, 1919). His achievements are, first, to attempt a meeting between art, craftsmanship, and mass production; and second, to attract some of the world's leaders in their field to teach at the Bauhaus. At the moment of opening, Wassily Kandinsky is **53**; Lyonel Feininger is **48**, and has just completed the "Cathedral of Socialism" as part of the Bauhaus proclamation; Paul Klee is **40**; Mies van der Rohe, **33**; Johannes Itten, **31**; Josef Albers, **31**; László Moholy-Nagy, **24**; and Marcel Breuer is **17**. Note that not all of these were in the Bauhaus on the first day, but this date has been chosen to compare the ages of the main faculty. After a brilliant success, the school is closed under the new regime of Adolf Hitler (**44**), when Gropius is **50**. At **55**, Gropius is appointed a professor at Harvard University. For the later career of Mies van der Rohe, cf. architecture, **43***. One of the earliest Bauhaus students is Marcel Breuer, who goes on to design the classic chromium-plated tube chair; but later, in his work in North America (**35** onward), his imagination deteriorates, even as his Bauhaus-derived reputation increases. Finally, at **64**, he is chosen as architect of the prestigious Whitney Museum, in New York, and he responds with a design which is almost wilfully lacking in ideas. Josef Albers is another early student at the Bauhaus, beginning there at **32**, having originally worked as an elementary schoolteacher. He is quickly invited onto the faculty, and becomes a "Bauhaus master." After the Bauhaus, he teaches at Black Mountain College, U.S.A., from **41–61**; at **60**, one of his students is Robert Rauschenberg (**23**). Albers's lifelong interest in geometry and painting reaches a climax with another modern classic, "Homage to the Square," from **62** onward.

ARCHITECTURE

Robert Smythson: Longleat House, Wiltshire, England (1572).

Pierre L'Enfant: plans for the new Federal capital of Washington, D.C. (1791). His client is, in effect, George Washington (**52**). On completing the outline design for the city, he is dismissed after less than a year, by direction of Thomas Jefferson (**48**). L'Enfant proves to be an impossibly demanding architect for any client, and the capital city is almost his only design to be completed. He dies at **70**, in poor circumstances.

Mies van der Rohe: outline drawings for a concrete office building (1922); this is the definitive construction system for a modern office block. (cf. **43***)

Alison (**34**) and Peter (**39**) Smithson: headquarters for the *Economist* magazine, London (1962–65).

Renzo Piano (**34**) and Richard Rogers (**38**): Pompidou arts center, Paris—competition now won in July 1971; constructed by 1977.

ART

Thomas Hoving: new director of the Metropolitan Museum of Art, New York City (1967–77).

MUSIC—CLASSICAL

Georges Bizet: *Carmen* (1875). He had written *L'Arlésienne* at **33**, but he dies at **36**—partly from the strain of *Carmen,* which is a failure at its first performances.

Alban Berg: *Wozzeck* (1921). Also *Lulu* is written from **43** until his death at **50**.

LITERATURE

Giovanni Boccaccio: *The Decameron* (1349–51).

Jane Austen has her first book published, *Sense and Sensibility* 1811)—she had started writing at **20**. She now writes *Mansfield Park*, and *Emma* (**39**), and *Persuasion* (**40**). She dies at **42**.

Washington Irving: *Rip van Winkle* (c. 1819). Rip van Winkle awakes after a sleep of twenty years. This has two effects: (1) he is suddenly made aware of vast political changes that have gradually taken place over the years; and (2) he has passed painlessly from the licensed idleness of youth, into the licensed idleness of old age, without spending too much time—he is glad to note—in the demanding years of adulthood.

Walt Whitman publishes at his own expense twelve of his poems, *Leaves of Grass* (1855), and it is an instant success. He keeps revising it, and adding to it all his life, and has a deathbed edition just before he dies at **72**.

George Eliot begins writing her first novel, *Amos Barton* (1856). Later, *Adam Bede* is at **39**; *The Mill on the Floss* at **40**; and *Middlemarch* at **52**. She lives until **61**, having married at **60** and honeymooned in Venice.

John Updike: *Couples* (1968).

John Irving: *The World According to Garp* (1978).

PLAYS, DANCE

Jean-Baptiste Molière and his theater company perform the play *Le Docteur amoureux* in front of King Louis XIV (**20**, in 1658) and it is well received—this is the beginning of Molière's central career. Previously Molière's company had been on the fringe, trying to make a living in the provinces of France. At **39**, he writes *The School for*

 Husbands. At **40** he marries Armande Béjart (**18**), sister of his former lover Madeleine (**44**); and he writes *The School for Wives*. Molière writes *Tartuffe* at **42**; *Le Médecin malgré lui* at **44**; and *Le Bourgeois Gentilhomme* at **49**. Molière dies after collapsing during the fourth performance of *Le Malade imaginaire* at **51**.

Oscar Wilde: *Lady Windermere's Fan* (London, 1892). This is his first play. As an undergraduate, Wilde had been brilliant, and had written the poem "Requiescat." Afterward, he becomes a journalist and self-publicist. At **27–28** he went on a tour of America, to lecture on the new fashions in art. On arrival there, he complained about the Atlantic Ocean. He married at **29**, and published his novel, *Dorian Gray*, on the subject of aging, at **35**. His own lifestyle became his major focus of attention. It is in his early **30**s that Wilde becomes committed to homosexuality. Now at **36**, Wilde has a great success with his play; at the first night he wears a green carnation—his new trademark—and congratulates the audience for applauding the play. At **38**, he writes *A Woman of No Importance;* this contains the line "Those whom the gods love grow young." At **40**, he completes *An Ideal Husband* and *The Importance of Being Earnest*. But now follows the greatest change in circumstances ever to happen to a playwright. Thirteen weeks after his fourth successful premiere, Wilde is convicted of indecent acts with males **18** and younger. Wilde has allowed himself to be caught up in a family quarrel between his lover, Alfred Douglas (**25**) and the latter's father, the Marquess of Queensberry (**50**). Wilde is sent to prison for two years, the judge (**77**) commenting on homosexuality: "People who do these things must be dead to all sense of shame." In the climate of the times, Wilde's career is now terminated. It becomes impossible to see his plays or to buy his books. After prison, he moves to Paris, where he dies in obscurity at **46**.

J. B. Priestley: *The Good Companions* (1931).

Antonin Artaud: first pronouncement on the "Theater of Cruelty" (1932). He exemplifies these ideas in his own play, *Les Cenci* at **39**, but becomes insane shortly afterward, and spends nine years in a hospital, until **50**. He lives until **52**.

Robert Bolt: *A Man for All Seasons* (1960).

Neil Simon: *Barefoot in the Park* (1963). Until now, he has been mainly a scriptwriter for TV, "Phil Silvers (**46–47**) Show" at **31–32**. Simon's plays include *The Odd Couple* at **38**; *Plaza Suite* at **41**; and *The Last of the Red Hot Lovers* at **42**. At **46**, his second marriage is to Marsha Mason (**31**). Afterward he writes *California Suite* at **49**, and *Chapter Two* at **50**.

FILMS

D. W. Griffith: *Enoch Arden* (1911)—the first American two-reel film.

W. C. Fields is in his first film—*Pool Sharks* (1915).

Douglas Fairbanks, Sr., starts United Artists (1919), with D. W. Griffith (**44**), Charlie Chaplin (**30**), and Mary Pickford (**26**).

Charlie Chaplin: *The Gold Rush* (1925).

Cedric Gibbons: design for the Oscar, the Academy Award trophy (1929).

Walt Disney: *Snow White and the Seven Dwarfs* (1937).

Leni Riefenstahl: *Olympia*—about the Munich Olympic Games of 1938; the film is premiered at the birthday party of Adolf Hitler (**49**).

Cary Grant: *The Philadelphia Story* (1940).

Greta Garbo: *Two-Faced Woman* (1941); this is not a success, and she retires to live on her earnings for the rest of her life.

Elia Kazan: *A Tree Grows in Brooklyn* (1945)—his first feature film.

Christopher Lee makes his film debut, as *Dracula* (1958).

Alain Resnais: *Le Chant de Styrène* (1958)—a film about the manufacture of polystyrene.

Marcello Mastroianni: *La Dolce Vita* (1960); and *La Notte*, at **37**.

Marilyn Monroe dies of a barbiturate overdose (1962).

Andy Warhol: *Empire* (1964)—an 8-hour shot of the Empire State Building.

Mike Nichols: *The Graduate* (1967), with Dustin Hoffman (**30–31**), and the older woman is Anne Bancroft (also **36**).

Francis Ford Coppola: script of *Patton* (1969).

Jane Fonda goes to Hanoi (July 1972), and campaigns against the Vietnam War.

MUSIC—NON-CLASSICAL

George Gershwin: *Porgy and Bess* (1935), which includes the song "Summertime." He has been writing successfully since **21**, and his best-known songs include "Someone to Watch over Me" at **28**, and "I Got Rhythm" at **32**. He now goes on to write the music for *An American in Paris* before his death at **38**. His "Rhapsody in Blue" was at **26**.

Debbie Harry, and Blondie: "Rapture" (1981).

TV, ETC.

Alan Alda: as a doctor in "M*A*S*H" (1972); at **19**, he had intended to be a medical student, but did poorly in a chemistry test. At **43**, he writes and stars in *The Seduction of Joe Tynan*.

Evel Knievel attempts to ride his motorbike over Snake River Canyon, Twin Falls, Idaho (1974). The attempt fails, but makes him a celebrity—or a curiosity.

John Cleese: "Fawlty Towers" (1975). At **30**, he was a star in "Monty Python's Flying Circus"; and he is in *The Life of Brian* at **40**.

LOVE, LIFE

Paul Harris, with three others: first meeting of the Rotary Club (Chicago, 1905). All four come from small-town backgrounds, and are trying to make their careers in the big city. By the time of Harris's death (**78**), there are 300,000 Rotarians throughout the world.

Burt Reynolds: nude centerfold for *Cosmopolitan* magazine (1972).

EXPLORATION

Hernando Cortez: conquest of the future site of Mexico City (1521).

Samuel de Champlain: exploration of the St. Lawrence River, Canada (1603). At **41**, he founds the Quebec colony. At **43**, he marries Hélène Boullé (**12**). After setbacks, he establishes a significant number of settlements in Quebec, and dies there at **68**.

Miles Standish: voyage of the *Mayflower,* to establish the Plymouth colony, in New England (1620). The youngest person to set sail is **−1,** and is born during the voyage. But half the settlers die within three months of arrival.

PRESS

W. T. Stead enters prison to serve a three month sentence (London, 1885). In order to expose Victorian sexual practices, he had himself purchased a virgin girl of **13**, and exposed this trade in a series of revealing articles entitled "The Maiden Tribute of Modern Babylon." His methods annoy the authorities, and this leads to his imprisonment. The prison is called "Coldbath-in-the-Fields," and Stead, who is a spiritualist, spends his time there in a state of religious ecstasy. But his campaign is entirely successful, and an act of Parliament raises the ages of consent. Reformers admire his journalism for its "scathing exposure of moral leprosy."

LAW

John Wayne Gacy's Illinois house is searched (1979) after a boy (**15**), who had asked to do a summer job there, is never seen again. Police discover 28 skeletons of murdered young men in the house, and Gacy confesses to having killed four others. In another case in 1978, Patrick Kearney is convicted of murder, having confessed to killing 32 homosexual boys and young men.

SPORTS

Geoffrey Boycott (1977) returns to international cricket, after two years self-exile from the England team, and he scores his 100th century in the match against the Australians.

In a recent typical international cricket team (England, 1978), the captain was **36**, and the other players were **36, 35, 34, 32**; and **29, 29, 27, 26, 23**, and **21**.

Muhammad Ali (1978) regains his world heavyweight boxing championship, for the third time—a record. He had first won it at **22***. Between **25** and **29**, he had been kept out of boxing because of his draft refusal. The greatest fight of his career is said to have been at **33**—his third battle with Joe Frazier (**31**). A series of televised fights in Zaire, Manila, and other exotic locations have made him one of the most famous people in the world. He is instantly recognizable, wherever he goes. But he loses a fight at **38***, and fans beg him to retire.

37

HISTORY—WORLD

Lenin: the London conference (1907) of 300 revolutionaries. Lenin now establishes his ascendancy over the others. For the next ten years, he lives mainly in Paris and Switzerland. At **47***, he travels to Russia, to take charge of the revolution, plotted since he was **17***. At **37**, the qualities which gain him leadership include: dominance both in face-to-face groups and in large crowds of people; complete giving of his time; a clear theory to guide his actions, showing how his forthcoming success is an inevitable feature of history; both a massive long-term plan for the country (and for the whole world) and short-term plans for his group's immediate needs; practical and realistic, without false heroism or useless gestures toward revolution; skilled timing; ability to establish a hierarchy of jobs and fill posts with the most appropriate people; ready to be vicious if necessary, even to the extent of getting rid of decent old-timers in his own movement.

Lech Walesa: "Solidarity," the independent trade union in Poland (1980).

HISTORY—U.S.A.

Franklin Pierce resigns from the Senate (1842). But returns to public office, at **47**, by being elected President—he is nominated at the convention on the forty-ninth ballot.

Thomas Jackson holds off a strong Union attack at the first battle of Bull Run (July 1861); acquires the name of "Stonewall" Jackson.

Richard Nixon: as a member of the House Un-American Activities Committee, he becomes a national figure (1950), by forcing the further investigation of Alger Hiss (**45**), which leads to Hiss's imprisonment of three years eight months. Also at **37**, Nixon is elected to the Senate. (cf. **45***)

HISTORY—U.K.

Mary I becomes the first-ever Queen of England in her own right (July 1553). But at **38** she begins the practice of burning numbers of her religious enemies—thus becoming "Bloody Mary." She is married at **38** to Philip II of Spain (**27**), but never has any children; she dies at **42**.

Sir Alec Douglas-Home has to spend two years on his back (1940–42), recovering from tuberculosis of the spine. At this time, he is quite a minor politician. He afterward says that most of his time was spent in reading, much of it about the great Victorian political figures.

RELIGION, PHILOSOPHY

Elijah Muhammad becomes head of the tiny nation of Islam (1934)—the Black Muslims. The community expands considerably from his **50**s onward; by his death (**77**), it has its own religious, educational, and economic network.

SOCIAL SCIENCE, EDUCATION

Edward Sapir: *Language: An Introduction to the Study of Speech* (1921).

A. A. Berle, and G. C. Means: *The Modern Corporation and Private Property* (1932).

Arthur Laffer: first publications on the "Laffer Curve" (1977) which he is said to have first formulated in a Washington restaurant at **34**. In effect, according to Laffer, increasing tax rates beyond a certain point leads to decreasing tax revenue, since high taxation becomes a disincentive to work.

SCIENCE, TECHNOLOGY

Johannes Kepler publishes his discovery that the planets travel in elliptical not circular paths (1609). At **29**, he had been assistant to Tycho Brahe (**54**) at the latter's death, and had inherited his data on the movement of the planets. Kepler now spends the rest of his life in detailed astronomical observations. He also, at **37** onward, writes a pioneering science fiction work about a journey to the moon. This *Dream* journey story is in press at the time of his death (**58**).

Francis Crick and James D. Watson (**25**): the concept of the DNA molecule as a double helix (1953). Watson obtained his Ph.D. at **22**, and publishes his memoirs at **40**. At the moment of the discovery in 1953, Linus Pauling is **52**, Erwin Chargaff (**48**), Max Perutz (**39**), Maurice Wilkins (**36**), J. C. Kendrew (**36**), and Rosalind Franklin is **32**.

Herbert Boyer, and Stanley N. Cohen (**38**): gene splicing methodology (1973). At **41**, Boyer and Robert Swanson (**28**) set up a genetic engineering company, Genentech. At **44**, the company gains a public quotation, and Boyer's share is worth $37 million.

MONEY, WORK

Josiah Wedgwood, the pottery manufacturer, decides to have his right leg amputated (1768) as it has always been giving him trouble. Lives until **64**.

Francis Cabot Lowell: the Boston Manufacturing Company, at Waltham, Massachusetts (1812)—a milestone in the development of the modern factory.

Andrew Carnegie switches all his business interests into steel (1873); previously he had been in Western Union, and in railroads. He is the first to cash in on the new Bessemer process. By **57**, he controls virtually the whole of the U.S. steel industry. From this is formed United States Steel Corporation, when he is **65***.

Frederick W. Taylor leaves salaried employment (1893), and sets up a consultancy to promote his ideas of "scientific management"; publishes *The Principles of Scientific Management* at **55**; dies on the day following his **59**th birthday.

Jean Paul Getty: his father dies (1930), and he inherits his share of the $15 million estate; forms the Getty Oil Company at **40**. Getty invests heavily in oil leases (1931–32) during the Depression—at the time, everyone thinks he is crazy. (cf. **56***)

Y. K. Pao buys his first ship, an old freighter (1955). He left China at **31**, at the beginning of the Communist government. Since then, he has been working in the export-import business in Hong Kong. By **57**, he owns more tankers than anyone else in the world.

RENAISSANCE

Michelangelo: completion of his frescoes on the ceiling of the Sistine Chapel, Rome (1512). He had begun this work at **33**. At **30**, he had begun work on the tomb of Pope Julius II (**62**) and this project lasts, on and off, until Michelangelo is **67**. At **43**, he is architect for the facade of San. Lorenzo, Florence, but this design is never built. At **49**, he works on the Laurentian Library, and at **54** he designs fortifications for the defense of Florence. At **56**, his father (**87**) dies. At **58**, Michelangelo makes the unfinished sculptures of slaves imprisoned in stone, later displayed in the Academy Museum, Florence. He leaves Florence for the last time at **59**, and completes his work at the Sistine Chapel with the "Last Judgment," **61–66***.

John Vanbrugh, in 1701: he now starts his career as an architect, and his first design is Castle Howard, a beautiful palace in the north of

England. At this time, he is a leading figure in the theater world. He has had two permanent successes as a playwright—*Relapse, or Virtue in Danger* at **32**, and *The Provok'd Wife* at **33**. At **41**, Vanbrugh starts work on the titanic Blenheim Palace. At **54**, Vanbrugh marries Henrietta Yarburgh (**25**), partly "to keep myself warm," and he lives until **62**.

Denis Diderot: prospectus and first volume of the *Encyclopédie* (Paris, 1750). This is a complete review of the arts, sciences, and technology during the Age of Reason. Diderot writes many of the entries, and edits the whole enterprise. In his late **20**s and early **30**s, he had gained employment in the translation of English books into French. This had brought him into contact with a wide range of new ideas, for example, on medicine, on morality without religion, and on Greek history. At **32**, he published a small but influential book on philosophy. At **35**, he published a pornographic novel, *The Indiscreet Jewels* about a ring which can make any part of the body begin to speak; by chance, the ring is often placed on sexual parts. Diderot is briefly jailed for this. While in prison, he is visited by his friend Jean-Jacques Rousseau (**37**, in 1749); Diderot encourages him to enter the Dijon essay competition, which becomes the fateful break in Rousseau's career (cf. philosophy, **38***). Diderot at **37** now suffers immense difficulties with the encyclopedia. Owing to its anti-royalist and anti-clerical tinge, it is censored when he is **45**, but the project is finished at **58**. Diderot lives until **70**.

ARCHITECTURE

George Dance (younger): Newgate Prison, London (1768).

Philip Johnson qualifies as an architect (1943).

ART

Velazquez: equestrian portrait of Prince Balthasar Carlos (**5**) (1635).

MUSIC—CLASSICAL

Rossini: *William Tell* (Aug. 1829). This is the last of his 38 operas. He now virtually retires, owing to exhaustion and desire for the good life—he has made a great deal of money from royalties. At **38**, he is given a good pension and appointed Inspector General of Singing in France, a sinecure. His health seems bad, and a doctor recommends leeches on his hemorrhoids—but Rossini in fact lives till **76**. In the last 39 years of his life, he finishes only *Stabat Mater* (**49**), and *Petite Messe Solennelle* at **72***.

Wagner: first performance of *Lohengrin* (1850, Aug. 28). He has first thoughts of the Ring, and a special opera house in which to perform it. This ambition occupies him on and off until he is **63**. At **40**, he meets his future wife, Cosima Liszt (**16**). (cf. **50***)

Verdi: *Rigoletto* (Mar. 1851)—his sixteenth opera. The previous works have nearly all been well received, but *Rigoletto* is the first to become a permanent success. He follows it with *Il Trovatore* at **39**; *La Traviata* also at **39**; *Sicilian Vespers* at **41**; and *Un Ballo in Maschera* at **45**. (cf. **60***)

Tchaikovsky gets married (1877)—it lasts only nine weeks. He is currently very poor (he comes from a "new poor" family), but a rich widow, Nadezhda von Meck (**46**) starts helping him. She begins a regular subsidy, and takes an interest in every aspect of his life—later, even to the extent of dying immediately after him. Tchaikovsky is a nervous person, who takes a comparatively long time to produce the work for which he becomes famous. With perhaps one exception, all his memorable compositions come after his **35**th birthday, for example, his Piano Concerto no. 1 at **35**; *Swan Lake* (**36**); *Eugene Onegin* (**38**); *1812* Overture (**40**). (cf. **53***)

LITERATURE

AGE 37 YRS

Samuel Johnson starts on his *Dictionary of the English Language* (1746)—it takes him and his assistants nine years until publication.

Robert Burns dies (July 1796), probably from endocarditis (not from women and drink, as in legend).

William Wordsworth: "Intimations of Immortality" (1807). He had contributed to the "Lyrical Ballads" at **28**, and married at **32**. (cf. **43***)

James Fenimore Cooper: *The Last of the Mohicans* (1826).

A. E. Housman publishes "A Shropshire Lad" (1896). Many of the poems were written while he was a clerk in the London patent office, where he had gone after virtually failing his finals at Oxford. His major public career is as a professor of Latin, having made his name while doing academic work in the evenings after working in the patent office.

T. S. Eliot now earns enough money to pursue his literary career on a full-time basis (1925). Previously he had worked in a bank. He is baptized into the Church of England at **38**. (cf. **55***)

Thomas Wolfe dies (1938), with three novels unpublished (and unedited), including *You Can't Go Home Again*. He had had his break with *Look Homeward, Angel* at **29**.

John Steinbeck: *The Grapes of Wrath* (1939); and *Cannery Row* at **43**.

Humbert Humbert moves into 342 Lawn Street, somewhere in New England, and meets Dolores "Lol" Haze (**12**), and her mother, "the Haze woman" (also **mid-30**s). After traveling around the U.S.A. with Lol, Humbert is arrested, and dies in prison, at **42**. —in *Lolita* (1955), by Vladimir Nabokov (**56**); also in *Brigitte Bardot and the Lolita Syndrome* (1959), by Simone de Beauvoir (**51**).

PLAYS, DANCE

Aristophanes: *Lysistrata* (411 B.C.), in which women throughout Greece go on a sex strike, as a protest against the continued wars between the city-states.

Jean Cocteau: *Orphée* (1926).

FILMS

Douglas Fairbanks, Sr., marries Mary Pickford (**26**) (1920), and they live at "Pickfair"—but divorce sixteen years later.

Fritz Lang: *Metropolis* (1927).

Edward G. Robinson: *Little Caesar* (1930)—first major success in his typical gangster role.

Irving Thalberg dies (1936), with his last two productions not yet shown—*Camille*, and *The Good Earth*.

Humphrey Bogart: *The Petrified Forest* (1936). This is his breakthrough, and he is a star from now until his death. He goes on to make *Dead End* at **38**; *High Sierra* and *The Maltese Falcon* at **42**; and *Casablanca* at **44***. His private life improves dramatically at **45***.

Marlene Dietrich: *Destry Rides Again* (1939).

Laurence Olivier: *Henry V* (1944).

Alec Guinness: *The Lavender Hill Mob* (1951).

Gregory Peck: *Roman Holiday* (1953).

Ingmar Bergman: *Smiles of a Summer Night* (1955).

Simone Signoret: *Room at the Top* (1958); Oscar; she is the loving woman left behind by ambitious Laurence Harvey (**31**).

Alain Resnais: *Hiroshima, mon amour* (1959).

John Schlesinger: *A Kind of Loving* (1962)—his first big feature.

Bo Widerberg: *Elvira Madigan* (1967).

Donn A. Pennebaker: *Don't Look Back* (1967).

Jean-Luc Godard: *La Chinoise* (1967).

Frederick Wiseman: *Titticut Follies* (1967). With his cinema verité method, Wiseman now proceeds to make the same kind of film about a variety of organizations and institutions. These are uniformly interesting, and they cover, for example, high school at **38**, the police at **39**, a hospital at **40**, and so on. Wiseman at **37** has now established his own personal vision with which he explores familiar places in a new and revealing way.

Jack Nicholson: *Chinatown* (1974).

Michael Cimino: *The Deer Hunter* (1978).

Martin Scorcese: *Raging Bull* (1980), starring Robert De Niro (**35**).

Marquis de Sade: imprisoned, for numerous evil acts with neighboring children (France, 1777). He now gradually begins his writing career. At **44**, he is transferred to the Bastille prison where he writes *The 120 Days of Sodom*. At **47**, he writes *The Adversities of Virtue*; at **49–50**, he is placed in the lunatic asylum at Charenton, but released. He spends ten years as a playwright and a participant in the French Revolution. In his **50**s, he writes *Justine* and *Juliette*. At **60**, he is returned to Charenton where he organizes performances of his plays, with fellow mad people as participants. De Sade is kept at Charenton until his death at **74**. His family are ashamed of him, and burn his manuscripts. The boom in de Sade's reputation as a writer comes decades after his death. His name is given to a perversion, in *Psychopathia sexualis* (1886) by Richard Krafft-Ebing (**46**).

Friedrich Wilde: invention of the cervical cap (1838).

Clarence Birdseye: first mass production of frozen food (1924). At **25–29**, he has been a fur trader in Labrador, and has seen native people freezing food to preserve it. He has spent his time since then in developing large-scale methods of copying this idea.

Peter C. L. Hodgson: invention of "Silly Putty" (1949).

EXPLORATION

Francis Drake: circumnavigation of the world (1577). He starts with 200 men and five ships, and he returns with one ship, 56 men, and a large amount of gold which he has stolen from the Spanish. Drake lands to the north of San Francisco, and he is the first European to see the west coast of Canada. He is the first captain to achieve the circumnavigation without, as did Magellan, dying in the attempt. Later, at **47**, Drake attacks Spanish ships in their home port of Cádiz, and at **48** he is instrumental in defeating the Armada sent by King Philip II (**61**) of Spain. Drake dies at sea, from a fever, at **56**.

James Wilson Marshall: discovery of gold at Sutter's (**44**) Mill, California (1848); this is the cause of the great Gold Rush of '49. Marshall is unable to cash in on his discovery—other prospectors simply overrun his territory, and take everything. Later, Marshall goes mad at times, and dies in poverty at **74**. John A. Sutter has been a successful frontiersman and developer of the new lands. Paradoxically, the discovery of gold is the end of his career—his workers desert him, and he goes bankrupt, unable to enforce any claims against those who mine gold on his lands. Sutter also dies in poverty, at **77**.

Louis Blériot: first flight across the English Channel (1909).

George Mallory: death, on Mt. Everest (1924). He is last seen 800 feet from the summit and he is observed to be climbing strongly; but he is never seen again, and his body is presumed to be encased in ice on Everest. When asked why he wished to climb Everest, he explained, "Because it's there."

PRESS

John Wilkes starts his journal *The North Briton* (1762) in answer to a government publication *The Briton*. Up to this time, Wilkes has been a sex-maniac, spendthrift, pamphleteer, and very minor political figure. Issue No. 45 contains a fairly routine attack on the king and government, but arouses them to attempt its suppression. Wilkes is put in the Tower of London, but he becomes a hero of the crowds—"Wilkes and Liberty." The ineffective campaign to suppress Wilkes is a turning point in press freedom. By **49**, Wilkes is Lord Mayor of London, though always a supporter of unpopular causes.

C. H. Dow (**37**) and E. D. Jones (**33**): the *Wall Street Journal* (1889).

Roy Thomson opens his first radio station (1931)—it is in the Canadian wilderness. His main purpose is to stimulate demand for the radio sets which he has been trying to sell. This moment is the beginning of take-off for his career; previously he has tried a number of small business ventures and failed. By **59***, he is rich, but unknown; by **67**, he is very rich, and very well known.

LAW

Billie Sol Estes is arrested for allegedly embezzling $22 million through government farm support schemes (Texas, 1962). By switching identification plates on a handful of tanks of fertilizer, he gives the illusion of possessing vast amounts of fertilizer, and thus obtains loans and grants against these "assets."

SPORTS

Jersey Joe Walcott (1951) beats Ezzard Charles and so wins the world heavyweight boxing championship—for the first time. Walcott is the oldest person to do so, and wins with a knockout.

Lee Genud: world backgammon champion (1981). In the final, she beats Joe Dewek (**41**).

38

HEALTH

William Harvey: discovery of the circulation of the blood (London, 1616). This is not published in book form until **50**, with his *Exercitatio* *anatomica de motu cordis et sanguinis in animalibus.* For his medical training, Harvey had gone from England to Padua, then the world center of medical research. He gained his M.D. there at **24**. Harvey dies at **79**, suffering from gout.

Joseph Lister: first operation using antiseptic principles (1865). Previously, "hospital disease" (infection) had killed many of those who had survived the operation itself. Lister lives until **84**.

Ernest H. Starling: discovery of hormones (1904–05).

HISTORY—WORLD

Louis XVI is executed (1793) during the French Revolution. Shortly afterward, Marie Antoinette (**37**) is also guillotined. Danton, formerly on the Committee of Public Safety, is executed at **34**, as is Robespierre (**36**); Marat is murdered at **50**. At the time of the king's death, Napoleon is **23**; the future King Louis XVIII is **37**, being restored to the throne at **59**; and Louis XIV would have been **154**. The chief executioner at this time is Charles Henri Sanson (**54**); he records 2,918 public executions in Paris. The danger age for victims is **25–50** (57 percent of the total); only two percent are **20** and under; while 318 victims are **60** and over, including nine who are guillotined when **80+**.

President Nasser of Egypt: nationalization of the Suez Canal (1956), and subsequent failed intervention by Britain, France, and Israel. At this moment, David Ben-Gurion is **70**, John Foster Dulles is **68**, Anthony Eden is **59**, Guy Mollet of France is **50**, Dag Hammarskjold of the United Nations is also **50**, and Moshe Dayan is **41**.

HISTORY—U.S.A.

Patrick Henry says, "Give me liberty or give me death" (Mar. 1775)—in fact, he dies at **63**.

HISTORY—U.K.

Queen Victoria: presentation of the first-ever VCs (1857, June 26)—the Victoria Cross. (cf. **68***)

Anthony Eden is appointed Foreign Secretary (Dec. 1935)—youngest ever. But he resigns at **40**, over the appeasement policies of Neville Chamberlain (**68**).

Tony Benn disclaims his peerage (1963); previously he was the second Viscount Stansgate.

RELIGION, PHILOSOPHY

Aristotle: marriage (c. 346 B.C.).

St. Thomas à Kempis: *The Imitation of Christ* (1418).

Jean-Jacques Rousseau enjoys sudden overnight fame (1750) on receiving a prize for an essay which attacks recent developments in art and science. Previously, he has had to work in obscurity, supporting himself as a waiter, secretary, and gigolo. Now, his self-evaluation (genius) is confirmed by the outside world. About his "break" he later comments: "I surrendered myself completely and unreservedly to the pleasure of savoring my glory." Between **40–50**, he writes his *Social Contract;* and *Confessions* between **53–59**. He dies, still pretty famous, at **66**. In his personal career, Rousseau is an early pioneer in radical chic. His writings are about earthiness, revolution, and an attack on the jaded, artificial society around him; privately, he is a snob, sexist, and general hanger-on to the titled elite. (cf. **50***)

Bertrand Russell and A. N. Whitehead (**49**): *Principia mathematica* (1910–13). (cf. **49***)

Martin Heidegger: *Sein und Zeit* (1927).

Jean-Paul Sartre: *Being and Nothingness* (1943).

SOCIAL SCIENCE, EDUCATION

Michel de Montaigne: retirement (1571)—he later goes on to become the famed essayist and writer on life in France. He now writes that he ". . . long weary of the servitude of the court and of public employments, while still entire, retired to the bosom of the learned Virgins [the muses], where in calm and freedom from all cares he will spend what little remains of his life, now more than half run out. If the fates permit, he will complete his abode (his family chateau), this sweet ancestral retreat; and he has consecrated it to his freedom, tranquillity, and leisure." Montaigne publishes his first volume of *Essays* at **47**, and second volume at **55**; he dies at **59***. The essays touch on all aspects of the world around him, from education to criminology, on age and on happiness.

SCIENCE, TECHNOLOGY

G. W. Leibniz: publication of his calculus (1684).

J. C. Doppler: prediction of the Doppler Effect (1842).

Richard Owen: first use of the word "dinosaur" (1842).

Harold C. Urey: discovery of heavy hydrogen (1931).

William Shockley, W. H. Brattain (**46**), and John Hardeen (**40**): invention of the transistor (1948). By the time Shockley is **61**, transistors overtake valve/tubes in quantity sold in the U.S.A.

MONEY, WORK

Henry Ford starts his second new company—the Henry Ford Company (1901, Nov. 30). But it lasts only four months; his backers desert him, and start their own company—Cadillac. Ford starts his third company at **40***.

Asa G. Candler: sole proprietor of Coca-Cola (1889), an interest which he buys for $2,300. He now builds up the company. At **68**, he and his family sell out for $25 million. The second great wave of expansion starts under Robert W. Woodruff (**33**) in 1923.

John D. MacArthur borrows $2,500 to start his own insurance company (1936)—it is later worth at least $1 billion.

RENAISSANCE

Albert Schweitzer leaves Europe to settle in Lambaréné, Gabon, Africa (1913). At **24**, he had received his doctorate in philosophy, with a thesis on Kant. He then took another doctorate, which was published at **31**, *The Quest of the Historical Jesus.* He was also becoming a distinguished organist and at **30** he published a book on the mysticism of J. S. Bach. At **30**, he decided to become a medical missionary and he has been a medical student since then. Now, the rest of his life is spent in building up his own hospital, but he maintains his other interests by publishing books on theology and philosophy, and by making best-selling records of organ music. He receives the Nobel Peace Prize at **79**, and dies in his Lambaréné hospital at **90**.

ARCHITECTURE

Mumtaz Mahal dies (1631) in childbirth (fourteenth child); her husand, Shah Jahan (**39**) starts building her tomb—Taj Mahal—which is finished when he is **61**.

John Soane: Stock Office, Bank of England (1791); the approximate beginning of his own style.

McKim, Mead, and White: Boston Public Library (1887–95).

Antonio Gaudí: beginning of the towers of Sagrada Familia church, Barcelona (1890), in his own characteristic style. (cf. **73***)

Louis H. Sullivan: Guaranty Building, Buffalo, New York (1894–95) (cf. **40***)

Le Corbusier: Pavillon de L'Esprit Nouveau (1925); virtually his first project to be built.

Eero Saarinen wins competition for the Jefferson Westward Expansion memorial, at St. Louis, Missouri (1948). Another contestant is his father, Eliel Saarinen (**75**). The design is built, and consists of an arch 630 feet high, with an observation tower at the top, reached by a special elevator that travels inside the curve of the arch. At **38**, Saarinen also starts work on the giant General Motors Technical Center (1948–56).

Jørn Utzon wins the Sydney Opera House competition (1956); built 1960–73.

James Stirling: History Building, Cambridge University (1964–68).

Norman Foster and associates: Willis Faber office building (1973–75).

James Wines and SITE: the Best store at Richmond, Virginia

(1971–72)—the brick facade is peeling off the face of the building. This is their first built design for Best. At **41**, he and SITE build a store in Houston in which the brick facade appears to be crumbling down the front of the building.

Ricardo Bofil, with Peter Hodgkinson (also **38**) and others: Marne La Vallée, Versailles (1978)—the Greek revival apartment buildings made of precast concrete. Bofil's Walden-7 apartment tower was at **28**.

MUSIC—CLASSICAL

J. S. Bach becomes director of music at the Thomas School, Leipzig (1723, Apr. 22). This is the beginning of his major period in choral composition—almost the first item is the St. John Passion. He maintains this job for the rest of his life, dying in Leipzig at **65***. (cf. **44***)

Mendelssohn dies (1847, Nov. 4), from a series of strokes. At **37**, he had had a gigantic success with his *Elijah*, and had always been extremely busy as a musical entrepreneur as well as composer. His beloved sister Fanny (**41**) dies just before him, and they are buried side by side, in Leipzig. His wife Cecile later dies from consumption at **34**. Their son Paul dies also at **38**, having founded Agfa, which becomes the well-known photographic business.

Hans Werner Henze: *The Bassarids* (1965).

ART

Giotto: frescoes at the Arena Chapel, Padua (1304–06). (cf. **43***)

Grant Wood: "American Gothic" (1930).

Robert Indiana: "LOVE" (1966).

LITERATURE

Sydney Carton volunteers to be guillotined, to save the life of the condemned Charles St. Evremonde (also about **38**), husband of Lucie (about **33**) whom Carton has always admired. Previously, he had promised Lucie that he would make any sacrifice to bring her happiness. Sydney Carton, a romantic idiot, has wasted his life in drinking, and he now performs the only great act of his life. His last thoughts are: "It is a far, far better thing that I do, than I have ever done; it is a far, far better rest that I go to than I have ever known."—*A Tale of Two Cities*, 1860, by Charles Dickens (1812–1870).

Ralph Waldo Emerson: first volume of essays (1841); and second volume at **41**.

Robert Louis Stevenson travels to Samoa in order to recover his health (1888), but he dies there at **44**. He had written *Treasure Island* at **33**, *A Child's Garden of Verses* at **35**, and *The Strange Case of Dr. Jekyll and Mr. Hyde* at **36**.

Joseph Conrad completes his first important book, *An Outcast of the Islands* (1896); he is also married this year, to Jessie George (**23**). Previously, he has been a traveler, adventurer, and seaman, and has risen to the rank of captain. He now begins a full-time career as a writer. He has little money, but possesses (1) a mass of tensions resulting from his disastrous childhood, cf. **3***; and (2) enough shipboard memories to provide settings in which to work out these tensions. His work is full of loneliness and caring; violence and cowardice; love and claustrophobia. See, for example, *Heart of Darkness* at **41**; *Lord Jim* at **42**; and *Nostromo* at **46**. He writes *Under Western Eyes* at **52**; this is the only book to deal with his homeland, and he immediately has a nervous breakdown. Although he continues to write until his death at **66**, he is never again able to show the emotional daring which he displays at **38–52**.

Lytton Strachey: *Eminent Victorians* (1918).

Aldous Huxley: *Brave New World* (1932).

Ayn Rand: *The Fountainhead* (1943); also, *We, the Living* at **31**, and *Atlas Shrugged* at **52**.

Nicholas Montserrat is an information officer (1950) in the British High Commission in South Africa; he starts writing his twelfth book, in "the eighteenth year of trying." None of his previous eleven books had earned him more than £400 ($800). Two years later, he completes *The Cruel Sea*—which goes on to sell ten million copies.

James Baldwin: *The Fire Next Time* (1963).

Philip Marlow, the private detective, (1939 onwards) is permanently **38**.

The heroine of *The Women's Room* (1977) is a housewife of **38** who decides to go to college—in the book by Marilyn French **(47)**.

PLAYS

William Shakespeare, in 1602: about this time he writes *Twelfth Night;* followed by *All's Well That Ends Well*. At **40–42**, he writes *Measure for Measure*; *Othello*; *King Lear*; and *Macbeth*. At **43–45**, he writes *Antony and Cleopatra*; *Coriolanus*; and *Pericles*. At **46–47**, he writes *Cymbeline*; and *The Winter's Tale*. (cf. **28*** and **48***)

Ben Travers: *A Cuckoo in the Nest* (1925); this is the first of nine brilliant farces which he writes in the next eight years—the Aldwych farces. Travers lives until **94**, and his last play is at **89***.

FILMS

Jack Warner: producer, *Little Caesar* (1930).

Busby Berkeley: *Gold Diggers of 1933* (1933), which includes his sequence "We're in the Money."

Paul Robeson: *Showboat* (1936).

Spencer Tracy: *Boys' Town* (1938)—gets his second Oscar in two years.

Clark Gable: *Gone with the Wind* (1939); with Vivien Leigh **(25)**, directed by Victor Fleming (**56**), from the original book by Margaret Mitchell (**35**).

James Cagney: *Yankee Doodle Dandy*; Oscar.

Marlon Brando: *Mutiny on the Bounty* (1962).

John Schlesinger: *Billy Liar* (1963).

Peter Sellers first plays Inspector Clouseau (1963); later, for the sixth time, at **53**.

Steve McQueen: *Bullitt* (1968).

Richard Harris: *A Man Called Horse* (1970).

Francis Ford Coppola: *The Godfather* (1971).

Jack Nicholson: *One Flew over the Cuckoo's Nest* (1975).

MUSIC—NON-CLASSICAL

Cole Porter: *Fifty Million Frenchmen* (1929). This is the beginning of his main career, which extends until *Silk Stockings* at **64**. He had written "Let's Do It" at **37**. Previously he has always been talented, but inherited wealth has allowed him to be relatively unproductive. He now rushes into action, and at **38** three Cole Porter musicals open within five weeks of each other. Even his well-known songs are too numerous to list here, but they include "Anything Goes," in the musical of that name, at **43**; "Begin the Beguine" and "Just One of Those Things" at **44**; and "My Heart Belongs to Daddy" at **47**. (cf. **57***)

Jerry Bock (**36**) and Sheldon Harnick (**40**): *Fiddler on the Roof* (1964).

Chuck Berry comes out of prison (1964) after a two-year sentence imposed after an alleged offense at his nightclub. Now follows at least five years in which his work, when he produces any at all, is poorly reviewed. But at **46** he has an international hit, with "My Ding-a-Ling" which owes its fame partly to action against it by purity groups. Chuck Berry has been one of the greatest rock pioneers, for example, "Roll over Beethoven" at **30**, and "Johnny B. Goode" at **32**.

Joan Baez goes on a twenty-three-city concert tour (1979) to protest human rights violations in Vietnam and to raise money for the "boat people" who are trying to escape from the Communist regime in Vietnam. Previously, in her mid-**20**s, she had been a supporter of communism in that country, hoping that it would achieve complete power, which it indeed did. Despite attacks, Baez sticks to her position, that she is right to change her view of the Hanoi government and that it would be simple-minded not to revise the opinions formed in a previous decade.

Bob Dylan: "Slow Train Coming" (1979)—an album heavily influenced by Jesus Christ, and well received. At **37**, he had made a film, *Renaldo and Clara*, often reviewed as tedious and self-indulgent.

John Lennon, the former Beatle (cf. **22***) publishes an advertisement in the *New York Times* (1979) about the current interests of himself and Yoko Ono (**46**). Most fans are disappointed by the text, and believe that Lennon has been softening in the mind. His last album had been at **35**. The *Times* message is called "Spring Cleaning of the Mind" and includes this news: ". . . we are writing in the sky instead of on paper—that's our song." This writing is said to take place as three angels look over his shoulder. At this time, the other Beatle genius, Paul McCartney (**37**) is touring with his group Wings, which includes his wife Linda (**37**). He has made nine LPs since the break-up of the Beatles. His income from Wings and Beatles songs is estimated to be somewhere between $10 million and $44 million each year, because of his 43 songs which have each sold one million copies. Paul McCartney had his first burst of creativity from **20** to **27**, and then has had almost another career in Wings. He comments on the process of aging: "When I was **18**, I thought that **25** was about as far as you could go." When reading a history book which belongs to his daughter (**16**) he sees his own name in it, under the heading "media." John Lennon is shot dead at **40**, by a fan (**26**); in contrast to Lennon's own approach to life, his death is marked by a wave of sentimentality. Pete Best, at **39** (1981), is deputy manager of an employment exchange in Liverpool; at **20**, he had been asked to leave the Beatles, after their time in Hamburg and shortly before their breakthrough. Best, sometimes known as the Fifth Beatle, now lives in a three-bedroom terrace house with his wife, a former fan; he says of his luck: "Do you know, it's nearly nineteen years from that time and I still feel kind of shocked. I'll never know exactly why it had to happen to me."

Mick Jagger, Bill Wyman (**40**), and Charlie Watts (**40**): sell-out tour of the U.S. (1981).

TV, ETC.

Florenz Ziegfeld: start of the "Ziegfeld Follies" (1907).

LOVE, LIFE

Fanny Farmer: *Boston Cooking School Cook Book* (1896). She pays the production costs of this book as the publishers do not expect it to succeed. But the book is never out of print from now on.

Marie Stopes: *Married Love* (1918). This is a famous pioneer manual on sex and contraception. At the time of writing, Stopes is both a virgin and a divorcée. Now at **38** she marries again, and loses her virginity; she goes on to have a son. She scandalizes the world by advocating contraceptive practices—even the word is controversial. Stopes always believes that she will live to **120**; at **70**, she is still agile enough to put her big toe in her mouth. Within her family, the convention is maintained at birthdays that she is **26**, year after year; when her son reaches **26**, he observes that next year he will be older than his mother. Stopes lives until **77**, and suffers a little in later life—the cause to which she has devoted her life has become so successful that it is no longer of much interest.

Phillipe Junot: marriage, to Princess Caroline of Monaco (**21**, 1978).

Georges Blanc: third star from Michelin Guide, for his restaurant (France, 1981).

PRESS

John Peter Zenger is tried for publishing a criminal libel (1735) but acquitted by a jury—an important moment in the development of press rights in the U.S.A.

Thomas Paine: *Common Sense* (1776).

James Wilson: start of the *Economist* magazine (London, 1843). At his death (**55**), he is succeeded as editor by Walter Bagehot (**33**).

H. L. Mencken (in 1918): these are said to be the peak years of his influence as a writer on American life.

Ann Landers starts writing her advice column on personal problems (1955). Her sister (also **38**) is her assistant. Soon afterward, the sister moves to another paper and starts her own column—"Dear Abby, by Abigail Van Buren." Ann Landers (originally Esther Pauline Friedman) had been born seventeen minutes ahead of Abigail Van Buren (originally Pauline Esther Friedman). They now go on to become the most provocative advice columnists in journalism. At **62**, Abigail Van Buren asks if women at **50** on enjoy sex—she receives 227,000 letters, half of them saying yes.

EXPLORATION

Robert LaSalle: voyage down the Mississippi (1681–82), and the naming of Louisiana, in honor of King Louis XIV (**43**).

Richard Byrd: first-ever flight over the North Pole (1926). At **42**, he makes the first flight over the South Pole. He later makes flights over the South Pole at **59** and at **68**—on both occasions he is in charge of large expeditions to survey Antarctica.

LAW

Charles Ponzi inaugurates the Securities and Exchange Company (Boston, 1919), to make foreign exchange dealings. He pays interest of fifty percent after 45 days deposit, and thus attracts $200,000 per day. Often people bring him their entire life savings. But this is a pure pyramid operation, and he is arrested at **39**. The swindle lasts only nine months, but loses millions of dollars. Before and after this time, Ponzi is an unsuccessful minor dealer and con man. He dies in poverty in Rio de Janeiro, at **66**.

Willie Mays: retirement. His career in the majors begins at **24**.

Bob Hewitt is one of the pair to win the doubles championships at Wimbledon (1978). His partner is Frew McMillan (**36**) who is known for always playing in a white cap. One of their opponents in the semifinal was **3** when Hewitt first played at Wimbledon.

Mario Andretti: world racing champion (1978).

Jack Nicklaus (golf, 1978) makes a comeback. He is fourth in the list of money-earners, gaining one quarter million in this year. His career total is now $3.3 million. He wins the British Open, at St. Andrews, his seventeenth major title. At **19**, Nicklaus had been U.S. Amateur champion; at **22**, he had beaten Arnold Palmer (**33**) to win the U.S. Open. At **35**, Nicklaus had won the Masters for the fifth time.

Muhammad Ali (boxing, 1980): he is forced to retire after the tenth round in his title fight with Larry Holmes (**30**).

In a typical recent year (1978), the top ten money-earners in golf were **25–39**.

39

HEALTH

Gabriel Fallopius: death (1562). He had discovered and named certain genital organs, including the fallopian tubes.

For first-time mothers at **39** and over, there is a forty-three percent chance that the child will be left-handed, according to research by Carole Jeffery and others (Manchester University, 1981).

HISTORY—WORLD

King Henry IV of France decides that "Paris is worth a Mass" (1593)—although brought up as a strict Protestant, he sees that a change in religion will consolidate his regime. He is then welcomed on his entrance into Paris. The Edict of Nantes is at **44**, and he dies at **56**.

Eamon De Valera: the creation of the Irish Free State (1922). By holding out for a fully independent nation, he does not become head of the government until **49**. He serves as Premier (taoiseach) from **49–65**, **68–74**, **74–76**, and President from **76–90**.

Benedict Arnold: as commander of West Point (1780), he treasonably plots to surrender the fort to British forces; he escapes to England, where he lives until his death at **60**.

Thomas "Stonewall" Jackson: death, while commanding Confederate infantry during the Civil War (1863). His last words are "Let us cross over the river and rest under the shade of the trees."

Theodore Roosevelt: in charge of the Rough Riders (1898). This is an amateur cavalry regiment which he has enrolled and trained on his own. Within two months, he wins the Battle of San Juan, in Cuba, and returns home a national hero. At **23**, he had become a member of the New York State Assembly. At **30–36**, he had been a civil service commissioner in Washington. At **36–38**, he is president of the New York Board of Police Commissioners. At **40**, he is elected Governor of New York. At **42**, he is elected Vice-President, and becomes President also at **42**, following the death of President McKinley (**58**). Roosevelt does well because (1) he possesses an almost superhuman mental and physical energy; and (2) he believes in an anti-big business policy, at a time of the mammoth trusts which are frightening the electorate. At **41**, before the presidential campaign, Roosevelt suffers from exhaustion, and so takes off a month from work. He says: "I don't mean to do one single thing except write a life of Oliver Cromwell." This is in fact what he does, and it is his thirteenth book. He dictates 63,000 words to one secretary, while simultaneously dictating to another secretary on policy matters affecting the nation.

Franklin D. Roosevelt has polio (1921), and is crippled for the rest of his life; becomes President at **51***.

Malcolm X is assassinated while addressing a public meeting (1965). His *Autobiography of Malcolm X* is published after his death.

Martin Luther King, Jr.: killed while supporting a garbage-workers strike in Memphis, Tennessee (1968, Apr. 4).

HISTORY—U.K.

William I wins the Battle of Hastings (1066, Oct. 14) and is crowned King of England. He defeats and kills Harold (**44**). (cf. **58***)

Robert Bruce wins the Battle of Banockburn (June 1314). He defeats Edward II (**30**), and kills 30,000 English.

Oliver Cromwell in 1638: after a number of years of religious doubt, he has a resurgence of his faith, and becomes prominent in the cause of Parliament, versus the King (**37**). By **45**, he is instrumental in founding the New Model Army; and at **49*** he causes the execution of the King.

William III conquers Irish forces at the Battle of the Boyne (1690, June 30)—he thus become "King Billy" as he is later remembered in Northern Ireland.

Lord John Russell leads in the passage of the Great Reform Bill (1832, June 7)—the first proper organization of the voting system. His partner, Earl Grey, is **58**. Russell had first been elected an MP while just under the qualifying age of **21**.

RELIGION, PHILOSOPHY

St. Thomas Aquinas: completion of *Summa Contra Gentiles* (1259–64).

Dietrich Bonhoeffer, the theologian, is hanged (1945) for association with a plot to blow up Adolf Hitler (**55**)—only months before the end of World War II.

SOCIAL SCIENCE, EDUCATION

E. B. Tylor: *Primitive Culture* (1871). This book opens with the first-ever definition in anthropology of "culture."

C. S. Pierce: *Illustrations of the Logic of Science* (1878)—first steps in his "pragmatic" thinking.

Freud: *Studies on Hysteria* (1895), with Josef Breuer (**53**); this is the first book on psychoanalysis. Previously Freud has been researching the physiological basis of nervous diseases. At **36**, he begins letting a patient speak her thoughts "without censorship"; he is amazed at what this reveals. Soon Freud realizes that half these stories are fantasy. He is only momentarily stopped by this "error." Around now, this is a highly creative period in which he suddenly puts together the basics of psychoanalysis, for example, the psychic reality of wishes, repression and defense, denial, Oedipus complex, regression, and so on. From now on, Freud has ten years of "intellectual isolation"; he is mildly notorious in Vienna for his apparently filthy views on children and their sexuality. It is not until **52*** that he achieves any major reputation.

Émile Durkheim: *Suicide: a Study in Sociology* (1897); at **35**, *The Division of Labor in Society;* and at **37** *The Rules of Sociological Method.*

Werner Sombart: *Modern Capitalism* (1902).

Lewis M. Terman: *The Measurement of Intelligence* (1916)—on the IQ, and on IQ testing. At **48**, he selects 1,500 children of top IQ, and follows them for the rest of their, and his, life. He dies at **79.**

Lewis Mumford: *Technics and Civilization* (1934).

David Riesman: *The Lonely Crowd* (1950).

SCIENCE, TECHNOLOGY

Rudolf Diesel: invention of the diesel engine (1897).

Thomas J. Watson loses his job with National Cash Register (1913) where he has been a leading salesman since joining at **21**. At **40** he becomes president of the new Computing-Tabulating-Recording Company, which at **51** he turns into International Business Machines. When he is **61**, the U.S. Social Security Administration is formed and results in a vast demand for data-processing equipment. By **66**, he has made IBM into the dominant supplier of office equipment. Watson lives until **82.**

Edwin P. Hubble: the concept of the Hubble radius of the universe (1929).

John W. Maunchly and J. Presper Eckert (**27**): ENIAC (1946), the pioneer in electronic computing. And, UNIVAC, when they are **43** and **31**.

MONEY, WORK

George Hearst: having worked as a marginal gold prospector since **30**, he strikes it rich (1859) in western Nevada—foundation of the family's huge fortune.

Charlie Schwab: first president of the new United States Steel Corporation (1901); but resigns at **41**, to head the small Bethlehem Steel Company—transforming it within ten years into a giant. He dies at **77***.

Henry Ford II: the Edsel car (1957). This is a famous failure, but the Mustang, when he is **46**, soon becomes a classic.

John S. Samuels III is worth almost nothing, but invests in coal mine options just before the energy crisis (1972). By **42**, *Fortune* magazine says that he is worth $100 million.

RENAISSANCE

Giorgio Vasari: *The Lives of the Painters, Sculptors, and Architects* (Florence, 1550). This is the result of his lifelong interest in biography, and it shows the arts culminating in the work of his friend and hero, Michelangelo (**72**). The book is the single most quoted source of information about Renaissance artists. Vasari has supported himself by his work as a painter. Later, at **49** onward, he is the architect for the Uffizi, the new administrative center in Florence. From **53** on, he is architect in charge of the rebuilding of St. Peter's, Rome. He is also well known for the posthumous portrait of Lorenzo de' Medici (1464–92). Vasari dies three days before his **63**rd birthday.

ARCHITECTURE

Palladio, having studied in Rome for two years, enters his first architectural competition, and wins (1547). This, his first building, is started two years later—the Basilica, Vicenza. (cf. **69***)

James Gibbs: St. Martin-in-the-Fields, Trafalgar Square, London (1721–26).

William Kent changes careers, from painter to architect (1724).

John Wood (the younger): Royal Crescent, Bath (1767–75).

Robert Adam: Kenwood House, London (1767–69).

James Gandon: Customs House, Dublin (1781).

Rudolph M. Schindler: Lovell Beach House, Los Angeles (1926).

Charles and Ray Eames: first mass production of the Eames chair (1946). They had designed this molded plastic chair at **30**, and it has taken them almost a decade to work out the production method. Their lounge chair and ottoman is at **49**.

ART

Benozzo Gozzoli: frescoes—procession of the three kings—in the Palazzo de' Medici, Florence (1459).

Domenico Ghirlandaio: "Adoration of the Magi" (Foundling Hospital, Florence, 1488).

W. P. Frith: "Derby Day" (1856–58).

Rodin: "The Gates of Hell" (1880). This is an endless project which is never fully completed. It contains a large number of figures that become distinguished in their own right, for example, "The Thinker." Rodin now becomes a social and sexual celebrity. He begins work on "The Burghers of Calais" at **43**; and "The Kiss" at **45**. (cf. **50***)

Thomas Eakins: "The Swimming Hole" (1883).

John William Waterhouse: "The Lady of Shalott" (1888).

MUSIC—CLASSICAL

Chopin: death (1849, Oct. 17). His heart is buried in Poland, his homeland; the rest of his body is buried in Père-Lachaise, Paris. The music at the funeral includes his own "Funeral March," from the Sonata in B-flat Minor (**29**).

Engelbert Humperdinck: *Hansel and Gretel* (1893).

LITERATURE

John Galsworthy publishes *The Man of Property* (1906), the first in the Forsyte saga. The last Forsyte book is produced at **63**.

Marcel Proust has his bedroom lined with cork (1910), so that he can more easily write *À la recherche du temps perdu*. He now has a short draft, but the complete seven volumes take him the rest of his life, three being published after his death at **51**. The first volume has to be published on a vanity basis, at **42**, but it is then well received. Before *A la recherche* he has been something of a socialite and has only published one novel, a translation, and a few short pieces.

Capt. W. E. Johns: *The White Fokker* (1932)—the first Biggles story. Johns had flown in World War I, and is now a journalist specializing in aircraft matters. He writes over 200 books.

Dylan Thomas supervises the first performances of his *Under Milk*

 Wood (1953), but dies just afterward, from the effects of a lifetime of drinking.

PLAYS

Ibsen: *Peer Gynt* (1867). (cf. **49***)

Strindberg: *Miss Julie* (1888).

George Bernard Shaw: *The Man of Destiny*, and *You Never Can Tell* (1895–96).

Chekhov: *Uncle Vanya* (1899).

Eugene O'Neill: *Strange Interlude* (1929, Jan. 29)—a play of nine acts, which runs nearly six hours, from about 5:15 to 11:00 P.M. Later, he marries for the third and last time—his wife is **40**.

Tennessee Williams: *The Rose Tattoo* (1950).

Peter Brook directs *Marat/Sade* (1964). (cf. **48***)

FILMS

James Cagney: *Angels with Dirty Faces* (1938).

Walt Disney: *Fantasia* (1940).

Douglas Fairbanks, Jr.: *Sinbad the Sailor* (1947).

Ingmar Bergman: *The Seventh Seal*; and *Wild Strawberries* (1957).

Federico Fellini: *La Dolce Vita* (1960).

Alain Resnais: *Last Year at Marienbad* (1961), with Delphine Seyrig (**29**), and script by Alain Robbe-Grillet (also **39**).

John Cassavetes: *Rosemary's Baby* (1968).

Michael Ritchie: *Smile* (1975)—a sweet satire about a beauty competition.

Jane Fonda: *Fun with Dick and Jane* (1976); in this, she is the first female American star to be filmed while urinating.

"When I was **17**, I wanted to be a film director, but by accident I spent most of my life on the production side. One morning I woke up, realized that I was approaching **40**, and had not achieved what I wanted. . . ."—Alan J. Pakula, director of *The Sterile Cuckoo* at **40**, and of *All the President's Men*, at **48**.

MUSIC—NON-CLASSICAL

Leonard Bernstein: *West Side Story* (1957). The choreography is by Jerome Robbins (**37**) and the lyrics are by Stephen Sondheim (**27**).

Galt MacDermot: *Hair* (1967).

TV, ETC.

Jack Benny reaches **39** (1933) and remains **39** for the rest of his life. His career had taken off only the year before, at **38**, with his new weekly radio program This lasts for 23 years, and he then moves over into TV where he wins an Emmy at **65**. His two central jokes against himself are his miserliness, and his permanent youth, being **39** until his death 41 years later.

Ken Russell leaves BBC-TV (1966) where he has made a series of wonderful features on musicians and composers. He now moves up to the film world, but loses all sense of proportion, never again repeating his early critical success. His lavish new resources lead him astray, and he is denounced for self-indulgence and for aggravating his audiences.

LOVE, LIFE

Lady Caroline Lamb accidentally sees the funeral procession of her former lover, Lord Byron (d. **36**, 1824) and she is mentally ill for the rest of her life (d. **42**). At **28**, she had had a brief but passionate affair with the poet, and described him as "mad, bad, and dangerous to know."

John Ruskin falls hopelessly in love with Rose La Touche (**10**, in 1860). Ruskin is the distinguished art critic and writer on Venice. Rose calls him "St. Crumpet"; he likens her to "Sleeping St. Ursula" by Carpaccio, (**35**, 1495) in Venice. At **29**, Ruskin had married Euphemia Gray (**20**) but the marriage was never consummated, and it was broken up after six years. At **48**, Ruskin proposes marriage to Rose; later, she (**21**) declines. She dies at **27** from natural causes. Ruskin lives until **80**, forever affected by his great love for Rose. Both John Ruskin and Rose La Touche are virgins when they die.

Baba Ram Dass: Dr. Richard Alpert's acquisition of a new name, as a guru, after a year's study in India (1967). He had first taken psilocybin at **31**, and had been removed from teaching duties at Harvard University at **35**, for encouraging students to go on hallucinogenic trips.

Jacqueline Bouvier Kennedy, in 1968: marriage to Aristotle Onassis (**62**). At **22**, she had won first prize in the *Vogue* magazine talent contest. At **24**, she married John F. Kennedy (**36**); she was widowed at **34**. At **43**, her stepson, Alexander Onassis (**24**), dies in a plane crash. At **45**, she is a widow again, at the death of Aristotle Onassis.

Stephen Gaskin, and others: creation of an ideal community at The Farm, Sumertown, Tennessee (1971).

EXPLORATION

Captain Samuel Wallis: first European to land on Tahiti (1767). Native girls are hired to give pleasure to his crew—the fees are iron nails, and gradually these are stripped from his ship.

Roald Amundsen: first person to reach the South Pole (1911). At **54**, he is the first person to fly over the North Pole in an airship.

Neil Armstrong: first person to walk on the moon (1969, July 21). His fellow astronauts are Edwin "Buzz" Aldrin (also **39**) and Michael Collins (also **39**). At this moment, James E. Webb, head of NASA, is

63; Wernher von Braun, the rocket pioneer, is **57**; Christopher C. Kraft, head of Mission Control, is **45**; and Rocco A. Petrone, supervisor of the Apollo 11 launch, is **43**. The first person in space has been Yuri Gagarin (**27**, in 1961), and the first American in space is Alan B. Shepard (**37**, also in 1961). Astronauts have typically been **28–45**, with Americans being in the **32–45** range. The average age of all U.S. astronauts on take-off is **38.6**. The initial U.S. specification for astronauts had **40** as the upper age limit. In 1968, the Russians sent up Colonel G. T. Beregovoiy (**47**). The age range of 19 people entering NASA's astronaut training program in 1980 is **28** to **38**.

Gerry Spiess: solo journey across the Atlantic, in a yacht (1979). The remarkable feature of this trip is that the yacht, "Yankee Girl," is only 10 feet long and 5 feet wide. He completes the 3,200 mile voyage in 54 days.

LAW

Wild Bill Hickok dies from a gunshot wound while playing poker (1876). In his hand, he has two pairs—aces and eights—ever afterward known as Deadman's Hand. At **33**, he had briefly held office as marshal of Abilene. He has been a vicious killer, responsible for at least 36 deaths.

Charles Guiteau shoots President James A. Garfield (**49**) (1881), who dies two months later. Guiteau is hanged, still believing himself to be an instrument of the Deity.

SPORTS

Janet Guthrie (1977): first woman driver to race in the Indianapolis 500. She had originally trained as a pilot, and had taken up sports car racing at **25**.

Ken Rosewall gets to the finals of the men's singles at Wimbledon (1974). He had won the U.S. championship at **36**, having previously won it at **22**.

40

HEALTH

Howard Florey decides to have one big throw (1940) and concentrate all his research effort on penicillin. In the previous year, he has published eight research papers, none of them on this topic. Since its discovery by Alexander Fleming (**47**, in 1928), almost no use has been made of penicillin, partly because of the great difficulty in manufacture. Florey, with Ernst Chain (**34**) and others, now perform clinical trials and also devise a production process. Penicillin is both benign to healthy tissue, and lethal to bacteria; this is the beginning of the "Age of Antibiotics."

Jonas Salk: polio vaccine (1954). The first oral vaccine against polio is made by Albert Sabin (**49**, in 1955).

The risk giving birth to a baby with Down's syndrome is one in 1,500 for mothers in their **20**s; one in 750 for mothers **30–35**; one in 600 for mothers **35–40**; one in 300 for mothers **40–45**; and one in 60 for mothers at **45**.

NOTE: *the following entries are on late mothers, late first-time fathers, very late fathers, and families in which there is a tradition of late parents. There has recently been a hypothesis that late parents can lead to senility in the children when the latter are older—this is clearly not necessarily true. Another theory is that creative people regard children as a threat to their own creativity, and so put off the formal acceptance of parenthood for as long as possible.*

Late mothers include the following:

—the mother of Rudolf Nureyev is **35** (1938) when she gives birth to the future dancer—on a train which is traveling between Lake Baikal and Irkutsk;
—the mother of the poet John Milton (1608–74) is about **36** at his birth;
—Lawrence Alma-Tadema, the painter: at his birth, his mother is **36** (1836). He lives until **76**.
—Yoko Ono has her son Sean Ono Lennon at **37** (1975);
—Jean Shrimpton, the model, has her first baby at **37** (1979).
—Helena Rubinstein, the cosmetics empress, says that she is **38** (1909) and **41** at the birth of her two children;
—Marie Stopes the contraceptive pioneer, loses her virginity at **38** (1918) and goes on to become a mother;
—Diana Rigg, the actress, has her first baby at **39** (1977);
—Claudia Cardinale, the film star, has a baby at **40** (1979);
—Alice Roosevelt Longworth has her only child at **41** (1925); she is later remembered for her brisk approach to medical problems—because of her two mastectomies, she refers to herself as the "topless wonder of Massachusetts Avenue," and when President Johnson (**59**) shows his appendix operation scar to the press, she (**83**) comments, "Lucky it was not an operation on his prostate." Alice Roosevelt Longworth lives in her birthplace, Washington, until her death at **96**;

—Lucille Ball has a baby at **42**, as part of her TV program, "I Love Lucy";
—Johanna Christiane Brahms is **43** at the birth of her second child, the composer, in 1833;
—Ursula Andress, the film star, has her first child at **44** (1980) and the father is **28**.

Late first-time fathers, and very late fathers include:

—Joseph Conrad, the novelist, fathers his only child at **40** (1898), and this son at **73** publishes an interesting book on his upbringing;
—William Godwin, the philosopher, is a first-time father at **41** (1797), and his wife is then **38**—this child, Mary, goes on to write *Frankenstein* at **20**, and she lives until **53**;
—Alfred Tennyson, the poet, fathers his first child at **41** (1851); he had lost his virginity also at **41**, on the occasion of his marriage to Emily Sellwood (**37**) to whom he had first become engaged fourteen years previously;
—Leland Stanford, of Stanford University, fathers his only child at **45** (1869);
—Peter Mark Roget (1779–1869), the creator of *Roget's Thesaurus* at **73***, is a first-time father at **46**;
— C. P. Snow, of "two cultures" fame, is a first-time father at **46** (1952);
—the painter Mark Rothko is said to be a first-time father at **47** (1950)—the baby is called Kate after Rothko's mother who had died in about the same month in which the baby is conceived; Rothko's second and last child is at **60**;
—James Montgomery Flagg, creator of the brilliant U.S. recruiting posters during World War I, has his one and only child at **48** (1925);
—Bertrand Russell is a first-time father at **49** (1921);
—the painter Fra Filippo Lippi is a father for the first and only time at **50** (1406);
—Robert Baden-Powell, founder of the Scouts, is first married at **52** (1909) and his wife is then **25**—they go on to have three children;
—Sir John Vanbrugh, the polymath architect, first marries at **55**, and he and his wife (about **24**) later have two children, one of which survives until adult life;
—Arnold Bennett, the novelist, is a first-time father at **59** (1926).
—Benvenuto Cellini is a father once only, at **60** (1560);
—Edward G. Robinson, only child in his **40**s;

—Humphrey Bogart, first-time father at **49** (1948);
—Ronald Colman, who marries at **46** (1938) and his only child is at **53**—Colman's father and mother had been **43** and **40** at his birth;
—Roger Corman, the director, is a first-time father at **49** (1975);
—Charlie Chaplin marries for the last time at **54** (1943) and goes on to have an additional eight children, the last at **73**;
—Clark Gable's only child is born after Gable's death at **61** (1960); and Cary Grant's daughter is born when he is **62** (1966).

These are distinguished people who happen to have been born to older parents:

—Mozart's father is **37** at the composer's birth (1756);
—Oscar Wilde's father is **38** at the playwright's birth (1854);
—at the birth of Stephen Potter (1900), the inventor of "gamesmanship" and other "one-up" behavior, his father is **41** and his mother is **36**; Potter lives until **69**;
—George Bernard Shaw, the playwright, is born in 1856, when his father is **40** and his mother is **25**—Shaw himself lives until **94**;
—at her birth, Helen Keller's father is around **42** and her mother is **22** (1880); Helen Keller lives until **87**;
—Eugene O'Neill, the playwright, is born in 1888 when his father is **42** and his mother is about **34**—at **55**, his daughter Oona (**18**) marries Charlie Chaplin (**54**, above);
—the father of Richard Wagner is **43** at the composer's birth (1813) and the mother is **34**—Richard Wagner lives until **69**, completing his last opera at **68**.
—Otto von Bismarck, the German chancellor and pensions pioneer—at his birth, his father is **43**, and his mother is **25**. Bismarck lives until **83**.
—T. S. Eliot, the poet—at his birth, his father is **47**, and his mother is **45** (1888).

Here are some other families in which there is a sometime tradition of late parents:

—John Tyler, President of the U.S.A., marries for the second time at **54** (1844) and goes on to have seven children, in addition to the seven he has fathered already; when the president was born, his father was **43**;
—the wife of Denis Diderot (**39**), the encyclopedist and poly-

math, gives birth to Angélique, their only child to survive to adulthood, when she is **43** (1753)—coincidentally the mother of Diderot was also called Angélique, and she was **35** at the birth of her first child and **42** at the birth of her sixth and last child;

—J. W. Goethe (1749–1832), the German poet and polymath, is a first-time father at **40**, and grandfather at **68**—Goethe's father had been a first-time father at **39**, the child being the poet himself; also, Goethe's grandfather had been **53** at the birth of Goethe's father;

—the father of Christopher Wren, the polymath architect, is **43** (1632) at the birth; Christopher Wren's grandfather had been **37** at the father's birth; Christopher Wren's children are born when he is **39**, **42**, **44**, and **46**, but the last child is mentally retarded; the son born when Wren is **42** himself has sons at **37** and **46**, and this last son goes on to become the family historian;

—at the birth (1880) of Sean O'Casey, the Irish playwright, his father is **43** and his mother is **43** also; O'Casey lives until **84** and his own children are born when he is **48**, **55**, and **59**;

—the mother of the naturalist Charles Darwin (1809–82) is Susannah "Sukey" Wedgwood Darwin, and she is **44** at his birth; Charles Darwin's own wife, Emma Wedgwood Darwin, gives birth to her ninth child at **43** and this is her last baby to survive to adulthood—she has another baby at **48** but he lives for only two years; Emma Wedgwood Darwin lives until **88**—she herself is the ninth and last child of Elizabeth Allen Wedgwood who had been **44** at Emma's birth.

—Tolstoy's last child to survive into adult life is born when the author is **55** and the mother is **39** (1884); this child, Sasha, lives until **95**, and publishes her last book at **69**; at Leo Tolstoy's birth, the father had been **33** and the mother was **38**; at the birth of Tolstoy's wife, Countess Sonya Tolstoy, the father was **38** and the mother was **20**. Coincidentally, both Sonya Tolstoy and her mother had thirteen children. Leo Tolstoy lives until **82**, and Sonya Tolstoy lives until **74**.

For those now **40**, life expectancy in the U.S.A. (1976) is until **72.7** for males, and until **78.7** for females. The causes of death for people **25–44** are for males: (1) accidents; (2) diseases of the heart; (3) cancer; (4) suicide; (5) cirrhosis of the liver; (6) cerebrovascular; (7) pneumonia. For females: (1) cancer; (2) accidents; (3) diseases of the heart; (4) suicide; (5) cerebrovascular; (6) cirrhosis of the liver.

You can now expect to live until **77.9** (female) and until **72.3** (male)

(England and Wales, 1975). Out of total deaths in all ages, only 2 percent (male) occur in the ages **35–44**, and 1.35 percent (female).

The age group **30–44** is expected to grow by 20 percent between 1976 and 1991, in England and Wales. The only other age group to have such a large increase is **75+**. (cf. **80***)

Some countries with a fairly low life expectancy include Afghanistan, where males at birth can expect to die at **39** and females at **40**; Laos, **39** and **41**; India, **41** and **40**; Bhutan, **42** and **45**; Zaire, **42** and **45**; and Kampuchea, **44** and **46**.

The life expectancy in the Plymouth colony has been estimated to be around **45.5**.

In 1876, the life expectancy at birth of a Swiss male was **40**; in 1958, it was **68**. For females, the figures were **43** (1876) and **74** (1958).

In Scotland in the 1790s, the expectation of life was typically in the early **40**s. It varied from **36.2** in one geographical area, to a high of **48.5** in one favored location. The life expectancy of males in England and Wales in 1841 was **40.2**, and **42.2** for females. In 1871, these figures had improved somewhat to **41.4** male, and **44.6** female.

Animals' maximum life span: the brown bear can live until **37** years old; and the parrot until **39**. The hippopotamus typically lives until **40**. The emu might live to a maximum of **40**, and the macaw to a maximum of **43**.

HISTORY—WORLD

Marcus Aurelius: Roman emperor (161 A.D.) until his death at **59**.

Constantine the Great: creation of the capital city Constantinople (328 A.D.), from the old town of Byzantium. He had become Roman Emperor at **20**.

King Louis XIV of France: the successful ending to the Dutch War (1678), begun at **34**. These are his peak years as the "Sun King." His palace of Versailles is almost ready to be the seat of government—its designers include Mansart (**31**) and Le Nôtre (**64**). His court includes the writer Racine (**39**), and the composer Lully (**46**). His mistress is Mme de Montespan (**37**). But by the end of his life (**76***), much of this "gloire" has been dissipated.

Adolf Hitler, in 1929: the Depression provides the conditions in which his medium-sized National Socialist party can flourish. Until now he has been a forceful leader of one out of many political groups. He now moves to a central position—he becomes Chancellor at **43**, and uses the Reichstag fire as an excuse to limit democratic controls. At **45**, he purges his own extremist supporters, the Stormtroopers. At **48**, he occupies Austria; the Munich agreement is at **49**; by **51**, he controls most of Europe, and forces France to reverse the 1919 Treaty of Versailles. At **52***, he overreaches himself with his attack on Russia.

HISTORY—U.S.A.

Senator Joe McCarthy becomes a national figure overnight, by announcing (Feb. 1950) that the U.S. State Department is infested with Communists, of whom he has a list of 205 names; McCarthyism is a powerful force for almost the next five years. Up to this time, McCarthy has been an ineffective first-term senator, and he discovers this issue almost by accident. (cf. **42***)

HISTORY—U.K.

Emily Wilding Davison, in 1913: to bring public attention to the cause of women's suffrage, she flings herself under the horse of King George V (on his **48**th birthday) at the Derby, and she dies shortly afterward.

Winston Churchill, in 1915: having been a leader in an unsuccessful initiative in Turkey, he is now forced to leave the government. Although he has had a brilliant career (cf. **20***) up until now, he has antagonized many people with his ambition and with his fondness for almost any new idea. In the eyes of both friends and enemies, he has failed to make the jump from boyish enthusiast to reliable political leader. At **42–47**, he is in the government again, but he is distrusted for his ambition and self-absorption. At **49**, he is Chancellor of the Exchequer where he pursues an old-fashioned hard money policy which is the opposite to that preferred by J. M. Keynes (**41**). Churchill's policies intensify the Depression, and he leaves office at **54**. From **55–64**, he concentrates on reacting to the development of nazism; having established himself as untrustworthy and opportunistic, his warnings on Hitler (**41–50**) tend to be dismissed as warmongering. Even during the Munich crisis (**63**), he is not followed. But events overwhelm his opponents, and he becomes Prime Minister at **65***.

Eligibility: you can now retire from the military services on a pension, at any time after completing 22 years service which has begun from **18** on.

RELIGION, PHILOSOPHY

When a man at **40** is the object of dislike, he will always continue what he is.—Confucius.

Muhammad, in 610 A.D.: he receives a vision that he is to be the messenger of God. At **43**, he starts preaching these messages, and after his death (**62**), his teaching is collected to form the Koran. At **52**, he moves from his birthplace, Mecca, to Medina; this marks the beginning of the Islamic Era. At **54**, a vision comes to him that in prayer Muslims must face toward Mecca. At **58**, he makes the first annual pilgrimage to Mecca. Muhammad lays the foundation of the Islamic religion and of Arab power.

St. Theresa of Avila: beginning of her life as a mystic (1555). Previously she had been an unenthusiastic nun. She founds her own ascetic convent at **47**, and has her "mystic marriage" at **57**.

Rev. H. W. Baker: *Hymns Ancient and Modern* (1861).

Nietzsche writes on his birthday: "Everything comes in its own good time. I am **40**, and I find myself at the very point I proposed, when **20**, to reach at this age. It has been a fine, a long, and a formidable passage" (1884). He is now writing *Thus Spake Zarathustra*, the aphorisms of a superman: full of Olympian vision, domination of the rabble, sublimation, and the idea that suffering and power are the only realities. Nietzsche himself lives an entirely nondescript life, and has little personal success—*Zarathustra* is first published at his own expense, in an edition of 40 copies. While writing, he suffers from poverty, loneliness, insomnia, poor vision, and acute headaches which he relieves with Javanese narcotics. At **44**, he has an intimation that he is about to become a world-famous cult figure; but he goes mad, and dies at **55**, never experiencing any reward for his own Olympian efforts.

Idries Shah: the book *The Sufis* (1964).

SOCIAL SCIENCE, EDUCATION

From the middle of life onward, only he remains alive who is ready to *die with life.* For in the secret hour of life's midday, the parabola is reversed, death is born. The second half of life does not signify ascent, unfolding, increase, exuberance, but death, since the end is its goal. The negation of life's fulfillment is synonymous with the refusal to accept its ending. Both mean not wanting to live; not wanting to live is identical with not wanting to die. Waxing and waning make one curve.—Carl Jung, in *The Meaning of Death*. Jung himself dies at **85***.

F. A. Mesmer: the concept of "animal magnetism" (1774). This is the beginning of his career in "mesmerizing," or hypnosis. Previously he has been working as an M.D. At **50**, he is labeled a charlatan, and has to return to conventional medical practice, having made his name only in this period **40–50**.

Auguste Comte: first use of the word "sociology" (1838).

Lewis Henry Morgan (1858) accidentally hits on the subject of examining kinship terms (the equivalent to our "uncle" or "aunt") in native American tribes. At this time, he is a lawyer in the railroad business, with an amateur interest in native peoples. At **53**, he publishes *Systems of Consanguinity and Affinity of the Human Family*—a pioneer work of research in systematic anthropology. His amateur interests are elevated into a key social science volume when discovered and discussed by Engels (**64**), three years after Morgan's death.

Henry George: *Progress and Poverty* (1879).

Karl Pearson, the statistician: invention of the product-moment correlation coefficient (1897); also, first use of the term "standard deviation" at **37**; and "chi-square" at **43**.

John Dewey: *The School and Society* (1899), and *Democracy and Education* at **57**.

Max Weber: *The Protestant Ethic and the Spirit of Capitalism* (1904). This is his first major work. At **30**, he was appointed a professor of economics, but at **36** he had a nervous breakdown and never does routine teaching again. (cf. **49***)

Oswald Spengler: *The Decline of the West* (1918–22), two volumes published at **38** and **42**.

Simon Kuznets: *National Income and Its Composition: 1919–38* (1941).

Margaret Mead: *Balinese Character: a Photographic Analysis* (1942). (cf. **69***)

C. Wright Mills: *The Power Elite* (1956). Also, *White Collar: the American Middle Classes* (**35**); and *The Sociological Imagination* at **43**. He dies at **45**.

T. S. Kuhn: *The Structure of Scientific Revolution* (1962).

R. D. Laing: *The Politics of Experience, and the Bird of Paradise* (1967).

Susan Brownmiller: *Against Our Will: Men, Women, and Rape* (1975).

SCIENCE, TECHNOLOGY

Anders Celsius: invention of the centigrade scale (1742). The mercury thermometer is invented in 1714 by Gabriel Fahrenheit (**28**) who devises his own temperature scale.

G. S. Ohm: Ohm's Law (1827).

Michael Faraday: invention of the electricity generator (1831). At **42**, he revises the nomenclature of electricity and with friends he devises such words as "electrolyte," "anode," and "cathode." In the rest of his life, he becomes a government adviser on matters of science and technology, and he develops interests in subjects which are even larger than those he has tackled so far. (cf. **67***)

William Fox Talbot: first photography using a negative to produce any quantity of positives (1840). He has been working on this since about **35**. Here, necessity is very much the mother of invention, since he has been a keen traveler whose lack of sketching skills has made him frustrated at his inability to record buildings and landscapes. In his **20**s and **30**s Talbot has done creative work in calculus; in spectrum analysis in chemistry; and in classical history. He now goes on to exploit his invention by becoming a distinguished photographer and he lives until **77**.

J. J. Thomson: discovery of the electron (1897).

Paul Müller: first use of DDT as an insecticide (1939).

Enrico Fermi: first chain reaction in atomic physics (1942). His first experiment in fission had been at **32**. He is **43*** at the completion of the first atomic bomb.

MONEY, WORK

Robert Owen: after twenty years in the cotton industry, he gives the first lecture that touches on his later views on industrial relations (1812). At **44**, he takes first concrete step, by opening New Lanark's "new institution for the formation of character" (1816, Jan. 1). (cf. **49***)

Henry Ford starts the Ford Motor Company (1903, June 13) with the help of James Couzens (**31**) and money from Alexander Malcolmson (**38**) and others. They revolutionize the market by making their cars first, and then selling them to the lower end of the market. At this time, the majority of cars are made to order, after the customer has inspected a sample model. Although Ford has been so far a creative engineer, this is his first real commercial success; at **41**, he pays his first-ever annual dividend—68 percent. (cf. **45***)

Aristotle Onassis is worth about $30 million (1945–46); marries for the first time—to Tina (**16**); buys 16 war-surplus ships, and this is the beginning of the huge growth in his wealth. (cf. **48***)

Between **40** and **70**, an employer may not discriminate against you on account of your age. You are now protected by the Age Discrimination in Employment Act (U.S.A., 1967). If you believe that you are suffering discrimination, you should check with your local Equal Employment Opportunity Commission. Discrimination on age grounds is no more moral or legal than discrimination on account of gender or skin color. There are a small number of jobs, however, such as airline pilot, in which age may be used as a job qualification.

ARCHITECTURE

Inigo Jones makes a second visit to Italy, for a year of study (1613–14).

Robert Adam: the Adelphi, London (1768); a huge urban complex of houses, warehouses, and riverside wharves.

John Soane: Tyringham House, Buckinghamshire, England (1793).

A. W. N. Pugin dies (1852, Sept. 14) with his Houses of Parliament interiors unfinished; he is buried in St. Augustine's, Ramsgate designed by himself (**38**).

James Renwick: St. Patrick's Cathedral, New York City (1858–79).

Louis H. Sullivan lays down the dictum that "form follows function" (1896). (cf. **47***)

Peter Behrens: AEG Turbine Hall, Moabit, Germany (1908–09); an unattractive building, but one which occurs in every history of modern architecture.

Gerrit Rietveld: Schröder House (1924); this design establishes De Stijl once and for all.

ART

Sandro Botticelli: "Primavera," about this time (1486). (cf. **60***)

Hans Holbein: portraits of Henry VIII (**46**) (1537).

Mathew Brady takes photographs of the American Civil War (1862). At the end of the war, he overextends himself in his portrait business, and goes bankrupt at **50**. He dies in poverty at **73**, though his Civil War negatives have already become a national treasure.

James McNeill Whistler: his first one-man show (1874). His best-known paintings are done around now: "Arrangement in Gray and Black: No. 1—the Artist's Mother (**68**)" at **38**; and "Nocturne in Blue and Gold—Old Battersea Bridge" at **39**. At **44**, he goes bankrupt from the legal expenses of his battle with Ruskin (**59**). After this, he becomes more of an artistic personality than a painter; he is influential as a teacher and friend to other artists.

Dorothea Lange joins the historical division of the Farm Security Administration (1935). The next eight years as a photographer of the New Deal are the peak of her career. She had been a photographer since **20**, and afterward continues in similar work for the rest of her life. In 1935, Walker Evans (**32**) and Ben Shahn (**37**) also join the FSA. Evans coauthors *Let Us Now Praise Famous Men* when he is **38**.

Judy Chicago, and others: completion of "The Dinner Party" (1979).

MUSIC—CLASSICAL

Gounod: *Faust* (1859).

LITERATURE

To live beyond **40** is bad taste.—Fyodor Dostoevsky (1821–1881).

It is in the **30**s that we want friends. In the **40**s we know they won't save us any more than love did.—F. Scott Fitzgerald (1896–1940).

Approaching **40**, I am about to heave my carcass of vanity, boredom, guilt, and remorse into another decade. . . . Both my happiness and unhappiness I owe to the love of pleasure; of sex, travel, reading, conversation (hearing oneself talk), food, drink, cigars, and lying in warm water.—Cyril Connolly (1903–74).

Samuel Johnson tells the actor David Garrick (**32**) that he can now no longer visit Garrick in the Green Room of the Drury Lane Theater—"The silk stockings and white bosoms of your actresses do make my genitals to quiver" (1749).

Thomas Carlyle (1835, Mar. 6): the manuscript for much of *The French Revolution* is used by a maid to light a fire, and it takes him six months to rewrite. At **46**, he publishes *On Heroes, Hero-Worship, and the Heroic in History*, defining a hero as having "a God-created soul which will be true to its origin." He says that "History . . . is . . . the History of Great Men." (Women tend to be a "necessary evil" in his scheme.)

Anthony Trollope publishes *The Warden* (1855), and *Barchester Towers* at **42**. These are the first of his Barsetshire novels, and the beginning of his immense popularity. He writes the Palliser series between **48** and **65**. His typical day begins at 5:30 A.M. when he puts his watch on the desk and forces himself to write 250 words every 15 minutes. After breakfast, he leaves the house, and begins a regular day's work, as a senior civil servant in the post office (where he claims to have invented the pillar-box). After completing one novel, he would start the next on the following day, thus he writes a total of 65 books. (cf. **63***)

James Joyce: completion of *Ulysses* (1922), which he began at **32**. "Bloomsday," the day which the book describes, occurred at **22** when Joyce first knew Nora Barnacle (**20**).

Franz Kafka dies (1924, June 3), from tuberculosis. He has never married; none of his major works have been published—*The Trial* or *The Castle*.

Constantine Cavafy, in Alexandria: almost all his poetry is written after **40** (1903). Cavafy is employed in the Egyptian Irrigation Service, from **29** to **60**. During his lifetime, his poetry is never formally published, but only sent out to friends at his own expense. At **47**, he writes "The City," his sad but persuasive poem on the impossibility of changing one's life. Cavafy dies in Alexandria, twelve days after his **70**th birthday.

J. P. Marquand surveys his life up till now, and makes the conscious decision that he will stop being a hack writer and will become a serious artistic force in the world (1934). Since about **25**, he has made himself wealthy by his writings for magazines. Within limits, Marquand now succeeds in his ambition. *The Late George Apley* is the first of the new works, at **43**. *H. M. Pulham, Esquire* is at **47**. *Point of No Return* is at **55**. J. P. Marquand transforms himself into one of the best-known semiserious novelists of his day.

PLAYS, DANCE

When an actress gets to **40** there's really nothing new to stretch her until she reaches **60** and can start on the old ladies, and in some curious way the fact that nobody writes great parts for middle-aged women also affects their standing in the theater generally. Nobody thinks of us as leaders because we don't get to play leaders.—Glenda Jackson (**40**, in 1976).

FILMS

If you're only young enough in America, you can demand the world, and they'll give it to you. Now I'm over **40**, so America lost interest in me.—Orson Welles (**40** in 1955).

Groucho Marx (to a woman): How old are you?
Woman: Approaching **40**.
Groucho Marx: From which direction?

D. W. Griffith: *The Birth of a Nation* (1915).

Mae West signs her first film contract (1932), and is an instant success in *Night After Night;* and at **41** in *She Done Him Wrong*.

John Ford: *The Informer* (1935).

Busby Berkeley: *Gold Diggers of 1935* (1935); this is the one with 56 white pianos; he makes a similar Gold Diggers film at **41**.

John Grierson: his visit to Canada (1938) results in the setting up of National Film Board.

Sergei Eisenstein: *Alexander Nevsky* (1938).

Gene Kelly: *Singin' in the Rain* (1952).

Jose Ferrer in *Moulin Rouge* (1952).

Alan Ladd: *Shane* (1953).

Yul Brynner: *The King and I* (1956).

Lindsay Anderson: *This Sporting Life* (1963).

Sidney Poitier: *Guess Who's Coming to Dinner;* and *In the Heat of the Night* (1967).

Stanley Kubrick: *2001: a Space Odyssey* (1968).

Andy Warhol: *Lonesome Cowboys* (1968)—this is also the year in which he survives a stabbing.

Gene Hackman: *The French Connection* (1971).

Michael Caine: *Sleuth* (1973).

Robert Redford and Dustin Hoffman (**39**): *All the President's Men* (1976). Redford says at **40** that he has never cheated on his wife.

Margaret O'Brien now benefits from a trust fund (1977) which had been set up to deal with her earnings of $1 million as a child star.

MUSIC—NON-CLASSICAL

Florenz Ziegfeld: *Follies of 1907* (1907). He is the greatest producer in Broadway history and his aim is to produce a "National Institution Glorifying the American Girl." This is his first Follies; the twenty-first and last are at **64**, and he dies at **65**. At **60**, having been associated with one era for most of his life, he helps inaugurate another era by presenting *Show Boat* by Kern and Hammerstein (both **32**).

"Life Begins at **40**"—this song is originally associated with Sophie Tucker, the vaudeville star (**40** in 1924). For her, life had begun at **22** with her first professional appearance in New York City. She had left school at **13**, and joined the Ziegfeld Follies at **25**. She is prominent in show business from about **26** until her last professional engagement at **81**, again in New York. Perhaps her most famous song is "My Yiddisher Momma," at **41**. At **69**, she makes this comment on life: "I've been rich and I've been poor, and believe me, rich is best." Another song about **40** is "Life Made Me Beautiful at **40**," written for herself by Eartha Kitt.

Stephen Sondheim: *Company* (1970); and *Follies* at **41**; *A Little Night Music* at **43**; *Pacific Overtures* at **46**; and *Sweeney Todd* at **49**. He had written the lyrics for *West Side Story* at **27**.

Charlie Rich: "Beyond Closed Doors" (1973). This is his first gold record; previously he has struggled with a career of minor hits and various recording contract difficulties.

TV, ETC.

Raymond Burr: "Perry Mason" (1957–65). He has to work incredibly hard to make the 245 episodes of this series—during the week he has his home on the studio lot, and he gets up every day at 3:30 A.M. to learn his lines. At **37**, he had been the murderer in the film *Rear Window*. At **50**, he starts on "Ironside."

Eric Porter: as Soames Forsyte in "The Forsyte Saga" (1968), with Kenneth More (**54**), Susan Hampshire (**30**), and Nyree Dawn Porter (**28**).

LOVE, LIFE

Elizabeth Barrett: marriage, to Robert Browning (**34**, in 1846).

Of U.S. women **40** to **44**, 4.7 percent have never married (1977).

PRESS

Norman Podhoretz: editor of *Commentary* (1970). His interesting book on ambition, *Making It*, was at **38**.

EXPLORATION

Ferdinand Magellan: first person to sail around the southern tip of South America (1519–20). He gives the newly discovered ocean the name of Pacific Ocean, owing to its calm and pacific nature, after the horrors of Cape Horn. Magellan is killed at **41**, in the Philippines, but remnants of his expedition reach home later, and are the first people to sail around the world.

Tenzing Norkay and Edmund Hillary (**33**): first people to reach the summit of Mt. Everest (1953). Hillary goes up the mountain as an elite person within the comparatively small community of mountaineering people; when he descends, he has temporarily become one of the most famous people in the world. Among those who later climb Everest are Pierre Mazeaud (**49**), who in 1978 has companions of **32** and **25**; he is a former French cabinet minister, for youth and sports, and he climbs Everest at his third attempt. In the same year, Everest is conquered by a West German party of **34**, **34**, and **28**. Also in 1978, Reinhold Messner (**34**) and Peter Habler (c. **39**) climb Everest without oxygen. The mountain should more properly be known as Mt. Everest **75***, incidentally.

LAW, CRIME

Judge Jeffreys conducts the "Bloody Assize" in the west of England (1685). Following a local rebellion, he orders 200 hangings, 200 whippings, and about 1,000 to be transported. Jeffreys had got his first judicial appointment at **33**, and had risen rapidly by always following the political leadership. At **40**, he now becomes Lord Chancellor. But at **44**, following a change in the political climate, he is imprisoned for his vicious sentences, and dies in the Tower of London.

James Earl Ray kills Martin Luther King, Jr. (**39**) (1968). He is sent to prison until **139**. Ray comes from "poor white trash," and his family has a history of crime and violence. At **31**, Ray gets a 20-year sentence for some robberies, and he is sent to Jefferson City jail. Here, the chaos, violence, and race hatred is so bad that the warden himself commits suicide. Ray escapes from here at **39**, and stays free until months after killing Dr. King.

Joseph (Specs) O'Keefe (and others): the Brinks robbery in Boston (1976); $2.7 million is stolen from the security firm, and much of it is never recovered. At **46**, O'Keefe tells the FBI of his accomplices. They get life sentences, and O'Keefe is moved to California under an alias. He stays there till his death at **67**.

About 11 percent of the murderers who are sentenced to death are aged **40** or over. The peak years for murderers receiving the death sentence are **20–24**, and decline continuously after that.

SPORTS

Babe Ruth (baseball, 1935): in his last-ever game, he hits three consecutive home runs.

Hank Aaron (baseball, 1974) breaks the record for home runs, the record having previously been set by Babe Ruth (also **40**,) in 1935. At **42**, Aaron is still playing and earns $240,000 in this one year. In 1979, Carl Yazstremski (also **40**) gets his 3,000th hit; he had gained his 400th home run at **39**. Ty Cobb reaches the 3,000 hit mark at **34**

(1921); also Stan Musial reaches it at **37** (1958), and Cap Anson at **46** (1897). Pete Rose (1978) has his 3,000th hit at **37**, as well as a streak of hitting safely in 44 straight games.

Don King (1971) leaves prison after serving four years for manslaughter—during a street fight his opponent had died. King now starts out on a new career, as a boxing promoter. He later gets to sign up Muhammad Ali, and is able to promote such fights as the "Thriller in Manila," at **43**, between Ali (**32**) and Joe Frazier (**30**). It is claimed that one billion people watch this fight.

Jack Nicklaus: winner, U.S. Open golf championship (1980). He is now the only person to have won a major golf championship in four separate decades of his life. He goes on to win the PGA championship shortly afterward.

Men's track and field records now at **40**:

100 meters in 10.8 seconds;
400 meters in 49.5 seconds;
1,500 meters in 3 minutes 52.0 seconds;
10,000 meters in 28 minutes 33.4 seconds;
10 mile walk in 1 hour 22 minutes.
The high jump record is 6′8″ and the
long jump record is 24′ 4¾″.

Women's track and field records now at **40**:

100 meters in 13.1 seconds;
200 meters in 27.5 seconds;
400 meters in 62.7 seconds;
800 meters in 2 minutes 32.2 seconds;
the mile in 5 minutes 24 seconds;
10,000 meters in 35 minutes 51 seconds.
The long jump record is 13′2″.

41

HISTORY—WORLD

Metternich: the Congress of Vienna (1814–15), for the remaking of Europe after the fall of Napoleon (**45**). Prince Metternich is Austrian Foreign Minister from **36** to **74***.

HISTORY—U.S.A.

Huey P. Long: as a senator, he publishes *My First Years in the White House* (1935), setting out his views on his "share our wealth" plans; but is assassinated at **42**.

HISTORY—U.K.

Henry VIII: five weddings within the next 10½ years (1533). At **18**, he had married Catherine of Aragon (**23**); at **41**, he now marries Anne Boleyn (**26**); at **45**, Jane Seymour (**27**); at **48**, Anne of Cleves (**23**); at **49**, Catherine Howard (**18**); and at **52**, he marries Catherine Parr (**31**). At **42**, excommunication proceedings are begun against him. At **44**, he executes Sir Thomas More (**57**). Henry VIII dies on his **56**th birthday.

William Pitt the Younger leaves office of Prime Minister (Mar. 1801) which he has held since **24**. He regains office at **44**, and dies as Prime Minister at **46**.

RELIGION, PHILOSOPHY

St. Ignatius Loyola: foundation of the Society of Jesus (1534), the Jesuits.

René Descartes: *Discourse on Method* (1637). He starts with his Method of Doubt, and proceeds onward from the only proposition of which he is certain—*cogito ergo sum*. Also, in this book he develops Cartesian coordinates, to fix any position on a plane or in space. (cf. **53***)

SOCIAL SCIENCE, EDUCATION

Jeremy Bentham: *Introduction to the Principles of Morals and Legislation* (1789).

Lewis Namier: *Structure of Politics at the Accession of George III* (1929).

J. William Fulbright sponsors law to give travel grants—"Fulbright scholarships"—to graduate students (U.S.A., 1946).

Simone de Beauvoir: *The Second Sex* (1949).

Thomas Szasz: his first book *The Myth of Mental Illness* (1961). He continues to promote this theme, best summarized by the title of a later book *The Manufacture of Madness: a Comparative Study of the Inquisition and the Mental Health Movement* (**51**).

Alvin Toffler: *Future Shock* (1970).

George Gilder: *Wealth and Poverty* (1980).

SCIENCE, TECHNOLOGY

John Dalton: *New System of Chemical Philosophy* (1808). This is the first use of particle weights in a systematic way to form a general theory about the quantities by which elements combine. He sets forth the concepts of atom and molecule. This work is not the result of a sudden brilliant insight by Dalton: instead he has been inching toward this achievement since about **37**, when he first published his ideas on particle weights. This is only a part of his wide-ranging interests in technology, meteorology, teaching, and grammar. At **32**, he published the first systematic study of color blindness. Dalton now carries on with the same wide interests until his death at **77**, but he never again achieves the quality of work done between **32** and **41**. He promotes his own symbolic notation for the elements, but this work is superseded by that of J. J. Berzelius (**31**, in 1811) who proposes O for oxygen, and so on.

John James Audubon: prospectus of *Birds of America* (1827). He had published his first drawing of a bird at **39**. Audubon's late start is probably due to the muddle in his life, as even his conception had taken place within a highly ambiguous relationship. He lived both in France and the U.S.A., and he went bankrupt at **33**. At **41**, he now begins on his life's work, but lack of progress is caused by the great ambition of his birds project. It is not finished until **54**. At **55**, he starts on *Vivaporous Quadrupeds of America* and he finishes his work on this at about **63**. He lives until **65**.

Elisha Otis demonstrates his new safety elevator (1852); he gets into the elevator, cuts the cable which is suspending it, and it does not fall to the ground.

James Clerk Maxwell: completion of his work on equations for electromagnetic theory (1873). His peak years are roughly **32** to **41**, and he dies at **47**.

Elisha Gray is the coinventor of the telephone (1876). But he believes that it will have no commercial future, so he immediately pursues other interests.

William Ramsay: joint discovery of the gas argon (1894). At **45** he produces neon, as later used in neon tubes. The development of neon lighting is attributed to Georges Claude (**40**, in 1910).

John von Neumann: the proposal that an electronic computer should have a stored program (1945).

Peter Goldmark: invention of the long-playing record (1948).

Samuel C. C. Ting (**38**) and Burton Richter (**43**): discovery of the Psi or J molecule, and "charm" (1974).

MONEY, WORK

Charles Lewis Tiffany: Tiffany & Company (1853). He had opened his first store in New York at **25**; this is the first time that the store carries only his own name. He lives until **90**.

Henry Royce: the first car (1904, Apr. 1) to be designed and built by himself. Up to this time, he has had a skilled medium-small electrical business, making dynamos. After making two more cars, he is introduced to a London sports-car dealer, the Hon. C. S. Rolls (**27**); a few months later, they decide to go into business, forming Rolls (**27**)-Royce (**41**) Ltd. Two years later, he makes the first Silver Ghost.

RENAISSANCE

Sergei Diaghilev: his ballet company puts on the first performance of *The Rite of Spring* (1913). The choreography is by his lover, Vaslav Nijinsky (**23**) and the music is by Igor Stravinsky (**30**). This is the most famous of many events at which Diaghilev antagonizes those who are unsympathetic to the avant garde; arguments and fights break out on the first night, and the police have to be called in the interval. But enthusiasts in the audience include the composers Maurice Ravel (**38**) and Frederick Delius (**51**). Diaghilev had grown up in a rich and cultured vodka-producing family in Russia. As a youth, he had met some of the leading personalities of the times. His first public work was to organize an art exhibition at **25**, and at **26** he started an art magazine. In both of these he brought the new foreign art styles to St. Petersburg. Between **26** and **29**, he is on the staff of the Imperial Theaters, where the ballet is still run by the pioneer choreographer, Marius Petipa (**70–73**). In his early **30**s, Diaghilev continued to organize international art exhibitions; from this grew a season of Russian opera, in Paris at **36**. His first season to include ballet is at **37**, and this is the start of his main contribution to the world. At **38**, he puts on *The Firebird.* From **37** onward he directs his own touring ballet company; at **50** he achieves a stable base for the organization through a contract in Monte Carlo. He dies at **57**, in Venice. His greatest gift is to discover geniuses and to persuade them to work for the company. For example, at **41** he works with the composer Richard Strauss (**49**); at **42**, with Serge Prokofiev (**23**); at **44**, with Pablo Picasso (**34**), Jean Cocteau (**27**), and Erik Satie (**50**); at **46** he works with Sonia and Robert Delaunay (both **46**); at **47**, with the painters André Derain (**39**) and Henri Matisse (**49**); at **51** he works with Georges Braque (**41**); at **55** with Stravinsky again and with George Balanchine (**24**); and at **57** he starts a collaboration with the composer Paul Hindemith (**33**).

ARCHITECTURE

Philibert Delorme: gallery over the river, château de Chenonceaux (1556–59); seen on a million travel posters, it is perhaps the most beautiful château of the Loire.

Jules Hardouin-Mansart: the Grand Trianon, Versailles (1687).

Sir Charles Barry wins the competition for the new Houses of Parliament, London (1836).

Peter Behrens: his office staff (1909–10) includes Walter Gropius

(**26**), Ludwig Mies van der Rohe (**23**), and Charles-Édouard Jeanneret (Le Corbusier) (**22**).

Raymond Hunt (with others) wins the competition for the Chicago Tribune building (1922)—defeating Eliel Saarinen (**49**), and Walter Gropius (**39**).

ART

Henry Rousseau retires from the French Customs and Excise service (1885) and starts his painting career. By **61**, "Douanier" Rousseau is able to tell Picasso (**24**) that they are the two greatest artists of the period.

Alfred Stieglitz opens his gallery for photography at 291 Fifth Avenue (1905), with Edward J. Steichen (**26**).

František Kupka: "Vertical Planes III" (1912–13)—perhaps the first true abstract painting.

Willem de Kooning: first solo show (1948).

Christo constructs a fence 18 feet high and 24 miles long, in Sonoma County, California (1976).

MUSIC—CLASSICAL

Edward Elgar: the *Enigma Variations* (1898). This is the beginning of a burst of creativity: *The Dream of Gerontius* at **43**; *Cockaigne* Overture at **44**; *Land of Hope and Glory* at **45**. He later writes his first symphony at **53**, and Violin Concerto at **55**. Previously, he had in his **30**s been only a well-known musician in the Worcester area; *Enigma* is his first permanently remembered work. After **55**, he hardly writes anything that is performed later. And at **62**, he is devastated by the death of his wife (**71**). He lives another fourteen years, as a public figure in the music world, but composing hardly anything. After his wife's funeral, he writes: "All I have done was owing to her, and I am at present a sad and broken man—just stunned. My daughter does everything and is wonderful about the hideous ghoulish business which civilization makes necessary. Death we know and expect and try to bear like men, but I cry out 'Leave me with my dead.' " The *Nimrod Variation* is a thank-you to August Jaeger (**38**), who has helped bring Elgar out of obscurity.

Puccini is later remembered chiefly for the three operas which he writes around now: *La Bohème* at **37**; *Tosca* at **41** (1899); and *Madame Butterfly* (**15–18**) at **45**. He is an opera composer all his life, and he dies at **65**, still working on *Turandot.*

Gustav Holst: *The Planets* (c.1915); and *I Vow to Thee My Country* at **47**.

Carl Orff: *Carmina Burana* (1937).

LITERATURE

Alexandre Dumas: *The Count of Monte Cristo* (1844–45).

Harriet Beecher Stowe: *Uncle Tom's Cabin* (1852).

Robert Frost returns to America from England (1915), and becomes a full-time poet for the first time. Previously he had been a farmer and a teacher. Afterward he says that editors who kept rejecting his early work made him bitter at the time. Later on, when he met them and saw what they looked like, he forgave them. For poor poets, he advises a job as far away from writing as possible. (cf. **52***)

James Joyce begins work on *Finnegan's Wake* (1923, Mar. 10).

Truman Capote: *In Cold Blood* (1965). He wrote *Breakfast at Tiffany's* at **34**.

Allen Ginsberg is chief guru at the Human Be-In, in Golden Gate Park, during the San Francisco "Summer of Love" (1967). He had written "Howl" at **30**, and had been a market researcher at **27**.

PLAYS

Thornton Wilder: *Our Town* (1938); and *The Skin of Our Teeth* at **45**.

Jean Anouilh: *Ring Round the Moon* (1948).

Christopher Fry: *The Lady's Not for Burning* (1948).

Neil Simon: *Plaza Suite* (1968).

FILMS

D. W. Griffith: *Intolerance* (1916)—narrative titles by Anita Loos (**23**).

Douglas Fairbanks, Sr.: *The Thief of Baghdad* (1924).

George Cukor: *The Philadelphia Story* (1940), with Katharine Hepburn (**31**), Cary Grant (**36**), and James Stewart (**32**).

Humphrey Bogart: *High Sierra;* and *The Maltese Falcon* (1941)—his transformation from "well known," to "great" and "star."

Kirk Douglas: *Paths of Glory* (1957).

Judy Garland: *I Could Go on Singing* (1963); this is her last film, and she dies at **47**.

Lee Marvin: *Cat Ballou* (1965); makes him a star.

Jean-Luc Godard is seriously hurt in a car crash (1971).

François Truffaut: *Day for Night* (1973).

Vanessa Redgrave makes an unprogrammed speech about the Middle East, at the 50th Academy Awards ceremony (1978); she has recently completed a 2½ hour documentary on *The Palestinians*, financed by moving into a smaller home.

MUSIC—NON-CLASSICAL

Richard Rodgers and Oscar Hammerstein II (**48**): *Oklahoma* (1943). Now follows an unbelievable string of successes, such as *Carousel* at

43 and **50**, which includes the soccer fan's anthem, "You'll Never Walk Alone"; their *South Pacific* is at **47** and **54**; and *The King and I* is at **49** and **56**. (cf. **64***)

TV, ETC.

Stanley Siegel: "Stanley and the Shrink" (1977). Once a week, Siegel is psychoanalyzed during his own TV show. He also visits his psychoanalyst three other times each week, but these sessions are not shown on TV.

Ted Turner: Cable News Network (1980).

LOVE, LIFE

Duke (**42**) and Duchess (**40**) of Windsor: marriage (1937). This is his first marriage; she was previously married at **20** and at **32**.

EXPLORATION

Marco Polo arrives back in Venice (1295) which he had left at **17**. His friends and neighbors are amazed to see him. He had been taken traveling by his father and uncle, and had spent about 16 years at the court of the emperor of China. Now, he gradually begins to write descriptions of his travels; his stories are so amazing that for a long time people cannot believe them. Marco Polo lives until he is about **70**.

Christopher Columbus, in 1492: this is his approximate age at the discovery of the New World, when he arrives at San Salvador, in the ship *Santa Maria.* At this moment, his patron Queen Isabella is **41**, and her husband Ferdinand is **40**. Columbus leads further voyages across the Atlantic, at **43** and **47**. At **49**, when he is a colonial administrator, he has to be brought back home in chains, as his high-handed behavior has been virtually insane. He leads his fourth and last voyage at **51–53**, and dies at **55**.

Valery Ryumin, and Leonid Popov (**34**): 185 days in orbit above the earth, a record (1980).

Jaromir Wagner: he is carried across the Atlantic on the top of an airplane (1980)—a bizarre but unique achievement.

LAW, CRIME

Bugsy Siegel is shot to death in Beverly Hills (1947). In his **20s**, he was a leader in illegal liquor supply in New York, and had a suite in the Waldorf-Astoria Hotel. At the end of Prohibition (**30**), he moved to California. At **39**, he was a pioneer in the development of a Las Vegas hotel into a gambling resort—thus helping with the city's transformation from a small town into a major vacation center. But his killing occurs before this becomes profitable. J. Edgar Hoover (**52**) calls him "criminal scum."

John White is murdered in Ohio by a killer (**19**) who has been hired by White's own children (**14** and **17**) (1979). The killer's fee is $60, and the reason for the quarrel is that White has been too strict as a father.

SPORTS

Manuel Dominguez (1857): during a bullfight, the bull's horn damages Dominguez's eye. The matador scoops the eye out of its socket, throws it away, and carries on with the bullfight.

Bobby Simpson (cricket, 1977): captain of Australia.

42

HISTORY—WORLD

Napoleon: war against Russia (1812). This is the beginning of the end. Since **30***, he has been dictator of France, and gradually acquired control of nearly all Western Europe. But his campaign against Russia is a disaster, and he is forced to abdicate at **44**. He makes his "Hundred Days" comeback at **45**, but his defeat at Waterloo means that he is sent to live on a tiny island, St. Helena, in the middle of the South Atlantic. He dies there at **51**.

Simón Bolívar: land which he has freed in his guerilla campaigning is formed into the new country of Bolivia (1825). This is the high point of his career; but he is unable to maintain unity among the countries which he has freed from Spanish occupation. He therefore flees to Europe, and dies in Spain at **47**.

Czar Alexander II of Russia: the great emancipation of 50 million serfs (1861). This and other acts of modernization do not bring him personal popularity—he is assassinated by reformers at **62**.

HISTORY—U.S.A.

John Winthrop becomes Governor of the Massachusetts Bay Colony (1630).

Julia Ward Howe: "Battle Hymn of the Republic" (1862).

Sitting Bull kills George A. Custer (**36**) and all his forces at Little Big Horn (1876, June 25), but surrenders at **47**. He is later settled on a reservation, and dies at **56**.

Joseph McCarthy: the height of McCarthyism (1952)—he attacks, with impunity, General George C. Marshall (**71**). (cf. **45***)

Robert F. Kennedy: killed while campaigning for the presidency (1968, June 6). Robert Kennedy was U.S. Attorney-General at **35**, and a member of the U.S. Senate at **39**.

RELIGION, PHILOSOPHY

Thomas Bray: foundation of the Society for Promoting Christian Knowledge (1698).

Søren Kierkegaard: death (1855). At **25**, he had met the love of his life, but "I was 1,000 years too old for her." At **31**, he publishes *The Concept of Dread* which leads to the widespread use of the word *Angst.* At **32**, he writes *Stages on Life's Way.* His book at **33** is a starting point in existentialism. At **36**, he publishes *The Sickness unto Death.* Kierkegaard is also later remembered for this quotation: "Life must be lived forward, but it can only be understood backward."

Bhagwan Shree Rajneesh: opening of his ashram in Poona, India (1974).

SOCIAL SCIENCE, EDUCATION

Jacob Burckhardt: *The Culture of the Italian Renaissance* (1860).

Thorstein Veblen: *The Theory of the Leisure Class* (1899).

John B. Watson is fired from Johns Hopkins University (1920) for having an affair with a graduate student (**23**). Watson had become the professor of psychology there at **29**, and his experiments are later seen as classics in behaviorism. His lectures at **34** at Columbia University were a major event in the development of psychology. At **36**, he published *Behavior,* and was made president of the American Psychological Association. But from now onward, he is shunned and despised by his academic colleagues. He is unable to secure any position or research funds. He turns to the field of advertising, and obtains work in market research. His first project is a study of the rubber boot market along the Mississippi; his second project is on the purchase of instant coffee. Watson goes on to revolutionize market research, and in effect to create a new discipline. At **42** he divorces his first wife (**37**) and marries the graduate student, Rosalie Rayner—he is said to never have another affair. He lives until **80**, and she until **88**. At **79***, he is awarded the Gold Medal of the American Psychological Association, but he chooses not to attend the presentation ceremony.

Lester C. Thurow: *The Zero-Sum Society* (1980).

SCIENCE, TECHNOLOGY

Simon Marius: naming of the Andromeda nebula (1612).

William Herschel: discovery of Uranus (1781).

Max Planck: quantum theory, and Planck's Constant (1900).

Rita Levi Montakini: work on NGF, nerve growth factor (1951).

Karl Friedrich Schinkel: Berlin Museum (1823).

Sir Robert Smirke: British Museum (1823–47).

Capt. Francis Fowke: Royal Albert Hall, London (1865)—but dies immediately after construction begins.

G. E. Street: wins competition for the Law Courts, London (1866).

Alfred Waterhouse: the Natural History Museum, London; and Girton College, Cambridge (1872).

Sir Aston Webb: Victoria and Albert Museum, London (1891).

Le Corbusier: Villa Savoie (1929–31).

Frei Otto: the German Pavilion, Montreal World's Fair (1967).

ART

Thomas Gainsborough: "The Blue Boy" (c.1770).

Bernard Berenson completes the fourth and last part of his history *Italian Painters of the Renaissance* (1907; begun at **29**). He is now established as the unique expert on his subject, and no major painting purchase can take place without his comments. This fact brings him great wealth in the succeeding 52 years of his life.

Henry Moore: now able to support himself as a full-time sculptor (1940). Previously he had earned his living as a teacher. (cf. **60***)

MUSIC—CLASSICAL

Smetana: *The Bartered Bride* (1866).

Fauré: *Requiem* (1887).

Hugo Wolf dies in a mental asylum (1903, Feb. 22). At **39**, he had gone mad, and told his friends that he was in charge of the Vienna Opera. His first "action" had been to dismiss the reigning chief, Gustav Mahler (then also **39**). Nearly all the lieder for which Wolf is later famous were written in a brief period between **27** and **29**. His death causes a flood of interest in his work, and his copyrights are sold for a huge sum of money.

John Cage: *4'33"* (1954)—four minutes, thirty-three seconds, of silence.

LITERATURE

Henry Fielding: *Tom Jones* (1749).

Sir Walter Scott anonymously publishes his first novel, *Waverley* (1814), beginning his very successful career as a novelist. In the next six years, he writes fourteen novels. (cf. **54***)

Lord Macaulay: *Lays of Ancient Rome* (1842); and *Essays* at **43**.

Henry Miller: *Tropic of Cancer* (Paris, 1934), his first book. *Tropic of Capricorn* is at **47**. *Sexus* and *Plexus* are both at **57**. He goes on to have a vigorous old age, playing table tennis with naked Japanese girls.

He lives until **88**. He suffers from censorship problems, and this first book at **42** is published in the U.S.A. when he is **69**.

FILMS

Eadweard Muybridge is asked by Leland Stanford (**48**) to photograph horses in motion (1872) to determine how they move their legs; a pioneering moment in the history of motion pictures.

Charlie Chaplin: *City Lights* (1931).

Marx Brothers: *A Night at the Opera* (1935).

Frank Capra makes *Mr. Smith Goes to Washington* (1939).

Alfred Hitchcock: *Suspicion* (1941).

Spencer Tracy and Katharine Hepburn (**33**): *Woman of the Year* (1942); this is the first of their nine films together.

Walt Disney: *Bambi* (1943).

Clark Gable gets the Distinguished Flying Cross for flying five missions over war-time Germany (Oct. 1943).

Dalton Trumbo: his career wrecked by being one of the "Hollywood Ten" (1947)—but wins an Oscar at **52**, having collaborated on a script, using a pseudonym.

John Huston: *The Treasure of Sierra Madre* (1948), starring his father, Walter Huston (**64**), and Humphrey Bogart (**48**).

Jack Hawkins: *The Cruel Sea* (1952).

Saul Bass: the film credits for *Walk on the Wild Side* (1962).

Federico Fellini: *8½* (1963).

Pier Paolo Pasolini: *The Gospel According to St. Matthew* (1964).

Richard Burton: *Who's Afraid of Virginia Woolf?* (1967).

Jack Lemmon: *The Odd Couple* (1967), with Walter Matthau (**47**).

George C. Scott: *Patton* (1969); Oscar, which Scott refuses to accept.

Marcel Ophuls: *The Sorrow and the Pity* (1969)—the favorite film of Woody Allen (also **42**) in *Annie Hall* (1977).

Louis Malle: *Lacombe Lucien* (1974).

Francis Ford Coppola: *The Godfather, Part II* (1975).

Woody Allen and Diane Keaton: *Annie Hall* (1978); four Oscars.

Natalie Wood: *The Last Married Couple in America* (1980). She herself had first been married at **19**, to Robert Wagner (**27**). At **33**, her third marriage is also to Robert Wagner (**41**). Her death, by drowning, is at **43**.

TV, ETC.

Lucille Ball gives birth to Desi Arnaz, Jr. (**0** in 1953)—the entire gestation has been incorporated into her "I Love Lucy" show, and the interest which this creates has pushed the show to highest-ever ratings. She had begun the show two years previously, and then earned the title "Most Promising TV Star." At **58**, she sells the company—Desilu—to a conglomerate for $17 million.

LOVE, LIFE

King Louis XIV of France is secretly married to his last mistress, Mme de Maintenon (**45**, in 1680). He was married at **21**, to Maria Theresa (also **21**). His mistresses have included: at **22**, Louise de la Vallière (**17**); at **28**, Mme de Montespan (**25**); at **41**, Marie-Angélique de Fontages (**18**). Both La Vallière and Fontages later die in convents. Louis XIV writes: "[T]he time allotted to a liaison should never prejudice our affairs [of state] since our first object should always be the presentation of our glory and authority, which can only be achieved by steady toil." The mistresses of his successor, Louis XV, include: at **35**, Mme de Pompadour (**24**); at **43**, a number of prostitutes (c. **14**); at **52**, Mlle Tiercelin (**15**); and at **59**, Mme du Barry (**25**).

Ruth Handler: design of the Barbie doll (1959).

Kenneth Tynan: *Oh Calcutta!* (1968).

Yves Saint Laurent: the fragrance "Opium" (1978).

PRESS

Lord Northcliffe acquires control of the *Times* (London, 1908). (cf. **57***)

Walter Lippmann: start of his column "Today and Tomorrow" (1931).

EXPLORATION

David Livingstone: first European to see Victoria Falls, in Africa (1855).

SPORTS

Ted Williams (baseball, 1960): he is up to bat for the last time, in his last-ever game—he hits a home run.

Gary Player (1978) wins three championships in a row—the U.S. Masters, the Tournament of Champions, and the Houston Open. He had previously won the Masters at **25** and **38**. At **42**, he finishes the season ninth in the final standings. He lists himself even higher—"I am the greatest player in the world."

Joyce Smith is the first woman to finish the Tokyo Marathon (1980); she is first woman in the London Marathon, at **43**.

43

HEALTH

Alois Alzheimer: identification of the senile dementia known as Alzheimer's disease (1907). He himself lives only until **51**.

Virginia Apgar: the Apgar scoring system (1952) to rate the health of the newly born.

HISTORY—WORLD

General Franco: beginning of the Spanish Civil War (1936). Franco had been a brilliant young army officer, and by **33** was promoted to brigadier-general. Later, during a change of government, he had been effectively demoted by a left-wing administration. As the country becomes more unstable, Franco now seeks to impose an authoritarian and Fascist regime. Around the world, supporters of both right and left sides see the war as vitally important. Franco and his Fascist army gain complete control when he is **46**. He goes on to kill any remaining opponents, and stays in office until his death at **82***.

Sheikh Yamani: the OPEC oil price rise (1973).

HISTORY—U.S.A.

Sam Houston wins the battle of San Jacinto (1836, Apr. 21), and later becomes president (also at **43**) of the Republic of Texas.

George F. Kennan: his "Mr. X." article in *Foreign Affairs* (July 1947), setting out a policy for containment of the U.S.S.R. and its leader, Josef Stalin (**67**).

John F. Kennedy becomes President (1961, Jan. 20); Joseph P. Kennedy is **72**; Rose Kennedy is **70**; Averell Harriman, ambassador-at-large, is **69**; Dean Acheson **67**; Adlai Stevenson **60**; J. K. Galbraith **52**; Lyndon Johnson also **52**; Dean Rusk **51**; Robert McNamara **45**; Arthur Schlesinger, Jr., **43**; Robert Kennedy **35**; Ted Sorensen **33**; Jackie Kennedy **31**. Nikita Krushchev is **66**, and George Washington's (**57**) first cabinet is younger on average than Kennedy's. (cf. **46***)

Cesar Chavez and UFWOC win grape boycott (1970) against California grape growers; Chavez turns to supporting next the lettuce workers.

King Edward II: murdered, in 1327, by order of his wife (**32**)—red hot poker up his anus.

RELIGION, PHILOSOPHY

St. Francis Xavier: arrival in Japan to establish a Christian mission (1549).

SOCIAL SCIENCE, EDUCATION

Machiavelli loses his civil service job in Florence (1512). He had been secretary to the Council of Ten. He is suspected of taking part in a plot against the Medici. Although innocent, he is tortured, suffering six drops of the strappado, and being kept in prison for twenty-two days, shackled and manacled. During the next thirteen years, he is in exile; he writes *The Prince,* and *The Art of War* during this time. At **56**, he has a brief return to office, but dies at **58**, with his work still circulated only in manuscript.

Karl Popper: *The Open Society and Its Enemies* (1945).

Benjamin Spock: *Baby and Child Care* (1946), with Jane C. Spock. At publication, they have two children—**13** and **2**.

SCIENCE, TECHNOLOGY

Henry Bessemer: the first Bessemer converter, for making steel (1856). He sets up his own steelworks at **47**, and becomes extremely rich.

Hiram Maxim: first true automatic machine gun (1883).

Robert Watson-Watt: the first effective radar (1935).

Donald W. Douglas: the DC-3 airliner (1935). He goes on to build 11,000 of this design.

Christopher Cockerell: first experiments in the invention of the hovercraft (1953).

At the first explosion of an atomic bomb, Enrico Fermi is **43** (1945); Lise Meitner is **66**; Otto Han (**66**); Niels Bohr (**59**); Vannevar Bush (**55**); James Chadwick (**53**); Arthur Compton (**52**); Harold Urey (**52**); John Cockcroft (**48**); Leo Szilard (**47**); and J. Robert Oppenheimer is **41**—he is later denounced as a security risk, at **50**.

MONEY, WORK

John D. Rockefeller: Standard Oil Trust (1882), the peak of his power. (cf. **69***)

Henry Royce and C. S. Rolls (**29**): the Rolls-Royce Silver Ghost (1906).

W. O. Bentley: his Bentley car company gets into difficulties during the Depression (1931), and has to be bought up by Rolls-Royce. Bentley does not fit in with the new management, and leaves at **47**—continues with the successful design of new engines.

ARCHITECTURE

Filippo Brunelleschi, in 1420: this is the great time in his life when he designs two of the world's most influential buildings. At **42–43**, he designs the Innocents building in Florence; and now he designs the dome of Florence Cathedral. Construction of the dome lasts until **59**, and he lives until **69**.

Inigo Jones: the Queen's House, Greenwich, London (1616–17).

Sir Christopher Wren: St. Paul's Cathedral (1675); his designs are approved by the clients.

Dankmar Adler and Louis H. Sullivan (**31**): the Auditorium Building, Chicago (1887–89), later Roosevelt University.

Sir Edwin Lutyens begins his design work on the capital city of New Delhi (1912).

Mies van der Rohe: the German Pavilion at the Barcelona Exhibition of 1929, and the Barcelona chair (1929). (cf. **44***)

Philip Johnson: all-glass house for himself, New Canaan, Connecticut (1949).

John Portman: Hyatt Regency Hotel, Atlanta (1967)—the first of his hotels with wonderful huge full-height atriums, around which he puts the bedrooms. Portman is both the architect and his own developer/client.

ART

Giotto: "Madonna and Child Enthroned" (c.1310). In the Uffizi museum, this is placed next to two other large paintings of the same subject, by Cimabue (**42**, painted in 1282), and by Duccio (c.**27**, in 1285).

On his **43**rd birthday, Paul Gauguin arrives at the island of Tupuai, not far from Tahiti (1891). He has now escaped from the "disease" of civilization. He stays here for the next two years—the times of his best work. He then goes back to Europe; he returns to the Pacific at **47**, and dies there at **54**.*

Mark Rothko: between now (1946) and **46**, he hits on his mature style, in Abstract Expressionism. Up till now, he has been a figurative painter who is interested in surrealism and in myth.

Joseph Beuys: formation of the Fluxus group (1965).

MUSIC—CLASSICAL

Claudio Monteverdi writes *Vespers of the Blessed Virgin* (1610), in Mantua. At **46**, he is appointed Maestro di Capella, at St. Marks, Venice, and continues in office until his death at **76**. (cf. **75***)

Robert Schumann writes his last piece of musical criticism (1853), saying that Brahms (**20**) is the man of the future. Schumann then becomes psychotic, and is taken away to a mental asylum, dying there at **46**. His wife Clara (widowed at **36**) pursues a distinguished career as concert pianist, and lives till **76**.

Brahms: Symphony no.1, in C Minor (1876).

Arthur Sullivan: the music for *The Mikado* (1885).

Havergal Brian composes the first of his 32 symphonies (1919) (cf. **72***)

Zoltán Kodály: *Háry János* (1926).

LITERATURE

Dante Alighieri now starts work (1308) on the *Divine Comedy.* He drops a lesser project in order to concentrate on this great work. It takes him the rest of his life (d. **56**). The poet, who is **35** in the poem, experiences *Inferno* ("abandon hope, all ye who enter") and then *Purgatorio.* Finally he is lead to *Paradiso* by Beatrice (**24***) who takes her place with figures from the Bible and classical legend. In Florence, there is a portrait of Dante by Giotto, who is a year older than the poet.

William Wordsworth receives a job in the government post office, and moves to Grasmere (1813), where he lives for the rest of his life, dying at **80**.

Elizabeth Gaskell: *Cranford* (1853). Her first published work was at **38**. On the conflicts between motherhood and writing, she says: "When I had *little* children I do not think I could have written stories, because I should have become too much absorbed in my *fictitious* people to attend to my real ones."

Arnold Bennett: beginning of the *Clayhanger* series (1910). His first major novel was published at **41**, and he had previously worked on *Woman* magazine. This is the time at which his career takes off—at **45**, he makes as much money in one year as he had in his entire previous life.

D. H. Lawrence: *Lady Chatterley's Lover* (1928); but he dies two years later.

William Golding: *Lord of the Flies* (1954).

Aleksandr Solzhenitsyn completes *A Day in the Life of Ivan Denisovich* (1962). (cf. **55***)

Leon Garfield, an American, publishes his first book (1964). A subsequent book is a Book of the Month Club selection, and at **55** he publishes four books in one year.

PLAYS, DANCE

Arthur Wing Pinero: *Trelawney of the Wells* (1898).

Sean O'Casey: first production of one of his plays (Abbey Theater,

Dublin, 1923). O'Casey's education ended at around **13**, and since then he has been a laborer, trade union organizer, and has written some poems and songs. At **34**, he drafted the constitution of the Irish Citizen Army, but he has had so little money that he has been to the Abbey Theater on only two or three occasions. At **40–42**, the theater had rejected four of his manuscripts. Now at **43** his first successful play is *The Shadow of a Gunman.* Later this year he completes *Juno and the Paycock.* At **45**, the premiere is held of *The Plough and the Stars,* certainly one of the great artworks of the twentieth century. In these three Dublin plays O'Casey both discusses great universal themes and also creates real characters in real settings. But at **46** he moves into an expressionist-symbolist-fantasy style, the first example of which is *The Silver Tassie.* This is rejected by his former colleagues, W. B. Yeats (**61**) and Lady Gregory (**74**). O'Casey leaves Dublin never to return, and pursues his own line. Later he returns to the Dublin of his childhood when he writes his autobiography, at **59*** onward. At **46**, for the London production of *The Plough and the Stars,* he meets Eileen Carey (**26**) when he is looking for an actress to play Nora Clitheroe; he persuades her to take the part, and they are married in the following year—the first and only marriage for both of them.

FILMS

Busby Berkeley: *Gold Diggers of Paris* (1938)—the last of the series. He continues with musicals, but they become repetitive.

Jacques Tati: *Les Vacances de Monsieur Hulot* (1951)—the creation of this character.

Katharine Hepburn: *The African Queen* (1952).

Alec Guinness: *The Bridge on the River Kwai* (1957).

Sergio Leone makes the first of his three spaghetti westerns (1964), with Clint Eastwood (**34**).

Stanley Kubrick: *A Clockwork Orange* (1971).

Shirley MacLaine and Anne Bancroft: (**47**): *The Turning Point* (1978).

Robert Redford, director: *Ordinary People* (1980), starring Mary Tyler Moore (also **43**), Donald Sutherland (**46**), and Timothy Hutton (**19**).

Warren Beatty: *Reds* (1981).

TV, ETC.

Phil Silvers: as Sergeant Ernie Bilko (1955). This series stops when he is **46**, but is remembered forever.

Johnny Speight: the script of "Till Death Us Do Part" (BBC-TV, 1964–74), starring Warren Mitchell (**38**) as a hilarious bigot, and Dandy Nichols (**57**) as the doormat wife who always wins in the end. In the U.S.A., "All in the Family" (1971–77) is by Norman Lear (**49**), with Carroll O'Connor (**47**) as Archie Bunker.

Phil Donahue: now the leading talk-show host on U.S. TV (1979).

LOVE, LIFE

Lord Sandwich: eating of the first sandwich (1762). He invents this form of fast food so that he can gamble continuously without interruption by meals.

Eleanor Marx: suicide (1898). She has been the sixth child of Karl Marx (1818–83). Marx's second child, Laura, also commits suicide, at **66**. Coincidentally, the children of Leon Trotsky (1879–1940) also have unhappy endings; Zinarda Trotsky kills herself at **32** (1933); Sergei Trotsky is presumed to be killed by the Russians, at **29**; and Lyova Trotsky dies in mysterious circumstances at **32**. Also, the suicide of Nadiezhda Stalin is at **31** (1932); she had married Josef Stalin (**40**) at **18**.

Charles Stewart Parnell is named in a divorce action by Captain William O'Shea (**49**, 1889). Parnell has been a leading figure in the fight for Irish independence, and his Kilmainham Treaty, at **36**, was a dramatic step forward for that cause. But since **34** Parnell has been having an affair with Kitty O'Shea (then also **34**), wife of a fellow member of Parliament. By persisting in this affair, Parnell has put at risk the whole independence movement. Now, when the affair is publicized, a wave of controversy causes confusion to his own supporters. O'Shea's divorce is in the following year. Parnell marries Kitty O'Shea when they are both **45**—but he dies four months after the wedding. Their love affair has set back the Irish political cause by perhaps two decades; and the power of the Catholic priests' attacks on Parnell has a permanently chilling effect on Irish Protestants.

PRESS

Helen Gurley Brown: editor of *Cosmopolitan* magazine (1965). She had made her name at **40** with *Sex and the Single Girl*.

EXPLORATION

Captain Robert Falcon Scott: death, in Antarctica (1912). He has been leading a party to be the first people at the South Pole, but on arrival he finds that Roald Amundsen (**39***) has arrived there first, 32 days previously. Scott had decided that his expedition should pull their own equipment, but Amundsen has used teams of dogs and sledges; these dogs are killed at intervals, and form a useful addition to the food for the men and the remaining dogs. On the return journey from the Pole, Scott's expedition becomes overwhelmed by the poor conditions. When Scott realizes that the end is inevitable, he completes his diary and writes 12 letters—to his wife (**31**), friends, to the playwright J. M. Barrie (**52**), and even to some of the expedition's sponsors. He and two remaining companions lie in their tent for nine days, gradually freezing to death. Shortly before Scott's death, one of his party had committed suicide so that his ill-health would not impede the progress of the expedition. This was Captain Laurence Oates, who on his **32**nd birthday awoke to find that his frostbite had almost crippled him; he left his tent and walked into a blizzard, saying, "I am just going outside and may be some time." Months later, the bodies are discovered, and left inside the tent. They gradually become swallowed up by ice. Sixty-seven years later, this ice begins to break away from the land mass, and to form an iceberg which drifts out to sea.

LAW, CRIME

Eligibility: now old enough to retire on pension from the London police force. You can join at **18½**; the pension is available after 25 years, and must be taken up after 30 years, unless you are very senior. The current chief was appointed at **53**. In Massachusetts, policemen must retire from uniform at **50**.

SPORTS

Hashim Khan: winner for the last time of the world squash championship (1959). He has won this seven times since **35**.

Renee Richards plays in the U.S. women's singles championships at Forest Lawn (1977); she had previously played in the U.S. men's singles championships when he was **26**.

44

HEALTH

Louis Pasteur resigns from administrative duties (1867) which have come to him because of his great success as a researcher (at **25**, he had produced a paper which led to the foundation of stereochemistry). He now returns to full-time lab work, and first looks at the causes of decay in fresh food. Having proved the existence of bacteria, he invents the process of briefly heating milk so that certain microorganisms are killed—thus, pasteurization. His most spectacular work is against rabies, at **62***.

Sun Yat-sen: first-ever president of the Republic of China (1911), after 4,000 years of dynastic rule.

Stalin takes gradual control in Russia (1924), following the death of Lenin (**53**). Stalin is only one in the main leadership, but he establishes his supremacy through his total ruthlessness toward even the most loyal of revolutionary supporters. At **50**, he starts on the 100 percent collectivization of the agricultural sector. His opponents believe that the resultant famine will lead to Stalin's collapse. But at **55**, he begins the show trials, in order to purge the party of any critical thinking. By the beginning of World War II (**61**), Stalin has caused the death of 10–20 million of his fellow Russians. About the age of these purge victims: they are almost invariably **30–55**; very few are under **30**, and children of **12** and below are always exempt. Stalin dies in office at **73**.

HISTORY—U.S.A.

George Washington is **44** at the Declaration of Independence (1776, July 4). Benjamin Franklin is **70**; Richard Henry Lee also **44**; Paul Revere **41**; John Adams **40**; John Hancock and Thomas Paine both **39**; Benedict Arnold **35**; Thomas Jefferson **33**; Mad Anthony Wayne **31**; John Paul Jones **28**; James Madison **25**; Alexander Hamilton **21**; Pierre L'Enfant **21**; Aaron Burr **20**; James Monroe **18**; Andrew Jackson **9**; John Quincy Adams **8**. King George III is **38**; Lord North is **44**, and William Pitt, Lord Chatham, is **67**.

Andrew Young: U.S. ambassador to the United Nations (1977), until **47**.

Jane Byrne: mayor of Chicago (1979).

HISTORY—U.K.

Mary Queen of Scots is executed at Fotheringay Castle (1587, Feb. 8), having been in prison since she was **25**.

Robert Walpole is Chancellor of the Exchequer and First Lord of the Treasury (1721, Apr. 3)—gradually becoming in effect the first-ever Prime Minister. Prior to Walpole, government members were directly responsible to the sovereign; now they become responsible to one senior member of the government, who is then responsible for the whole team to the sovereign. Walpole builds Houghton Hall (**45–58**), his gigantic country house, using profits gained from the South Sea Bubble. (cf. **65***)

William Pitt the Younger becomes Prime Minister (1804, May 10), for the second time.

Margaret Thatcher has her first cabinet position (June 1970), as Secretary of State for Education and Science. She has been an MP since **33**. One of her jobs now is to abolish subsidized milk for older children, and she is subject to vicious personal criticism because of doing this—though her opponents never reintroduce it when they later get the chance. Mrs. Thatcher becomes party leader at **49**, and first-ever woman Prime Minister at **53**.

RELIGION, PHILOSOPHY

John Bunyan: first part of *Pilgrim's Progress* (1672), written in Bedford jail, where he has been kept since **32**. Bunyan dies at **60**.

SOCIAL SCIENCE, EDUCATION

Robert Burton: *Anatomy of Melancholy* (1621).

Herbert Spencer: *Principles of Biology* (1864). In this, he is the first to use the phrase "survival of the fittest." (cf. **76***)

T. H. Huxley: first use of the word "agnostic" (1869).

Sir James Frazer: *The Golden Bough* (1890).

Robert Redfield: *The Folk Culture of Yucátan* (1941).

B. F. Skinner: *Walden Two* (1948).

SCIENCE, TECHNOLOGY

John Napier: invention of logarithms (1594). He is a Scottish landowner whose interests include theology, agricultural experiments, the military, and mathematics. He now works for over 20 years part-time, to calculate his logarithmic tables, which are published when he is **64**. At **65**, he invents rods ("Napier's bones") which can be used in calculations. He dies at **67**. The development of natural logs is by Henry Briggs (**53**, in 1614), who publishes his results when he is **63**.

Isaac Newton: *Principia* (1687). This is written in Latin, and brings together his work since **23*** on gravity, force, and so forth. As well as these interests, Newton has been doing a great deal of work on chemistry-alchemy, but this is much less influential. At **50**, Newton has a nervous breakdown, and he comments: "I am extremely troubled at the embroilment I am in, and have neither ate nor slept well this twelve month, nor have my former consistency of mind." At **53** he is given a high administrative appointment at the Mint, in London; this involves a great amount of detailed work on coin manufacture and on the pursuit of forgers and criminals. From about **50** onward Newton's creative work is separate from the mainstream of scientific development, as his interests turn to theology and other topics. At **60**, he becomes president of the Royal Society, and there becomes perhaps the first scientific administrator—he is the go-between linking politicians and businessmen with the emerging sciences which are affecting manufacture, navigation, and so on. Newton's publication at **44** starts a revolution in thought—first in astronomy (infinitization of space), and more widely in the Age of Enlightenment. Since Newton had taken on the problems of the universe and solved them, it is obvious that a similar rational approach will be adequate to cure earthly problems. At the moment of publication in 1687, Galileo would have been **123**, but had died at **78**; Descartes has been dead for 37 years; Robert Boyle is **60**; Christiaan Huygenz (**58**); Samuel Pepys (**55**); John Locke (**55**); Christopher Wren (**54**); King James II (**53**); King Louis XIV is **49**; Harvard University (**48**); Leibniz (**41**); John Flamsteed (**40**); Edmund Halley (**30**); Reverend Cotton Mather (**24**); Thomas Newcomen, steam engine pioneer, is **24**; George Berkeley, the future philosopher, is **3**; Gabriel Fahrenheit is **1**; G. B. Vico, the philosopher, is born a year later; Montesquieu is born two years later, and Voltaire is born seven years later.

Robert Bunsen: invention of the Bunsen burner (1855). At **49**, he initiates the science of spectroscopy, with Gustav Kirchhoff (**36**).

R. J. Gatling: the first machine gun (1862).

G. F. Fitzgerald: the hypothesis that objects contract as their speed approaches the speed of light (1895). At this moment, Hendrik Lorentz is **42,** and the concept is later known as the "Lorentz-Fitzgerald contraction."

Edward Teller: first explosion of an H-bomb (1952).

MONEY, WORK

William Stern goes bankrupt (1978), with personal debts of £104,390,248 (about $208 million), a record. He had been the leading speculator in the London property boom of the early 70s; belief in his skill was so great that he raised huge loans on the strength of his personal guarantee only. He now agrees to pay back £6,000 per year, and he will be able to pay off his debts by the time he is **17,000**.

ARCHITECTURE

Philip Hardwick, Sr.: the Euston Arch, at Euston Station, London (1836–39).

John Carrère and Thomas Hastings (**42**): New York Public Library (1902).

Mies van der Rohe becomes head of the Bauhaus school (1930). (cf. **52***)

ART

Jan van Eyck: "The Arnolfini Wedding" (1434); and "The Madonna with Chancellor Rolin" at **45**.

Franz Hals: "The Laughing Cavalier" (1624).

Peggy Guggenheim: opening of her pioneer art gallery, "Art of This Century" (1942).

J. S. Bach: St. Matthew Passion (Apr. 1729). (cf. **56***)

LITERATURE

Virgil: the *Aeneid* (26 B.C.)

Henry David Thoreau dies (1862, May 6), from tuberculosis.

Ivan Turgenev: *Fathers and Sons* (1862).

Charles Kingsley: *The Water Babies* (1863).

A. A. Milne is later known only for his three works written between **42** and **46**—though he is a successful journalist all his life. He writes *When We Were Very Young* (1924) at **42**, *Winnie-the-Pooh* at **44**, and *The House at Pooh Corner* at **46**.

R. D. Blackmore: *Lorna Doone* (1869).

Sir Arthur Conan Doyle revives Sherlock Holmes (Oct. 1903), amid worldwide rejoicing, having killed him off at the Reichenbach Falls, three years previously. Doyle regarded the Holmes stories as somewhat of a diversion from his other interests, such as divorce law reform, historical novels, the Boer War, the Channel tunnel, and spiritualism.

F. Scott Fitzgerald dies in Los Angeles (1940) with his *The Last Tycoon* unfinished. The tycoon is Irving Thalberg, of MGM, who had died recently at **37**. Although Fitzgerald had been a heavy drinker, he dies not from alcoholism, but from a heart attack, while reading the *Princeton Alumni Weekly*. His wife, Zelda Sayre Fitzgerald is burned to death at **47**, in a fire in the mental hospital where she is a patient—she is survived by her mother (**87**).

Paul Gallico: *The Snow Goose* (1941).

PLAYS

Shakespeare's mother dies when he is **44** (1608). His father had died when Shakespeare was **37**. At **44**, he is now a grandfather for the first time, following the marriage in the previous year of his daughter Susanna (**24**). (cf. **38*** and **48***)

John O'Keefe: *Wild Oats* (1791).

Anton Chekhov: death (1904), from a heart attack. Chekhov grew up in a provincial town 600 miles south of Moscow. He qualified as a doctor at **24**. During his **20**s, he quickly made a national reputation for himself as a short story writer. His best-known plays start with *The Seagull* at **36**; this is not well received at first, but at **38** it is revived by Stanislavsky (**35**) who establishes it as a favorite work. *Uncle Vanya* is at **39**. Chekhov is married for the first time at **41**, to Olga Knipper (**32**), and he completes *Three Sisters* in the same year. On his **44**th birthday he attends part of the first night of *The Cherry Orchard,* but dies six months later. Olga Knipper lives until **89**.

J. M. Barrie: *Peter Pan* (1904). The story concerns a number of children who learn to fly and thus make their way to Never-Never Land. All the children except Peter later return to ordinary life and the process of growing up. But Peter Pan refuses to leave boyhood—"I'm youth—eternal youth! I'm the sun rising—I'm poets singing—I'm a little bird that has broken out of the egg—I'm joy, joy, joy!" The play is an instant success. The number two role is Wendy, and the play quickly establishes Wendy as a girl's name, plus the idea of a Wendy House. On the first night, Peter Pan is played by Nina Boucicault (**37**); Wendy (**9**) by Hilda Trevelyan (**24**); and Captain Hook, the pirate, by Gerald du Maurier (**31**). In a revival nine years later, the part of Slightly is played by Noel Coward (**13**). For J. M. Barrie, a key experience in his life occurred at **6** with the death of his brother David (**13**); his mother (**47**) then transferred all her love and favoritism to Barrie, seeing him as the consolation for her loss; Barrie's father (**52**) was an austere figure and a workaholic. Now at **44**, Barrie is still married to Mary Ansell (**42**) but they have never had sex in the ten years of their marriage. Barrie has a surrogate family including Peter Llewellyn Davies (**7**) and his mother Sylvia (**38**) whom Barrie regards with unconsummated excitement. J. M. Barrie lives in a circle which sometimes behaves outside the average expectation of aging. At his birth, his father was **46**. Nina Boucicault's father, Dionysius, was also **46** at her birth, and at **64** he married an actress, Louise Thorndyke (only **21**). The most distinguished American Peter Pan is Pauline Chase—she plays the part from **21** to **28**; she is baptized at **20** (1906) and her godmother is the actress Ellen Terry (**58**) who at **16** had married the Michelangelesque painter and sculptor G. F. Watts (**47**). Barrie's wife divorces him when he is **49**; and shortly afterward, at **47**, she marries a playwright over twenty years younger than herself. Later, she writes a book about the love of dogs—but when Barrie (**77**) is on his deathbed, she (**75**) crosses Europe to be with him.

FILMS

D. W. Griffith: *Broken Blossoms* (1919); and *Way Down East* at **45** and *Orphans of the Storm* at **47**. (cf. **49***)

Al Jolson: *The Jazz Singer* (1927)—the first talking picture.

Boris Karloff: *Frankenstein* (1931)—he suddenly becomes world famous.

Marx Brothers: *A Day at the Races* (1937).

John Ford: *Stagecoach* (1939).

Humphrey Bogart: *Casablanca* (1943), with Ingrid Bergman (**28**) and Claude Rains (**54**). Playing the piano is "Sam"—Dooley Wilson (**49**). In the film, Rick, the owner of the bar, is **37**.

Johnny Weismuller is fired from his role as Tarzan, as being too old

(1948); later he becomes vice-president of a Florida swimming-pool company.

Billy Wilder makes *Sunset Boulevard* (1950), with Gloria Swanson (**52**); and Buster Keaton (**55**), Hedda Hopper (**60**), Erich von Stroheim (**65**), and Cecil B. DeMille (**69**).

Fellini: *Juliet of the Spirits* (1965).

Paul Scofield: *A Man for All Seasons* (1966) about the events leading up to the execution of Sir Thomas More (**57**).

Charlton Heston: *Planet of the Apes* (1968).

Paul Newman and Robert Redford (**33**): *Butch Cassidy and the Sundance Kid* (1969).

Dudley Moore: *10* (1980), also starring Bo Derek (**23**).

TV, ETC.

Lorne Greene: "Bonanza" (1959–71).

Peter Falk: "Columbo" (1971–77).

LOVE, LIFE

Lady Hamilton: last meeting with Admiral Nelson (**47***), on his way to the Battle of Trafalgar (1805). She had first made love to him at **37**, with the apparent consent of her husband, William Hamilton (then **68**), and since that time Nelson had been passionately attached to her. Before his death in battle, Nelson expresses the wish that Emma Hamilton should receive state support from Britain, but this is never granted. The nation is embarrassed to find that its hero has had this romance, and Emma spends some time in a debtor's prison, before her death at **54**.

Roman Polanski, the film director: guilty of unlawful sexual intercourse with a minor (about **13**, in Los Angeles, 1977).

PRESS

Ida Tarbell publishes chapter three of a study (1903) of Standard Oil and John D. Rockefeller (**63**). This appears in *McClure's* magazine, edited by Sam McClure (**45**). The event is a key moment in the history of muckraking; other articles in it are by Lincoln Steffens (**36**) and Ray S. Baker (**32**).

Theodore H. White starts work on his first book in the series *The Making of the President* (1959).

EXPLORATION

Jacques Cartier: exploration of the St. Lawrence River, Canada, and of the future locations of Quebec City and Montreal (1535).

James Cook: first person to sail south of the Antarctic Circle (1773). His schooling had finished at **12**, and he commanded his first ship at

20. His first voyage of discovery was at **39–42**, and led to the naming of Botany Bay and New South Wales, and to the discovery of the Great Barrier Reef. In his second voyage, **43–46**, he makes perhaps his greatest contribution to sailing, by making his crew eat limes; this voyage is therefore the first in which a substantial portion of the crew does not die of disease. His third voyage starts at **47**, and he is the first European to visit Hawaii. He is killed there at **50**, in a fight with its inhabitants. Cook's widow survives him for another 56 years, dying at **93**.

LAW, CRIME

The Earl of Lucan disappears (1974) shortly after his employee, Sandra Rivett (**29**) is found battered to death in his home. Lucan is never seen again.

SPORTS

Willie Shoemaker (1976), the jockey, wins his five thousandth race. Another champion jockey, Johnny Longden, is said to continue racing until **59**, having won 6,032 races since **19**.

45

HEALTH

Christiaan Barnard: first heart transplant (Dec. 1967). At this time, the heart operation pioneer Norman Shumway is **44**.

F. Gowland Hopkins: experiments leading to the discovery of vitamins (1906–07).

In England and Wales, 1977, there were 282 births in which the mother was **45+**. Three of these mothers produced multiple births, that is, twins, or more.

HISTORY—WORLD

Julius Caesar: invasion of Britain (45 and 44 B.C.). This is an incident in his nine years of war in northern Europe. At **50**, Caesar is told by Rome to resign command of his army, but he refuses. He leads his army across the river Rubicon, and starts a civil war—which he wins by **52**. But at **56*** he is assassinated, having turned from being a reformer into a tyrant.

Kublai Khan becomes the Great Khan, or Chief, at Shang-tu, "Xanadu" (1260). He now becomes the most enlightened and conciliatory of the Mongol rulers of China. He continues in office until his death at **79**.

Pierre Trudeau becomes a Canadian member of Parliament for the first time (1965). Previously, he had been an assistant professor of law (**41–45**) after spending his life up till then as a traveler who educates himself about world problems. At **48**, Trudeau becomes Prime Minister, establishing his position as a fresh young face among a lot of tired old rivals. (cf. **60***)

HISTORY—U.S.A.

George Washington, in 1777, is in charge of the revolutionary army of the new United States (**1**). His army is not strong, and it is not sufficiently well supported by the states' administrations. At **45**, Washington sets up winter quarters at Valley Forge, at a time when the war seems indecisive and endless. It is not until **49**, with the surrender of Charles Cornwallis (**42**) at Yorktown, that the revolutionary forces have triumphed. At **51**, Washington resigns his commission and returns home to his estates at Mt. Vernon. (cf. **55***)

Abraham Lincoln, in 1854: this is perhaps the time when he changes his central attention from his statewide legal work to a career as a politician. He is aroused by the controversy over the Missouri Compromise, now at **45**. At **47**, he becomes prominent in national politics for the first time with a speech that is both abolitionist yet not extremist in tone. At **49**, in his unsuccessful campaign for the Senate, he has seven powerful debates with Stephen Douglas (**45**), and these mark Lincoln as a major figure. At **51**, he is selected as presidential candidate, and elected. His inaugural speech (**52**) is pro-Union but conciliatory on the slavery issue; but he has to take almost dictatorial powers at the start of the Civil War. He announces his Emancipation Proclamation at **53**. His Gettysburg Address is at **54**; Lincoln describes its initial effect as "like a wet blanket." He wins a second presidential term at **55***.

Lyndon Johnson (1953) continues as a senator. He becomes Vice-President at **52**.

Joseph McCarthy: the end of McCarthyism—he is censured by the Senate (1954, Dec. 2) and dies at **47**.

Ronald Reagan, in 1956, continues to work for the "General Electric Theater," on TV, in which he is the host and sometimes a player. He continues to lecture in GE plants on the capitalist system. At **47**, he is president again of the Screen Actors Guild. Also at **47**, he makes his first trip abroad, when he goes to England to star in a film. At **48**, he fathers his last child, Ronald, later the ballet dancer. At **51**, he leaves General Electric, and until **54** he works on TV in the weekly drama, "Death Valley Days." Following his political work for GE, he is chosen at **53** to make a speech in support of presidential candidate Barry Goldwater (**55**); Reagan so electrifies his audience that immediately some wealthy and influential Republicans form a supporters' club for him. He is chosen as the Republican candidate for governor of California, at **55***.

Richard Nixon, in 1958, continues as Vice-President. At **47**, he is Republican presidential candidate, but loses the election. At **49**, he is the Republican candidate for governor of California, but he also loses this election. He decides to leave politics. He says to the press: "You won't have Nixon to kick around any more, because, gentlemen, this is my last press conference." He moves away from his home state of California, and obtains a lucrative position with a New York law firm.

John F. Kennedy, in 1962, continues as President, since **43***; but he is assassinated at **46***.

Jimmy Carter, in 1969, continues as a peanut farmer in Plains, Georgia. He holds two local county positions. He is elected Governor of Georgia at **46**, and serves for one term. At **46**, he becomes a national figure briefly when he puts forward anti-racist views, in contrast to his predecessor Lester Maddox (**55**). At **47**, during the presidential election, he meets a number of candidates on their visits to Georgia, and he decides that he is their equal. He therefore determines to be a presidential candidate at the next election. At **50**, he is a forgotten one-term governor of Georgia; at **52**, he is elected President of the United States.

Henry Kissinger: Special Assistant for National Security to President Nixon (**56**, in 1969). Kissinger is Secretary of State, **50–54**.

HISTORY—U.K.

William Gladstone has to resign as Chancellor of the Exchequer (Aug. 1855) and is so unpopular that a friend advises him to look for another occupation besides politics. He is regarded as brilliant, but lacking in judgment—liable to go after obscure ideas with extremist thinking (and feeling). But he becomes Chancellor again at **49**, and Prime Minister at **58**. (cf. **64***)

Sylvia Pankhurst, daughter of Mrs. Pankhurst (**69**), has her first and only child (1927, Dec. 3) and as a matter of principle she never names the father. Since campaigning for women's suffrage (when she was **36**), she has become increasingly left-wing, going at **38** to meet Lenin (**50**) in Moscow. She is a fierce anti-Fascist. Her elder sister Christabel has become increasingly religious since women's winning of the vote (when she was **38**) and is a leader in the fundamentalist Christian group, the Second Adventists. Both Pankhurst sisters live till **78**.

Plato: *The Symposium* (c. 384 B.C.). Plato is continuously productive throughout his life. He dies at about **82**. He had been born into the upper class of Athens, and in his youth attached himself to the leading philosopher of the day, Socrates, until the latter's death at **70***. (cf. **60***)

John Knox: "First Blast of the Trumpet Against the Monstrous Regiment of Women" (1558).

Martin Buber: *I and Thou* (1923).

SOCIAL SCIENCE, EDUCATION

David Ricardo: *Political Economy and Taxation* (1817).

Jung completes *Psychological Types* (1920). He had entered psychiatry at **25***, and had done well, following then the influence of Freud. Although always a success, Jung is very much a late developer as far as his own unique ideas are concerned. His first visit to primitive peoples is at **49**, when he goes to the Pueblo Indians of New Mexico, and there meets the "sons of Father Sun." His publication on the collective unconscious is at **59***.

Arnold Toynbee: *A Study in History* (1934); the first volume. The last is at **72**, and he produces a very interesting book on death at **79***.

Gunnar Myrdal: *An American Dilemma* (1944).

Ivan Illich: *The Celebration of Awareness*, and *Deschooling Society* (1971). He goes on to write *Tools for Conviviality* at **47**; *Medical Nemesis* at **49**; and *Vernacular of Gender* at **55**.

SCIENCE, TECHNOLOGY

André Ampère: pioneer work on electrodynamics (1820). He has had a long career in science; he is now galvanized into action by the work of H. C. Oersted (**42**, in 1819) whose experiments show that an electric current affects a magnet.

MONEY, WORK

Leland Stanford, Collis P. Huntington (**47**), and others: the "golden spike" (1869, May 10), the completion of the final link for rail travel across the U.S.A. At **61**, Stanford uses his railroad fortune to start Stanford University (1885).

Henry Ford: the Model T, and the assembly line (1908). He sells 10,000 cars in the first year, at $850 each.

Lord Rank starts the Religious Film Society, in order to better promote his work as a Methodist Sunday School teacher (1933). His main work is currently as a very rich flour miller. But he becomes interested in the film industry—by **55**, he has become the number one figure in

 British film industry. His trademark is what appears to be a naked man hitting a 10-foot-high gong.

In societies where manual labor was/is common, a person is worn out around now, and has to take a less stressful job. This is the early form of retirement. Factories would employ the fit young people on the rushed productive jobs; and then fire people as they moved into their **40**s, or else move them into floor sweeping, nightwatchman jobs, and so on.

A note on relationships between aging and salary: (1) the idea that the older you are, the greater your earnings should be—age=seniority—and you are either more useful or it is morally right to pay you more, or both; (2) alternatively, performance is the only criterion, and age should be irrelevant; if your performance deteriorates after a certain age, then you should receive less money.

RENAISSANCE

Paul Robeson: appearance in the title role of *Othello* on Broadway, New York (1943). This performance is perhaps the high point of his stage career, and the production runs for almost a year. Robeson had always shown extreme ability in a number of different fields—at Rutgers University (**18–21**) he had gained a national reputation in football, as well as being selected for Phi Beta Kappa, and becoming the class valedictorian. He then earned his way through law school by professional football appearances. After a short time practicing law, he acted from **26** onward in plays by Eugene O'Neill (**36**) and others. He appeared in the musical *Show Boat* at **30**. Now in his late **40**s he becomes increasingly prominent in political controversy. He had first visited the U.S.S.R. at **36**, and he now holds up Russia and communism as ideals. He is a pioneer in arguing publicly that blacks, his own race, are colonized within the U.S.A., and that there is a war relationship between blacks and whites. By about **48** his career as a performer is subordinated to his political work. At **50**, he campaigns for the Progressive party in the 1948 presidential election. From **51–60**, his passport is withdrawn, and his inability to travel abroad makes him almost an international martyr. Robeson retires at **60**, and lives until **77**.

ARCHITECTURE

Louis Le Vau: Vaux-le-Vicomte (1657), with gardens by André Le Nôtre (**44**).

Robert Adam: Osterley Park, London (c.1773).

Sir Charles Barry: the layout of Trafalgar Square (1840).

Decimus Burton: Palm House, Kew (1845).

Charles Rennie Mackintosh resigns from his architectural practice

(1913) owing to the strain and to his drinking. He leaves Glasgow the next year, and hardly designs another building, dying at **60**.

Eero Saarinen: U.S. Embassy, London (1955–60). (cf. **46***)

ART

John Constable: "The Hay Wain" (1821), and "Flatford Mill" at **41**; and views of Salisbury Cathedral at **47**. Constable is a slow developer who receives only grudging support from the art world (for example, Royal Academy at **53**, versus Turner, Royal Academy at **27**). He is never able to support himself as a painter, but lives off his own and his wife's inheritances.

Alfred Gilbert: the statue "Eros" (1899) in Piccadilly Circus, London.

Alberto Giacometti: first sculptures in his mature style (1946).

Graham Sutherland: first major portrait painting (1949). Until now he has been known for his landscapes and religious work. He now paints a portrait of the writer Somerset Maugham (**75**) and this is the beginning of his best-known work. He goes on to become the leading portrait painter of the very rich and conspicuous.

Francis Bacon: portrait of a pope, with meat in the background (1954).

Eligibility: it is now time for your mid-career retrospective exhibition.

MUSIC—CLASSICAL

Gaetano Donizetti: *Don Pasquale* (1843). He writes sixty-eight operas from **20** onward, and most are never performed again. But at **34** he wrote *L'Elisir d'amore* in two to five weeks, and *Lucia di Lammermoor* at **37**. He goes mad at **47**, from the effects of a venereal disease, and dies at **50**.

Richard Strauss composes his best-known operas during his **40**s; for example, *Salome* at **41** (1905); *Elektra* at **44**; *Der Rosenkavalier* at **45**; and *Ariadne auf Naxos* at **48**. (cf. **70***)

Respighi: *The Pines of Rome* (1924). This is highly successful, and he calls his new home "The Pines."

Prokofiev: *Peter and the Wolf,* and *Romeo and Juliet,* the first two suites (both, 1936).

LITERATURE

Alfred Lord Tennyson: *The Charge of the Light Brigade* (1854).

Feodor Dostoevsky: *Crime and Punishment,* and *The Idiot* (1866); and *The Devils* at **50**. (cf. **59***)

Virginia Woolf: *To the Lighthouse* (1927). (cf. **47***)

Sinclair Lewis gets the Nobel Prize (1930), but his work is now said to deteriorate. His reputation had been made with *Main Street* at **35**, and *Babbitt* at **37**.

Alan Paton: *Cry, the Beloved Country* (1948)—his first novel, written during his time as a teacher.

Ian Fleming: *Casino Royale* (1953), his first book on James Bond. About some other escapist fiction: Edgar Rice Burroughs writes his first Tarzan book at **39** (1914). Frank Baum writes the *Wonderful Wizard of Oz* at **44** (1900). Bram Stoker writes *Dracula* at **50** (1897). And Raymond Chandler writes his first Philip Marlowe book, *The Big Sleep* at **51*** (1939). *The Scarlet Pimpernel* is by Baroness Orczy (**40**, in 1905).

Laurie Lee: *Cider with Rosie* (1959).

Yukio Mishima: ritual suicide (1970), after trying to arouse Japanese Self-Defence Forces against their own impotence. He had made his literary reputation with a novel at **24**, but since **40** his writing has been said to have declined in quality. At **42**, he sets up the Shield Society, to provide a shield to defend the emperor (**66**). In the same year, he brings out a book on an old Samurai text; it includes these words: "One who chooses to go on living having failed in one's occupation will be despised as a coward or bungler. . . . One cannot accomplish feats of greatness in a normal frame of mind. One must turn fanatic and develop a mania for dying. By the time one develops powers of discernment it is already too late to put them into effect. In the Way of the Samurai, loyalty and filial piety are superfluous; all one needs is a mania for death. Within that attitude, loyalty and filial piety will come to reside."

PLAYS, DANCE

Arnold Wesker: *Love Letters on Blue Paper* (1977)—an incredibly moving play.

FILMS

Mauritz Stiller dies in a charity ward of a Stockholm hospital (1928, Nov. 8)—he is clutching a photograph of his protégée Greta Garbo, taken at **19** when they had both just arrived in New York.

Jean Renoir: *La Règle du jeu* (1939).

John Ford: *The Grapes of Wrath* (1940).

Humphrey Bogart meets Lauren Bacall (**19**, 1944) when they start making *To Have and Have Not*. They are married in the following year—his fourth and last marriage. Bogart carries on making films at the same brilliant level he has shown since his breakthrough at **37***. Later films include *The African Queen* at **52**, and *The Caine Mutiny* at **55**. He dies at **57**.

Bob Hope: *Paleface* (1948).

John Huston: *The Red Badge of Courage* (1951).

James Stewart: *The Glenn Miller Story* (1953), and *Rear Window* at **46**.

Ingmar Bergman: *The Silence* (1963).

Walter Matthau: *The Odd Couple* (1965). He has been a stage actor until now, and this is the moment at which he becomes a star.

Arthur Penn: *Bonnie and Clyde* (1967), with Faye Dunaway **(26)** and Warren Beatty **(30)**.

Lindsay Anderson: *If* (1968).

Franco Zeffirelli: *Romeo and Juliet* (1968), with Olivia Hussey **(15)** and Leonard Whiting **(16)**; script by William Shakespeare **(31)** and music by Nino Rota **(57)**.

John Schlesinger: *Midnight Cowboy* (1970), with Dustin Hoffman **(33)**, and Jon Voigt **(31)**.

Robert Altman: *M*A*S*H* (1970)—his first big breakthrough. *Nashville* is at **50**.

Norman Jewison: *Fiddler on the Roof* (1971).

Sam Peckinpah: *Straw Dogs* (1971).

Nicholas Roeg: *Don't Look Now* (1973).

MUSIC—NON-CLASSICAL

It's a sobering thought that when Mozart was my age, he had already been dead for ten years.—Tom Lehrer (1973).

TV, ETC.

Ed Murrow and Fred Friendly: "See It Now" (1953). This news documentary begins the questioning of the current McCarthy anti-Communist posture of America.

Broderick Crawford: "Highway Patrol" (1955).

Walter Cronkite: "The CBS Evening News with Walter Cronkite" (1962). At **57**, a poll reveals him to be the most trusted man in America. Walter Cronkite retires from this weekday program at **64**.

Barbara Walters moves to ABC (1976) from NBC, and earns $1,000,000 per year.

PRESS

Rupert Murdoch acquires control of the *New York Post* (1976), and also *New York* magazine and the *Village Voice*. Born into a rich Australian family, he inherited at **21** control of a small newspaper, the *Adelaide News,* on the death of his father **(66)**. At **24**, he started a Sunday paper in Perth, and went on to build a chain of publications. At **38**, he moved to London, and acquired the *News of the World,* followed by the *Sun.* At **42**, he sets up a U.S. subsidiary which now at **45** makes its mark on New York. At **49**, Murdoch buys the London *Times* from the Canadian newspaper lord, Kenneth Thomson (**57**).

LAW, CRIME

Mary Ann Nichols is murdered (1888) in the East End of London. She is the first of the five victims of Jack the Ripper. All are prostitutes, and aged **45**, **45**, **45**, and **43**. All have their throats slashed in a single left-to-right motion, and usually the body is disemboweled or otherwise mutilated ("ripped") with a knife. The murderer is never found. Out of a large number of plausible theories, the most alarming is that the women are murdered because they have incriminating evidence about a member of the Royal Family—the bisexual Prince Albert "Eddy" Victor (**24**) who frequented the notorious Cleveland Street brothel.

Eligibility: This is the last year is which you may be a member of the Young Lawyers International Association.

SPORTS

Alexander Alekhine (1937)—world chess champion again. He has been champion from **34–43**, and from now until **53**.

Joe Davis (1946): World Snooker Champion, for the twentieth and final year. At **52**, he scores his 500th century snooker break. And at **54**, he scores 147, the maximum possible snooker break. He retires at **62**, having scored 689 century breaks, and he lives until **77**.

Scientific Creativity, and Age

Jacob Bronowski (1976) echoed the conventional view when he linked scientific creativity with youth. He baldly stated that we know that physicists do their best work before **30**, mathematicians even earlier, and biologists slightly later. This view suggests a bizarre picture of Bronowski watching the young talent move up to their peak age, perform, and then flop exhausted into a sideline administrative position for the rest of their lives. What is frightening is: (1) that such ideas have typically been accepted; (2) that they may have inhibited those outside the "magic" age from attempting creative work; and (3) that, despite its apparent precision, the proposition may not be adequately supported by data.

Support for the conventional viewpoint came from H. C. Lehman (1953) who graphed individual scientific achievements of the past against the age of the individuals involved. The careers of numerous achievers were amalgamated into one single line for each branch of science. The lines obtained by Lehman often showed dramatic peaks in the late 20s, with a clear falling-off from 30 onward. This led inescapably to the conclusion that there is an age of high creativity, followed soon by loss of ability, even before middle age has begun. Lehman's work became a classic on thinking about age and performance.

But in what might be a highly upsetting article, Stephen Cole (1979) suggested that the conventional view, and Lehman in particular, had ignored the effect of difference in life span. It is quite possible that the apparent productivity of younger people was due to the greater number of people in that age group, at a time when the expectation of life was markedly less than today's. In the past, the older generations may have seemed less creative simply because there were fewer individuals of that age at work.

Cole examined careers in mathematics, physics, and other sciences and found that there was an increase in both quality and quantity as people came to 35–45, and then a reduction. But the effect was so small that he says, "Age explains very little variance in productivity." This same conclusion applies to quality, as measured by citations received.

Instead of lumping together all scientists and finding average ages of achievement, Cole hypothesized three career patterns in science—the strong publisher, the weak publisher, and the nonpublisher. He suggested that to get a career in science some attempt at publishing was necessary; so, early on, there is an emphasis on productivity. But rewards go only to those whose work is of higher quality, and the lower quality researchers drift out of the game. Incidentally, rewards are both psychic (prizes and citations) and physical (assistants, money, and time off for research).

The sensation that much publishing is done by younger people may again be true—because such people need to establish themselves. But the corollary, that aging necessarily reduces creativity, is not proven, and is likely to be untrue. Medium and low quality workers are channeled away from publishable research, as they grow older. And high quality workers now appear to be productive until late in life.

What is less explored here is the possibility of changing from one career pattern to another within your working life. Crudely, if you are now in the medium grade, is there any chance of moving upward? Cole suggests that in practice such moves do take place but that they are comparatively rare. However, we do not know how much an individual's stability within one grade or pattern is due to a constancy in inherent ability, or is due to a tracking phenomenon—having once been placed in a medium track because of your performance at **25–30**, then it may well be administratively impossible for you to obtain the time and other resources necessary to do work of the top standard.

As with any tracking pressure, the most alarming thought is that the individual takes on board the label or evaluation which the outside world places on him or her; that is, you begin to accept that you are irredeemably mediocre and a nonpublisher.

So, aging is a proxy for other variables, for example, professional tenure or access to resources, that happen to coincide, in certain institutional frameworks, with chronological age.

It is easy to show that our efficient career channeling, with its careful documentation of past performance, would have excluded some distinguished researchers in the past from pursuing their careers. Charles Darwin, for example, would not have done well if he had applied to UCCA London, the university clearing house on admissions, for his third attempt at training for a career. Even the switch to his second career training would be difficult today. It is depressing to realize that our efficient-style career procedures are (1) based on a model of career development that may simply be wrong, and (2) would have had the effect of excluding some of the greatest talents of the past.

46

HEALTH

Edward Jenner: the first inoculation—of cowpox, in order to prevent smallpox (1796). The patient is James Phipps (**8**). Jenner now meets with indifference and skepticism; people fear that this injection will cause them to have cowlike characteristics, such as horns. But by **50** he is so accepted that he is called upon to vaccinate an entire regiment. In his early **50**s, he becomes an international celebrity, and he lives until **73**. Jenner had originally noticed that certain milkmaids had acquired an immunity from smallpox; they had caught cowpox through the cow's diseased teats.

Peter the Great, in 1718, watches as his own son (**28**) and heir is flogged to death—for not being dynamic enough to continue the newly modernized Russia which Peter is trying to create. Similarly, Ivan the Terrible (**51**) in 1581 kills his son and heir (**27**), during an argument.

Louis XV is stabbed (1757) by Damiens (**43**). The king survives, but Damiens is tortured to death. Other French assassinations: Jean Paul Marat (**50**) is stabbed to death in his bath, by Charlotte Corday, a Royalist virgin of **25** (1793); and Robespierre (**36**) is shot in the face by gendarme Merda (**20**)—the dying and unpopular Robespierre is quickly guillotined.

Lenin tells followers that the revolution may be years away. "We of the older generation may not live to see the decisive battles. . . ." But the czar falls, and at **47*** (1917) Lenin is in charge of the Russian government.

Abdul Aziz Ibn Saud: formation of Saudi Arabia (1926).

Alexander Dubček: the "Prague Spring" (1968)—the Czechoslovak experiment of communism "with a human face." This lasts for eight months. After invasion by 200,000 Russian troops, Dubček is forced to resign. He is never again mentioned in public; as a nonperson, he is reassigned to duties in a provincial office of the Forestry Department.

HISTORY—U.S.A.

Peter Minuit: purchase of Manna-hata Island (1626) for sixty guilders, or approximately $24, to create the settlement of New Amsterdam. Later, the city is surrendered by its governor, Peter Stuyvesant (**72**, in 1664) and given the name New York (**30**) City, in honor of James, Duke of York (**30**).

President Kennedy is shot (1963, Nov. 22)—by Lee Harvey Oswald (**23**). After his death, it is revealed that he has often been ill and that "at least one-half of the days that he spent on this earth were days of intense physical suffering," according to Robert Kennedy (now **38**). This ill-health has led the president to say that he never expected to live beyond **45**.

HISTORY—U.K.

William Pitt the Younger: death (1805). His doctor had previously told him that he could cure his gout by drinking a bottle of port a day. Cirrhosis of the liver is a cause of his last illness.

The Duke of Wellington, and General Blucher (**73**) win the Battle of Waterloo (1815, June 18). They defeat Napoleon (**45**).

Lord Palmerston becomes Foreign Secretary for the first time (1830, Nov. 22) and continues in office on and off between now and

66. This is the "Age of Palmerston." He becomes Prime Minister at **70**. (cf. **80***)

RELIGION, PHILOSOPHY

Girolamo Savonarola: hanged and burned (1498, May 23). He has been too forceful in applying an ascetic regime to the wonders of Renaissance Florence.

SOCIAL SCIENCE, EDUCATION

Antonio Gramsci, the Italian writer on communism, dies (1937) from natural causes, on the day he is due to leave prison—where he has been since **37**, sentenced by a Mussolini court.

Claude Levi-Strauss: *Tristes Tropiques* (1955); and *The Savage Mind* (**53**), and *The Raw and the Cooked* (**55**).

Louis Althusser: *Pour Marx* (1965).

Arthur Jensen: "How Much Can We Boost IQ and Scholastic Achievement?" Harvard Educational Review (1969).

E. O. Wilson: *Sociobiology* (1975).

SCIENCE, TECHNOLOGY

Oscar Barnack: first sale of a Leica, the pioneer 35mm camera (1925). He made the prototype at **35**.

MONEY, WORK

William C. Durant: foundation of General Motors (1909).

David Rockefeller becomes president and chairman of the Executive Committee, Chase Manhattan Bank (1961).

Henry Ford II: the Mustang car (1964).

RENAISSANCE

Benjamin Franklin: experiment with a kite in a thunderstorm, to prove that lightning is the same as the newly discovered electricity (1752). As part of his wide-ranging interests, Franklin has always had a scientific turn of mind; he speculated on earthquakes at **31**, and designed his famous stove at **38**. He acquired his first electrical equipment at **40**, and immediately began experiments, which he writes up in a professional manner. At the same time, Franklin maintains his political interests, and at **48** he is the Pennsylvania representative to the Albany Congress. From **51–56**, he is the representative in London of the colonies, and tries to avert the break between the two sides. After a visit to America, he appears before the House of Commons in London at **60**, and again is a virtual ambassador there. The greatest moments of his public career come in his **60**s and **70**s, and he lives until **84***.

John Nash marries Mary Ann Bradley (**25**) (Dec. 1798), who has five children by an unknown other man—he was probably Nash's principal client, the Prince Regent (**36** at the time of the wedding). (cf. **59***)

Gordon Bunshaft and Skidmore, Owings and Merrill: Lever House, New York (1952).

Eero Saarinen receives commissions from both IBM and Bell Telephone to design research campuses (1956). He also starts work on the TWA building at Kennedy airport, New York. (cf. **48***)

MUSIC—CLASSICAL

Debussy: *La Fille aux cheveux de lin* and *La Cathédrale engloutie* (1909). He had written *La Mer* around **40**, and *Golliwog's Cake-Walk* and other children's pieces at **43**. His only child, Chouchou, is born when he is **43**, and he dies at **55**.

LITERATURE

Charles Dickens moves to a country house, Gad's Hill (1858). He leaves his wife of twenty-two years, and starts on *A Tale of Two Cities*. This is followed by *Great Expectations* at **48**, the "most completely unified work of art that Dickens ever produced"—Angus Wilson. At **46**, Dickens starts a new career, of public readings of his books. These one-night stands bring in vast profits, but contribute to his death at **58**.

Kate Douglas Wiggin: *Rebecca of Sunnybrook Farm* (1903). Also, *Pollyanna* is by Eleanor Porter (**44**, in 1913). *A Child's Garden of Verses* is by Robert Louis Stevenson (**35**, in 1885). *Anne of Green Gables* is by L. M. Montgomery (**33**, in 1908). *National Velvet* is by Enid Bagnold (**46**, 1935).

George Orwell: *1984* (1949). At **34**, *Homage to Catalonia* is his first book to set out his most dramatic theme, that the left can be totalitarian in the same way as the right. *Animal Farm,* at **42**, is published after receiving twenty-three rejections, including one by T. S. Eliot (**57**). George Orwell dies at **46**.

Anthony Powell writes the first book in his *Music of Time* series, and finishes with the twelfth volume at **71**.

PLAYS, DANCE

Samuel Beckett: first production of *Waiting for Godot* (Paris, 1953). Up till now, he has been a relatively unknown figure, except to a small group who read his novel *Molloy,* published at **44**. Now almost overnight he becomes the best-known dramatist of the day. Beckett had published a novel, *More Pricks than Kicks* at **28**, and had been a wanderer for much of his **30**s. He had been an agricultural laborer in France during World War II. At the end of the war, he returned to

 Paris, at **40**, and there began the most fruitful years of his life. Now he goes on to write *Endgame* at **51**, and *Krapp's Last Tape* at **52**.

Jean Genet: *The Balcony* (1956).

John Osborne: *Watch It Come Down* (1976); this is not much of a success, and critics see it as repetitive of his early work, for example, at **26***.

Jill Bennett, the actress, in 1979: when asked her age, she answers, "Between Tatum O'Neal and death—and nearer death."

FILMS

John Huston: *Moulin Rouge* (1952); and *The African Queen,* with Katharine Hepburn (**43**), and Humphrey Bogart (**53**) and a script by James Agee (**43**).

Henri-Georges Clouzot: *The Wages of Fear* (1953).

Trevor Howard: *Mutiny on the Bounty* (1962), with Marlon Brando (**38**).

Gregory Peck: *To Kill a Mockingbird* (1962).

Gillo Pontecorvo: *The Battle of Algiers* (1965).

Walter Matthau: *The Fortune Cookie* (1966).

John Schlesinger: *Sunday, Bloody Sunday* (1971), with Peter Finch (**55**) and Glenda Jackson (**35**).

Shirley Temple is appointed U.S. Ambassador to Ghana (1974).

TV, ETC.

Ed Sullivan is hired by CBS-TV (1948) as host for a variety show; Sullivan is a newspaper columnist and this is a temporary appointment as his stage manner is so wooden. However he always manages to pick the great new acts, and he retains this position until **69**. His wooden delivery gradually becomes a lovable trademark.

LOVE, LIFE

Catherine the Great, Empress of Russia, in 1776: she has fifteen lovers between now and her death at **67**. These are always men between **22–25**; they are obtained by her ex-lover Prince Potemkin (**37**). These young army officers perform only a physical function, while Potemkin and the empress maintain a lifelong friendship.

King Mongkut becomes the king of Siam (1851). Until now he has been a Buddhist priest and lived under a vow of celibacy. Within the next few months he acquires a large number of wives, and children soon appear. Mongkut has had twelve children as a priest; but between now and his death at **63** he fathers 82 royal children, with 27 mothers. He is afterward commemorated in the musical *The King and I*. According to a 1931 survey, Mongkut is the first person in Thailand to follow the Western custom of annually celebrating one's birthday; previously each person had known their birthdate, because of its significance within the astrological system. But a repeat celebration each year was wholly unknown.

PRESS

Katherine Graham: in charge at the Washington *Post* and at *Newsweek* (1963), following the death of her husband, Philip Graham (**48**). At **61**, she retires, and is succeeded by her son Donald (**33**).

LAW, CRIME

Captain Kidd: hanged for piracy (1701).

Louis Werner organizes a robbery at Kennedy Airport, New York (1978) in which $5.8 million is stolen from Lufthansa Airlines. Werner has accumulated immense gambling debts, and as a Lufthansa employee he supplies inside knowledge of the movement of valuables.

SPORTS

Juan Fangio (1957): world champion motor racing driver for the fifth and last time. He retires at **47**. He had won the championship at **40**, **43**, **44**, and **45**. The earlier part of his career was interrupted by World War II.

Vince Lombardi (1959) is appointed coach and general manager of the Green Bay Packers, a team which is not doing very well. Lombardi pursues his philosophy—"Winning is not the most important thing; it's everything"—and his team becomes league champions when he is **48**; and also at **49**, **52**, **53**, and **54**. They are also in the Super Bowl at **53** and **54**.

Gary Player (golf, 1981): winner of the South African open championship, for the thirteenth time.

47

HEALTH

Ignaz Philipp Semmelweis: death, in a mental hospital (1865). He has been the first person to suggest that the routine dangers of childbirth were due to lack of cleanliness in the delivery room. He advises obstetricians to wash their hands before touching patients. This advice so insults the doctors that at **37** he has to leave his job in Vienna, and go to Budapest. Here he continues to promote his views, but the indifference and enmity of his fellow professionals drives him to madness. Semmelweiss contributes to his own unpopularity by calling doctors "murderers," "assassins," and one "a medical Nero." In the year of his death, Joseph Lister (**38**) begins his similar work on the curtailment of hospital infection through antiseptic procedures.

Carlos Finlay: the discovery that yellow fever is transmitted by a mosquito (1881). Practical application of this discovery has to wait until its proof again by Walter Reed (**49**, in 1900). This leads to the eradication of yellow fever by W. C. Gorgas (**50**, in 1904), and the start of the construction of the Panama Canal.

HISTORY—WORLD

Lenin travels from exile in Switzerland (1917) in a sealed train, across Europe, to the Finland Station. He is now in charge of the revolution; with only 5,000–10,000 committed supporters, he becomes leader of the world's largest country—30 years after his brother (**21**) had been hanged as a terrorist, when Lenin was **17***. Now, Russia's war with Germany makes the opportunity for revolutionary changes. Lenin negotiates peace in this war, and gradually wins a civil war against his rivals both left and right. At **51**, Lenin inaugurates a temporary retreat from full socialism, with the New Economic Policy. But at **52***, he has his first stroke, and soon loses control of the government. At the start of the Russian Revolution (1917), Lenin is **47**; Maxim Gorky (**49**); N. K. Krupskaya (**48**); Alexandra Kollontai (**45**); A. Lunacharsky (**42**); Trotsky (**38**); Stalin (**37**); G. E. Zinoviev (**34**); Nikolai Bukharin (**29**). Karl Marx would have been **99**, but he had died earlier at **64**. Rasputin had been killed in the previous year, at **44**. Czar Nicholas II and Alexandra are both **49**. The interim prime minister, A. Kerensky, is **36**. Also, Nikita Khrushchev is **23**, Leonid Brezhnev is **10**, and Aleksandr Solzhenitsyn is born a year later.

HISTORY—U.K.

Lord Cornwallis becomes Governor-General of India (1786, Feb. 24)—at **42**, he had lost the important Battle of Yorktown to George Washington (**49**). He resigns this position at **54**, but is re-appointed at **66**. He dies in India, at **66**.

Admiral Nelson wins the Battle of Trafalgar (1805, Oct. 21) but is killed. At **42**, he had won the Battle of the Nile, partly through ignoring an order signaled to him—he "turns a blind eye." He had lost the eye at **35**, and lost his right arm at **38**, both accidents happening in battle.

Mrs. Pankhurst organizes the first disturbances in support of women's suffrage (1905, May 12). She organizes a small riot outside Parliament, after a women's suffrage bill had been talked out (in favor of a bill which forces rear lights to be put on carts). She had been widowed at **40**, and starts her own national organization at **45**. She is egged on by her daughters, Christabel (**25**), Sylvia (**23**), and Adela (**20**). Violence increases for the next ten years, and Mrs. Pankhurst goes on hunger strike on at least ten occasions, the last being at **56**. Votes for women are first achieved when she is **60***.

Ramsay MacDonald (MP since **40**) makes pacifist speeches at the beginning of World War I (1914); he is abused throughout the country—and thrown out of Lossiemouth Golf Club.

RELIGION, PHILOSOPHY

Brigham Young leads the Mormons (1848) in a great trek across North America, to the new world of Utah, where they set up their own state. Young lives until **76**, and is said to have 56 wives.

Wittgenstein: beginnings of his *Philosophical Investigations* (1936). This is the second wave in his philosophy, and it occupies him until his death at **62**. His *Tractatus* was at **29**, after which he gave up philosophy, and worked as a primary school teacher, architect, et al. None of his work from now on is published during his lifetime; instead, it is given out in virtual secrecy, and Wittgenstein becomes a cult figure, whose influence grows and grows.

Jim Jones: suicide, of himself and about 900 followers (1978), at Jonestown, Guyana. He shoots himself, and the followers drink potassium cyanide, prepared by a doctor (**30**). The dead include about 260 children, **0–15**, including Jones's own son (**6**). Jones had given his first sermon at **14**; at **34**, he had arrived in California as head of his own tiny sect; by **46**, this was big enough for him to set up his own community, named after himself, in South America.

SOCIAL SCIENCE, EDUCATION

Samuel Smiles: *Self-Help* (1859).

Francis Galton: *Hereditary Genius* (1869). Now follows a long period in which he develops the subject of statistics, and this reaches its climax in *Natural Inheritance* at **67**. Galton is impressive proof that creativity in statistics is not necessarily confined to young people. His most spectacular work is at **70***, *Finger Prints.* Other achievements in statistics include: Pierre Simon Laplace's *Analytical Theory of Probabilities* at **63** (1812); Poisson's work on distribution, published at **56** (1837); Karl Pearson's product-moment correlation coefficient at **40** (1897) and chi-square at **43**; C. E. Spearman's work on factor analysis at **41** (1904); and Markov chains, by A. A. Markov at **51** (1907).

Elton Mayo: the Hawthorne effect (c.1927). At Western Union's Hawthorne plant, near Chicago, he is surprised to find that even diminishing the physical comfort of workers can increase output—if the workers know that they are engaged in a cooperative enterprise with management.

Ortega y Gasset: *The Revolt of the Masses* (1930).

T. W. Adorno: *The Authoritarian Personality* (1950).

Milton Friedman: *A Program for Monetary Stability* (1959). And, Nobel Prize at **64**.

SCIENCE, TECHNOLOGY

James Watt: definition of horsepower (1783).

Elmer Sperry begins his famous work on the design of gyroscopes (1907) and he sets up his own company at **50**. Up to this time, he has been an independent inventor, particularly working in electrical engineering.

Cesar Milstein and Georges Kohler (**28**): first manufacture of monoclonal antibodies (1975).

Hyron Spinrad: discovery of a galaxy 10,000 million light years from earth (Lick Observatory, California, 1981). This galaxy may contain the equivalent to a million million stars such as the sun, and it is the farthest point from earth that has yet been observed.

MONEY, WORK

William C. Durant forms General Motors (1909), out of the Cadillac, Oldsmobile, Pontiac, and Buick car companies.

ARCHITECTURE

Thomas Walter: the dome of the U.S. Capitol, Washington D.C. (1851–67).

H. H. Richardson: Marshall Field Wholesale Warehouse, Chicago (1885–87).

Louis H. Sullivan: Carson, Pirie, Scott (1903–04)—the Chicago department store. (cf. **51***)

Julia Morgan begins work at Hearst Castle, San Simeon, California (1919, until 1947).

Frei Otto: suspension roof for the Munich Olympic Games (1972).

ART

Rembrandt: "Aristotle Contemplating the Bust of Homer" (1653). (cf. **50***)

Francisco Goya suffers a severe illness (1792–93) which brings him close to death. It leaves him deaf by **49**. But it is also the moment when he begins to turn from being a very distinguished court portrait painter into one of the geniuses of art; for example, his frescoes at San

Antonia de la Florida, at **52**; "The Family of Charles IV" at **55**; and "Naked Maja" around **56**. (cf. **62***)

Antonio Canova: "Pauline Borghese" (1804). Later, this statue of Venus is the subject of a famous photograph, showing the nude figure (**24**) being admired by Bernard Berenson (**90**, in 1955).

MUSIC—CLASSICAL

John Stainer: *The Crucifixion* (1887).

Arthur Sullivan: *The Gondoliers,* with W. S. Gilbert (**53**, in 1889). The Gilbert and Sullivan partnership now begins to break up, ostensibly over an extravagant carpet in the Savoy Theater, but in fact because they both want to pursue grander objectives in their work. These objectives bring them virtually nothing, however. Sullivan also has a minor career as an official composer; for example, at **44** "Ode for the Opening of the Colonial and Indian Exhibition."

LITERATURE

Geoffrey Chaucer (1387): he resigns from his position as Controller of the Customs and Subsidy of Wools, Skins, and Hides in the Port of London. It is about this time that he starts writing *The Canterbury Tales.*

Virginia Woolf publishes *A Room of One's Own* (1929), her feminist book; she believes that women are equal but different from men; and she believes that creative people should be androgynous, using both the sexes that are within you. At **43**, she had published *Mrs. Dalloway,* and *The Common Reader;* and she publishes *The Waves* at **49**. (cf. **59***)

Seicho Matsumoto starts writing (1956)—21 years later, he is Japan's richest and most famous living author.

Robert Lowell: *For the Union Dead* (1964); and *Waking Early Sunday Morning,* at **50**.

PLAYS, DANCE

Eugène Ionesco: *Rhinocéros* (1959); and *Exit the King* at **50**.

Margot Fonteyn dances Juliet (**14***) with Rudolf Nureyev (**28**) as Romeo (**16**) in a film of the ballet (1966). Fonteyn at **42** had almost retired when her main partner Michael Somes (**44**) announced his retirement. But shortly afterward she became partner to Nureyev (**23**) after he had defected from the U.S.S.R. Fonteyn's career has therefore been extended in an unforeseeable way—an opportunity which she seizes with enthusiasm.

Peter Shaffer: *Equus* (1973). *The Royal Hunt of the Sun* was at **38**, and *Amadeus* is at **54**.

Hugh Leonard: *Da* (1973).

Cecil B. DeMille: *The Ten Commandments* (1928).

Charlie Chaplin: *Modern Times* (1936). He marries for the third time—to Paulette Goddard (**25**), his only nonteenage wife.

Humphrey Bogart: *The Big Sleep* (1946).

Marlon Brando: *The Godfather* (1971).

Bob Fosse: *Cabaret* (1972), starring Liza Minelli (**26**) and Joel Grey (**40**).

Paul Mazursky: director, *An Unmarried Woman* (1978).

Roman Polanski: *Tess of the d'Urbervilles* (1980).

MUSIC—NON-CLASSICAL

Irving Berlin: the music for *Top Hat,* including "Cheek to Cheek" (1935).

TV, ETC.

Gordon Jackson: as Hudson, the butler, in "Upstairs, Downstairs" (1970–75). Rose, the maid, is played by Jean Marsh (**36**), a joint creator of the series. Nicola Pagett (**24**) plays the luscious but spoiled daughter of this rich family household. Hudson is the solid center that every home needs; Rose is always trying to break out of the constraints of life, and she is always welcomed back when she fails.

PRESS

Stephen Potter: *Gamesmanship* (1947). Potter shows how you can win when your opponent is more able than yourself. This one joke now keeps him going for several books, as well as a large number of articles and lectures. He had had the initial idea at **31** when an old professor had partnered him in a tennis match, and they had beaten two undergraduates—"without actually cheating."

EXPLORATION

John Cabot: first European to see Newfoundland (1497). Owing to lack of navigational knowledge, Cabot believes that he has now arrived in China. Cabot is lost at sea, when he is about **49**.

V. J. Bering: discovery of the Bering Strait (1728). He dies at **60**, while leading the first modern Russian expedition to Alaska.

Don Ida and Max Anderson (**46**): journey in a hot-air balloon from Luxor, Egypt to New Delhi, India (1981). They had hoped to be the first people to make a nonstop balloon trip around the world.

LAW, CRIME

Estes Kefauver: chairman, U.S. Senate committee to investigate organized crime (1950–51). He becomes a national figure as the hearings are televised and as a number of underworld figures come forward to testify.

SPORTS

Viktor Korchnoi (1978) is defeated in his attempt to take the world chess championship from Anatoly Karpov (**27**). The contest is held in the Philippines, and lasts for 32 games, spread over three months. Karpov is allegedly assisted by a psychiatrist who conducts long-range hypnotism against Korchnoi. The latter trains by meditating with two yoga gurus. As a Soviet exile, he is trying to get his wife (**46**) and son (**19**) out of Russia. Three years later, Korchnoi again is beaten by Karpov.

Bobby Unser: first to complete the 1981 Indianapolis 500. But he suffers a penalty, and is given second place. The race is awarded to Mario Andretti (**41**).

Eligibility: soccer referees in England must now retire; but in Scotland you can continue.

48

HISTORY—U.S.A.

Aaron Burr shoots and kills Alexander Hamilton (**49**) in a duel (1804, July 11). At **51**, Burr is tried for treason, but is acquitted; he travels outside the country until **56**, when he returns to a successful law practice. At the time of the duel, Burr had been Vice-President; Hamilton had been first-ever Secretary of the Treasury, and had prevented Burr's chances of higher office.

HISTORY—U.K.

King John is forced to sign Magna Carta (1215, June 15), and dies a year later.

William Pitt the Elder becomes in effect the Prime Minister (1757–61). The next four years are his period in history; for example, the battles of Minden and Quebec, both at **50**. He is premier again from **57** to **59**, and dies at **69**.

Harold Wilson becomes Prime Minister (1964), the youngest in the twentieth century.

St. Thomas Aquinas stops work on *Summa Theologica* (1273), begun at **40**.

George Santayana leaves Harvard (1911). It is said that he is in the middle of a philosophy class; suddenly he sees the futility of it all, and he walks out. He lives until **89**.

SOCIAL SCIENCE, EDUCATION

William James: *The Principles of Psychology* (1890).

Alfred Marshall: *Principles of Economics* (1890).

Erik Erikson: *Childhood and Society* (1950)—his first major book. See also: *Young Man Luther* (**56**); *Gandhi's Truth* (**67**); and *Life History and the Historical Moment* (**73**, in 1975).

SCIENCE

Galileo: first observation of Neptune (1612). The planet is later rediscovered by Johann Galle (**34**, in 1846).

Edmund Halley: prediction that a well-known comet will return (1705). He dies at **85**, and the comet returns when he would have been **101**—it is then named Halley's comet, and it will return again in 1986. In 1758, the first person to identify Halley's comet is Charles Messier (**28**).

Otto Lilienthal: killed in a gliding accident, flying in one of his bird-like gliders (1896).

Edwin Armstrong: the completion of his major work on frequency modulation in radio, that is, FM as opposed to AM (1939). Armstrong kills himself at **63**, a victim of endless patent lawsuits, all of which his executors later win.

MONEY, WORK

Aristotle Onassis: launching of the largest oil tanker yet built; buys the casino at Monte Carlo—Société des Bains des Mers; acquires extravagant new yacht (1953–54). At **50**, his shipping business is dangerously overextended, but he is saved by the closure of the Suez Canal (fall of 1956). Oil tanker rates zoom upward, and Onassis becomes one of the richest men in the world. But the rest of his business life is an anticlimax, as his pre-Suez fright causes him to be conservative. (cf. **62***)

RENAISSANCE

André Malraux: the book *Museum Without Walls* (1949). During World War II (**38–43**), he has been a central figure in the French Resistance.

André Le Nôtre: the beginning of his most spectacular work—he is appointed garden designer at Versailles (1661). His previous work includes the extension of the Champs Elysées at **24**, and the gardens at Vaux-le-Vicomte, at **43** onward. Le Nôtre is now in charge of 15,000 acres, and he works here until his death at **87**.

James Wyatt: Fonthill Abbey (1795–1807).

Ebenezer Howard: publication of *Tomorrow* (1898), the pioneer text in the garden city movement. At this time he is a shorthand reporter. Soon afterward, *Cité industrielle,* another influential text on this theme, is by Tony Garnier (**32**, in 1901).

Henry Bacon: Lincoln Monument, Washington D.C. (1914–22).

Charles Holden designs thirty classic London Underground stations between **48** and **53** (1923–28).

Eero Saarinen: Dulles Airport (1958–62).

ART

AGE 48 YRS

Julia Margaret Cameron receives a camera (1863) from one of her married daughters and takes photographs for the first time. Soon she is producing masterpieces of the early history of photography. She portrays a number of famous Victorians who visit her neighbor Tennyson (**54**). Previously, Mrs. Cameron had been a high-powered housewife and hostess. At **60**, she and her husband (**80**) emigrate to Ceylon, and her twelve-year period as a major artist comes to an end.

The organizers of the New York Armory Show (1913) are Robert Henri (**48**), John Sloan (**42**), and Alfred Stieglitz (**49**). The show brings the new art to the U.S.A.; Man Ray (**23**) meets Marcel Duchamp (**26**), and together they work on the Dadaist movement.

Piet Mondrian: "Composition in Grey, Red, Yellow, and Blue" (1920)—his first painting in the full mature style for which he later becomes famous.

Marino Marini: "Horse and Rider" (1949). In this, he hits on the best-known theme and style of his life's work.

Diane Arbus, the photographer of freaks and others, kills herself (1971).

MUSIC—CLASSICAL

Gluck: *Orfeo ed Euridice* (1762); and *Alceste* at **53**.

Stravinsky: *Symphony of Psalms* (1930). (cf. **69***)

Benjamin Britten: *War Requiem* (1961). He had written *Billy Budd* at **37**, and *Noye's Fludde* at **43**. (cf. **59***)

Noah Webster publishes his first dictionary—*A Compendious Dictionary of the English Language* (1806). At **25**, he had published his first book, an educational text on grammar and spelling.

Henry W. Longfellow: *The Song of Hiawatha* (1855).

Mark Twain: *The Adventures of Huckleberry Finn* (1884). He had written *Tom Sawyer* at **40**; and at **53** he writes *A Connecticut Yankee at King Arthur's Court*.

Edith Holden dies (1920, Mar. 16), accidentally drowning at Kew Gardens, London, "while gathering buds from chestnut trees." She is a hardly-known illustrator, whose works have been published in a small number of books. But at **35** she had spent one year making a diary of poems and watercolors about her life in the country; 57 years after her death, this diary is resurrected and published—*The Country Diary of an Edwardian Lady* (1977), an international best-seller.

Laurence Durrell publishes the fourth and last volume (1960) of *The Alexandria Quartet*.

Norman Mailer: *The Prisoner of Sex* (1971). He had written *The Armies of the Night* at **45**—about anti-Vietnam War protests—and *An American Dream* at **42**.

PLAYS

William Shakespeare: *The Tempest* (1612). He dies in his hometown of Stratford-on-Avon at **52**, having left most of his property to the children of his daughter Susanna (**32**). Later, comparatively little is known about the events in his own life, but the years of his plays are listed at **28*** and **38***.

Peter Weiss: *The Persecution and Assassination of Marat As Performed by the Inmates of the Asylum of Charenton Under the Direction of the Marquis de Sade* (1964).

FILMS

Sergei Eisenstein finishes cutting *Ivan the Terrible,* Part 2, but has a heart attack, and never makes any more films (1946). He dies at **50**. *Potemkin* was at **27**; *Alexander Nevsky* was at **40**.

Walt Disney: *Seal Island* (1949)—the first of his nature documentaries.

Errol Flynn: *The Sun Also Rises* (1957).

Michelangelo Antonioni: *L'Avventura* (1960).

Alec Guinness: *Lawrence of Arabia* (1962).

Ingmar Bergman: *Persona* (1966).

Marlon Brando: *Last Tango in Paris* (1972).

Paul Newman and Robert Redford (**37**): *The Sting* (1973).

Mel Brooks: *Blazing Saddles* (1974).

Alan J. Pakula: *All the President's Men* (1976).

Robert Benton: *Kramer vs. Kramer* (1980), with Dustin Hoffman (**43**).

John Boorman: *Excalibur* (1981) starring Nicol Williamson (**43**).

MUSIC—NON-CLASSICAL

Scott Joplin: death (1917), from the effects of syphilis. At **30**, he had written the most entrancing piece of ragtime music, "The Maple Leaf Rag." But for the last few years, he has been wholly neglected as a composer, and from his death onward his music is forgotten—until 57 years after his death, when his rags are used for the film *The Sting*. This provokes the greatest interest in his work, far greater than he has ever enjoyed in his lifetime. Two years after the film, he receives a posthumous Pulitzer Prize, when he would have been **105**.

Irving Berlin: "There's No Business like Show Business" (1946).

TV, ETC.

Larry Hagman: as J. R. Ewing, in "Dallas" (1978). Hagman has had a long career, but this is his moment of take-off. His success comes from being contracyclical; he is against all the trends which currently define decent conduct. His J. R. is capitalist, manipulative, success-crazy, sexist, and even anti-ecological—and he becomes the key figure in the series.

LOVE, LIFE

John Profumo: forced to resign as Britain's Secretary of State for War (1963) because of his affair with Christine Keeler (**20**). The latter has simultaneously been having a friendship with Captain Ivanov, the military attaché at the Russian Embassy. It has been suggested that Ivanov has asked Christine Keeler to ask Profumo about nuclear weapons secrets. These relatively undetected relationships throw doubt on the efficiency of the Secret Service. John Profumo and Christine Keeler had been introduced at Cliveden House, the property of Lord Astor (then **54**). Their affair had taken place mainly at the home of Dr. Stephen Ward (**50**), an osteopath; Ward is the only person in the incident to be prosecuted, and he commits suicide. The Profumo scandal is indirectly a boost to the career of Harold Wilson (**47**), an opponent of the government, who says that "the disclosures . . . have shocked the moral conscience of the nation"; he promises to build a new nation in which such a "diseased excrescence" will never occur again. The Prime Minister, Harold Macmillan (**69**), is asked to resign by a supporter who quotes this poem, The Lost Leader:

> Let him never come back to us!
> There would be doubt, hesitation and pain,
> Forced praise on our part, the glimmer of twilight,
> Never glad confident morning again!

 Afterward, John Profumo builds a new career as a charity worker and he is helped by the permanent support of his wife, Valerie Hobson (about **45**); Harold Macmillan resigns a few months later; Cliveden House becomes an overseas campus of Stanford University; and Christine Keeler goes on to lead a life of dignity and seclusion, having retired from public view at **21**.

Gay Talese: *Thy Neighbor's Wife* (1980). He starts research on this at **39**. Talese lost his virginity at **19** and married at **27**.

The menopause is typically at **48–51**.

PRESS

Tom Wolfe: *The Right Stuff* (1979).

EXPLORATION

Amerigo Vespucci: voyage from Europe to the country later known as Brazil (1499–50). He had been brought up in Florence, and at **40** had been sent to Seville by Lorenzo de' Medici (**42**) to work in the Medici family bank there. At **51**, Vespucci asserts that the new land he visited is not Asia but a new continent. And at **56**, this continent is named America, in his honor.

Francisco Pizarro, in 1523: he now begins preparation for a journey of discovery, south from central America. He has been one of several successful administrators in the new Spanish colonies there. At **49–52**, he is the first European to see Peru, and he has a glimpse of its vast potential wealth. He fails to obtain local approval for a large expedition south, and has to return to Spain for a royal decision. Approval is obtained, and at **56** he sails again for Peru with 180 men. By **58**, he has gained control of the Peruvian empire, by viciously tricking and then strangling its chief, Atahualpa (**31***). Also at **58** he takes possession of Cuzco. Pizarro dies at **66**, during a fight with his family over the division of spoils in the new Spanish territory. If Pizarro had died at **49**, he would have been entirely unknown; instead, rightly or wrongly, he has changed the nature of South America.

Ben Abruzzo (**48**), Max Anderson (**44**), and Larry Newman (**31**): first balloon journey across the Atlantic (1978). The three people all come from Albuquerque, and complete the 3,100 mile trip in 5 days, 17 hours. At one point, they reach a height of 20,000 feet and have to use oxygen equipment. Newman had first flown solo in a plane at **12**; Abruzzo and Anderson both began ballooning seven years ago. Later, Max Anderson at **45** makes the first nonstop balloon trip across North America, and he is accompanied by his son Kris (**23**).

John Marshall: *Marbury* v. *Madison* (1803). As Chief Justice of the U.S. Supreme Court, he sets out the doctrine that the courts can review legislative acts.

Boss Tweed is arrested for corruption (1871), having defrauded New York State out of $13 million in the construction of a courthouse. Tweed dies in jail at **55**. The beginning of his Tammany Hall power period was at **43**.

Joseph Colombo, the Mafia leader, is shot at an Italian-American rally (1971), which is held to protest that the FBI unfairly associates the Mafia with people of Italian-American origin. Colombo's attacker is instantly shot dead by a bodyguard. Due to injury, Colombo is never able to speak or move again, until his death at **55**.

Stanley Goldblum is president and chief executive of the Equity Funding Corporation of America, on the day that fraud is revealed (1973). The original company was started with assets of $10,000 when he is **35**, and it moves rapidly ahead. At **40**, to further increase the rate of growth, Goldblum and associates start inventing people, then insuring them and selling this business to legitimate insurance companies. Equity Funding at one time carries a market valuation of $1 billion. By **48**, he and others (and their data processing equipment) have invented 64,000 people.

49

HISTORY—WORLD

General de Gaulle: leader (1940), of the Free French—fighters who have escaped from France after its conquest by Hitler (**51**). Previously, de Gaulle has held staff positions in the army, and written a number of books on warfare. Recently, he had been appointed to a middle-rank position in the Paris government. In the 1940 crisis, he sets himself up as leader, without anyone to appoint him or to approve of him; he has foreseen this moment, and developed a theory as to why this crisis is inevitable. At **53**, allied victory over the Nazis establishes de Gaulle as leader in Paris. But he resigns at **55**, owing to bickering by politicians. He gradually goes into complete exile, at his country house, Colombey-Les-Deux-Églises. At **67***, he becomes leader again, in another crisis.

HISTORY—U.S.A.

George Washington defeats Lord Cornwallis (**42**) at the battle of Yorktown (1781, Oct. 19), thus ending the American War of Independence. Washington becomes President at **57**—and Cornwallis becomes Governor-General of India at **47***. (cf. **55***)

HISTORY—U.K.

Oliver Cromwell: execution of Charles I (**48**, 1649, Jan. 30). But Cromwell almost immediately arrests the greatest supporters of his revolution, the Levelers; and at **50** he leads a cruel expedition against the Irish. He becomes Lord Protector at **54**, having previously held power by being the military chief of the Parliamentary forces. He dies in office at **59**.

Neville Chamberlain is an MP for the first time (1918)—and Prime Minister at **68**. Other late MPs include Andrew Bonar Law, MP at **42**, and Prime Minister at **64**; Stanley Baldwin—MP at **41**, and Prime Minister at **55**; Ramsay MacDonald—MP at **40**, and Prime Minister at **57**; Stafford Cripps—MP at **40**, and Chancellor of the Exchequer at **58**.

Harold Macmillan is knocked unconscious by a bomb (1943); on recovery, his first words are "Tell my mother I'm alive and well"—even though she had in fact died when he was **43**. (cf. **57***)

SOCIAL SCIENCE, EDUCATION

Karl Marx: *Capital,* Vol. I (1867). This book "summons as foes into the field of battle the most virulent, mean, and malignant passions of the human breast, the Furies of private interest." Marx dies at **64**, with his last two volumes of *Capital* still unpublished.

Max Weber finishes *The Agrarian Sociology of Ancient Civilization* (c.1913), and begins work on his major synthesis, *Economy and Society.* It is not fully complete at the time of his death (**56**). About age, Weber briefly mentions gerontocracy and primogeniture, but has nothing to say on age rules, even though these are a central feature of bureaucratization.

SCIENCE, TECHNOLOGY

Charles Coulomb: Coulomb's Law (1785).

J. M. Jacquard: first exhibition of his programmable weaving loom (1801). This has been the result of several years' part-time work.

Ernst Mach: research work on the speed of sound (1887). This is later commemorated in the phrase Mach-1, Mach-2, and so forth.

E. W. Morley: the Michelson (**34**)-Morley experiment (1887).

Konrad Lorenz: *King Solomon's Ring* (1952); also *Man Meets Dog* at **51**, and *On Aggression* at **63**.

Charles Weissman: first person to make Interferon by gene splicing (1980).

MONEY, WORK

Robert Owen: "Report to the County of Lanark" (1820)—a basic text in the development of industrial relations, and of the cooperative movement; it includes a discussion on the relief of unemployment caused by technological innovation.

George Pullman: his personal company town, of Pullman, Illinois (1880).

William Morris (Lord Nuffield): beginning of mass sales of his cars (c. 1926).

Bruce Henderson: formation of the Boston Consulting Group (1964).

RENAISSANCE

Luca Pacioli: *Summa de arithmetica, geometria, proportioni et proportionalita* (Venice, 1494). This is one of the earliest printed books on mathematics. Pacioli emphasizes that mathematics is related to astrology, architecture, painting, sculpture, business, war, theology, and law. After his death, the book is best remembered for its section on double-entry bookkeeping, and it is seen as the pioneer textbook in the development of accountancy. At **53**, Pacioli completes *De Divina Proportione,* on mathematics, God, proportion, architecture, and the use of the human body as a model for proportion in architecture. The well-known illustrations are by his friend Leonardo da Vinci (**46**).

ARCHITECTURE

Sir Joseph Paxton wins the competition for the design of the Great Exhibition of 1851, with his Crystal Palace—he enters at the last minute, and takes nine days to produce the competition drawings.

Alfred Waterhouse: Prudential Assurance Building, Holborn, London (1879).

ART

Velazquez: "The Toilet of Venus"—the Rokeby Venus (London) (1648).

Manet: "Bar aux Folies-Bergères" (1881).

MUSIC—CLASSICAL

Johann Strauss the Younger: *Die Fledermaus* (1874).

Leoš Janáček: *Jenufa* (1903); and—more surprisingly—*The Cunning Little Vixen* at **69**. (cf. **337***)

Daniel Defoe: *Robinson Crusoe* (1719); and *Moll Flanders* at **52**.

Edward Fitzgerald: translation of the *Rubaiyat* of Omar Khayyam (1859).

Tolstoy finishes *Anna Karenina* (1873–77), and suffers from exhaustion and depression. This ends when he has a rebirth of his religious feelings, at **53**. (cf. **61***)

Kenneth Grahame publishes *The Wind in the Willows* (1908), written while he is secretary in the Bank of England, where he has worked since **19**. The book began in bedtime stories to his son Alastair "Mouse" (now **8**). Grahame has been well known as a part-time author, but *The Wind in the Willows* is by far the most imaginative piece that he ever writes—and it gets a rejection slip from his regular publishers. He now resigns from the bank to be a full-time writer—but writes hardly another line. Mouse later kills himself, by lying down on a railway track, five days before his **20**th birthday. (One of the originals for *Peter Pan,* Peter Llewellyn Davies, also kills himself under a train, at **63**.)

Mario Puzo publishes *The Godfather* (1969). This is his fourth book—previous novels have had good reviews but poor sales. He gets a $5,000 advance, but sales later go to 13 million copies. At **54**, he does screenplays for *The Godfather Part 2,* and for *Earthquake,* for which he gets $1 million. At **57**, he sells the paperback rights for his new novel *Fools Die* for $2.2 million.

PLAYS

Henrik Ibsen: *Pillars of Society* (1877). This is the first play in the realistic style in which he goes on to create many of the classics of world theater. Ibsen had a lonely childhood; at **8**, his father (**39**) had been financially ruined; at **16**, Ibsen left school and began self-education. In his early **20s**, he had a job at Norway's new and only professional theater, at Bergen. At that time, he put on some of his own plays, none of which attracted audiences. At **38**, he gained a large Scandinavian audience with *Brand* and at **39** with *Peer Gynt.* These were epic verse dramas, full of symbolism, in which Ibsen tries to discuss timeless questions in an almost metaphysical setting. But to later audiences these plays are bewildering. Now at **49** he writes an entirely different type of play. He focuses on the modern world, and its conflicts between public integrity and private self-fulfillment. Paradoxically Ibsen now creates a universal world, in a way that his earlier work has never provided. From **49** onward, having found his unique style, he completes a major play at approximately two-year intervals: *A Doll's House* at **51**; *Ghosts* at **53**; *An Enemy of the People* at **54**; *The Wild Duck* at **56**; and *The Master Builder* at **64**. His last play is at **73***.

Arthur Schnitzler: *Undiscovered Country* (1911); and, *La Ronde* was at **35**.

FILMS

D. W. Griffith: *Isn't Life Wonderful* (1924). He has been the pioneer in the film industry, at **33*–41**. This film at **49** is the last in which he can claim to be abreast of developments in the industry. He now enters a long and permanent decline. He makes his last film at **56** and it is ignored. At **61** he marries Evelyn Baldwin and they divorce after eleven years. He dies at **73**, almost unknown to the then leaders of the industry. From his **mid-40**s onward Griffith has suffered a loss of confidence in his ability to contribute new ideas. His own innovations in film have become so taken-for-granted that no one can conceive of the imaginative leap that was necessary to create them. From **49** onward Griffith now spends the next twenty-four years as an outmoded and irrelevant figure, until the new interest in film history elevates him to the status of artist and master—shortly after his death.

Will Hay: *Oh, Mr. Porter* (1937).

Mike Todd: *Around the World in Eighty Days* (1956); he marries Elizabeth Taylor (**24**), but dies in a plane crash at **51**.

David Lean: *The Bridge on the River Kwai* (1957)—his first big, big film and his first Oscar; with Alec Guinness (**43**) and Jack Hawkins (**47**).

David Niven: *Separate Tables* (1958); Oscar; with Deborah Kerr (**37**).

Michelangelo Antonioni: *La Notte* (1961).

Burt Lancaster: *Bird Man of Alcatraz* (1962).

MUSIC—NON-CLASSICAL

Leadbelly: his first concert (1935)—he has been "discovered" in prison, by a visiting folk-music historian. His time in jail has been **33–39**, for murder, and **45–49**, for attempted murder. Now at **49** he goes on to become a world figure in music, until his death at **64**.

Frank Sinatra: "It Was a Very Good Year" (1965); also, "Strangers in the Night" at **50**, and "My Way" at **53**. At **48**, Sinatra was briefly married to Mia Farrow (**19**).

TV, ETC.

Mark Goodson and Bill Todman (**49**): "Call My Bluff" (1965).

Telly Savalas: "Kojak" (1973). During the run of this series, until **53**, he accumulates a large number of fans who regard him as sexy and desirable. He has been shaving his head daily since **41**.

LOVE, LIFE

Julia Child: *Mastering the Art of French Cooking* (1961, with two co-authors). This is her first book, and it gradually moves to best-seller status. When she was **36**, her husband had got a job in Paris; she traveled with him from the U.S.A., and took a six-month Cordon Bleu course.

EXPLORATION

J. Bruce Ismay: sinking of the *Titanic,* in the Atlantic Ocean (1912). He is chairman of the company which owns the ship. 1,400 people die. Ten millionaires drown in the disaster, including the recently married Colonel J. J. Astor (**47**), and Benjamin Guggenheim who puts on formal clothes as a preliminary to death. The Captain is E. J. Smith (**62**) who goes down with the ship. The hero of the tragedy is Wallace Hartley (**33**), the bandmaster, who continues to play cheerful music while the waters overcome the ship. Hartley receives worldwide fame, though he too is drowned. The piece which he allegedly plays last, "Nearer My God to Thee," becomes an international hit. J. Bruce Ismay is a passenger on the *Titanic* and manages to save himself. This earns him great contempt, since many believe that he should have done the decent thing and drowned with his customers. Ismay survives until **74** and his wife until **96**, but they live in obscurity, having been the scapegoats of the event. The lookout who first gives warning of the fatal iceberg hangs himself 53 years later.

LAW, CRIME

Hammurabi, ruler of Babylon, issues his legal code (1799 B.C.), the first to survive. Coincidentally, Justinian's law code is also written when Emperor Justinian is approximately **49** (528 A.D.). The Code Napoleon is put into effect in 1804 when Napoleon is **35**.

This is the average age of judges on appointment to U.S. District courts. There is no minimum age for appointment, but in practice judges are appointed at **45–55**. There is no maximum age at appointment, but very few judges are appointed at **60+**. A Federal judge may retire from active service at **70** after ten years service, or at **65** after fifteen years service.

50

HEALTH

Wilhelm Roentgen: discovery of X rays (1895). He has had a career in physics and is a person of solid competence. One day at **50** he notices the glow produced by X rays, during a routine experiment on the cathode ray tube, which he has been studying for seventeen months. Now, having discovered a completely new and inexplicable phenomenon, he is almost in a state of shock. He writes up his experiments within seven weeks, and illustrates his paper with an X-ray photograph of the hand of his wife (**56**). By his **51**st birthday, Roentgen has become a worldwide sensation. Some other discoveries include: the first barium meal is devised by Walter B. Cannon (**26**, in 1897). And later, Computerized Axial Tomography, body scanning, is due to Godfrey Hounsfield (also **50**, in 1969) and to Allan Cormack (**39**, in 1963).

John H. Gibbon: first use of a heart-lung machine (1953).

Life expectancy in the U.S.A. (1976) is now until **74.2** for males, and until **79.8** for females.

In the U.S.A., 1900–02, the life expectancy at birth for the white population was until **48.2** (male) and until **51.1** (female). By 1976, the comparable figure, of expectancy at **0**, was **69.7** and **77.3**.

You can now expect to live until **78.7**, female, and until **73.4**, male (England and Wales, 1975). Out of total deaths at all ages, 9.25 percent (male) occur from the ages **45–54**, but only 4.12 percent (female) in the same age group.

The causes of death for males **45–54** in England and Wales, in 1977, are: (1) ischemic heart disease; (2) lung cancer; (3) miscellaneous other cancers; (4) cerebrovascular disease; (5) bronchitis, asthma, emphysema; and (6) pneumonia, stomach cancer, and suicide. The causes of female deaths are: (1) breast cancer; (2) miscellaneous other cancers; (3) ischemic heart disease; (4) cerebrovascular disease; (5) lung cancer; (6) cancer of the cervix, uterus.

Forty-three percent of all male deaths between **45** and **64** result from coronary heart disease; men who take vigorous exercise run about one third of the risks of such disease compared with those men who do not exercise—according to the Royal College of Physicians, and the British Cardiac Society.

 Animals' maximum life span: the hippopotamus, orangutan, and the pilot whale can live until now. Also, the wandering albatross, the ostrich, and condor.

HISTORY—WORLD

Eligibility: you are now old enough in ancient Rome to be head of the Curia (c. 200 B.C.), the original assembly and a forerunner of the Senate. At **42**, you became eligible to be one of the two consuls, the leading officers of the state. At **25**, you were eligible to be one of the decuriones, a local councilor. At **16**, the males began wearing the *toga virilis*. Marriage was allowed at **14** (males) and **12** (females).

Eligibility: in Italy, now old enough to be president.

HISTORY—U.S.A.

Nelson Rockefeller: Governor of New York (1959) until he is **64**; becomes Vice-President at **65**.

The average age of President Carter's (**52**) first cabinet is **50.7**, on the announcement of their appointment.

Lieutenant General Edward C. Meyer: Army Chief of Staff (1979), the top position in the army.

HISTORY—U.K.

Henry VIII has his fifth wife, Catherine Howard executed (1542, Feb. 13) and marries again at **52**, dying at **55**. His sixth and last wife is Catherine Parr (**31**), who is already a widow twice over; she later dies at **36**, following childbirth, after her fourth marriage.

Keir Hardie is the first-ever chairman of the Parliamentary Labour party (1906). He had been the first and only independent Labour MP at **36**. The Labour party is still a tiny force in politics, getting around 8 percent of the national vote in his lifetime. He dies at **59**, partly through strain from being a pacifist at the beginning of World War I.

Field Marshal Haig: end of World War I (1911, Nov. 11). David Lloyd George, the Prime Minister, is **48**.

Shirley Williams, Roy Jenkins (**60**), William Rodgers (**52**), and David Owen: the Social Democrat party (1981).

RELIGION, PHILOSOPHY

Jean-Jacques Rousseau: publication of both *Émile,* on childhood (cf. **13***), and *The Social Contract* (1762). (cf. **66***)

SOCIAL SCIENCE, EDUCATION

Cardinal Richelieu: foundation of the Académie Francaise (1635).

Edward Gibbon completes the 6th and final volume of *Decline and Fall of the Roman Empire* (1787). He had the initial idea at **27**, and started writing at **31**. His interest in Roman history began around **14**, and though he studied widely he never completed a degree. His life has been devoted to "scribble, scribble, scribble."

Marquis de Condorcet is sentenced to death (Paris, 1793) by the revolutionary tribunal—he has offended the new ruling elite. He now goes into hiding and writes *Esquisse d'un tableau historique.* In this, he shows the continuous sequence of improvement in the human condition, from the distant past, and inevitably into the future. He says that the future will be perfection—no disease, no social inequalities, no starvation, and no problems of any kind. The French Revolution will lead to this. On completion of this book, Condorcet is captured, and dies the next day—in a revolutionary prison.

John Kenneth Galbraith: *The Affluent Society* (1958). And, *The New Industrial State* at **59**.

Barbara Tuchman: *The Guns of August* (1962), about the beginning of World War I. This is her first best-seller. She also writes *The Proud Tower* at **54**; on China and General Stilwell at **59**; and *A Distant Mirror,* on the fourteenth century, at **67**.

John Rawls: *A Theory of Justice* (1971).

Michel Foucault: *History of Sexuality* (1976); and previously, *History of Madness* at **35**; *Archaeology of Knowledge* at **43**; and *On the Birth of the Prison* at **49**.

SCIENCE, TECHNOLOGY

[There is] a conflict of conscience that in some form or other is spared no university teacher who has passed, say, his **50**th year.—Albert Einstein (1879–1955).

Antoine Lavoisier: execution (1794). From **28*** onward he has worked on the discovery of oxygen. Also at **28**, he had married Marie Paulze (**13**), daughter of a tax farmer. Fraud in the collection of tax was a regular feature of the system, and it became an important source of funding for Lavoisier's experiments. Now, during the French Revolution, he is one of a batch of tax gatherers, including his father-in-law, who are publicly executed in Paris. His widow is afterward supported by the family which goes on to form the Du Pont Company in Delaware. She lives until **78**, a widow for 42 years.

Charles Darwin: *On the Origin of Species, by Means of Natural Selection, or, the Preservation of Favoured Races in the Struggle for Life* (1859). At **49**, Darwin had presented a paper on natural selection, jointly with A. R. Wallace (**25**) who had independently produced the same concept. Darwin has been developing his ideas since **29** or **30**; having hit on the general principles, he has spent 20 years gathering and presenting supporting data, so that his revolutionary views will have the correct impact. Wallace at **22** had been in Malaysia, and had noticed the line differentiating the animals of Asia and Australia. At **25**, he had had a fever, and in a flash he saw that evolution proceeds by natural selection. Darwin always emphasizes that his insights have been the result of steady cumulative work, or perhaps a moment of insight embedded in years and decades of observation. His slow work habits are helped by his illness, real or imaginary—". . . ill-health, though it has annihilated several years of my life, has saved me from the distractions of society and amusement." Darwin's last book is at **72***.

Georg Cantor: *Beiträge* (1895–97). This is the culmination of his work on transfinite set theory, on which he has been working continuously since his **20**s. This book marks the end of his major work in mathematics, but paradoxically it marks the beginning of his main reputation. Up till now, he has received very little support from his professional colleagues. In his **50**s and **60**s, he acquires an international reputation. Cantor suffers from depression, and from now onward spends significant time in mental hospitals. He lives until **72**.

Vladimir Zworykin: first scanning electron microscope (1939).

MONEY, WORK

Sir Richard Arkwright decides (England, 1782) to remedy his early lack of education—so he sleeps two hours less per night, and studies grammar and handwriting.

ARCHITECTURE

Pheidias: the sculpture on the Parthenon, Athens (c.450 B.C.).

Sir Christopher Wren: Chelsea Hospital, London (1682)—home of the Chelsea pensioners.

John Wood, the elder: the Circus, Bath (1754).

Sir George Gilbert Scott: St. Pancras Station Hotel, London (1861).

Bernard Maybeck: Palace of Fine Arts, San Francisco (1912).

Cesar Pelli: Pacific Design Center, Los Angeles (completed 1976); and the Winter Gardens, Niagara Falls, completed at **54**.

ART

Simone Martini: "Annunciation" (Uffizi) (c.1333).

Rembrandt: bankruptcy (1656). Since opening his own studio, he has been both a commercial and an artistic success. The bankruptcy is due to his own extravagance and to the changing taste of his patrons. His possessions are sold. He lives until **63***. Many of his self-portraits date from this time.

Katsushika Hokusai says that "I was born at the age of **50**" (1810)—it took him this long to develop his own personal style. His best-known work is published at **63**—"Thirty-six views of Mount Fuji." These are the instantly recognizable pictures of the mountain with trees or huge waves in the foreground. Until **32**, Hokusai had been confined to illustrations for the theater; he then began teaching himself a wide variety of painting styles. He lives until **89**, but believes that he would have achieved perfection as a painter if he could live until **110***. (cf. **74***)

Degas comments: "Everyone has talent at **25**; the difficulty is to have it at **50**." Around **45**, Degas had begun a new theme, as a sculptor. From now onward (1884), until near his death at **83**, he is a pretty vigorous sculptor and painter, though he uses subjects that he has already explored.

Rodin said that he was poor until **50** (1890). (cf. **60***)

Claude Monet in 1890: a stream is diverted through his garden, thus creating a small water garden. This becomes the stimulus for a complete new style or theme in his work. These new paintings, the "Water Lilies," occupy him on and off until **86**. His paintings of Rouen Cathedral are done between **52** and **54**. At **59–61**, he goes to London, and this visit results in 100 canvases. His last development is at **77***—an entire room of water lilies.

Andy Warhol: screenprints of ten star athletes (1978).

MUSIC—CLASSICAL

Wagner is introduced to King Ludwig II (**18**) who now agrees (1864, May 4) to free him from financial worries, so that he can return to work on the *Ring*. The premiere of *Tristan und Isolde* is at **52**; the last music for the *Ring* is finished at **61**; first complete performance at **63** (cf. **56*** and **57***). Wagner is unusually conscious of birthdays. At **54**, during the birth of his daughter Eva, he goes into an adjoining room and plays the "Morning Dream" theme from *Die Meistersinger*. And for his patron, King Ludwig, he endeavors to celebrate the latter's birthday in a special manner. Between **20** and **28**, the king usually receives birthday presents of the latest Wagner composition, and often has a poem in his honor. On one occasion he is also given a cushion embroidered with Wagnerian themes. At **57**, Wagner arranges for his second marriage to be held on the king's **25**th birthday. King Ludwig had originally been called Otto, but his name was changed to Ludwig because he was born on the birthday of his grandfather, King Ludwig I (**59**). (cf **23***).

Camille Saint-Saëns: *Le Carnaval des animaux: fantaisie zoologique* (1886).

Gustav Mahler: Eighth Symphony, *Symphony of a Thousand* (1910). He dies this year, with his Ninth Symphony unperformed, and his Tenth Symphony not yet finished. His death is in Vienna.

LITERATURE

At **50**, everyone has the face he deserves.—George Orwell (d. **46**, 1950).

John Donne becomes Dean of St. Paul's Cathedral, London (1621), and stays in office until his death at **60**.

Matsuo Basho: *The Narrow Road to the Deep North* (1694).

Bram Stoker: *Dracula* (1897).

Herman Hesse: *Steppenwolf* (1927).

Ernest Hemingway: *Across the River and into the Trees* (1950). This is widely seen as a deterioration, since *For Whom the Bell Tolls* at **40**. His *The Old Man and the Sea* restores his reputation at **52**, but he publishes little before his suicide at **61***. Also, on his birthday, he has sex three times.

Evelyn Waugh goes mad on a cruise (1954), and subsequently writes this up as *The Ordeal of Gilbert Pinfold* (**53**). At **43**, he had visited the U.S.A. for the first time—discovered "Forest Lawn," and written *The Loved One.*

Aleksandr Solzhenitsyn completes *Cancer Ward* (1969).

James Herriot, a veterinarian in Yorkshire, has his silver wedding, (1966) and a week later his wife says, "You're never going to be a writer"—so he starts writing, in the evenings while the rest of the family is watching TV. Three years later, his first book *If Only They Could Talk* is published, and he subsequently sells at least five million copies of his various titles. Unfortunately, his example encourages most other veterinarians to deluge publishers with their memoirs, and extra supplies of rejection slips have to be printed.

Toni Morrison: *Tar Baby* (1981).

PLAYS, DANCE

George Bernard Shaw: *Major Barbara* and *John Bull's Other Island* (1906). He later says that "Life is at its worst between **50** and **60**." His *Man and Superman* was at **49**; and Shaw continues to write with amazing energy, for example, *Androcles and the Lion* at **56**; *Pygmalion* at **57**, later the musical *My Fair Lady; Heartbreak House* is at **63**; *Back to Methuselah* at **65**; *Saint Joan* at **67**; and *The Apple Cart* at **73**. In his **70**s and **80**s, Shaw continues to be a vigorous public figure, issuing pronouncements on most topics of the day. He lives until **94***.

FILMS

Tod Browning: *Freaks* (1932); only two of the cast lack deformities.

John Barrymore: *Rasputin and the Empress* (1932), also starring his distinguished siblings, Ethel Barrymore (**53**) and Lionel Barrymore (**54**). John Barrymore has been a leading actor, for example, in *Rich-*

ard III at **38**, and *Hamlet* at **40**. At **49**, he earned $460,000. But now at **50** he is in the early stages of perhaps the most public collapse ever seen. Barrymore and alcoholism become indissolubly linked in the public mind. By **53**, he needs to spend a whole day doing fifty-six takes to produce one scene. His deterioration is so spectacular that it becomes the subject of films in which he himself plays the part of a drunken actor. John Barrymore lives until **60**, and in his last days works in radio shows in order to pay off his taxes. His brother afterward explains that John had never recovered from the death, when he was **15**, of his grandmother Mum Mum (**77**), the only person who had provided him with a stable home.

Howard Hawks: *The Big Sleep* (1946).

Errol Flynn: death (1959). Perhaps his best-known film is *The Adventures of Robin Hood* at **29**. But soon afterward he begins his public deterioration so that he dies at **50** as a drunk and a drug addict. Flynn is also known for his obsession with teenage girls. At **50**, his constant companion has been a girl of **17**, and he has survived two charges of statutory rape. Flynn's last film is, appropriately, about another famous wreck, John Barrymore (see above).

Jacques Tati: *Mon Oncle* (1958).

Anthony Quinn: *Zorba the Greek* (1965).

Charles Bronson, who is a character actor (though one of the highest paid) becomes a national star with *Chato's Land* (1971).

Ken Russell: *Valentino* (1977); this is the film debut of Rudolf Nureyev (**39**).

TV, ETC.

"This Is Your Life"—you are surprised to enter a TV studio where you find all the people of your past. You get to review your life, from childhood onward. As you talk to old friends, tears flood your eyes.

LOVE, LIFE

Joy Adamson: *Born Free* (1960), the story of her work with the lion cub, Elsa.

Jeremy Thorpe: acquittal from the charge of incitement to murder (London, 1979). In his trial, it is alleged that at **32** he had had an affair with Norman Scott (**21**); and that the blackmailing demands of Scott since that time have caused Thorpe to plot the removal of Scott from the face of the earth. Jeremy Thorpe, an old Etonian, had become an MP at **30**, and had plausibly seen himself as a future prime minister. But following his acquittal, he retires from public life.

It is said that half of American women are now divorced, widowed, or single.

In 1977 in England and Wales, there were 2,933 births in which the father was **50** or over.

The peak years for female suicide are **45–54**; but the male suicide rate rises steadily throughout life, and peaks at the oldest years. The overall male rate is twice the female rate.

PRESS

John Baskerville: completion of his Baskerville typeface (1756).

EXPLORATION

There are old divers, and there are bold divers, but there are no old, bold divers.—industry saying.

Robert Baden-Powell: start of the "Scouts" movement (1907). He is an army officer and at **42** had been in charge of Mafeking, during its siege in the South African Boer War. Immediately before this, he had published *Aids to Scouting,* a textbook on living in the wilds. Now at **50** he holds the first Boy Scouts camp, and it lasts eight days. This is such a success that he retires from the army at **53** and also then founds the Girl Scouts/Guides. The Cub Scouts are started at **59**. An international jamboree at **63** creates him Chief Scout of the World, and he lives until **83**.

John W. Young and Robert L. Crippen (**43**): flight crew of Columbia, the space shuttle, on its first flight (1981). The back-up crew is Joe Engle (**48**) and Richard Truly (**43**). Also, one of the astronauts, who dock in space with the Russian *Soyuz* craft is Donald Slayton (**51**, in 1975).

LAW, CRIME

About five percent of inmates of state prisons are aged **50** and above. The peak years are **20–24** and fall away after that.

The peak years for earnings as an English barrister (trial lawyer) are **50–54**. Earnings under **30** are not much over the average industrial wage, but climb steadily till now. Earnings at **60–64** are diminished, but still good.

SPORTS

W. G. Grace (cricket, 1898)—his last international match. He now becomes keen on bowls. At **47**, he had scored his 100th century, and had scored 2,346 runs, his third highest annual total. At **58**, he is still playing some cricket, and scores 74 in the "Gentlemen versus Players."

Stanley Mathews (U.K., 1965) retires from league soccer. He had started at **17**, and has played in 54 internationals.

Inez Finch cycles 50 miles in two hours four minutes, at the Veterans Time Trials (U.K., 1976). At **51**, John C. Shyne cycles 3,600 miles across the U.S.A., by himself, in 50 days (1977).

Arnold Palmer (golf, 1980): winner, Canadian PGA championship.

Willie Shoemaker (horseracing, 1981): winner of the first Arlington Million race.

Men's track and field records now at **50**:

100 meters in 11.4 seconds;
400 meters in 53.6 seconds;
1,500 meters in 4 minutes 15.0 seconds;
the mile in 4 minutes 32.2 seconds;
10,000 meters in 32 minutes 30.4 seconds;
10 mile walk in 1 hour 24 minutes.
The high jump record is 5′7″ and the long jump record is 19′11½″.

Women's track records now at **50**:

100 meters in 15.9 seconds;
200 meters in 29.6 seconds;
400 meters in 80.2 seconds;
800 meters in 3 minutes 0.8 seconds;
the mile in 6 minutes 31.4 seconds; and
10,000 meters in 46 minutes 17.0 seconds.

51

HEALTH

Luther L. Terry: as Surgeon General (**50–54**) of the United States, he initiates the report (1962) which determines that cigarette smoking can damage your health.

HISTORY—WORLD

Ali Bhutto: hanged (1979). He had been Prime Minister of Pakistan, from **45** to **49**.

Franklin D. Roosevelt: President (1933, Mar. 4); initiates the Hundred Days of the New Deal. Louis D. Brandeis is **76**; Harold Ickes **58**; Felix Frankfurter **50**; Frances Perkins (first-ever woman in cabinet) is **50**; Eleanor Roosevelt **48**; Robert F. Wagner **45**; Henry A. Wallace and James A. Farley both **44**; Rexford Tugwell and Harry Hopkins both **42**; Dean Acheson **39**; and A. A. Berle **38**; Herbert Hoover had been President from **44** to **48**. (cf. **59***)

Admiral Hyman Rickover is twice passed over for promotion (1951), and is therefore due for mandatory retirement, from his job directing U.S. nuclear submarines. But President Truman (**67**) and others support him—Rickover continues in office until **80*** and beyond.

Eugene McCarthy almost wins New Hampshire primary (Mar. 1968), and precipitates withdrawal of Lyndon Johnson (**59***) from possible campaign for reelection as President.

RELIGION, PHILOSOPHY

Confucius—K'ung Fu-tzse—becomes chief magistrate of the city of Chung-tu (500 B.C.). Previously he had been a private citizen, developing his ideas on government. He now has the chance to put these ideas into practice. But by **55** his reforming zeal has made him unpopular; he loses office, and becomes a wanderer again. He returns home at **68**. Confucius does not write books; his later influence comes from the books written about him by his disciples. He dies at **72***. Confucius later records his own development: "At **15**, my desire was toward learning. At **30**, my mind was fixed. At **40**, I had no doubt. At **60**, my ear received every thing with ease. At **70**, my desires did not transgress the law . . . without effort, (I) remained in the path of virtue."

SOCIAL SCIENCE, EDUCATION

Milton Friedman: *A Monetary History of the United States* (1963).

MONEY, WORK

Henry Ford: the $5 per day minimum wage (1914).

RENAISSANCE

Leonardo da Vinci, in 1503: in his early **50**s he now does some of his greatest paintings—"Virgin and Child with St. Anne," the "Mona Lisa (**23**)," and the "Battle of Anghiari." At **47**, he had left Milan, (cf. **16***) where he had been since **30**, and at **50** he became a military adviser to Cesare Borgia (**27**) during one of the latter's most vicious and effective campaigns. (This campaign is observed by Niccolò Machiavelli (**33**) and Borgia becomes the model for *The Prince;* Borgia's peak years end at **28** with his capture, followed by his death at **32**.) Leonardo returns home to Florence at **51**, and now begins probably the greatest years of his creativity. For the "Mona Lisa (**23**)" portrait, he "engaged people to play and sing, and jesters to keep her merry; and remove that melancholy which painting usually gives to portraits." At this time he does intense work on the dissection of corpses, and this leads to his famous drawings of the womb, coition, and the arteries. He is a pioneer at **54** in the identification of arteriosclerosis. In his **50**s, he also sketches the helicopter, the glider, and designs for bridges, windmills, ships, hulls, canals, and compasses. His designs for machinery are so far ahead of his time that they are not fully appreciated for decades or even centuries after his death. Leonardo must have worked at high speed, remorselessly following up the manufacturing implications of each design. One cost of his working method is that he leaves relatively few finished projects and the chaos and inaccessibility of his manuscripts makes his ideas far less influential than they should have been. Leonardo goes to Rome at **61**, and then to France at **64**, where he dies at **67***. His creativity is not in one burst, but is a continuous force of the highest intensity through his **30**s, **40**s, **50**s, and early **60**s. His public reputation is mainly due to his art and his military skills; he leaves an overwhelming quantity of scientific material that is never known in his lifetime. Faced with being so far in advance of his contemporaries, he develops his scientific theories for a readership whom he will never meet.

ARCHITECTURE

Louis Henry Sullivan: National Farmers Bank, Owatonna, Minnesota (1907)—about this time, Sullivan's career disintegrates, partly owing to his drinking; he never designs another large building, but instead does a few of these small (but beautiful) local banks. (cf. **68***)

Eero Saarinen dies (1961, Sept. 1) with the following designs still under construction: two colleges at Yale; Deere offices, Illinois; CBS building, New York City; TWA building, Kennedy airport.

ART

Albrecht Dürer: "The Triumphal Chariot of Maximilian I" (1522).

Titian: "Venus of Urbino" (Uffizi) (1538). (cf. **99***)

LITERATURE

Honoré de Balzac dies (1850, Aug. 18) after calling out for a doctor who is in fact a character in one of his own novels. A few months previously, Balzac had married an enormously rich Polish landowner, whom he had been pursuing for the past 17 years.

Maxwell Perkins is editor for *Of Time and the River* (1935) by Thomas Wolfe (**35**)—which Wolfe dedicates to him. Perkins is also editor to Ernest Hemingway (**36**) and F. Scott Fitzgerald (**39**) at this time.

Raymond Chandler: *The Big Sleep* (1939). This creation of the detective, Philip Marlowe, is the breakthrough in his career, and he goes on to write six more novels about Marlowe, the last being at **70**. Chandler dies at **70**; Philip Marlowe is always **38**.

Mary McCarthy: *The Group* (1963).

PLAYS, DANCE

Ibsen: *A Doll's House* (1879).

Eugene O'Neill: completion of *The Iceman Cometh* (1939). He also writes *Long Day's Journey into Night;* he decides that this should not be performed until twenty-five years after his death, as it is too revealing about his parents and family. At **61**, he hears that his son (**40**) has killed himself by slashing his wrist. O'Neill dies at **65**.

FILMS

Douglas Fairbanks, Sr., retires (1934).

Charlie Chaplin: *The Great Dictator* (1940).

Gary Cooper: *High Noon* (1952).

James Cagney: *Love Me or Leave Me* (1955).

Cary Grant: *To Catch a Thief* (1955).

Robert Altman: *Nashville* (1976).

Marlon Brando now weighs 250 pounds (1976).

TV, ETC.

Fred Friendly resigns from CBS-TV (1966) when the network shows the fifth rerun of an "I Love Lucy" episode, instead of live testimony by George F. Kennan (**62**) at a congressional hearing on the Vietnam War.

EXPLORATION

Samuel Cunard: formation of the British and North American Royal Mail Steam Packet Company, or Cunard Line (1839). This is a pioneer in offering regular scheduled transport across the Atlantic, and Cunard has had to work until now to provide the four ships which are required for the service.

LAW, CRIME

William Marwood performs the first long-drop execution in England with a scientifically calculated length of drop (1871). The aim is to instantly break the neck without wrenching off the head. In the old short-drop method, the victim was turned off the back of a cart, and choked to death; relatives would sometimes tug at the victim's feet so that he or she would die more quickly. Before being hangman, Marwood had been a cobbler, and developed an amateur interest in hanging. He himself dies of natural causes at **63**. His predecessor is William Calcraft (**75**) who has been in office since **31**. In 1815, William Brunskill (**72**) had retired from the job, having held it since **32**.

Sandra Day O'Connor: first woman member of the U.S. Supreme Court (1981).

SPORT

Cornelis van Rietschoten: organizer and captain of "Flyer," the yacht which wins the 1978 Round the World race. Another amazing yachting achievement is that of Eric Tabarly who at **48** (1980) sails across the Atlantic in the record time 10 days, 5 hours, and 13 minutes.

52

HISTORY—WORLD

Attila the Hun: the invasion and terrorizing of northern Italy (452 A.D.). This is the climax of his campaigns against the Roman Empire. He dies at **53**.

François Toussaint L'Ouverture becomes head of state in Haiti (1795). He was born a slave in Haiti, and had been freed at **34**. He took over the leadership of a slave revolt, from **48** onward, and the revolt is now successful. He goes on to defeat French, Spanish, and British forces, and to resist the reintroduction of slavery. But he is tricked into being captured by the French at **59**, and dies of disease in a French prison at **60**.

Sir John Macdonald: first-ever Prime Minister of Canada (1867).

Lenin: first stroke (1922), and death at **53**. Since **47***, he has been leader of the Soviet Union. Watching the revolution he has helped to create, he suffers remorse at its exaggerated nature. "I am, I believe, strongly guilty before the workers of Russia." His own ruthlessness has led to a government style that is cruel at its worst, and highly bureaucratic at its best. Lenin is too sick to prevent the disaster which he sees ahead—the rise of Stalin (**44***). After his death, Lenin becomes a cult figure, useful to the next generation of rulers. Only his widow, Krupskaya (**54**) protests that this is against his lifelong ideals.

Adolf Hitler: the beginning of the end (1941). Having now avenged himself for the 1919 Treaty of Versailles, he now invades the U.S.S.R. This is an impossible project for him, and the U.S.A. joins in war against him, a few months later. Around this time, he accelerates his attack on Jews and other non-Aryans into the frenzy of the Holocaust. By **56***, he commits suicide, as Berlin is about to be conquered.

Moshe Dayan: Six Day War (1967).

HISTORY—U.S.A.

Fiorello LaGuardia is Mayor of New York for the next eleven years (1934–45). Also, Richard Daley becomes Mayor of Chicago (1955), and continues in office until his death at **74**.

George Wallace is confined to a wheelchair for life, after a bullet wound in an assassination attempt (1972); but he continues as Governor of Alabama.

HISTORY—U.K.

Sir Arthur "Bomber" Harris: Anglo-American firestorm raid on Dresden (1945).

RELIGION, PHILOSOPHY

Thomas à Becket is taken from the altar at Canterbury Cathedral (1170), and murdered, after a chance remark against him by King Henry II (**37**). Afterward, the king is so filled with remorse that he goes to the same altar, and has himself whipped by each of the Canterbury monks—all 70 of them.

Alec McGowen: first stage performance of his recital of St. Mark's Gospel (1977).

SOCIAL SCIENCE, EDUCATION

Adam Smith: *The Wealth of Nations* (1776); on the benefits of a market economy to "public opulence." This is only his second book (cf. **14***). Smith's book is an immediate success, and he now goes into semiretirement. He lives, peacefully, until **67**.

Freud: first public fame (1908)—formation of the Vienna Psychoanalytical Society, visit to the U.S.A., honorary doctorate, and first conference on psychoanalysis. The conference lasts only one day, and nine people attend, including Jung (**33**), and Adler (**38**). At **54**, Freud has a distinguished client, the composer Gustav Mahler (**50**). (cf. **67***)

J. M. Keynes: *The General Theory of Employment, Interest, and Money* (1936). Keynes now continues with his career as an international policymaker. (cf. **61***)

Erving Goffman: *Frame Analysis* (1974). He had written *Presentation of Self in Everyday Life* at **34**; *Asylum* at **39**; and *Interaction Ritual* at **45**.

SCIENCE, TECHNOLOGY

James Watt: invention of the centrifugal governor (1788) for use in his steam engine (cf. **29***). This is a pioneer work in cybernetics. At **48**, Watt had invented the sliding-wheel gearbox, similar to that later used in automobiles. He lives until **83**.

Gail Borden: the invention of condensed milk (1853). His first career as a surveyor had made him interested in easy-to-carry food.

An Wang, and Wang Laboratories, start work on the development of word processing (1972); by **60**, he has become the world leader in a huge new market. At **28**, Wang had invented the core storage which was at the heart of computers for twenty years.

MONEY, WORK

Ray Kroc catches sight of the first McDonalds takeout restaurant, in San Bernardino, California (1954). He is thrilled, because the business needs eight milkshake mixers, the machine for which he is a salesman. The operation is beautifully organized, and Kroc sees its potential. Gradually he hits on the idea of franchising McDonalds throughout the world, and he negotiates the rights to do this. Kroc had never graduated from high school, and has previously been a salesman for disposable paper cups. All his energy and creativity have gone into salesmanship and the fast food industry. His efforts have brought him a decent income but at **52** his relentless trying begins to have a giant payoff. He now takes a year to organize his own first McDonalds and to develop its procedures. Expansion quickly follows. By **54**, he has sold eight franchises. At **59**, his training school, Hamburger University, graduates its first students. At **64**, he sells his two billionth hamburger. At **72**, he buys a baseball team, the San Diego Padres. At **74**, he opens the four thousandth McDonalds. Kroc makes himself rich, but he is not obsessed by money itself. He comments on his millions: "So what! I can still only wear one pair of shoes at a time."

ARCHITECTURE

Brunelleschi: Pazzi Chapel, Florence (1429–61).

Leon Battista Alberti: the entrance facade of Santa Maria Novella, Florence (1456–70).

Mies van der Rohe emigrates to the U.S.A. from Nazi Germany, and becomes head of the school of architecture (1938), in the future Illinois Institute of Technology, Chicago. (cf. **59***)

 Wallace K. Harrison (and many others): United Nations building, New York City (1947–50).

Alvar Aalto: municipal buildings, Säynätsala, Finland (1950).

MUSIC—CLASSICAL

Ludwig van Beethoven: *Missa Solemnis* (1823); also Symphony no. 9. Since **32***, he has been acknowledged throughout the world as a composer of unparalleled force. Beethoven never marries; he never has children; he has very few friends; he has permanent money problems; he is deaf; and he is constantly changing house. He dies at **56**, of cirrhosis of the liver, and thousands attend his funeral. His last complete work is the Quartet in F Major, op. 135, at **55**. Now, at the moment of the completion of the Ninth Symphony, Goethe is **74**; Carl von Weber is **37**; both Carl Czerny and Meyerbeer are **32**; Rossini is **31**; both Franz Schubert and Donizetti are **26**; Felix Mendelssohn is **14**; both Robert Schumann and Frédéric Chopin are **13**; Franz Liszt is **12**; Richard Wagner is **10**; César Franck is **1**; and both Smetana and Bruckner are **−1**. Mozart had died thirty-one years previously, at **35**. Brahms is born ten years afterward; Saint-Saëns is born twelve years afterward; and Tchaikovsky is born seventeen years after this moment.

Brahms: Symphony No. 4 (1885).

Dvořák: Symphony in E Minor, *From the New World* (1893)—written on seeing North America for the first time.

LITERATURE

George Eliot: *Middlemarch* (1871).

Robert Frost sets the final exam for a course he is teaching (1926): "Do anything appropriate to this course that you think would please me." He gives only one A, to the student who merely signs his name. (cf. **86***)

Graham Greene: *The Quiet American* (1956).

Ayn Rand: *Atlas Shrugged* (1957).

Doris Lessing: *Briefing for a Descent into Hell* (1971).

PLAYS

August Strindberg: *The Dance of Death* (1901). This is another play in his naturalistic style. But at this time he is also working in a poetic expressionist manner; for example, *To Damascus* at **49**, and *A Dream Play* at **53**. Now at **52** Strindberg is married, for the third time; his bride is an actress, Harriet Bosse **(21)** but they divorce when he is **55**. To the end of his life (d. **63**) he is productive as a playwright, and continues to be controversial, mad, and unapproachable. It is only at his impressive funeral that he can at last receive an unambiguous tribute from the world.

FILM

Alfred Hitchcock: *Strangers on a Train* (1951).

Henry Fonda: *Twelve Angry Men* (1957).

Orson Welles: *A Man for All Seasons* (1967)—the part of Cardinal Wolsey.

Kirk Kerkorian: control of MGM (1969).

MUSIC—NON-CLASSICAL

Ivor Novello: "We'll Gather Lilacs" (1945). His six great musicals are written between **42–56**. His song, "Someday My Heart Will Awake" is in the last of these, *King's Rhapsody,* at **56**.

Frederick Loewe and Alan Jay Lerner (**38**): *My Fair Lady* (1956), perhaps the best-known musical of all time. These two are responsible for six other musicals, including *Brigadoon* (**43** and **29**); *Gigi* (**54** and **40**); and *Camelot* (**56** and **42**).

LOVE, LIFE

Stanford White: death (1906). He has been a partner in McKim (**58**), Mead (**59**), and White, and he has been the lawgiver for architecture and interior design in upper-class New York circles. White is shot and killed by Harry Thaw (**35**) as a result of White's alleged intimacy with Thaw's wife, Evelyn Nesbit (**21**), a person of overpowering beauty. At the trial, Thaw is released on the grounds of temporary insanity. Stanford White is considered by the public to have received poetic justice, and Thaw is something of a celebrity for the rest of his life. Thaw lives until **76**; Evelyn Nesbit lives until **81** and dies in Hollywood. Another passionate killing is by the pioneer photographer Eadweard Muybridge, who at **41** (1871) shoots the lover of his bride (**19**); he also is acquitted.

Gregory Pincus: discovery of a production method for the contraceptive pill (1955).

Alex Comfort: *The Joy of Sex* (1972).

EXPLORATION

Robert Edwin Peary: first person at the North Pole (1909). He has prepared for this journey by living among Eskimos, from **42–46**, and following their methods of adaptation to the harsh climate.

LAW

Henri "Bluebeard" Landru is guillotined in France (1922). He had put advertisements in lonely-hearts columns of newspapers, and thus corresponded with hundreds of women. Eleven of them travel to his village home, where he kills them, and burns them in his kitchen oven.

53

HEALTH

Jacques Lordat, a dean of medicine (1825) has a stroke which causes him profound difficulties in reading, listening, and talking, but which makes "not the least change in his innermost intelligence." Lordat makes a slow recovery but eventually resumes his academic career, and publishes widely. He lives until **98**. Another example of recovery is Woodrow Wilson, who suffers a severe stroke at **49** (1906) but recovers. He carries on as president of Princeton University until **53**, and is President of the U.S.A. at **56**. (cf. **61***)

HISTORY—U.S.A.

Jefferson Davis is elected (Feb. 1861) first-ever and only President of the Confederacy, the southern states which secede from the Union.

Abraham Lincoln: Emancipation Proclamation (effective Jan. 1, 1863), announcing freedom for all slaves in the U.S. (cf. **55***)

Edward Koch: Mayor of New York City (1978).

The average age of twentieth century presidents on entering the White House is **53.5**, with the exception of Ronald Reagan. Theodore Roosevelt is President from **42** to **50**; John F. Kennedy **43–46**; William H. Taft **51–55**; Calvin Coolidge **51–56**; Franklin D. Roosevelt **51–63**; Jimmy Carter **52–56**; Herbert Hoover **44–48**; Warren Harding **55–57**; Lyndon B. Johnson **55–60;** Woodrow Wilson **56–64**; Richard Nixon **56–61**; Harry Truman **60–68**; Gerald Ford **61–63**; Dwight D. Eisenhower **62–70**. Theodore Roosevelt had been Vice-President, and moved up on the assassination of William McKinley (**58**). John F. Kennedy (**42**) is the youngest person to have won a presidential election.

HISTORY—U.K.

Admiral John Byng is shot for neglect of duty (1757), which Voltaire (**65**) said (1759) was to encourage the others.

Lord Castlereagh: suicide (1822); he slashes his throat with a penknife. He has been Britain's Foreign Secretary since **42**. Coincidentally, his nephew, Robert Fitzroy, Captain of HMS *Beagle* on its famous voyage (**26–31**), also commits suicide, at **59**.

RELIGION, PHILOSOPHY

Descartes: he is now internationally famous (for work at **41***) and he is invited, or summoned, to Sweden by the polymath Queen Christina (**23**, in 1649) to be her teacher, and to set up an academy. Descartes, has to begin teaching at five in the morning; he soon gets pneumonia, and dies.

SOCIAL SCIENCE, EDUCATION

Marshall McLuhan: *Understanding Media* (1964); also *The Gutenberg Galaxy* at **51**.

Garrett Hardin: *The Tragedy of the Commons* (1968).

SCIENCE, TECHNOLOGY

Samuel F. B. Morse: the sending of the first message "What Hath God wrought!" by electric telegraph (1844). Morse's first career had been as a painter, and his work was accepted at the Royal Academy, London, at **32** and **34**. At **41** he was appointed professor of painting at the future New York University. In the same year, he became interested in electricity for the first time, and in a flash he designed the basics of his telegraph—the Morse code, and instruments for receiving and sending the message. For seven years, he worked to develop and promote his invention. His first patent was at **46**. Now at **53**, he teams up with Amos Kendall (**55**) who makes a career switch away from journalism and government work. Morse provides the invention and Kendall's job is to exploit it. There is a ten-year gap before they have fully secured their rights on the telegraph, and they then become rich. Samuel Morse's domestic life falls into three parts: he is married from **27–34**, and a widower for the next 23 years. At **57**, he marries Sarah Griswold (**25**) and they go on to have four children. He fathers his last child at **65**, and this son himself dies at **63**. Both Morse and Kendall live until **80**. On the day of Morse's funeral, all the telegraph offices in North America are draped with rosettes of black crepe, as a symbol of international mourning.

William H. Bragg receives the Nobel Prize in 1915—as does his son (**25**), for their joint work in chemistry.

Alec Issigonis: design of the Mini Minor (1959), the pioneer car which has front wheel drive with the engine placed at right angles to the direction of movement.

Paul Berg and Walter Gilbert (**47**): 1980 Nobel Prize, for their work in genetic engineering.

C. P. Snow: *The Two Cultures and the Scientific Revolution* (1959).

ARCHITECTURE

Giorgio Vasari: the upper-floor corridor across Florence, that joins the Palazzo Vecchio to the Pitti Palace (1564) for the use of the Medici family.

Sir William Chambers: Somerset House, London (1776).

Gustave Eiffel: Statue of Liberty, New York City (1885)—the internal supporting structure; the base is by Richard M. Hunt (**58**), and the original sculpture is by Bartholdi. (cf. **57***)

McKim, Mead, and White: Morgan Library, New York City (1902–07).

François Spoerry, in 1966: start of Port Grimaud, his own "fishing village" and vacation center in the South of France—a pioneer in the reaction against the Modern movement.

ART

Fra Angelico: "Annunciation" (upstairs corridor, San Marco) (c. 1450).

Andrea del Verrocchio: the equestrian monument (1488) in Venice to Bartolomeo Colleoni (d. **75**, 1475); Verrocchio dies this year.

Louise Nevelson: beginning of her unique sculptural style, using found timber objects and painted matte black (1953). Nevelson had her first solo show at **41**.

MUSIC—CLASSICAL

Tchaikovsky dies from cholera (1893), caused by his drinking a glass of unclean water—a self-destructive act which is typical of his moody approach to life. At **49**, he had written *Sleeping Beauty; Nutcracker* at **52**; and Symphony no. 6 (*Pathétique*) at **53**.

Maurice Ravel: *Bolero* (1928)—this is the piece which is one long crescendo.

LITERATURE

Thomas Hardy writes *Tess of the d'Urbervilles* (1842) at **52**, and *Jude the Obscure* at **53**. He now gives up novels, and concentrates on poetry. (cf. 77*)

William Styron: *Sophie's Choice* (1979).

PLAYS

Luigi Pirandello: *Six Characters in Search of an Author* (1921). Pirandello has been a minor literary figure since his early **20**s. At first, he was supported by the fortune of his wife (now **49**) but at **36** this money was lost; he had to work as a teacher, and his wife became mentally unstable. His work is heavily affected by the experience of living with madness. At **51**, his wife goes away to an asylum, and Pirandello is influenced by the Futurist movement. After *Six Characters,* he immediately writes *Henry IV.* Later, he writes twenty-six more plays, and also supports the dictatorship of Benito Mussolini (now **37**). Pirandello lives until **69**. In his great work at **53**, Pirandello manages to show how social life exists on the edge of chaos; and he makes a play which is revolutionary in format but which is full of live, sympathetic characters. This is the one moment of his life that all aspects of his ambition and experience work together in harmony for him.

FILMS

Max Ophuls: *Lola Montes* (1955)—later said to be his best work.

Carol Reed: *Our Man in Havana* (1959), with an appearance by Nöel Coward (**60**), and screenplay by Graham Greene (**54**).

Charles Bronson: *Death Wish* (1974)—he is the private citizen who patrols New York, shooting at muggers.

Pier Paolo Pasolini is bludgeoned to death by a boy prostitute, near Rome (1975, Nov. 22).

Paddy Chayefsky: *Network* (1976).

MUSIC—NON-CLASSICAL

Cole Porter: "Ev'ry Time We Say Goodbye (I Die a Little)" (1944).

Burton Lane and Alan Jay Lerner: *On a Clear Day You Can See Forever* (1965).

TV, ETC.

Johnny Carson threatens to leave the "Tonight" show (1979) and the effect is to cast doubt on the profitability of his employers, the NBC network. Carson currently works only three nights per week, earning an astronomic income. At **36**, Carson had become host on the "Tonight" show, replacing Jack Paar, who held the position from **39–44**, and whose public career seems to have ended on leaving "Tonight." Now at **53** Carson gains a new contract under which he will receive $5,000,000 per year. His program goes out late at night, and he has described it as "NBC's answer to foreplay." Johnny Carson's assistant is Ed McMahon (**39**, at the start in 1962) who introduces him every night. McMahon is not ashamed to say that his later success is due to his working on the show—"Everything I do stems from my fifteen-year relationship with Johnny Carson." Ed McMahon got his big break when he attended a party and became the unofficial master-of-ceremonies; unknown to him, one of the guests is a TV producer, who immediately introduces him to Johnny Carson.

Alfred C. Kinsey: *Sexual Behavior of the Human Male* (1948); this is a landmark study of sexuality. Kinsey had first come upon this topic at **44** when he was a professor researching wasps. He was asked to become faculty adviser to a noncredit course on marriage, and he went to the library to check out the literature on human sexuality. He was surprised to find nothing descriptive and systematic. In the first year of the course, he has each student write out a straight description of their sex life. At **45**, he realizes that he has chanced upon a highly innovative topic, and the "sex history" becomes the core of his approach. After this book at **53**, he begins work on *Sexual Behavior of the Human Female,* published at **59**. The next generation of sex research is exemplified by *Human Sexual Response* (1966), by William Masters (**50**) and Virginia Johnson (**41**). Masters had begun this phase of his life at **38**; and at **39** he met Johnson (**30**). Another important text is published when they are **54** and **45**; they marry in the following year.

PRESS

Johann Gutenberg now has a print shop, and has completed his invention (c.1450) of movable type in printing. Previously he had trained as a goldsmith. Not much is known about Gutenberg. The first English language book to be printed is by William Caxton (**50**, in 1475)—he had left London at about **17**, and had been a businessman in Bruges, then a leading commercial center. Caxton begins his new career in book publishing at about **48**, and is famous not only for printing but also for his imagination as a publisher. Two other printing inventions are: Linotype, by O. Mergenthaler (**30**); and the first rotary press by R. Hoe (**34**).

LAW

Dr. Joseph-Ignace Guillotine promotes the use of a machine for performing executions—the "guillotine." The detailed design is by Dr. Antoine Louis (**69**), and the first execution is performed in 1792. The executioner, Charles Henri Sanson, is also **53**. The machine is a huge success—80 are constructed at once, and 160 executioners are trained throughout France. Executions tend to be performed regardless of age; in 1793, four victims are **14**, **14**, **13**, and **13**. Dr. Guillotine himself dies from a carbuncle on his shoulder, at **76**.

SPORTS

Bill Tilden (1946): having turned professional at **37**, after a career as the leading U.S. tennis player (cf. **27***), he works as a coach in Los Angeles. He gains pleasure from illicit relationships with "a harem of ballboys," and is convicted for an offense with a boy of **14**. He now goes to prison. He is disgraced, and shunned by the public. Even his old university, the University of Pennsylvania, destroys all records of his membership in the Alumni Club. He is unable to earn any money, and dies at **60**, broke and forgotten.

54

HEALTH

Henry J. Heimlich: the Heimlich maneuver, to save the life of someone who is choking to death on a piece of food (1974). Previously, the leading authority has been Samuel D. Gross (**49**), who wrote a treatise on the subject in 1854. Heimlich develops his idea after focusing on the problem at **53**.

HISTORY—WORLD

Idi Amin: end of his rule in Uganda (1979). He had seized power at **45**. Previously, at **21**, he had joined the King's African Rifles, and become a corporal at **24**. As President, he had begun expelling Asians, the economic elite, when he was **47**. At **51**, he made himself President-for-Life. During his presidency, his "State Research Bureau" and "Public Safety Unit" have killed between 300,000 and 500,000 people, out of a total population of about 11 million. Afterward, Amin is briefly succeeded by Yusufu Yule, a psychiatrist of **67**.

HISTORY—U.S.A.

Spiro T. Agnew is forced to resign as Vice-President (1973, Oct. 10), owing to corruption while in office.

HISTORY—U.K.

Elizabeth I: defeat of the Spanish Armada (Aug. 1588). Lord Howard of Effingham is **52**, and Sir Francis Drake is about **48**.

The Duke of Marlborough wins the Battle of Blenheim (1704, Aug. 13); and Ramillies (**56**), Oudenarde (**58**), and Malplaquet (**59**). He lives till **72**.

RELIGION, PHILOSOPHY

Mary Baker Eddy: *Science and Health* (1875). She opens her first Christian Science church at **58**, and lives until **89**. She starts the *Christian Science Monitor* at **88**.

SOCIAL SCIENCE, EDUCATION

Ivan Pavlov: *Experimental Psychology and Psychopathology in Animals* (1903), on the concept of the conditioned reflex—a basic text in behavioral psychology.

Émile Durkheim: *The Elementary Forms of Religious Life* (1912).

Edmund Husserl: *Ideas: General Introduction to Pure Phenomenology* (1913).

Eric Berne: *Games People Play* (1964).

SCIENCE, TECHNOLOGY

Friedrich Bessel: the first use of the concept "light year," as a measure of distance in astronomy (1838).

J. A. Fleming: invention of the rectifier, or valve/tube (1904). He has been working in electrical engineering for the whole of his adult life.

John Wheeler: *Gravitational Collapse* (1965)—this book publicizes the term "black holes," in astronomy.

Paul MacCready: "Gossamer Penguin," the first solar-powered airplane (1980).

ARCHITECTURE

Jacopo Sansovino: the library of St. Mark's, Venice: (1540).

Baron Haussmann is appointed prefect of the Seine département (1853–70), and he sets about organizing the characteristic wide boulevards of Paris.

Cass Gilbert: Woolworth building, New York City (1913)—the outstanding Gothic-style skyscraper.

Lucio Costa wins the competition for the masterplan of the new city of Brasilia (1956).

James Stirling: projects for the Fogg Museum, Cambridge, Massachusetts, for Bayer Laboratories; and for a science center in Berlin (1980). These are all in his new quasi-classical style, and form a second peak in his career. His first major impact had been with a high technology style, exemplified in his collaboration on Leicester University science building, at **33**, and Cambridge University history block at **38**. Stirling comments on his own output: "I've been accused of having created only five building types; well, that's three more than Mies and five more than Gropius."

Paul Gauguin dies at Atuana on the island of Hiva Oa, in the Marquesas, in the Pacific (1903). He is in debt and not well known. The local Catholic bishop writes about him: ". . . the sudden death of a contemptible individual named Gauguin, a reputed artist but an enemy of God and of everything that is decent."

Abby Aldrich Rockefeller, and others: the Museum of Modern Art, New York (1929).

LITERATURE

Sir Walter Scott loses £130,000 in the failure of a publisher and printer in which he had invested (1826, Jan. 17), but he writes more than ever, in an attempt to pay off the debt. He had finished the main building of his Scottish baronial home, "Abbotsford" at **52**, and he dies at **61**.

Theodore Dreiser: *An American Tragedy* (1925); he had written *Sister Carrie* at **29**.

John Betjeman: *Summoned by Bells* (1960)—his autobiography in verse.

Robert A. Heinlein: *Stranger in a Strange Land* (1961); and *The Moon Is a Harsh Mistress* at **58**.

Richard Adams resigns as assistant secretary, the Department of the Environment, in London (1974), his senior civil service post—two years previously, he has published *Watership Down*.

PLAYS, DANCE

Sarah Bernhardt plays the title role in *Hamlet* (1899).

FILMS

Charlie Chaplin marries (1943, June 16) Oona O'Neill (**18**), daughter of playwright Eugene O'Neill (**55**). Mr. and Mrs. Chaplin subsequently have eight children.

Fred Astaire: *The Band Wagon* (1953).

Walt Disney opens Disneyland (1955).

Cary Grant takes LSD for the first time, given to him by a psychiatrist (1958). "I have just been born again," he says.

Billy Wilder: *The Apartment* (1960), with Jack Lemmon (**35**) and Shirley MacLaine (**26**).

Groucho Marx, and others: *Love Happy* (1959). This is the last Marx Brothers film. At **56**, he moves into TV quiz shows, and starts a new career. At **58**, he marries Eden Hartford (**24**). This marriage breaks up at **74**, and he meets Erin Fleming (**39**). She helps him start on a third career—one-man stage shows. This is another success, until shortly before his death at around **81**.

James Stewart: *The Man Who Shot Liberty Valance* (1962).

Bette Davis and Joan Crawford (also **54**): *Whatever Happened to Baby Jane?* (1962).

David Lean: *Lawrence of Arabia* (1962), with Peter O'Toole (**30**) and Alec Guinness (**48**).

Joseph Losey: *The Servant* (1963), with Dirk Bogarde (**42**), and screenplay by Harold Pinter (**33**).

Ingmar Bergman: *Cries and Whispers* (1972).

Paul Newman is one of the three drivers of the car which comes in second in the Le Mans 24-hour race (1979). This is his first attempt at the race. Earlier, in his **20**s, he had been a stage and TV actor. His film breakthrough was at **30** in *Somebody Up There Likes Me.* His best-known work includes *Hud* at **38**, and *Butch Cassidy and the Sundance Kid* at **44**, with Robert Redford (**32**).

MUSIC—NON-CLASSICAL

Irving Berlin now creates the best-selling song of all time, ("I'm Dreaming of a White Christmas"); this goes on to sell 113 million single records. Berlin writes *Annie Get Your Gun* at **58**, and *Call Me Madam* at **62**. His first major score has been at **26**, and he has been producing memorable work continuously since then.

TV, ETC.

Benny Hill, in 1979, becomes a minor cult figure on U.S. television; he is notable for unashamedly staring at girls (**18–25**). Hill's programs are now being run twice nightly on a New York TV channel.

LOVE, LIFE

Gloria Vanderbilt: start of her "designer jeans" empire (1978).

EXPLORATION

Joshua Slocum completes the first-ever solo sailing trip around the world (1895–98). At **65**, he sets sail again on another long voyage, but he is lost and is never seen again.

LAW

Adolf Eichmann is captured while getting off the bus (1960) after a day in the Buenos Aires car factory where he works as a foreman. He is taken to Israel where he is tried and executed. Between **34** and **39**, he had been in charge of the extermination of six million Jews. At the end of World War II, he is briefly held under false names, but escapes capture. He works for three years as a forester in Germany, before traveling to Argentina, under the auspices of the ODESSA network.

Congressman John M. Murphy is found guilty of conspiracy, after being photographed accepting bribes during the "Abscam" operation

(1980). Other Abscam guilty verdicts affect Congressman Frank Thompson (**62**), U.S. Senator Harrison A. Williams, Jr. (**61**) and Alexander Feinberg (**73**). The latter two hoped to gain $12.6 million from help with a government contract for military hardware.

SPORTS

Walter F. O'Malley (baseball, 1958): as owner of the Dodgers, he moves the team from Brooklyn to Los Angeles. He had acquired the team at **46**, and relinquishes command at **66**. This move at **54** brings huge crowds to Dodger games, and makes him the sport's best-known owner.

Betty Cook (1977): world champion in offshore powerboat racing. In 1978, a survey of this sport listed the age of leading competitors, including Don Aronow (**50**) of Florida; and Derek Pobjoy (**42**), Ken Cassir (**42**), and Tim Powell (**40**) of Britain.

John Thorne (horseracing, 1981): he rides the horse that comes in second in the Aintree Grand National. Amazingly, he also bred the horse and trained it.

55

HEALTH

Theodore Tuffier: first operation on the aortic valve (1912).

HISTORY—WORLD

Otto von Bismarck: unification of the German states (1871), under a new German emperor.

Mao Tse-tung: formation of the People's Republic of China (1949). He has been a guerilla fighter since **33***. Chou En-lai is now **51**. At **62**, Mao organizes the campaign for "Let a Hundred Flowers Bloom"; at **64**, the Great Leap Forward; and between **72–75***, the Red Guards and the Cultural Revolution.

Robert Mugabe: first Prime Minister of Zimbabwe (1980).

HISTORY—U.S.A.

George Washington, in 1787, is a landowner in Virginia. At **51** he had left his position as head of the revolutionary forces, and he is now again developing his Mt. Vernon estate, of 3,250 acres. Washington is careful and innovative, though facing considerable difficulties in farming. He returns to the national scene when, toward the end of **55**, he attends the Constitutional Convention. As the former commander in chief, he is the most conspicuous and admired member, and he becomes the presiding officer. After the adoption of the resultant constitution, Washington becomes the first-ever President, and takes office at **57**, working in New York and later in Philadelphia; in the same year, **57**, his mother (**81**) dies. At **58**, he chooses the site of the new Federal capital. At **59**, the Bank of the United States is floated, and the capital city's plan is adopted. Washington is reelected at **60**, and serves until **65***.

Abraham Lincoln, in 1864: he wins reelection as President. At **56**, the Civil War ends with the surrender of Robert E. Lee (**58**). But Lincoln is shot at **56**, by John Wilkes Booth (**26**), during a performance of *Our American Cousin* by Tom Taylor (**41**, 1858).

Lyndon Johnson, in 1963, moves from Vice-President to President, and wins the office by election at **56**. But his war policy in Vietnam reaches a climax at **59***.

Ronald Reagan, in 1966, campaigns to become Governor of California. His opponent is Pat Brown (**61**) and Reagan's campaign consists of giving the same speech up and down the state—cynical newsmen say that this is the same speech that he gave in support of Barry Goldwater (**55**) at **53**, which itself may have been the same speech that he gave in General Electric factories at **43–51**. Reagan wins the election, and goes on to become a fair, nonextremist, and respected governor. He leaves office after two four-year terms. He then attempts to enter presidential politics, but fails at **65***.

Richard Nixon, in 1968: elected President of the United States. At **59**, he visits China, where he meets Chairman Mao (**79**). But the Watergate break-in occurs during his reelection campaign, also at **59***.

Jimmy Carter continues as President (1979). But he loses his reelection campaign at **56**, and retires home to Georgia.

Warren M. Christopher: negotiations to free U.S. hostages at the Teheran embassy (1981). The hostages themselves range from **20** to **64**.

HISTORY—U.K.

General Montgomery: the Battle of El Alamein (Oct. 1942). His defeated opponent is Erwin Rommel (**51**).

Enoch Powell visits the U.S.A. for the first time (1967), and is said to be horrified by the hatred shown between different races over color. He decides that integration of the races is one of the great myths of our time. A few months later, he is both a hero and a villain for his "rivers of blood" speech (1968, Apr. 20), saying that nonwhite immigration into Britain should be curtailed. He now loses his cabinet-level position in the Conservative party. Through his early **50**s, Powell seems to attempt to systematically knock conventional thinking—he attacks the Commonwealth as a delusion, and he is the earliest public figure to take up monetarism. But until **55**, he is not very well known; his anti-immigration speech transforms him into perhaps the most famous individual at the time.

The average age of the British cabinet (Nov. 1978) is **55**—ranging from **40** to **69**.

Eligibility: All ranks in the Army, Navy, and Air Force must now retire. If you have an Army pension, you are now old enough to become a Chelsea pensioner.

SOCIAL SCIENCE, EDUCATION

Alfred Adler: first use of the term "inferiority complex" (1925).

Kurt Hahn: opening of the first "Outward Bound" course (1941). The first Outward Bound in the U.S.A. is opened when he is **75**.

Roman Jakobson, with others: *Preliminaries to Speech Analysis* (1952).

SCIENCE, TECHNOLOGY

Alessandro Volta: invention of the electric battery (1800)—he began experiments on this subject at **51**, having worked in electricity since **18**.

Rachel Carson: *Silent Spring* (1962), a leading book in the revival of interest in ecology. After receiving numerous awards, and after seeing that she has changed the consciousness of the world, she dies two years later.

MONEY, WORK

J. Pierpont Morgan creates four gigantic corporations over the next ten years (1892–1902), by a process of mergers and rationalization. They are General Electric, American Telephone and Telegraph, International Harvester, and United States Steel. (cf. **64***)

Roger B. Smith: chairman of General Motors (1981); he succeeds Thomas A. Murphy who has reached the mandatory retiring age of **65**. The new chief executive of NBC is Grant Tinker (also **55**, in 1981).

MUSIC—CLASSICAL

Clifford Curzon, the pianist, later says, "I was still taking lessons from (Artur) Schnabel well into my **50**s. There is nothing more exciting than a lesson."

LITERATURE

Charles Dickens makes his second reading tour of the U.S.A. (1867–68).

Emily Dickinson dies (1886, May 15), and her sister is amazed to find a locked box containing over 1,000 poems. Though the two sisters had lived in the same house all their lives, the sister knows almost nothing about the poems—only four were published during the poet's lifetime. The major years of her secret creativity were about **28** to **35**, though she continued to write for the rest of her life.

Another secret poet is Andrew Marvell (d. **57**, 1678) who is a prolific publisher on political questions during his lifetime and is a member of Parliament. His serious verse is completely unknown to his contemporaries, and it is published two years after his death by his housekeeper. The real impact of his work is delayed until the year when he would have been **300**, when T. S. Eliot (1888–1965) holds him up as a great example of the Metaphysical poets. Marvell is perhaps best remembered for the poem "To His Coy Mistress," and for the lines "But at my back I always hear/Time's winged chariot hurrying near." Coincidentally, the best-known poems of John Donne (1572–1631) are never shown to his contemporaries; he believed, not unreasonably, that publication would hinder his career within the established church.

T. S. Eliot completes the last of the "Four Quartets" (1943) which he had begun around **46**. This is the end of his poetry writing, but he has already written two plays, and later writes three more. (cf. **68***)

Aleksandr Solzhenitsyn completes volume two of *The Gulag Archipelago* (1974), and is expelled from the U.S.S.R.

Alex Haley publishes *Roots* (1976) which he had begun around **43**. He had established himself with *The Autobiography of Malcolm X* at **44**; until **38**, he had worked in the U.S. Coast Guard.

FILMS

Buster Keaton comes out of retirement for a guest appearance in *Sunset Boulevard* (1950). At **57**, he has a similar spot in *Limelight.* Keaton had made his last feature at **33**.

Alfred Hitchcock: *Rear Window* (1954), with Grace Kelly (**26**).

George Cukor: *A Star Is Born* (1954), with Judy Garland (**32**).

Cary Grant: *North by Northwest* (1959).

John Huston: *The Misfits* (1961).

Antonioni: *Blow-Up* (1967).

Don Siegel: director, *Coogan's Bluff* (1968), starring Clint Eastwood (**38**). This is the start of a successful partnership, and they go on to make such films as *Dirty Harry* when Siegel is **58**.

MUSIC—NON-CLASSICAL

Sidney Bechet: "Petite Fleur" (1952).

Lee Marvin, in 1979: a court ruling by Judge Arthur Marshall (**57**) orders him to pay $104,000 to his former unmarried live-in lover, Michelle Triola Marvin (**46**). She has sued him for $1.3 million, as her share of his earnings while they had a relationship for five years. Michelle Triola is represented by Marvin Mitchelson (**50**) who asks the court for $.5 million, in legal fees. Soon afterward, Mitchelson advises Soraya Khashoggi (**33**) to sue for $2 billion from her former husband, Adnan Khashoggi (**43**), the arms dealer and businessman. Soraya Khashoggi at **15** had won a newspaper competition for a trip to Paris from her obscure home town. In Paris, she met Khashoggi, and married shortly afterward.

About 15 percent of arrests for drunkenness are of people in their **50**s (U.S., 1977).

SPORTS

Bobby Riggs (1973) challenges Margaret Court (**31**) to a tennis match, so that he may invalidate the claims of Women's Lib. Court is currently holder of both the U.S. and French women's singles titles. Riggs wins, 6–2, 6–1. He goes on to play Billie Jean King (**29**), in a contest at the Houston Astrodome, before a TV audience of about 50 million people. Riggs loses, 6–3, 6–3. At **21**, he had won the men's singles at both Wimbledon and Forest Hills, and he had been a professional since **23**.

DEFINITIONS

AGE: [1] **chronological age:** the years-months-days since the moment of birth (cf. Social Sciences, **0***); [2] **biological age:** the same; [3] **calendar age:** the same; [4] **functional age:** physical, mental, sexual, or social ages; how one aspect of you has matured relative to the norm; you may have a reading age of **13**, and a swimming age of **9**; one research team has found 137 functional ages; [5] **perceived age:** how old you see yourself—often there are significant leads or lags between your chronological age and this perceived or [6] **psychological age;** [7] **visual age:** how old you look to others; [8] **professional age:** the years since you adopted your career and meaning in life; for example, Charles Darwin (**22***, in 1831), when about to commit himself to work as a naturalist, wrote: "My second life will then commence and it shall be as a birthday for the rest of my life"; this is analogous to the years since you became a born-again Christian or had some similar change; [9] **bone age:** estimating the chronological age from changes in teeth or bones.

AGE-CONSCIOUSNESS: attaching importance to age, by favoring one age range as the source of power, wisdom, or vitality.

AGE DECREMENT: in statistics, the extent to which performance deteriorates with age.

AGE-IRRELEVANT SOCIETY: an exaggerated view in which age ceases to have meaning. In its less extreme form, the concept is an attempt to separate (1) the inevitable facets of aging, or the journey toward death, from (2) events which are culturally linked to aging, such as entry to undergraduate study at **18–20**.

AGE OF MAJORITY: the age at which you cease to be restricted legally on the basis of age; typically, many age rules in a society cease to apply at one age (usually **18** or **21**); but there are variations, so that, for example, the MEDICAL AGE OF MAJORITY may well be younger, and you can make decisions about operations, abortions, and so on, without reference to any other ADULT.

AGE RULES: determining eligibility on the basis of age.

AGE-SET: in anthropology, people of the same age who form a group. For many writers, AGE-SET, AGE-CLASS, and AGE-GROUP are virtually interchangeable terms. You join an age-set, and move with it through society. Members of an age-set belong to a defined age-range; they can belong to only one set; an age-set cannot overlap with another; there is a sequence of age-sets, from junior to senior; members cannot resign from their age-set unless they leave the entire society. Members of the set, AGE-MATES, typically have comradely feelings toward each other, and provide help to one another. The age-set is typically given a name—perhaps that of one of its members; in classical Greece, the age-sets were named after (EPONYMOUS with) the archon, chief magistrate, at the time of the set's inception. An **AGE-GRADE** is a position and status in society, based on age. An age-grade system includes a sequence of grades, though which individuals move; you belong to only one grade at a time; when you leave one grade, you automatically enter the next. Members of an age-grade share tasks, behavioral styles, and privileges. The difference between the age-set and the age-grade is analogous to university life; the class/SET/group of 1985 moves through the GRADES of freshman, sophomore, junior, senior. TRANSITION RULES govern your movement from one grade to the next; RITES OF PASSAGE mark this transition. An age-graded society typically has an elite grade, the ruling generation, who are not always the very oldest, and who exercise the chief political functions. It is possible for the age-grades to cover only a part of the total life span; adolescence is a suitable subject for age-grading. In primitive societies, women were often less represented in age-grade systems, probably because the basic events in their life, for example, childbearing, were so graphic as not to need any other focus. Age-grading is a horizontal grouping in society, and it balances the vertical groupings of family connections.

AGE-SPECIFIC: statistics include age as a variable.

AGED: either seen positively, as in wine that has been aged in wood, acquiring maturity, patina, and so on; or seen negatively, aged, exhausted, worn out.

AGIST, AGISM: prejudiced, and denying opportunities/rewards to people on account of their age; believing that age in itself limits abilities and attractiveness.

ANNUS MIRABILIS: one year in which a lifetime's achievements are performed; for example, Newton at **23***, or Einstein at **26***.

CAREER ORIENTED, versus WORK ORIENTED: the former see the career as central to their identity, and the latter see work instrumentally, for example, to make money in order to pursue a leisure interest which gives a sense of identity.

CAREER MATURITY: knowledgeable and decisive about actions affecting career choice; CAREER IMMATURITY: confused and ignorant about career decisions, options, and alternative payoffs.

CLIMACTERIC: in classical Greek theory, the person undergoes profound changes of life at **7**, **21**, **49**, **63**, and **81**. Ages **63** and sometimes **81** are seen as GRAND CLIMACTERICS. There is an adjective to describe these years, CLIMACTERICAL. These years were designed on the basis of combinations of the numbers three and seven. Alkmaion, a disciple of Pythagoras (580–500 B.C.) listed seven ages, each seven years long; **49+** was the final stage. In China and Japan, rites were performed at **3**, **5**, and **7**, on the basis that odd numbers are positive numbers. In Japan today, **7** still marks the beginning of emergence into the adult world; years of danger are **25**, **42**, and **61**, for men, and **19**, **33**, and **37** for women. Unusually worrying years are **33**, for women, and **42**, for men. The end of worry occurs at **61** and **77**. The same attention to specific years also applies in Japan when you are dead; the key years are the first, third, seventh, thirteenth, twenty-third, twenty-seventh, and thirty-third anniversaries of your death—and also the one hundredth.

COUP DE VIEUX: suddenly becoming old and decrepit.

CRITICAL PERIODS: the age at which you may be most susceptible to learning a certain skill.

DECRUITMENT: almost the opposite to recruitment—toward the end of a career, the individual stays in the organization, but gradually moves down from their high position.

DEMOGRAPHICS: statistics of birth, marriage, disease, and death. EPIDEMIOLOGY is the science of inferring causal models about disease, often from such statistics.

DEVELOPMENTAL PSYCHOLOGY: the behavioral science whose subject is the changes in the early years of life; and also at the end of life, and perhaps in the middle years.

DISENGAGEMENT THESIS: that old age consists of contentedly disengaging from this world and its ties, until no ties remain at the moment of death. The opposite thesis may well be an "activity" approach, that activity perpetuates liveliness. In practice, it is likely that old people illustrate numerous theses.

DYING TRAJECTORY: dying. There is also END-STAGE.

EARLY RETIREMENT: is at **40–50** (the military and the police). VERY EARLY RETIREMENT is in the **mid-30**s or earlier (rock stars and ballerinas. (cf. **35***)

EMBRYO: in the first four weeks after CONCEPTION; then you become a FETUS, until birth, becoming a NEONATE, and being NEONATAL. The first, second, and third TRIMESTERS are three-month periods of PREGNANCY or GESTATION.

FERTILITY RATIO: the number of babies born to the average woman in her lifetime. The FERTILITY RATE is the number of babies born in a given year, divided by the number of women of fertile age, usually assumed to be **15–49**. The BIRTH RATE is the number of births, divided by the total population.

FIXATION: not fully moving through the stages of development, but remaining fascinated by, or attached to, or FIXATED on, an object from a previous stage.

FLEXILIFE: a general purpose word to describe alternatives to one-life/one-career; analogous to FLEXITIME, in which you contribute a set amount of production at any time within your life span.

GENERATION: either a group of people who are roughly of the same age, the "baby boom generation", or a COHORT; or, an age group who have been subject to the same formative experience, such as the "Lost Generation," after World War I; or, more ambitiously, generation has been used as a major explanation of historical change, whereby generational consciousness may be as powerful as, say, class consciousness. Organizations can have age-classes, differentiated not by their members' chronological age but by their year of entry into the organization; for example, you joined during the pioneer days, and thus form part of a generation.

GENERATIVITY: in Erik Erikson, the extent to which you still desire to produce children, or to produce public works.

GEROKAMY: for an old person to lie with a younger person, so that the elder will absorb some of the younger's YOUTHFUL vigor. (cf. Health, **100***)

GERONTOCRACY: political or economic power is held by only the elders of society. In a full gerontocracy, power is due to the elders, the bulls, because they have a sacred aura, associated with the basic identity of the society. Gerontocracy is often associated with POLYGYNY, whereby powerful older men can continue to acquire wives as they get older. A certain stability in society is associated with gerontocracy since everyone can look forward to a period in the elite group, as long as they merely survive; and gerontocracy balances nature, by providing increasing distinction as people become physically weaker through age.

GERONTOLOGY: the study of old people in all aspects; GERIATRICS deals only with the medical side.

GERONTOPHOBIA: hatred of the old.

HUBRIS: success leads the individual to believe that he or she is now beyond the rules that govern ordinary people.

IMPRINTING: a thing or living object is seen when you are young, and it is forever fixed in your mind.

INFANT: **0–3**; and CHILD, **4–10**.

IQ: ratio of mental age divided by chronological age; and the DQ is the developmental age over the chronological age.

JOB SHARING: two or more people share the same job. In WORK SHARING, a set amount of work is divided among the people available, even if no individual thus works full-time.

LATE START: your achievements begin when your peers are retiring; the LATE, LATE START occurs when your peers are dying.

LIFE CRISIS: two or more of the fundamentals of your life—love, career, finances—fall apart at the same time; being forced to make changes, either by breaking out of the circumstances which limit you, or by adjusting your expectations.

LIFE CYCLE: seeing your life in broad stages which are defined by such fundamentals as birth, marriage, and death; or, technically, the stages from conception to reproductive capacity.

LIFE PATTERN: alternative models of the shape of your life; a CAREER PATTERN is an alternative shape for your career.

LIFE TABLE: shows the number of people who, starting with a group of 100,000 at **0**, are SURVIVORS to various ages. From this can be found the MORTALITY RATE at any age; and the average number of years to be lived by people at any age, the EXPECTATION OF LIFE. Since health standards can change dramatically during a lifetime, it is important to note the COHORT to which the life expectancy figure applies.

MANPOWER PLANNING: in an organization or society, planning that there is a sufficient flow of appropriate personnel into all levels of work, over the next decade or more; manpower planning contains conscious and unconscious models of its subjects' career and life patterns.

MEDIAN EXPECTATION OF LIFE: age at which half of a population group has died.

MORATORIUM: a period of life in which society leaves you alone for exploration, without your having to enter into any lifelong commitments (Erikson).

MORTALITY: the propensity to death; and MORBIDITY, the propensity to illness. NEONATAL MORTALITY: deaths within the first four weeks after birth; and INFANT MORTALITY, deaths within the first year of birth. The PERINATAL DEATH RATE is the number of deaths between the seventh month of pregnancy and the first week after birth, per 1,000 live births, per year. A STILLBIRTH is born after the twenty-eighth week of pregnancy, and is not breathing.

MOZART'S FATHER: giving up a good career, to help an infant genius.

NYMPHET: preteen girl admired by Humbert Humbert. (cf. Literature, **37***)

OLD: the YOUNG OLD versus the FRAIL OLD—the latter implies that only a fraction of the old are functionally old; there are also YOUNG OLD, MIDDLE OLD, and the OLD OLD.

OMNIPOTENCE: in children and infants, the sensation that the world is organized entirely for your benefit; gradually REALITY intervenes.

PEAK AGE: in a sport, the age range at which the absolute top performance is achieved; before and after the peak age, sporting fixtures may be organized in prepeak (novice, futures) or postpeak (veterans) age groupings. (cf. Sports, **35***)

PEDOPHILIA, and GERONTOPHILIA: the loving, or lusting after, those who are much younger or much older than yourself.

PETER PRINCIPLE: in an organization, rising to just above your level of competence.

PRODIGY: originally a portent or a monster; now, a person who is amazingly skilled, relative to their age; thus, INFANT PRODIGY, or a PRODIGY OF OLD AGE.

PSYCHOHISTORY: the application of psychology to history and biography; for example, why the psychological conflicts of one person match those of an entire community, and so produce the leader of the people.

PUBERTY: the physical changes from child to adult; ADOLESCENCE: the social and emotional changes that result from puberty.

REGRESSION: moving back to an earlier stage of life; as a defense, you move back to a stage which you did not sufficiently work through at the time.

RITES OF PASSAGE: ceremonies to mark your entry into the next stage of life.

SENIORITY SYSTEM: in organizations, you rise in power, influence, and reward as you become older; such as in traditional Japanese companies.

SETTLING DOWN: an adjustment, seen positively; and SETTLE FOR, an adjustment, seen negatively.

STAGES, in Freud: oral, anal, genital; with early and late variations; and with Oedipal and latent, before the mature stage of genital.

STAGES, in Erik Erikson: (1) trust, versus mistrust; (2) autonomy, versus shame and doubt; (3) initiative, versus guilt; (4) industry, versus inferiority; (5) identity, versus role diffusion (adolescence); (6) intimacy, versus isolation (the prime of life); (7) generativity, versus stagnation (middle age); (8) ego integrity, versus despair (old age).

STAGES of life according to Paolo Zachia (1584–1659), the medical expert at the Court of Rota, Rome: *infantia; pueritia; pubertas; juventus; virilitas; senectus;* and *decrepitas.* In this system, "senectus" begins at **60**, and retirement for public officials is at **70**.

STAGES of musical life, according to the critic, Bernard Levin. First, Beethoven; then, Wagner; then, Schubert and Mozart. With Beethoven, your affections start with the symphonies and move to the (late) quartets; and there is also the move from the concertos to the sonatas. With Wagner, you move from *Tristan, Lohengrin,* and *Parsifal*, towards *The Mastersingers*. At last, permanent love is felt towards Mozart—"All life is a progress towards Mozart."

STROKE: an interruption to the supply of blood to the brain, caused by a hemorrhage or clot; CORONARY THROMBOSIS is a stoppage in the supply of blood to the heart muscle, and is caused by a clot in an artery around the heart. ARTERIOSCLEROSIS is loss of ability to deliver oxygen to the brain.

TERMINALLY ILL: dying. THANATOLOGY is the study of death and dying.

THIRD AGE: in France, the old; and FOURTH AGE, the old who are unable to look after themselves, the FRAIL OLD.

TRACKING: a whole society may be organized so that your freedom is minimal to change the direction of your life. Labeling, caste, and class can help to achieve this, but so can more recent developments such as manpower planning. In a highly tracked society, you are allocated to your track early in your life—at birth, at school, or at entry into university. In an apparently meritocratic society, a small extra increment of talent or effort early in life can be built up into an overwhelming advantage by middle age; early performance is the basis of the track allocated to you, and so has leverage over the rest of your life.

TRANSITIONS: the change to the next stage of life. Transitions appear to be fixed to those to whom they apply. But over long periods of time, transitions (retirement) can be moved backward or forward, to accommodate bulges or deficiencies in the population. Transitions can also be scrapped as no longer significant, and other transitions can be created (—from the researcher Daniel J. Levinson).

The words for people nearly always have an age connotation. Sometimes such a word can be flattering or insulting, depending on the relative age of the speaker and the person described. KID or GIRL may seem friendly to someone of the same age, but insulting if used by a much older person. You may happen to be a CHILD, but you do not want to be called CHILDISH: Similarly with SOPHOMORE and SOPHOMORIC.

Words for children include BABIES, BABES, INFANTS, WEE BAIRNS, BAMBINO, and those OF TENDER YEARS.

Next we find TEENAGERS, TEENS, KIDS, GUYS, GALS, BOYS, GIRLS, TEENYBOPPERS, and FELLAS; also, THE LADS.

After, or during, the PRIME OF LIFE, we come upon the MIDDLE AGED, who are either **43+**, or people of an overly settled attitude. You are ON THE WRONG SIDE OF **40**. Now is the time to change from MADEMOISELLE to MADAME, whether you are married or not. But you should avoid being PREMATURELY MIDDLE AGED.

Somewhere before old age there is the GOOD OL' BOY, which is similar to the French VIEUX GARÇON, later followed by the VIEUX GAGA. Afterward, we enter the world of the OLD, the OLD FOLK, those who are OVER THE HILL, the OLD FOGIES, and the GRAYBEARDS. Such people can be found in retirement homes, or sunset communities, or rest homes, or just "homes" of one kind or another. Now is the time to accept that YOU'RE NO SPRING CHICKEN. Be a SENIOR CITIZEN. With any luck, you won't end up a SHOPPING BAG LADY, or an 800, as unfortunates are known to the police. Don't get OUT OF THE SWIM or ON THE SHELF. You may already be OF A CERTAIN AGE.

Job descriptions can have an age feeling to them. Jockeys are always called BOY in America, however old they are; and LAD is a stable helper of any age. GARÇON is a French waiter of any age; and sometimes you hear of the OFFICE GIRLS, including the GIRL FRIDAY. It may be significant that a PERSON FRIDAY has fewer overtones.

In reading through this list, it is surprising how many age-related words can have an unpleasant tinge to them. Clearly there are pressures to keep to our age-related slots in society. So, any attempt to move out of an age-related, or age-stigmatized, role will have to be pursued with cunning and vigor.

56

HISTORY—WORLD

Julius Caesar: death (44 B.C.). Having become excessively powerful as head of state, he is assassinated on the Ides of March, by Marcus Brutus (**42**) and Cassius. Later, Caesar is deified, and Brutus kills himself at **43**, after losing a battle.

Adolf Hitler: suicide (1945, Apr. 30). At this moment, Mussolini has just died at **61**, Goering is **52** and kills himself at **53**; Rommel has recently been forced to kill himself at **52**; Goebbels now commits suicide at **47**; Willy Messerschmitt is **47**; Eva Braun is **33**, and she also commits suicide. The war had begun (1939, Sept. 1), when Lieutenant Adolf Galland (**27**) flew from Germany to Poland, and began the blitzkrieg there.

Admiral Yamamoto: the Japanese attack on Pearl Harbor (1941). At **57**, he loses the Battle of Midway, and is killed by American forces at **58**. Paradoxically, Yamamoto always had a clear idea that the industrial power of the U.S.A. would eventually defeat Japan. He justifies his actions by saying, "I am the sword of my Emperor (**40**)."

HISTORY—U.S.A.

Robert E. Lee narrowly loses the Battle of Gettysburg (1863, July 1–3), to General G. G. Meade (**47**).

At the end of World War II (1945), Douglas MacArthur is **65**; George C. Marshall **64**; Franklin D. Roosevelt had died shortly before, at **63**; President Truman celebrates his **61**st birthday; George S. Patton is **59**; Dwight D. Eisenhower is **56**, and Adolf Hitler had just killed himself, also at **56**; Omar Bradley is **52**. Richard Nixon is **32**, serving in the U.S. Navy in the Pacific—he leaves at **33** with the rank of lieutenant commander; John F. Kennedy is **27**; Jimmy Carter is **20**, and at the U.S. Naval Academy, Annapolis.

Alexander Haig: Secretary of State (1981). Almost all the cabinet-level appointments of the new administration are in their **50**s only, with the exception of the Director of the CIA, William Casey (**67**) and the Director of the Office of Management and Budget, David Stockman (**34**)—and also with the exception of the President, Ronald Reagan (**69***). Also, James Watt (**43**) becomes Secretary of the Interior.

HISTORY—U.K.

At the end of World War II (VE Day, 1945, May 8), Adolf Hitler had just died at **56**. Winston Churchill is **70**; Sir Hugh Trenchard is **72**; Lord Beaverbrook **65**; General Alan Brooke **62**; Clement Atlee also **62**; Admiral Andrew Cunningham also **62**; Professor Henry Tizard **60**; Professor Frederick Lindemann **59**; General Montgomery **57**; Ernest Bevin **56**; Arthur Tedder **55**; Dame Myra Hess also **55**; General William Slim **54**; "Bomber" Harris **53**; Robert Watson-Watt also **53**; Sir Charles Portal **52**; Vera Lynn is **29**, and Group Captain Leonard Cheshire VC (chosen only as one example of the actual fighters) is **27**.

Typical pilots in the Battle of Britain (1940) are Richard Hillary (**22**), "Ginger" Lacey (**23**), and Douglas Bader (**30**). The chief of Fighter Command is Hugh Dowding (**58**). The "Dambusters" raid (1943) is led by Guy Gibson (**25**), with bombs designed by Barnes Wallis (**53**). Most of the pilots in the Battle of Britain are **18–24**—2,900 flew, and about 500 were killed.

SOCIAL SCIENCE, EDUCATION

Max Weber: death (1920). His *Economy and Society* is incomplete, and the bulk of his work is not yet published. In the last year, he has attended the Versailles Peace Conference, and helped to draft the constitution of the new (and short-lived) Weimar Republic of Germany.

Herbert Marcuse: *Eros and Civilization* (1954); and *One-Dimensional Man* at **67**. (cf. **70***)

Erich Fromm: *The Art of Loving* (1956).

SCIENCE, TECHNOLOGY

William Gilbert: *Of the Magnet and Magnetic Bodies* (1600); this is the first book on electrical effects, and it is the first to use the word "electric."

William Oughtred: first publication to use the mathematical signs *x*, *sin*, *cos*, and *tan* (1631). At about **45**, he had invented the slide rule. He is a creative mathematician all his life; at **82**, he publishes three books, and he lives until **85**, owing to his "temperance and archery."

Erwin Schrodinger: *What Is Life* (1944), an influential book on molecular biology.

Louis Leakey: discovery of the remains of *Australopithecus boisei*, at Olduvai Gorge, Tanzania (1959). This is the culmination of a lifetime's searching for the predecessors of *Homo sapiens*. Leakey had led his first expedition in Africa at **23**, when his ideas had been dismissed as irrelevant. Now, in 1959, the actual discovery is made by his second wife Mary (**46**), while he has turned gradually to the work of fund-raising and writing up the results of their discoveries.

Norman Borlaug: Nobel Prize (1970) for his work on the "green revolution." He had first gone to Mexico City at **30** and begun work on the development of new strains of wheat and maize.

MONEY, WORK

Thomas Mellon resigns as judge in the court of common pleas, Pittsburgh (1869) and sets up his investment interests as a bank. One of his first customers is Henry Clay Frick (**21**). By **60**, the Mellons purchase the Pittsburgh National Bank of Commerce. The judge retires from banking at **71**, and moves to Kansas City, Missouri. His son Andrew (**33**, in 1888) participates in the $20,000 start-up costs of the new Pittsburgh Reduction Company, later Alcoa; at **46**, Andrew Mellon participates in the beginning of Gulf Oil.

Gottlieb Daimler: start of his own car company, making the Mercedes car (1890). At **51**, he had made his first motorbicycle.

Jean Paul Getty purchases huge oil leases from Saudi Arabia (1948–49). By **62**, these yield oil, and become the biggest break in his career. Around **61***, he learns Arabic, his sixth foreign language.

John Z. Delorean: the first Delorean sports car (1981).

ARCHITECTURE

Étienne-Louis Boullée: design for a cenotaph for Isaac Newton, in 1784. This is a giant sphere which is surrounded by tiers of stone and of trees. Boullée is remarkable in that his great creative work begins at around **50**. With the revolutionary changes in France, Boullée's imagination is liberated, and with his designs he enters architectural history. At this time he proposes an amphitheater for Paris, and it would hold 300,000 people. Like all his best work, it is never constructed, but it influences designers for years to come. A typical Boullée design consists of Egyptian and classical forms which are repeated endlessly until they disappear into the distance. He lives until **70**.

Sir Charles Barry: Cliveden House (1851).

Eduard Reidel: Neuschwanstein (1869–81)—the Wagnerian castle built for King Ludwig II (**23***) of Bavaria.

Daniel H. Burnham: the Flatiron building, New York City (1902); the wedge-shaped office building, the tallest building in the world when constructed.

Louis Kahn: medical research laboratories, Philadelphia (1957–61). He also does the Concrete Foundation studies for diagonally-supported office buildings—a pioneer megastructure concept. At **58**, he does the Salk Institute, La Jolla, California.

Gordon Bunshaft and SOM (Skidmore, Owings, and Merrill): Chase Manhattan Plaza, New York (1962).

Oscar Niemeyer: Parliament buildings, Brasília (1962–67), and the cathedral there, at **58**.

ART

Cézanne has his first solo show (1895). He is "discovered" and immediately becomes a father-figure to the new painters. He had been working on his own in his home town of Aix-en-Provence for most of his life. He continues to work steadily and creatively until his death at **67**.

Pablo Picasso: "Guernica" (1937). (cf. **76***)

MUSIC—CLASSICAL

J. S. Bach fathers the last of his 20 children, Regina Susanna (1741–1809). Her mother, Anna Magdalena Bach, is **41** (cf. **65***). Richard Wagner also is father for the last time at **56** (1869); at **57**, Wagner wakes up his wife (**33**) exactly one year after the birth—at 4:30 A.M. he plays the piano to her. (cf. **57***)

Handel: *Messiah* (1741). This is written in about twenty-four days, and he immediately starts on another huge oratorio, *Samson*. Previously, he had been seen by his public to have exhausted his ideas in his late **40**s, and at **50** he was ill with perhaps a mild stroke. But at **52**, he wrote both *Saul* and *Israel in Egypt.* He now continues his lifetime of composition, until forced to stop by blindness at **67**. He lives till **74**. (cf. **61***)

LITERATURE

John Milton completes *Paradise Lost* around now (1665) and it is published at **58**. He later writes both *Paradise Regained,* and *Samson Agonistes.* He dies at **66**. He had gone blind around **40**, and had spent the middle part of his life as a senior civil servant.

PLAYS, DANCE

Sophocles: *Antigone* (440 B.C.).

Ibsen: *The Wild Duck* (1884).

Jean Renoir: *The River* (1950).

Lilian Gish: *The Night of the Hunter* (1955).

Ingmar Bergman: *Scenes from a Marriage* (1974), with Liv Ullman (**36**).

Walter Matthau: *The Bad News Bears* (1976), with Tatum O'Neal (**12**), directed by Michael Ritchie (**37**).

Federico Fellini: *Fellini's Casanova* (1977).

TV, ETC.

"Sixty Minutes": this is the leading newsmagazine program on U.S. TV, and at the beginning of its twelfth season (1979) its staff includes: Dan Rather (**48**); Harry Reasoner (**56**); Mike Wallace (**61**); in charge, backstage, is Don Hewitt (**56**).

LOVE, LIFE

Stavros Niarchos: marriage to Charlotte Ford (**24**, in 1966). They soon divorce, and at **28** she is featured by *Look* magazine as "America's Most Eligible Divorcée."

PRESS

William Randolph Hearst starts building his castle at San Simeon, California (1919). The building site is on acreage half the size of the state of Rhode Island. The gardens are later filled with giraffes and other animals. Besides his work in running his newspaper chain, he now takes an interest in promoting the film career of his companion, Marion Davies (**20**). By his early **60**s, his Hearst Castle has become an important social center for Hollywood, and a symbol of paradise and extravagance. (cf. **74***)

57

HISTORY—WORLD

Hammurabi: the conquest of Larsa (1763 B.C.). This is the foundation of Babylon as the major city of the Middle East for the next 2,000 years. Hammurabi now calls himself "Ruler of the Four Quarters of the World."

HISTORY—U.S.A.

Geronimo finally surrenders to the white man (1886, Sept. 4)—this is the end of the Apache attempt to resist the white settlers. After prison, Geronimo himself takes up farming; he becomes a "legend in his own time," as a living symbol of the old Indian resistance; dies at **80**.

James Forrestal: suicide (1949); he throws himself out of a kitchen window at Bethesda Naval Hospital. He has had a spectacular career on Wall Street, and at **45** had become president of Dillon, Read, bankers. At **48**, he became Under Secretary of the Navy, and Secretary at **52**. After World War II, he becomes the first-ever Secretary of Defense, serving from **55–57**. Forrestal has been driven by a sense of excellence and perfection. His depression has resulted from the ingratitude, as he sees it, of politicians and the military for the super-achieving pace that he has set at the Pentagon. Before dying, he copies out these words of Sophocles:

> Better to die and sleep,
> The never-waking sleep, than linger on
> And dare to live, when the soul's life is gone.

HISTORY—U.K.

Earl of Cardigan: the Charge of the Light Brigade (1854). He had previously been an unpopular and inefficient general, who maintained his position only through his wealth. He now becomes a national hero. At **70**, he dies, after falling off a horse.

Harold Macmillan: has his first effective cabinet job (Oct. 1951), as Minister of Housing. With Ernest Marples (**45**), he helps organize the building of 300,000 houses per year. This is his first national success, and reached at **60**. He had had his first break at **48**, during World War II, when he was representative of Winston Churchill (**68**) in the Mediterranean. Between **30** and **46**, Macmillan had been an almost unknown backbench MP, working mainly in the family publishing company. He is Prime Minister, **62–69***. (Clement Atlee also has his first cabinet position at **57**, and he is also Prime Minister at **62**. Another late developer is Derrick Heathcoat Amory who first enters Parliament at **45**, 1945, and is Chancellor of the Exchequer at **58–60**.)

RELIGION, PHILOSOPHY

Sir Thomas More: execution, at the Tower of London (1535). He has been "a man for all seasons."

Immanuel Kant: *The Critique of Pure Reason* (1781). This is the start of the second wave in his writing—the first had ended at **46**, and he has been silent since then. He now continues to elaborate the *Critique* until **73**, and dies at **79***.

Suzanne Langer: *Feeling and Form* (1953).

Karl Popper: *The Logic of Scientific Discovery* (1959).

RENAISSANCE

Gianlorenzo Bernini: start of the construction of the Piazza and Colonnade in front of St. Peter's, Rome (1656–67). At **25**, he had designed the baldacchino inside the basilica. At **46**, he began his sculpture, "The Ecstasy of St. Theresa (**57**)", and at **49** he designed the fountains in the Piazza Navona. He goes to Paris at **65** to present designs for the Louvre; these are not accepted but at **66** he creates perhaps his most memorable sculpture, a bust of King Louis XIV (**26**). Bernini, who had been an infant prodigy, lives until **81**.

Robert Ardrey: *The Territorial Imperative* (1966). Though not fully admired by specialists, this is a powerful book in the emerging interest of sociobiology. At **52** he had published his first book in this field, *African Genesis.* Previously he had had careers as a playwright in his **20**s, and as a scriptwriter in his **30**s. He wrote the scripts for the film *They Knew What They Wanted* at **31**; *The Lady Takes a Chance* at **34**; and *The Three Musketeers* at **38**. But this book now at **57** is the peak of his reputation.

ARCHITECTURE

C. G. Langhans: Brandenburg Gate, Berlin (1789–93)—prototype of similar triumphal gateways throughout Europe.

Gustave Eiffel: the Eiffel Tower (1889).

Le Corbusier, in 1945: at the end of World War II, he retains his immense reputation as a provocative thinker on architecture, but he still has yet to complete a significant number of built works. His output has been mainly ideas, not constructed buildings. Now at **57**, he is asked to design housing in Marseilles, and at **58** work starts on "Unité d'Habitation." The chapel at Ronchamp is at **62**, and the monastery at La Tourette is at **66** onward. His housing at **57**, and the monastery at **66**, are probably the forms most often used by other architects. At **63**, he begins work on the new city of Chandigarh, in India. The Carpenter Arts Building, Harvard, is at **72**, and his Venice hospital project is at **73**. He lives until **77**.

Kenzo Tange: the huge and wonderful central megastructure at the Japanese World's Fair (1970).

ART

Velazquez: "Las Meninas" (1656)—a picture of the maids of honor to a princess, the Infanta Margarita (**5**).

MUSIC—CLASSICAL

Richard Wagner, in 1870, for the birthday of Cosima (**33**): she comes downstairs in the morning to find an orchestra playing the first-ever performance of the *Siegfried Idyll.* Among those present are Hans Richter (**27**) and Friedrich Nietzsche (**26**). (cf. **63***)

LITERATURE

Anna Sewell completes *Black Beauty* (1877), but dies in the following year. She had been crippled for most of her life, and she had been unusually dependent on horses in order to get around.

Mario Puzo: *Fools Die* (1978). U.S. paperback rights bring him $2.2 million.

PLAYS

George Bernard Shaw: *Androcles and the Lion;* and *Pygmalion* (1913–14), starring Mrs. Patrick Campbell (**49**). In the musical version, *My Fair Lady,* the lead actress is Julie Andrews (**20**) (1956, Mar. 15).

FILMS

Howard Hawks: *Gentlemen Prefer Blondes* (1953).

William Wyler: *Ben-Hur* (1959), starring Charlton Heston (**35**) and Jack Hawkins (**47**). The script is adapted from the book by Lewis Wallace (**53**, in 1880), written while he served as Governor of New Mexico Territory. The first version of *Ben-Hur* was made by Fred Niblo (**51**, in 1925) and starred Ramon Novarro (**26**) and Francis X. Bushman (**42**).

Luchino Visconti: *The Leopard* (1963), with Burt Lancaster (**50**).

John Wayne has lung cancer (1964).

MUSIC—NON-CLASSICAL

Cole Porter: *Kiss Me, Kate* (1948). This is another of his hit musicals, and the songs include "Wunderbar," "Always True to You in My Fashion," and "So in Love."

PRESS

Lord Northcliffe dies from blood poisoning (London, 1922)—he had started the *Daily Mail* at **30*** and controlled the *Times* from **42**. Northcliffe's mind is disturbed toward the end, perhaps unbalanced by the huge power and instant gratification that his empire has given him. On his deathbed, he dictates instructions as to how the *Times* should write up his obituary; and he asks to be buried as close as possible to his mother (still alive at **84**).

Stewart Alsop, *Newsweek* columnist (1971), is told that he has leukemia, and will die within one to two years. He continues to write his column, and describes his experiences as a dying patient. He publishes a successful book about this, *Stay of Execution.* His death comes nine days after his **60**th birthday. In his book, Alsop concludes: "Sooner or later, there comes a time when a dying man has to die, as a sleepy man has to sleep."

New York Times in 1979: the senior journalist is Managing Executive Editor Abe Rosenthal (**57**).

SPORTS

Rear Admiral Nicholas Goodhart (Retd.) holds the U.K. gliding distance record, for a trip of 360 miles (1977).

58

HISTORY—WORLD

Anwar Sadat flies to Israel (1977) to meet Prime Minister Begin (**64**). The Camp David talks on peace in the Middle East are later organized by Jimmy Carter (now **53**).

HISTORY—U.S.A.

Robert E. Lee surrenders at Appomattox (1865, Apr. 9), thus ending the American Civil War. The victor is Ulysses S. Grant (**42**). Lee dies at **63**. Grant is President, **46–54**, and also dies at **63**.

President William McKinley: assassinated (1901, Sept. 14).

HISTORY—U.K.

William I orders a complete survey of England (1085), for purposes of taxation and military service—this is the Domesday Book. He dies at **60**.

The Duke of Wellington becomes Prime Minister (1828, Jan. 9)—he had won the Battle of Waterloo at **46**. But he is unsuccessful as Prime Minister because of his opposition to reform of the archaic voting system; he resigns at **61**.

William Gladstone: Prime Minister, for the first time (1868, Dec. 4). (cf. **64***)

Edward Heath loses election (Feb. 1974) and resigns as Prime Minister, following campaign by the National Union of Mineworkers. His opponents are Harold Wilson (**57**), and Arthur Scargill (**34**).

In the twentieth century, the average age for first becoming Prime Minister is **58.8**. Harold Wilson (1964 onward) **48–54**, and **57–60**; A. J. Balfour (1902) **53–57**; Lloyd George (1916) **53–59**; Mrs. Thatcher (1979) **53**; Edward Heath (1970) **54–58**; H. H. Asquith (1908) **55–64**; Stanley Baldwin (1923) **55–56**, **57–61**, **67–69**; Ramsay MacDonald (1924) **57–58**, **62–68**; Anthony Eden (1955) **57–59**; Alec Douglas-Home (1963) **60–61**; Clement Atlee (1945) **62–68**; Harold Macmillan (1957) **62–69**; Bonar Law (1922) **64**; James Callaghan (1976) **64–67**; Winston Churchill (1940) **65–70**, **76–80**; Neville Chamberlain (1937) **68–71**; and Sir Henry Campbell-Bannerman (1905) **69–71**.

John Paul II: Pope (1978). He has been promoted at each decade of his life—Priest at **26**; Bishop at **38**; Cardinal at **47**; and Pope at **58**. Before ordination, during World War II, he had been a factory worker and freedom fighter. He was a curate at **28**, and university professor at **34**. His book *Love and Responsibility* was published at **38**.

SOCIAL SCIENCE, EDUCATION

John Locke: *An Essay Concerning Human Understanding* (1690), his best-known work; and *Some Thoughts Concerning Education* at **61**.

RENAISSANCE

Ignace Paderewski: appointment as the Prime Minister of Poland (1919). He resigns at **59**, leaving Poland and never returning. He then resumes his first career, as a concert pianist. But he has had a powerful effect on Polish history, as at **57** he persuaded President Woodrow Wilson (**61***) to include the independence of Poland in the Fourteen Points which were to form the basis of the new order after World War I. Paderewski had made his concert debut at **27**, and his first tour of America at **31**. At that time, the role of concert pianist was the greatest in the performing arts, and Paderewski had often met the leading politicians of the time. These contacts, as well as his sheer fame, give him a base for his second career as a Polish patriot.

Isaac Asimov: publication of his 200th book (c.1978). His subjects have included astronomy, history of science, catastrophes, the Bible, the Greeks, jokes, and he has also been a novelist. He continues with his duties as an associate professor of biochemistry. His first book was published at **30**; his 55th book at **44**; and his 100th book at **49**.

ARCHITECTURE

Palladio: Villa Capra, La Rotonda (1566–67).

Sir Jeffrey Wyatville starts on the restoration of Windsor Castle, and the enlargement of the Round Tower (1824).

Gio Ponti: Pirelli building, Milan (1955–58), with engineering by Pier Luigi Nervi (**64**).

Arne Jacobsen: St. Catherine's College, Oxford (1960).

Philip Johnson: New York State Theater, Lincoln Center (1964).

ART

Paolo Uccello: "The Battle of San Romano" (London, Louvre, and Uffizi) (c.1455). Uccello lives until **78**.

Pierre Bonnard buys a villa in the south of France (1925); a large number of his best-known paintings are done from now onward. At **48**, he said that he "goes back to school," and had started all over again. Bonnard continues working until **78**.

MUSIC—CLASSICAL

Haydn in 1790: on the death of his patron, Prince Esterházy (**75**), Haydn leaves Hungary, and travels to London. He now composes the first six of his London symphonies, and on a second visit, the second six, including his 104th and last symphony. In London now, he is extremely popular—this is his first experience of mass adulation, as the major part of his adult life, from **29** onward, has been spent at the Esterházy estate in Hungary. At **66**, Haydn writes *The Creation.* (cf. **69***)

Béla Bártok: String Quartet no. 6 (1939). His other quartets were at **27**, **36**, **46**, **47**, and **53**.

LITERATURE

Ebenezer Brewer: *Dictionary of Phrase and Fable* (1870). He completes the second edition at **84**. He had first married at **46** and he lived until **86**. (For *Roget's Thesaurus,* cf. Renaissance **73***).

Dashiell Hammett spends six months in jail for refusing to cooperate with Senator Joe McCarthy (**43**). Hammett had written *The Maltese Falcon* at **36**.

Georges Simenon: start of his 180th book (1961, Aug. 16). On the previous night, his wife/agent had cleaned his pipes and his typewriter; he himself has carefully arranged his desk, checking that all his writing equipment is in place. In the morning, he makes coffee and puts a "Do Not Disturb" sign on his door. By seven, he has already written five pages, and the book is finished within twenty-five days. He is not thrilled at this speed, as he remembers the time when he could write 80 pages a day. His hard work has made him rich, but he gives this interesting warning about wealth: "A man can be content with the necessary, with the indispensable, and be almost happy. But when one gets into the realm of the superfluous, luxury or near luxury, there are no limits, therefore no satiety, no satisfaction."

PLAYS

Ibsen: *Rosmersholm* (1886).

George Bernard Shaw publishes a pacifist pamphlet about World War I—"Common Sense About the War" (1914). He turns from being a popular playwright into a hated public figure.

FILMS

David Lean: *Dr. Zhivago* (1966).

Katharine Hepburn: *Guess Who's Coming to Dinner* (1967).

EXPLORATION

David Livingstone: meeting in central Africa with H. M. Stanley (**30**, in 1871). Stanley introduces himself with the words, "Dr. Livingstone, I presume."

SPORTS

James Counsilman (1979) swims the English Channel—21 miles in 13 hours. He is the oldest person to do so (youngest is **12***). The second oldest is William Barney (**55**) in 1951.

59

HEALTH

Denton Cooley, the surgeon, continues to do at least eleven heart operations per day (Texas, 1979). He grosses $30,000 for each day in the operating theater.

HISTORY—U.S.A.

Commodore Matthew Perry sails into Tokyo Bay (July 1853)—first stage in the opening up of Japan to contemporary Western ideas, and to trade.

John Brown liberates slaves at Harpers Ferry, Virginia (1859), a continuation of his life-long work for abolition. He is captured by Robert E. Lee (**52**) and executed—"but his soul goes marching on."

Franklin D. Roosevelt declares war, after the Japanese attack on Pearl Harbor (1941, Dec. 7). (cf. **62***)

Robert Welch: The John Birch Society (1958).

Lyndon Johnson: the Vietnam War is now the longest war in U.S.

history (1968, June 22). About 520,000 U.S. personnel are in Vietnam. Dean Rusk is **59**; General William C. Westmoreland **54**; Richard Nixon also **54**; Robert McNamara **52**; W. W. Rostow **51**; William P. Bundy **50**; Henry Kissinger **45**; the draft age is from **18** to **26**, with a legal limit of **36**; Cardinal Spellman, leading supporter, had recently died at **78**, and John Wayne (**61**) makes the film *The Green Berets.* Wayne Morse is **67**, having at **64** been one of two people to vote against the Tonkin Gulf resolution; Eugene McCarthy is **52**. Ho Chi Minh is **78**. President Johnson is forced to leave the White House at **60**, and dies at **64***.

Richard Nixon, as President, visits China (1972, Feb. 21), after a preliminary visit by Dr. Henry Kissinger (**48**). They meet Chairman Mao (**78**).

Richard Nixon is **59** on the night of the break-in at the Democratic National Headquarters, Watergate (1972, June 17-18). J. Edgar Hoover is **77**; Senator Sam Ervin **75**; Judge John J. Sirica **68**; John Mitchell **58**, and Gerald Ford also **58**; E. Howard Hunt **53**, and Martha Mitchell also **53**; Henry Kissinger **49**; Alexander Haig **47**, and John Ehrlichman also **47**; H. R. Haldeman **45**; Jeb Stuart Magruder **37**; Ron Ziegler **33**, and John Dean also **33**; Robert Woodward is **29** and Carl Bernstein is **28**.

Richard Nixon is reelected President; in a landslide, he defeats George McGovern (**50**) and carries every state but one. (cf. **61***)

HISTORY—U.K.

Edward VII becomes King (1901, Jan. 22), on the death of his mother, Queen Victoria (**81**). He has been Prince of Wales since the age of **1 month**. The first-ever Prince of Wales was created Prince at **16**, and became King Edward II at **23**. Edward the Black Prince dies at **46** (1376), without ever succeeding to the throne. He had fought at the Battle of Crécy, and there used the Prince of Wales feathers and motto for perhaps the first time. Frederick Louis, Prince of Wales, dies at **44** (1751), without ever succeeding his father, George II, who lives till **76**. George IV, when Prince of Wales, becomes Prince Regent at **48** (1811, Feb. 5), owing to the madness of his father, George III (**72**), and becomes King at **57**. He had become Prince of Wales when only **5 days** old.

David Lloyd George is forced to resign as Prime Minister (1922, Oct. 19). He is the last Liberal prime minister. He is admired for winning the war (**54** onward) and for his part in the creation of an independent Ireland (at **58**). But he is disliked for his authoritarian personal manner, and his corruption over the honors list. He now continues as an active politician and journalist, but never holds office again, living until **82**. (cf. **80***)

Montaigne: death (France, 1592). He has suffered for some years from kidney stones, but has not complained. Illness is nature's way of preparing you to leave this world; every time you are ill, you see a little of death—therefore "being so often led to the port, confident that you are still within the accustomed limits, some morning you and your confidence will have crossed the waters unawares."

Montesquieu: *The Spirit of the Laws* (1748).

Jung: *The Archetypes of the Collective Unconscious* (1934). Also *The Relation Between the Ego and the Unconscious* at **53**. Jung goes on his first visit to India at **62**. At **68**, he has a severe heart attack, but recovers—his **70**s and early **80**s are perhaps his most dynamic period. (cf. **70***)

SCIENCE, TECHNOLOGY

James Hutton: first outline of *Theory of the Earth* (1785); this is the first nonmystical book about geology, in which the evidence of rocks is used to give a scientific picture of the earth's origins. Hutton now spends ten years in collecting data to support his views, and he publishes his two main volumes, the culmination of his career, at **69**.

Henry Thomas: first commercial decoder, to allow a standard television to show videotext systems (1981).

MONEY, WORK

Henry J. Kaiser moves into the field of ship construction (1941) and later produces a new freighter every week. He has previously been in the construction business; for example, the Hoover Dam, at **49**.

ARCHITECTURE

Charles Le Brun and Jules Hardouin-Mansart (**32**): Galerie des Glaces, Versailles (Hall of Mirrors) (1678).

John Nash: Blaize Hamlet, near Bristol, England (1811)—here he invents the Picturesque style. (cf. **60***)

Mies van der Rohe: the first phase of the campus for Illinois Institute of Technology is complete (1940–45); Mies starts work on the Farnsworth House (1945–50). (cf. **62***)

Minoru Yamasaki: completion of the World Trade Center, New York (1972); but, in the same year, part of the Pruitt-Igoe housing project is demolished in St. Louis.

ART

Winslow Homer: "The Northeaster" (Metropolitan Museum of Art, New York City) (1895).

Edward Hopper: "Nighthawks" (1942)—his best-remembered

painting. The picture of the deserted street "Early Sunday Morning" is at **48**. Hopper lives until **84**.

MUSIC—CLASSICAL

Berlioz: *Les Troyens* (1863). In 1830, Mendelssohn (**21**) said about him, "[W]ith all his efforts to go stark mad, [he] never once succeeds." Berlioz lives until 1869.

George Grove: *Dictionary of Music and Musicians* (1879). At **63**, he is instrumental in the opening of the Royal College of Music, London.

Benjamin Britten: *Death in Venice* (1973); and String Quartet no. 3, at **61**. He dies at **63**.

LITERATURE

Daniel Defoe: *Robinson Crusoe* (1719).

Jonathan Swift: *Gulliver's Travels* (1726).

Feodor Dostoevsky: *The Brothers Karamazov* (1880); he dies in the following year.

Gertrude Stein: *The Autobiography of Alice B. Toklas* (**53**) (1933).

Virginia Woolf finishes *Between the Acts,* but drowns herself (1941). (cf. **9*** onward)

Aleksandr Solzhenitsyn: speech at Harvard on the decline of the West (1978).

PLAYS

Sean O'Casey: first volume of his autobiography (1939). From his breakthrough (**43***) as a dramatist onward, O'Casey is almost always productive. Now, his autobiography runs to six volumes, starting with *I Knock at the Door,* and *Pictures in the Hallway* to *Sunset and Evening Star* at **74**. He continues to write plays, *Purple Dust* at **60**; *Red Roses for Me* at **61**; and *Figure in the Night,* first published at **81**. Until his death, O'Casey continues to take part in the controversies that his plays arouse. For example, at **77**, one of his new plays is banned in Dublin as obscene, so O'Casey stops his plays being performed in Ireland. He lifts his ban shortly before his death at **84**.

FILMS

Buster Keaton: a cache of his early films is found (1954) in his former home, currently owned by James Mason (**45**). These and others are rescued, and a Keaton revival ensues.

Clark Gable dies of a heart attack (1960, Nov. 16), two weeks after completing *The Misfits.* The attack is said to have been brought on by the unprofessional conduct on the set of his costar, Marilyn Monroe (**34**). Four months after his death, his only child is born.

Katharine Hepburn wins her second Oscar in two years—for *The Lion in Winter* (1968).

Art Carney: *House Calls* (1978).

PRESS

Roy Thomson leaves Canada (1953) and starts buying *The Scotsman* newspaper in Edinburgh. This is beginning of the "Thomson Organization," a giant empire of newspapers, TV, and oil exploitation companies. Up to this time, Thomson has owned sixteen local newspapers in Canada, and "a small string of radio stations." He later divides his life up into three parts: "Young manhood—repeated nonsuccess until I was **40**. [From] **40** to **60**—success at last. [From] **60** onward—the curious urge to step into the top class"; this latter is what he now begins to achieve. His change in life at **59** is precipitated by the death of his wife, his failure to be elected a member of Parliament, and the departure of his top aide for a better paying job. (cf. **67***)

60

HEALTH

Life expectancy in the U.S.A. (1976) is now until **76.8** for males, and until **81.5** for females. The causes of death for people **45** to **64** are for males: (1) diseases of the heart; (2) cancer; (3) accidents; (4) cerebrovascular; (5) cirrhosis of the liver; (6) suicide. And for females: (1) cancer; (2) diseases of the heart; (3) cerebrovascular; (4) cirrhosis of the liver; (5) accidents; (6) diabetes. Note that the rates for the first two causes are much larger than for any of the others.

You can now expect to live until **80.3** (female) and until **75.7** (male) in England and Wales, (1975). Out of total deaths at all ages, 27 percent (male) occur in the ages **55–64** and 9.8 percent (female).

The causes of death for males **55–64** in England and Wales, (1977), are: (1) by far the most important, ischemic heart disease; (2) lung cancer; (3) cerebrovascular; (4) miscellaneous "other" cancers; (5) bronchitis, emphysema, asthma; (6) stomach cancer and pneumonia. The causes of female death are: (1) ischemic heart disease; (2) miscellaneous "other" cancers; (3) breast cancer; (4) cerebrovascular; (5) lung cancer; (6) pneumonia; bronchitis, emphysema, asthma; and cancer of the large intestine.

In Britain, only around 7.2 percent were **60+** until 1911; this proportion was very steady until 1911 when it expanded quite markedly. Previously 6.8 percent of males were **60+**, and females 7.4 percent. (cf. **65***)

In Calcutta (1976), the census showed that only 4.8 percent were **60+**.

Once you get to **65**, your life expectancy has not increased much since Victorian times.

Here are the causes of death as recorded in London, 1843–47, for people dying at **60+**: old age, 28 percent; diseases of the respiratory organs, such as bronchitis, 24 percent; diseases of the nervous system, for example, apoplexy, 13 percent; digestive system, 6 percent; circulatory system, 5 percent; diarrhea, 2 percent; and other causes, mainly typhus and some dysentery, cancer, gout, and so forth, 19 percent.

Animals' maximum life span: alligators can live until **56**: the snapping turtle, **59**.

Trees produce their best seed during middle age, typically 10–20 years after the principal height growth is complete. For oak and beech, you should collect seeds when the tree is **60**; hornbeam, **40**; sycamore and Norway maple, **35**; and alder, **25**.

HISTORY—WORLD

Miltiades: in charge of the forces of Athens (490 B.C.). He halts the westward expansion of the Persian empire by defeating its army at the battle of Marathon. He sends the news back to Athens with a (marathon) runner.

Trotsky is killed in exile (1940). His assassin is a man of **27**, who is punished by imprisonment between **27** and **47**. Trotsky had exactly ten years of power—at **38**, he celebrated his birthday by being a leader in the 1917 Russian Revolution. At **41**, as a field marshal, he had been instrumental in crushing the Kronshtadt rebellion which had aimed for a more democratic left-wing government—35,000 die. But at **48**, Stalin (**47**) had forced him out of the party. Trotsky is in exile from **49** onward. He spends his time in writing about theories of social change.

Jean Drapeau: Mayor of Montreal during the 1976 Olympic Games. He became Mayor at **38**, and was **51** at the time of the Montreal World's Fair.

Pierre Trudeau announces that he will resign as head of his party (1979). At **59**, he had been defeated by Joe Clark (**40**) and had lost the position of Prime Minister of Canada which he had held since **48**. Now at **60** his political obituary is written by commentators. He comments on his resignation: "I feel like an orphan." But Joe Clark, Canada's youngest ever premier, stumbles in office; another election is set, and Trudeau is called upon to lead his party. Trudeau wins at **60** and continues in office as Prime Minister. At **62**, he is responsible for the patriation of the Canadian constitution.

Eligibility: in the ancient Greek city-state of Sparta, you could now become a member of the "Gerontes," a small council of elders with limited formal powers but high prestige and influence.

HISTORY—U.S.A.

Woodrow Wilson: entry of U.S. into World War I (1917, Apr. 2). The commander of U.S. forces in Europe is John J. Pershing (**57**). (cf.**61***)

Harry S. Truman: Vice-President (1944), and President (1945, Apr. 12). (cf. **61***)

Eleanor Roosevelt is widowed by the death of Franklin D. Roosevelt (**63**) (1945); she becomes U.S. delegate to the new United Nations, and at **61** she helps to draft the Declaration on Human Rights.

Although it is commonly believed that people become more right-wing as they get older, this is probably not the case. Research by Karen Oppenheim and Richard F. Hamilton suggests that there is no such thing as a "right-wing drift" with aging. Research by John Crittendon suggests that there is a small movement toward the Republican party, but this movement is much smaller than would be expected from popular prejudice. Richard Hamilton believes that as many people move left as move to the right.

HISTORY—U.K.

Mrs. Pankhurst: "Representation of the People Act" (1918). This gives votes to women for the first time—if they are over **30** and have a property qualification. (In 1928, this voting restriction was lowered from **30** to **21**, the same as for men.) Christabel Pankhurst, her daughter, is **38**, Sylvia Pankhurst **36**, and Adela Pankhurst **33**. Charlotte Despard is **74**, Millicent Fawcett **71**, Emmeline Pethick-Lawrence **50**, and Frederick Pethick-Lawrence **46**. (cf. **67*** and **74***)

Eligibility: this is the mandatory retiring age for anyone in the Foreign Office. No ambassador or other member of the service can be employed on the exact day following his or her **60**th birthday. Therefore the top appointments are held between **55** and **60**. Members of the security or espionage services retire on full pension at **55**. For the Home Civil Service, top administrators retire at **60**. There is some provision for working at **60–65**, but this can usually be done only at a reduced rank, and few people take much advantage of this facility.

RELIGION, PHILOSOPHY

Plato is invited to put into effect his political ideas (the philosopher-king) in the city of Syracuse (367 B.C.), but the experiment is a failure. Plato had always wanted to be a statesman, but the weakness of Athens in his lifetime would have given him little power. Between **67** and his death (c. **82**), he writes *The Laws,* a long and influential blueprint for the good society, covering everything from the legal system to the promotion of ambidexterity. Plato sets great store by age rules; for example, membership in the cabinet, the Curators of Laws, is for **50–70** only; Prime Minister, **50+**, marriageability—for males, **30–35**, and females **16–20**. Minimum age for any public office—males at **30**, and females at **40**. In the education field, exercise begins at **−1**, as mothers should exercise you by themselves running around; discipline begins at **3**; reading at **10**; lyre playing at **13**. Judges of musical soloists must be **30+**; choirmasters **40+**; and judges of poetry **50+**. In order to keep check on eligibility within these age rules, Plato proposes a state register of births and deaths—here he is the first-ever person to make such a proposal.

Almost certainly, Plato's *The Laws* (above), contains the earliest and most elaborate set of age rules ever made (and it immediately shows the arbitrariness and foolishness of most such enterprises). Here are some further items about the development of age rules:

Where documents from ancient Egypt have survived, they do not contain age rules as a basis for eligibility in achieving office—though they do have words which differentiate between infants, children, adults, and old people. Census lists of the twelfth dynasty seem to give the names of infants, but not their age. Where we would record age, they did not do so, for example, on tombstones, and in descriptions of an official's progress from one job to another, as he progressed up the hierarchy. Despite a great skill at recording data (on taxes, battles, and the height of the River Nile, for example), birthdays were hardly ever recorded. Where the age of a pharaoh is given in a modern book, it is typically calculated from X rays of mummies and/or length of time on the throne. Dates were reckoned by the year of the reign, so that a certain year would be "Year 16, under the majesty of King XYZ . . . ." The year of nomination as crown prince was recorded, and commemorated until becoming ruler. Perhaps in some sense, adults waited before recording the existence of a person, to see which individuals would survive the health hazards of childhood.

Michel de Montaigne (**47**, in 1580) comments unfavorably on both higher and lower age limits for eligibility: "To send men into retirement before the age of **55** or **60** seems to me a little unreasonable. It would be my opinion that our vocation and employment should be extended as far as possible, for the public good; but I find the fault on the other side, that they do not employ us early enough. Here was a man [Augustus] who was arbiter of the whole world at **19***, and yet he would have a man to be **30** before he was qualified to determine the position of a gutter." Augustus had become Roman Emperor at **19***;

30 was the minimum age for a local government official in Rome.

In the formalization of the French Revolution, males with a property qualification had the vote at **21**. They could only vote for electors (**25**+) from whom came the much smaller number of legislators. There were two assemblies: the Council of Ancients (**40**+), and the Council of 500 (**30**+). These two assemblies agreed on the executive cabinet, the Directory (**30**+). This constitution was part of a rationalization of France's institutions. Previously, the king was released from control of a regency at **13**, and could gradually take full executive power by his late teens. His advisers might be from **73*** up till **90**.

Mao's original draft constitution of Communist China (c.1930) fixed **16** as the voting age; but it was not until **18** that you were a full adult in terms of rules about employment, for example, in restrictions on the hours you could work.

Where age cannot be calculated from records, some aspect of bodily development is often used as a substitute—an obvious example is the apparent age of your face, or number of grey hairs, and so on. At a public swimming pool, half-price tickets may be available to those under **12**; but since such people are unlikely to carry identification cards, the management may allow everyone under a certain height to have a cheap ticket. A grisly example of the same principle comes from Genghis Khan (c.1162–1227)—desiring to destroy the enemy's adult population, he once killed every prisoner who was taller than the axle of a cart.

Another perception on age in politics is that the elite are seen as full adults, while the lower orders are youths, whatever their chronological age. For example, in old Russia, the landowner would be "Father" and the serf would be a child in relation to the owner; this was independent of the chronological age of either party. Similarly, Hobbes (1588–1679) wrote of the newly emergent lower class as a "robust but malicious child."

Exactly the same comments could be made about China, after reading the records of the "Grand Historian of China" (c.100 B.C.). Although filial piety was a basic principle, there was only an age rule for conscription (**19–23**, see under **18***); in the archetypal system of the scholar-bureaucrat ("mandarin," cf. **24***), there were no age rules during the greater part of the system's existence. Promotion was by examination, and you could take the exam at any time. If you failed, you could take it again next time, three years later. If, after a lifetime, you still had not passed, at **80** or **90**, you were eligible for an honorary degree, according to Victorian observers of the tail end of the system. There was no set age at which a young emperor was free of a regency's control; that is, no fixed majority. But boys were "capped" at **20** (our **19**, cf. **0***), and then wore the "cap of manhood." Confucius, in his designs for a good society, does not mention any formal age rule—neither does Mencius, nor does the Tao—except for his broad assumption of respect for elders, and the idea that the ruler-ruled relationship should mimic the good parent-child relationship, with its obligations in both directions. For example, "There is government when the prince is prince, and the minister is minister; when the father is father, and the son is son."

Records of birth do not occur in the numerous cuneiform clay tablets of Babylon, even though this was a highly bureaucratic society, with detailed records of taxes, and so forth.

In ancient Greece, males were liable for military call-up at **18**. They were then eligible to attend the "ekklesia," the meeting of all adults, held in the agora; this attendance was equivalent to gaining the vote in modern societies.

Emperor Charlemagne (**59**), in his formalization of the feudal system (802 A.D.), fixed **12** as the age at which you must swear fealty.

Venice: the republic had a constitution which was widely admired for promoting both stability and wealth. The republic lasted for six centuries, and the elaborate voting rules were designed to stop the formation of any parties or factions. A basic feature of the system was an individual's slow progression to the top positions. The head, the Doge, was typically about **70** (cf. **75***) on election; you were eligible for the Senate at **40**; eligible to vote in the election of a Doge, at **30**; admissible to take part in the Greater Council at **25**; admissible as an observer only at the Greater Council, at **20**. Where voting procedures had to be arranged by lot, these lots were drawn by boys of **11**, brought from an orphanage. Middle-class institutions were also organized with age rules similar to those of the central political system.

In Florence in 1480, members of the new Council of Seventy had to be **40** or over.

SOCIAL SCIENCE, EDUCATION

G. Stanley Hall: *Adolescence* (1904).

SCIENCE, TECHNOLOGY

Albert Einstein: the Einstein-Szilard (**41**) letter to President F. D. Roosevelt (**57**) in 1939. This is instrumental in advancing the start of U.S. research on the atomic bomb. Einstein, since **40**, has been the most famous scientist in the world, and he has accepted a large number of public duties. At **52**, he had a correspondence with Sigmund Freud (**76**) on the possibility of ending war; Einstein's solution has been world government, but Freud is discouraging about this. More practically, Einstein helps numerous Jewish scientists to escape from the Nazis, and he raises support for the future state of Israel. At **73** he is offered the position of President of Israel. In physics, he has been working on unified field theory—in his previous work on relativity (**26***–**36***) he had united space, time, and matter; now, in a unified field theory, he hopes to bring together gravity, electricity, and quantum phenomena. Rightly or wrongly this approach is not seen by others to be successful. His new approach is believed to be overambitious or even impossible, and the subject of physics moves elsewhere. But he continues to work all his life and never stops in his effort to answer the largest possible questions. Einstein has an instantly recognizable personal style, and to avoid the distractions of life he wears a leather jacket, which never needs cleaning, and he never wears socks. He has lived in Princeton since **54**, and he dies there at **76**. (cf. **75***)

Lewis Thomas: *The Lives of a Cell* (1974).

MONEY, WORK

O death, how bitter is the remembrance of thee to a man that liveth at rest in his possessions.—Ecclesiasticus 40:1

F. W. Woolworth consolidates (1912) the chain of stores run by himself, his relatives, and by his former employers where he had started the "five cents" idea. The new company carries only his name; at **61**, he opens his new headquarters, in the world's tallest building, the Woolworth building. At his death (**66**), he controls 1,000 branches, and has a number of chains imitating him.

William Zeckendorf: his huge real estate operation, Webb & Knapp, goes bankrupt (1965, May 7). He had been in the forefront of the movement to revitalize city centers; for example, at **51**, he had started on the Place Ville Marie site, in downtown Montreal. After bankruptcy, he starts up again.

"Success over Sixty" is one of many employment agencies that specialize in this age group.

RENAISSANCE

Francis Bacon: dismissal as Lord Chancellor (London, 1621), a position he has held since **56** and in which he has reached the peak of his career as a lawyer. His dismissal has arisen from the struggle for power between crown and Parliament. Although deeply frustrated at being unable to influence political life, he survives because of his other interests—his literature and his science. His first *Essays* were completed at **36**, and he adds to them at **41** and **64**. His writings on science form a landmark in the development of the new empiricism. His *The Advancement of Learning* was at **44**; his *Novum Organum* had been published at **51**, and in his retirement he now writes *New Atlantis* (**63**) which is a highly influential description of a utopian community of scientists. Also in his retirement he writes on the winds, on health, and a history of England during the previous century. At **45**, Bacon had been married to Alice Barnham on her **14**th birthday; at the time, no comment is made on their age difference. Coincidentally or otherwise, Bacon describes a legendary woman in these terms: "That lady had the face and countenance of a maiden, but her loins were girt about with yelping hounds." The death of Bacon comes from his pursuit of science—he tests a theory of his that the freezing of food will lead to its preservation; he catches a cold from stuffing a newly-killed chicken with ice, and he dies shortly afterward. In being so active at **65** he has ignored his own previous advice: "Discern of the coming on of years, and think not to do the same things still; for age will not be defied."

ARCHITECTURE

John Nash begins work on Regent Street, and on Regent's Park, London (1812). (cf. **73***)

ART

Sandro Botticelli serves on a committee (1504) to decide on a position in Florence for the new statue of David by Michelangelo (**29**).

Ando Hiroshige dies (1858); he had done "Fifty-three Stages of the Tokaido Highway" at **36**—the famed scenes from Japanese life. Just before his death, he writes:

> I leave my brush at Azuma
> I go to the Land of the West on a journey
> To view the famous sights there.

Auguste Rodin continues as the best-known sculptor of his day (1900). He had produced his powerful statue of Balzac at **57**. His wealth and reputation allow him to indulge himself as a sex maniac. He explains: "A woman undressing, how dazzling! It is like the sun piercing through clouds. . . ." (cf. **72***)

Alfred Stieglitz, the photographer, marries Georgia O'Keeffe (**36**), the painter (1924). This produces a huge burst of energy in him, and he makes an endless series of portraits of her; he lives for another 22 years.

Henry Moore, in 1963: perhaps his most widely known work is done in his **60**s: "Large Torso: Arch" (**60–67**); "Knife Edge Two Piece" (**60–63**); "Reclining Figure" (Lincoln Center) (**63**); and "Nuclear Energy" (**64**). His piece "King and Queen" was made at **54**. (cf. **80***)

Guillaume de Machault: start of his work on the words and music of "*Le Livre du voir dit*" (France, 1360). This is a 9,000 line poem in honor of Peronne (**18**), "Toute-Belle," the last of six teenage girls who have been Machault's central inspiration. The work is in the form of letters which are sent to Peronne. The relationships ends at **64**, and the work is complete at **65**. Machault lives until **77**. In *Voir dit,* Machault now creates one of the leading musical and romantic works of the fourteenth century.

Verdi: *Requiem* (1873). This is written at the death of the novelist Alessandro Manzoni (**89**). Verdi had written *Don Carlos* at **54**, and *Aïda* at **58**. He now considers that he has done enough composing, and tells everyone that he has retired. But he writes *Otello* at **73***.

LITERATURE

> Still as death approaches nearer,
> The joys of life are sweeter, dearer.—Thomas More,
> "Odes of Anacreon."

Izaak Walton: *The Compleat Angler* (1653).

Henry James: *The Ambassadors* (1903). He had written *The Wings of the Dove* at **59**; and *The Golden Bowl* at **61**.

FILMS

W. C. Fields: *You Can't Cheat an Honest Man* (1939). At **58,** he had given up drinking, and did not do any work for the next two years.

Irving Berlin: the music for *Easter Parade* (1948).

Katharine Hepburn: *Madwoman of Chaillot* (1969). In the same year, she stars in the Broadway musical *Coco.*

TV, ETC.

Hours spent watching TV per week: 19.7 hours at **15–34**; 18.7 hours at **35–54**; 22.6 hours at **55+**.

On TV programs and age: for commercial channels the program makers are clearly influenced by the varying discretionary purchasing power of the different age groups. TV and radio is segmented along age lines in these ways: (1) certain stations or even channels may concentrate on an audience of a specific age range; (2) within a wide-range channel, certain programs are highly age specific, whereas others are family viewing, or for all age groups; (3) within the 24 hours of the day, time zones are thought appropriate to certain ages, for example, there is a "toddlers' truce" in the afternoon and early evening, when the more provocative—adult—violent programs are not shown.

LOVE, LIFE

Andrew J. Volstead: the Volstead Act, bringing Prohibition to the U.S.A. (1920). Prohibition is ended when he is **74**, and he lives until **87**.

In the age group **60–64**, there are 87.9 males for every 100 females (U.S.A., 1976).

In a typical recent year in England and Wales (1977), there were 297 births in which the father was **60** or over. In one case, the father was **60**+, and the mother was **19** or younger.

EXPLORATION

St. Brendan: according to medieval reports, he now begins the first of three voyages across the Atlantic, from Ireland, and leading to the discovery of North America.

Commercial airline pilots in the U.S.A. must now retire. Flight attendants retire at **65**. Age has been ruled to be a legal occupational qualification for flight personnel.

PRESS

Joseph Shuster and Jerry Siegel (also **60**): a twelve-year court case finally establishes that the current owners of "Superman" have no obligation toward them—even though these two had invented the character when they were both around **24**. They had sold their rights, and been replaced by salaried cartoonists and scriptwriters. At **60**, they witness a vast revival of interest in Superman. Both are now poor: Shuster is going blind, and Siegel is working as a filing clerk. After press interest in their fate, they receive a favorable offer of money.

LAW, CRIME

In Colorado, there are extra penalties if an assault victim is aged **60** or over.

Eligibility: now too old to be appointed an English magistrate for the first time.

Eligibility: in ancient Greece, you would now be old enough to be an arbitrator, which, as later, was an alternative to going to court. But Plato regarded **60** as the correct minimum age for a judge.

SPORT

Cricket umpires: for the international panel of umpires (U.K., 1979), the ages of six of the eight members were obtainable and were: **69**, **66**, **47**, **46**, **46**, and **42**. Two first-class umpires retired at the beginning of the season; they were **68** and **66**.

Men's track and field records now:

100 meters in 12.0 seconds;
400 meters in 59.1 seconds;
1,500 meters in 4 minutes 50.3 seconds;
the mile in 5 minutes 18.8 seconds;
10,000 meters in 36 minutes 16.0 seconds;
10 mile walk in 1 hour 36 minutes.
The high jump record is 5 feet 0 inches and
the long jump record is 17 feet 8 inches.

Women's track records now:

100 meters in 16.8 seconds;
200 meters in 37.6 seconds;
400 meters in 91.1 seconds;
800 meters in 4 minutes 16.7 seconds;
the mile in 8 minutes 8.4 seconds.
The record at **61** for the 10,000 meters is 53 minutes 33 seconds.

61

HISTORY—WORLD

Nikita Khrushchev: speech at the 1956 Party Congress in Moscow, denouncing Stalinism. Khrushchev is party leader and effectively number one from **59–70**.

Aldo Moro: kidnapped (1978). He had worked to promote the "historic compromise" between Italy's Roman Catholic political party and the Italian Communist party. Two months after being captured in Rome, he writes to his wife, "I kiss you for the last time. Kiss the children for me," and he is killed.

Ahmed Ben Bella is released from prison in Algeria (1979); he has been held since **47**, without charges ever having been made against him. At **44**, Ben Bella was head of the newly independent state of Algeria—he had fought against the French occupation and had been imprisoned by them for eight years. At **47**, a new government deposed him, and placed him in prison.

John Adams becomes President (1796–1800), as does Andrew Jackson (1828–36).

Harry S. Truman: atomic bombs on Hiroshima and Nagasaki (1945, Aug. 6 and 9). (cf. **64***)

Richard Nixon resigns as President (1974, Aug. 9), because of Watergate. His successor is Gerald Ford (also **61**). (cf. **65***)

SOCIAL SCIENCE, EDUCATION

Karl Marx: end of writing of *Capital* (1879), the first volume of which was published at **49***.

J. M. Keynes: at the Bretton Woods Conference (1944). He dies at **62**, and is survived by his father **(94)** and mother **(85)**.

SCIENCE, TECHNOLOGY

Gregor Mendel dies (1884) without ever knowing that he has been a major scientist. Between **34–49**, he did careful experiments on the inheritance of characteristics in plants. At **43**, he published some conclusions and they were ignored. At **46**, he was appointed head of the monastery in which he has been a member, and gradually the pressure of this work, and the lack of any recognition, lead to his relaxing the precision of his experiments. In the year in which he would have been **77**, researchers in heredity catch up with his ideas, and resurrect his paper of **43**, which is elevated to landmark status. Mendel had always been an outsider in the academic system, having failed his teacher's exams at **28** and probably again at **34**.

Count Zeppelin: the flight of the first dirigible balloon or Zeppelin (1900). At **53**, he had retired from the army with the rank of lieutenant general. He had always been interested in ballooning, but his main career begins on his retirement. His innovations are to give the balloon an engine and a metal frame. He lives until **78**.

Henry Kaplan **(61)** and Lennart Olsson **(31)**: first production of human monoclonal antibodies (1980).

MONEY, WORK

Leland Stanford: the foundation of Stanford University (1885), in memory of his son, Leland Junior (died at **15**). Stanford had made his money as a robber baron in the railroad business.

Thomas J. Watson, Sr.: the new Social Security Administration (1935) creates a vast need for data-processing; this is the take-off for his IBM Corporation, which up to this time has not had its now-characteristic spectacular growth. Watson has always spent heavily on research and development, and on integrating his equipment into the customer's total system. He dies at **82**.

Woodrow Wilson: as President of the United States, he arrives in Paris at the end of World War I (1918) and is greeted by the largest crowd ever seen in the city. A banner in the Champs Elysées says "Honor to Wilson the Just." He is accompanied by his famous assistant, Colonel House (**50**). The President's Fourteen Points for a fair and permanent settlement of the war seem to raise him to superhuman heights. Previously, Wilson had had a distinguished career as a scholar and as a university administrator, before he entered politics. He was head of Princeton University, **45–53**, and had there introduced educational reforms which were later widely adopted. His first elective office was at **53** when he became Governor of New Jersey, on a reform ticket; he went on to start a powerful clean-up administration. At **55** he was elected President, and reelected at **59**. The U.S.A. entered the World War when he was **60**. But now at **61** he is outnegotiated by his allies, and the peace treaty is later seen as virtually the start of World War II. Wilson is instrumental in the foundation of the League of Nations, but is unable to obtain the support he wants for American membership. His rigidity (or idealism) leads him to make a suicidally demanding campaign tour of the U.S.A., and causes a thrombosis of the brain. For eighteen months he lives in the White House but is unable to exercise any presidential function. He is insulated from all responsibilities by his second wife, Edith Galt Wilson, **47** at the time of his attack. At **64** Wilson is succeeded by Warren G. Harding (**55**) and Wilson dies at **67**. He is convinced to the end that American membership in the league, or a similar organization, is part of Providence's plan. After death, he is preyed upon by psychobiographers, for two main reasons: (1) he has been a confusing mixture of megalomania and moralizing; and (2) though effective in the major part of his public career, he has showed a fatal inability to compromise at certain key moments of his life. Mrs. Edith Wilson survives as a widow for 35 years; she dies at **89** on what would have been her husband's **105**th birthday.

ARCHITECTURE

Daniel H. Burnham: masterplan for the city of Chicago (1907)—about which he says, "Make no little plans; they have no magic to stir men's blood."

Louis Kahn: Government Assembly complex, Dacca, Bangladesh (1962).

ART

Benvenuto Cellini: *Auto-biography* (1562).

MUSIC—CLASSICAL

Handel: *Judas Maccabeus* (1746—first performed at **62**). Handel composes continuously throughout his life, from late teens till late **60**s. Most of the work for which he is later famous is written in his **50**s.

Jacques Offenbach dies (1880, Oct. 4) during rehearsals of his new opera *Tales of Hoffmann.* The first night comes four months after his death, and it is a great success.

LITERATURE

Tolstoy publishes *The Kreutzer Sonata* (1888–89). He had written "The Death of Ivan Ilyich" at **57**. They show him becoming more and more pessimistic about life and marriage. But at **60** he had celebrated the birth of his last and thirteenth child by walking home from Moscow, covering 130 miles in five days. (cf. **67***)

Giuseppe di Lampedusa: death (1957). He leaves a brilliant unpublished manuscript, which becomes the one great work of his life, *The Leopard*. At the end of the book, the Leopard, the Prince of Salima, dies; on his deathbed, he is pleasantly surprised to find that when Death comes to collect him she is in fact a lovely young woman—"chaste but ready for possession."

Ernest Hemingway: suicide (1961). At **29**, his father (**67**) had also killed himself.

FILMS

W. C. Fields: *The Bank Dick;* and *My Little Chickadee* (1940), the latter with Mae West (**48**).

Lillian Gish: *The Unforgiven* (1960).

Celia Johnson is the headmistress in *The Prime of Miss Jean Brodie* (1969).

Peter Finch: *Network* (1977)—he gets the whole country to lean out of the window and shout: "I'm sick and tired and I'm not going to take it anymore"; receives Oscar posthumously.

EXPLORATION

John Franklin: death (1847). He has been probably the first person to prove the existence of the Northwest Passage, at the north of Canada. His ship is caught in ice, and he is frozen to death. Ten years later, the bodies of Franklin and his crew are found by a search party, the fifth to be sent out by his widow (then **65**). Franklin previously led Arctic expeditions at **39** and **41**; in his **40**s and **50**s, he has been a colonial administrator.

LAW, CRIME

Sir Edward Coke is first-ever Lord Chief Justice of England (1613–16). At **55**, he had asserted the independence of the judiciary from the political system, by denying the claim of King James I (**44**) that the sovereign was still head of the judiciary. At **58**, he becomes famous for asserting the independence of Parliament from the king. From **68** to **77**, Coke is a member of Parliament. In his last speech (**77**), he is instrumental in promoting parliamentary independence from the attempts of King Charles I (**29**) to limit Parliament's right to set its own agenda. (cf. **79***)

SPORTS

Joe DiMaggio (baseball, 1976): immortalized at **26***, he is now famous again, for his TV commercials which advertise coffee, and also the Bowery Savings Bank. He has gained only ten pounds since he stopped playing baseball at **36**. He refuses to play at oldtimers games, owing to the possibility of injury.

Alec Stock (U.K., 1979) is appointed manager of the Bournemouth soccer tream, a member of the fourth division. He had retired, with honors, as a first division manager at **59**—but could not stand the idleness of retirement.

62

HEALTH

Louis Pasteur: the first injection against rabies (1885). The patient, Joseph Meister (**9**), survives, and this is another in a long line of Pasteur successes. At **54**, he had begun studying chicken cholera; by chance, he had injected chickens with a weakened form of the cholera, and noticed that this gave them immunity. This leads him to the general principal of vaccination. Pasteur later comments on his luck: "In the field of investigation, chance favors only the prepared mind." Pasteur dies at **72**, having survived a serious stroke at **45**. Joseph Meister later returns to Paris, and works for the rest of his life at the Pasteur Institute as chief gatekeeper.

HISTORY—WORLD

David Ben-Gurion: first Prime Minister of the new state of Israel (1948). At this moment, Chaim Weizman is **73**, Rabbi Herzog (**59**), Golda Meir (**50**), Menachem Begin (**34**), and Moshe Dayan is **32**.

Dred Scott: following Supreme Court decision that he is still legally a slave (1857), he is bought by a sympathizer, and given his freedom. He dies a year later, having spent that last year as an employee of a hotel. The principal decision in the Dred Scott case is written by Chief Justice Roger Taney (**80**).

Franklin D. Roosevelt wins his fourth presidential campaign (1944); attends Yalta Conference at **63** (Feb. 1945) with Winston Churchill (**70**) and Joseph Stalin (**65**); but Roosevelt dies of a stroke at **63**.

HISTORY—U.K.

Edward I fathers his fifteenth and last surviving child (1301). He had married a second time, at **60**, and lives till **68**.

RELIGION, PHILOSOPHY

Tomás de Torquemada: assistant inquisitor of the Spanish Inquisition (1482)—he is appointed by Ferdinand (**30**) and Isabella (**31**), the country's rulers. Torquemada becomes Grand inquisitor at **63**, and at **64** he writes a handbook on how to proceed with an inquisition. Previously, he had been head of a monastery. He had achieved power by being confessor to the new queen. It is likely that the Inquisition is to Torquemada the fulfillment of a lifetime ambition.

Martin Luther: death (1546).

Wittgenstein: death (1951), with all his later philosophical work still unpublished.

SOCIAL SCIENCE, EDUCATION

Piero Sraffa: *Production of Commodities by Means of Commodities* (1960).

Studs Terkel: *Working* (1974). Also, *Hard Times* at **58**. He started having his own TV show at **38**.

SCIENCE, TECHNOLOGY

Robert Goddard: death (1945). He has been a rocket pioneer since about **43**, but he dies a few years before the great boom in U.S. rocket programs.

Frederick Sanger: Nobel Prize (1980) for his work in microbiology. This is his second Nobel Prize—his first was awarded at **40**.

MONEY, WORK

Paul M. Warburg publishes *The Federal Reserve System: Its Origin and Growth* (1930). Previously he had warned of the possibility of a great crash. The reforms which he wanted to prevent this did not happen until after his death (**63**).

Aristotle Onassis is married (1968, Oct. 20), on his own private island, to Jacqueline Kennedy (**39**).

Eligibility: under a scheme of Robert McCrindle, MP, both women and men would retire at **62½**; the current U.K. retirement ages would be adjusted gradually, so that male and female retirement ages meet in the middle.

RENAISSANCE

Linus Pauling: Nobel Peace Prize (1963). This is his second Nobel Prize. At **53**, he had received the Nobel Prize in chemistry, for his work at **38**, *The Nature of the Chemical Bond.* At **52**, he had just missed the discovery of the double helix in molecular biology.

ARCHITECTURE

Mies van der Rohe: 860 and 880 Lake Shore Drive, Chicago (1948–51)—his apartment blocks. (cf. **68***)

I. M. Pei: completion of the John F. Kennedy Memorial Library (1979); and of the East Building, National Gallery of Art, Washington.

ART

Goya in 1808: the French occupation of Spain brings on a liberalized regime, which pleases Goya, but obviously at the expense of his nationalist feelings. Though previously a court portrait painter, he now produces his most frightening and earthy and well-known work *The Disasters of War* (**63**). (cf. **73***)

Josef Albers: "Homage to the Square" (1950 onward). This is the culmination of his lifelong interest in color and geometry.

MUSIC—CLASSICAL

Ludwig von Köchel publishes his *Chronological and Thematic Catalogue of Mozart's Works* (1862). He had begun this at **50**; previously he had been a botanist and tutor.

PLAYS

Ibsen: *Hedda Gabler* (1890).

FILMS

John Wayne: *True Grit* (1969); Oscar.

Joseph Losey: *The Go-Between* (1971), with Julie Christie (**31**).

David Niven: his autobiography *The Moon's a Balloon* is a best-seller and he starts on a new career as a writer (1971). His first Hollywood film had been at **27**, and his career includes *Wuthering Heights* at **30**; and *Separate Tables* at **49**.

Richard Burton: translation of the *Kama Sutra* (1883). At **64–67**, he translates *Tales of the Arabian Nights.* Most of his life has been spent as an explorer and as a failed diplomatic official.

LAW, CRIME

Louis Calland sees a Manchester policeman being kicked unconscious by a gang (**18, 18, 19**, and **19**). Calland attacks the gang who are subsequently arrested. At their trial (1978), the judge, Sir Rudolph Lyons (**66**), leaves the bench to shake the hand of Calland, saying, "I would like the privilege of shaking hands with a very brave man."

SPORTS

Fiona Colquhoun Arran (power boat racing): first woman to travel at more than an average 100 mph in an offshore boat (1980).

63

HEALTH

Chang and Eng, the Siamese twins: death (1874). They have spent the whole of their lives together, joined at the chest. They had married two sisters and slept in a bed for four people. They fathered 21 children. Later, the sisters set up homes a few miles apart, and the twins commute between the two places. At **59**, Chang had become paralyzed after a stroke, and Eng had been forced to lie in bed with him since then. Chang dies first, and Eng follows a few hours later.

HISTORY—WORLD

Menachem Begin: Prime Minister of Israel (1977). He had come to Jerusalem at **29**, having been imprisoned both in his country of birth, Poland, and in a Siberian labor camp. At **30**, he is head of Irgun Zva'i Leummi, probably the most feared of the freedom-fighting movements before independence. At **34**, at the beginning of the state of Israel, Begin turns the IZL into the Herut political movement. Except for three years as a minister without portfolio, Begin is in opposition between **34** and now.

HISTORY—U.S.A.

John Quincy Adams: though a former President (**57–61**), he is elected member of the House of Representatives (1831), and continues as congressman until his death (**80**) in the House itself.

Dwight D. Eisenhower: the effective end of the Korean War (July 1953). The secretary of state is John Foster Dulles (**65**), and the agreement with the Communists is opposed by South Korean President Syngman Rhee (**78**).

HISTORY—U.K.

Disraeli becomes Prime Minister for the first time (1868, Feb. 28). (cf. **66***)

Winston Churchill warns against the Munich agreement (1938), but is generally ignored. (cf. **65***)

RELIGION, PHILOSOPHY

Thomas Hobbes: *Leviathan* (1651).

SOCIAL SCIENCE, EDUCATION

Friedrich Engels: on the death of Karl Marx (**64**, in 1883), Engels completes the editing of volumes two and three of *Capital.* Engels himself dies at **75**. (cf. **70***)

E. F. Schumacher: *Small Is Beautiful* (1973).

SCIENCE, TECHNOLOGY

Alfred Nobel: death (1896). In his will, he establishes the Nobel Prizes. He had made his fortune from the invention of dynamite at **32**.

Konrad Lorenz: *On Aggression* (1966).

ARCHITECTURE

John Roebling: Brooklyn Bridge (New York, 1869). He has been working since **51** to promote this construction, but he dies now at **63**, in the early days of the bridge building. His death is a result of an industrial accident and so he never lives to see the major achievement of his career.

Hans Scharoun: first prize in the competition to design the Berlin Philharmonic Concert Hall (1956). He completes this building at **70**. Although always a "rising star of the Modern movement," Scharoun's major break does not occur until **61** with the start of his expressionist "Romeo and Juliet" housing scheme, completed at **66**. Scharoun continues to stretch himself with architectural competitions. Between **56–66**, he enters nineteen competitions, and gains four first prizes and three second prizes. At **70**, he wins the Berlin Mehringplatz competition; at **71**, he wins the Berlin State Library competition; and at **72** he wins the theater competition at Wolfsburg, defeating, among others, Alvar Aalto (**67**) and Jorn Utzon (**47**). At his death (**79**), Scharoun has three major buildings under construction.

ART

Rembrandt: last self-portrait, and death (1669).

J. M. W. Turner: "The Fighting Téméraire" (1838).

MUSIC—CLASSICAL

Wagner: first-ever performance of the Ring cycle (Aug. 1876) in the new festival theater at Bayreuth. Wagner has been working on this since his late **30**s, with a long break from **44** onward. His patron, King Ludwig II, is now **31**. (cf. **69***)

LITERATURE

Anthony Trollope (1878) writes another eight and one half books before his death at **67**.

J. R. R. Tolkien publishes the third and last volume of *The Fellowship of the Ring* (1955). He had written *The Hobbit* at **45**.

Anaïs Nin: publication of the first volume of her *Diaries* (1966). Although always known in literary circles for her novels, this is the beginning of her great popular reputation. She dies at **73**, working on the seventh volume of the *Diaries*.

PLAYS, DANCE

Konstantin Stanislavsky: the book *An Actor Prepares* (1926). This sets out his Method which he has been developing since he organized the Moscow Arts Theater at **35**.

FILMS

Charlie Chaplin: *Limelight* (1952)—he produces, directs, and stars in it, using his own screenplay and own music. Guest spots are given to two stars from his past, Buster Keaton (**57**) and Edna Purviance (**58**).

Walt Disney: *Mary Poppins* (1964).

Henry Fonda: *Once upon a Time in the West* (1968).

Otto Preminger: *Tell Me That You Love Me, Junie Moon* (1969).

David Lean: *Ryan's Daughter* (1971).

Alec Guinness: *Star Wars* (1977).

TV, ETC.

Jim Davis: "Dallas" (1979). He has had a solid career in films and TV, but between now and his death at **65** he shoots to worldwide fame in the role of the family chief, Jock Ewing.

LAW, CRIME

Chief Justice Earl Warren: *Brown* **(9)** v. *Topeka Board of Education* (1954).

64

HISTORY—WORLD

François Mitterrand wins his third attempt to become President of France (1981). He had previously contested presidential elections at **49** and **55**.

HISTORY—U.S.A.

Former President Theodore Roosevelt creates the "Bull Moose" or Progressive party (1912), to the left of his own Republican party—but loses in the presidential election to Woodrow Wilson (**55**).

Eugene V. Debs, while in prison, receives almost one million votes as Socialist candidate in the presidential election (1920); at **63**, he had been sentenced to prison for ten years, for attacking U.S. involvement in World War I; but he is released at **66**.

Harry S. Truman wins whistlestop election (1948), against the favorite, Thomas E. Dewey (**46**).

Lyndon Johnson: death (1973)—one mile from the place where he was born.

William Proxmire, in 1980: his daily morning exercise program is 100 push-ups, 200 sit-ups, and other calisthenics for a total of thirty minutes. He then runs to work, five miles in 35 minutes, to the U.S. Senate, where he has been a senator since **41**. He had his famous hair transplant at **57**, and inaugurated his "Golden Fleece" award, for government wastefulness, at **59**.

HISTORY—U.K.

William IV becomes King (1830, June 26); he has previously been a naval commander, and reigns for seven years.

William Gladstone resigns as Prime Minister (Feb. 1874—since **58**), and as part of his intention of resigning from politics, he also resigns later as leader of his party. But at **66**, he comes out of retirement with his pamphlet on the "Bulgarian Horrors . . ." (an Amnesty International-type investigation of an atrocity) and he begins almost another career, as public speaker at open-air mass rallies. At **69**, he successfully campaigns to be MP for Midlothian, and later becomes Prime Minister for three more times. (cf **75***)

SCIENCE, TECHNOLOGY

John Ray: first book to set out a systematic taxonomy of animal species (1693). This is the culmination of Ray's life. He has been a vigorous observer of plant and animal species, and he now refines their arrangement into a powerful system. From about **62** onward, he has started on a new interest, the study of insects; here again, he makes notable contributions, before his death at **76**.

MONEY, WORK

J. Pierpont Morgan: United States Steel is formed (1901).

RENAISSANCE

Leone Battista Alberti: (Florence, 1468)—*On the Man of Excellence.*

Sir Walter Raleigh: public execution, by decapitation (1618). He had published his first poems at **22**, and after legal training he had become a soldier and an adventurer. At **31**, he was instrumental in setting up the expedition that later results in the colony of Virginia. At **32**, he is said to bring the tobacco and potato plants to Europe for the first time. At **38**, he is briefly in prison for his secret marriage to Elizabeth Throckmorton (**27**), a courtier to Queen Elizabeth I (**59**). Raleigh is sentenced to death at **49** for alleged treason and since then he has spent most of his time in the Tower of London. There he occupies himself in writing an influential *History of the World.* On the night before his execution Raleigh takes his well-known poem, "Even such is time . . ." and finishes it with these two lines:

> And from which earth and grave and dust
> The Lord shall raise me up I trust.

Raleigh, always the adventurer and explorer, takes his execution calmly, and his last words are of God: ". . . as I hope to see Him in His Kingdom, which I hope will be within this quarter of an hour." His body is buried in a neighboring church, but his head is kept by his widow, in a velvet bag, for the remaining 29 years of her life.

ARCHITECTURE

Arnolfo di Cambio: Santa Maria del Fiore, the Cathedral of Florence (1296–1462). (cf. **66***)

Jacques-Ange Gabriel: the Petit Trianon, Versailles (1762).

Sir Aston Webb: the entrance front to Buckingham Palace (1913).

MUSIC—CLASSICAL

Carlo Maria Giulini: conductor of the Los Angeles Philharmonic Orchestra (1978). He succeeds Zubin Mehta (**42**) who was originally appointed at **26**. A guest conductor of the orchestra is Simon Rattle (**23**).

LITERATURE

Samuel Johnson goes on a journey around the Western Isles of Scotland (1773), accompanied by Boswell (**33**).

PLAYS, DANCE

Henrik Ibsen: *The Master Builder* (1892).

FILMS

Edith Evans: *The Importance of Being Earnest* (1952).

Alfred Hitchcock: *The Birds* (1963).

MUSIC—NON-CLASSICAL

Oscar Hammerstein II: the lyrics for *The Sound of Music* (1959). At **63**, he had written both the libretto and the lyrics for *Flower Drum Song*. In both of these, the music is by Richard Rodgers, seven years younger than he. (cf. **41***)

Louis Armstrong: "Hello Dolly" (1964).

TV, ETC.

Alistair Cooke: "America: A Personal History of the United States" (1972–73). Every week since **38** he has been doing a fifteen-minute radio talk, "Letter from America" for British listeners—his original contract had been for only thirteen weeks.

LOVE, LIFE

Kay Summersby: she is told by doctors that she has cancer and that she has only six months to live (1973). She spends this remaining time in writing about her secret relationship at **33–36** with Dwight D. Eisenhower (**51–54**); he had been in charge of allied forces in Europe during World War II and she had been his driver. Six years before Summersby's illness, Eisenhower had died, at **78**. Kay Summersby lives for another twelve months, and her memoirs are published two years after her death.

The Duke of Gualtieri Avarna, in Sicily, 1981: a court rules that he is free to ring the bell of his private chapel whenever he has had sexual intercourse. His estranged family had complained that it was noise pollution, that he did it to annoy them, and that the bell rings at all times of the day and night.

PRESS

I. F. Stone: end of *I. F. Stone's Weekly* (1971), which he had begun at **46**, and run almost by himself since then.

LAW, CRIME

Eligibility: you are now too old to be appointed a U.S. judge for the first time, according to the American Bar Association.

65

HEALTH

Florence Nightingale, on her birthday (1885): she writes in her diary "Today, Oh Lord, let me dedicate this crumbling old woman to Thee." In fact, she is not crumbling, and has fifteen more years of public service ahead of her. She lives until **90***.

Patrick Steptoe and Robert Edwards (**52**): the world's first conception outside the body, in 1978—the test-tube baby (**–1***). The two doctors have been working together for the past ten years. They have great difficulty in obtaining research grants, and much of Steptoe's work has had to be financed by doing legal abortions.

Life expectancy at birth in the U.S.S.R. (1977): males can expect to live until **64**, and females until **74**.

Life expectancy in the U.S.A. (1976): males who are alive now can expect to live until **78.7**, and females until **82.7**.

In the U.S.A., 28 percent of total medical expenditure goes to people **65+**.

"Bed-disability days" measures the number of days in which you are forced to stay in bed owing to health problems. The rate for people **64** and below is 6.2 days per year. The rate for **65+** is only 15.1 days per year (U.S.A., 1977).

In the U.S.A. (1977), the people aged **65+** form 10.9 percent of the population, and they are 23 million in number. In 1950, there were only 12 million, and in 2000 there are expected to be 32 million, which will be about 12 percent of the population. In the whole world (1977), 6 percent of people are **65+**; 36 percent are **0–15**, and 58 percent are **15** to **64**. In South Asia, only 3 percent are **65+**, but the corresponding figure in Western Europe is 14 percent. If we take Indonesia as an example of a developing country, it is interesting to note that only .66

 percent are **75+**. The corresponding figure for the U.S.S.R. is 1.12 percent being **75+**.

The idea that people are more likely to die because of retirement is probably not true, and SRDS, Sudden Retirement Death Syndrome, may well be a mistaken view. It is likely that poor health precipitates retirement, and this would affect the statistics of death linked to retirement. But studies show normal death rates in the year after mandatory retirement, according to the research of Haynes and others.

If we assume that the dependent population is roughly those under **18** and over the retirement age (**65** male, and **60** female) then in England and Wales these dependent groups are 44 percent of the population.

In Britain, there are different retiring ages per sex—males at **65**, and females at **60**. Using the life expectancy figures at those ages, males can expect 12.4 years of retirement, until **77.4**; and females can expect 20.3 years of retirement, until **80.3**.

On the fixing of **65** as the retirement age: if we take England and Wales in 1871 in order to obtain a rough picture of demographic conditions at the time of Bismarck's legislation, the life expectancy at **0** was **41.4**, male, and **44.6**, female. This compares with **69** and **75.3** in 1970. It was not until the 1940s that the male life expectancy at **0** extended beyond the retiring age. In 1871, even if you were healthy enough to survive childhood, you still could not expect to enter retirement; the life expectancy of a male at **15** was until age **58.4**. The comparable figure in 1970 was **70.8**.

If we take current retiring ages (male **65**, and female **60**, in England and Wales), then in 1871 6.17 percent of the population was in this pensionable group—though of course there was no pension to be obtained. In 1931, the comparable figure was 9.4 percent, and in 1976, 17.2 percent. If we follow the standards used in the development of the original pensions, then we should raise the retirement age to around **73–77**.

Retirement age in the Chinese bureaucracy of mandarins was fixed in 1757 at **55**, by Emperor Ch'ien-lung (**46**). Later, when he was **57**, the emperor changed this rule to **65**—but retirement was not strictly enforced. Ch'ien-lung retired himself at **84**, but was a considerable influence until his death at **87**. The mandarin retirement rule of 1757 was the first in the 2,000 year history of the mandarin system; perhaps it is relevant to note that China experienced a doubling of population around that time, from 150 million (1700) to 313 million (1794).

HISTORY—WORLD

Ivan the Great: death (1505). He has had the longest reign of any ruler of Russia, having held office since **22***. Also: Catherine the Great dies at **67*** (1796), having been Empress since **33**. Alexander II dies at **62**

(1881); Ivan the Terrible dies at **53** (1584); and Peter the Great dies at **52** (1725). The last-ever Czar, Nicholas II, is killed at **50**.

HISTORY—U.S.A.

George Washington, in 1797: retirement, from the presidency. His Farewell Address (**64**) is a landmark statement. He now returns home to Mt. Vernon. At **67**, it is proposed that he should become head of the army again, but no military action follows. George Washington dies at **67**, and is buried at Mt. Vernon.

President James Monroe: the Monroe Doctrine (1823, Dec. 2), seeking to limit and end European expansion in America.

William Jennings Bryan dies (1925), a few days after surviving intense cross-examination by Clarence Darrow (**68**) at the Scopes "Monkey" trial. Darrow's side is for the Darwinian theory of evolution; Bryan is a literal believer in the Book of Genesis.

Douglas MacArthur, in 1945: at the conclusion of the war in the Pacific, he is appointed the effective ruler and "Shogun" of Japan during its occupation. MacArthur had gained distinction during World War I (**37–38**) and at **40** became Superintendent of West Point. At **50** he was Army Chief of Staff; at **52**, he was ordered by President Herbert Hoover to drive the Bonus Marchers out of Washington. His brilliantly successful leadership in the Pacific campaign is at **61–65** and is later seen as a supreme achievement of generalship in World War II. Now at **65** he organizes the rebuilding and democratization of Japan; his regime helps to lay the foundations of the country's future wealth. At **70**, he becomes commander of U.S. forces in Korea, and has another brilliant success at the Inchon landing. But he exceeds his authority by attempting to extend the scope of the fighting, and at **71** he is stripped of his command by President Harry Truman (**66**). On his return MacArthur looks to the future, and says, "Old soldiers never die. They just fade away." He spends the rest of his life as a heroic figure, until his death at **84**.

Ronald Reagan, in 1976: having been Governor of California **55–63**, he now attempts to become the Republican candidate for the presidency. But Gerald Ford (**62**) is preferred. To the surprise of many, Reagan does not give up his presidential ambitions, and makes another attempt at **69***.

Richard Nixon continues in retirement (1978), having recently published his memoirs; becomes a grandfather for the first time.

John F. Kennedy would have been **65** in 1982.

HISTORY—U.K.

Robert Walpole resigns as the first-ever Prime Minister (Feb. 1742). He receives an earldom, and £4,000 per year. He lives until **68**, and has held power from **44** until now.

 Winston Churchill becomes Prime Minister for the first time (1940). Between **63–65**, his reputation is transformed from (1) a formerly brilliant young man who has become an irrelevance, to (2) the genuine savior of his country. By leading the country in a war for survival, he is living out the self-image that he gave himself in his **20***s, as a person of destiny who will inevitably affect history. Events now at last provide him with his great opportunity. His speeches at **65–66** are instrumental in preventing the success of Adolf Hitler (**51–52**). At **67**, he is Premier during the war in North Africa, the last successful independent action by the British Empire. The war is concluded at **70**, but Churchill's reputation as a romantic imperialist and anti-Socialist lose him the subsequent election. He occupies his time out of government by writing a history of the war. At **71**, he identifies the "Iron Curtain" between Russia and the West, and encourages a policy of European union. At **76**, he is elected Prime Minister again. He survives a stroke at **78**, but resigns at **80***.

RELIGION, PHILOSOPHY

Voltaire: *Candide* (1759).

John Paul I: Pope, for 33 days (1978).

SOCIAL SCIENCE, EDUCATION

Charlotte Buhler, the researcher, has grouped people now into four types: (1) want to rest and relax; (2) want to keep active; (3) dissatisfied with their past, but resigned; (4) life has been meaningless, and now feel frustrated.

SCIENCE, TECHNOLOGY

Jean Baptiste Lamarck: *Philosophie zoologique* (1809): this is the first book to put forward a coherent theory of evolution. After a career as a botanist, he was appointed professor of invertebrate zoology at **49**, and this was perhaps the beginning of the peak years of his life. He publishes his last book at **78**, and survives until **85**, outliving four wives.

MONEY, WORK

Andrew Carnegie sells out his business interests to the new United States Steel Corporation (1901). In the next 18 years, he spends $350 million on such projects as public libraries, the Carnegie Hero medal, and so on.

Andrew Mellon: Secretary of the Treasury (1921–29), for the next eight years; by **73**, he reduces the U.S. national debt to $16 billion.

Henry Ford: the Model A Ford (1928)—but this is the end of his total domination of the car market, as others offer a greater choice. At

65, he keeps fit by running three miles per day. At **69**, Ford is extensively featured in *Brave New World* by Aldous Huxley (**38**).

Jean Paul Getty's fifth marriage ends (1957), and he decides to be a bachelor for the rest of his life (lives for almost another 20 years). He had fathered his last child at **53**.

Otto von Bismarck (**68**) chose **65** as the age for receiving retirement benefits when he initiated the pension and benefit system in 1884.

The U.S. Social Security Act (1935) is associated with Senator Robert F. Wagner (**48**).

In a survey (1968) of the 66 centimillionaires in the U.S.A., the average age was found to be **65** (—*Fortune*).

In the U.S.A. (1977), there are 1.7 million males and 1 million females in employment in the age group **65**+. This is out of a total labor force of 97 million people.

RENAISSANCE

Thomas Jefferson: end of his presidency (1809). After writing the Declaration of Independence at **33*** he has served as U.S. representative in France, **41–46**. His wide-ranging *Notes on the State of Virginia* had been completed at **39**. He traveled extensively in Europe, and observed the beginnings of the French Revolution. In Paris, as a widower of **44**, it is possible that he fell in love with one of his slaves, Sally Hemings (**14**); she is said to have seven children by him, the last when he is **61**. From **50–53**, Jefferson is the first Secretary of State, and then returns to Monticello. In his early **50**s, he redesigns the house in its permanent form, using ideas gained abroad, and he pursues a policy of scientific estate management; he institutes a small factory to manufacture nails, and staffs it with slaves, aged **10–16**. He is Vice-President at **53**, and President **57–65**. The Louisiana Purchase occurs at **60**. After retiring from national government, his main achievement is the development of the University of Virginia. From **77** onward, he designs both the buildings of the university and its curriculum. He also supervises the hiring of faculty. Jefferson lives until **83**, in full possession of his faculties; his old age is spent at Monticello, surrounded by a constant stream of visitors who are eager to meet such a figure from history.

ARCHITECTURE

Richard M. Hunt: The Breakers, Newport, Rhode Island (1892–95).

Le Corbusier: Chandigarh—the Palace of Justice, and the Secretariat (1952–56).

ART

The Japanese scheme for "Living National Treasures" is part of the Cultural Assets Protection Law, which originally had the conventional conservation aim of preserving historic paintings and buildings. But a Living National Treasure is someone whose skill, not artifacts, is the "intangible cultural property" which must be preserved. Typical of these intangibles are traditional methods of dyeing, and the religious ritual dances performed by mendicant mountain priests. A Living National Treasure receives a grant of one million yen per year. From 1951 to 1975, only 72 people received this designation. The last four were two Kabuki actors, Kanzaburo Nakamura XVII (**65**) and Koshiro Matsumoto VIII (**64**); and two sword polishers, the first-ever to be so designated, Nisshu Honami (**67**) and Kokei Ono (**61**).

MUSIC—CLASSICAL

J. S. Bach dies (1750, July 28), working to complete *The Art of Fugue.* Although well known in his native area, his memory now fades away quite rapidly, as his children go on to produce new kinds of music. Bach's manuscripts are even said to be used for scrap paper. But 50 to 80 years after his death, interest revives, and he is seen as virtually a saint, as well as a genius. His later fame is far greater than anything he has known in his lifetime.

Dame Nellie Melba: her farewell performance at Covent Garden (1926, June 8). She finishes with the last act of *La Bohème,* and her Rodolfo is **35**, and her Marcello is **30**. Melba lives till **69**.

LITERATURE

Boris Pasternak: completion of *Dr. Zhivago* (1955); publication at **67**; Nobel Prize at **68**.

F. R. Leavis receives an honorary fellowship from Downing College, Cambridge. Although arguably the best critic in English literature at Cambridge, it was not until his **mid-50**s that he was even granted a lectureship.

PLAYS

Ben Travers: *She Follows Me About* (1975).

FILMS

George Cukor: *My Fair Lady* (1964). The designer is Cecil Beaton (**60**); with Audrey Hepburn (**35**), Rex Harrison (**56**), and Wilfred Hyde White (**61**).

Walt Disney dies (1966), with his Florida Disneyworld still under construction.

Luchino Visconti: *Death in Venice* (1971); and *Ludwig* at **67**; *Rocco and His Brothers* was at **53**.

Richard Brooks: director, *Looking for Mr. Goodbar* (1977).

Alec Guinness: *Tinker, Tailor, Soldier, Spy* (1979). He starred in the film *Bridge on the River Kwai* at **43**, and in *Star Wars* at **63**.

Richard Salant is forced to leave the presidency of CBS News (1979) because of reaching the network's mandatory retiring age. He immediately moves across to NBC and does well for himself. Only one administrator is allowed to break the retirement age rule—William S. Paley (**78***), the chairman and founder.

LOVE, LIFE

Giacomo Casanova starts writing his memoirs (1790). (cf. **15***)

In the U.S. population **65+**, there are 68.4 males to every 100 females.

Of people **65+** in the U.S.A. (1977), 52 percent are widowed, 37 percent are married with the spouse present, 6.4 percent single, 2.8 percent divorced, and 1.8 percent married but separated.

Although it is often believed that old people are likely to be in institutions or homes, this is in fact not the case. For example, a survey in the U.S.A. (1970) showed that the population of homes for the aged and dependent was 928,000 out of a total population of 203 million. Out of all people **65+** (U.S.A., 1976), only 4.48 percent live in institutions.

In Victorian England, the only state equivalent to our pensions was entry into a workhouse. In 1868, the Boards of Guardians categorized their population first into male and female, and then into aged, able-bodied, children, and sick. The guardians were specifically warned, by the Poor Law Board, not to regard **60** as the threshold of being aged. Instead, they had to take a function approach, and judge each individual on his or her personal fitness. Presumably a fixed pension age grew up later because of the difficulties and abuses that could surround this functional definition of the aged. The Victorian workhouse had a punitive atmosphere so as to actively discourage drifting and unemployment, and to stimulate the elderly into having made their own provisions for themselves. Three details show the repelling atmosphere of the workhouse: (1) married couples could not live together, but had to go separately into the male and female wards; (2) in the wards, beds were 2 feet 6 inches wide, and there was only 1 foot 6 inches space between beds; (3) in the diet, meat was hardly plentiful since it had to be served "at least once per week."

In Britain at the beginning of the twentieth century, 10 percent of the **65+** lived in workhouses; 20 percent of the **70+**; and 33 percent of the **75+**. These workhouses were the old Poor Law institutions for those without any resources, and were the bottom of society. Fear of the workhouse was designed to promote thrifty and industrious habits among the working class.

PRESS

At *Le Monde,* Paris, the editor must now retire—but if the journalists vote a special approval, then he or she can stay until **68**.

EXPLORATION

Francis Chichester: completion of his recordbreaking solo sailing trip around the world (1967). Previously he has had a number of careers, including pioneering work in aviation; at **28** he had made a solo flight from England to Australia. At **44** he had started a map business. He started ocean yachting at **52**, and won the first solo transatlantic yachting race at **59**. Now at **65** he achieves his greatest fame, and he goes on to do another solo crossing of the Atlantic at **69**, completing 4,000 miles in 22 days. He dies at **70**. Chichester stops at only one port in his trip around the world; the first solo sail without stopping at any port is by Robin Knox-Johnston (**30**, in 1968–69).

LAW, CRIME

John Mitchell leaves prison (1979) after serving 14 months for his part in Watergate. During the Nixon administration, he had been the chief law officer, the Attorney General.

Fear of crime is said to increase as people get older. But most statistics show that chances of being a crime victim diminish steadily from **25** onward. The only two crimes where this is not the case are purse-snatching and pickpocketing; here, the chances of being a victim diminish after **24**, but increase again around **65**.

SPORTS

Woody Hayes (1979) is fired as coach of Ohio State's football team, after he has hit an opposing player (**20**). Hayes has been the autocrat of the Ohio team since **37**, and has been brilliantly successful. But recently his obsessions about winning have led to an increasingly bad temper—this assault at **65** is just the last in a series of embarrassing incidents. In the same year, "Bear" Bryant (also **65**) continues as football coach at the University of Alabama, running the "Crimson Tide."

Phil Weld: winner of the 1980 Singlehanded Transatlantic Yacht Race. The runner-up is Nick Keig (**44**). Phil Weld is a former Massachusetts newspaper owner and he is the oldest competitor in the race. At **57**, he had finished twenty-seventh in the transatlantic race. At **61**, he had capsized in the Atlantic, and had had to wait four days on the upturned hull before he was rescued.

Finishers and Non-finishers

To be intelligent enough to read this book is to be intelligent enough to have your own entry in it. Each person of our acquaintance has within them at least one project which would be good enough for an entry here. But out of a million readers, only a few will finish a project which is good enough for the next edition. Many will start, but few will finish. We asked Zarathustra to speak on the differences between finishers and nonfinishers.

To finish is to transform yourself. To be a finisher is to enter the adult world; to nonfinish is to baby yourself. Finishers live on the sunny mountaintop; nonfinishers are wan and sunless, and they linger half-heartedly at the midpoint.

Nonfinishers come near to the end, and then stop. Finishing causes them fear. Nonfinishers like to be in the world of production, but without going to the end of the race. Finishers know that there is only one dignity—to finish. Nonfinishers are afraid of conquest. To finish is to conquer the mass of nice ordinary nonfinishers. Nonfinishers decline to hurt other nonfinishers. But finishers see only one imperative—finishing.

Finishers have a style, or a channel, or an organization, through which they can express their ideas. Nonfinishers are full of ideas—but have no easy manner of expression. Nonfinishers are searching around for the vehicle that will carry their ideas. Nonfinishers are at war with the organization, style, or other channel through which they are currently trying to work. Finishers already have the paradigm/vehicle/channel/organization through which they are now in action, even at this present moment.

Finishers are, roughly, satisfied with themselves now. Long-term ambitions are temporarily put aside, while they finish. Finishing expresses themselves at this moment—and this is right. Nonfinishers are dissatisfied with themselves. For a nonfinisher to finish would be to make permanent an unsatisfactory view of him or her self. To be a nonfinisher is to continue the endless search for the ideal self. Nonfinishers have the luxury of putting off any decision about themselves.

Finishers are always starters; some nonfinishers never even start. Other nonfinishers start too much—they start and start again. The nonfinisher is the dilettante; at first acquaintance, the nonfinisher is more fascinating than the finisher. Later, this fascination turns to ashes.

Nonfinishers are operating within systems of rules, regulations, obligations by others to them, and general doctrines of fairness. Finishers are finishing. Finishers use whatever rules or people are necessary so that they can finish. Nonfinishers would have finished if only the circumstances were right; finishers create their own opportunities for finishing. Finishers will finish whether or not the circumstances are favorable.

Both finishing and nonfinishing are equally addictive. Nonfinishers are the victims of their own cycle of nonfinishing. Nonfinishers set up overlarge projects, and so never have the sensation of finishing. Finishers aim for smaller goals, and know that one finish leads to the next. To finish is a sweetness beyond any temporary pain.

Nonfinishers are anxious to get the right conditions before they can begin to finish. Nonfinishers are good at getting things out of the way, getting the mood right, getting ready, and clearing the desk so that they can have a free run at finishing. Nonfinishers must get important issues out of the way before they can start finishing. Nonfinishers must get clear in their relationships with all the people involved. True finishers put finishing first; and all these preliminaries come last. To get ready for finishing is to be a nonfinisher.

For finishers, the best is enemy of the good. To postpone finishing until you have perfection is, in practice, to be always a nonfinisher. Ambition leads to finishing; but to be consumed with overwhelming ambition leads only to the ranks of the nonfinishers. Nonfinishers hate to draw the line; they never have an end in sight; they cannot understand the benefits of beginning-middle-end. A finisher's project is finite; a nonfinisher's project is infinite and unfinishable.

Nonfinishers will finish when they can find a project that will solve all their problems in one go. Finishers are more incremental and aim to finish a series of projects. Nonfinishers want to avoid this gradual process and they look lovingly at the people (all two of them) who have managed to be instant finishers. Nonfinishers fear a step-by-step approach. Nonfinishers aim to be free in one leap; years and years go by, and the nonfinisher is still looking for this instant success.

Nonfinishers like to help others. Nonfinishers help good causes with their time and dilettante support. Nonfinishers are good supporters. Finishers are clear on this issue: to finish is your main contribution to the world.

Nonfinishers are keen on advice—both the giving and the receiving of advice. Nonfinishers like to sit around in meetings. Late night discussions show commitment to a project. Finishers spend this time in finishing. Nonfinishers want advice on themselves and their progress. Nonfinishers sit around with other nonfinishers, and set up more discussions. Finishers know that to finish is worth a million conferences.

Nonfinishers are held in place by friends. Finishers have friends who are stimulated by your finishing. The friends of a nonfinisher like you to be the way you are—dependent. Nonfinishers have no idea how much their acquaintances would be disturbed by their finishing. Nonfinishers are surrounded by other nonfinishers. These nonfinishers may even despise finishing; they find failure more authentic than finishing. To finish is to disturb the balance of relationships—better to postpone finishing for a little longer. Nonfinishing friends collude in your nonfinishing; while finishing friends look forward to your finishing.

Nonfinishers must be driven away from you; when you walk with a nonfinisher, you must carry a whip.

Nonfinishers are afraid of the judgments that their finished work will cause. The project, once finished, becomes an object to be evaluated. Other people, often the nonfinishers of our society, will act as critics. To finish is to be aggressive. To be a nonfinisher is to avoid this aggression, but to be rewarded with nothing. Finishing is aggression, but is rewarded by serenity.

66

HEALTH

Major Reginald Bristow dies (Scotland, 1977) after being in a coma since **48**. He had been in a road accident and had never recovered consciousness. Soon after the accident, his last son was born, and had grown up normally during the father's time in coma. In a similar case, David Bisset survives in a coma until his death at **49** (England, 1979) after a road accident had injured him at **40**.

HISTORY—WORLD

Abdulhamid II is thrown out of office as head of the Ottoman or Turkish Empire (1909). Although a reforming sultan, he has created enemies through his autocratic manner. The opposition has grouped itself under the banner of the Young Turks, and they now take over the running of the country. Abdulhamid is not executed, but lives under supervision until his death at **75**.

Hu Yao-bang: chairman of the Chinese Communist party (1981).

HISTORY—U.K.

Disraeli publishes *Lothair* (1870), a novel. He had resigned as Prime Minister at **64**. (cf. **75***)

RELIGION, PHILOSOPHY

Thomas Cranmer is literally stripped of his vestments as Archbishop of Canterbury (1556) and later burned to death, for his support of the Reformation. At **59**, he had been instrumental in the writing of the Book of Common Prayer. Following the success of counter-Reformation forces, he wavers in his beliefs, and signs documents renouncing some of his earlier statements. When being burned, he suffers remorse at this self-betrayal, and he holds his right hand in the flames, so that it is burned first.

Jean-Jacques Rousseau: death (1778). One version of his last words is "God! See how pure the sky is. There is not a single cloud. Don't you see that its gates are open and that God awaits me?"

This is both the approximate average age of popes on election, in the twentieth century; and the average age of the Conclave of Cardinals. Out of 115 cardinals eligible to vote in 1978 (**80** and under), the youngest twenty-two were **50–60**; and the oldest fifty-four were **71–80***.

SOCIAL SCIENCE, EDUCATION

Richard Gough: *The History of Myddle* (1701).

W. G. Sumner: *Folkways* (1906)—first use of the word "ethnocentric."

MONEY, WORK

Colonel Harlan Sanders: start of Kentucky Fried Chicken (1956). At **40**, he had opened his first restaurant, as a sideline to his service station. Up till then, he had not been able to stick to any single career. From **40** onward, his restaurant earns a statewide reputation, but at **64** new roads cause the isolation of his restaurant and the collapse of its value. Now at **66**, he travels the U.S.A., selling his private method of speedy but attractive frying of chicken. He franchises the name and the method, in return for a four percent royalty. By **70**, he has 400 franchises, and 638 by **74**. (cf. **86***)

Roy Williams: elected president of the Teamsters union (U.S.A., 1981), for a five-year term of office.

Michelangelo: completion of the "Last Judgment" on the altar wall of the Sistine Chapel (Rome, 1541). He had begun this at **61**, and his work on the ceiling there had been from **33–37***. His sonnets and other poems are written mainly between **55–70**. At **71**, he produces designs for the Capitoline Hill square in Rome, and at **72** he designs the dome of St. Peter's Basilica; this is not completed in his lifetime. His "Pietà" in Florence Cathedral, with its self-portrait of an old man holding Christ, is finished at **75**. For Michelangelo, the last twenty years of his life are as busy as ever; he is now producing some of the best-known visual images in history, before his death at **88***.

ARCHITECTURE

Arnolfo di Cambio: Palazzo Vecchio, Florence (1298).

Giovanni and Bartolomeo (**47**) Buon: Ca' d'Oro (1421–40)—the most beautiful house in Venice. Giovanni dies at **87**, two years after the building is completed.

William Kent: Horse Guards, Whitehall, London (c. 1751)

Frank Lloyd Wright, in 1935: "Falling Water," the Pennsylvania house built over a waterfall. At this time, he publishes *Broadacre City*, his urban planning proposals. The Johnson Wax office building, Wisconsin, is at **67**, and the adjacent laboratories are at **75**; Wright, never a shy person, says that these are "one of the world's most remarkable structures." Many people agree with him. At **69** onward he designs Taliesin West, his monastery for architects in the wilds of Arizona. His Price Tower, combining offices and apartments, is completed at **87**, the same year in which construction starts on the Guggenheim Museum, New York; this had been designed at **74**. Frank Lloyd Wright designs his largest-ever and perhaps most attractive building at **89***. (cf. **-1***)

LITERATURE

Hermann Hesse: *Magister Ludi* (1943). *Demian* was at **42**, and *Der Steppenwolf* at **50**. Hesse lives until **85**.

FILMS

Will Hays retires from the "Hays Office" (1945), where he has enforced a morality code on Hollywood since he was **42**.

John Huston: *Fat City* (1972), a film about failed boxers.

Gingers Rogers performs on a nightclub tour of North America (1978).

TV, ETC.

Kenneth Clark: "Civilization" (1969).

Michael Killanin (1980): chief administrator of the Olympic Games. He has held this position since **58**, and now retires. His predecessor, Avery Brundage, becomes chief administrator at **65** (1952), and continues in office until **85**, dying at **87**. Brundage has himself been successful as an athlete, winning the then equivalent of the decathlon, in the U.S.A, at **27**, **29**, and **31**. Also, at **28**, he started his own construction company in Chicago, and becomes a multimillionaire. In a third career, Brundage is one of the most distinguished collectors of oriental art, and endows a large collection in San Francisco.

67

HISTORY—WORLD

K'an-hsi, Emperor of China, in 1721: he celebrates his 60 years of rule—roughly, he has been China's Peter the Great—and holds a "Festival of Old Men." From all over China, old men come to Peking. At a feast, everyone **90+** receives a present from the hands of the emperor; younger people get a present from an official. Throughout the Empire, presents are given to the old—**90+** get 30 bushels of rice and two pieces of common silk; **100+** get 50 bushels of rice, one piece of common silk, and one piece of fine silk. The emperor's grandson, Ch'ien-lung (**12**), "Lasting Glory," witnesses this event, and himself repeats it when he is **76**. He then comments:

> Grandfather and grandson
> Twice feasted with thousands of elders
> In all of history
> There is no parallel.

Catherine the Great: death (1796). She has a heart attack while urinating. She had become ruler of Russia at **33**. At **50**, she made a list of her achievements so far: these included 78 victories in battle, 144 cities built, and 123 edicts to improve the lot of the people.

General de Gaulle: Prime Minister of France (1958). During the failure of the war in Algeria, de Gaulle offers to be head of government, if he can have a free hand to promote a new constitution which would centralize power in the presidency. De Gaulle wins a referendum on the constitution, and himself becomes President. In his late **60**s, he resolves the war in Algeria. In his early **70**s, he pursues a new and vigorous foreign policy; and at **77** he successfully rides out the riots of 1968. In effect, at **67**, de Gaulle comes out of his self-imposed exile entirely on his own terms, because people see him as the last hope for ending the crisis. De Gaulle had made his name at **49*** by seizing leadership during another crisis. At **78**, he resigns as President, and he dies at **79**, in Colombey-les-Deux-Églises.

Jiang Qing: death sentence, suspended (1981) for her crimes during China's Cultural Revolution, when she was **53–63**. She has been one of the Gang of Four.

Menachem Begin wins reelection as Prime Minister of Israel (1981). He beats Shimon Peres **(57)**.

HISTORY—U.S.A.

Harry Smoler: election, for the first time, to the New York State Assembly (1978). He beats candidates of **24**, **25**, and **26**.

William Casey: Director of the Central Intelligence Agency (1981).

HISTORY—U.K.

Henry I dies (1135, Dec. 1); he had been King since **32**. His bowels are buried in France, and the rest of his body is buried in England.

Mrs. Pankhurst opens an English tea shop (1925) at Juan-les-Pins, in the South of France, but it stays open for only a few months. She stands unsuccessfully as a Conservative MP at **68**, and dies at **70**. Votes for women had come when she was **60**.

Michael Foot: elected leader of the Labour party (1980); as the new leader of the opposition, he is in effect the alternative prime minister.

SOCIAL SCIENCE, EDUCATION

Sir Francis Galton: *Natural Inheritance* (1889)—a key book in the development of statistics. (cf. **70***)

Freud: *The Ego and the Id* (1923). Freud has the first of his 36 operations for cancer of the jaw. With so much bone removed, he has to wear upper and lower prostheses inside his mouth. By his death at **83**, his cheek is eaten away by the disease. Freud has always been a heavy smoker, and finds it impossible to give up smoking. He continues to smoke four cigars per day, even though he is advised of the dangers of doing this. (cf. **73***)

B. F. Skinner: *Beyond Freedom and Dignity* (1971).

Barbara Tuchman: *A Distant Mirror: the Calamitous 14th Century* (1979). This has taken her seven years, but immediately sells 500,000 copies.

Milton and Rose Friedman (both **67**): *Free to Choose* (1980).

SCIENCE, TECHNOLOGY

Michael Faraday: experiments to convert the force of gravity directly into electricity (1859). To do this he drops weights of 280 pounds from a tower 116 feet high. The weights are tested for an electrical current at the end of the fall, but none is found. This work is part of Faraday's attempt to provide a unified theory of the forces of the universe, but in this he has attempted too much. At **60**, he published *On the Physical Character of the Lines of Force*, which forms the origin of field theory, and which is a development away from his earlier views (cf. **15*** and **40***). In his **50**s and **60**s, he advises the government on such problems as the design of lighthouses and the preservation of paintings in the National Gallery, London. Faraday's memory and physical health gradually deteriorate, but he husbands his energy by (1) concentrating only on central tasks, to the neglect of secondary matters, and (2) refusing all honors; at **65**, he writes, "I must remain plain Michael Faraday to the last; and let me now tell you, that if I accepted the honour [presidency] which the Royal Society desires to confer on me, I could not answer for the integrity of my intellect for a single year." Faraday lives until **75**.

MONEY, WORK

John Sherman: the Sherman Anti-Trust Act (1890).

Charles Revson: marketing of the fragrance "Charlie" (1974).

RENAISSANCE

Leonardo da Vinci: death (France, 1519). Previously he has said this about life and creativity: "See: one's hopes and wishes to return to one's homeland and origin—they are just as moths trying to reach the light. And the man who is looking forward with joyful curiosity for the new spring, and the new summer, and always new months and new years—and even if the time he is longing for ever comes, it will always seem to him to be too late—he does not notice that his longing carries in it the germs of his own death. But this longing is the quintessence, the spirit of the elements, which through the soul is enclosed in the human body and which craves for return to its source. You must know that this very yearning is the quintessence of life, the handmaid of Nature, and that Man is the model of the world."

LITERATURE

Tolstoy has his first bicycle lesson (Mar. 1895). The machine is a gift from the Moscow Society of Velocipede-Lovers, and Tolstoy quickly gains skill at this new activity. He finds that cycling gives him a sense of boyish pleasure. Another advantage is that scientists have recently proved it to be good exercise. However, Tolstoy's secretary and disciple, Vladimir Chertkov (**41**) feels that such a frivolous pursuit is not consistent with Tolstoy's current position as a world leader of morality. (cf. **23***, **35***, **49***, **61***, **70*** and **82***)

H. G. Wells: *The Shape of Things to Come* (1933).

PLAYS, DANCE

Aeschylus: the trilogy, *Oresteia* (458 B.C.).

Euripedes: *Electra* (c. 413 B.C.).

George Bernard Shaw: *St. Joan* (1923).

FILMS

W. C. Fields dies (1964) on Christmas Day, a day that was one of his pet hates.

John Ford: *The Man Who Shot Liberty Valance* (1962).

Spencer Tracy: *Guess Who's Coming to Dinner* (1967), with Katharine Hepburn (**58**), and Sidney Poitier (**40**). Tracy dies shortly after filming ends.

PRESS

Roy Thomson is one of the first from the West to meet Nikita Khrushchev (also **67**) (1962, Feb. 9). Later, he answers his own question: Why did a **67**-year-old do so well? "Experience is a very important element in the management side of business. . . . To be good at anything at all requires a lot of practice, and to be really good at decisions you have to have plenty of practice at taking decisions." Ten years later, he is an early and very successful entrepreneur in North Sea oil.

SPORTS

Juan Fangio (1978) comes in second in a veteran drivers' "Race of Champions," just behind Jack Brabham (**52**). During the race, Fangio reaches 165 mph. He had last won the world championship at **46***.

68

HEALTH

Girolamo Fracastoro: *De contagione et contagiosis morbis* (1546)—the first book on the contagion or germ theory of disease, as opposed to either the religious theories of disease, or the theory of miasma.

Jean Monnet, and others: the Treaty of Rome (1957), establishing the European Economic Community.

Masayoshi Ohira: Prime Minister of Japan (1978), in succession to Takeo Fukuda (**73**). At this date, Emperor Hirohito is **77**.

HISTORY—U.S.A.

William H. Harrison becomes President of the United States, shortly after his **68**th birthday (1841). But he dies from pneumonia after one month in office. He is succeeded by his Vice-President, John Tyler (**51**), the youngest person to hold this office up till this time. Tyler marries for the second time at **54**; he dies at **71**, in bed next to the cot of his fourteenth child Pearl (c. **1**).

Lillian Carter joins the Peace Corps (1966) and spends the next two years working as a nurse at a clinic near Bombay, India. At **70–72**, she is a lecturer, traveling around the U.S.A., in support of the Peace Corps. At **78**, "Miss Lillian" works for the election of her son, Jimmy Carter (**52**) to the presidency.

HISTORY—U.K.

Queen Victoria starts learning Hindustani (1887), as part of her continuing interest in India—of which she has been Empress since **57**. (cf. **81***)

SOCIAL SCIENCE, EDUCATION

Gregory Bateson: *Steps to an Ecology of Mind* (1972).

Studs Terkel: *American Dreams: Lost and Found* (1980).

MONEY, WORK

Commodore Cornelius Vanderbilt: purchase of shares in the New York and Harlem Railroad (1862). This is the beginning of his interest in railroads; although rich, he now starts on the creation of a gigantic fortune. He leaves behind him the world of shipping, in which he has spent all his adult life. At **69**, he takes his first management action, and extends the railroad. At **73**, he secures control of the New York Central, which, at **75**, he unites with the Hudson River Railroad. At **78**, he brings together all his rail interests into one system—this is the dominant transport organization in what is currently the world's most rapidly expanding economic region. At **79**, he begins work on Grand Central Station, New York. At **68**, he is worth $15 million; at his death, **82**, he is worth $100 million.

Giotto: the campanile next to the Cathedral, Florence (1334).

Borromini commits suicide with a sword (1667).

Louis H. Sullivan, just before he dies (1924), hands over his life's collection of drawings of ornament to Frank Lloyd Wright (**57**).

Mies van der Rohe: Seagram Building, New York City (1954–58). (cf. **74***)

Le Corbusier: Maison Jaoul (1955–57).

Buckminster Fuller publishes "Untitled epic poem on the history of industrialization" (1963). (cf. **69***)

ART

Mark Rothko commits suicide (1970) by taking a drug overdose and slicing his elbow veins with a razor. He had hit on his abstract-expressionist style at around **43—46**. Rothko leaves 798 paintings. He writes his controversial will at **65**; after his death, the legal fees for disputes over this will are over $3 million.

MUSIC—CLASSICAL

Thomas Tallis composes *Spem in Alium*, the 40-part motet, probably written in 1573 to celebrate the birthday of Queen Elizabeth I (**40**). Tallis lives until **80**.

Hubert Parry: *Jerusalem* (c. 1916).

Peter Pears sings the role of Captain Vere, in *Billy Budd*, at the Metropolitan Opera House, New York, 1978.

LITERATURE

Victor Hugo returns to France (1870), from where he has been in political exile for the past 19 years.

T. S. Eliot marries his secretary, Valerie Fletcher (**30**) (1956). At **67**, he had lectured on poetry to 13,000 people in a Milwaukee football stadium, and earned $2,000. At **69**, he writes the play *The Elder Statesman*.

Lillian Hellman: *Pentimento* (1973); and *An Unfinished Woman* at **64**.

PLAYS

Ibsen: *John Gabriel Borkman* (1896).

FILMS

C. Aubrey Smith: his first talking picture (1931). This is the take-off point for his major career. In Hollywood, he now becomes the all-purpose representative of British imperialism, and he is eventually cast in almost all the authority positions of that system. For example, he plays Lord Chatham, the Prime Minister, at **72**; the Duke of Wellington at **71** and **75**; the head of Scotland Yard at **82**; and the Lord Chief Justice at **84**. Even in his **80**s, he is renowned for always knowing his lines at the commencement of each day's shooting. At **85**, he plays Lord Caversham in *An Ideal Husband*, but dies shortly before he is due to act in *The Forsyte Saga*.

Cecil B. De Mille: *Samson and Delilah* (1949).

Charlie Chaplin: *A King in New York* (1957); this is a bit of a failure. *A Countess from Hong Kong*, at **77**, is even worse.

Samuel Fuller: *The Big Red One* (1980).

Ginger Rogers: three weeks of shows with the Rockettes, at Radio City Music Hall (1980). She still spends over half the year performing in nightclubs. Her film career took off at **22**, in *Flying Down to Rio*, with Fred Astaire (**34**).

PRESS

Charles Addams: marriage (1980) to Marilyn Mathews Miller (**53**). He is the cartoonist who has specialized in the bizarre and the spooky. This wedding takes place in a dog cemetery, and the bride wears black.

EXPLORATION

Guy Touzeau: walk from Menton, in the South of France, to Edinburgh (1978). He covers the 1,500 miles in about 15 months, and his possessions are in a cart pulled by a donkey, "Rose" (**12**). Touzeau is a former advertising executive, and he does the journey in tribute to *Travels with a Donkey in the Cevennes*, by Robert Louis Stevenson (**28**, in 1878).

LAW, CRIME

Albert B. Fall is sentenced to one year in prison, and fined $100,000, for his part in the Teapot Dome scandal. At **60**, as Secretary of the Interior, he had directed that U.S. Navy oil reserves at Teapot Dome, Wyoming, be leased to companies run by acquaintances. Coincidentally, Fall receives $100,000 from these acquaintances to improve his ranch. On appointment as Secretary, Fall had been promised the first vacancy on the U.S. Supreme Court. After prison, he never pays his fine, but dies broke.

Judge John J. Sirica is instrumental in exposing the Watergate scandal (1973). At **74**, he retires and sells his memoirs for over $500,000.

Teddy Tinling continues as a leading designer of tennis dresses. For example, at Wimbledon (1978), four players wear his creations—Billie Jean King (**34**), Virginia Wade (**33**), Martina Navratilova (**22**), and Tracy Austin (**15**).

69

HISTORY—WORLD

Zenko Suzuki: Prime Minister of Japan (1980); he had entered Parliament at **37**. He succeeds Masayoshi Ohira (**70**) who has died in office. A few months previously Hirokichi Nadao (**79**) and Haruo Okada (**65**) had been elected Speaker and Deputy-Speaker of the House of Representatives. In the recent election, the candidate with the greatest number of votes has been Fusae Ichikawa (**87**). Now, Zenko Suzuki's new Japanese cabinet is aged **71, 71, 69, 69, 67, 67, 66, 63, 61, 61, 60, 58, 57**, and **56**. In the following year, the Minister of Home Affairs (**71**) becomes ill, and his place is taken by Tokichi Abiko (**76**).

John Bjekle Petersen: reelection as Prime Minister of Queensland, Australia (1980). He has held this office since **57**.

HISTORY—U.S.A.

Ronald Reagan is elected fortieth President of the United States (1980). He is the oldest person to enter office, and he defeats Jimmy Carter (**56**). At this moment, his supporters include: Earle Jorgensen (**82**); Holmes Tuttle (**75**); Justin Dart (**73**); Senator Paul Laxalt (**58**); his wife, Nancy Reagan (**59**); Vice-President George Bush (**56**); James A. Baker III (**50**); and Ed Meese (**48**).

At **70**, Reagan survives a bullet from a would-be assassin (**25**).

HISTORY—U.K.

Neville Chamberlain: Munich agreement (Sept. 1938), with Adolf Hitler (**49**), and Mussolini (**55**). This agreement guarantees "peace in our time."

Harold Macmillan resigns as Prime Minister (Oct. 1963), and arranges to be succeeded by Sir Alec Douglas-Home (**60**), the fourteenth Earl of Home, thus excluding R. A. Butler (**60**). Macmillan had said that you have "never had it so good" at **63**; "wind of change" speech in South Africa at **66**. But he had fired seven cabinet members on one day at **68**, and had been damaged by the scandal of John Profumo (**48***). (cf. **85***)

RELIGION, PHILOSOPHY

Swami Prabhupada arrives in New York with about $6; he has a struggle to survive, but later founds the Hare Krishna movement.

SOCIAL SCIENCE, EDUCATION

E. Yale sends books and other gifts to a new college (1718), and the college then calls itself "Yale."

Gunnar Myrdal: *Asian Drama: an Enquiry into the Poverty of Nations* (1968). He had written *An American Dilemma* at **45**.

Margaret Mead: *Culture and Commitment: a Study of the Generation Gap* (1970); also *A Rap on Race* at **70**, with James Baldwin (**47**). She dies at **76**, and takes notes about the process of her own death.

SCIENCE, TECHNOLOGY

Nicolas Copernicus: *De revolutionibus orbium coelestium* (1543), with introduction by Andreas Osiander (**45**) and dedication to Pope Paul III (**76**). This is his first complete book, apart from a translation. Note that this book is published sometime around his **70**th birthday, and it is shown here at **69** so that the entry can be read with Galileo (**69***). This book is the starting point of modern astronomy, and leads to the eventual overthrow of earth-centered models of the universe. Copernicus had gone to university in Poland, **18–22**, followed by seven years study and travel in Italy, which was then the most exciting place in the world. He trained to be an M.D. and this involved detailed study of the planets, whose movements caused disease, according to the prevailing medical-astrological theory. Copernicus first circulates his heliocentric views at **37–41**, in manuscript. This provoked almost no interest whatsoever. After that, Copernicus, a church property administrator in a small town, spends much of the rest of his life gathering and reworking data to support his views. By his **60**s, he has gained a small reputation as a potential revolutionary. At **70**, he dies in Poland, just after a copy of his first and last book has been rushed to him from his Nuremberg printer. Though influential, the new book is not a best-seller; the second edition comes 22 years later, and the third edition is produced after another 52 years.

Galileo is forced by the Inquisition (Rome, 1633) to recant the views expressed in his book *Dialogue* (**68**). This book reports a conversation between supporters of the two sides in the intellectual dispute of the era; viz., is the earth or the sun at the center of the physical universe. He now has to travel to Florence where he dresses in a white robe, and publicly tells of the error of his ways. At **25**, Galileo had been a professor at Pisa University, and had there made his famous observations on the pendulum, and on the same acceleration of different falling objects. He had been **36** when Giordano Bruno **(52)** was burned to death for opposition to church doctrines. At **45**, Galileo built the first effective telescope and thus revolutionized the study of astronomy. He then became convinced of the Copernican heliocentric view, and the *Dialogue* is the culmination of his campaign to promote Copernicanism. The theory is unpopular because (1) it is counterintuitive to suggest that the earth is merely a flying object in space; (2) the theory suggests a new view, that planets are made of earthlike rock, instead of, in the old view, being fluid spheres whose movements make music and which are made of a semimystical substance, linked to Heaven itself; and (3) the theory appears to threaten the prevailing social order. After his setback at **69**, Galileo in the following year begins work on an important text about the mathematics of bodies in motion, and this is published at **74**. He lives until **77**. Galileo's assistant in his last days is Evangelista Torricelli **(33** at Galileo's death) who at **34** demonstrates the Torricelli vacuum, and thus the barometer. Following on from Galileo's work in Pisa, the first pendulum clock is made in 1656 by Christiaan Huygens **(27)**.

Isaac Newton has commented on aging: "The boyling blood of youth puts the spirits upon too much emotion or else causet too many spirits. But could age makes the brain either two dry to move rapidly through or else is defective of spirits." At **69**, in 1711, Newton forces the Royal Society to adjudicate in his quarrel with Leibniz **(66)** over priority in devising calculus. Newton wins the battle, only partly because he has stage-managed the committee. Newton had done his calculus work at around **23***, and Leibniz at around **26–27**. Both of them are intellectual giants, and for both the invention of calculus has been only one achievement out of many. Leibniz dies at **70** when Newton is **73**. In his **70**s, Newton keeps working hard on his obsessions, which include the chronology of ancient civilizations, the Bible, and the nature of God. At **80**, he still does not need spectacles and he retains all but one of his teeth. But it is now too difficult for him to work on gravitational theory since it had "made his head ache and kept him awake so often that he would think of it no more." Newton lives until **83**, and presides over a meeting of the Royal Society shortly before his death.

MONEY, WORK

John D. Rockefeller: the Rockefeller Foundation (1909, June 19); he starts it with a gift of $50 million. In his life his charitable gifts total $244,608,309.74.

 Henry Clay Frick dies (1919); leaving his house as the Frick Museum, New York City.

ARCHITECTURE

Palladio: Church of the Redentore, Venice (1577).

Jacques-Ignace Hittorff: the Gare du Nord, Paris (1861–65).

Pier Luigi Nervi: three stadia for the Olympic Games, Rome (1960).

Alvar Aalto: Finlandia Hall, Helsinki (1967–71).

Buckminster Fuller: dome for the U.S. pavilion, Expo '67, Montreal (1967); his largest-ever geodesic dome. (cf. **74***)

ART

Claude Lorrain: "Landscape with Dancers" (1669). Claude slowly developed his own style from his **40**s onward, and he produces major work into his **70**s.

J. M. W. Turner: "Rain, Steam, and Speed" (1844).

Balthus: "The Cat with the Mirror" (1977–80)—perhaps the best known of his studies, done throughout his life, of the adolescent figure.

Korczak Ziolkowski continues work on the largest sculpture in the world (1978)—a statue whose height is 563 feet, and which shows Crazy Horse, who defeated General Custer at Little Bighorn (1876). Mr. Ziolkowski started work at **39**, and has since then blasted away nearly six million tons of rock. The site of his sculpture is 20 miles from Mount Rushmore, where he had originally trained.

MUSIC—CLASSICAL

Haydn: *The Seasons* (Apr. 1801). At **66**, he had written *The Creation*, as well as the Nelson and the Theresa masses. After a lifetime of writing symphonies, he had been influenced by hearing choral music in London. At **58**, he had heard the Hallelujah chorus for the first time, and burst into tears.

Wagner: *Parsifal* (1882, July 22). His wife Cosima is **45**, and their son Siegfried is **13**. Wagner dies a few months after the first performance, and Cosima and Siegfried keep up the Bayreuth Festival until they both die 47 years later.

Stravinsky: *The Rake's Progress* (1951); and *Cantata on Four Poems by Anonymous English Poets* (1952). Stravinsky had moved to the U.S.A. at **58**. He seems to have had an amazing quality of self-regeneration throughout his life. For example, *The Firebird* at **28**; *Symphony of Psalms* at **48**; and so on. He lives till **89**.

LITERATURE

Czeslaw Milosz: Nobel Prize for literature (1980). In the past ten years, the average age of the recipients of this prize has been **69**. The literary Nobel Prize committee is, by chance, **65** and over (there is no rule that this should be the case). The dominating influences are believed to be Artur Lundkvist (**74**) and Anders Osterling (**96**) who has served on the committee since **35**.

PLAYS

Aeschylus is killed by a tortoise falling on his head (456 B.C.). The tortoise is dropped by a passing eagle which believes the playwright's bald head to be a rock.

Sophocles: *Oedipus Rex* (c. 425 B.C.).

Sarah Bernhardt has a leg amputated (1914) but at **71–72** she goes on her last acting tour of the U.S.A. She lives until **78**, working as an actress until only four days before her death. At **78**, she is so ill that she cannot get out of bed; so, film cameras are brought to her house, and she acts the part of someone lying in bed.

FILMS

Harold Lloyd puts together pieces of his early films, into *Harold Lloyd's World of Comedy* (1962); this is so successful that he does a second version at **71**.

LAW, CRIME

Carmine Galante is shot dead at a Brooklyn restaurant (1979). Galante is said to be a Mafia leader who has aimed to be the Boss of Bosses. Mafia leadership is a crime practiced into old age. For example, a Los Angeles court convicted five men for conspiracy (1980)—they were **68**, **66**, **61**, **59**, and **52**, and were described as leaders of the city's organized crime. After Carmine Galante's death, speculation names his successor as Frank "Funzi" Tieri (**74**).

Dr. Herman Tarnower is shot dead in an argument with Jean Harris (**56**) in Purchase, New York. He has made a fortune from his slimming diet, and has been having an affair with Harris for the past fourteen years. But during this time, despite having "the appearance of a lizard," he has been seeing numerous other women. Harris, a headmistress with a reputation as a disciplinarian and opponent of marijuana, has recently become intensely angry over Tarnower's affection for his medical assistant, Lynne Tryforos (**38**). Tarnower is now shot five times at his $500,000 estate, and dies shortly afterward. Later, Jean Harris is sent to prison until she is at least **72**.

70

HEALTH

Galen: approximate age at death (c.199 A.D., probably in Rome.) His medical theories are dominant in Europe for another 1,300 years.

At birth, the U.S.A. life expectancy (1976) is until **69** (male) and until **76.7** (female). And for those alive now at **70**, the expectancy is until **81** for males and until **84.1** for females.

In England and Wales, you can now expect to live until **82.9** (female) and until **79.6** (male) (1975). Out of total deaths at all ages, 33 percent (male) occur in the ages **65–74**, and 23 percent for females.

The causes of death for males **65–74** (England and Wales, 1977) are: (1) ischemic heart disease; (2) lung cancer; (3) cerebrovascular; (4) bronchitis, emphysema, asthma; (5) pneumonia; (6) miscellaneous other cancers. The causes of female death are: (1) ischemic heart disease; (2) cerebrovascular; (3) miscellaneous other cancers; (4) pneumonia; and (5) breast cancer.

Animals' maximum life span: the Asiatic elephant can live until now. The maximum life span of a raven is until **69**.

HISTORY—WORLD

Empress Tz'u-hsi continues to be the effective ruler of China (1905). Since **25**, she has been perhaps the most powerful woman in China's history—but also one of the most rigid and maladaptive to the modern world. She dies at **72**, and 4,000 years of dynastic rule are ended by revolution three years later.

Mackenzie King continues as Prime Minister of Canada (1945). In all, he holds this office longer than anyone else—**46–51**, **51–55**, and **60–73**.

Golda Meir: Prime Minister of Israel (Mar. 1969), until she experiences a reverse at **75**, and leaves office at **76**.

HISTORY—U.S.A.

S. I. Hayakawa: U.S. Senator from California (1976); this position is obtained in his first run for an elective office. At **49**, he had become a professor at San Francisco State College, after distinguished work in semantics. He makes his reputation at **62**, during student riots at the college. After two college presidents have resigned, he takes charge and defies the rebels. As himself a member of an ethnic minority, he believes that he has the moral strength to stand up to those radicals who are using minority grievances to promote their own ends. Hayakawa now goes on to become a prominent member of the Senate Foreign Relations Committee. Some other old election winners include James Rhodes (**69**) who is reelected Governor of Ohio, in 1978. Daniel Flood is reelected a congressman at **74** (1978). Strom Thurmond is reelected to the U.S. Senate at **75** (1978). Jennings Randolph is reelected to the U.S. Senate at **76** (1978). Barry Goldwater is reelected to the Senate at **71** (1980).

Nelson Rockefeller: death, from a heart attack (1979). He had been Governor of New York from **50–65**. He had unsuccessfully entered presidential election campaigns at **51**, **55**, and **59**, but had been nominated as Vice-President at **66**. In the last year, he has been setting up a business to sell reproductions from his art collections. Rockefeller's death arouses curiosity since his last hour is spent with an art assistant, Megan Marshack (**25**).

HISTORY—U.K.

Neville Chamberlain declares that Britain is at war (1939, Sept. 3). Winston Churchill (also **70**) declares that the war is over (1945, May 8). (cf. **65***)

RELIGION, PHILOSOPHY

The great man is one who never loses his childlike touch.—Mencius (c. 350 B.C.).

Socrates is forced to poison himself with hemlock, having been condemned to death for leading astray the youth of Athens (399 B.C.). He dies at sunset, having had a last dialogue with the tearful Plato (**30**).

Bishop Hugh Latimer and Nicholas Ridley (**55**) are burned to death in Oxford (1555) for their support of the Reformation. Previously, Latimer had taken part in the burning of counter-Reformation supporters. Also, Archbishop Cranmer is burned at **66***; Archbishop Laud is beheaded at **71*** (1645), the last archbishop to be executed; and Father John Southworth is hanged at **72** (1654) for activities as a Catholic missionary within England.

Pope Paul VI: *Humanae vitae* (1968)—this is the document which fixes Catholic opposition to all nonnatural forms of birth control. In effect, the Pill and other methods are banned in favor of the rhythm method. The previous directive on the subject had been *Casti conubii* by Pope Pius XI (**73**, in 1930).

 Eligibility: Anglican bishops must now retire.

This is often accepted as the life span decreed in the Old Testament. Psalm 90 says: "The days of our years are **Threescore Years and Ten;** and if by reason of strength they be **Fourscore** years, yet is their strength labor and sorrow; for it is soon cut off and we fly away." But Genesis 6.3 has this statement: "And the Lord said, My spirit shall not always strive with man, for that he also is flesh; yet his days shall be an **Hundred and Twenty** years." Many biblical figures lived a long time. Sarah had her only child at **90**, when her husband was **99**; and Methuselah fathered his first male child at **187**. It is important to remember that all these ages, even **70**, would be markedly outside the usual expectation of a person living at that time.

SOCIAL SCIENCE, EDUCATION

Friedrich Engels (1890) continues to read seven daily newspapers, in three languages; and he reads nineteen weeklies, in eight languages. He has one of the first telephones, and employs three servants.

Francis Galton: *Finger Prints* (1892), in which he points out the uniqueness of the print of each finger. This leads almost immediately to the first collection of criminal fingerprints.

Jung: *The Phenomenology of the Spirit in Fairy Tales;* and *The Psychology of Transference* (1945 and 1946). At **72**, the C. G. Jung Institute is founded in Zurich. He works hard on his books, viz. *Answer to Job* at **75**, and *Mysterium coniunctionis* at **79**. His most widely known work is written at **85***.

Herbert Marcuse suddenly becomes world famous (1968) when his books are taken up by leaders of student revolt. Previously Marcuse has been admired as a relatively obscure philosopher who has worked on a synthesis of Marx and Freud. He did not become a professor until **56**. His major books are *Eros and Civilization* (**57**), and *One Dimensional Man* at **67**. By his death (**81**), he has almost returned to his original obscurity.

Eligibility: It is now time for your "Festschrift," a collection of papers by your admirers, on the topic(s) which you have spent your life investigating.

MONEY, WORK

Taizo Ishizaka, in 1956: president of the Federation of Economic Organizations, Japan (the leading business group). He resigns at **82**, and is president of the Osaka World's Fair at **84**. Note: Japanese business is remarkable in that one of the "Three Sacred Emblems" of labor policy is the seniority system. In this, part or the whole of your salary is calculated on the basis of your age. Depending on your company, another part is paid on the basis of your performance. The company is thus like a family in which increasing years bring increasing respect and rewards—"The worker exists only with the company." A survey in 1975 showed that, in medium and large Japanese companies, wages and salaries rose consistently from **18** to a peak at **50–59**; but, in small companies, wages peak at **35–39**, and salaries peak at **40–49**.

The average life span of the leading entrepreneurs of the Industrial Revolution was nearly **70**; the current average for their class would have been close to **40**, according to Neil McKendrick, the business historian.

There are about 1.6 million workers in the U.S.A. who are aged between **65** and **70**.

A 1977 act of Congress has raised, from **65** to **70**, the mandatory retiring age that a private company can impose. The Federal government cannot now impose any retiring age at all though tests of competence are of course allowed. A leading sponsor of this legislation is Claude Pepper (**77**), who had become a freshman representative to Congress at **62**.

RENAISSANCE

Howard Hughes: death (1976). He had his first nervous breakdown at **39**, owing to his immense work load and to the overwhelming variety of projects which he had initiated (cf. **2***). At **31**, he had acquired control of TWA, the airline, and because of his incompetent management style he was later forced out of power. At **51**, he had to sell RKO studios which had become a loss-maker during his ownership. At **60**, he receives approximately one half billion dollars for his share in TWA, and he moves to Las Vegas. He lives in a sealed hotel bedroom and sees no one; he buys seven resort-casinos, plus a local TV station whose programing he alters to suit his taste. Hughes gradually loses touch with even his closest associates, and he takes up a number of health fetishes (storing his own urine in glass jars, for example), which insulate him from all normal relationships. At **67**, he sustains a fall and never walks again, due to his disobeying of doctors' instructions concerning his recovery treatment. In his late **60**s, he starves himself and weighs 90 pounds at the end. Hughes dies from drugs and malnutrition; at the moment of his death, he is being transported in his own airplane, without the company of any friends, lovers, or even business colleagues.

ARCHITECTURE

Sir John Soane retires from architectural practice, owing to blindness (1833), but sets up his home and collections and drawings as a permanent public museum.

Richard Strauss: the opera *The Silent Woman* (1934). (cf. **77***)

Toscanini conducts the new NBC Symphony Orchestra at their first-ever performance (1937). He continues to work with them till he is **87**. (cf. **85***)

Sir Henry Wood agrees that he is now no longer fit enough to conduct every night of the Promenade Concerts (1939), so for almost the first time he shares the load with another conductor. He carries on conducting for another five years. Sir Malcolm Sargent, also **70**, conducts 23 of the 1967 Proms.

LITERATURE

Tolstoy writes: "The moral progress of mankind is due to the aged. The old grow better and wiser." He is still overwhelmed by "the tragedy of the bedroom," that is, his sexual desires which invalidate his public antisex philosophy. But he celebrates his birthday (1898) by riding twenty miles, and making love to his wife (**62**). (cf. **82***)

Frank Richards is said to write 38 more books about Billy Bunter, from **70** onward.

Dorothy Parker says on her birthday (1963): "Promise me I won't get old." (cf. **73***)

Enid Blyton writes eleven books this year, including five about Noddy.

Alberto Moravia publishes *The Inner Life* (1978), his first novel in seven years.

FILMS

Now, they say, you should retire at **70**. When I was **70**, I still had pimples.—George Burns (**82**, in 1978).

Maurice Chevalier: *Gigi* (1958); includes his singing "Thank Heaven for Little Girls."

Lillian Gish publishes her memoirs: *The Movies, Mr. Griffith, and Me* (1969).

George Cukor: *Justine* (1969).

Helen Hayes is a stowaway in *Airport* (1970); Oscar.

Pola Negri is brought out of retirement by Walt Disney (**63**), and given a cameo part in his *The Moonspinners*.

Fred Zinnemann: *Julia* (1977), with Jane Fonda (**40**) and Vanessa Redgrave (**40**).

Laurence Olivier: *The Betsy* (1977).

Rex Harrison: wedding to Mercia Tinker (**40**, in 1978)—his sixth marriage.

Akira Kurosawa: *Kagemusha* (1980).

I'd rather have ten years of super-hypermost than live to be **70**, sitting in some goddam chair watching TV.—Janis Joplin, who has died at **27** (1970) from the effects of drugs and overstimulation. (cf. **35***)

Marlene Dietrich is touring Australia (1976).

TV, ETC.

Raymond Massey: last episode of "Dr. Kildare" (1966), also starring Richard Chamberlain (**31**). The series has been running for five years.

Robert Young: last episode of "Marcus Welby, M.D." (1977), begun at **61**. His "Father Knows Best" was between **47–52**.

Joseph Murray, founder of the Irish League of Decency, forces himself to watch the first-ever nude scene on Irish television (1978). But he suffers a heart attack five minutes after the end of the program.

Barbara Woodhouse: "Training Dogs the Woodhouse Way" (1980).

Danny Thomas: "I'm a Big Girl Now" (1981).

LOVE, LIFE

To be **70** years young is sometimes far more cheerful and hopeful than to be **40** years old.—Oliver Wendell Holmes (**79**, in 1889) on the **70**th birthday of Julia Ward Howe.

In the age group **70–74**, there are 73.5 males for every 100 females (U.S.A., 1976).

PRESS

William Loeb continues as publisher of the *Manchester Union Leader* (New Hampshire, 1975).

William Shawn continues as editor of *The New Yorker* (1977).

James Reston continues his column in the *New York Times* (1979).

Betty Kenward continues her London society column under the name "Jennifer" (1976).

Arthur Marshall continues his column for the *New Statesman* (1980).

LAW, CRIME

Simon Weisenthal continues in his work as Nazi hunter (1979), tracking down all those responsible for the Holocaust. He is head of the Jewish Documentation Center in Vienna.

Eligibility: you are now too old to continue as a chief judge, or senior administrator, of a U.S. Federal court; but you can continue as a judge.

Eligibility: you are now too old to be appointed a judge in Idaho or

Michigan. The maximum age for new judges to be appointed in Iowa is **71**.

About four percent of murder victims are **70** or over (U.S.A., 1977).

SPORTS

Dan Maskell continues as the BBC's chief commentator at the Wimbledon tennis championships (1978). He has attended every single day of Wimbledon since **21**.

Colonel Vaughan arrives thirty-third in the Iditarod (1981), the thousand mile dogsled race in Alaska.

Men's track and field records now:

100 meters in 14.6 seconds;
400 meters in 68.4 seconds;
1,500 meters in 5 minutes 30.8 seconds;
the mile in 5 minutes 42.2 seconds;
10,000 meters in 41 minutes 21.0 seconds;
10 mile walk in 1 hour 48 minutes;
high jump of 4 feet 3¼ inches;
and long jump of 14 feet 7½ inches.

Women's track records at **67**:

200 meters in 35.1 seconds;
the mile in 8 minutes 19 seconds;
and the 10,000 meters in 67 minutes 45 seconds.

71

HISTORY—U.S.A.

Leon Jaworski is appointed head of an investigation into alleged corruption in the U.S. House of Representatives (1977).

HISTORY—U.K.

William Gladstone, in 1881: Prime Minister (second time), and Chancellor of the Exchequer (third time). (cf. **75***)

Winston Churchill: his speech at Fulton (Mar. 1946), on the new "Iron Curtain" that is dividing the world. (cf. **80***)

Archbishop William Laud is publicly executed (1645). He had been Archbishop of Canterbury since **62**, but the past five years have been spent in the Tower of London, in the period leading up to the English Civil War.

SOCIAL SCIENCE, EDUCATION

George Herbert Mead: *Mind, Self, and Society* (1934).

Dr. Spock: article in *Redbook* magazine (1974), arguing somewhat against permissiveness. This is said to be his recanting of views expressed at **43***, in his celebrated book on baby care. A new edition is published at **73**, and purged of the original's sexist thinking. Dr. Spock is married for the second time, at **73**, to Mrs. Mary Councille (**35**).

ARCHITECTURE

Philip Johnson designs a New York skyscraper, for the American Telephone and Telegraph Company, in the style of a Chippendale bookcase (1978).

LITERATURE

Lord Kinross completes a five-year book project *The Ottoman Empire* (1976). It is sent to the printers, he chooses the illustrations, and dies.

FILMS

Cecil B. De Mille: *The Greatest Show on Earth* (1952).

Edward G. Robinson: *The Outrage* (1964).

John Houseman gets his first Oscar—best supporting actor in *The Paper Chase* (1973).

Luchino Visconti: *L'Innocente* (1977).

Jack Warner: producer, *My Fair Lady* (1964); and *Camelot* at **74**.

Henry Hathaway: director, *True Grit* (1969).

TV, ETC.

Bette Davis: "Strangers" (1979)—this receives an Emmy Award.

LOVE, LIFE

Coco Chanel: reemergence as a major force in the fashion world (1954). She had been a leader in dress design from around **35** until her retirement at **55**. Her fragrance "Chanel No. 5" is at **39**. She now invents the Chanel suit, a design which is widely copied. She maintains her position until her death at **87**, in the Ritz Hotel, Paris.

Glynn Wolfe: marriage, in Los Angeles, to Donna Maria Hessee (**17**, in 1980)—her first, his twenty-fourth. He had divorced his previous wife (**21**) because of her age. Wife number 22 had also been **17**.

72

HISTORY—WORLD

Pietro Nenni: Deputy Prime Minister of Italy (1963), until **77**. He is Foreign Minister at **77–78**, and lives until **88**. Because of his exile following his break with the Fascists, his government career did not begin until after World War II, when at **54** he first held national office.

Chairman Mao swims in the Yalu River (1965)—nine miles, in sixty minutes. (cf. **75***)

HISTORY—U.S.A.

Emmanuel Celler: Civil Rights Act of 1960. This is the most comprehensive of many such acts which he guides through Congress. He is a congressman until **84**, and lives until **92**.

Philip M. Klutznick: Secretary of Commerce (1979, until 1981).

Clark Clifford: chairman of a panel of "Wise Men" (1979), to advise President Carter (**55**) on ways of handling the presence of Soviet troops in Cuba. Clifford first became counsel in the White House at **39**, after sixteen years as a trial lawyer and a period in the Navy. At **61**, he was Secretary of Defense. Now, his advisory panel includes Averell Harriman (**87**), John McCloy (**84**), John McCone (**77**), Roswell Gilpatric (**72**), David Packard (**67**), and Henry Kissinger (**56**).

HISTORY—U.K.

George III is removed from his duties, owing to madness (Jan. 1811); he lives until **81**, under the regency of his son (**48–57**).

RELIGION, PHILOSOPHY

St. Augustine: completion of *City of God* (426 A.D.), the book which he had begun at **59**.

Bertrand Russell: *A History of Western Philosophy* (1945). (cf. **89***)

Father Pedro Arrupe indicates his desire to resign as head of the Jesuits (1980). But this proposal leads to opposition, because in the 439 years of the Jesuits no General has left office except through death. Arrupe now wants to introduce the concept of retirement, whereas the Jesuit General has always been elected for life. At **73**, Arrupe is incapacitated by illness. Pope John Paul II (**61**) appoints a new chief who is to be the Pope's personal representative; this is Father Paolo Dazza (**79**). The Pope's action is likened to the suppression of the Jesuits by Pope Clement XIV (**67**, in 1773).

SOCIAL SCIENCE, EDUCATION

Confucius dies (479 B.C.);

> The great mountain must crumble,
> The strong beam must break,
> The wise man must wither away like a plant.

SCIENCE, TECHNOLOGY

Charles Darwin: publication of his last book (1881). This is on earthworms, and it has been described as a pioneer in quantitive ecology. The initial idea came to him at **28**. Since **29**, he has published twenty-one volumes of research, roughly 230 pages per year. At **62**, he published *The Descent of Man,* on the effect of sexual selection; at **63**, he published *The Expression of the Emotions in Man and Animals.* His method of working depends on insights which are preceded by long observation, and followed by the detailed accumulation of evidence. For example, at **51** he had been intrigued by insect-eating plants, and he publishes a book on this at **66**. Darwin lives until **73**; by living in the country, and by surrounding himself with children, grandchildren, plants, and pets, he has insulated himself from the intellectual ferment which his ideas have caused. In death, he is placed close to Isaac Newton (d. **83**, in 1727).

MONEY, WORK

John D. Rockefeller is forced to break up his Standard Oil Trust (1911). He is worth $815 million, excluding the charitable foundations that he has already set up. (cf. **97***)

John D. Rockefeller III is killed (1978), when a learner driver (**16**) smashes into Rockefeller's 1965 Ford Mustang. He had been a prime mover in the creation of New York's Lincoln Center at **56** onward.

In the U.S.A., government Social Security pensions go to everyone at **72** or more, without any earnings rule. Under **72**, $1 is deducted from the benefits, for every $2 earned over $3,000 a year.

In the U.S. labor force, there are 750,000 people who are aged **72** or more.

ARCHITECTURE

Le Corbusier: Carpenter Arts Building, Harvard University (1959).

ART

Rodin: sculptures of Nijinsky (**22**) (1912). Rodin lives until **76***.

MUSIC—CLASSICAL

Rossini: *Petite Messe solennelle* (1864). This work surprises his public, since he has written almost nothing since **37**. He goes on to write *Hymn to Napoleon and his Valiant People* at **75**, for 800 instrumentalists and 400 singers. He lives till **76**.

Meyerbeer dies (1864), while completing *L'Africaine*, probably his best-known work. It is not produced until after his death, and he had been working on it intermittently since around **47**.

Adelina Patti gives her final concert (1915). She had given her first farewell in New York at **45**; and she had a farewell season at Covent Garden when she was **52**, then publicly retiring to her castle in Wales. From **53** onward, she went on a series of farewell tours, which last up till now. She lives till **76**. By way of comparison, Maria Callas retired from opera performances at around **41** (1965); gave a number of recitals at **49**; and died at **53**.

Havergal Brian begins the most productive 25 years of his life (1948). He has just retired, and a BBC producer now takes an interest in his work. Brian writes 25 symphonies from **72** onward, and the first-ever performance of his *Gothic* symphony (**51**) is given at **90**. Brian had done reasonably well in his **30**s; his work was performed, and critics talked of his promise. But his **40**s, **50**s, and **60**s were lean periods, partly owing to changes in musical taste, and partly due to his continued self-portrayal as an outsider. At **69**, he begins to be rediscovered, and he becomes, in effect, famous for not being famous. (cf. **80***)

LITERATURE

Herman Melville dies (1891, Sept. 28), virtually unknown, with his last book, *Billy Budd,* unpublished. The plates for *Moby Dick* (**31**) had been lost in a fire, two years after publication, and no new edition was ever prepared in his lifetime. From **46** onward, he has to obtain routine employment as a customs officer.

Paul Gallico: *The Poseidon Adventure* (1969).

PLAYS, DANCE

George Bernard Shaw: the book *An Intelligent Woman's Guide to Socialism;* and the play *The Apple Cart* (1928). (cf. **93***)

George Balanchine: *Union Jack* (1976), his 149th ballet, and danced by the New York City Ballet, which he has been directing since he jointly started it at **44**. (cf. **75***)

Dame Judith Anderson: *A Man Called Horse* (1970); she has to learn to speak the Sioux language throughout the film.

PRESS

Ambrose Bierce, the newspaper columnist, goes on an expedition to Mexico (1914), and is never seen again.

Roy Thomson buys the *Times* (London, 1966).

SPORTS

Karl Wallenda, the circus tight-rope walker, walks on a high wire strung between the top floors of the Eden Roc and the Fontainebleau hotels, at Miami (1977). But he is killed in a high-wire accident soon afterward.

73

HISTORY—WORLD

Cardinal Fleury is appointed (1726) chief minister to King Louis XV (**16**) of France. Fleury holds this position until his death at **90**. Coincidentally, also at **73**, the Comte de Maurepas is appointed chief minister to King Louis XVI (**19**) in 1774; Maurepas continues in office until near his death at **80**. In 1981, Pierre Dreyfus (also **73**) is appointed Minister for Industry, and Gaston Defferre (**70**) becomes Minister of the Interior.

HISTORY—U.K.

Stanley Baldwin, in 1940: the ornamental gates of his country house are taken away—ostensibly as part of a wartime drive for scrap metal, but also as revenge for his ineffective foreign policy when Prime Minister last, **67–69**.

SOCIAL SCIENCE, EDUCATION

Freud: *Civilization and Its Discontents* (1929). Freud is extremely energetic throughout his life; he writes and sees patients until close to his death at **83**. (cf. **80***)

SCIENCE, TECHNOLOGY

Isaac Newton receives a difficult mathematical problem in the mail (1716), and he stays up all night to solve it. The problem has been sent to him by Leibniz (**69**).

RENAISSANCE

Peter Mark Roget: *Roget's Thesaurus* (1852). He has been compiling this since his retirement at **69**. He sees the *Thesaurus* as more than a literary device; it is a way of showing how everything connects, and it is thus the culmination of his truly renaissance life. Roget had originally trained as a doctor, and had lectured at medical school. In addition, from **37–45**, he contributed some 300,000 words to the *Encyclopaedia Britannica*. From **48–69**, he has been secretary of the principal scientific group of his time, the Royal Society. At **49**, he wrote a significant public health report on the probable connection between London's epidemics and the poor water supply. Now at **73** he finds that he has an international success on his hands. He lives to see twenty-five reprints, translations, and new editions, and he works to update the *Thesaurus* until shortly before his death at **90**. Roget is a late-developer in his family life. His only marriage is at **45**, to Mary Hobson (**29**); he is a widower from **54** on, owing to her death from cancer. Roget is a first-time father at **46**, and a first-time grandfather at **89**.

ARCHITECTURE

John Nash: enlargement of Buckingham Palace (1825) but dismissed at **78**, as his designs fall into disfavor. (cf. **75***)

Antonio Gaudí dies (1926, June 7), after being run over by a trolley car. He is buried in his own design, Sagrada Familia, Barcelona.

ART

Goya, in 1819: he now has his second deathlike illness, but he recovers, and goes on to paint the "Black Paintings." These are nightmares, and are literally black with horror. At **78**, Goya leaves Spain and settles in Bordeaux with Leocardia Weiss (**36**) and their daughter Rosaria (**10**). Goya continues working as a painter and lithographer until just before his death at **82**. One remarkable feature of Goya is that he never seems blocked; with each change in himself, or in Spain, he simply reacts in the most appropriate way. He keeps producing; he is open to any mood, from the darkest to the most ceremonial. (cf. **79***)

Renoir: "The Judgment of Paris" (1914). He had previously defended his interest in the nude by saying, "A painter who has the feel for breasts and buttocks is saved."

Verdi composes the opera *Otello* (1887). (cf. **79***)

Vladimir Horowitz goes on a concert tour of Japan (1976).

LITERATURE

W. B. Yeats dies (1939, Jan. 28)—he had chosen the following lines for his gravestone:

> No marble, no conventional phrase;
> On limestone quarried near the spot
> By his command these words are cut:
> Cast a cold eye
> On life, on death.
> Horseman, pass by!

Dorothy Parker dies in poor circumstances in a New York hotel (1967, June 7), accompanied only by her dog Cliché whom she allows to mess on the carpet. Friends afterward discover a two-year-old check for $10,000 which she had mislaid. From about **40** to **50**, she and her ex-husband had earned almost $500,000 as Hollywood scriptwriters; and at **25*** she had started the Round Table at the Algonquin Hotel.

Ezra Pound is released from mental hospital (1958); he has been arrested at **60**, for his Fascist-sounding broadcasts during World War II. He now moves back to Italy, and lives until **87**.

Graham Greene: *The Human Factor* (1978). It is said that he writes two hundred words per day, and stops—even if he is in the middle of a sentence.

PLAYS, DANCE

Henrik Ibsen: *When We Dead Awake* (1899). This is his last play, and he lives until **78**. The "we dead" are those who are so close to death that they have given up on life. The awakening occurs when an old and successful sculptor meets a former model; and when his wife meets a vigorous and nonartistic lover. The sculptor regrets that he never allowed himself to fall in love with the model. In retrospect, his love for her should have had priority over his career. They now stay together, and the model says that they will go "through all the mists, and then right up to the summit of the tower that shines in the sunrise." In the background, the sculptor's wife shouts with excitement, because of the new pleasures in her life. Ibsen's question: how many people have lost out because of the artist's devotion to his art?

Alfred Hitchcock: *Frenzy* (1972).

Billy Wilder: *Fedora* (1979).

John Huston: *Wise Blood* (1979). At **74**, he publishes his memoirs, and starts work on the film *Annie*.

MUSIC—NON-CLASSICAL

Bing Crosby does a tour of Europe (1977); in Spain, he dies, immediately after completing a round of golf. His best selling record has been "White Christmas," made at **38**, and selling forty million copies.

Rex Harrison: eleven month tour in *My Fair Lady* (1980–81). The part of his mother is played by Cathleen Nesbitt (**92**).

TV, ETC.

Bette Davis: "Family Reunion" (1981).

EXPLORATION

Dorothy S. Bailey: oldest person on the first journey of the "Central Kingdom Express" (1979), a new scheduled railway service between London and Hong Kong. The train covers 9,300 miles in 42 days, and calls at Warsaw, Moscow, Irkutsk, and Shanghai. The second-oldest person on board is Denis Haviland (**68**).

LAW, CRIME

Judge Learned Hand: his landmark ruling on the Alcoa antitrust suit (1945).

Earl Warren: the Warren report (Sept. 1964), on the assassination of John F. Kennedy (**46**).

SPORTS

George McCulloc is the oldest parachutist at the annual skydiving displays at Zephyrhills, Florida (1978). He now completes his 875th jump.

Walt Stack is the oldest person to complete the International Triathlon in Hawaii (1981). This contest consists of (1) a 2.4 mile ocean swim; (2) a 112 mile bicycle race; and (3) a full-length marathon run. Stack completes the event in 26 hours 20 minutes. The winner is John Howard (**33**) whose time is 9 hours 38 minutes. The contest results are organized into age divisions. The youngest person to finish is Robin Tain (**14**), and for people **56–60**, the winning time is 14 hours, 46 minutes.

74

HISTORY—WORLD

Prince Metternich is forced to resign as Foreign Minister of Austria (1848). Coincidentally, Otto von Bismarck is forced to resign as German Chancellor (1890) also at **74**. Metternich has held office since **36**, and Bismarck effectively since **47**.

HISTORY—U.S.A.

Richard Daley dies in office, as Mayor of Chicago (1976).

Paul Nitze: U.S. Chief at the Soviet-American arms control talks (Geneva, 1981); and T. E. Cummings (**72**), U.S. Ambassador to Austria.

HISTORY—U.K.

Sylvia Pankhurst emigrates to Ethiopia (**56**), and dies there at **78**. In her **40**s and **50**s, she has been a strong supporter of Ethiopia, against its invasion by Italy. After the success of their campaign for votes for women, Mrs. Emmeline Pankhurst became increasingly conservative; her daughters Sylvia and Adela became increasingly left-wing, and Christabel became increasingly religious.

RELIGION, PHILOSOPHY

Pierre Teilhard de Chardin: death (1955); none of his religious work has been yet published—permission had not been given by the church authorities. *The Phenomenon of Man* is published shortly after his death.

SOCIAL SCIENCE, EDUCATION

Dr. Wilhelm Stekel: suicide, with aspirin (1940). He had been an associate of Freud, and was the first person to define "thanatos," the death instinct, versus "eros," the life instinct.

Ernest Jones: *The Life and Death of Sigmund Freud* (1953)—the first volume; the last volume is published at **79**, and he dies at **80**.

ARCHITECTURE

Cass Gilbert: U.S. Supreme Court building, New York City (1933).

Frank Lloyd Wright: first drawings of the Guggenheim Museum, New York City (1943)—finished just after he had died at **89***.

Mies van der Rohe: office building at Charles Center, Baltimore (1960–63). (cf. **76***)

Buckminster Fuller publishes *Operating Manual for Spaceship Earth* (1969). (cf. **80***)

Philip Johnson: completion of the Crystal Cathedral, Garden Grove, California (1980).

ART

Donatello: two pulpits or cantoria for the Cathedral, Florence (1460). He also begins work about now on his statue of Mary Magdalene—"the first style of old age in the history of art." At around **54**, Donatello had made the bronze statue of David, also in Florence. He lives until **80**.

Katsushika Hokusai: "One Hundred Views of Mount Fuji" (1834). (cf. **110***)

Henry Moore: "Sheep Piece" (1972).

LITERATURE

S. J. Perelman, with two companions, (1978–79), drives from Paris to Peking, in an old MG.

PLAYS

Euripides dies (406 B.C.), with his last play *The Bacchae* unproduced. It later wins first prize when staged at Athens.

FILMS

Leni Riefenstahl publishes a book of her photos and writings about an African tribe, *People of Kau* (1976).

Joan Blondell: *Grease* (1978).

PRESS

William Randolph Hearst, in 1937: his publishing empire is in debt to the extent of $126 million, and he is forced to relinquish financial control—though he maintains editorial control. Hearst has had a lifetime of overindulgence; spending $25,000 per week. At **78**, the film *Citizen Kane* makes him out to be an eccentric ogre. But he keeps fit and active until his death at **88***. At **71**, he had celebrated his birthday by playing tennis against his three sons, aged **30**, **27**, and **25**.

Stanley Marcus: publication of his memoirs, *Quest for the Best* (1979). For fifty years, he has worked at the family store, Neiman-Marcus. He divides the people and objects of life into two categories: (1) the best; and (2) less than the best. He quotes Somerset Maugham: "It is a funny thing about life, if you refuse to accept anything but the best you very often get it."

Lord Bath, Lieutenant Colonel Robert Henderson (**75**), Peter Bull (**67**), and others: organization of the 1979 Arctophiles Congress for the Good Bears of the World, the charity for lovers of teddy bears. People come from all over the world to attend the congress and to share their teddies—named after Theodore Roosevelt (**44**, in 1902).

Felix Grucci: winner of the 1979 Monte Carlo annual international fireworks competition.

75

HEALTH

Three fourths of accidents in the home are said to occur to people **75** and over.

HISTORY—WORLD

Eamon De Valera continues as head of the government of Ireland (1958).

General de Gaulle continues as President of France (1966).

Mao Tse-tung: the climax of the Cultural Revolution (1969), begun at **72** by the Red Guards. Mao has been party chairman since **55***. Now his writings and this campaign—against the creation of a new managerial elite—make him a cult figure in China and throughout the world. By the time of his death (**82**), he is virtually deified.

Morarji Desai, an Indian politician, starts on a new health habit (1971)—he drinks a glass of his own urine every morning. By **81***, he is Prime Minister of India.

Habib Bourguiba continues as President of Tunisia (1979).

Nikolai Tikhonov: premier of the Soviet Union (1980). He replaces Alexei Kosygin (**76**) who has held the position since **60**. Tikhonov became a deputy Prime Minister at **60**; First Deputy Prime Minister at **71**; and a full member of the Politburo at **74**. At this moment, Leonid

 Brezhnev (**73**) continues as President; the control commission chief is Arvid Pelshe (**80**); the Party Secretary is Andrei Kirilenko (**73**); the Defense Minister is Dmitri Ustinov (**71**); the Foreign Minister is Andrei Gromyko (**70**); and the head of the KGB is Yuri Andropov (**65**).

In 1981, the average age of the Russian Politburo is **69**. There are four members in their **50**s; nine in their **60**s; seven in their **70**s; and two in their **80**s.

HISTORY—U.K.

Disraeli resigns as Prime Minister, for the second and last time (Apr. 1880—since **69**). At **70**, he had arranged for the purchase of the Suez Canal; and at **72** he had made Queen Victoria (**57**) Empress of India. He had written his most recent novel *Lothair* at **65**. Now, after retirement, he writes a best-seller, *Endymion,* also at **75**. (cf. **76***)

Gladstone resigns as Prime Minister, for the second time (1885, June 9). (cf. **76***)

RELIGION, PHILOSOPHY

Eligibility: In the Roman Catholic Church, priests and resident bishops must now offer their resignation to the pope.

SOCIAL SCIENCE, EDUCATION

F. A. von Hayek: Nobel Prize (1974), in the same year as Gunnar Myrdal (also **75**). Other Nobel Prizes include: Milton Friedman, **64** in 1976; Herbert A. Simon, **62** in 1978.

Bernard Rudofsky: *Now I Lay Me Down to Eat* (1980)—a provocative view of the basic human bodily processes as performed in different societies.

SCIENCE, TECHNOLOGY

Albert Einstein, in 1954: his birthday is marked by worldwide celebrations and Einstein writes to a friend about this: "Once again you have thought of me in such a friendly way on this strange occasion. Actually, unless an individual has already departed, he automatically turns **75** without any particular effort. But, having reached that stage, he feels bewildered and awkward since he is quite incapable of proving himself worthy of the many demonstrations of affection—especially when he has, through no will of his own, become a kind of legend in his own time."

MONEY, WORK

Henry Ford is still fit enough to do handstands (1938); he gets into convertibles by leaping over the door.

Elizabeth Arden, founder of the beauty empire, is still able to do a yoga headstand (1954). Her can-do image is so firmly established that when she dies (**87**), one of her beauty assistants exclaims, "But it's so unlike her."

ART

Alexander Calder: exterior design for a Braniff Airlines DC-8 (1973).

ARCHITECTURE

Nicholas Hawksmoor completes designs for the west (entrance) towers of Westminster Abbey (the towers seen in all the postcards), but dies immediately afterward (1736).

John Nash: Carlton House Terrace, the Mall, London (1827).

MUSIC—CLASSICAL

Monteverdi: *L'Incoronazione di Poppea* (1642). This opera is his last major work, and is perhaps his most daring and influential work. At **70**, an opera house had opened in Venice, and Monteverdi is stimulated to a rush of creativity. He dies at **76**, still the Maestro di Capella at St. Mark's.

Saint-Saëns gives three concerts (1910), playing Mozart's twelve clavier concertos.

Claudio Arrau, the concert pianist, gives 110 concerts this year (1978), all over the world. He continues to learn new works, and to play them in his programs.

Vladimir Horowitz celebrates his birthday (1978) by dancing at Studio 54, New York, and playing with the New York Philharmonic Orchestra in a concert which is transmitted by satellite to European TV.

LITERATURE

Reginal Goodall: conductor of the first-ever digital recording of *Tristan and Isolde* (1981).

Christopher Isherwood: *My Guru and His Disciple* (1980).

PLAYS, DANCE

William Wycherley marries for the second time, but dies eleven days later (1716).

George Balanchine continues as artistic director of the New York City Ballet (1979). At **20**, he had worked for Serge Diaghilev (**52**) and had become a ballet master at **30**. At **44**, his company became the New York City Ballet, and at **60** its home was established at Lincoln Center. The great choreographer/ballet masters have all been long-lived: Auguste Bournonville is in charge at the Royal Danish Ballet from **24** (1830) until **72**. Filippo Taglioni is a choreographer at least until **63** (1841) and he lives until **93**; at **54**, he choreographs *La Sylphide*, starring his daughter Marie Taglioni (**28**). Marius Petipa is a dancer at St. Petersburg from **29** (1847) onward; he becomes ballet master at the Imperial Russian Ballet at **44**, and retires at **85**, living until **92**. Jean Coralli lives until **75** (1854); at **62**, he had choreographed *Giselle* in association with Jules Perrot who himself lives until **82**. Jean-Georges Noverre, the codifier of classical ballet, lives until **83** (1810). Leonide Massine choreographs until **64** (1960) and lives until **82**. Bronislava Nijinska's last work is at **69** (1960) and she lives until **81**. Now, when George Balanchine is **75**, other great living ballet figures include Merce Cunningham (**60**); Jerome Robbins (**61**); Lincoln Kirstein (**72**); Frederick Ashton (also **75**); Ninette de Valois (**81**); Marie Rambert (**91**); and Martha Graham (**85**) who is still traveling with her own company. Tamara Karsavina has died in the previous year at **93**.

FILMS

Cecil B. De Mille: *The Ten Commandments* (1956)—a remake of his earlier film (at **47**).

Busby Berkeley revives *No, No Nanette* on Broadway (1970).

Helen Hayes: *One of Our Dinosaurs Is Missing* (1975).

Bob Hope is master of ceremonies at the Academy Award Oscar prize giving (1978).

Henry Fonda (**76**) and Katharine Hepburn (**74**): *On Golden Pond* (1981), with Jane Fonda (**43**).

EXPLORATION

George Everest: naming of Mount Everest, in his honor (1865). Everest had been in charge of the pioneer surveys of India, from **33** to **53**. Until now, Mount Everest has been called either "Goddess Mother of the World" by its neighboring peoples, or "Peak XV" by the surveying team. The world's second-highest mountain continues always to be known by the survey name "K2." George Everest dies at **76**.

LAW, CRIME

In New York (1979), a man attacks his wife (**73**) with a knife, and then jumps out of their apartment window. The wife survives, but the husband dies.

Eligibility: judges in Britain must now retire, if they were appointed after the Judicial Pensions Act of 1959.

76

HISTORY—WORLD

King Louis XIV of France: end of the War of the Spanish Succession (1701–14). Between **50–59,** Louis had been fighting against the "Grand Alliance." These two wars have weakened the economy of France, and led to famine and unnecessary taxation. Louis has lived on into another age, from his great days around **40***. At his death, **76**, the crowds are happy.

Deng Xiaoping continues as effective leader of the People's Republic of China (1980). In 1981, after a reshuffle of the government, the new Defense Minister is **72**; the new Minister of the State Capital Construction Commission is **69**; the new Secretary-General of the State Council is **66**; and the new Minister of Agriculture is **65**. There are, however, younger ministers—for Textiles (**45**), and for Power (**52**).

HISTORY—U.S.A.

Howard Jarvis and Paul Gann (**65**): Proposition 13 (1978), the unilateral cut in the money-raising powers of local property taxes in California.

HISTORY—U.K.

Disraeli dies (1881, Apr. 19)—six weeks after a heroic speech in the House of Lords, defending the empire in India, saying that "The key of India is in London."

Gladstone becomes Prime Minister, for the third time (1886, Feb. 1). (cf. **82***)

Winston Churchill becomes Prime Minister, for the second time (1951). (cf. **80***)

RELIGION, PHILOSOPHY

John XXIII: Pope (1958). He is elected on the 12th ballot. The expectation is that, as an old man, he will take little action; the Church will therefore be able to postpone settlement of its differences until the election of the next Pope. However, he immediately persues his own modernizing policy, and he holds the innovative second Vatican Council at **80**. By the time of his death, **81**, he is one of the most admired figures in the world.

SOCIAL SCIENCE, EDUCATION

Herbert Spenser: last volume of his *Principles of Sociology* (1896), begun at **56**. He lives until **83**.

SCIENCE, TECHNOLOGY

Hiram Maxim: death during World War I (1916) which the invention of his machine gun (**43**) had done more than anything else to create. Both sides use the machine gun to kill soldiers who are given no defensive armor.

ARCHITECTURE

Antonia da Ponte: the Rialto bridge, Venice (1588–91).

Mies van der Rohe: New National Gallery, Berlin (1962–68). (cf. **81***)

ART

Sir Lawrence Alma-Tadema paints his last self-portrait, and dies shortly afterward (1912). In the background of this last picture, he shows another picture painted by himself—a portrait of his mother (**52**), done when he was **16**.

Auguste Rodin marries Rose Beuret (**72**) (1917). They had first met when they were **23** and **20**, and had lived together since then. Rose dies two weeks after the wedding, and Auguste a few months later.

Edward J. Steichen organizes the huge photographic exhibition, "The Family of Man" (1955). This exemplifies the two main themes of his life—his work as a photographer, and his desire to show photography as an art form. Steichen dies on the day before his **94**th birthday.

Pablo Picasso, in 1957: forty-four variations on the painting "Las Meninas" by Velazquez (**57**, 1656).

MUSIC—CLASSICAL

Arnold Schoenberg: death (1951). His atonal compositions were from **34** onward; his twelve-tone compositions were from **49** onward. Though he has aroused opposition in the musical world for all his professional life, his birthday at **75** is marked by great celebrations in which he is reconciled to other musicians, and vice versa. Schoenberg is superstitious about the number 13, and has been convinced that he will die at **76**, since $7 + 6 = 13$. In fact, he dies on Friday the thirteenth of July, at thirteen minutes before midnight.

H. G. Wells completes his doctoral dissertation (1942), and receives the D.Sc. from London University. He had left school at **14**.

Richmal Crompton publishes *William and the Masked Ranger* (1966); this is her thirty-sixth book about William (still **11**).

Lord David Cecil: *A Portrait of Jane Austen* (1978). He wrote *The Young Melbourne* at **37**, and *Lord M* at **52**.

PLAYS

George Bernard Shaw: *Too Good to Be True* (1932).

Diana Trilling: *Mrs. Harris: the Death of the Scarsdale Diet Doctor* (1981). (cf. **69***)

FILMS

Charles Foster Kane dies; his last word is "Rosebud."

LOVE, LIFE

Sir James Innes (Scotland, 1812): the House of Lords decides that he is the right person to become the new Duke of Roxburghe. The previous duke had died at **77**, seven years ago, without leaving an obvious heir; he was a distant relative of Sir James. Much of the family fortune has been spent on legal costs in establishing Sir James's right to be the new duke. Now, at **76** he has yet to have a child. At **71**, his first wife had died, and eight days later the duke had married again. At **76** there is considerable family pressure on him to produce an heir, so as to prevent further costly litigation at his own death. At **80**, his first child is born. At **87**, he dies; his title and estates go directly to this only son, who himself lives until **63**.

SPORTS

Norman Preston (1979) continues as editor of *Wisden's Cricketer's Almanack,* the annual bible of the game.

77

HISTORY—WORLD

Mahatma Gandhi: the independence of India (1947). He had entered national politics at **49**, with his plan for passive resistance to the colonial power. But he is assassinated at **79**, by a Brahmin (**37**).

Empress Nagako of Japan: on her **77**th birthday she becomes the first empress to reach this age while her husband is still alive.

HISTORY—U.S.A.

Averell Harriman: head of the U.S. delegation to the Paris peace talks of 1968, in an attempt to end the Vietnam War.

RELIGION, PHILOSOPHY

Pope Pius IX: first campaign for the "immediate animation" theory of gestation (1869), that the soul enters the fetus at the moment of conception, so that abortion is no less than murder. He thus moves the Catholic Church into opposition against all abortions, instead of (as previously) only those after the fortieth day. (cf. **70*** and **78***)

SCIENCE, TECHNOLOGY

Charles Babbage: death (1871). The main aim of his life has produced no results which are accepted by his contemporaries; he has spent decades on the design of a mechanical computer. His design would be programmable and have memories. In the attempt to build his design, he has had to become an expert on metallurgy. But he is widely regarded as a crank. Twenty to fifty years after his death he comes to be revered as one of the greatest of computer pioneers.

MONEY, WORK

George Eastman (founder of Kodak) kills himself (1932).

Charlie Schwab dies insolvent (1939)—even though he had had the highest-ever salary while at United States Steel. Cause: personal extravagance.

Arnold Batliner continues as the coin washer at the Hotel St. Francis, San Francisco (1981). And, Alice Lynch continues as a switchboard operator at the St. Regis Hotel, New York (1978); she started this job at **26**. And, at the Oriental Club, London, Alice Moores continues to work as a waitress until shortly before her death at **90** (1979). And in Moscow, Semyon Grishin (**97**, in 1981) continues as a chef in a cafe opposite the Mayakovsky Theater.

ART

Claude Lorrain: "Port, with Villa Medici" (Uffizi) (1677).

Claude Monet begins work on a complete room of paintings of water lilies (1907). These are created between now and **86**; they become the "Sistine Chapel of Impressionism."

Louise Nevelson: chapel in white wood, at St. Peter's Lutheran Church, New York City (1977).

Richard Strauss composes five operas in his **70**s. The last is *Capriccio* (1941) at **77**. He continues to work as a composer until **84**, and dies at **85**.

LITERATURE

Thomas Hardy publishes (1917) a book of 159 poems, nearly all of which have been written in the past four years, since his wife died. Her death releases energy in him and he writes love poems about their early, happy days together. These poems are among his most admired work, and he keeps writing and publishing poetry for another ten years. (cf. **86***)

Paul Gallico dies in Monte Carlo (1974). Sometime previously, he had said about death: "I shall deeply regret not getting my *New York Herald Tribune*."

Barbara Cartland is writing her 254th romantic novel (1979). She dictates every afternoon, between 1:15 and 3:15, to one of her four secretaries. She also answers 10,000 letters per year, to people asking for her advice on health, diet, vitamins, and longevity.

Marguerite Yourcenar: first woman to become a member of the French Academy (1981).

FILMS

Mae West: *Myra Breckinridge* (1970), with Raquel Welch (**30**), and earning her $350,000 for ten days' work.

Luis Buñuel: *That Obscure Object of Desire* (1977). His first film was *Un Chien Andalou*, at **29**, with Salvador Dali (**25**). Recently Buñuel has made twelve films from **60** on, including *Belle de Jour* at **66**, and *The Discreet Charm of the Bourgeoisie* at **72**.

Marlene Dietrich: *Just a Gigolo* (1978).

LOVE, LIFE

Admiral Jackson R. Tate: first meeting with his daughter, the Russian Viktoriya Fyodorova (**19**, in 1975). She was conceived when the U.S. admiral was on a week-long visit to Moscow, during World War II. About this first meeting, she comments: "The only thing I expect from this visit is to finally get to know my father. He is my admiral and I am his little soldier."

In Japan, this birthday is called "kiju." You have now reached the state of pleasure.

LAW, CRIME

J. Edgar Hoover dies in office as Director of the FBI (1972). He had been appointed acting director at **29**, having been assistant director at

26. Hoover lives long by keeping to a strict diet, eating only grapefruit and cottage cheese for lunch. He is never married, but keeps two dogs, whom he allows to mess the carpet.

William O. Douglas resigns from the U.S. Supreme Court (1975). He had been appointed at **40**, and he has a record term in office—thirty-six years, seven months. At **68**, he had suffered an attempt at impeachment, owing to his moral character—he had just married for the fourth time, and his wife was **23**. (cf. **78***)

According to the *New York Times,* the preeminent U.S. trial lawyer in the field of compensation for accidents and compensation is Harry Liepsig (**77** in 1979). He believes that compensation payments, if anything, are too low. Since **57**, he has had only three cases in which he fails to collect any money for his client.

W. A. Boyle receives three life sentences for murder (1979). At **67**, as president of the United Mine Workers Union, he had arranged for the death of an election rival, Joseph Yablonski (**57**), and Mrs. Yablonski (**57**) and their daughter (**25**).

78

HISTORY—WORLD

Giovanni Giolitti becomes Prime Minister of Italy (1920), for the fifth time.

HISTORY—U.K.

Winston Churchill has a second stroke (1953, June 23), but continues in office as Prime Minister for another two years. (cf. **80***)

RELIGION, PHILOSOPHY

Pope Pius IX: he and all other popes are pronounced infallible—under certain conditions—by the Vatican Council of 1870.

Ayatollah Khomeini takes over the government (1978) from the Shah of Iran (**59**). Previously, Khomeini has been exiled by the shah since **63**. Members of the new government include Ayatollah Shariet-madari (**76**) and Ayatollah Taleghani (c.**74**), and Prime Minister Bazargan (c.**72**). One of the new government's first acts is to shoot some members of the previous administration, including the head (**65**) of

SAVAK, the old secret police, a former prime minister (**61**), and a former foreign minister (**67**).

SOCIAL SCIENCE, EDUCATION

G. Stanley Hall: *Senescence* (1922). He had virtually invented "adolescence" in a book at **60**.

Karl Pearson: *Tables of the Incomplete Beta-Function* (1934).

F. A. von Hayek: having been rediscovered as a right-wing economist, he now goes on a round-the-world lecture tour, stopping off to advise government leaders on their economic policy (1977).

Lily Pincus: *Death and the Family: the Importance of Mourning* (1976)—on her thoughts since the death of her husband, when she was **65**.

Erich Fromm: *To Have or To Be* (1978).

MONEY, WORK

Jean Mantelet continues as head of Moulinex (1978), the kitchen appliance firm which he started at **38**.

Mr. Joseph Schwarz gets a job (two days per week) at S.R.I., California, checking references on job applications (1976). He got the job through Retirement Jobs Inc., one of about 70 jobs-for-the-retired agencies in the U.S. Their office manager is Alyce West (**70**) and the office junior is Joseph Himes (**67**).

ART

Matisse: designs for the Chapel of the Rosary, Vence, France (1952—until **81**). (cf. **82***)

PLAYS

Euripides: *Bacchae* (405 B.C.); and *Iphigenia in Aulis*. He dies this year, and these two plays are given their premieres two years later.

FILMS

Edith Evans: *The Whisperers* (1966). Also at **78**, she asks that her age be deleted from reference books as "It may stop me getting work."

TV, ETC.

William S. Paley: as chairman of the board of CBS, he arranges for the dismissal of his chief executive officer, John D. Backe (**47**, in 1980). This is the third time that Paley has dispensed with the services of a man who was marked to succeed him when he eventually retires. Paley had become president of CBS at **27**, and has been chairman of the board since **45**. At **75**, he sets up and finances the Museum of Broadcasting, in New York, and he publishes his autobiography at **77**. The mandatory retiring age at CBS is **65**, except for Paley—his current contract runs until **86**. Another great TV pioneer, David Sarnoff of NBC, does not fully retire until he is **78** (1970).

PRESS

William Randolph Hearst unsuccessfully tries to stop the premiere of *Citizen Kane* (1941) by Orson Welles (**25**), as it is widely seen as an attack on the whole of Hearst's career.

LAW, CRIME

Justice Oliver Wendell Holmes in 1919 gives his definition of free speech (no right to shout "fire" in a theater), in the case of the Espionage Act of 1917.

Earl Warren retires as Chief Justice, U.S. Supreme Court (1969). His successor is Warren Burger (**62**). The first-ever Chief Justice, John Jay (1745–1829) serves only from **43** to **49**. John Marshall (1755–1835) is Chief Justice from **45–79**; Roger Taney (1777–1864) **58–87**. Oliver Wendell Holmes is an Associate Justice from **61** to **90** (1932); John M. Harlan **44–78** (1911); and Hugo Black **51–85** (1971). On Independence Day, 1976, the Supreme Court justices were **51, 59, 61, 68, 68, 69, 69, 70**, and **77**.

Pieter Menten is sent to prison (1977) by a Dutch court until **93**, for his part in a massacre of Poles and Jews at **41**. He had evaded the legal system since then, and had become a millionaire and well-known art collector. Owing to legal technicalities, he is released at **79**, but faces another full trial.

79

HEALTH

Giambattista Morgagni: *On the Seats and Causes of Diseases as Investigated by Anatomy* (Padua, 1761). Morgagni has been the pioneer in the science of morbid anatomy, and this book summarizes his life's work. He lives until **89**.

Voltaire is told by his doctor that coffee is a poison; but he replies, "I've been poisoning myself for 80 years."

Ho Chi Minh: death (1969)—with his lifelong aim of a unified Vietnam some way from fulfillment.

HISTORY—U.S.A.

Lewis B. Hershey: resignation, as head of the draft (1973). At **43**, he had been secretary to the committee which devised the draft system. At **48**, at the beginning of World War II, he was appointed Director of the Selective Service System, and he has held this position since that time. Hershey now lives until **83**.

HISTORY—U.K.

Admiral Lord Cochrane volunteers for active service at the start of the Crimean War (1854). But he is turned down, as he might lead his force into some "desperate enterprise," according to the Admiralty.

RELIGION, PHILOSOPHY

Kant: death (1804). He has promoted his own longevity by avoiding medicine, and living a life of extreme regularity. He dies in the same town in which he was born, educated, had his professorship, and wrote his books. (cf. **57***)

SOCIAL SCIENCE, EDUCATION

John Dewey: *Experience and Education* (1938). Having published revolutionary ideas on education at **40***, he has lived long enough to see them implemented on a fairly wide scale. In this book, he reviews this implementation with a certain amount of doubt.

J. B. Watson is awarded the gold medal of the American Psychological Association (1957). At **42***, he had been hounded out of the psychology world, owing to his affair with a graduate student (**23**). He never again attended a meeting of the APA, whose president he had been at **36**. Since that time, Watson has made a second career himself, as a vice-president of J. Walter Thompson, the advertising agency. Now at **79**, many psychologists are surprised that Watson is still alive; he is a figure who seems to come out of the history books. He himself appears to be pleased by the gold medal, as a gesture of apology and reconciliation.

Arnold Toynbee, with others: *Man's Concern with Death* (1968)—an excellent and intelligent book. Toynbee himself dies at **86**. At **24**, Toynbee had been exempt from conscription during World War I, owing to illness. A vast number of his friends had been killed. He now describes his own time alive since **24** as his "bonus time"—so "I shall therefore have no excuse if, when my turn comes to die—and, at my age, death cannot be far off—I fail to face death readily and cheerfully. . . . If I do flinch and quail and repine, I shall feel deeply ashamed, because I shall be unable to forget the bonus-time that I have enjoyed."

ARCHITECTURE

Sir Christopher Wren: St. Paul's Cathedral is finished (1711).

ART

Goya: "The Bulls of Bordeaux" (1825). When autographing work, Goya now tends to put his age next to his signature.

MUSIC—CLASSICAL

Verdi: *Falstaff* (Feb. 1893). He had written *Otello* at **73**. His mother had lived till **64**; his father till **81**; and his second wife till **82**. Verdi spends his last years building a large retirement home in Milan for musicians. He dies at **87**, and 200,000 people attend his entombment.

Andrés Segovia fathers his last child (1970). His wife, Emilia, is **30**.

FILMS

George Cukor: *The Corn Is Green* (1978—for TV), with Katharine Hepburn (**69**).

TV, ETC.

Fred Astaire: *A Family Upside Down* (1978).

LAW, CRIME

Judge Edward Coke (1631) resists an offer of medicine, on the grounds that he has never "taken physic since he was born, and would not now begin." Coke dies at **82**; he had been first-ever Lord Chief Justice of England at **61**. The previous head office of the judiciary was the Chief Justice of the King's Bench. This position was first held by Robert the Bruce VI (**58**) in 1268; Bruce lives until **85**. In the fourteenth century, the best-known chief justice was Sir William Casgoigne—in office **50–62**, and dying around **70**. In the eighteenth century, Lord Mansfield is Lord Chief Justice from **51** to **83**, dying at **88**; Mansfield is said to have told a criminal, "There's nothing wrong with you that a good hanging won't cure." In 1920, the newly appointed Lord Chief Justice is Mr. Justice Lawrence (**77**).

Harold Jaggard commits suicide (1978) while still in office as chairman of an English building society (savings and loan institution). Investigation shows that he owes the organization £7 million ($14 million), due to theft in his 40 years employment. At **79**, he has still been taking £300 per day. The money is obtained by not returning housing loans to the institution (when the borrower sells his house) but pretending that the loan is still outstanding. The returned capital is then used as income for himself. This income is devoted to a number of girlfriends, and to a very extensive gambling career.

80

HEALTH

The causes of death (U.S.A., 1976) in people **65+** are (male): (1) diseases of the heart; (2) cancer; (3) cerebrovascular; (4) pneumonia and flu; (5) accidents; (6) arteriosclerosis. The causes of female death are: (1) diseases of the heart; (2) cancer; (3) cerebrovascular; (4) pneumonia and flu; (5) arteriosclerosis; (6) diabetes.

Life expectancy at birth—some countries with a high life expectancy include Japan, with **72**, male, and **77**, female; Norway, **71.8** and **78**; Sweden, **72.1** and **77.8**.

You can now expect to live until **87.3** (female) and until **85.8** (male) (England and Wales, 1975). Out of total deaths at all ages, 27 percent (male) occur in **75–84**, and 35 percent (female). This is the first and youngest age group in which female deaths outnumber male deaths—the men are already gone.

(Note that in the following figures cancer deaths have been split up into separately listed cancers for each major site, such as lung, breast, etc.). The causes of death for males **75–84**, in England and Wales in 1977 are: (1) ischemic heart disease; (2) cerebrovascular; (3) pneumonia; (4) bronchitis, emphysema, asthma; (5) lung cancer; (6) other heart diseases. The causes of female deaths are: (1) ischemic heart disease; (2) cerebrovascular; (3) pneumonia; (4) other heart diseases; (5) miscellaneous other cancers; and (6) breast cancer. In both sexes, the first two causes are far more important than the following four causes.

Animals' maximum life span: the finback whale can live until now.

In 1821 (England and Wales), only about .6 percent of the population was **80+**; and only 2.9 percent was **70+**. In 1907 (France), 5 percent was **70+**. The number of the very old is increasing. For example, in 1986, there are expected to be 22 percent more **75–84**s than in 1976; and 24 percent more **85+**. By 2011, the **75–84**s will be 12 percent more than in 1976, and the **85+** will be a giant 75 percent more. (England and Wales). A contrasting trend is that by 1991 there will be 6 percent fewer aged **45–74**. By 1991, the **15–29**s will probably be up 4 percent, and the **30–44**s will be up 20 percent. The explanation of these figures includes the greater longevity, changes in the birthrate, and changes in the number of those in the fertile age groups—which is a product of birthrates in the previous generation.

Historically, the greatest effect of increased longevity has been on young people. If you could get past the early years, then your remaining expectancy was pretty much the same as today. For example, if we take males in England and Wales, and compare 1910 versus 1970, there has been an increase of life expectancy of 17.5 years at **0**; but only .97 of a year at **70**.

Some possible symptoms of aging may include the following: decrease in muscle weight and strength, so that physical strength at **70** is half that at **20**; hardening and narrowing of the arteries—you are as old as your arteries, since the delivery of oxygen, through blood, is the basis for healthy cells everywhere in your body; less efficient lungs, and diminished vital capacity; gradual lessening of heart function; increase in blood pressure; deterioration in circulation and so more susceptible to cold; less blood going to the skin; less calorie intake; increase in body fat; lower metabolic rate; less elasticity and more stiffness in the body; pain in the joints; less short-term memory, and longer response to questions, but not necessarily any less memory if given time to answer; shakiness; deterioration in the condition of the feet; baldness and/or gray hair; mental confusion and even senile decay, with inability to concentrate or think; less ability to walk or run; lessening sexual activity; some loss of vision, hearing, and sense of taste; loss of teeth; dried-up skin; perhaps a more cautious style of behavior, and perhaps less creativity; in general, less able to quickly adjust to changes in your environment.

There is no single known cause of aging. Also, it is difficult to tell the difference between (1) aging which is caused by social pressures or expectations; or (2) aging caused biologically, and independent of any action that we may take; or (3) biological aging which is avoidable through health-conscious habits. Some causes of aging symptoms include: perhaps part of the genetic program, since for example, cell divisions continue to approximately **50** and then no more; living creatures must at least live long enough to reproduce the species, and by implication having reproduced you are no longer needed; greater longevity, comparing one species with another, is associated with greater brain weight, and less body weight, and slower metabolic rate; you suffer an accumulation of cell mutations, and/or other defects of the cell; continuous exposure to the chances of disease means that eventually you will be unlucky; hardening of the arteries, which is either thickening of the blood vessel walls, or deposits on the inside wall of the artery; decrease in water content of the body, and this is the cause of the shrunken appearance of the aged; bones become lighter and more brittle; a change in the nature of collagen in your skin leads to changes in appearance; nerve cells are not replaced, and diminish in quantity; parts of the brain suffer loss of cells; nonrenewal of certain cells; the amount of blood pumped by the heart decreases 40 percent between **30** and **90**. A number of systems gradually suffer a reduction in their capacity, and we respond by lowering our demands on the body and by a sharing of the load between systems. So we then live for years at just above the threshold level for each system. But suddenly there is an overload on one system, perhaps caused by an accident. The high demand causes a breakdown, and there is a cascade effect as high demands are placed on other systems, straining each beyond tolerance. So a broken bone leads to complications which lead to death.

Not only is your longevity correlated with your occupation and social class, but a wife's longevity is influenced by the job of her husband. Machine tool operators live significantly less than machine tool setters; and employees in coke and natural gas works live longer than laborers and bricklayers. The wives' longevity mimics these patterns.

HISTORY—WORLD

Cardinal Fleury continues as first minister of France (1733).

Prince Talleyrand resigns as French Ambassador to London (1834), and dies at **84**. His career is a monument to survivalism, as he is one of the elite during both revolutionary and counterrevolutionary administrations. He is Foreign Minister during the French Revolution, from **43–45**; Foreign Minister to Napoleon (**30**), at **45**, and until **53**; and Foreign Minister to the restored king between **60–61**. In the following regime, he receives his last post, as London ambassador, at **76**.

Konrad Adenauer continues as Chancellor of West Germany (1956).

Eamon DeValera continues as President of Ireland (1963).

Jomo Kenyatta continues as President of Kenya (1972).

Marshal Tito continues as President of Yugoslavia (1972).

General Franco continues as Spanish head of state (1975).

John Diefenbaker, former Canadian Prime Minister, continues as a member of Parliament (1976).

Marshal Yeh Chien-ying becomes Chairman of China's National People's Congress (1978), virtually China's head of state. And, in China's invasion of Vietnam (1979), the command is held by General Hsu Shih-yu (**73**).

King Sobhuza II continues in office as King of Swaziland (1979). He has held this position since **21**. He is regarded as "The Lion," and he has had 200 children with 70 wives. He maintains the traditional custom in which each year a new corral is built for the Queen Mother by all the female citizens who are at puberty age and who have not yet had children.

U. K. Kekkonen continues as President of Finland (1980).

HISTORY—U.S.A.

Former President John Adams dies on Independence Day, 1826, as does Thomas Jefferson (**83**). Former President James Monroe (**73**) dies on Independence Day, 1831.

Admiral Hyman Rickover continues in charge of the U.S. Navy's nuclear submarine program (1979). He is sixteen years over the maximum legal age for military service, and receives dispensation. The president is his former subordinate, Jimmy Carter (**56**). Rickover continues until his retirement at **82**.

HISTORY—U.K.

Youth is a blunder; manhood a struggle; old age a regret.—Disraeli (1804–81).

Lord Lovat is beheaded outside the Tower of London (1747, Apr. 9), for his part in the Scottish rebellion of 1745—he is the last person ever to be beheaded in England.

Lord Palmerston wins election (July 1865), and continues as Prime Minister. But he dies in office, a few months later. He had first been Prime Minister at **70**. At **78**, he had been cited as corespondent in a divorce trial, for adultery that year, with a journalist's wife (**30**). At **80**, his eating at a banquet is noted—twelve courses—and at **79** he rides 12 miles in 55 minutes. On his deathbed, he imagines that he is Foreign Secretary again, dictating a treaty; his last words are "That's Article 98; now go on to the next."

Mary Anne Disraeli dies (1872, Dec. 15), and her husband (**67**), the Victorian Prime Minister, discovers that every time she had cut his hair, she had saved all the hairs—for their 33 years of married life.

David Lloyd George, now widowed, marries (1943) his secretary, Frances Stevenson (**55**). At **77**, he had been offered a cabinet position, but declined—perhaps in the hope of later getting an even more important job. As Chancellor of the Exchequer, he had first made love to Miss Stevenson when she was **25** and his secretary, and he was four days past his **50**th birthday. Frances Stevenson never has any complaints; she finishes her memoirs with the words "My cup runneth over." Sir Robert Walpole, first-ever Prime Minister, also marries his mistress immediately after his first wife dies (1737)—he is **61**, and his second wife, Maria "Molly" Skerrett, is **35**.

Winston Churchill resigns as Prime Minister (Apr. 1955), for the second and last time. His birthday is a national celebration. In the public memory, all his faults have been forgiven, and his career (cf. **20***, **40***), is seen as leading inevitably to his leadership at **65***. He receives a portrait which shows him having a touch of arrogance; this gift so angers him that his wife (**70**) directs a servant to destroy it. Churchill continues to appear in the House of Commons until **89**, and lives until **90**.

There are about 70 members of the House of Lords who are **80** or over (1978). The oldest is the Earl of Albemarle (**95**). One of the newest members is the Duke of Portland (**89**), who joined at **88**, when he succeeded to the title on the death of a distant relative. In 1979, one of the Government whips in the House is Lord Jacques (**74**). The chairman of the House of Lords committee which looks into Britain's defense is Lord Shinwell (**94**).

RELIGION, PHILOSOPHY

When I was young I liked mathematics. When this became too difficult for me, I took to philosophy, and when philosophy became too difficult I took to politics.—Bertrand Russell (1872–1970).

Old age is defined at **80**+, in *Essay on Old Age* (Rome, 44 B.C.), by Cicero (**61**). Aging is clearly associated, for him, with changes in behavior—infancy is the time of imbecility; youth, of ardor; manhood, of gravity; and old age, of experience, discretion, and judgment. There are four objections to old age: (1) it incapacitates you for public life; (2) its bodily infirmities; (3) it stops sensual gratification; (4) it threatens you with death. Cicero disproves (1) and (2) with stories of great Romans at **80** and **90**. He is pleased about (3), since declining desire stops you making a fool of yourself. And (4), death is not to be feared: if there is a spirit world, then death is good, and if there is no spirit world, then death is nothingness. Old age is therefore "the last scene in the great drama of life." Good-tempered people will enjoy it; only the petulant will dislike old age. Cicero himself dies at **63**, killed in one of the disputes following the assassination of Julius Caesar (**56***).

Pope Gregory XIII: establishment of the Gregorian calendar (1582), as used today.

Pope John XXIII: inauguration of Vatican Council (1962).

Here are some long-lived popes; they are shown in chronological order, with their ages at election and death, and the year of their death: Urban II, **46–57** (1099); Celestine III, **85–92** (1198); Innocent III, **38–56** (1216); Martin IV, **71–75** (1285); Boniface VIII, **60–69** (1303); John XXII, **67–85** (1334); Urban III, **53–61** (1370); Paul IV, **79–83** (1559); Gregory XIII, **70–83** (1585); Urban VIII, **55–76** (1644); Innocent X, **70–81** (1655); Innocent XI, **65–78** (1689); Alexander VIII,

 79–81 (1691); Benedict XIII, **75–81** (1730); Benedict XIV, **65–83** (1758); Clement XIII, **65–76** (1769); Pius VII, **60–83** (1823); Pius IX, **54–86** (1878); Leo XII, **68–93** (1903); Pius X, **68–79** (1914); John XXIII, **76–81** (1963). Pope John Paul II is elected at **58** (1978).

Eligibility: Roman Catholic cardinals can no longer vote, after **80**, for the new pope; and they must resign from their full-time positions in the Vatican.

SOCIAL SCIENCE, EDUCATION

Freud writes about his birthday celebrations (1936): "What is the secret meaning of celebrating the big round numbers of one's life? Surely a measure of triumph over the transitoriness of life, which, as we never forget, is ready to devour us. Then one rejoices with a sort of communal feeling that we are not made of such frail stuff as to prevent one of us victoriously resisting the hostile effects of life for **60**, **70**, or even **80** years." Freud in fact resists until **83**.

F. A. von Hayek is writing his fifty-fourth book (1979), and witnessing a swing in economic fashions, back toward the views that he had developed in his **40**s onward. At **78**, he had gone on a round-the-world lecture tour, advising governments on their economic policy. His right-wing views are now influential, having been dismissed in his **50**s to early **70**s, in favor of Keynesianism. A current best-seller is *The Road to Serfdom,* written at **45**—centralized planning is seen as leading to a more general loss of freedom in noneconomic matters. Keynes himself had died at **62** (1946), having seen a gradual and steady increase in his own influence in the last ten to twenty years of his life.

Jung: death of his wife Emma (**73**, in 1955). They have been married for 52 years, and Jung himself dies at **85***. In his bereavement, Jung now takes up a project in stone—he carves on three stone tablets the names of his male relatives, his paternal ancestors, and his son's sons. The series begins with the motto from Delphi—"Called or not called, God will be present."

Samuel Eliot Morison: *The European Discovery of America* (1967). He next publishes a book (**82**) on Samuel de Champlain, the Canadian explorer. Morison had become Harvard professor at **38**, and he dies at **88**.

Alice Pearce: elected Homecoming Queen, at Methodist College, Fayetteville, North Carolina (1977).

Now is the time to do "oral history," that is, contributing to social sciences by being an informant about events in your early life. For example, veterans of the 1914–18 war were interviewed in 1975–78 in an oral history project. This led to the book *They Called It Passchendaele,* by Lyn MacDonald.

On the effect of failing memory upon scientific creativity: "As long as memory lasts, a crowd of people are working together as a unity: the **20**-year-old, the **30**-year-old, and so on. As soon as it fails, one begins to be increasingly alone and the whole generation of selves stands back and mocks the helpless old man."—G. C. Lichtenberg.

MONEY, WORK

Dr. Armand Hammer negotiates a giant chemical fertilizer deal between the West and Comecon (1978). Asked for the secret of his success, he says: "Some people call me lucky, but when you work between ten and fourteen hours per day for seven days a week, you get lucky."

ARCHITECTURE

Buckminster Fuller publishes his magnum opus: *Synergetics: Explorations in the Geometry of Thinking* (1975).

ART

Grandma Moses: first solo show (1940). Although she had done a painting at **58**, she started serious work in her **70**s. Grandma Moses now lives and paints for another twenty years.

Josef Albers continues to work as a painter (1968). He says, "That's my secret—stay a student and don't get old."

Henry Moore: large exhibition in Kensington Gardens, London (1978)—retrospective, and work in progress.

Hans Feibusch has a birthday show of his paintings and sculpture (1978), put on by the Greater London Council. The catalogue foreword is written by the architect Sir Clough Williams-Ellis (**94**).

MUSIC—CLASSICAL

Leopold Stokowski injures his leg while playing football with his grandson, but continues conducting in New York, Philadelphia, and London, in the same year (1962). At **80**, he is the founder of the American Symphony Orchestra. (cf. **94***)

Havergal Brian composes twenty-two symphonies from **80** onward. (cf. **89***)

Pablo Casals: marriage, to a pupil, Maria Montanez.

Arthur Fiedler continues as the conductor of the Boston Pops Orchestra (1974).

LITERATURE

Alfred Tennyson: "Crossing the Bar" (1889).

FILMS

Growing old is what you do if you're lucky.—Groucho Marx (1895–1977).

Boris Karloff: *Targets* (1967)—directed by Peter Bogdanovich (**27**).

MUSIC—NON-CLASSICAL

Maurice Chevalier: final farewell tour (1968). His first success was at **20**, in the Folies Bergères, Paris. The song "Louise" is at **41**. And the film *Gigi* is at **70**.

TV, ETC.

Jack Warner: last episode of "Dixon of Dock Green" (U.K., 1976), the longest running TV series in the world. In this, he plays the part of a London policeman. The series had begun twenty-one years previously, when Warner was already past the London police retiring age.

"Dad's Army" (U.K., 1977)—the tenth and last year of this comedy series. It shows part-time soldiers preparing to defend the country during World War II. Not only are the characters old, but so are the stars; Arthur Lowe (now **63**) as the officer in charge; and John Le Mesurier (**64**) as the sergeant. In the ranks, the men include Arnold Ridley (**82**), and John Laurie (**80**) as the gloom-laden town undertaker. It is fair to say that all of these actors have had solid working careers, but in this series each one hits on exactly the perfect part.

"Coronation Street" (U.K., 1980)—the twentieth year of twice-weekly shows about life in a poor industrial district of northwest England. Many of the stars have grown old with the series and have become part of the viewers' family life. For the public at least, the stars are completely identified with their TV characters, which they have had to play to the exclusion of any other acting role. The permanent members of "The Street" include Violet Carson (now **79**) who plays the part of a lovable old harridan—she is famous for always wearing her hair in a net; Doris Speed (**75**) whose part is bossy, snobbish, but fascinating; Patricia Phoenix (**56**) whose character is still being led astray by men and who never learns her lesson; and Jack Howarth (**83**), solid working class of the old sort.

"The Archers: an Everyday Story of Country Folk"—its 29th year (U.K., 1980). This fifteen-minute, five times per week radio series is a record breaker. It describes the activities of Doris Archer (now **80**), Dan Archer (**84**), their son Phil (**52**), and others in their village. This series continues to be a marking point in the daily routine of millions of listeners. It is probably impossible for the scriptwriters to kill off any of the characters; despite the decades of happy listening, most listeners still have not forgotten the day, twenty-five years ago, on which the Archers' new daughter-in-law, Grace (**26**), was burned to death in a stable fire. In fact, the actress (**75**) playing Doris Archer (**80**) becomes too ill to continue her work, and the character has to die—she has a heart attack at Sunday teatime.

Ruth Gordon continues to be a TV star. She first appeared on Broadway at **19**, in *Peter Pan,* and was a distinguished stage actress throughout her **30**s. At **46**, she married Garson Kanin (**30**). Her first film part was at **44**; her first Oscar nomination was at **70**; and first Oscar award at **72**, for her part in *Rosemary's Baby*. At **75**, she starred in *Harold* (**20**) *and Maude* (**79**). At **80** (1976), she appears in "The Great Houdini."

LOVE, LIFE

There are few persons who, in the first decline of old age, do not give evidence in what respect their body and mind must fall away.

Few people know how to be old.

Old age is a tyrant who forbids, under pain of life, all the pleasures of youth.—La Rochefoucauld (1613–80).

[Healthy males have] a capacity for sexual performance that frequently may extend beyond the **80** level.—Masters and Johnson.

In times of famine, the natives of Tierra del Fuego kill and eat the old women before they touch their dogs. When they were asked why they did this, they said that dogs could catch seals, while old women could not do so.—the gerontologist Elie Metchnikoff. (Note that most stories of cannibalism turn out to be untrue.)

G. R. Talbert has reported spermatogenesis in males **80+**. There is probably no worthwhile data on sexual activity at **60+** because (1) self-reporting is the prime source of data and it is open to self-delusion and embarrassment; and (2) sexuality at **60+** may be heavily influenced by cultural and generational pressures so it would be impossible to say what is the basic potential for sexual activity in the age group.

Alfred Kinsey (1949) found a male (**70**) who had seven ejaculations per week, and a married couple (**88** and **90**) who often had sex once a week. Kinsey said that at **70**, 25% of males were impotent; the corresponding figure at **80** was 75%. For married men, there were 1.8 emissions per week at **50**; 1.3 at **60**; and 0.9 at **70**. The angle of erection reached a peak at **26—30** and declined from then onward. In general, male sexual performance declines from the **late teens** onward; female sexual performance peaked at **30**s and **40**s, according to Kinsey. William Masters has said that anxiety, not a physical change, is the main reason for decreasing sexual activity among older males. Anxiety itself is caused by being unwilling to accept a slightly less dramatic sexual performance, and so giving up altogether—even though one does not set the all-or-nothing standard for other activities.

The *Los Angeles Times* recently (1979) published an anonymous letter from a woman (**84**) in which she said: "I pray that I might die." Having a chronic medical condition, she was living in a convalescent home and seeing a doctor for only five minutes per month. Not all the staff spoke English, and few were in the slightest bit interested in her as a person. She had little choice of food. She had to go to bed early, for the convenience of the institution. There was nothing to live for; no friends, no pleasures, no kindnesses to her, and no possibility of improvement.

According to research by gerontologist Ethel Shanas, the proportion of people living with an adult child (in the U.S.A.) has gone down, but if we include the elderly living within ten minutes of an adult child, then the figures have not changed in the past 20 years. Another way of measuring family relationships is to look at the number of elderly who saw one of their children in the past week; again, this figure has not deteriorated recently, whatever the popular misconception may be about a mass breakdown in family life and responsibility.

In Japan, September 15 is a national holiday, "Keiro-no-Hi," in honor of old people.

PRESS

Richard Strout continues to write the "TRB" column at the *New Republic* (1978)—his thirty-fifth year on the magazine. He also writes every week for the *Christian Science Monitor*.

LAW, CRIME

Roger Brooke Taney: judgment in the Dred Scott case (1857). Taney dies in office, as Chief Justice of the U.S. Supreme Court, at **87**. Dred Scott is about **62**, and dies at **63**.

George Waters continues as a prisoner in California (1962). He had entered San Quentin at **44**, having murdered his wife. No body was ever found; the main evidence against him was given by his daughter (then 7). At **69**, Waters had received a long-service pin, for having been a model inmate for 25 years.

Lord Denning continues as Master of the Rolls (1979), the third most prominent position in the English courts system. He is famous for his views that trade unions have switched from an underdog role into a position of overbearing power and monopoly. On his birthday, he publishes a book *The Discipline of the Law,* which sells well. He had become Master of the Rolls at **64**. At **78**, he had overturned government objections to the cut-price air travel plans of Freddie Laker (**55**).

SPORTS

Duke of Beaufort continues to ride to hounds, three days each week (1980). On his birthday at **11**, he received his own pack of foxhounds, and he has been a foxhunter ever since then. Having his own pack has meant that he has been addressed as "Master" since **11**.

Paul Spangler (track,1980) creates the following records:

100 meters, 19.7 seconds;
800 meters, 3 minutes 27.2 seconds;
mile, 7 minutes 4.2 seconds;
5,000 meters, 25 minutes 9.8 seconds;
10,000 meters, 49 minutes 22.7 seconds.

In one hour, he runs 6 miles 1,408 yards. Spangler was not an athlete in his youth and had never been more than a "weekender" as far as exercise is concerned. At **67**, he was 40 pounds overweight and took no regular exercise. He then began systematic running as he was afraid of atherosclerosis. He now weighs 150 pounds, and his blood pressure is 100/60.

The male long jump record at **80** is 11 feet 7 inches; and the high jump record is 3 feet 1 inch.

81

HISTORY—WORLD

Marcus Cato, in 153 B.C., visits Carthage, and determines on his policy that the city must be destroyed before it becomes a threat to the Roman Empire. Carthage is the rich Phoenician city in the Gulf of Tunis. From now onward, whenever Cato makes a speech, on any topic, he adds the rider—"Carthage must be destroyed." At **17**, Cato had been a soldier in the Roman army when Hannibal (**30**), the Carthaginian general, crossed the Alps with a herd of elephants and attacked Italy. The attack was eventually repulsed. Since then, Cato has had a distinguished career as orator and magistrate. At **84**, his policy is adopted by Rome, but Cato dies at **85**, four years before Carthage is utterly destroyed. Cato's life story is later described by Mestrius Plutarch (c.50–c.120 A.D.), the priest at Delphi whose *Parallel Lives* describe pairs of famous personalities—for example, Julius Caesar and Alexander the Great—and draw conclusions about the nature of greatness and about the interaction of private behavior with public achievement.

Morarji Desai: Prime Minister of India (1977). His home minister is Charan Singh (**74**). Desai replaces Indira Gandhi (**59**), who has recently kept him in jail for 18 months. He looks after his health carefully, and keeps to a strict diet, as well as daily drink of his own urine.

Alessandro Pertini: President of Italy (1978). He is the country's first Socialist president. From **32–47**, he had been in prison during the Fascist period. Among his friends in jail was Antonio Gramsci (**46***), the writer on communism, who died then from ill health.

HISTORY—U.K.

Queen Victoria makes her fourth visit to Ireland (1900), to thank the Irish people for providing the bulk of the soldiers used in fighting the Boer War. Her last discussion with a minister is about the war, and she dies at **81**. Her reign is a longest-ever 63 years 7 months. The second-longest reign is that of George III—59 years 96 days, and he also dies at **81**. Elizabeth I dies at **69** (1603); Edward I, **68** (1307); Henry I, **67** (1135); George I also **67** (1727); George IV also **67** (1830); and Edward III dies at **64** (1377).

RELIGION, PHILOSOPHY

Krishnamurti publishes his fourteenth book (1976).

MONEY, WORK

Jean Paul Getty continues as president of Getty Oil; opens his classical museum at Malibu, California (1974, Jan. 15). At **83**, he gives no one reason for his success, but says that he must have "had a reserved seat in life."

ARCHITECTURE

Mies van der Rohe: Museum of Modern Art, Berlin (1967–68). His enormous Federal Center, Chicago, is finished about this time.

FILMS

Howard Hawks: *A Hell of a Good Life* (1977)—his filmed memoirs.

Ruth Gordon and Lee Strasberg (**76**): *Boardwalk* (1978).

Fred Astaire: marriage, to the jockey, Robyn Smith (**37**, in 1980).

James Cagney: *Ragtime* (1981).

Harold Bennett: as Young Mr. Grace, in "Are You Being Served?" (U.K., 1978).

PRESS

Samuel Newhouse acquires Booth newspapers (1976) at a cost of $300 million.

SPORTS

Amos Alonzo Stagg: named as "College Coach of the Year" (1943). He had been football coach at the University of Chicago from **29** to **70**, at a time when the team achieves huge success. He then serves as head coach at the College (later University) of the Pacific, at Stockton, California. Stagg lives until **102**.

Honus Wagner: death (1955). At **66**, he had been one of the first five members of the Baseball Hall of Fame. The others die at the following ages: Christy Mathewson (at **45**, in 1925); Babe Ruth (at **53**, in 1948); Walter Johnson (at **59**, in 1946); and Ty Cobb (at **74**, in 1961). Also, Willie Mays dies at **79**, in 1971.

Nellie Brown (1975) wins her first swimming race, at the Washington D.C. Masters Swimming Club. She goes on to win six events in her age group of **80**+ at the U.S. National Masters Championships. At **84**, she becomes YMCA national woman of the year; between **81–85**, she collects 30 gold medals, 16 blue ribbons, and 23 trophies. Her lifestyle at **85** includes a half-mile swim per day, and 30 minutes on an exercise bicycle. Previously, she had been a public school first grade teacher, until mandatory retirement at **70**. She then taught in a private school until **77**. As a child, she had had no athletic success, owing to an attack of polio.

82

HISTORY—WORLD

General Franco: death (1975). He has been Spanish head of state since about **43***. Later, it is said that for seventeen days he is kept alive while clinically dead, so that his cabinet can complete the negotiation of a complex treaty with Morocco. Coincidentally, Antonio Salazar, dictator of Portugal, had also reached office at **43**, and dies at **81**

(1970). He had had a stroke at **79** (allegedly precipitated by an accident in putting up a deck chair) and was no longer able to take any part in administration. However, his aides are too scared of him to tell him that someone else has had to be appointed prime minister. Consequently, at his death, he still believes that he is running the country. Similarly, President Tito (d. **87**, 1980) of Yugoslavia is kept in a dying state for several months, so that his country can gradually learn to live without his presence. Tito suffers a leg amputation and is kept on life-support equipment in a coma for much of this time.

HISTORY—U.K.

William Gladstone becomes Prime Minister (Aug. 1892) for the fourth time; and pushes his Irish Home Rule Bill through the House of Commons. He and his wife Catherine (**80**) are still in love; and at **81** she finishes a letter to him: "You never saw such a brilliant day, brilliant sunshine, clear views, but I am longing to get back to *somebody*. Who can that be? God bless you. Be very good." At **80**, Mrs. Gladstone gives up her habit of a cold bath every morning; but they both continue to attend church before breakfast. (cf. **84***)

RELIGION, PHILOSOPHY

Plato: death (347 B.C.).

SOCIAL SCIENCE, EDUCATION

Lewis Mumford is working on two new books (1977)—his twenty-seventh and twenty-eighth.

Mr. Irving Kantor appears in the *New York Times* (1977) as he is a freshman at Brooklyn College, New York. At Harvard, one of the freshmen in 1977 is Harry Gersh (**63**). At Manchester University, a final-year undergraduate is John Lawrence Hogan (**68**, in 1977). Eric Reader (**69**) receives a degree in modern languages from Trinity College, Cambridge (1976). William Alin graduates from University College, Swansea (Wales, 1973) with a B.A. Hons. in geography; he begins work on an M.A. thesis. Mrs. Rae Toffler earns her B.A. from the Open University (U.K., 1976) at **81**; she began it at **75**, and had originally left school at **13**. In 1935, the Rev. J. E. McSkate receives his Ph.D. from St. Andrews University, Scotland, at **87**, with a thesis on the book of Jonah, having begun at **83**.

MONEY, WORK

Andrew Mellon gives paintings and money (1937) to set up the National Gallery of Art, Washington D.C.

Matisse: "Papiers-découpés" (1952). The artist is too ill in bed to paint, so instructs an assistant to cut out papers in the shapes that Matisse desires. These cutouts are new, startling, and attractive. In the last two years of his life, he becomes influential once again.

LITERATURE

Tolstoy leaves home (Nov. 1910) and gets on a train; he has no particular destination in mind, except the intention of getting away from people. His home has been full of money and children, thus (allegedly) invalidating the communist and Puritan philosophy which he has been publishing for the past 30 years. But he becomes ill on the train, and dies in the stationmaster's cottage in an obscure country town.

PLAYS, DANCE

Richard Goolden is "Mole" in the play *Toad of Toad Hall* (1977), for the twenty-second Christmas season in succession, in London.

FILMS AGE 82 YRS

George Burns plays God in *Oh, God* (1977). This is a success, and he signs a contract for a sequel, *Oh, God II*. Burns had a brilliant career in TV with his wife, Gracie Allen (d. **58**, when Burns was **68**). After a period in which he was also a producer, he starred in the film *The Sunshine Boys* at **76**, and gained an Oscar. This was the start of an immensely popular second career. At **84**, he becomes a hit singer with his record "I Wish I Was **18** Again," and he also publishes his memoirs. George Burns's daily routine starts early, with thirty minutes of exercising, followed by a fifteen minute walk. At ten he meets his scriptwriters. At noon, he has lunch, followed by a rest. He gets up again at five-thirty and goes out socializing. He goes to bed at ten and reads for an hour. He comments on aging: "As soon as I get to be **85** I'm going to give up golf. And skiing."

George Cukor: *Rich and Famous* (1981), starring Jacqueline Bisset (**36**) and Candice Bergen (**34**).

Fred Astaire: *Ghost Story* (1981), also starring Melvyn Douglas (**80**), John Houseman (**79**), and Douglas Fairbanks, Jr. (only **71**).

PRESS

Norman Rockwell attends a Norman Rockwell parade (1976) in which his best-known covers for the *Saturday Evening Post* are reenacted as living tableaux by 2,000 people. He had started painting these covers at **22**.

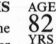

83

HISTORY—WORLD

Emperor Haile Selassie of Ethiopia is smothered to death (1975) by order of a new government, shortly after a coup d'etat. At **43**, he had made a dramatic personal appeal to the League of Nations when he asked for help against an invasion of Ethiopia by Mussolini (**52**). He received no assistance, but Ethiopia was liberated at the end of World War II (**48**), and Selassie then returned to his throne.

HISTORY—U.K.

Duke of Wellington: death (1852). His funeral is a national event; the procession includes a detachment of 83 Chelsea Pensioners, one for each year of his life.

RELIGION, PHILOSOPHY

Spencer W. Kimball: as President of the Mormon Church (1978), he hears a revelation from God that the church must remove the color bar at entry into the church.

MONEY, WORK

Gordon Selfridge: owing to his extravagance, his Selfridges store is in difficulties (London, 1940)—Gordon Selfridge is deposed as chairman; but lives until he is **90**.

LITERATURE

Alfred Lord Tennyson continues publishing poetry until now, the year of his death (1909).

FILMS

Charlie Chaplin gets an Oscar (1972) for his *Limelight* (**63**), which had been banned in the U.S.A. for the past twenty years.

MUSIC—NON-CLASSICAL

Mabel Hunter sings at the Kennedy Center, Washington, D.C. (1978) and is featured in an exhibition, "Great Women in Jazz." In the same month, another great singer is still performing—"Bricktop" (**84**) has a season at the Playboy Club, London. When she was **40**, Cole Porter (**43**) had written for her the song "Miss Otis Regrets She's Unable to Lunch Today." She says that she owes her longevity to eating black-eyed peas and cornbread, and avoiding frustration—"I've spent all my life running away from any situation which might disturb or upset me."

LOVE, LIFE

Miss Mildred Thomson: death (Scotland, 1975). She leaves £50,000 ($100,000) to a hospital "in memory of my late fiancé," Captain John Lauder who had died at **22**, in World War I, when she was **24**.

LAW, CRIME

Vicente Sunza, oldest U.S. Federal prisoner, is paroled from prison, but having no place to go, parole is rescinded, and he returns to prison hospital (1976). He had been jailed at **33** for second degree murder.

84

HEALTH

Cecile Tischler (**84**) dies (New York, 1977)—her husband William (**87**) tells the doctor that he will "soon follow"; sixteen hours later, William Tischler dies of a heart attack. In a similar case, Frederick and Mary Ward (both **71**) die only twelve minutes apart (Maine, 1979)—they were twins who had lived together all their lives. Another case of parallel deaths is that of the two men who built up Levi Strauss into a leading position in the jeans business. These men were Walter Haas and Daniel Koshland. In 1922, Haas (**33**) invites Koshland (**30**) to join the business, when it was only of regional importance, and they proceed to transform it into an international enterprise. Later, Haas dies at **90**, and Koshland (**87**) dies on the day of Haas's funeral.

HISTORY—WORLD

President Tito of Yugoslavia (1977): his first visit to China. On this trip, he also travels to Moscow. Tito had become head of state at **53**, after being a guerilla leader during World War II. At **56**, he successfully defied Joseph Stalin (**80**) and maintained a Communist but independent country. Tito in his **80**s keeps fit; at **86**, he is married for the fourth time, to an opera singer (**35**); and he outlives his most obvious successor as President, Edvard Kardelj, who dies at **69**. At **84**, on his return from his world travels, he is greeted at Belgrade airport by a crowd of 500,000. He lives until **87**.

HISTORY—U.K.

William Gladstone retires as Prime Minister (Mar. 1894); works on his translation of Homer's odes. He dies at **88**.

RELIGION, PHILOSOPHY

St. Luke, writer of the third gospel: death.

RENAISSANCE

Benjamin Franklin: death (Philadelphia, 1790). He has been famous as a writer and printer (cf. **0***) and as a scientist (cf. **46***). His great public roles are in his **50**s onward, when he is the representative of the colonies to the London government. As the revolutionary break becomes inevitable, he leaves London at **64**. At **69**, he is a member of the second Continental Congress, and at **70** he is on the committee to draft the Declaration of Independence. Later in 1776, he goes to Paris as U.S. minister there. He is the representative of the new country to the leading European powers. Recognition by France comes when he is **71**, and he negotiates peace with Britain when he is **75–77**. He leaves Europe at **78**. His years in Europe, **70–78**, are probably the culmination of his life, since his formal political duties are of international importance, and his vast popularity in France is due to his brilliant renaissance career, as writer and scientist. He is also admired for his straightforward personal style, in which he has made no attempt to become an aristocrat as he has become more prominent. In his **70**s, many see him as the ideal person of the times—rational, scientific, and democratic. On returning home, he is a delegate to the Federal Constitutional Convention at **81**, and also works for the abolition of slavery. His *Autobiography* is written at various ages, **65**, **78**, **82**, and **84**. Franklin has come from a long-lived family—his mother survived until **85**, and his father until **89**. At **84**, Benjamin Franklin is asked his theological views, and he replies on the divinity of Christ: "It is a question I do not dogmatize upon, having never studied it, and think it needless to busy myself with it now, when I expect soon an opportunity of knowing the truth with less trouble."

MUSIC—CLASSICAL

Pablo Casals gives a cello recital at the White House (1961).

Voltaire returns to Paris (1778) from his home on the Swiss border (located so that he would be able to escape from France) and is suddenly the talk of the town, in his last year.

W. Somerset Maugham: *Points of View* (1958), his last book.

Henry Miller (who wrote *Tropic of Cancer* at **40**) is now quoted as saying: "It's amazing how young women will allow themselves to fall in love with old men. Sometimes my rivals are 25 years old. I tell these women I'm decrepit and falling apart. But they say the young guys can't teach them anything."

85

HISTORY—WORLD

Rudolph Hess continues in solitary confinement (1979) at Spandau Prison, Berlin. He is the only prisoner; Spandau contains 599 empty cells, and its costs are at least $1 million per year. The prison is administered by the victorious powers of World War II, each having one month in control. Hess has been a captive since **47**, when he flew to Britain, apparently to privately negotiate the end of the war; he had been deputy to Adolf Hitler (**52**). Now at **85**, new medical evidence suggests that this prisoner may not even be Hess after all.

HISTORY—U.K.

Harold Macmillan gives the main speech at the annual conference (1979, Feb. 10) of the Young Conservatives (**15–35**).

RELIGION, PHILOSOPHY

Pastor Niemöller is asked to become a hostage in a kidnapping case involving the Baader-Meinhof gang (1977). He would have stood in for the original captive.

SOCIAL SCIENCE, EDUCATION

Jung: last days (1961). He completes work on his contribution to *Man and His Symbols;* out of all his publications, this is his best known. He has a dream about his death, on returning to Bollingen, his home on the edge of the lake at Zurich—"He saw the 'other Bollingen' bathed in a glow of light, and a voice told him that it was now completed and ready for habitation. Then far below he saw a mother wolverine teaching her child to dive and swim in a stretch of water." To him, the "other Bollingen" is his future home; mother nature will teach him the new ways of life there. He dies a few weeks before his **86**th birthday. One of his biographers, Barbara Hannah, attends his funeral and writes: "When I stood by his infinitely peaceful and yet very remote dead body, I could only say 'thank you' again and again. And that is how I still feel toward this life which was lived so fully and that we were privileged to know: a profound and boundless gratitude."

MONEY, WORK

Daniel K. Ludwig continues with the development of his three million acre estate on the Amazon River (1978). At a cost of $1 billion he has cleared 200,000 acres, and had a complete instant wood pulp plant towed on barges from Japan.

George Meany: retirement as President of the AFL-CIO (1979), the 14-million-member federation of labor. At **46**, he was secretary-treasurer of the American Federation of Labor, and when the AFL combined with the Congress of Industrial Organizations, he became the first president, at **61**. Another long-lived labor leader is Fidel Velazquez who at **78** (1978) continues to head the Confederation of Mexican Workers. Labor leaders in Britain typically have to retire at **65**, but they often have the benefit of lifetime employment on reaching the top position in their union; if elected at **45**, they can hold this position for twenty years without having to face a reelection campaign. When George Meany retires at **85**, he is succeeded by Lane Kirkland (**57**). When Meany (**61**) negotiated the combining of the AFL and the CIO, his rival for the top position was Walter Reuther (**48**, in 1955) who accepted the number two slot, expecting to move upward in the natural course of events. Meany neither retired nor died, and later Reuther at **60** led his own union, the autoworkers, out of the AFL-CIO. Reuther was killed in a plane crash at **62**.

ART

Joan Miró moves back to Spain (1978) after the death of Franco (**82**). Miró is doing a sculpture for Chicago, murals for Barcelona, and a tapestry for Washington's National Gallery.

MUSIC—CLASSICAL

Toscanini: last performance of Beethoven's (**52***) Ninth Symphony, with the NBC Symphony Orchestra (1952).

Karl Boehm continues as the star conductor of the Salzburg Festival and conductor of the Vienna Philharmonic Orchestra (1979).

FILM

Mae West: *Sextette* (1978).

86

HISTORY—WORLD

Field Marshal Hindenburg, in 1933: as President of Germany, he appoints Adolf Hitler (**43**) as Chancellor.

Louise Weiss: election to the parliament of the European Economic Community (1979). She is the oldest member; the youngest is Sile de Valera (**24**).

SOCIAL SCIENCE, EDUCATION

Edward H. Carr, of Cambridge University, publishes the fourteenth and last volume (1979) of his history of the Soviet revolution. He had begun the project at **53**.

Muriel St.-Clare Byrne: *The Lisle Letters* (Chicago, 1981). This project is two million words in length, and she began it at **36**.

SCIENCE, TECHNOLOGY

Francis Rous receives the Nobel Prize (1966), for the identification of a virus which causes tumors in chickens. He completed this work at **31**.

MONEY, WORK

George Kraft is the oldest worker that the *Wall Street Journal* could find in U.S. factories (1977). He was hired in 1907, at **16**, by the grandfather of the firm's current president.

Colonel Harlan Sanders, wearing a white linen suit, eats take-out Kentucky Fried Chicken at the 21 Club in New York City. On the previous day, he toured company outlets, testing the food. Most were okay, but some were "finger-lickin' bad" (1976). On his **88**th birthday, Colonel Sanders opens a museum about chickens at the firm's headquarters.

LITERATURE

Walter Savage Landor: *Imaginary Conversation*, "Virgil and Horace," and "Milton and Marvell" (1861). This finishes a series which he had begun at **49**.

Thomas Hardy: death (1928). His body is buried in Westminster Abbey, but his heart is taken out and buried in Dorset.

Robert Frost recites his poem "The Gift Outright" from memory (1961), at the inauguration of President John F. Kennedy (**43**). He publishes his last book of verse, *In the Clearing* at **89**.

SPORTS

Sir Michael Sobell (U.K., 1979): joint owner of Troy (**3**), the horse that wins the 200th Derby. Sobell has been trying to do this since **64**.

87

ARCHITECTURE

Frank Lloyd Wright: proposal for a building which is one mile high, for Chicago (1956).

88

HEALTH

Charles Saint-Évremond, a French writer, explains his current good health: "I eat oysters every morning, I dine well; I don't sup badly. People less worthy than I become heroes, provided they have enough wit to put into practice this excellent motto of the school of Salernius: Good humor, rest (after work), and a moderate diet." This quotation comes in a nineteenth century book on longevity.

Mr. Walter Southgate and Mrs. Rebecca Holbrook appear on the platform of the Labour party's annual conference (1978), to get awards from the Prime Minister (**66**) for their lifetime of work for the party.

RELIGION, PHILOSOPHY

Mary Baker Eddy: the *Christian Science Monitor* (1909).

Reverend W. Keble Martin: *Concise British Flora in Colour* (1965). This project has been his hobby since **22**. At **91**, he continues to celebrate Holy Communion, and he publishes his autobiography.

RENAISSANCE

Michelangelo: death (Rome, 1564). The last twenty years of his life have been almost as productive as any other period (cf. **66***). At **82**, he designs the staircase of the Laurentian Library in Florence, receiving the design in a dream. At **84**, he designs a chapel in Rome; at **85**, he makes a design for the Porta Pia, and at **86** he produces a design for Santa Maria degli Angeli. He is at work on the "Rondanini Pietà" until six days before his death. His funeral is in Florence, and it is organized by a committee including Benvenuto Cellini (**63**), Bartolomeo Ammanati (**52**), and Giorgio Vasari (**52**). Apart from the sheer quality of his work, Michelangelo's life has had three extraordinary features: (1) he has had the company of the world's elite since **13***; (2) for at least sixty years he has continued to produce work that is among the greatest ever achieved; and (3) throughout his life, he has suffered from wholly ordinary problems, such as difficult relations with clients, inability to obtain the right materials for his work, and difficulties with his assistants—the last being often due to his own touchy nature. At his funeral, the tributes include this lovely Roman verse:

> You are father, you are creator of things, you are our home.
> Your designs, great man, supply models in abundance.

PRESS

William Randolph Hearst dies (1951, Aug. 14); ten weeks later, his friend Marion Davies (**50**) is married, for the first time. His granddaughter Patty Hearst is born when he would have been **90**.

SPORTS

Elizabeth "Bunny" Ryan (1979) dies on the second-last day of the Wimbledon tennis championships—the day before she would have seen the end of her own record, for winning the greatest number of Wimbledon titles. Ryan had won 19 championships between **22–40**. Her record is now broken by Billie Jean King (**34**) who gains her twentieth title by winning the women's doubles. Coincidentally, Bunny Ryan's great doubles partner, Suzanne Lenglen, had died just before another Wimbledon, at **39** (1938). Also, Maureen Connolly, Wimbledon champion at **18**, dies just before the 1969 Wimbledon championship, at **35**.

89

HISTORY—WORLD

Marshal Pétain is sentenced to death (1945) for collaborating with Hitler's troops who had been occupying France. Pétain had finished World War I, at **62**, as a French national hero. But as President **(84)** after France's defeat in 1940, he believed that accommodation with Hitler was the only reasonable option. Now at **89**, he is not executed, but kept in solitary confinement on a small island, until his death at **95**.

HISTORY—U.K.

Winston Churchill: last appearance in the House of Commons (1964, July 27). (cf. **90***)

RELIGION, PHILOSOPHY

Bertrand Russell is put in prison for one week (London, 1961), as a result of his civil disobedience in support of the Campaign for Nuclear Disarmament. At **80**, he had married, for the fourth time; his new wife was **50**. At **85**, he had helped start the Pugwash East-West conferences. (cf. **93***)

Philip W. Whitcomb: degree of M.Phil., at the University of Kansas (1980). At his graduation, he says that he hopes this degree will lead other old people into the universities "from which they have been barred for the last 100 years or so."

MONEY, WORK

Alfred P. Sloan, and others: publication of *My Years with General Motors* (1964). He had joined at **40**, and become president at **48**. He retired as chief executive officer at **71**, and retired as chairman of the board at **81**. Sloan's regime brought consolidation and a degree of centralization to the company—plus expansion. At **48**, GM produced .7

million cars; by **81**, it produced 4.09 million cars. Sloan lives until **90**, and William C. Durant, founder of GM, lives until **85** (1947).

Marcel Boussac has to sell his giant French textile empire (1978)—it is losing 15 million francs per month.

ARCHITECTURE

Frank Lloyd Wright: death (1959). He has recently completed the design of the Marin County Civic Center, California, which is constructed posthumously. Wright comes from a long-lived family: his mother died at "only **83**," and his grandfathers live until **87** and **99**. Wright has had, in effect, a wonderful second career since **66***.

MUSIC—CLASSICAL

Havergal Brian writes 10 symphonies between **89** and **92** (1965). (cf. **90***)

Artur Rubinstein, on a concert tour, gives a recital to celebrate the **75**th birthday of the Wigmore Hall, London (1976).

PLAYS

Ben Travers: *The Bed Before Yesterday* (1975). This is popular with audiences who make no allowances for the author's age. Shortly afterward his farce *Plunder,* written at **41**, is successfully revived. Travers lives until **94**, having at **92** demonstrated his daily exercise routine on a television talk show.

90

HEALTH

Florence Nightingale: death (1910). Her family have been long-lived—her mother had died at **92**, and of nine uncles and aunts, the earliest death was at **69**, with six going beyond **80**. As a legendary figure in medical history (cf. **30***, **34***), she has been given many honors. And at **87**, she receives a proclamation which is signed by thousands of people called Florence—each named after her.

Out of total deaths at all ages, 8.6 percent (male) in the years **85–94**, and 22 percent (female) (England and Wales, 1977). The causes of death for males **85+** are: (1) ischemic heart disease; (2) pneumonia; (3) cerebrovascular; (4) other heart diseases; (5) bronchitis, emphysema, asthma; (6) lung cancer. The causes of female death are: (1) ischemic heart disease; (2) pneumonia; (3) cerebrovascular; (4) other heart diseases; (5) bronchitis, emphysema, asthma; (6) lung cancer. Male and female causes of death have now become identical, using this measuring system.

As societies have longer surviving populations and life expectancy moves from **45** to **70**, so the causes of death change too. In the "**45**" society, you die of infection and parasites; flu, pneumonia, and bronchitis; other respiratory problems; or diarrhea. In the "**70+**" society, you die from neoplasms or from cardiovascular failure. People today survive to be threatened by the new fears of cancer and heart attacks. In the past, you would not have survived to be threatened by cancer—you would already have died from tuberculosis or typhoid.

Alex Comfort has suggested that the vast majority of the population will live to **90** but be dead by **100**, in societies of the near future.

James F. Fries has said that the average age at death will be **85**. Two thirds of all deaths will occur at **81–89**, and 95 percent would be from **77–93**. Deaths before **85** he calls "premature."

Medicine has gone a long way in eliminating diseases that cause deaths in the early years. Now, we are up against an underlying restriction on the life span, and this is perhaps caused by the death of cell lineages. Cells typically cease reproducing themselves after 50 divisions. Although the calendar age of a cell lineage may be extended, by varying the temperature, for example, the limit to the number of cell divisions is relatively constant. There is no single accepted theory as to why cells cease to divide. In this overall view, the human life span is as fixed as any other limit on human growth, such as the limit on height. It is similar to the other clock mechanisms in the body, such as the onset of puberty.

If the population will typically live until **85–90**, then an important public policy question revolves around the distinction between "old" and "frail old," that is, to what extent will this new mass group of the old be a burden on the rest of the population. It is typically assumed that aging is dependent on the lack of stimulus and the lack of use; crudely, the more you exercise, the longer you will be able to exercise. If this is true, then the dependency of the **80s** and **90s** is a function of decisions about age rules which limit the ability of older people to participate and to earn their way. If a whole age group is not allowed to take a prominent part in life, then it will become dependent and be a drain on the resources of the community. We therefore have a problem of our own making. But, although any dependency of the old is often a self-fulfilling prophecy, some authorities have argued there will be an absolute increase in the number of those who are dependent because of degenerative diseases.

The "dependency ratio" is an attempt to measure the dependent population as a proportion of the providers. Rightly or wrongly, the ratio in practice measures people **0–17** and **65**+, in relation to those **18–65.** In the period 1970–79, the dependents in the U.S.A. have declined. This has been caused by a decrease in children, not balanced by an increase in those **65**+. In 1979, the U.S.A. had 24 million **65**+, out of a total of 222 million (**0**+). In the period 1970–79, the numbers of those **85**+ increased from 1.4 million to 2.3 million. So although there was a dramatic percentage increase, the gain in absolute numbers was hardly excessive.

In 1970–79 (U.S.A.), there was an increase in the **65**+, but an even larger increase in those around **30**. The **65**+ increased 23 percent, while the **25–34** increased 40 percent.

HISTORY—WORLD

Not only do national leaders enjoy longevity but so do their spouses. For example, Song Qinling continues to live in Peking, until her death at **90**, in 1981; at **24**, she had married Sun Yat-sen (**48**) the founder of post-Imperial China; she has been a widow since **35**. Deng Yingchao (**77**, in 1980), widow of Chou En-lai, continues to serve on the Political Bureau in Peking; she had married Chou (**27**) at **22**. Donna Rachele lives until **89** (1979); at **16**, she had married Benito Mussolini (**25**), later the Fascist dictator of Italy, and she has been a widow since **55**. Clementine Churchill lives until **92** (1977); her husband Winston had died at **90** when she was **80**. Bess Truman (**96**, in 1981) continues to live in Independence, Missouri; at **87**, she had been widowed at the death of her husband, former President Harry S Truman (**88**). And, Yvonne de Gaulle dies at **79** (1979), one day before the ninth anniversary of the death of her husband, the French leader Charles de Gaulle, who also died at **79**.

RELIGION, PHILOSOPHY

The Reverend Edward Courtman continues as Rector of the village of Mildenhall, Wiltshire (England 1975). He serves from **51–94**.

Michael Gonzi continues as Archbishop of Malta (1976); he resigns at **92.**

The Rev. Sydney Stevens (**93**, 1981) continues as the vicar of Collaton St. Mary, Devon, a position which he has held since **60**. But all Anglican priests appointed after 1975 must retire at **70**.

SOCIAL SCIENCE, EDUCATION

Will Durant and Ariel Durant (**77**): *The Story of Civilization:* volume eleven (1975). This is their last volume. The project had started when they were **55** and **37**; by volume four, they had only got as far as 1300

 A.D., and they were aged **65** and **52**. At **69** and **56**, they tried to retire, but soon returned to work. They have now been married for 63 years—they married when she was **15** and a student in the school where he (**27**) was a teacher. They say that their success is due to a lifetime of working seven days per week. At **96** and **83**, his death occurs two weeks after hers.

MONEY, WORK

Robert Woodruff: gift of $100 million to Emory University, Atlanta, Georgia (1979). He had earlier been chairman of the Coca-Cola Company.

Helena Rubinstein continues as chief of her beauty products business (1961). If she is ill on the day of a board meeting, she stays in bed and has the other members gather around her bedside. She attends her office until two days before her death at **94**. She had opened her first salon at **31**, in Melbourne, and had been one of the first to link the science of dermatology with the cosmetics of the marketplace.

ARCHITECTURE

Sir Christopher Wren dies (1723, Feb. 25) and is buried in his own design of St. Paul's Cathedral (**43**). His tombstone advises if you wish for a monument, look around you: "Si monumentum requiris, circumspice."

Sir Ninian Comper: Royal Window, Canterbury Cathedral (1954).

ART

Pablo Picasso: to celebrate his birthday (1971, Oct. 25), a leading art gallery arranges for 90 children to release 90 doves from its front steps.

Georgia O'Keeffe: still at work as a painter (1977). The Metropolitan Museum of Art, New York, holds a famous example of her early work—"Black Iris" (**39**). At **42**, she had her first visit to the desert—an experience which has powerfully affected her work since then.

Imogen Cunningham: *After Ninety,* a book of photographs.

MUSIC—CLASSICAL

Leopold Stokowski records twenty albums after the age of **90**. (cf. **94***)

Havergal Brian: first-ever professional performance (1966) of his *Gothic* symphony, written at **51**. This giant work needs 700 singers, and up to four brass bands. Although he had been productive in his **30**s, his career really takes off in his **70**s, and he is now still energetic—he composes seven symphonies between **90** and his death at **96**.

Sophocles: death (406 B.C.). Greek dramatists appear to have been long-lived. Aristophanes dies at **68** (380 B.C.); Aeschylus dies at **69** (456 B.C.); and Euripides dies at approximately **78** (406 B.C.).

FILM

Abel Gance, in 1981: his heroic film *Napoleon*, made at **35–37**, is revived, and he suddenly becomes an international celebrity. At home in France, he receives a phone call so that he can hear the applause live from the 6,000 seat Radio City Music Hall in New York where *Napoleon* is being shown. Since **28**, Gance has continued in the film industry, but has been too experimental and erratic for public opinion. Now at **90** his rebirth is organized by the director Francis Ford Coppola (**47**) and the film historian Kevin Brownlow (**42**).

LOVE, LIFE

Pearl Taylor is chosen as Campus Queen at Long Beach City College, California (1978). She has been a part-time student since age **88**, and her duties include reigning over the college's Mardi Gras.

In the age group **85+**, there are 47 males for every 100 females (U.S.A., 1976).

PRESS

George Ryall continues to write about horses for *The New Yorker* (1977). His first column for the magazine had been at **38**, and his last is at **91**.

SPORTS

Reginald Honey, from South Africa, continues as a member of the International Olympic Committee (1977)—he is the oldest member.

Men's track records:

> Duncan McLean runs 100 meters in 19.9 seconds and 200 meters in 49.2 seconds (London, 1975). Robert Willis runs 800 meters in 8 minutes 54.2 seconds (California, 1977).

Women's track records:

> Eula Weaver (**88**) runs 800 meters in 7 minutes 28.6 seconds (California, 1977) and she runs 1,500 meters in 16 minutes 34.6 seconds.

91

HISTORY—WORLD

Konrad Adenauer: death (1967). He had been Chancellor of West Germany between **73–87**. So many world leaders make use of their time at his funeral to negotiate with each other that Willy Brandt (**53**) calls it a "working funeral."

RELIGION, PHILOSOPHY

Thomas Hobbes: death (1679). He had played tennis until **75**. He is best known for his quotation, at **63***, in which he describes human life as "solitary, poor, nasty, brutish, and short."

FILMS

Cecil B. De Mille's office is daily maintained and got ready by his secretary (1973), even though he has died at **77**.

John Cromwell: the bishop who performs the ceremony in *A Wedding,* directed by Robert Altman (**53**, in 1978). The dead grandmother is played by Lillian Gish (**79**).

LAW, CRIME

In California (1980), the oldest prisoner is **91**, a murderer who was convicted at **74**. However, the majority of prisoners are in their **20**s. The median age is **28.5** (male) and **29.4** (female).

93

RELIGION, PHILOSOPHY

Bertrand Russell resigns from the British Labour party (1965), as a protest against its acquiescence in the Vietnam War; he tears up his membership card at a public meeting. Russell continues as a prominent public figure until his death at **95**.

LITERATURE

P. G. Wodehouse: death (1975). He has published a *Jeeves* book at **90**; he published thirteen books during his **80**s.

PLAYS, DANCE

A. E. Mathews, the actor (1980) is asked how he starts his day: "I read the *Times* at breakfast, and if I am not in the obituary column I get up."

94

RELIGION, PHILOSOPHY

David O. McKay: as President of the Mormon Church (1968), he goes on his last world tour as a missionary. He had become President at **77**. He dies at **96**, and is succeeded by Joseph Fielding Smith (**93**)—succession is decided on the basis of seniority.

Catherine Bramwell Booth continues as a commissioner of the Salvation Army (U.K., 1978); she receives an award from the Guild of Professional Toastmasters, as "Best Speaker of the Year," and makes a speech at the presentation lunch.

MUSIC—CLASSICAL

Leopold Stokowski signs a six-year recording contract (1976), but dies in the following year. He had been conductor of the Philadelphia Orchestra, **30–54**. He collaborated on the film *Fantasia* at **58**. He fathered his fifth child at **69**, and founded the American Symphony Orchestra at **80**. It is not difficult to find other long-lived musicians. Among those who are not mentioned elsewhere are: Eugene Ormandy, who ceases to be full-time musical director of the Philadelphia Orchestra at **80** (1980), and Artur Rubinstein, the pianist, who retires at **90** (1977). Vaughan Williams, the composer, lives until **85** (1958); he had begun almost a second career when he started writing film scores at **68**. Georg Philipp Telemann, the composer, lives until **86** (1767). Igor Stravinsky lives until **88** (1971). Charles Vidor, the organist, lives until **92** (1937). Paul Paray (**93**, in 1979) is the conductor at the opening of

 Monte Carlo's new concert hall; Paray now goes on a fifteen-concert tour of Israel, and a tour of Sweden, before his death in the same year. And Pablo Casals, the cellist, lives until **96** (1973).

PLAYS

George Bernard Shaw: death (1950). He has been a dynamic public figure from his late **30**s onward (cf. **50***). At **72**, he wrote *The Intelligent Woman's Guide to Socialism,* and the play *The Apple Cart* at **73**. At **75**, he starts worldwide travel for the first time, having done little previously except for visits to the Mediterranean and to Bayreuth. He visits Russia, and is favorably impressed. He decides that "Unlike the other dictators, Stalin (**52**) has an irrepressible sense of humor." At **76**, he writes the play *Too Good to Be True* and, at **78** *The Millionairess.* He continues to swim in his **80**s, and thanks vegetarianism for his longevity. At **94**, he fractures his thigh while pruning a tree, and dies six weeks later. Previously, at **87** he had commented that the death of his wife (**86**) "has left him awaiting his own with perfect serenity." At **42**, he had planned that his funeral procession should include oxen, sheep, poultry, and an aquarium—the animals being there to thank him for having been a vegetarian.

SPORTS

Fred McLeod (1976): as honorary starter for the U.S. Masters golf tournament, he hits the first ball—for 120 yards. He is said to be still playing three rounds per week. He had won this tournament back at **26**.

96

HISTORY— U.K.

Dame Margery Corbett Ashby makes a speech in Westminster Hall (1978) at a meeting to celebrate the 50th anniversary of women's suffrage, which she had helped to promote.

MUSIC—CLASSICAL

Pablo Casals comments: "Age is a relative matter. If you continue to work and absorb the beauty of the world about you, you find that age does not necessarily mean getting old. At least, not in the ordinary sense. I feel many things more intensely than ever before, and for me life grows more fascinating." Casals dies at **96** (1973). At **81**, he had married Marta Montanez (**20**) and they went on to develop the Casals Festival.

EXPLORATION

Tesichi Igarashi: climbing of Mt. Fuji, 12,385 feet (1981). Each year, starting at **90**, he has made the ascent of the sacred mountain.

97

HISTORY—U.K.

Princess Alice: death (1981). She has lived longer than any other member of the Royal Family. At her birth, her father was **29**, and her mother was **22**. At her father's birth, his own mother, Queen Victoria, was **33**. Her father lived until **31** and her mother until **61**.

MONEY, WORK

John D. Rockefeller dies (1937, May 23). Jean Paul Getty has died at **84** (1976) and the first J. J. Astor also dies at **84** (1848). Henry Ford dies at **83**. Commodore Vanderbilt dies at **82** (1877), Andrew Mellon dies at **82** (1937), and Thomas J. Watson also dies at **82** (1956). J. Pierpoint Morgan dies at **75** (1913).

MUSIC—CLASSICAL

Sir Robert Mayer goes on a tour of the U.S.A. (1976) with the London Schools Symphony Orchestra, which he had founded at **72**. (cf. **100***)

98

SOCIAL SCIENCE, EDUCATION

W. N. Stocker dies (1949), having been a Fellow of Brasenose College, Oxford, for 72 years. He has been the last surviving member of the old system, in which fellows were appointed for life at Oxford colleges.

99

SOCIAL SCIENCE, EDUCATION

Martin Joseph Routh: death (1854). Since there are, at this time, no rules for compulsory retirement, Routh has continued in office as head of Magdalen College, Oxford; he has held this position since **35**. His only marriage is at **65**, to Eliza Blagrave (**30**).

Joel H. Hildebrand continues to work at the University of California, Berkeley (1980). His birthday is not much celebrated as he has already received most of the honors that the university could present to him; at **74** a building was named in his honor.

ART

It is unlikely that Titian lived until **99**, as is sometimes believed—he was probably born around 1487, and so lived until **89**. He kept working into his **80**s; for example, "Shepherd and Nymph" (Vienna) at **83**.

100

HEALTH

(Note that the next 10 stories are taken from a book on longevity published in 1799 by James Easton in Salisbury, England. Easton had collected notes about centenarians; his recipe for longevity was country life, exercise, love, and family life, plus moderation—"Nature is frugal, and her wants are few.") James Cuppage dies at **104** (1747) and his funeral is attended by, among others, four great-great-great-grandchildren. Samuel Street dies at **102** (1774) with preparations underway for his forthcoming marriage—his sixth. Prudence Hudson dies at **107** (1774) while at her spinning wheel. Henry and Bridget Townson die within a few minutes of each other, at **100** (1752), having been married in their **20**s. Frances Woodworth dies at **102** (1662); she had been a mother for the last time at **51**. Daniel Bull M'Carthy dies in Ireland at **111** (1751); at **84**, he had married for the fifth and last time. He and his wife (**14**) had gone on to produce twenty children. M'Carthy never wore a nightshirt, but slept naked, even on the coldest nights. In his book, James Easton often refers to the simple diet of centenarians; for example, Mrs. Watkins dies at **110** (Wales, 1790), having eaten only potatoes since **80**. At a time when hardly anyone lived beyond **50**, it would be possible to see the complete life cycle of your neighbors. For example, Frances Barton dies at **107** (Derbyshire, 1789), having been village midwife for 80 years; her husband had been sexton (gravedigger) for 70 years. So "this ancient pair frequently boasted that *she* had twice brought into the world, and *he* had twice buried, the whole parish."

Out of the total male deaths at all ages, .5 percent occur at **95** and over; the corresponding figure for females is 2.3 percent (England and Wales, 1977).

In 1821, England, Scotland, and Wales had 100 males **100+**, and 191 females **100+**. A later commentator (Bailey, 1857), noting this difference between the sexes, said of the women that "their sober, temperate habits, generally so much superior to those of men, enabled them to weather through all the chilling blasts of life, and arrive at last at the haven of an extreme old age."

There has always been interest in living a long life. For example, one ambitious publication was *De vita hominis ultra CXX annos* by Thomas of Ravenna, published in Venice in 1553, and explaining how to live until **120**. Typically, the main methods for achieving longevity were: (1) potions, elixirs, and alchemy, and (2) a lifestyle of sobriety and godliness. A more eccentric method was breathing the breath of young people; and in our own time interest has been aroused by "cell replacement treatment," an attempt to replace your dying cells with fresh cells from unborn lambs or monkeys. An elixir of life would be a drug of some kind; for example, the "mercury of life" was twenty grains of antimony to three grains of mercury. Other recipes included the eating of crushed stones. Sobriety was always advised—Bacon said that "Any agitation of the mind prevents the benefits which we ought naturally to derive both from food and rest." As with us today, old people were usually seen as active and hard-working, though one opposing and ironic theory was that "Trees live long because they take no exercise." Quite often, apart from the elixirs and crushed stones, the advice was very similar to our own today; viz., moderate living, exercise and living in the country, though the reasoning may be unfamiliar. Easton (1799) preferred the country because the city was full of the newly-discovered phlogiston. Lying with young people (gerocamy) was occasionally seen as beneficial; for example, "King David was old and stricken in years; and they covered him with clothes, but he gat no heat. Wherefore his servants said unto him 'Let there be sought for my Lord the king a young virgin; let her stand before the king and let her cherish him, and let her lie in thy bosom, that my Lord may get heat" (Kings 1:1). King David's young woman was Abishag the Shunammite; she slept with the king, and stayed a virgin.

Areas where perhaps great longevity may be found include Georgia in the U.S.S.R. and Vilcabamba in South America. Claims in such areas are now being examined by using tests on teeth. According to one writer, there are twelve *viejos* (**100+**) in the village of Vilcabamba; diet has very little meat or milk, but is mainly vegetables and beans, and provides about 1,700 calories per day, about half the U.S. average. The men are sexually vigorous until **100**. Unfortunately, these stories may not be true; it is possible that the old folk are suffering delusions of longevity.

A note on the lives of two theorists about longevity: first, Luigi Cornaro, who lived until **91** (1566). His early career had been as an architect. At **83**, in Padua, he published *Della Vita sobria,* a hymn to the life of moderation: "Sobriety purifies the senses, lightens the body, gives vivacity to the intellect, cheerfulness to the mind, strength to the memory, quickness to the movements, readiness and decision to the actions." Cornaro was famous for his minimal diet—12 ounces of solid food per day, and 14 ounces of wine. His interest in longevity had begun at about **35**, when either he was exhausted with extravagant living, or (another story) a doctor told him that he had only two more years to live. A second theorist on longevity, Elie Metchnikoff had been given the Nobel Prize for medicine at **63** (1908, for work on another subject); he noticed that longevity in the different species was inversely related to the length of the large intestine (with the inexplicable exception of the elephant). He theorized that slow putrefaction in the gut was dangerous to health. He recommended yogurt to counter this, and took it himself regularly, having studied it at the Pasteur Institute. He died at **71**.

The umbrella bamboo is a plant which produces flowers once in a century. After that, there are no more flowers for approximately 99 years.

The maximum life span of a giant clam is said to be **60–100**.

The possession of long-lived animals was often seen as a symbol of the owner's vigor and even sexual prowess. Turtles were kept in the Orient for this purpose. An ancient animal also indicated the stability of its owner's family or organization. For example, a griffon vulture lived in a Vienna zoo until **117** (1824). As such a bird would usually live until **30**, this Viennese bird may perhaps have had "understudies" to keep it going for over a century. If it was the same bird for all that time, it was initially owned by the distinguished general, Prince Eugene (1663–1736). In the early part of the twentieth century, the Rothschild family owned two giant salamanders which lived until **40** and **44**. And the Archbishop of Canterbury owned a land tortoise which lived until **128** (1753). A rival to this was a tortoise owned by the bishops of Peterborough; this lived until **220** (1813)—so they claimed.

HISTORY—U.K.

Eligibility: you are now eligible to receive a birthday telegram from the Queen. A friend should arrange this for you. Telegrams are sent to those of **100**, and at **105, 106, 107**, and so on. Approximately 1,800 telegrams are sent worldwide per year. This custom originated in 1917, at the Diamond Wedding of the then King (**52**) and Queen (**50**).

MONEY, WORK

Mary Moody continues as chairman of the board, Mark and Moody and Company (Stourbridge, England, 1981).

RENAISSANCE

Faust: death. Faust had originally desired to have a life of indulgence; his bargain with the Devil was to have this lifetime of pleasure but at death to pay for it with his soul reverting to the Devil. But in the most famous version of this legend, the dead Faust now enters Paradise as a little child, and is helped there by a woman he had cruelly seduced in his youth. Faust has had a journey of pleasure and discovery, but escapes from the cycle of sin-punishment-redemption, because he is a person who constantly strives. The act of genuinely striving for the truth frees you from any punishment, whatever the sins that have been committed during this striving. This *Faust* is completed by J. W. Goethe in his early **80**s, having begun it in his **mid-20**s, with a middle section in his **50**s. Goethe has been a world-famous figure since his second novel at **24***, and from his **20**s and **30**s he has been seen as the greatest poet in the German language. His heroic energy has kept him busy at poetry, drama, science, and public administration. From about **54**, his Weimar home has been a kind of living museum; at **60**, Napoleon Bonaparte (**41**) personally begs him to move to Paris, to add distinction to that city. At **74**, Goethe falls in love with Ulrike von Levetzow (**19**); he has just recovered from a serious illness, and he is thrilled to be with her. Her family reject his proposal of marriage, and Goethe goes on to write one of his most famous poems, "Trilogy of Passion." Goethe's loves include the following: at **24**, with Lili Schoenemann (**17**); at **25**, with Barbara Schulthess (**30**); at **26**, with Charlotte von Stein (**33**); at **38**, with Faustina (**23**); at **39**, with Christiane Vulpius (**23**); at **65**, with Marianne Jung (**30**); and at **74**, with Ulrike von Levetzow (**19**). About age, Goethe at **79** says that people of genius "experience a repeated puberty while other people are young only once." At **82**, Goethe writes his last poem for *Faust* and dies shortly afterward.

MUSIC—CLASSICAL

Sir Robert Mayer: the London Schools Symphony Orchestra gives a concert in London's leading concert hall, with Mayer as the sole member of the audience (1979). This is to thank him for his campaigns, since retiring from business at **50**, to provide classical music concerts for children. Other celebration concerts are also organized in his honor, and he goes on a lecture tour in the U.S.A. At **11**, he had met Johannes Brahms (**57**); together they attended *Die Meistersinger* and Brahms had stood throughout the performance, to increase his concentration. Robert Mayer now publishes his memoirs, entitled *My First Hundred Years.* When an interviewer points out how happy he looks, he replies, "I am a perfectly happy person. I think this is due very largely to the fact that I am a strong believer. I owe this to my wife. Until her death [when he was **95**] I felt that the most important thing in life was to try to serve society, a man-made affair, to be served with a man-made motivation. I learned from my wife's life, and after her death, to have a reason for being and striving—that what is man-made is not sufficient, you have to go outside that. And I have that faith. That is why I'm today a perfectly happy person. I believe there is a force outside this world which intervenes. I accept it. I make deductions about how to fit it."

Berta Ruck republishes (1978) her romantic novel *Her Official Fiancé;* it now appears in the Barbara Cartland (**77**) Library of Love.

FILMS

Adolf Zukor is appointed Honorary Chairman of the Board, Paramount Pictures (1973). He is in office until **103**.

EXPLORATION

Daisy Farrington celebrates her birthday (1979) by going on her first plane flight. She had told a neighboring policeman of her approaching birthday, and her desire to fly, and he arranges for her trip in a Piper Cherokee, from Birmingham airport.

101

HEALTH

Dr. W. L. Pannell continues to practice medicine in East Orange, New Jersey (1979) and he is one of eight centenarians who address a House of Representatives committee on aging. Dr. Pannell believes that "If you exercise your mind and your muscles, you'll live a long time." The meeting is organized by Representative Claude Pepper (**79**) who says that the U.S. has 13,000 centenarians in 1979, versus only 3,200 in 1969.

HISTORY—U.S.A.

There are approximately 91 army veterans remaining from the Spanish-American War (1898). The average age is **101** (1981), and the oldest is Harry J. Chaloner (**107**) of Florida.

102

LAW, CRIME

Mrs. Alice White wins an action in the High Court over her sister's will (England, 1976); she now inherits all the sister's estate of £6,000 ($12,000).

LOVE, LIFE

Jane Yanson: death (Scotland, 1799). She leaves a husband (**97**). They have been married for 63 years, and she has kept her wedding dress so that it may now be used as her shroud.

103

LOVE, LIFE

Harriet Orton (**102**) and John Orton (**104**): eightieth wedding anniversary (Cambridge, 1980).

LAW, CRIME

A woman is mugged in New York City (1976), and robbed of $2 worth of groceries. *Time* magazine speculates that she is the oldest person to have been mugged in New York.

John Davis celebrates his birthday in prison (South Carolina, 1979). At **46**, he received a life sentence for burglary, and is now the oldest prisoner in the state.

105

HEALTH

In one year in England and Wales (1977), 41 people died who were **105** or more.

106

HEALTH

Mme Robineau continues to live in Paris (1907) and is carefully examined by doctors interested in longevity. It is noted that the nail of her middle finger grows 2.5 millimeters in three weeks. The skin of her hands is so transparent that visitors can see her bones, blood vessels, and tendons. She retains her faculties, and takes a "vivid interest in those around her." Pulse is 70–84. She excretes 500 cubic centimeters of urine per day. She eats little, but chooses from a varied diet (—from Elie Metchnikoff). (cf. **100***)

LAW, CRIME

Moses Beckett is killed by a sniper (Philadelphia, 1979) as he is about to attend the birthday party of his sister, Mary Ellen Palmer (**104**).

110

ART

At **75**, Katsushika Hokusai (the most famous Japanese printmaker on the subject of Mount Fuji) writes as follows: "Although from about **50** I have often published my pictorial works, before **70** none is of much value. At the age of **73**, I was able to fathom slightly the structure of birds, animals, insects, and fish, the growth of grasses and trees. Thus perhaps at **80** my art may improve greatly; at **90**, it may reach real depth, and at **100** it may become divinely inspired. At **110**, every dot and every line may be as if living. I hope all good men of great age will feel that what I have said is not absurd." Hokusai dies at **89**.

113

HEALTH

Alex Comfort records these documented long lives: Philip Joubert, dying in Quebec at **113**, in 1814; John Turner, dying in London at **111**, in 1963; and Ada Roe, dying in London at **111**, in 1970. According to Dr. Comfort, only 1 in 1,000 births reach **100**, at this present time.

116

HEALTH

Jane Lewson: death (London, 1816). She had been widowed at **26**, but left with money. She became an eccentric, and is known to her neighbors as Lady Lewson. She never washes the windows of her house; and she never has a bath—instead she daily smears her face and neck with hog's lard. At **87**, she had cut two new teeth.

Shigechiyo Izumi continues his life in Kagoshima prefecture, Japan (1981). On September 15th, Japan's annual respect-for-the-aged day, he is visited by the Prime Minister, Zenko Suzuki (**70**, cf. **69***). Izumi is probably the oldest person in the world to have a fully documented birth and life. He has spent his years in the warm, south part of Japan.

117

SOCIAL SCIENCE

A **40**-year-old divorcée has been jailed for living with a **117**-year-old man in Malaysia. It is illegal for unmarried couples to live together. (—story in the *Sun* newspaper, 1977).

120

HEALTH

In commercial forestry, oaks are felled at **100–140**; beech at **90–120**; sycamores, **60–80**; and conifers, **40–80**.

RELIGION, PHILOSOPHY

Moses dies. "His eye was not dim, not his natural force abated" (in Deuteronomy). In 6 Genesis, God promises that the regular life span for a human being shall be **120**. Adam, the first human, at **130** "begat a son in his own likeness, after his image; and called his name Seth." Adam lives until **930**. Job dies at **140**.

143

HEALTH

Medzhid Agayev: death (1978), in Tikyaband, Azerbaijan. He is described as "one of the oldest" inhabitants in the Soviet Union.

150

HEALTH

Giant tortoises can stay alive until **150** in the Galapagos Islands, off Ecuador. Like many long-lived humans, their daily life is marked by careful routine. The infant tortoise hatches from its egg after 4–8 months. According to an informant of Charles Darwin, these giant tortoises never die of natural causes but only from accidents, such as a fall from a precipice. In 1923, a turtle was still alive at **150** in the Tonga Islands, having been marked by an expedition in the eighteenth century. At **150**, the turtle was blind, and "when walking creaks like an ox cart." Other long-lived tortoises live on the island of Aldabra, in the Indian Ocean, where they have thrived, owing to the absence of sailors and others who might use them for food. The Galapagos turtle lives to a maximum of **177**, and the maximum life of a common box turtle has been until **123**.

152

HEALTH

Thomas Parr: death (London, 1635). He had been a poor countryman who did not marry until **80**, when he fathered two children. At **102**, though still married, he fathered another child outside marriage, and so did penance in his local church, standing there in a white sheet. At **130**, he was still able to thresh corn. Now at **152**, he is brought to London to be exhibited as a sensation. His previous diet had been skimmed cheese, milk, coarse bread, small beer, and whey, but this is changed in London, and he dies—in the big city, he "fed high, and drank plentifully of the best wines by which, after a constant, plain and homely diet, the natural functions of the parts of his body were overcharged, his lungs obstructed, and the habit of the whole body quite disordered; in consequence, there could not but speedily ensue a dissolution." Old Parr is buried in Westminster Abbey, after he had had the honor of an autopsy performed on him by the discoverer of the circulation of the blood, William Harvey (**52**). The latter reports favorably on Parr's good internal condition.

161

TV, ETC.

Joice Heth is exhibited (U.S.A., 1835) as the nurse of the late President George Washington. Allegedly, in her youth, she had been a slave on the Washington family's estate. Heth is the first exhibit of Phineas T. Barnum (**25**), but she dies soon afterward, and dispassionate observers rate her age as about **80**. Barnum's show business career then comes to a halt, until at **32** he takes over a museum and fills it with freaks. These create enormous public interest. At **42**, he becomes an impresario for visiting European singers and actors. It is not until **60** that he opens his most famous venture, the three ring circus. And at **70** he amalgamates with a rival, J. A. Bailey (**34**) to establish a preeminent position in the circus world. Barnum lives until **80**, and the shy Bailey until **59**.

185

RELIGION, PHILOSOPHY

St. Mungo: death (Scotland, 600, Jan. 5). He had been the founder of Glasgow Cathedral.

237

FILM

In *Sleeper* (1973), Woody Allen plays a man waking up in the future, at **237**.

250

LITERATURE

In the blissful world of Shangri-La, the high lama is **250**, according to the book *Lost Horizon*, by James Hilton (**33**, in 1933).

337

MUSIC—CLASSICAL

Emilia Harty, in the opera *The Makropulos Affair:* by chance, a doctor has used her at **37** to demonstrate a new drug which gives life for 300 years. She finds that there is little pleasure in such a long life. But toward the end of her 300 years, she is afraid of death and she searches frantically for the doctor's formula, so that she can continue to live. At the end of the opera, she finds the formula and offers it to a young girl. This person is so horrified by the effect of immortality on Emilia that she burns the paper, and Emilia sinks to the ground. The opera is by Leoš Janáček (**71**, in 1925); he has had a local reputation as a composer with a special interest in the Moravian-Slovakian folk music of his homeland. Janáček's first great work has been *Jenufa* at **49**, but his main reputation does not begin until his **60**s. *The Cunning Little Vixen* is at **69**; *Glagolitic Mass* is at **72**; his opera *The House of the Dead* is at **73**; and he dies at **74**. The upsurge in his work at around **63** is due to the independence of his country toward the end of World War I, to a production of a revised *Jenufa* which establishes it as a classic, and to his romance with Kamila Stosslova (**25**) whom Janáček sees as the culmination of his lifelong search for the passionate gypsywoman.

600

RELIGION, PHILOSOPHY

Noah builds an ark to survive the flood of the world; by taking on board a pair of each species, Noah now saves the entire ecosphere. At **500**, Noah had fathered three children—Shem, Ham, and Japheth. Noah lives until **950**.

969

RELIGION, PHILOSOPHY

Methuselah: death. He is the longest-lived person in the Old Testament. At **930**, Adam had died.

1,000

LAW, CRIME

Paul Bryant, at **30**, is convicted of raping and murdering a woman (**59**) in Chicago, 1980; he is sent to prison until he is **530–1530**. In Spain, there is a convict, Eluterio Sanches, who is due to leave prison at **1,052**.

A recent FBI publication mentioned that a multiple murderer had been sentenced to 2,000 years in prison.

1,146

RELIGION, PHILOSOPHY

Muhammad al-Mahdi al-Hujjah: he is still absent from the world (1980) following his disappearance around **887**. Shiite Moslems believe that he will return; any current leader or Imam serves only in the temporary absence of this man, the twelfth great Imam.

4,000

HEALTH

General Sherman: still alive (1979). This is a tree, *Sequoiadendron giganteum* in California; it is 272 feet high, and 75 feet in circumference at breast height. The giant sequoia typically lives until **2,000** or **3,000**. Also, many species of hardwood and softwood live until **200** to **500**. It is possible that yew trees in country churchyards live until **1,000**. Oaks are lucky to reach **500**.

4,600

HEALTH

This is the approximate maximum life span of a bristlecombe pine tree.

10,000

HISTORY—WORLD

One of the titles of the Emperor of China was Wan Sui Yeh—"Lord of Ten Thousand Years."

11,700

HEALTH

A creosote bush in the Mojave Desert, California, may be **11,700**, according to botanist Frank Vasek (1980). These bushes grow in rings, and the current rings are clones from the original plant. The oldest ring has a diameter of almost eight meters, and is claimed to be the world's oldest living organism.

30,000

RELIGION, PHILOSOPHY

Ra, the god of ancient Egypt, lives until now.

311,040,000,000,000

RELIGION, PHILOSOPHY

In Hinduism, a Brahma lives until now.

HEALTH

Some definitions of death:

—cardiac death—no heartbeat;
—somatic death—the irreversible end of your personality, even though parts of your body may continue to have life;
—brain stem death—no reflexes;
—a flat EEG reading—no activity anywhere in the brain;
—all vital signs at zero;
—putrefaction—this was the old "final" sign which, although it took some time to register, was often adopted when fear of premature burial was significant.

With increasing urbanization, burial became a more specialized and anonymous process, performed by people who had no personal interest in the dead body. Fear of premature burial was one consequence of this. In the nineteenth century, French and German authorities even adopted "waiting mortuaries" where you were kept for twenty-four hours before being placed in the coffin. Elaborate tests for death were devised—for example, breath on mirror, pinching of the nipples, testing anal strength, placing snuff on the nose, or attaching a bell to a finger for 24 hours. Finally, plans were made for coffins which allowed communication between the potentially awakening corpse and the outside world.

About 50 percent of dying people today die in hospitals. Only 6 percent are said to be conscious in the moments before death.

Styles of dying: within the family, as a natural event; heroically; or "mechanical death" (—Ivan Illich) in the hospital.

The pioneer hospice for the dying is St. Christopher's Hospice, which was opened in London in 1967 by Dr. Cicely Saunders (**49**). She began medical school at **33**, having been a medical social worker. A custom of her hospice is that your room is left empty, except for flowers, for the day after you have died.

A "right to die" bill has been promoted in the New Hampshire

 House (1979) by Representative Everett Sackett (**77**). He said that he wanted medical help in an emergency, but did not want to be hooked up to machines in a hospital, and so merely in existence, not truly alive.

In England and Wales, there are 1,500 deaths per day.

Around 5,300 people die every day in the U.S.A. (1978). Here are the causes of death for all ages: diseases of the heart, 37.8 percent; cancer, 20.6 percent; cerebrovascular, 9 percent; accidents, 5.6 percent; influenza and pneumonia, 3 percent; diabetes, 1.7 percent; cirrhosis of the liver, 1.6 percent; arteriosclerosis, 1.5 percent; suicide, 1.4 percent; bronchitis, emphysema, asthma, 1.1 percent; homicide, 1.1 percent.

Mortality rates vary dramatically with your occupation. If you look at the death rate per 1,000 males at **15–64**, the comparable figures are 2.87 for university teachers, who benefit from a graceful lifestyle, but 16.44 for bricklayers, laborers, and 19.04 for electrical engineers. Occupations with a low death rate include civil servants, school teachers, managers, and local government officers. Occupations with unfavorable death rates include laborers, unskilled workers, fishermen, and coal miners.

Cryonic suspension is keeping your body at a very low temperature. The hope is that, when medical science has improved, your body will be unfrozen, and the disease that caused your death will be cured. You will then resume normal life. If opting for cryonic suspension after "death," it is essential to leave enough money for your maintenance—otherwise during an inflationary period you may have to be allowed to thaw, and then be buried.

Some hospital definitions:

DOA: dead on arrival
BID: brought in dead
GORK: God only really knows; typically, an unconscious patient whose brain damage is probably permanent
NTBR: not to be resuscitated
222: an emergency number to obtain the immediate services of the cardiac arrest unit (each hospital has a different number)
DWD: die with dignity; if you are very old and desperately ill, and if another heart attack will further incapacitate you, the nursing staff will ask for instructions—"222 or DWD?"

Live on through:

—a part of the body that is named after you; such as the fallopian tubes;

—a hospital or medical facility, or a part thereof, being named after you;
—donations to a sperm bank;
—the continuation of your genes;
—microorganisms, some of which never die; they merely split in two;
—part of your body used for organ transplant, such as heart, cornea, kidney, and so forth.

HISTORY—WORLD

Dulce et decorum est pro patria mori.—Horace (65 B.C.–8 B.C.).

Après nous le déluge.—Marie-Antoinette (1755–1793).

For this whole earth is but the cemetery of famous men, and their names shall live on, not merely graven in the stones above them, but far off, woven into the fabric of other men's lives.—Pericles (d. **66**, 429 B.C., in Athens).

AGE α YRS

I have heard that of all the countless beings beneath heaven which sprout or are brought to life, there is none which does not have its time of death, for death is a part of the abiding order of heaven and earth and the natural end of all creatures. How then can it be such a sorrowful thing? Yet in the world today, because all men rejoice in life and hate death, they exhaust their wealth in providing lavish burials for the departed, and endanger their health by prolonged mourning. I can in no way approve of such practices.—Wen the Filial, Emperor of China (died 157 B.C.).

The god entered his horizon, the king flew up to heaven and joined the sun's disc, the follower of the god met his maker. The palace was silenced and in mourning, the great gates were closed, the courtiers crouching on the ground, the people in hushed mourning.—upon the death of a king in twelfth dynasty Egypt.

Francisco Macias (**55**, in 1979): 101 death sentences. He has just been removed from office as President of Equatorial Guinea. Macias has been elected the country's first-ever President, at **44**, but with the help of his Fang tribe had turned the government into the most vicious on the face of the earth. In his small country, at least 50,000 citizens are killed. The first action of the new government is to put Macias and six of his Fang associates on trial. It is at this trial that the prosecution demands 101 death sentences, and the first of these is carried out shortly afterward.

Shih Huang Ti (d. **49**, in 210 B.C.): he is accompanied in his tomb-mountain by an army of thousands of life-size clay soldiers, who are buried in the earth with him, and arranged in military formation. Since **13**, he had been King of Ch'in; he had gained full power at **21**, and had become the first Emperor of unified Ch'in, or China.

In Imperial China, the Emperor—the Son of Heaven, the Celestial Countenance—was believed after death to "ascend upon the dragon to be a guest on high."

"Junshi," in Japan, is committing suicide at the time of the death of your lord and master. "Seppuku" is the ritual suicide. Two similar ideas were "dying well"; and "apologizing by dying," to wipe away the shame of a disgraceful event by committing suicide.

Live on through:

—the survival of your country; if you died as a soldier, you contributed to the country, so a part of you survives with it;
—your name on a war memorial, or in a book of remembrance;
—dying young for your country: "They shall not grow old as we that are left grow old. . . ."
—posthumous medals;
—memorial books, and other forms of war memorial; for example, at the Menin Gate every night . . . ;
—flags ("colors") hanging in a cathedral;
—kamikaze; you fight until your death, but your country lives on;
—being remembered forever as a hero; gods live forever. Roman emperors would often be apotheosized, being made into immortal gods by a vote of the Senate;
—fixing the succession to your own power;
—the administrative system that you have devised;
—a hereditary title (Duke, Lord, etc.) in Europe; these survive as long as you had (male) descendants; in China, hereditary titles were awarded for a fixed number of generations, from only one to a maximum of twenty-six generations.
—forbidding the discussion of your possible successor; for example, it was not legal in Kenya, under penalty of your own death, to discuss the successor to President Kenyatta (1892–1978).

HISTORY—U.S.A.

Death is un-American.—Arnold Toynbee (1889–1975).

To live on through:

—all your papers are kept in a presidential library.

HISTORY—U.K.

Death is only an incident, and not the most important which happens to us in this state of being. On the whole, especially since I met you my darling one, I have been happy, and you have taught me how noble a woman's heart can be. If there is anywhere else, I shall be on the look-out for you. Meanwhile look forward, feel free, rejoice in life, cherish the children, guard my memory.—Winston Churchill writes this at **40**, when serving in World War I, "to be sent to Mrs. Churchill in the event of my death."

RELIGION, PHILOSOPHY

Jesus Christ: forty hours after his death, he is resurrected. His soul and body are reunited, and he walks around his old homeland. He talks to his followers, and performs miracles. Forty days after the Resurrection, he is carried up to heaven in a cloud.

As in death, too, the world does not change, but ceases. Death is not an event in life. Death is not lived through.—Wittgenstein (1889–1951).

Death is "a great leap in the dark," according to the last words of Thomas Hobbes (d. **91***) in 1679.

The Grail was the cup used at the Last Supper, and it later contained the blood of the crucified Jesus Christ—thus, the search for the Holy Grail.

In the Roman Catholic Church, admired individuals may be beatified, and later perhaps canonized or created saints. The process takes several hundred years, and follows rules laid down by Pope Benedict XIV (**59**, in 1734).

"In my end is my beginning" and "In the midst of life we are in death," in the Book of Common Prayer.

In medieval Christianity, life after death follows these stages: first, immediately on dying, your soul is taken from your body by angels. You are judged, on your conduct in life; you are then (unless you have been incredibly saintly) sent to Purgatory, where you suffer extremes of heat and cold, in order to purge you of your sins. Later, on release from this, you may go to Abraham's bosom, a resting place. At the Last Day, or Final Judgment, your soul is put back with your physical body. Everybody now has to be judged in order to determine your place for the rest of time. St. Peter meets you at the gates of Heaven; a recording angel reads out the story of your time on earth; saints and angels may speak on your behalf; Jesus, or God the Father, makes the final decision—Hell or Heaven. Hell is a mass of suffering, organized by beasts. Heaven is bliss, Paradise; it means that you are united with the maker of the whole universe, with the person who loves us all. Paradise was often seen as a garden; the Fall, or the break with God, took place in a garden—now we return to be with God in a garden. Thus is completed the story of human life on earth.

Limbo is neither Heaven nor Hell. It is an intermediate place, for those who on earth never heard of God. They therefore never had the option of choosing to believe and to live the good life.

Ars moriendi (c.1418) was a pioneer, best-selling, and much imitated text on how to die "well and surely." At the core, there are five stages in dying, viz.: the temptations to (1) unbelief in God; (2) despair; (3) impatience with the suffering in dying that God has given you; (4) spiritual pride; (5) avarice, and continuing to care about worldly matters of success, money, and so on.

In medieval theology, the acceptance of pain on your deathbed was good; it was an offering by you to God.

Bodies in graves have traditionally been placed with the feet facing east, and the head at the west, so as to facilitate arousal at the Resurrection.

The bodies of certain medieval saints were said not to deteriorate in the coffin.

The Prophet Ezekiel described afterlife as a valley of bones; he foresaw that they should come together—the dry bones connected to the dry bones—and with Spirit breathed into them there will be the Resurrection.

Cotton Mather (Boston, 1692) worked out the space required for the Resurrection. He postulated a total population for all those who had ever lived in the earth—one billion people every 50 years, for 10,000 years between Creation and the Judgment Day. There would be enough space in just the country of England for all these resurrected people.

The Last Rites consist of (1) confession; (2) extreme unction; (3) viaticum; (4) papal blessing. This service has been simplified since 1972. The viaticum is the last communion; extreme unction was originally known as "sacramentum exeuntium," the sacrament for those who are leaving this life. According to one medieval theory, if you recovered after receiving this sacrament, you could never have sex again, as you were "dead to the world."

"Deathbed repentance"—in this life pattern, you have almost a full life span of self-indulgence, but immediately before the judgment of death, you adopt spiritual behavior, confessing your sins and promising to change.

If your descendants become Mormons, you can, after your death, be baptized by them through the Mormon church.

Burial in ancient Egypt: first, removal of your internal organs, including the brain, but excluding the heart which was believed to be center of wisdom and emotions; the body cavity is rinsed with palm wine; body left to dehydrate for 70 days. It is then packed with linen and resin; wrapped in linen, and placed in the coffin. The internal organs are kept in four jars beside the coffin. After death, your "ka" remains with your body, and your "ba" roams the underworld with the sun each night, returning to your body at dawn while the sun goes into an arc in the sky. To facilitate the meeting between ba and body, a model of your face is placed over the mummy. Since, in the new world after death, you will need supplies, your tomb is decorated with carvings of cake, beef, wife, children, servants, and even ships and herds of cattle and herdsmen. The images will supply your spiritual self. At the end of your burial service, the priest says to you, "You live again, you revive always. You have become young again, you are young again, and forever."

In the Hindu funeral, your body is burned, and the ashes scattered on the Ganges. The river flows down to the ocean, in the same way that your soul will eventually merge with the complete divinity of the world.

In Buddhism, true death is the ending of all desire. Only desire brings on suffering, and the end of desire is the end of suffering. Physical death is not the end of suffering as long as there is still desire. If desire persists, then karma exists; karma leads to rebirth, and a return to suffering. Gradually, by meditation, desire may wither away, and we reach nirvana—the end of this cycle of desire, death, and rebirth—"Passing beyond sorrow." Warning: to desire nirvana is, like any other desire, a form of suffering.

On the ancient and common idea that the last words sum up the wisdom of a lifetime: "When a bird is about to die, its notes are mournful; when a man is about to die, his words are good."—Confucius.

Flowers at a funeral: this is analogous to the cycle of human life and death. In a textbook on *Holy Dying* (1651), the reader was invited to look at the rose, which started "fair as the Morning, and full of the dew of Heaven." But later it "began to put on darknesse, and to decline to softnesse, and the symptoms of a sickly age"; finally, it "fell into the portion (place) of weeds and outworn faces."

In folklore, there are various signs that death is coming; for example, bells ringing; a black coach coming to collect you; a devil figure appearing to you.

The idea of a second burial—one year after your death. The first year is spent in full discussion of the dead person; after a year, a symbolic funeral takes place, and the dead person goes to their permanent home, with the other ancestors.

The Tikopia believed that thunder was the sound of dead people dancing.

A prayer that touches on death:

Support us all the day long of this troublous life, till the shades lengthen and the evening comes, and the busy world is hushed, and the fever of life is over and our work is done. Then in your mercy give us a safe lodging, and a holy rest, and peace at the last.—John Henry Newman (1801–1890).

To live on:

—as God, who is outside time;
—as a soul in Heaven;
—as a soul reborn in another body;
—through martyrdom;
—through a "chantry." This was a fund, set up to employ people to pray for your soul which, after death, is now in Purgatory. The more prayers were said, the more God would be influenced to reduce your suffering in Purgatory. A chantry should have been a part of your will. The chantry was a medieval custom in England until 1529;
—as a ghost. You return to visit (haunt) the place in life where you had either ecstasy or suffering. If you had been thwarted in a desire (failed in life), you return again and again, permanently seeking that thing.
—through a curse which falls upon your descendants. For example, Pope Gregory VII (1021–85) excommunicated descendants down to the seventh generation; they were therefore born unable to take communion or have social relations with Christians;
—through a memorial service;
—through choosing the hymns for your own burial service, or otherwise fixing similar details;
—in the words on your tombstone;
—in Japan, at the festival for ancestors, celebrated each year at July 13–16;
—like Jesus Christ in the ceremonial meal, the Sacrament or Communion which commemorates his own last meal before his execution.

Death dominates all of the living.—Auguste Comte (1798–1857).

People really die, not only some, but all, each of us in our turn. . . . and Towards the actual person who has died we adopt a special attitude; something like admiration for someone who has accomplished a very difficult task—Sigmund Freud (1856–1939).

[A] human being is torn from us, and what remains is the icy stillness of death.—Carl Jung (1875–1961).

Elisabeth Kübler-Ross's stages of dying (1969):

1. denial and isolation;
2. anger and resentment;
3. bargaining and attempt at postponement;
4. depression and sense of loss;
5. acceptance.

AGE α YRS

Mourning involves such feelings and events as these: grief; numbness; guilt; resentment, anger, relief; physical illness; alcoholism, suicide, stigma in the eyes of the rest of the world; loss of identity; deprivation, loneliness, financial loss, yearning, hallucinations about the dead person.

Living on through:

—lectureships, professorships, colleges, scholarships, library books, and other educational facilities named after you;
—a theory or concept that is always associated with your name;
—"life after life," a body-free consciousness, that is, the sense of floating away from your body, and watching the living people react to your death;
—research results still coming in from a research project that you originated;
—not living on at all; death is the end of your existence.

SCIENCE, TECHNOLOGY

A new scientific truth does not triumph by convincing its opponents but because its opponents die, and a new generation grows up that is familiar with it.—Max Planck (1858–1947).

What a good thing it would be, if every scientific man was to die when **60** years old, as afterward he would be sure to oppose all new doctrines.—the geologist Charles Lyell (1797–1875).

 Nicholas Copernicus: his book on the sun-centered theory of astronomy, published when he was **69***, is "forgiven" by the Roman Catholic Church in 1835, when he would have been **362**. His book had been banned early after publication, and in 1835 the ban is lifted. Galileo's book on the same subject is also removed from the banned list in 1835, when he would have been **271**. Galileo is publicly forgiven by the church in 1979, reversing a judgment made at his trial (**69***); Galileo would have been **415** at this moment of forgiveness.

Graffiti in the toilets of an undergraduate science lab: "Old chemists never die, they merely increase in entropy," and "Old physicists never die; they merely decay exponentially."

Live on through:

—having priority as the first person to make a key discovery;
—a species, or element, or some other aspect of the world being named after you.

MONEY, WORK

Following the story of Lazarus, rich people find it unusually hard to enter the Kingdom of Heaven. "Lay not up to yourselves treasures on earth: where the rust and moth consume, and where thieves break through, and steal. But lay up to yourselves treasures in heaven: where neither the rust nor moth doth consume, and where thieves do not break through, nor steal. For where thy treasure is, there is thy heart also."—Matthew 6:19–21.

A tontine was a scheme in which a group contributed to a fund; this capital sum became the property of the person who outlived the rest.

According to U.K. Social Security administrators, it is almost impossible to check that pensions are not being paid out to people who have died. In 1979, Mrs. Ada Tragenza was given a two-month suspended sentence for collecting a pension on her mother (**105**) who had in fact died at **88**. In France, two sisters in their **60**s kept their dead mother in the house for four years, so that they could continue to obtain her pension; the mother, Mme Barbaroux (d. **90**, 1976), was said to be too ill to go outside, and the daughters were admired for staying at home and looking after her so attentively.

You can live on through your will; this continues to be the instrument of your desires, even when you are dead. Ancient Egyptians made wills; one of the earliest known documents in the world is the will of Prince Nekure (eighth dynasty, c. 2800 B.C.) in which he distributes his 14 towns among his widow and four children. In ancient Greece, you had no choice in the disposal of your assets; inheritance rules directed your wealth to your family. In Rome, you had a little area of discretion, but again the family interest was paramount. Julius Caesar (d. **56***, in 44 B.C.) in effect willed control of the Roman Empire to his great nephew Augustus (**19***). The Emperor of China decided which of his sons would succeed him; the name of the chosen heir was left in a sealed box, which was kept behind a tablet of stone. Following Peter the Great (**50**, in 1722) new czars of Russia were appointed in the will of the previous czar. And, the will of King Charles II of Spain caused much of Europe to go to war for thirteen years, in the War of the Spanish Succession (1701–14).

You can also live on through:

—a trust, which can exist as long as the named beneficiaries are alive;
—a foundation, which may exist for ever;
—a shop or company, which bears your name, such as Tiffany.

RENAISSANCE

AGE α YRS

As a well-spent day brings happy sleep, so life well used brings happy death.—Leonardo da Vinci (1452–1519).

Men fear Death, as children fear to go into the dark . . . Death hath this also; That it openeth the Gate, to good Fame, and extinguishes Envy.—Francis Bacon (1561–1626).

Peace, sweet peace, come oh come into my breast.—J. W. Goethe (1749–1832).

Denis Diderot (d. **70**, in 1784), the editor of the great *Encyclopédie,* is a conspicuous example of a person consciously working for approbation after his death, that is, from posterity. As one of the new atheists, he sees posterity as the one true form of immortality, since for a truly advanced thinker it would be unlikely that contemporaries would offer adequate praise. As with Leonardo da Vinci (d. **67**, in 1519) and as with Samuel Pepys (d. **69**, in 1703), a full appreciation of Diderot's later life was not possible until long after his death; he expected and planned this to happen. For Diderot, there are some people who were ". . . too far advanced for the time in which they lived, were little read, little understood, not at all appreciated, and have long remained in obscurity, until the moment when the century that they were in advance of has elapsed, and another century, to which they had belonged before it arrived, catches up with them and finally renders justice to their merit."

The Great Pyramid is a tomb built for the pharaoh Cheops (c.2600 B.C.). Its mass is thirty times that of the Empire State building. Its height is exactly two pi (2 × 3.14) times the height. Its sequence of passages is perhaps an analogy of the soul's progress after death. The Greeks believed that the pyramid was constructed over 20 years, by 100,000 people. But even this concentration of manpower is trivial compared with the size of the pyramid.

When a mausoleum was being prepared for a still-living empress of China, it was given the euphemistic name "the Happy Land for a Myriad Years."

Methods of finding a home for your body:

(1) buried: in the earth; cemetery; tumuli or barrow; tomb; sarcophagus; jar (Minoan); family mausoleum; family vault; necropolis; sepulcher; shrine; catacomb; pyramid; or placed in your favorite car and then buried (California);
(2) burned; cremated and the ashes placed in a columbarium; in a glade of remembrance; distributed on the sea, or at some place which was significant in your life;
(3) the body is allowed to decay, and the bones placed in an ossuary;
(4) the body is exposed, so that birds peck at it;
(5) the body is left in a tree, or similar construction above ground, or in a mud hut;
(6) public mummification (Jeremy Bentham d. **83**, 1831).

We take it for granted that burial places should be set apart from everyday life. An alternative view has sometimes been taken, for example, in China, that you should be buried among familiar scenery. These lines, in *Helen* by Euripides (d. **78**, 406 B.C.), express the latter view: "All hail, my father's tomb! I buried thee, Proteus, at the place where men pass by, that I might greet thee often; and so, even as I go out and in, I, thy son, call upon thee, father."

Live on through:

—people living or working in a building which you designed.

ART

Giotto (**38**) shows four figures in Hell, each suspended by the part of the body which has brought them to evil habits while in their earthly life—a cord holds them up by the tongue, or the hair (for personal vanity), or the vagina, or the penis (in the Arena Chapel, Padua; 1304–06).

"The Last Judgment" (c.1431) by Fra Angelico (c. **34**) shows God dividing people into the Good (on His right hand) and the Bad (on His left hand). The people had previously come back to life by breaking out of their graves. Bad people are then placed in one of seven pits, where their permanent suffering is supervised by devils. Good people are shown playing in a field, dancing with angels.

On a tomb, a broken column signifies that the life was cut off in its prime. Bay leaves are a symbol of eternity.

Live on through:

—one of your works continuing to give pleasure and stimulus.

Ars longa vita brevis.

As André Malraux said, "Art escapes death."

MUSIC—CLASSICAL

Chopin's "Funeral March" is written at **27** (1837) and incorporated at **29** into his Sonata no. 2 in B-flat Minor; Chopin dies at **39**, from tuberculosis. The "Death March" from *Saul* is by G. F. Handel (**54**, in 1739), who dies at **74**.

The first complete performance of the opera *Lulu* takes place forty-three years after the death of the composer, Alban Berg (d. **50**, in 1935). His widow (**49**, in 1935) forbids the production of this story about "the streetwalker of love." In the story, Lulu dies on Christmas Eve—so did Berg.

It is said that 70 percent of the orchestral records sold in Japan are by now-dead conductors.

Live on through:

—one of your compositions continuing to be performed.

LITERATURE

A popular inscription for tombs:

I was
  that which you are;
What I am
  that will you be.

Death strikes all, but bright Fame triumphs over Death and keeps it trampled underfoot; after her victory Fame proclaims the great deeds of the dead, so that the actions of those, who by their greatness have deserved glory, shall be remembered after their death.—from *The Triumphs* by Petrarch, in the fourteenth century. There is the Triumph of Love; the Triumph of Chastity over Love; of Death over Chastity; of Fame over Death; of Time over Fame; and there is the Triumph of Eternity over Time.

As a philosopher he knew that at the termination of any allotted life only an infinitesimal part of any person's desires has been realized.—from *Ulysses* (1922), by James Joyce (1882–1941).

Time will pass away.
I shall no longer be there.
There will be no return to the days of our fathers or forefathers; nor is this either necessary or desirable.
But that which is noble, creative, and great, will, after a lengthy parting, reappear at long last.
That will be an epoch of creativity.
Your life will then be at its fullest, its most fruitful.
Remember me then.
—from a dedication by Boris Pasternak (**65**, in 1955) to *Dr. Zhivago*.

Each time, I feel perplexed. Can that be he, my dear, dear beloved Leovochka there under the ground? And every time I cry, cry, cry until I have a pain in my chest.—Sonya Tolstoy, on the daily visits which she makes to the grave of her husband.

"Consolations" were ancient Greek and Roman writings to help the bereaved person. Also, euphemisms for death included the word "cemetery" which is the Greek for sleeping place.

"Automatic writing" was a nineteenth century device by which living people tried to obtain the thoughts of the dead.

Live on through:

—funeral oration; panegyric; obituary; eulogy; tombstone inscription; "laudatio funebris;"
—posters announcing your death, in Italy;
—through a book that you have written; or, a character that you once created continues to have meaning.

PLAYS, DANCE

Children preserve alive a dead man's name and fame. They are like corks that hold the fisherman's net, and keep His knotted lines from sinking to the ocean bed.—Electra, in *The Choephori,* by Aeschylus (**67**, 458 B.C.).

Imperial Caesar, dead, and turned to clay might stop a hole to keep the wind away.—Hamlet.

It is difficult to be thoroughly popular until one is quite dead.—Herbert Beerbohm Tree (1853–1917).

No need to be scared of words, doctor. This is called dying.—Luigi Pirandello (1867–1936) on his deathbed.

FILMS

At the funeral of "King" Cohn (d. **66**, in 1958), there is a large crowd, even though he has been extremely unpleasant in his work as head of Columbia Studios. Red Skelton (**44**) explains this paradox: "Well, it only proves what they always say—give the public something they want to see, and they'll come out for it."

MUSIC—NON-CLASSICAL

Elvis Presley (d. **42**, in 1977): at the news of his death, the comment is made "good career move." Recently, his record sales have been diminishing. But in the six weeks following his death, his record sales enjoy a boom which is said to be worth $250 million.

Live on through:

—being featured in the Country Music Hall of Fame;
—bringing out new records after your death;
—people continuing to sing your compositions;
—annual meetings of your fan club;
—the continued sale of your records;
—two minutes silence annually to remember the moment at which you died, this is a ceremony organized by the Elvis Presley Fan Club.

TV, ETC.

Death has been described as "Being called to see the great casting director in the sky."

LOVE, LIFE

A man can no more look steadily at death than stare at the sun.—La Rochefoucauld.

"Suttee" was an Indian custom in which the widow placed herself on the funeral pyre of her late husband, and was burned to death. Suttee was abolished in 1829, by order of Lord William Cavendish Bentinck (**55**), the governor-general.

On the approach of the death of a king of France, the king's mistress would have to leave his chateau, and his wife would appear; the king would then begin his confession.

According to Pope John Paul II (**61**, 1981), there will be full experience of our earthly bodies after the resurrection—but no sex. We will exist for eternity in our male and female states, but without sex or procreation.

The body of a suicide was traditionally despised; it was buried at a crossroads, with a fencepost through the heart.

Suicide rates per 100,000 population: U.S.A., 12.1; France, 15.6; Japan, 18; Denmark, 26.

Names for death include: passing away; passing on; passing quietly into Eternity; his final exit from the stage of life; dissolution.

To accelerate death: old and decrepit people were helped toward death in societies in which it was easy to do this; for example, nomads could easily leave a person behind while the main group went on to the next camping ground.

Cremation is a relatively small, but growing custom. In 1976, 7.3 percent of dead bodies were cremated, and in 1978 the figure was 8.6 percent. This applies to the U.S.A. In Canada, the proportion of cremations is almost twice as large.

How people say good-bye to you:

—funeral service; memorial service; tributes; memorial silence;
—a wake, or other get-together;
— wreaths of flowers, analogous to the cycle of life and death.
—a message on a wreath, addressed to you, at your funeral.
—tombstone inscriptions.
—letters of condolence to your closest relative.
—mourning; wearing special clothes, or behaving more seriously, to mark your death.
—keeping an empty chair at mealtimes; keeping a desk or room exactly as you left it.
—thinking of you every night, for the rest of our lives.

Live on through:

—your lineage of children, grandchildren.
—love; love conquers everything, even death.
—a message or letter, to be read after you have died.

—a street is named after you; your name is placed on a park bench.
—finger rings—in the sixteenth to nineteenth centuries, these were rings with your name on them, and they were given out after a funeral, so that you may be remembered.
—leaving enough money so that your friends may have a party; or that someone may have a charitable donation as you specify.
—a plaque is fixed on the house in which you have lived; the house becomes a historic site.
—in Japan's Festival of the Dead, you return annually to the family shrine.
—being at one with nature; there is a Japanese saying "The state may collapse but the rivers and mountains remain."

PRESS

Note: in the press, you are commemorated with obituary notices, "In Memoriam's" and in books such as "Who Was Who." Also, everywhere in the world, local newspapers contain poems, in the classified sections, taking note of the anniversary of a death. Here are three examples from the west coast of Ireland:

We never cease to think of you,
We never cease to care;
We only wish we could go home
And find you sitting there.

God saw you getting tired
When a cure was not to be;
He closed His arms around you, dad,
And whispered: Come to me.
So keep Your arms around him
And give him special care,
Make up for all he suffered
And all that seemed unfair.

In a near Glenamaddy graveyard
Where the trees their branches wave
Sleeps a kind and loving father
In his cold and silent grave.

EXPLORATION

Death has often been seen as the final journey of exploration. In classical legends you now travel to the land of Hades. Corpses in ancient Greece were given a coin in the mouth to pay Charon for a crossing over the River Styx, and a honeycake for the guard dog Cerberus. Japanese coffins contained six coins to pay for crossing across a similar river. In other cultures, great kings were sometimes buried in a ship.

The folk legends of the Wild Hunt: at night living people can wake up and see the dead in black clothes, riding black horses, accompanied by black hounds, streaming across the countryside in the dead of night.

A rural tradition: at the moment of your death, the windows of the house should be opened, the doors unlocked, and any knots be loosened—so that your soul or ghost has an easy passage away. Otherwise you might stay to haunt the house; worse still, you might want to take someone with you.

Live on through:

—a feature of the earth—a place, mountain, or ocean current, is named after you, such as Vancouver, or America.

LAW, CRIME

In the U.S.A. (1978), there are roughly 58 homicides per day, or 21,080 per year. They form 1.1 percent of all deaths.

Bodies of executed criminals were buried within the prison walls, in the twentieth century, and covered with quicklime. In Tudor times and earlier, parts of the body would be exhibited in different parts of the country. Later, bodies of executed criminals would be hung in chains, as a warning; sometimes this would be done on the tidal reaches of a river.

In Italy, you cannot libel the dead with impunity; a libel action may be brought on behalf of a dead person.

SPORTS

Arrhachion of Philagia (564 B.C.): during his third attempt to become Olympic champion at wrestling, his opponent begins to strangle him (this was allowed in the rules of the original Olympics). But Arrhachion, though being strangled, manages to break off his opponent's toes, and force him to resign from the contest. Meanwhile, Arrhachion dies. The judges are forced to take note of the opponent's resignation, and they declare Arrhachion to be the winner. The champion's wreath is therefore put on the corpse.

King George V (d. **70**, 1936) of England had been a keen yachtsman; after his death, his personal racing yacht, "Britannia," is stripped of its fittings, taken out into the English Channel, and sunk.

Jochen Rindt becomes world motor racing champion (1970), having achieved the highest number of points—but he had died (**28**) at Monza, before the end of the season.

In boxing, there are about 11 deaths per year.

Death is central to these sports:

—shooting of game, such as pheasants, grouse;
—angling and deep-sea fishing in "kill" tournaments;
—fox-hunting, beagling, and coursing;
—falconry;
—big-game hunting;
—shooting of wild deer and other medium-sized animals;
—cockfighting; in the past, there was dogfighting and even horse-fighting; bear baiting was not outlawed in Britain until 1835.
—bullfighting;
—in Italy, the shooting or netting of songbirds as they migrate;
—the Aztec sacred ball game, in which the winner was given the privilege of death, so that he could immediately become a messenger to the gods;
—combat by gladiators in ancient Rome; this originated as the appropriate way of ending a funeral in early Roman times. For example, G. T. Lucanus commemorated the death of his grandfather in 145 B.C. by having combat for three days, with sixty men fighting to the death. Later, these fights were no longer associated with funerals, and instead they became general sporting events which were held on any exciting occasion. Before the combat, gladiators could indulge in limitless feasting; during the parade through the amphitheater they would say, "Hail Caesar, we who are about to die salute you." Winners would become great heroes; they earned sexual favors and their freedom from slavery, and they would be given bowls full of gold coins. Losers would be "whipped with rods, burnt with fire, and killed with steel"; if they persisted in dying in a reluctant or sullen manner, they would be jeered at by the spectators.

Death is an ever-present danger in these sports:

—rock climbing;
—motor racing;
—skydiving, parachuting;
—circus acts;
—wrestling or boxing when performed in the original Olympic Games (added in 708 B.C.).

These sports were originally derived from the pursuit of death:

—javelin throwing;
—fencing;

—kendo;
—karate;
—aikido;
—perhaps boxing and wrestling;
—greyhound racing (from coursing);
—jousting tournaments;
—clay pigeon shooting;
—"release" tournaments in fishing, where the fish is released after being weighed;
—chess;
—although tennis is entirely peaceful, it does have a possible sudden-death ending.

Immortality in sport; to live on through:

—election to a hall of fame;
—a record which no successor can beat;
—a cup or trophy named after you; for example, the Stanley Cup, or the Derby, or the Capablanca chess tournament;
—a sports scholarship named after you;
—gates at a stadium named after you, or the stadium itself named in your honor;
—in chess, a sequence of moves being named after you; for example, the Damiano gambit, or the Greco Counter gambit;
—your picture on the walls of the sports club or the cricket pavilion.